SHENANDOAH COLL. & CONS. OF MUSIC LIBRARY

ADVERTISING RESEARCH

This is a volume in the
Arno Press collection

A CENTURY OF MARKETING

Advisory Editor
Henry Assael

Associate Editor
Larry J. Rosenberg

Editorial Board
Robert Bartels
Ewald T. Grether
Stanley C. Hollander
William Lazer

See last pages of this volume
for a complete list of titles.

SHENANDOAH COLL. & CONS. OF MUSIC LIBRARY

ADVERTISING RESEARCH

PERCIVAL WHITE

ARNO PRESS
A New York Times Company
New York • 1978

Editorial Supervision: JOSEPH CELLINI

Reprint Edition 1978 by Arno Press Inc.

Reprinted from a copy in the Newark Public Library

A CENTURY OF MARKETING
ISBN for complete set: 0-405-11156-8
See last pages of this volume for titles.

Manufactured in the United States of America

Library of Congress Cataloging in Publication Data

White, Percival, 1887-1970.
Advertising research.

(A Century of marketing)
Reprint of the ed. published by D. Appleton and Co., New York.
Includes index.
1. Advertising research. I. Title. II. Series.
HF5821.W5 1978 659.1'07'2 78-266
ISBN 0-405-111

HF 5821 .W5 1978 White, Percival
Advertising research
659.1 W585a

ADVERTISING RESEARCH

BY

PERCIVAL WHITE

MARKETING COUNSELOR

AUTHOR OF "MARKET ANALYSIS," ETC.

ILLUSTRATED

D. APPLETON AND COMPANY

NEW YORK LONDON

1927

COPYRIGHT, 1927, BY
D. APPLETON AND COMPANY

PRINTED IN THE UNITED STATES OF AMERICA

PREFACE

Advertising may be regarded as a science, but it is a science of to-morrow rather than of to-day. Advertising, though it bids fair to become one of the leading commercial sciences, must still be regarded primarily as an art, requiring, to a greater or less degree, those emotional qualities of genius which take flight into skies beyond the boundaries of mere science.

It is fully realized that advertising science is still in the embryo stage, and that no book on the subject can succeed in teaching any one how to *create* advertising. It is even conceded that creative advertising can never be taught, by this or any other method. It is not difficult to learn, from a book or a teacher, the principles and the technique of advertising, just as it is possible for any one of moderate intelligence to learn harmony, counterpoint, orchestration, and other branches of the *science* of music; but the creative impulse, though it may be quickened by suggestion or inspiration or example, cannot be learned by any processes of education yet developed.

Beginning with this assumption (and it is merely an assumption), the approach in this book has been frankly that of the scientist, attacking the problems of advertising as he would attack any other scientific problem. Previous books have presented advertising much after the plan followed by the person who enters an advertising agency and spends a certain length of time in each of its departments. That is, previous books, correctly considering advertising as primarily an empirical subject, have dealt with it empirically.

This text does not follow that precedent. It divides the study of advertising, not as the advertising man would divide it, but as the scientist would divide it. It endeavors to show the student how to deal with any advertising problem, except the supreme problem of creating advertising. An unimaginative mind, however well trained in the science of advertising, will never produce good advertising. A creative mind, even though not trained in the science, may or may not produce good advertising. But the best results will be the product of a creative brain scientifically trained.

This volume is offered as a text to students in advertising and is intended for use in college courses. It should also appeal to men professionally engaged in advertising, since its material is nothing more or less than the outgrowth of continued efforts to develop methods for obtaining the raw material from which advertising is fashioned, and for converting that raw material into a form best adapted to the requirements of those whose task it is to prepare the actual advertisements. The preparation of advertisements, however, is considered a matter of secondary importance and is discussed here only as an incidental.

Effort has been made to develop the theoretical aspects of advertising. There need be no discrepancy, however, between the theory and practice of this subject. Since the data used for illustrative purposes, as well as the inductions drawn from them, are the fruit of some years of practice in advertising research, marketing research, and sales research, the book should have that "practical" atmosphere upon which business men quite justly insist.

Realizing the limitations of his own experience, however, and fearing the dangers of applying the methods of a single man or class of men to a subject still so imperfectly developed, the author has, in the majority of cases, exhibited the work of others in preference to his own. Some examples have been included which do not at this moment seem entirely sound—some are, indeed, so unsound as to call forth rather severe criticism. Most of the cases cited, however, are considered representative of the best current practice.

It is hoped that the net result will prove more representative and better-rounded because of the policy of including illustrative material from all available sources. None of the research work here discussed is perfect, but every example used reveals something of originality and contributes something to the sum total of advertising science.

To those of his clients who have permitted the author to quote from their experiences he wishes to make acknowledgment. To other teacher-students and student-teachers, in schools, in advertising agencies, and elsewhere, thanks are also due. *In addition to those whose names appear in the text* (see index) special acknowledgment is due to Charles G. Wheeler, of Topsham, Maine, and Miss Clara L. Treyz, of New York City. To Walter S. Hayward, of Sharon, Conn., the greatest credit is due, since much of the creative work was his. Acknowledgment of assistance of various sorts is made also to the following:

Lawrence H. Adams, Washington, D. C.

Advertising and Selling Fortnightly, New York City: Frederick C. Kendall, editor.

Agricultural Publishers' Association, Chicago: Victor F. Hayden, executive secretary.

Aitkin-Kynett Co., Philadelphia: H. H. Kynett.

Alexander Hamilton Institute, New York City: D. E. Beebe and Frank Arkins.

American Legion Weekly, New York City: Gordon Hoge, advertising manager.

American Multigraph Sales Co., Cleveland: Tim Thrift.

American Newspaper Publishers' Association, New York City: T. H. Moore, assistant director.

American Statistical Association, New York City: Willford I. King.

Architectural Forum, New York City: Howard Meyers.

Architectural Record, New York City: J. D. Oakley, business manager.

Associated Business Papers, Inc., New York City: Donald Harris.

Atlantic Monthly, New York City: E. W. Bachman.

Audit Bureau of Circulations, Chicago: Art N. Apple, promotion manager.

Audit Bureau of Circulations, New York City: William F. Hoffman, New York manager.

Babson's Statistical Organization, Wellesley Hills, Mass., Roger W. Babson and C. N. Stone.

J. W. Barber, Advertising Agency, Boston: H. F. Barber.

Barton, Durstine and Osborn, New York City: C. E. Haring and Mary L. Alexander.

George Batten Co., New York City: F. M. Lawrence, secretary, and T. O. Grissell.

Edward L. Bernays, New York City.

Georg Birnbaum, ALA Anzeigen Aktiengesellschaft, Berlin, Germany.

The Blackman Company, New York City: J. K. Fraser.

Bromfield and Co., Inc., New York City.

Bureau of Business Research, New York University, New York City: Dr. Lewis H. Haney.

California Fruit Growers' Exchange, Los Angeles: Paul S. Armstrong, advertising manager.

Earnest Elmo Calkins, New York City.

Campbell Soup Company, Camden, N. J.: R. M. Budd, advertising department.

Chain Store Age, New York City: Godfrey M. Lebhar, Bertram Lebhar.

Chamber of Commerce of the United States, Washington: Alvin E. Dodd.

Fred E. Clark, Evanston, Ill.

Class, Chicago: G. D. Crain, Jr.

Colgate and Co., Jersey City: George S. Fowler.

Margaret Cone, New York City.

Coolidge Advertising Co., Des Moines: R. E. Broholm, vice-president.

The John Crerar Library, Chicago.

Critchfield and Co., Chicago: J. J. Hartigan.

Crowell Publishing Co., New York City: J. W. Hayes, Research Department.

Current Opinion, New York City: Romeyn B. Scribner.

Curtis Publishing Co., New York City: Earl M. Wilson, manager of the New York Office.

Curtis Publishing Co., Philadelphia: Charles Coolidge Parlin.

D'Arcy Advertising Co., St. Louis.

The Dauchy Company, New York City: George E. Harris, president.

Devoe and Reynolds, Inc., New York City: Theodore F. Damm.

Dennison Manufacturing Co., Framingham, Mass.: H. W. Hardy.

Reuben H. Donnelley, New York City.

C. S. Duncan, Association of Railway Executives, Washington, D. C.

Eastern Film Corporation, New York City: Frank O. Tichenor.

R. O. Eastman, Inc., New York City: Lenna V. Wallace.

Educational Magazine Publishing Co., Inc., Brooklyn: Henry S. Chapin.

Harriet Elias, New York City.

The Erickson Company, New York City: Guy Richards.

A. E. Fitkin Co., New York City: E. Paul Young.

Ford, Bacon and Davis, New York City.

C. W. Frerk, London, England, advertising consultant.

Fuller and Smith, Cleveland: Edward S. Swazey.

General Motors Corporation, Detroit: J. H. Dreibelbis and H. G. Weaver.

Greve Advertising Agency, Inc., St. Paul: S. Greve, president.

S. Roland Hall, Easton, Pa.

Hart, Shaffner and Marx, Chicago: C. W. Chapin, advertising manager.

Charles W. Hoyt Co., Inc., New York City: Roy H. Burrill, manager of the Contract Department.

Hupp Motor Corporation, Detroit: F. W. Munro, Advertising Department.

Illinois Power and Light Corporation, Chicago: Jennie L. Schram.

The *Inland Printer* Chicago: Harry Hillman.

International Business Machines Corporation, New York City: Clarence Snyder, advertising manager.

International Magazine Co., F. D. Wood, Research Department.

Iron Age, New York City: H. B. Todd, manager of the Department of Research.

Iron Trade Review, Cleveland: John Henry.

The C. Ironmonger, Advertising Agency, New York City: C. Ironmonger.

Jell-O Company, Inc., Leroy, N. Y.: A. L. LaBounty, advertising manager.

Johnson, Read and Co., Chicago: George A. Read, vice-president and A. Jenkins, manager of the Contract-Rate Department.

Ray D. Lillibridge, Inc., New York City: Otis Allen Kenyon.
H. E. Lesan Advertising Agency, New York City: Charles Lansdown, secretary and treasurer.
Library Bureau, New York City: E. E. L. Taylor, assistant manager.
Library of Congress, Washington, D. C., chief bibliographist.
Life Savers, Inc., Port Chester, N. Y.: M. B. Bates, advertising manager.
Wilmot Lippincott, New York City.
Thomas F. Logan, Inc., New York City: J. O. Bauer, manager of the Media Department.
Lord and Thomas, Chicago.
McCall Company, New York City: John Wenzel.
H. K. McCann, New York City.
McGraw-Hill Co., New York City: M. S. McGhie.
The Eugene McGuckin Co., Philadelphia.
McJunkin Advertising Co., Chicago: F. B. Avery, manager of the Space Department.
Macfadden Publications, New York City: P. L. Atkinson and C. A. Rheinstrom.
Mac Martin Advertising Agency, Minneapolis, Minn.
The *Mailbag*, Cleveland: Leonard W. Smith.
The Manternach Company, Hartford, Conn.: John Magee and O. C. Mosley.
The Meredith Publications, Des Moines, Iowa: L. W. Lane.
Metropolitan Life Insurance Co., New York City: R. W. Sparks, deputy manager.
Metropolitan Life Insurance Co., New York City: Lenore A. Tafel.
Mitchell Advertising Agency, Inc., Minneapolis: J. H. Mitchell.
William T. Mullally, Inc., New York City: F. Ehli, Space Section.
Condé Nast Publications, Greenwich, Conn.: Sara Hamilton Birchall.
The Nation's Business, Washington, D. C.: Victor Whitlock.
National Retail Dry Goods Association, New York City: William A. Fitzgerald.
Newark Public Library, Newark, N. J.
The *News,* New York City: L. E. McGivena.
Newspaper Advertiser Publishing Co., New York City.
New York Evening Journal, New York City: W. G. Hobson, advertising director.
New York Telephone Co., New York City: B. F. Young.
New York Times, New York City: Louis Wiley.
The 100,000 Group of American Cities, Chicago: L. M. Barton, secretary and treasurer.
The *Oregonian,* Portland: J. A. Davidson, manager of the Merchandising Service Department.
Outlook Company, New York City.
Pace and Pace, New York City: Homer S. Pace.

Parker Pen Co., Janesville, Wisc., Kenneth Parker, advertising manager.

Periodical Publishers' Association, New York City: R. E. Rindfusz.

Pictorial Review, New York City: B. A. Mackinnon.

Powers Accounting Machine Co., New York City: M. E. Gould and H. R. Russell, general sales manager.

John O. Powers Company, New York City.

Printers' Ink Publications, New York City: R. W. Palmer and John Allen Murphy.

The *Red Book Magazine,* New York City.

Ward G. Reeder, Ohio State University, Columbus, O.

Review of Reviews, New York City: F. W. Stone.

Joseph Richards Advertising Company, New York City: W. E. Randall, space buyer.

Jason Rogers, New Rochelle, N. Y.

Ruggles and Brainerd, New York City.

School of Commerce, Northwestern University, Evanston, Ill., L. D. Herrold.

Frank Seaman, New York City.

Horace Secrist, Northwestern University, Chicago.

A. W. Shaw Co., Chicago: C. C. Cummins, Advertisers' Service Bureau.

Carl Snyder, New York City.

Standard Oil Co., New York City: D. F. Brown.

Standard Paper Manufacturing Co., Richmond, Va.: J. S. Sutton.

Standard Rate and Data Service, Chicago: Walter Botthof, president.

The Stetson Press, Boston, Mass.: Henry Kuhns.

Street Railways Advertising Co., New York City: F. R. Barnard, national advertising manager.

The *Sun,* New York City: George Benneyan, manager of the Research Department.

David C. Thomas Co., Chicago: John M. McDonald.

Tracy-Parry Co., Philadelphia: E. S. Parry.

William C. Wales, Southern Methodist University, Dallas, Texas.

Artemas Ward, Inc., New York City: W. Harold Laughlin.

S. D. Warren Co., Boston: E. L. Johnson.

Westinghouse Electric and Manufacturing Co., East Pittsburgh: W. C. Koehler, Supply Sales Department.

PERCIVAL WHITE

CONTENTS

PART I

AN OUTLINE OF SCIENTIFIC PROCEDURE

PART II

THE PRODUCT TO BE ADVERTISED

PART III

THE AUDIENCE

PART IV

THE ADVERTISING CAMPAIGN

FIGURES

ADVERTISING RESEARCH

INTRODUCTION

THE SCOPE OF ADVERTISING RESEARCH

Advertising research is the application of the scientific method to advertising. Scientific method is the same whether applied to physics, biology, geology, or advertising. It begins with the gathering of facts, continues with the registration and measurement of the data thus obtained, and then arranges, charts, and tabulates them. Finally, it draws tentative conclusions. When these have been tested exhaustively and reduced to a workable hypothesis, they are generally termed "principles" or "laws."

To speak of a law in relation to so inexact a subject as advertising may, at first thought, seem presumption. Sciences, however, vary greatly in precision. Mathematics, it is true, is an exact or abstract science, the laws of which are obtained by deduction and are based on methods rather than on observations. Biology and psychology, on the other hand, are general sciences, using the methods and laws of other sciences as the basis of their principles. Advertising, like medicine and education, is an applied science, or, in the words of Huxley, the application of pure science to particular classes of problems.

The Scientific Approach to Advertising

The first step in approaching advertising scientifically (and to advertising men perhaps the most difficult step) is to divest one's self of preconceived notions, personal convictions, and confidence in one's mastery of the subject. The mind must be open to every new idea, whether it upsets previous theories or not. The mental mood must be objective, not subjective. Bias, prejudice, and persuasion must be cast out. Data must not be accepted at their face value, but investigated at their source. The aim must be to criticize, but not to condemn; to analyze, but not to destroy. The truth alone must rule. The first step, in other words, is to acquire the *scientific attitude.*

The second requisite for the scientific study of advertising is a working knowledge of the *scientific method.* This technique, this procedure, is substantially the same regardless of the subject approached, and it is simple enough for any intelligent person to master.

A third qualification for advertising research is the *scientific outlook.* This is merely an acquaintance with what science is doing in other fields of human activity, together with a grasp of the interrelated factors. A broad perspective of commercial and economic endeavor will simplify the task of studying advertising, which then assumes a position of relatvely minor importance. Once the awe is taken from advertising, its glamour disappears, and its workings, though less impressive, are easier to understand.

While it is difficult to approach the broader aspects of advertising in the entirely objective manner which is to be recommended, the student should at least attempt to do this; and such an attempt should be his first task. Perhaps it is safer to make one's entry as a skeptic rather than as a convert, since those who profess a knowledge of advertising, together with the overwhelming mass of literature which they have produced, place little stress on the unfavorable aspects of the subject.

Certain portions of this book, by erring in the other direction, aim to be an antidote for such propaganda and to suggest some of the avenues of inquiry which may be followed in the more critical approach. But it should be realized that an attitude which is iconoclastic, or even wholly critical, will defeat the ends which science sets itsef. Once aware of the shortcomings of advertising, the student should bend his efforts to improve it and should take measures to apply it more effectively than can be done by those who have not been trained to recognize its limitations.

What Is Advertising?

Advertising, like storing, financing, transporting, and selling, is one of the fundamental marketing functions. Normally it is no more important than some of these functions, and is less important than others. As an aid to distribution, it informs, it educates, it establishes concepts of value, and it creates and directs demand. Advertising has been called one of the most vital forces, for good and evil, in this country. Its uses fall chiefly under the following heads:

1. *Information.*—Advertising, by broadcasting news to the consumer, serves to coördinate supply and demand. For example, the California orange growers can sell their crop in the East because of the contact estabished between producer and consumer by their coöperative advertising. Furthermore, mass production of staple articles is possible because of the informative powers of the manufacturer's advertising, which links together a waiting demand and a ready supply, for mutual profit.

2. *Education.*—Advertising is often used as an educational force. A new product is introduced, and meets prejudices born of tradition and ignorance. But it may attain to popularity through the educational effect of advertising. The manufacturer is constantly educating his prospective buyers. When he has once convinced them of the utility of his product, he goes on to show them new uses and better ways to take advantage of old uses.

3. *Conception of Values.*—Advertising is often considered a part of selling. Its sole justification is as an adjunct to selling. Unlike selling, however, it is an impersonal force. It must be judged at its face value, minus much of the emotional appeal which it is possible to develop in personal salesmanship. To this extent, perhaps, its service is more real. It establishes the ideas of the institution that it represents, it creates good will for the advertiser, it builds up a personality for him, it serves to associate his reputation with his goods. It goes without

saying that should the accomplishments of the advertiser fail consistently to substantiate his claims, the concept of value created by his advertising will not endure.

4. *Creation and Direction of Demand.*—Advertising cannot increase the ability of the individual or of the group to buy. The resources of the buying public remain the same regardless of advertising. If advertising increases the consumer's expenditure for one product, it tends to reduce his ability to purchase other products. What advertising does is to increase and direct the will to purchase, by appealing to the fundamental buying motives of the individual or group.

The Rise of Advertising

It has been claimed, by some of those who help to spend the money, that over a billion dollars are appropriated annually for advertising in the United States. Despite its meteoric development, however, and the publicity it has brought upon itself, advertising is still one of the least scientific of all business activities. There are several reasons for this:

In the first place, the rapidity with which advertising has grown, and the profit it has brought to its supporters, have made them consider it unnecessary to carry on any widespread collection of basic data. Advertising has thus far been cultivated extensively; the period of its intensive cultivation is only just beginning.

In the second place, the ignorance concerning advertising has been profound, except on the part of advertising agents and publishers. Much advertising has been done because the business man said to himself: "My competitors are advertising; therefore I also must advertise." As in similar cases, ignorance has been accompanied by reverence. To some minds advertising bears a remote likeness to religion.

In the third place, advertising has hitherto been accepted largely upon faith. Not a few advertising men are endowed with that same faith that, in earlier days, sufficed to move mountains. The miracles they have performed have increased their confidence and their veneration. The lifeless businesses that they have quickened are numbered in the hundreds and are proclaimed far and wide. The failures of advertising, to be sure, are seldom recorded, except perhaps in the archives of a university or in some other convenient burial place. This condition is natural and excusable.

The Applied Science of Advertising

In order to give the reader an idea of the field which this book is to cover, and to indicate in a general way the methods of approach to the subject, a summary of all the chapters will be given at the outset.

Advertising problems may be approached either empirically or scientifically. The empirical method is that based on experience, without conscious attempt to formulate principles. Plans and judgments are based upon precedents, guesses, and recollections, which, though they may be unrelated and unorganized, are often shrewdly and profitably applied. The empirical method deserves credit for bringing all of business, and especially advertising, to its present state of development.

The scientific approach to advertising problems is that based upon organized and systematized observation, subjecting all data to scrutiny and comparison, and testing every finding for its validity and truth. Though this approach is more satisfying than empiricism, it normally requires painstaking study, often resulting in apparent delay and expense which do not always seem to be justified.

Scientific procedure may be divided into four processes: *observation, comparison, generalization,* and *verification.* The whole approach to advertising research falls into this fourfold division, and the subject will so be treated here.

Scientific observation and comparison vary widely in different branches of study. Where conditions can be controlled, as in a laboratory, one sort of observation may be used. In advertising research controlled conditions may to some extent be realized, as in the practice of experimental psychology; but where it is impossible to control conditions, observations are more difficult. Here, economic and statistical methods of research may be applied. Chapter I will discuss "The Applied Science of Advertising."

Methods of Observation

In making observations the methods of sociological and economic research are for the most part depended on, but in certain areas of investigation the methods of psychological research are used. In work of the latter sort original sources may usually be tapped directly; while in the former type true observation is rare and difficult. Data are usually secondhand. Whereas the psychologist performs his own experiments and records the results, the economist ordinarily makes use of material which he himself did not originate.

An important objective of advertising psychology is the study of the consumer of advertised goods. Such studies, if carried on in sufficient number, serve to measure features about advertising which would otherwise defy scientific analysis.

Ordinary reporting is another method of making first-hand observations. Reporters, field men, interviewers, or enumerators, as they are variously called, travel about among consumers and among various marketing functionaries, recording facts.

Still another method of observation of original sources is through correspondence. Letters from interested parties, such as buyers, sellers, or authorities, constitute a practical and easily utilized fund of information. Questionnaires, also mailed in, are useful indicators, if skillfully handled.

The various "Methods of Observation" are described in Chapter II.

Methods of Analysis and Comparison

As various items come in from the field, they must be assembled, sorted, and classified. If the investigation has been carefully planned, this task will not be extremely difficult; but there are sure to be factors not allowed for in advance, and these when discovered must be given their proper weight.

The mere recording of qualitative data gives an idea of what the marketing situation is; but no adequate conception can be had without considering the data quantitatively. This requires statistical treatment. Statistics, in fact, are used mainly for the purpose of comparing data. In order that this work be done intelligently, facts must be reduced to a mathematical, or at least a measurable, basis. They must be standardized. They must be grouped. They must be so arranged that they may be readily compared and made easily understandable. Graphic representation is of assistance in doing this.

The assembling and analysis of facts is usually a tedious undertaking. The routine work involved is exacting. It cannot ordinarily be reduced to a mechanical basis without danger of missing some point, seemingly minor, which is indicative of an important opportunity for profit. Only through contact with the actual work of analyzing facts can the advertising investigator become imbued with the problem at hand. "Methods of Analysis and Comparison" will be examined in Chapter III.

Methods of Generalization

When the work of analysis has been ably done, the conclusions will often become self-evident. In practice, however, data are seldom complete enough to warrant sweeping or unqualified generalizations. Many allowances and exceptions have to be made.

The obtaining and comparing of advertising data often call for the application of several sciences; but the process of generalization is simply a matter of reasoning from these data as premises, and theoretically this requires no specialized knowledge. Though this would hold true if all the facts were available, business research is usually so crude that the process of generalization calls for the exercise of the keenest discrimination.

An understanding of logic in its more formal aspects is, naturally, of much assistance. Logic is of two kinds, inductive and deductive. Induction consists in the formulation of a principle as the result of a wide number of observations. It consists in reasoning from the specific to the general. Deduction is the converse process. It consists of applying a general principle to a particular case.

Both induction and deduction are used in advertising research. A wide number of observations must be made, the resultant data must be compared, and general principles must be established. These principles are to be used as advertising policies, subject to modification as individual conditions may require. The process of generalization is probably the most difficult task in advertising research, owing to the complexity of conditions and to the lack of development in this line of investigation. Chapter IV will treat of "Methods of Generalization."

Methods of Verification

Scientific procedure may often be distinguished from empirical procedure by the method used for testing results. Scientific procedure does not tolerate unsubstantiated inferences. No work can be termed scientific which is not susceptible of proof.

Proof in the more exact sciences calls for little comment, because it is usually effected without difficulty and is performed as a matter of course. But in so inexact a field as advertising it is frequently easier to establish a conclusion than it is to prove it. The problem of testing results becomes, therefore, of paramount importance, especially in view of an increased demand for accuracy on the part of those who finance research work.

To corroborate or to disprove findings requires not only a knowledge of the technical principles and process which have been used, but also of logic. Testing, furthermore, has developed a technique of its own, wherein the subject of error and its detection plays an important part. Chapter V describes "Methods of Verification."

Product Analysis

The first five chapters of this book treat of the scientific methods used in approaching certain specialized problems with which advertising research has to deal and to which the remainder of the book will be devoted. Of these specific problems those connected with the analysis of the product are first to be considered. The product is whatever is to be marketed, whether it be a raw material, an agricultural product, a manufactured article, or a service. It may even be, paradoxically, a market: for example, a newspaper or magazine may consider its product to be a market, *i.e.,* the market which the readers of the publication comprise. This is all the publication has to sell to its advertisers.

In modern marketing the product is the tangible echo of a demand. As demand changes, so the product changes, otherwise it is superseded. A major aim of research is, therefore, to know demand intimately, that the product may always be adapted to it.

Accordingly, while the average product has been, consciously or unconsciously, fashioned in response to the needs of the public, the properties of the product which have been developed in order to fulfill those needs are usually easier to define and to analyze than are the needs themselves. This is because the product is a definite, tangible thing, while demand itself is intangible, illusory, and capricious. The province of advertising is to show the pubic that it needs this product, and to create a call for this product, in preference to others of its class. In order to accomplish such a purpose, product analysis is necessary. The thing to be marketed must be examined, tested, criticised, discussed, and put to the various uses for which it was designed. Only through an intimate acquaintance with the product and its performance after being marketed can consistently successful advertising be prepared. Chapter VI is a discussion of "Product Analysis."

Determination of Appeals

Product analysis is the term usually associated with the study of the product, its uses, and its performance. Following upon this, a study must be made of the product in relation to those who are to buy it and of their reasons for buying it. What are the outstanding characteristics of this product which make it especially desired? What *appeal* does this product possess?

Obviously, these questions bring in many factors other than the product itself and lead to the realization that every element with which advertising research has to deal is inextricably connected with every other element. To determine which are the most effective appeals calls for an engineering knowledge of the product and of all its possible uses and advantages, translated into terms which are eminently human, which strike deeply a responsive chord, and which create an active desire for possession. Psychological experiment is often used in determining the appeals of a given product and in estimating their relative weights. Such experiments are, for the most part, simple and easy for anyone of scientific training to carry out. They must, however, be conducted with the greatest care, since chances for mistake occur at every step. Especial pains must be taken in the interpretation and application of results. Here, as elsewhere, a first-hand knowledge of people and a grounding in selling are a necessary balance to laboratory experiment. The "Determination of Appeals" will form the subject matter of Chapter VII.

The Product as Its Own Advertisement

There is no advertisement quite so good as the product itself. An automobile rolling down the street attracts more attention and creates more desire, for the most part, than any number of printed descriptions. The value of the product for self-advertisement is exemplified in *display,* which is the basic advertising form, requiring no medium, so-called, for carrying the message.

It is a principle of display to make the product appear in its most prepossessing guise. Articles on display are therefore usually shown in their very best manner, and quite commonly are ornamented and decked out to enhance the illusion of desirability. A further step in this direction has resulted in the development of the package. Packaging has become a matter of great consequence in the sale of many goods. The package can often present the merchandise in its most favorable light and at the same time serve other purposes, such as protecting it from damage and offering it in neat, standardized units of weight or number. The package also permits the direct application to the product of the advertising message.

Another topic which is germane is the trade mark. This is a device normally applied direct to the product, whereby it is identified with its maker or seller. These questions will be taken up in Chapter VIII, "The Product as its Own Advertisement."

Consumer Analysis

The advertising man must know the consumer just as the salesman must know his prospect. In order to arouse a desire for the product, it is necessary to learn as much as possible of the character, habits, abilities, disabilities, prejudices, and finances of the possible purchaser or user.

Just as in the product appeals must be looked for, so in the consumer buying motives must be sought. The one set of elements balances the other. What sort of man is the logical consumer of this product? What sort of man, in practice, does buy it? How closely does this product meet his requirements? How nearly able is he to make the purchase? What possibilities are there of discovering in him a response which has not yet been appealed to? In other words, how can he be reached, better than at present, by advertising?

Although the deep-lying psychological product-consumer relationship is the fundamental problem here, there are other matters of moment. Assuming a definite and successful product appeal and a correctly analyzed predisposition towards the product, there is still the delicate task of reaching the consumer through advertising. Where and how can he be found? By what means can the advertising appeal be brought home to him most successfully, and at the most auspicious time? These are all matters for experiment and study, the methods of which will be enumerated in Chapter IX, "Consumer Analysis."

Market Analysis

Markets consist of consumers in the aggregate. Psychological studies serve to delineate the consumer as an individual; statistics are used to appraise consumers as a group. Markets must be divided and subdivided in various ways before the advertising campaign can effectively be planned. Markets may be divided geographically, for example, with a view to finding some advertising medium which will reach prospects without undue waste. Consumers, again, may be divided by social status, since an appeal which will prove effective in one social stratum may be weak in another. Markets, too, may be divided according to the channels of distribution available: it is necessary to advertise in one way to those who may be reached through department stores and in another way to those who buy through chain stores.

By methods of marketing research it is possible to obtain specific knowledge as to the location of buyers and the best methods of distributing merchandise to them. Market analysis makes plain what sales obstacles are to be overcome and indicates how advertising may be used to facilitate the flow of goods from producer to consumer. "Market Analysis" is the subject of Chapter X.

Classes of Media

Advertising must reach consumers through some sort of *medium*. Where ideal conditions exist, the medium and the market are, from the advertiser's point of view, coincident. Unfortunately, conditions are usually rather far from being ideal, so it becomes necessary to select one of several possible types of medium, none of which can be expected to give complete "coverage."

Shall the advertising be run in a newspaper, a magazine, on outdoor bulletins, or on car cards? Or shall direct mail, specialty, radio, or other form of advertising be employed? Or, again, may a combination of several of these be desirable? Media research presupposes an acquaintance with the various generic types of media, their advantages and disadvantages, their potentialities and limitations. Chapter XI describes the various "Classes of Media" and gives examples of media research as it has been successfully applied to each class.

Essential Characteristics of Media

The first point that comes up in the discussion of any particular class of media or any special medium has to do with the essential characteristics which make it fitted or unfitted for the purposes in hand. What elements must the medium have in order best to carry the message of the product under consideration?

If the medium is a publication, there will be many facts about it to be ascertained and recorded in quantitative terms, such as its content, the interest which readers have in its content, its editorial policy, and various other matters. Second, the research must examine the ability of the publication to cover successfully the market sought. This is usually done by a study of its circulation. Third, the cost of the medium, in relation to the results obtained, must be considered. Chapter XII will discuss these "Essential Characteristics of Media."

Duplication of Media

Duplication is one of those words glibly used by advertising men which no one seems fully to understand. The methods of determining duplication have been fairly well developed, but what to do with the resultant information is largely a matter of guesswork.

It is necessary to compare various media *in the same field,* such, for example, as those in the general magazine field. It is also necessary to attempt to determine which of several publications is best suited to carry the advertising. Often it is desirable to use more than one. It now becomes apparent that the two or more magazines have a great deal of circulation in common. The amount of duplication, its character, and the effect thereof is a matter which research, and research only, can determine. This subject, "Duplication of Media," is treated in Chapter XIII.

Selection of Media

The real objective of media study is to select and to combine those media which will most nearly "cover" all of the market which is being sought, with the minimum of waste. To find the best possible combination of media is a matter for research and for good business judgment.

Space-buying is the logical outgrowth of media research. The media must be selected and combined to meet certain requirements of the market. But they must also be chosen with reference to the money available for the purchase of blank space. Here the problem is brought to a sharp financial focus. The cost of reaching customers will vary widely in accordance with the schedule of media selected. "Selection of Media" is treated in Chapter XIV.

Analysis of the Marketing Facilities

Prior to the actual planning of the advertising campaign a study must be made of the means for marketing the product. The advertising is merely a part of the machinery for doing this. Coördination of advertising with the selling plan is of vital importance. If jobbers are used, a given type of advertising may be effective, while if sales are made direct this type might prove unsuccessful. Where distribution is local, national magazines would be unsatisfactory media, except in unusual cases.

Research considers advertising as an aid in selling and accordingly builds advertising upon a study of the market and of the trade channels feeding that market. Half the task of advertising lies in getting ready to advertise. A study of the marketing facilities requires a different sort of research from the other studies made, and it is less a matter of psychological and statistical analysis than of judgment based on economic facts and laws, of current practices in marketing, and of the personal and practical aspects of the situation. The problem is, none the less, one for research. Chapter XV will deal with the "Analysis of the Marketing Facilities."

Planning the Campaign

All the factors thus far considered are fundamental. They must be analyzed preparatory to the planning of the campaign. Nor are even these all-sufficient. Other circumstances must be taken into account, such, for instance, as the forecasting of business conditions, with a view to seasonal changes, cyclical fluctuations, and the secular trend. As in making any other major company plans, a knowledge of the future policies to be pursued is a prerequisite. In practice the sales programme is ordinarily laid down first, the advertising being made to conform with it. The ideal method is, of course, to make all marketing plans at the same time.

No consideration having as yet been given to the definite form which the advertising is to take, the present task will also include the rough shaping of the advertisements to be used, the amount of space for each, the periodicity of insertion, the planning of series of advertisements, and the other general arrangements which must be handed on, in the form of instructions, to the man in charge of the production of advertising. "Planning the Campaign" is treated in Chapter XVI.

Computing the Value of Advertising

Both before and after the planning process, it is desirable to compute the value of the advertising. It is an important function of research to reckon the results of advertising which has already been run and of that which is to run in the future. So poorly developed is the science of advertising at present that many companies have only a hazy idea of the benefits which their advertising brings them, while some do not even attempt to measure the results.

It is true that this is a difficult thing to do, but much has been done and advertising research can do more. In mail-order advertising or other *keyed* advertising, so-called, the results of any given advertisement can be appraised with a considerable degree of definiteness, if not with complete accuracy. In retail advertising, also, the sales of an advertised article bring the store definite and measurable returns, though these returns are not so easily computed as might be supposed. By analogy with the results obtained in the more easily measured returns, and by other means, approximate methods may be developed for checking other types of advertising. Methods of "Computing the Value of Advertising" are described in Chapter XVII.

Budgets and Appropriations

All along the line the man in charge of advertising will have been confronted with limitations imposed by cost. These are ever present. It is in keeping with the scientific approach to advertising to decide in advance what these limitations shall be and to set aside a budget or appropriation which shall be divided and subdivided as a regular part of the programme. The advertising plan as submitted to the executives who disburse the moneys for the campaign is far more convincing when it contains a detailed schedule of the advertising, an itemized statement of the various costs to be met, and a calculation of the net results, in dollars and cents, which the advertising may be expected to bring in. All this is perfectly possible of accomplishment. This subject, under the heading of "Budgets and Appropriations," will be taken up in Chapter XVIII.

Experimental Campaigns

In accordance with a practice which was first developed in the scientific laboratory, of experimenting on a small scale in order to determine what results will come about when a plan is put into effect on a large scale, the method of trial campaigns has been inaugurated. Here a miniature marketing plan is conducted in a limited territory or is otherwise restricted in field or extent. Although the amount of money and the lapse of time is small, a basis can often be arrived at for determining what profit may be expected from a complete and full-sized campaign. Another advantage of the trial campaign is that it permits various experiments, modifications, and novel schemes to be attempted at small expense. The trial campaign is parallel to the plan of experimenting with a few models of a new manufactured device before going into production with it.

The trial campaign is nothing more or less than the application, under practical business conditions, of the method of test described in Chapter VII. It is the next best thing to putting the plan into complete operation and judging by what happens —this being, after all, the only absolute test. "Experimental Campaigns," in their relation to advertising, are discussed in Chapter XIX.

Planning the Advertisement

The nearer one comes to the point of actually producing advertisements, the more difficult it is to apply methods even approximating those of pure science, and the more the element of creative art enters. Thus, while it is feasible through psychological tests to determine the most compelling advertising appeals inherent in a given product, it is not possible through mere laboratory experiment to put this appeal into vital and living form. The appeal for a certain canned product may be to the appetite, but it requires a good deal more than a statement of this fact to make the buying public hungry enough to go and buy the can.

As a matter of fact, nearly every product has a number of possible appeals. The force of each of these will be found to have been modified by a complex array of factors, such as the consumer's buying habits, the methods of distribution, the money available, the results of the test campaign, and the media chosen (which usually reserve the right to say what appeals they will permit to be used in the advertising which they carry).

Research may be of assistance, however, in selecting the theme of the advertising, and this is the preliminary step in the actual work of production of advertisements. The problem is that of translating the appeals in a way which will prove effective and practical and which will meet with the countless limitations imposed by conditions as they happen to be. The theme is the graphic outcome of the advertising plan. The theme is usually the creation of the "idea man," an individual who is supposed to have the faculty for taking the whole merchandising development, as brought to this point through research, and of kindling it with life. Chapter XX tells how research is used in "Planning the Advertisement."

Research as Applied to Copy

The copy, that is, the verbal message which the advertisement carries, is merely the theme put into words, accompanied by such information as may be necessary to assist the reader to satisfy the want which the advertisement is supposed to arouse, such as the name of the advertiser, the source from which the product may be obtained, the selection of lines, sizes, and models, and so on.

Research can make and analyze observations from which conclusions may be drawn as to the most effective form of copy. Tests of copy may also be made to advantage, and this is a function of research capable of much development. "Research as Applied to Copy" is treated in Chapter XXI.

Research as Applied to Layout

For the most part, the idea man must gain his effect through the use of the printed page, or by an outdoor bulletin on which displays are posted or painted, or by the use of a letter. The media which do not impose this particular limitation upon him impose others so much more irksome that they are less extensively used. The problem of layout is, therefore, one of the first with which the producer of advertisements has to deal.

By this time research, at first the prime mover in the steps of advertising procedure, has taken a passive and secondary place. Research cannot show how the layout should be made, but through it generalizations may be reached as to the most effective plans for the layout, the masses of light and shade, the introduction of art work, and so on. Furthermore, research methods can be used effectively to test the validity of any given layout, and its adequacy as an interpretation of the theme selected. Chapter XXII is an exposition of "Research as Applied to Layout."

Research as Applied to Illustration

Copy writing is a development of the science of rhetoric. Commercial illustrating is based upon the science of outline, color, and chiaroscuro, the three elements of graphic art. Research may be used to develop a knowledge of such science and to indicate what principles may most forcefully be applied in any given instance.

Whether color may be used to advantage and how it should be used, for example, may be determined by scientific methods. Color has been found to make definite psychological imprints and to call forth certain responses. It is therefore important to know what color or combination of colors brings a favorable reaction and which colors bring an unfavorable association or negative effect. There is hence much to be learned from "Research as Applied to Illustration." This subject is treated in Chapter XXIII.

Research as Applied to Color

Strictly speaking, color is a subdivision of the study of illustration, but it is of such increasing importance, and is being so much more widely used every year, that it deserves special treatment. Color and its effect upon the mentality and the emotions of the subject may be studied to excellent advantage by the methods of the newer psychology. The question of "Research as Applied to Color" is discussed in Chapter XXIV.

Research as Applied to Typography

Type faces, like color or words or a picture, have an immediate and primary effect upon the mind. That is, they carry a *denotation*. They also have a secondary, subconscious effect, or *connotation*. A line of type may convey an idea to the reader's mind which is quite apart from the message which the words themselves seek to impart. It is important for the advertiser to know what this secondary and often hidden effect may be. Research can be the guide here, but only (as in all other problems of producing advertisements) as an aid to the creative artist or artisan. Chapter XXV deals with "Research as Applied to Typography."

Conclusion

The scientific approach to any subject is of necessity critical. But it is extremely difficult to be critical and to preserve, at the same time, an attitude of scientific impartiality. The aim of his book is to provide the reader with some of the equipment necessary in order that he may criticize advertising intelligently. Its aim is not to criticize, but to aid in the development of criticism. At the end of the book, however, where they will not obtrude unduly, have been inserted some personal opinions of the author, carrying the caption, "A Critique of Advertising." These observations are offered by way of conclusion to the book.

PART I

AN OUTLINE OF SCIENTIFIC PROCEDURE

CHAPTER I

THE APPLIED SCIENCE OF ADVERTISING

Modern science has now developed to the point where artificial barriers are breaking down. Its various methods of approach are coalescing. The accumulated experience of one department of science, together with the special methods which it has developed, suddenly becomes available for other departments. Since the object of science is to find connections between phenomena, and thus to correlate them, the rapid increase of scientific knowledge is leading to the solution of many problems hitherto deemed unsolvable.

The Field of Science

The growth of science during the past fifty years has been called greater than all its previous growth. Since Pasteur's time, astonishing advances have been made. But, even then, the importance of science was realized. "In our century," he said, "science is the soul of the prosperity of nations and the living source of all progress. What really leads us forward are a few scientific discoveries and their application."

Dr. Arthur D. Little, one of the country's foremost chemists, states: "It is difficult to speak of the commercial possibilities of research without conveying to those who are unfamiliar with them an impression of exaggeration. They are as great as those of industry itself. . . . Industry and finance are to-day so organized that industrial developments of the successes of the laboratory follow with a speed incomparably greater than that possible even twenty years ago."

In science, there is no limit to the amount of search which may be necessary in order to obtain the desired information. It requires scrutiny of every phase brought out in the search, and the significance of each phase to the problem in hand must be studied. Given the problem and its known elements, research is used solely in order to find out something, to add something to the known.

Good technique, keen analysis, and sound reasoning are the required qualities for scientific work; truth and reliability are essential. For performing any kind of research work, an individual must be equipped with a good education and the ability to use it. A research is valueless if performed carelessly, without regard for every fact brought to light.

Investigative research departments in the field of advertising may be likened to industrial research laboratories, such as are maintained by many large concerns for the solution of problems relating to their own lines. New facts discovered in advertising research are the source of ammunition for advertising campaigns.

Methods in Advertising Research

Advertising research may be carried out according to the empirical method, the scientific method, or a combination of both. This is a decided improvement over the intuitional procedure which antedated them and which still exists in many quarters.

The Empirical Method

The empirical method is the purely practical plan of procedure. It is a direct descendant of the original method of making observations and then drawing from them any acceptable conclusions which seem to fit the case. In each instance, a direct connection is made between the cause and the result. Thus, the original and primitive method of empirical reasoning was to explain phenomena by assigning them to the intervention of some superior being, because no other reasoning seemed to satisfy the facts as they appeared.

The empiricist of to-day must always be careful to state that he does not lay down an infallible law; he says merely that

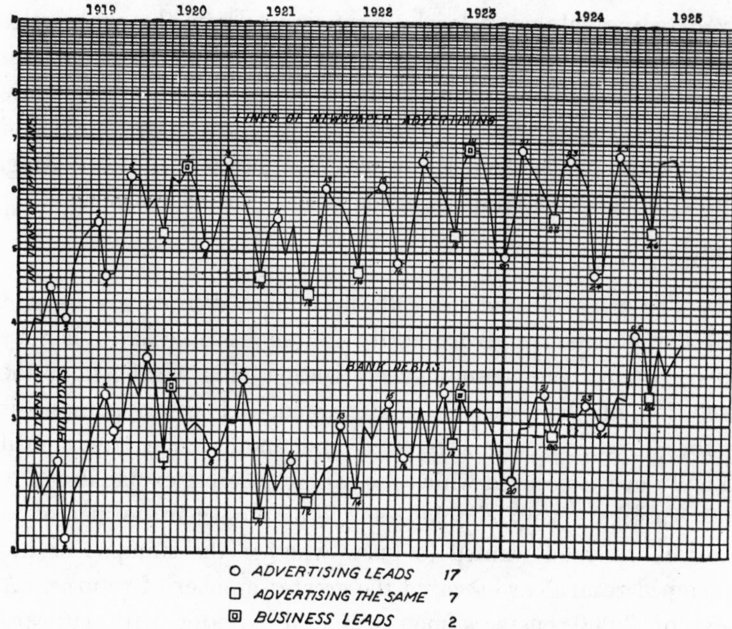

FIG. 1. AN EXAMPLE OF EMPIRICAL ANALYSIS

The upper line indicates the high and low points of the total number of lines of newspaper advertising in ten leading cities of the United States. The lower line represents the swings of bank debits in the same group of cities. The points marked by circles indicate the number of times advertising led business. The squares indicate the number of times business led advertising, and the "squares within squares" indicate that advertising turned the same month with business.

(Babson's Statistical Organization.)

from all his observations of experiences, such and such results have come about. The great value of the empirical method to the scientific investigator is that it points to certain possible conclusions which he can use as the basis of investigation. The objection to it lies in the fact that it offers no explanation of *why* a certain set of experiences should give rise to certain results.

Figure 1, drawn by Babson's Statistical Organization, is an example of empirical analysis. Through a study of business statistics, it was noted that there was a close relationship between a locality's amount of general business and the corresponding volume of local advertising. From the experiences charted on the graph, it appears that advertising leads business 17 times out of the 26 observations, is the same 7 times, while business leads twice. Phenomena may thus be compared and the results of the comparison used for purposes of forecasting, even though no attempt be made to show causal relations.

The Scientific Method

The scientific method calls first for a definitive statement of the problem, and ordinarily for an hypothesis. Then by observation, comparison, generalization, and verification, the solution of the problem is attempted. If the hypothesis is proved incorrect, it is rejected and another one tried, until finally one is secured which fits all the possible explanations.

To take a very simple example of the scientific method, a certain railroad wanted to know whether the stamped or unstamped return card secured the greater number of returns. A list of 2,000 business men was sent a letter with postcard enclosed. Half the names on the list were sent stamped cards, and half unstamped. The results were as follows:

PERCENTAGE OF RETURNS

Business	Stamped	Unstamped
Bankers	10.63	5.68
Lawyers	8.16	5.20
Contractors	7.44	3.74
Physicians	7.44	3.23
Dentists	5.85	2.71
Commission Men	5.00	2.61
Architects	4.49	1.06
Coal Dealers	2.65	1.78
Average	6.70	3.43

The observation and comparison being as above, the conclusion or generalization is that stamped envelopes secured a greater percentage of returns under every classification studied.

A number of firms doing research work act under the assumption that the methods which they use are peculiarly their own, and they take the position of not wishing to divulge any of their information. Obviously, such a spirit is contrary to the conceptions of modern science. A policy of secrecy is almost certain to retard progress, because if the results of one investigation are withheld from other investigators, the advance in method and in resulting data is unnecessarily retarded. Each investigator must then devise his own methods from the ground up, and is not able to make use of an accumulated body of information.

The Combined Empirical and Scientific Method

In actual practice, advertising research is usually a combination of the empirical and scientific methods. For example, the Joseph Richards Company, Inc. (Stanley I. Clark), uses them both in the following case:

As soon as a new client is secured, a questionnaire is submitted to him, consisting of about 100 questions, classified under the following headings:

1. Organization
2. Product
3. Production
4. Market
5. Demand
6. Distribution
7. Competition
8. Merchandising
9. Sales
10. Advertising

The experience of the client is used as the empirical basis of the recommendations given to the client. To fill in any gaps in the information, or to clear up some doubtful point, special analyses are made. In one instance, a large manufacturer was distributing entirely through his own retail stores, located in the principal cities from coast to coast. The agency felt that there was a large volume of business to be secured in smaller localities not covered by the manufacturer's stores. These smaller cities were covered only by traveling representatives calling directly upon the consumer at infrequent intervals. The agency recommended that an authorized dealer be secured in each of these localities, and submitted estimates of what the securing of this additional distribution would cost. The manufacturer authorized an investigation to determine whether the hypothesis of the agency was correct, the result of which was to substantiate it in every respect. In fact, the survey showed that the business obtainable by the new policy would be greater than estimated by about 10 per cent.

The agency knew from its experience that certain conditions existed, and on the basis of these made certain recommendations. In order to prove whether or not its recommendations were correct, a survey was made. Thus the empirical and scientific methods were combined.

As a matter of fact, most modern scientific work is such a combination. The method of Bacon is too "theoretical," the empirical method is too "practical," to use a distinction which perhaps is unsound. In any event, modern science depends largely upon empiricism. To this extent, empiricism is scientific.

Error

Scientific procedure emphasizes the need for accuracy at every step. Error is defined as a departure from what is true, exact, or right. It may occur at any point in the observation, comparison, generalization, or verification of the facts in question. To understand and guard against error, it is first of all essential to find out the reasons which most frequently cause its occurrence. These are:

1. *Insufficient Evidence.* There is often a great temptation to draw inferences when the evidence is insufficient to support them. For example, the observations made may not cover a wide enough range to be representative, or not be sufficient in quantity to form a true picture of conditions generally. Such error as this can be guarded against. It is a type of error, however, which is to be found in much research work.

2. *Incorrect Method.* If error is to be excluded rigidly, it is necessary to make use of the scientific method of procedure as outlined in the remainder of this chapter. For example, it would be productive of error to correlate varying sets of factors which had no true relation to each other. Much error in mod-

ern research is due to forcing facts to fit the case. Examples will be shown in later chapters.

3. *Ignorance.* Research calls for a breadth of knowledge on the part of the individual or individuals in charge which goes beyond the mere subject under discussion. Ignorance of certain external, but modifying, factors might affect the results of research and bring about the introduction of error.

4. *Bias.* Research, to be free from error, must be unbiased. Bias may be either conscious or unconscious. To avoid the latter, the research staff should be composed of individuals without any personal interest in the outcome of the investigation.

There is, of course, a certain amount of error which will naturally creep in due to no fault of the research man himself. He cannot be responsible for over- or understatements by people whom he interviews. He cannot guard entirely against certain clerical errors on the part of his helpers, though he should, of course, check all such work. Mistakes of this nature, however, tend naturally to compensate each other. If the number of observations is sufficient, the error on one side will probably be nearly equal to that on the other side, while the total result will be substantially the same as though the errors had not been made. There is small comfort in this, however, unless the errors are known and are measured.

The subject of error is of such importance, when dealing with the raw material of advertising, that methods of coping with it will be considered throughout the remainder of the book.

Ways of Approaching Advertising Problems

There are a number of possible approaches to any given advertising research problem. For example, the economic approach deals with the factors affecting the wealth of the market, notably its buying power. The psychological approach concerns the behavior of the individual buyer and his response to various methods of attracting attention, arousing interest, and turning desire into action. The statistical approach takes the quantitative and qualitative data which have been gathered and formulates them into averages, or otherwise makes it possible to compare and generalize.

At times, other scientific approaches must be utilized. The sociological approach may be required in certain cases. Chemical and physical analysis often plays a part in research connected with the product. In all cases, however, the procedure will follow the four steps of observation, comparison, generalization, and verification.

The Economic Approach

Economics, of all sciences, is perhaps the most useful in formulating the principles and practice of advertising research. Economics is the study of wealth, its production, distribution, and use. Economics is, therefore, the science underlying all business activity, of which advertising is only a part. Economists, dealing with the subject of wealth, have developed the principles governing its production, consumption, exchange, and distribution. They have dealt with the activities of business concerns as a whole, such as financing, manufacturing, and marketing. Advertising is the demand-creating function of marketing, and to some extent the method of making demand effective.

The economic view of advertising, therefore, envisages it as creating demand for the generic product rather than for the specific product of any one manufacturer. The economist may study the demand for tooth paste, but he will be less concerned with the methods to increase the demand for any one brand over the rest. If advertising is to justify itself in an economic sense, it must increase demand for the whole class of products, rather than for a single product at the expense of others. Therefore, advertising which is purely selfish, that is, which is aimed to secure sales for one brand to the detriment of other brands, is uneconomic, however profitable it may prove to the advertiser, the agency, and the publication.

Economics reveals the basis of the market and the marketing functions. It is predicated on the economic wealth of the market in question, its ability to buy. Psychology teaches the method of formulating the advertising so that it will reach this economic market, with its complex of characteristics. As opposed to their ability to buy, psychology will stress the mental characteristics of buyers. Advertising psychology deals with individuals rather than with masses. Economics always observes people in the aggregate, and deals with them in groups.

The basis of the usual economic investigation is a community or a group of communities, and the scale of living there. The procedure followed in economic research has much to recommend its use in pure advertising research. For example, the following steps are required:

1. The economic functions which it is desired to investigate are isolated. This will avoid the collection of many facts which are irrelevant, and will help to establish an hypothesis.

2. Relevant facts are gathered about the group or groups to be investigated.

3. These facts are tabulated and charted.

4. Conclusions are drawn from the statistical compilations of these groups.

5. The conclusions are verified by test and comparison with the hypothesis.

6. Conclusions are correlated with other than pure economic facts. The political situation, for example, often directly affects economics. So also various social factors. Purely statistical methods alone are rarely sufficient for the solution of an economic problem. It usually requires a wide experience in several fields of knowledge.

The value of economic studies to advertising has not been sufficiently obvious to cause a wide pursuit of economic studies by advertisers; yet this approach to advertising is highly important. Carson S. Duncan, of the Association of Railway Executives, one of the leaders in commercial research, contributes the following, which illustrates admirably the bearing of economic studies upon advertising:

The advertiser needs first to know the economic story lying behind the marketing of his product. There are many splendid illustrations of the way in which advertising has adjusted itself to changing conditions. Probably the citrus fruit campaigns illustrate the point clearly, and possibly as simply as any. I am inclined to believe, however, that the most interesting story lies behind the advertising campaign by such large millers as Washburn-Crosby, of Minneapolis.

A few years ago, flour was made in New England by local mills, which have all, or practically all, vanished, just as the local shoe shops have. These mills were displaced by brokers or wholesalers who handled the product of mills located in such places as Buffalo or Rochester or points farther west. With the rise of the flour mills in Minneapolis, competition increased and the brokers or jobbers in New England handled more than one kind of flour, but fought a losing fight with the bakers, who were developing rapidly.

It was at this time that the Minneapolis millers undertook to appeal directly to the consumer. For several years the Gold Medal advertisements attempted to glorify the work of the housewife, particularly in the kitchen over the hot cookstove. Any advertisement of four or five years ago will illustrate this point.

This also was a losing fight. If you will examine the recent advertisements by Washburn-Crosby you will see that they have given it up and that they have joined with the bakers in their appeal to the consumer.

The same thought is stated in general terms by A. Heath Onthank, chief of the Domestic Commerce Division of the Department of Commerce:

More should be done to tie in the minor movements and changes with the big underground economic currents which are the basis for the life of our people. Too little attention has been given to this phase of the subject, and too much to the various details of statistics. The problem of marketing goods nationally is not only one of gauging consumer preference and purchasing power, but also of the great economic developments which are occurring in the various sections of the country, and which tend to limit or to expand the sale of products.

The Psychological Approach

As in the case of economics, psychology is valuable both for its principles and for its technique. An understanding of attention, of stimulus and response, of association, of memory, and of motive serves to facilitate the shaping of advertising which will help to make the merchandising plan effective.

Psychology is the science of mental behavior. The psychological method of analysis calls for the observation of the human mind under controlled conditions. The latter point is of special significance. Whereas in the economic method of research, the factors in the field of observation are more or less tangible and measurable, the psychological method deals with the extremely elusive action of the human mind. If this is to be measured with even approximate accuracy, the conditions of the test must be arranged to avoid any influence, conscious or unconscious, which might affect the result. The use of the ordinary questionnaire, for example, is almost inevitably attended with a certain inaccuracy of results, because the conditions are not controlled. It is often impossible to frame satisfactory questions in an ordinary questionnaire which asks the person to whom it is sent to select some preferred item. Even if truthful and rational responses are elicited, they will not necessarily reflect the actual state of affairs, since much buying is irrational, and many of the strongest appeals are to the emotions rather than to the mind.

Psychology as applied to advertising is largely concerned with the methods by which the attention of the prospective purchaser is secured. The attention is attracted, other things being equal, to the thing which is seen first, last, or most often, to the thing which, because of its form of presentation, makes a vivid impression, or to the thing which brings associations to the mind and thus secures interest. These five conditions for attention are ordinarily termed:

1. Frequency
2. Primacy
3. Recency
4. Vividness
5. Association

The following example illustrates the psychological method of approach. A paragraph containing 50 words is arranged on cards, one word on each card. One word in the paragraph is repeated five times (frequency); there is a beginning and ending word (primacy) (recency); there is one word in large and one in small type (vividness); and there is one word with local association. These cards are turned over one after another before a given group, which is told to write down the words it remembers. It was found that if there are 50 in the group, then 50 may be expected to remember the repeated word, and above 40 to remember the first and last word, the vivid words, and the one with the local association. The conditions of the test are controlled. The members of the group do not know in advance what the nature of the test is. Each one has an equal opportunity to observe and to tabulate.

A psychological test of the attention value of advertisements in the *Saturday Evening Post* was conducted by Professors George B. Hotchkiss and Richard B. Franken of New York University. A reading assignment of an article on merchandising was given to a men's class of 175 students. No intimation was given of any advertising test. A week after the assignment was given, the test was made, only the 104 who had read the assignment being tested. The conditions were equal, since all tested had had an opportunity to read the issue of the *Saturday Evening Post* in question, and none of them knew that they were to be tested, or the conditions of the test.

All advertisements of a quarter-page and over in the issue, together with an equal number of advertisements from year-old issues, were pasted on thin cardboard, and keyed with a number in the upper right-hand corner. Each student was told to write the number of all the advertisements he was fairly certain he had seen in the test issue, and to put a circle around this number if he was absolutely certain of having seen it. Each advertisement was given one point for a number and two points for a number circled.

By this simple expedient, it was possible to determine, with considerable accuracy, the degree of attention which the advertisements possessed, for this particular group of men.

The psychological approach is important, in advertising research, because it strips the mind of barriers and inhibitions which other approaches cannot penetrate. The mind of the subject is dissected, one might almost say, its contents and its methods of operation being revealed to the observer, regardless of the will of the person who is being examined. Since advertising deals with emotion as well as with reason, and since few people understand the workings of their own minds, psychological methods are essential to successful research.

The Statistical Approach

The critical problem in advertising research centers round the reactions of consumers. In order to obtain a quantitative expression of qualitative facts, recourse is had to statistics. Statistics are merely applied mathematics. Through their use, consumers may be viewed in the aggregate or, in other words, as a market. Similarly, approach to the market may be expressed and reckoned with in quantitative terms. Since modern advertising must deal with consumers in masses, a working knowledge of the statistical method is second only in importance to an understanding of economics and psychology. "Statistics," says Herbert C. Hoover, "are a counterpoise to psychology in business—an anchor of basic facts to tie to."

Statistics represent facts, in so far as they may be expressed numerically. The so-called statistical method consists merely of collecting, recording, and observing quantitatively the data which relate to a given problem.

The first step in statistical research, as in any research, is to determine the problem or field for investigation. The next step is to fix upon a unit by which the statistical facts may be expressed. This unit may be already established. For example, the list of telephone subscribers, of home owners, or of automobile drivers may supply the material desired. It may be best to classify the statistical field according to income, occupation, or race. In a survey of consumer demand for milk in Philadelphia, made by the Bureau of Agricultural Economics, United States Department of Agriculture, the field, that is, the city of Philadelphia, was measured by individual families. Since, however, there was such a great difference in the economic and racial status of the individual families, the population was divided into the following eight groups:

Poor	Colored
Middle class	Italian
Well-to-do	Jewish
Wealthy	Suburban (well-to-do)

After the field of investigation has been divided into groups possessing common characteristics, the statistical data must be secured, as indicated in the following chapters. The statistical method requires, however, that such data selected comply with certain fundamental provisions. In the first place, they must be chosen so that they will be representative of the group under investigation. Second, the observations must be numerous enough to insure that the essential characteristics of the group are secured and that the conclusions will reflect true conditions.

The statistical method often requires comparison of one set of statistics with another. The sets of statistical facts which may be brought to bear upon one advertising or marketing problem may be many. Their effect cannot be judged unless they can be reduced to some common denominator. Hence the use of the various kinds of averages and index numbers.

A good example of the statistical approach to a marketing problem is shown in the Department of Commerce investigation of electrical merchandising lines (Trade Promotion Series, No. 9). Careful investigation was made of all data bearing upon the purchasing power for electrical appliance lines, purchasing inclination on the part of the population, availability of electric service, and economic conditions favoring the use of electrical appliances. The following factors were chosen as being fundamental:

1. Ratio of state population to total United States population, expressed in percentage.

2. Ratio of the native white population of each state to the total native white population of country, with due weight given to the purchasing power of the foreign-born and other peoples in the area, expressed as native white population equivalent in buying power for electrical appliances. The buying power of the native white population was taken as normally 100 per cent. Further adjustment was made of this factor to allow for a well-known

FIG. 2.—AN EXAMPLE OF STATISTICAL TABULATION OF MARKET ANALYSIS DATA

Results of a Marketing Survey of the Domestic Market Possibilities for Electrical Merchandising Lines Made by the United States Department of Commerce (Trade Promotion Series, No. 9)

	Average		Average
NEW ENGLAND	7.6696	SOUTH ATLANTIC—*Con.*	
Maine	.7630	West Virginia	1.3500
New Hampshire	.4513	North Carolina	1.4830
Vermont	.3642	South Carolina	1.0896
Massachusetts	4.0514	Georgia	1.4732
Rhode Island	.6810	Florida	.7497
Connecticut	1.3587	EAST SOUTH CENTRAL	5.4797
MIDDLE ATLANTIC	22.5556	Kentucky	1.5895
New York	10.9889	Tennessee	1.5710
New Jersey	2.9961	Alabama	1.3494
Pennsylvania	8.5706	Mississippi	.9698
EAST NORTH CENTRAL	23.8007	WEST SOUTH CENTRAL	6.4624
Ohio	6.2906	Arkansas	.9075
Indiana	3.0775	Louisiana	.9940
Illinois	7.3187	Oklahoma	1.4191
Michigan	4.4269	Texas	3.1418
Wisconsin	2.6870	MOUNTAIN	3.5258
WEST NORTH CENTRAL	11.7527	Montana	.7607
Minnesota	2.2783	Idaho	.5213
Iowa	2.5685	Wyoming	.1999
Missouri	3.0056	Colorado	.9199
North Dakota	.4335	Utah	.4665
South Dakota	.4914	Nevada	.1663
Nebraska	1.2031	New Mexico	.2175
Kansas	1.7723	Arizona	.2737
SOUTH ATLANTIC	9.7085	PACIFIC	9.0450
Delaware	.2002	Washington	1.8549
Maryland	1.3139	Oregon	.8896
District of Columbia	.5536	California	6.3005
Virginia	1.4953		

variation in purchasing inclination in different sections of the country, with some consideration also of the rates for electricity.

3. Ratio of urban population in each state to the total urban population of the country, with due allowances made for electric service being more generally available throughout rural areas in certain states as compared with others.

4. Ratio of families in each state to total for the United States, with slight adjustments made for size of families, whether above or below the average for the country.

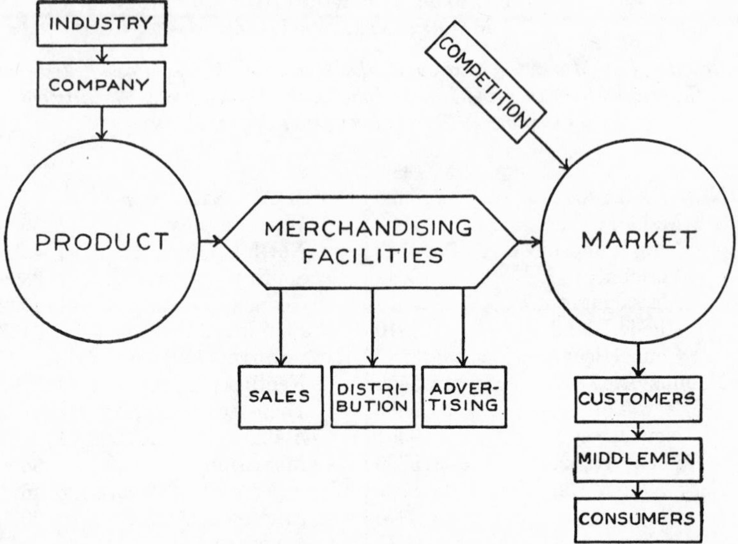

FIG. 3. THE THREE BASIC ELEMENTS OF THE MARKETING PROBLEM

The problem of marketing is to supply a market with a suitable product. In order to do this, certain merchandising facilities are necessary. This diagram shows the various elements in relation to each other.

5. Ratio of number of unencumbered homes in each state to total in country.

6. Ratio of passenger automobiles owned in each state to total for the country.

7. Ratio of incomes reported for each state to total income for country.

8. Ratio of number of residential electric-light consumers of each state to total for the country.

9. Ratio of kilowatt capacity of central light and power systems in each state to total for the country—with adjustments made to compensate for greater amount of power equipment serving industrial load in some states than in others.

10. Ratio of kilowatt-hours consumed in each state to the total for the country, with adjustment made to allow for an abnormal use of electricity for industrial purposes in some states as compared with an average proportion for the country as a whole.

The direct arithmetical average of the 10 factors as developed for each individual state is shown in Figure 2. This

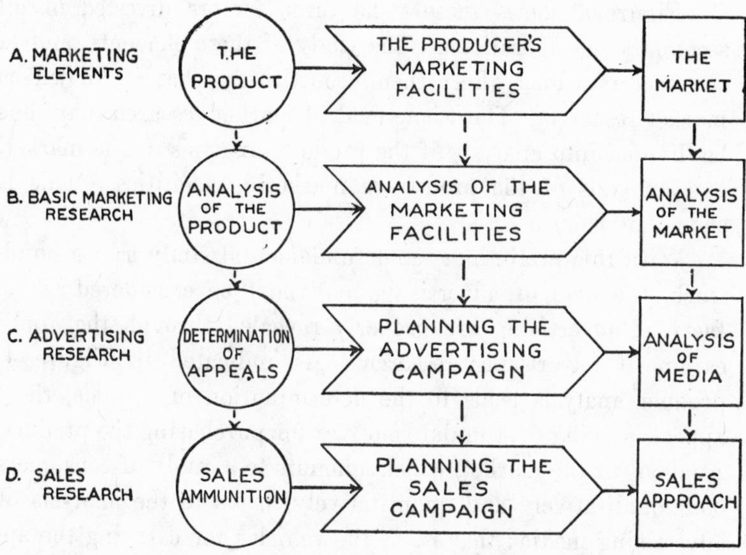

FIG. 4. PHASES OF MARKETING RESEARCH

Here the same elements shown in Figure 3 are again shown, in order to give an idea of the place of advertising research in relation to other marketing research.

study was based upon definite statistical data selected to make the analysis applicable to the problem in question.

The Field of Advertising Research

Advertising on a scientific basis is based on a knowledge of three things: First, a knowledge of the product in question; second, a knowledge of the logical market for that product; and third, a knowledge of the best manner of bringing product and market together. An understanding of these three elements implies an understanding of the whole marketing problem.

Figure 3 illustrates the relation of these three basic elements to each other. At one end of the scale is the product, which springs from the industry and from the company. At the other end is the market, with its various classifications of customers, middlemen, and consumers. Between the two is the distributive mechanism, supported by sales and advertising effort.

Figure 4 shows these same three factors divested of all secondary considerations. The study of these elements, and of the factors which affect them, constitutes what is known as market research. The whole field of market research may thus be divided into analysis of the product, analysis of the market, and analysis of the producer's marketing facilities. This is shown in Figure 4.

With this preliminary and fundamental study as a groundwork, the field of advertising may next be considered. The facts of advertising are properly revealed through the application of advertising research. As indicated in Figure 4, product analysis leads to the determination of appeals, these appeals serving to stimulate motives for purchasing the product. Analysis of the market, which amounts to a study of consumers both qualitatively and quantitatively, leads to the analysis of advertising media; that is, of the vehicles for carrying the appeals. Media, such as publications, are closely identified with the market. In fact, the advertising can get no nearer to the consumer than the medium. In many respects, the medium and the market occupy the same position. Analysis of the marketing facilities permits the planning of the advertising campaign.

When the medium of demand creation consists of personal conversation between the prospect and the representative of the seller, the process is no longer known as advertising, but as salemanship.

Figure 4 indicates the elements of sales research, which is analogous and parallel to advertising research. The analysis of the product results in the accumulation and the preparation of sales ammunition. The analysis of the market, *i.e.,* the consumer, indicates to the salesman how his prospect should be approached, and points out to him the psychology which he must employ. An analysis of the marketing facilities permits the planning of the sales campaign.

The sales campaign and the advertising campaign must, of course, be closely coördinated. Both of them are but parts of a single whole.

The breaking down of the problem of advertising, in accordance with the foregoing plan, is used because of its simplicity, as well as because it permits the relationship to be shown between marketing research, advertising research, and sales research. No sharp line of demarcation can be drawn, however, between these three subjects.

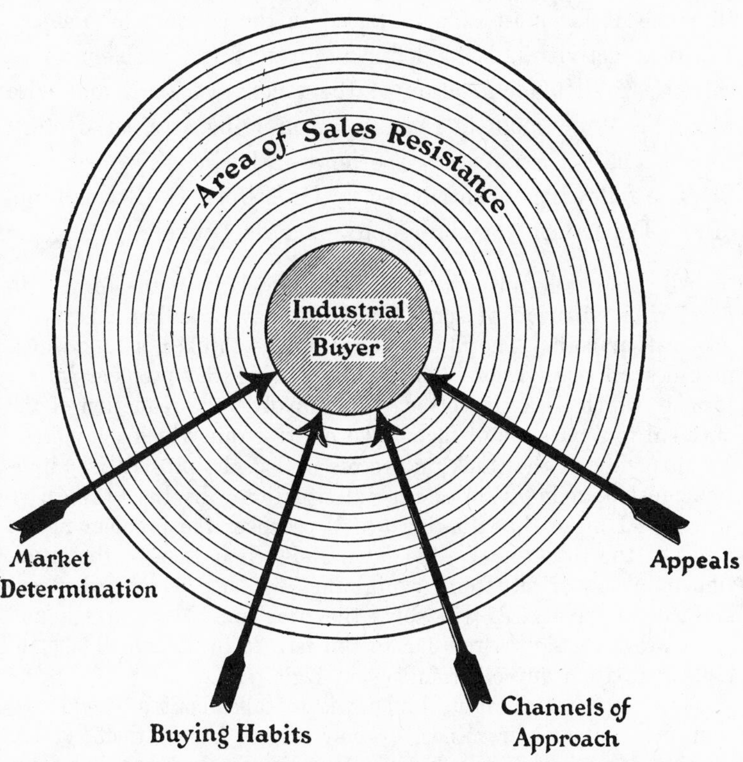

Fig. 5. Another Graphic View of the Marketing Problem

This diagram, from another source, discloses the same basic elements shown in the previous illustrations. Before any sale is consummated:

1. The worth-while markets must be analyzed.
2. Buying habits of these markets must be studied.
3. Channels of approach to the buyers must be selected.
4. The strongest possible appeals to buyers must be formulated.

(McGraw-Hill Company.)

Figure 5 illustrates another graphic method of analyzing the market problem. The basic conception is the same. Starting with the determination and analysis of the logical markets, and continuing on through the selection of the proper channels of direct approach, it ends with the formulation of the strongest possible appeal to buyers.

Determining the Problem

R. O. Eastman, a pioneer in advertising research, states that one of his most difficult tasks, in the conduct of his professional activities, is to define accurately the problem to be solved. Skillful delineation of the factors at issue, and wise planning of the steps to be taken in arriving at a satisfactory conclusion, call for a wide experience in business research.

The following is contributed by Dr. Filmer S. C. Northrop, of the Department of Philosophy of Yale University:

All thought begins with a problem which is in the form of a perplexing situation of some kind. It may be either mental or physical, or both. The first task facing the thinker, a task which precedes all observation—consists in getting the problem into a form in which it can be solved. This involves the reduction of the question to a question of fact. The positive rule which I lay down for this stage of the thinking process is that the provocative situation must be reduced to the factual situation. By the provocative situation I mean the situation which provokes the problem in the mind of the thinker. By the factual situation I mean the situation or group of situations containing the facts which, when examined and analyzed, will solve the problem. More breath and labor are uselessly wasted due to the failure to observe this principle than from any other fallacy in logic.

The tendency of most thinkers is to talk about any odd fact that may enter their minds, or may appear before them, rather than to take their thinking capacities directly in hand and focus them upon the task of determining what facts, if examined, will provide a conclusive solution to the problem in question. The fallacy involved here is the fallacy of irrelevance. In fact, irrelevance can usually be defined as thought about the provocative situation instead of about the factual situation.

A man may commit no fallacy in observing and describing the facts which he looks at, or in drawing inferences from his observation, and still reach a wrong conclusion, if the above rule is violated, for the simple reason that the solution of the question does not turn upon the facts which he picked out for observation.

GAINS and LOSSES of *Chicago Newspapers* in Advertising Lineage

the first ten months of this year against the corresponding period of last year

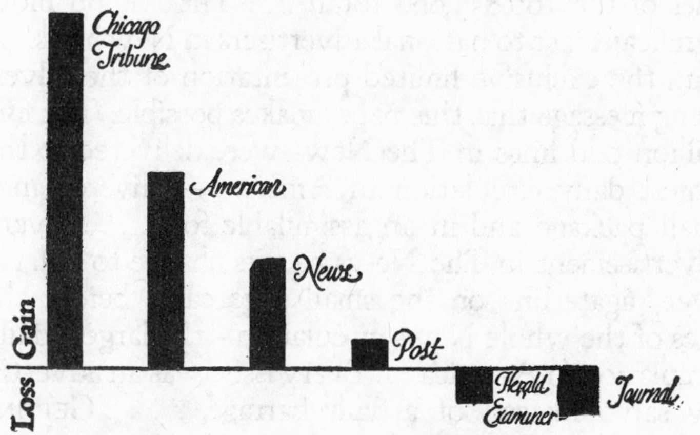

The Chicago Tribune

THE WORLD'S GREATEST NEWSPAPER

FIG. 6. INCREASE IN LINEAGE ADVERTISED

This appears to show an increase in the lineage of the *Chicago Tribune.* One seems expected to assume that such an increase is of advantage to the advertiser (see Figure 7).

THE NEWS carried less lineage!

than any other New York newspaper

for the twelve months of 1924 . . . . NOT because we couldn't get more, but because we couldn't print more in our tabloid paper . . . Only 3.6% of all the advertising run in seventeen New York and Brooklyn newspapers in the twelve months of 1924 appeared in The News—5,850,580 lines of the 160,853,666 total! . . . THERE IS no more significant fact to national advertisers in New York . . . than the exclusive limited presentation of the advertising message that this paper makes possible. The five million odd lines in The News were delivered to the largest daily circulation in America—delivered in a small package and in an assimilable form. . . . Every advertisement in The News had its chance to sell. . . . Every agate line on the small page came before the eyes of the whole News circulation—the largest daily circulation in America . . . Every issue was an advertising salvo instead of a daily barrage. . . . . GETTING copy into a paper isn't advertising necessarily, but getting copy into a reader's eyes is!

THE NEWS
New York's Picture Newspaper
25 Park Place, NEW YORK
7 S. Dearborn St., Chicago

FIG. 7. DECREASE IN LINEAGE ADVERTISED

The *News* makes capital of the very thing which the *Chicago Tribune* (in Figure 6) aims to disparage. Both papers have stated facts impressively. But the facts are antithetical. Are both claimants right? Research alone can give the answer.

Figures 6 and 7 bring out this point. In the former, facts are cited to prove that the *Chicago Tribune's* lineage has increased, the implication being that this increase is of advantage to the advertiser. In the latter, the reverse situation is claimed, and the opposite implication hinted at. It is for the advertiser to determine whether, from his point of view, increase in lineage is an advantage or a disadvantage.

Once the problem has been determined, the method of solving it may at once be put into effect.

CHAPTER II

METHODS OF OBSERVATION

Before taking up in detail the technique of observation, comparison, generalization, and verification, it may be helpful, even at the risk of being repetitious, to outline briefly the course of procedure in an ordinary advertising analysis.

The Analysis as a Whole

The research job begins with observation, which consists mainly in locating sources of data and obtaining information from them. It is customary to make a preliminary survey on the basis of the internal data available in the company's offices, because these will serve to point out more definitely the procedure to be followed later.

Advertising data are obtained chiefly from bibliographical work, questionnaires, interviews, and psychological tests. The bibliographical work should make available all the printed knowledge on the subject, whether in books, in periodicals, or in company records and reports. Questionnaires are used to obtain data and opinions from a wide area, the results of which should prove representative of the whole. Interviews are used for intensive field surveys, and also for obtaining opinions from specialists or authorities.

The analysis and comparison of the data secured constitute the second major step in the investigation. Facts which are susceptible of quantitative treatment are tabulated and presented in statistical or graphic form, so that they may be readily assimilated. Other facts are set forth in such a way as to permit ready comparisons.

The third step is to weigh the evidence as prepared and to

draw conclusions from it. If the weight of evidence leans strongly in one direction, it should be possible to make a positive judgment. If, however, the results seem doubtful, sweeping generalizations must be guarded against. Conclusions are usually embodied in a report.

The final step in advertising analysis is to test and check the findings. To put findings into effect without test is perhaps better than the usual procedure, which is to make no research at all; but some method of verification is highly desirable. Without it, the research will not have been scientific. One way to do this, and one which appeals to the business man as practical, is to carry on test campaigns in a restricted territory until the recommendations growing out of the research have been given a trial under working conditions. This often results in modifications of the original findings. The Westinghouse Electric and Manufacturing Company, for example, in trying out its new automatic electric iron, spent a year in testing, as the result of which it changed the name of the iron and varied the major merchandising appeal.

Where the results of the survey seem to call for a change in policy or a new plan of action, it is sometimes possible to submit these findings to a group of experts, or to the leaders of the industry. By securing their opinion, the consensus of evidence is secured. While this method costs little, as a rule, it is less likely to prove satisfactory than the more scientific method of checking by going direct to the market.

Sources of Data

The observation of experiences and the collecting of data bearing upon the problem is the primary step in scientific research. Observations fall into two great classes: first, those which have already been made, which provide the results of past experiences; second, those which must be made at first hand, which supplement the results obtained previously, or make discoveries along new lines.

Observations which have already been recorded should be considered first. They point the way to further research. Careful analysis of existing material often brings data to light which could not be obtained otherwise without great expenditure of time, money, and effort.

Recorded observations themselves are obtained from three principal sources:

1. The company's own library, records, reports, and files should provide internal statistics which bear particularly upon the specific problems under investigation. The results of an analysis of this material will often point out what additional facts must be secured at first hand.

2. The government, the chambers of commerce, and other organizations have a great volume of recorded experiences in statistical form which often proves of the utmost value. Such information is available to practically everybody who seeks it, being already in printed form.

3. Finally, the various trade associations and periodicals have material in their files which they are glad to give to those with a legitimate interest in it. Such information may be obtained by written request or personal visit to the offices of the association or periodical.

The gathering of recorded facts is essential to a successful investigation. As the sole method of obtaining information, however, it cannot hope to be successful. It lacks the color which is procured only from a first-hand analysis of present conditions as applied to the problem in question. Generalizations of value can seldom be drawn from purely academic observations. Hence, recorded experiences should be supplemented by the following methods:

1. Observation by personal interview is probably the best method of obtaining an accurate knowledge of conditions in a particular territory, or when it is desired to get accurate data from consumers. As a method of obtaining a wide view of a large market, it is probably inferior in practicability to the mail-questionnaire method.

2. Observation by means of the mail-questionnaire method has the advantage of providing a large volume of experiences at comparatively small cost. Where conditions are carefully

considered, it has proved highly satisfactory. It is often possible to combine the interview and questionnaire methods in order to check one against the other.

3. There is a third method of making observations which is coming into prominence in late years. The psychological test, made under controlled conditions, is of the greatest value in making analyses of the size of the advertisement, its position, the color to be used, the style of typography, and other factors based upon attention. It can also be used in the determination of buying motives and appeals.

Principles of Observation

From whatever sources the data are secured, there are ten principles which may well be observed. These are as follows:

1. *Accuracy* lies at the base of all observation. The investigator himself will be responsible for the accuracy of his subordinates who do the actual gathering of the data.

2. *Reliability* of data is also a fundamental requirement. The ordinary rule is to procure data as close to the original source as possible. In any case, it is advisable to find out by what method the observations used were originally made.

3. *Impartiality* must be absolute in obtaining data. For example, questionnaires should be so worded that no clue to the desired answer should be present. Investigations are often made anonymously to avoid possible prejudice or partiality in replies.

4. *Applicability* of facts gathered to the problem in hand is required. There should be no gathering of data for mere purposes of collection. All data should be pertinent to the specific case.

5. *Availability* of data obtained is an important point. The observations should be made in such a form that they will prove intelligible for purposes of analysis and comparison.

6. *Comprehensiveness* demands that all necessary data bearing on the subject be gathered.

7. *Representativeness* requires that the observations gathered should be fully indicative of conditions in the whole field.

Sufficient data from each group investigated must be secured to make the results representative.[1]

8. *Judgment* on the part of the investigator will be needed to see that the observations are made by trained analysts, that they should be accurate, reliable, impartial, applicable, available, and comprehensive.

9. *System* is needed to make observations expeditiously, thoroughly, and at a minimum expense.

10. *Control* of observations should be exercised in so far as possible. That is, care must be taken to see that observations made in a given case will produce authentic results. Decisions must be made as to the number of observations required, under what conditions they shall be made. Control is essential to the success of any organized survey.

Internal Statistics

The term internal statistics is ordinarily applied to the company's own records and reports. Such data are particularly valuable in giving a picture of the business, and in forming a background for the more specific aspects of the investigation. The sales records, for example, will define the geographical extent of the market already covered. They will show what products sell best and where. They will indicate the size of the average order, the sales per salesman, and sales fluctuations.

The company's books will show what financial condition it is in, and the profits which it is making and has made. Statistics as to the cost of selling may often be obtained, divided according to geographical location of territories, classes of product, and method of distribution.

---

[1] Speaking of the amount of research necessary to obtain a correct insight into a merchandising situation, Shaw Newton, one of the pioneer writers on advertising research, says: "The purpose of market studies is not necessarily to cover the whole market. In fact, from every standpint, an *adequate minimum* of field work is much to be desired. All that is required is sufficient information, collected from enough representative sources, to provide sound facts upon which a true conclusion may be premised. A field survey covering forty-eight states is not only unnecessary but would prove entirely too unwieldy and expensive in operation."

The advertising records will indicate what media have been used and how the advertising appropriation has been apportioned, the size of advertisements used, the position in the periodical, the appeals employed, and similar information.

Careful investigation of the internal statistics should present, for purposes of analysis and comparison, a complete history of the company's activities as related to markets and advertising.

Governmental Sources

The Superintendent of Documents, at the Government Printing Office, has over 75,000 pamphlets for free distribution or for sale at cost price. In addition, during a period of 12 months, 250,000 letters of inquiry are answered. In spite of this, the distribution of government statistical data is exceedingly limited, as compared with its activity in gathering and tabulating observations on almost every conceivable subject.

In the majority of cases, the collection of external statistics might well begin with inquiry into government sources. The Department of Commerce is naturally most closely connected with business subjects. Through the various divisions of the Bureau of Foreign and Domestic Commerce, it publishes a monthly "Survey of Current Business," a Domestic Commerce Series, and various other reports of primary interest to advertising men. For example, the Division of Domestic Commerce is making a study of domestic distribution along three main lines: first, it attempts to establish facts for the measurement of markets in important lines; second, it is making a series of regional surveys which attempt to explain the peculiar conditions affecting the sale and distribution of goods in these markets; and third, it attempts to formulate the best practice in such matters as establishing territorial boundaries and utilizing market information.

While the Department of Commerce deals principally with business subjects, there are a number of other government departments and bureaus which collect valuable and important data. The Bureau of the Census, for example, makes a census of manufactures every two years. This exhaustive study of industrial production classifies the various industries, tabulates the number of concerns in each, the number of workers employed, and a great volume of other information in regard to them.

The Bureau of Standards studies the mechanical process of industries, performs a great deal of testing for individual concerns, and makes confidential reports of its tests. It establishes standards and specifications for manufactured products, examines new processes, formulates standards for material, and performs various similar functions which are of value in product analysis.

The Federal Reserve Board publishes summaries of general business conditions; the Interstate Commerce Commission and the Federal Trade Commission also publish statistical reports. The Department of Agriculture has a wide range of information at the disposal of the public and publishes, in addition, a crop-reporting service.

Whatever type of product the advertiser desires to analyze, he is almost certain of finding some department of the government which will be helpful in supplying statistical material. In addition to those named, there are the Department of Labor, the Bureau of Fisheries, the Bureau of Chemistry, the Bureau of Plant Industry, the Bureau of Mines, and the Geological Survey, the Public Health Service, and the Tariff Commission, all of which publish the results of their observations.

As far as is possible under the limitations imposed, the government material bears the stamp of authenticity. In some cases, however, its value is impaired by the delay which occurs between the time of gathering the information and the time of making it public.

Other External Sources of Data

There are a number of sources of external data, in addition to the government, which should be searched for available material. In the first place, the public libraries in the larger cities are repositories for statistical information of all kinds. In many cases, these libraries maintain their own statistical departments for the purpose of assisting those in need of information on specific subjects.

The growth of special libraries in recent years has been noteworthy and, in many cases, these prove valuable sources for analyses and investigations.

There is often a wealth of material to be secured from periodicals which publish trade information in statistical form. The files of such periodicals should be consulted, as well as the classified indexes of articles appearing in trade journals.

The various statistical services which collect and tabulate observations as a regular business, such as Babson's, Brookmire, and the Harvard Economic Service, often have special information available, or can obtain such information on request.

Trade associations collect and publish statistical information as part of their service to members. Particularly active in this respect are the National Automobile Chamber of Commerce, the National Retail Dry Goods Association, the National Retail Clothiers' Association, the Direct Mail Advertisers' Association, and the Association of National Advertisers.

Many associations and periodicals have built up departments for the gathering of material as the result of frequent requests from advertising men for assistance. Although in some cases the information secured in this way is of excellent calibre, much of it is often poorly verified.

It is not uncommon for an agency to request of an association or publication a report on a given market. The association will, thereupon, circularize its members, attempting to find out what each particular field can sell and summarizing the results for the agency.

For example, the manufacturer of a pancake flour wanted to know the market situation in various parts of the country, whether it was decreasing or increasing. It submitted this question to the American Newspaper Publishers' Association, which sent the questionnaire illustrated in Figure 8 to its

FIG. 8.—AN EXAMPLE OF A DEALER QUESTIONNAIRE

Questionnaire Issued by The American Newspaper Publishers' Association to Investigate the Market for Pancake Flour

State__________ City__________ Newspaper Reporting__________

Q. 1. Please name brands of pancake flour sold in your territory in the order of volume of sales.

Name of Brand *Retail Price*

(*a*)
(*b*)
(*c*)
(*d*)
(*e*)

Q. 2. Which of these, if any, are put up by local millers or other local factors such as wholesale grocers?

A.

Q. 3. What brands, if any, are advertised in your territory in
Newspapers
Billboards and Signs
Street Cars

Q. 4. Please estimate the total volume of sales of pancake flour in your city annually.

A.

Q. 5. Is there a tendency toward increase or decrease in the consumption of pancake flour in your territory?

A.

Remarks:

American and Canadian members. Obviously, the opportunities for inaccuracies in such a procedure are very great. Nevertheless, it does suffice to present a general picture of market conditions. It brought out the fact that one brand only had a general sale, the rest of the market being sectional. It showed that in 58 per cent of the territory, consumption of pancake flour was increasing, while in 25 per cent there was a decrease, and in 17 per cent the demand was stationary. There were also a great many opinions as to why conditions were thus and so in a particular territory.

The Mail Questionnaire

Obtaining first-hand observations by means of questionnaires distributed by mail is, in spite of certain important objections, widely used. Compared with the interview method, it is inexpensive, costing no more to cover the opposite side of the continent than the home city. It is contended in many quarters, however, that the questionnaire is, in reality, more expensive than the interview method because it secures a low percentage of returns and with a high percentage of incomplete and useless data. Furthermore, it is stated that returns from mail questionnaires are not representative of the whole, since only one type of individual will answer a questionnaire.

The answer to these objections is that they can be overcome, to a large extent, by careful planning of the physical make-up of the questionnaire, the formulation of the questions asked, the copy appearing on the letter accompanying the questionnaire, and a careful selection of the persons circularized.

The first problem in preparing a questionnaire campaign is to plan for a sufficient number of replies to be representative of the whole field covered. This is a statistical question, as a general rule, varying with the particular case. Sometimes a large number is required; sometimes a relatively small number. When the number of recipients of a questionnaire is strictly limited, as in the case of cement manufacturers, it might be wise to send questionnaires to only half the list at first, and use the other half as a check.

The American Experience Table of Mortality is based on 100,000 observations. For an ordinary business investigation, 1,000 replies from consumers should be representative if they have been wisely chosen, while in a dealer questionnaire, a few hundred should be enough. After an advertiser has sent out several questionnaires, he should be able to gauge the number of replies he will receive from a given number sent. If he does not secure enough the first mailing, he can send out another and fill up the quota in this way. *The Literary Digest,* which has done a great deal of questionnaire investigation, finds that 40,000 letters mailed to names correctly apportioned among the 48 states, and among cities, towns, and rural districts, according to population, will give returns representing almost exactly the ratio received from a general mailing of 15,000,000.

The percentage of replies received from the mailing of a questionnaire will differ greatly, according to the type of person written to. Ten per cent replies from a consumer questionnaire is an excellent showing. In cases where the persons questioned have particular reasons for being interested, or are offered some special inducement, the replies may be 20 per cent or even higher. An instance is quoted in *Mailbag* (Wm. J. Reilly) where each member of a large organization was asked to suggest the name of a neighbor, and from 300 questionnaires sent to these names, 240 were returned properly filled in.

Factors in Securing Returns

The number of returns received from a questionnaire will depend on the nature of the individuals or firms to whom they are sent, the type of letter accompanying the questionnaire, the inducement for reply, the ease with which replies may be made, and the physical make-up of the questionnaire. The accuracy and value of the information secured will depend somewhat on the above factors, but mainly on the manner in which the questions are formulated.

1. *Sources of Information Questioned.*—It is a fundamental rule in sending out questionnaires to select the mailing list from those who will be able to answer the questions intelligently and accurately. Obviously, few people will answer questions about which they know nothing, nor are their opinions of any value in such a case. Obviously, also, a different type of questionnaire will be required for the expert authority, the dealer or distributor, and the consumer. Neither their interests nor their information will be identical.

The first point, therefore, in securing high returns, is to choose the mailing lists carefully. When any particular classification is desired, a directory of mailing lists may be consulted. Lists of dealers are, of course, available. It is often possible to use city directories, telephone directories, subscription lists, and other special lists.

2. *Incentive for Reply.*—The recipient of the questionnaire must be convinced that it is to his or her advantage to answer

ARCHIBALD M. CROSSLEY
Statistician
Box 103, Madison Square Station
NEW YORK CITY

February 14th, 1924

Dear Sir:

I have designed a thermometer method of getting information which, although novel and new, is most exact in its results.

I find, too, that getting information by letter is more reliable than obtaining it through personal conversation. If you are not at home when this letter arrives, I know that it will await your return whereas if you are out when I call, it is often inconvenient to call again.

I am taking the temperature of the public in order to gauge their interest in magazines. No magazines are listed so that it cannot be said that I am suggesting which you should vote for. You are asked to write on the dotted lines opposite each degree on the thermometer the names of the magazines you prefer.

You vote here just as you would in a national election, anonymously. You need not sign your name; in fact there isn't space on the card in which to do so. A stamped envelope is enclosed for your vote, and I shall be most grateful for a prompt reply.

Very truly yours
Archibald M Crossley

FIG. 9. LETTER TO ACCOMPANY QUESTIONNAIRE

A good example of the approach to a subject for observation. Skillfully handled, mail questionnaires are of inestimable value in advertising research.

it, or he or she must be asked, as a direct favor, to fill it out. The business firm is often glad to fill out a questionnaire if a digest of the findings is promised. It may complete it purely as a matter of coöperation and courtesy.

Experience has proved that a certain type of consumer or individual will fill out a questionnaire if approached courte-

CABLE ADDRESS "ERNSTAUDIT" NEW YORK

ERNST & ERNST

AUDITS AND SYSTEMS

TAX SERVICE

NEW YORK

87 CEDAR ST

NEW YORK
PHILADELPHIA
BOSTON
PROVIDENCE
BALTIMORE
WASHINGTON
RICHMOND
BUFFALO
PITTSBURGH
CLEVELAND
CINCINNATI
TOLEDO
DETROIT

CHICAGO
MINNEAPOLIS
ST. PAUL
INDIANAPOLIS
DENVER
ST. LOUIS
KANSAS CITY
NEW ORLEANS
ATLANTA
DALLAS
FORT WORTH
HOUSTON

September 5, 1923.

Dear Sir:

A large publishing house has engaged us to endeavor to secure unbiased facts on which to plan an important campaign to extend the use of certain kinds of machinery.

Hence this letter, which is addressed to a number of companies representative of the best practice in operating factories, mills, shops and industrial plants.

Will you help, please, by answering the three questions below and returning this letter in the enclosed envelope?

1. Who in your organization initiates the purchase of machinery such as conveyors, cranes, hoists, interplant transportation systems, power transmission equipment?

2. Of these men which one or ones actually specifies the equipment?

	(Check one or more) (Names not necessary)	(Check here)
Directors	____	____
President	____	____
Other officers (Please specify)	____	____
General Manager	____	____
Works Manager	____	____
Chief Engineer	____	____
Master Mechanic	____	____
Chief Electrician	____	____
Superintendent of Power	____	____
Purchasing Agent	____	____
Others (Please notify)	____	____

3. In what publication should advertising of such equipment appear to be most useful to your organization? (List one or more publications in order of preference) ____________________

Thanking you for your cooperation,

Yours very truly,

H. L. Davis

Ernst & Ernst.

FIG. 10. COMBINATION LETTER AND QUESTIONNAIRE

ously, and if his interest can be aroused. This is done particularly well in the letter illustrated in Figure 9. About 10 per cent returns were received from a mailing of 41,000.

In some cases, a souvenir or reward of some kind is used to secure a high percentage of returns. See the first page of the questionnaire illustrated in Figure 13.

3. *Ease of Reply.*—Experience has proved that the questionnaire which takes the least effort to fill out and mail will normally bring in the best results. For this reason, it is usually desirable to enclose a stamped, self-addressed envelope or return card. It should be made clear that all replies will be treated as confidential. The briefer the questionnaire, the more likely it is to receive adequate attention. Where possible, it is useful to combine the letter and the questionnaire, as in Figure 10. All that is required to answer this questionnaire is to make two check marks and write out two names of preferences, and return the letter in the enclosed envelope.

4. *The Approach.*—The approach to the person or concern questioned by mail is especially important. The letter which accompanies the questionnaire must convince the person questioned that he or she should take the time to answer it instead of throwing it in the wastebasket.

The letter should be brief, to the point, courteous, and should explain carefully just what is required of the recipient. Figure 11 brings out skillfully the method of approach which normally will prove most satisfactory in dealing with consumers. There is a frank admission that a favor is being asked. The questionnaire itself forms a part of the two-page letter, is carefully printed, and formulated most explicitly.

5. *Physical Appearance.*—The appearance of the questionnaire has much to do with the reception given it. The stationery should be of good or fair quality. Only one question should appear on a line, and space should be left for the answer. The questions should be as few in number as possible, and should preferably be connected in some way with the letter.

Make-up of the Mail Questionnaire

One important point to remember in sending out questionnaires is that the identity of the sender frequently must be concealed to avoid possible bias in answering questions. Thus in Figure 9 the mailing was under the name of a statistician, while in Figure 10, an accounting firm conducted the investigation. In neither case did the recipient of the questionnaire

JOSEPH RICHARDS COMPANY
INCORPORATED
247 PARK AVENUE · NEW YORK

OFFICE OF THE
DIRECTOR OF RESEARCH

April 23, 1925.

To the
Lady of the House.

Dear Madam:

Won't you do us a favor?

We are called upon from time to time to answer many questions about household products and we have always found that the best way to get such information is to put the matter up to the woman of the house.

So, if you will be good enough to answer the few short questions on the inside page we shall be a thousand times obliged to you. Since your answers will be used for statistical purposes only you need not sign your name. If you wish to do so, however, you may rest assured that it will be held strictly confidential.

Let us thank you in advance for any help you may give us.

Cordially,

Stanley I Clark

FM

Director of Research.

FIG. 11A. REQUEST FOR COÖPERATION

The "inside page" referred to is shown in Figure 11B.

Even though your experience with window shades may be very limited, we would greatly appreciate your answering as many of the questions as possible and returning them to us.

What make or makes of window shades are you now using?

....

....

When you last purchased window shades what make did you ask for?

I asked for ....

I did not ask for any make ....

If you did not ask for any make, why did you not do so?

....

....

Which do you consider more important, the cloth or the roller (check one).

Cloth .... Roller ....

Would you expect equal service and satisfaction from two different priced window shades made by the same manufacturer?

Yes .... No ....

With what makes of window shades or rollers are you familiar?

Shades	Rollers
....	....
....	....
....	....

Please check (√) that particular make of window shade and roller which you like best.

What are your three favorite magazines?

First ....

Second ....

Third ....

Do you live in the city or the suburbs—apartment or private house?

City........................ Apartment........................

Suburbs........................ Private house........................

If you own an automobile, what make is it?

Our car is a ....

We do not own a car ....

Fig. 11b. Questionnaire to Accompany Letter

This questionnaire is integral with the letter shown in Figure 11a.

Please write on the dotted line opposite each degree on the thermometer the names of the weekly or monthly magazines you prefer.

BLOOD HEAT — 98 Indispensable Literary Digest
A magazine I could not do without

SUMMER HEAT — 76 Necessary National Geographic
A magazine I read with regularity

NORMAL — 60 Interesting Saturday Evening Post
A magazine I enjoy, but do not read regularly.

ABOVE FREEZING — 40 Mild Interest ....
A magazine I approve and read occasionally

And mail in stamped envelope enclosed

The Thermometer Test. A. M. Crossley, Box 103 Madison Sq., New York, N. Y.

FIG. 12. QUESTIONNAIRE TO DETERMINE PREFERENCES

This questionnaire is interesting, not only for its method of approach, which is such as to arouse interest on the part of the subject, but also because of the conclusions which can be drawn from a study of this sort.

have an inkling of the identity of the firm actually concerned.

In formulating the questions for the questionnaire, the following points should be borne in mind:

Simplicity is fundamental. Normally speaking, the simpler the questions, the more valuable will be the answers received.

YOUR CHOICE FREE

January, 1925

Dear Friend:

Perhaps your name is among 17,000 of my friends who last year helped make a better Successful Farming.

I have planned to make the paper even more valuable to you this year and next, but will need your answers to the following questions in order to put it over 100%.

Several of the questions can be answered by making a simple check like this, (√) others can be answered by **yes** or **no.** It will save time for you and help me just as much if you use these short cuts for your answers.

Answers must be mailed within two weeks if you are to receive one of these rewards. Please use the enclosed envelope which is stamped and addressed.

Yours very truly,

E. T. Meredith

Which of the gifts shall I mail?... .... **How shall I address it?**

Name...............................**Town**.........................**R. F. D.**.. **.State**. ....

(BE SURE TO WRITE CLEARLY SO YOUR REWARD WILL REACH YOU)

B. M. A-45

FIG. 13A. AN INQUISITORIAL QUESTIONNAIRE

A high percentage of returns may be expected from a survey carried out with the use of such a questionnaire. But under such conditions the advertiser should inquire carefully into the accuracy of the results.

No question should be involved or be worded in such a way that it may be misunderstood. If the answer is to be "yes" or "no," the simplest method is to allow space for a check after the "no" or "yes."

(Please answer every question)

1. How many acres in your farm?..........2. Do you own your farm?........ (Yes or No) 3. About what is the value of your buildings including your home? $.............. 4. How many cows do you milk?.......... 5. Do you own an automobile?....... (Yes or No) 6. What make?......................

7. Are you expecting to buy a new automobile within the coming two years?........ (Yes or No) 8. What make do you plan on buying?.. 9. Do you do the repairing on your automobile, such as replacing piston rings, etc.?....... (Yes or No) 10. Do you have a tractor?........ (Yes or No)

11. What make?........................ 12. Are you expecting to buy a new tractor?........ (Yes or No) 13. Do you have a truck?........ (Yes or No) 14. What make?................. 15. What size? .....Tons.

16. Are you expecting to buy a new motor truck?........ (Yes or No) 17. What make?..........................

18. Is most of the repairing of your farm implements and machinery done on your farm?........ (Yes or No)

19. Do you have high line electric service?...... (Yes or No) 20. Do you own a farm electric lighting plant?...... (Yes or No)

21. What make?.................................. 22. Are you expecting to buy a new farm electric lighting plant?........ (Yes or No) 23. Do you have a furnace?........ (Yes or No) 24. What make?.................

25. What do you burn in it?.............. 26. Is it steam, hot water, or hot air?..............

27. Are you expecting to buy a new furnace?........ (Yes or No) 28. A new heating stove?........ (Yes or No) 29. Check (√) the finish you would most likely want on your heating stove: Mahogany enamel....Blue enamel.... Gray enamel....Plain black with nickel trimmings..... 30. Have you a heating stove now?........ (Yes or No)

31. What name?........................ 32. How old is it?......Years. 33. Check (√) the kinds of cook stoves you have: Wood....Coal....Gasoline....Oil....Gas....Name of wood stove........................Name of coal stove..........................Name of gasoline stove..................Name of oil stove.................Name of gas stove................

34. Do you have running water in your house?....... (Yes or No) 35. If so, check (√) the kind of a water system you pump with: Electric....Gas engine ....Windmill....Gravity.... 36. What is the make of your water system?.................................. 37. Are you expecting to buy a new water system?........ (Yes or No) 38. Do you have a bathroom?........ (Yes or No) 39. Do you have a radio?........ (Yes or No)

40. How many tubes has it?........ 41. If a home made set, how much did it cost? $............

42. If a manufactured set, how much did it cost? $................. 43. If a manufactured set, what make is it?............................ 44. What make of batteries do you use in your radio?.. 45. Are you planning to buy a new radio?........ (Yes or No)

46. What make?.......................... 47. About how many miles away is the nearest broadcasting station which can furnish you with market reports?........Miles. 48. Check (√) the names of

Fig. 13b. Inquisitorial Questionnaire, Page 2

If the question is such that several answers may be given, all possible answers are often tabulated. In order to express a preference, the recipient of the questionnaire merely makes a check mark. Note in Figure 10, where it is desired to know

(Please answer every question)

buildings you expect to erect within the next two years. Also tell us the principal materials you will use in each building.

	Check Here if Will Erect	Size of Buildings	Materials Will Use (Lumber, Brick, Hollow Tile, Cement, Stone, Wall Board, Plaster Board, etc.)
House	....	....x....	....
Barn	....	....x....	....
Poultry House	....	....x....	....
Hog House	....	....x....	....
Silo	....	....x....	....
Garage	....	....x....	....
Machine Shed	....	....x....	....
Milk House	....	....x....	....
Granary	....	....x....	....
Corn Crib	....	....x....	....
Other Buildings	....	....x....	....

49. How many rooms will your new house have?........ 50. Will new house have basement? .... (Yes or No) 51. Check (√) kinds of roofing you will use: Wood shingles....Metal shingles....Rubber or asbestos shingles....Tile....Slate....Metal Sheets....Rubber or asbestos rolls....Other kinds.......... 52. If you build a new house, check (√) the kind of wall finish you will have: Wall paper....Tinted walls......Painted walls...... 53. Which of your old buildings will need paint within the next two years?............................ 54. Check (√) the improvements you will make of cement. Walls....Troughs....Fence posts....Floors....Walks....Feeding platforms....Others.................. 55. Do you buy Minute Tapioca?........ (Yes or No) 56. How often do you serve it?......Times per month. 57. What brand of coffee do you buy?.................. 58. How many pounds do you use each month?............ 59. What price do you pay for this coffee?..........Cents per pound. 60. What kind of sirup do you use?.................... 61. Do you ever make sirup at home?........ (Yes or No) 62. Do you know about the uses of Mapleine?........ (Yes or No) 63. Do you use Mapleine as a sirup maker?....... (Yes or No) 64. Do you use it as a flavoring?........ (Yes or No) 65. What make of a shot gun do you have?........................ 66. How many boxes of shot gun shells do you use each year?........ 67. Do you buy your shells at local store?........ (Yes or No) Mail order house?...... (Yes or No)

FIG. 13C. INQUISITORIAL QUESTIONNAIRE, PAGE 3

who in the organization has the purchasing authority, that all officials are listed.

Figure 12 illustrates the so-called thermometer test, whereby the market is tested for degrees of preference. The

(Please answer every question)

68. How many men's suits of clothes are purchased in your family each year?........ 69. About what price do you pay? $............ 70. What brand do you buy?.................... 71. How many boys' suits of clothes are purchased in your family each year?............ 72. About what price do you pay? $............ 73. What brand do you buy? .... 74. How often do you buy a man's overcoat?................. 75. About what do you pay for it? $.............. 76. How often do you buy a boy's overcoat?.................... 77. About what do you pay for it? $............ 78. Do you buy these clothes from local store?........ (Yes or No) 79. If not, please give name of city or town where you do buy them............................. 80. Do you buy clothes from mail order houses?.......... (All, Part or None) 81. Check (√) the items most important to you when purchasing a suit or overcoat: Quality....Style....Price..... 82. How many pairs of men's **work shoes** do you buy each year?.......... 83. About what price do you pay? $............ 84. What brand do you buy?......................... 85. How many pairs of men's **dress shoes** do you buy each year?............ 86. About what price do you pay? $................ 87. What brand do you buy?.......................... 88. How many pairs of boys' shoes do you buy each year?........ 89. About what price do you pay? $........... 90. How many pairs of women's and girls' shoes do you buy each year?........ 91. What price do you pay? $............ 92. Do you buy your shoes from local store?........ (Yes or No) 93. Do you buy any of your shoes from mail order houses?.......... (All, Part or None) 94. What brand of rubber footwear do you buy?.................... 95. Where have you planned to travel outside your own state within the next three years?.. 96. How will you travel, by rail or auto?............ 97. How many people will go? Men?......Women?......Children?...... 98. Do you or any members of your family plan to locate permanently in another state within the next five years?.......... (Yes or No) 99. What state?.................... 100. What business will they probably engage in?............ .... 101. What kind of property insurance do you carry? (Fire, wind, hail, tornado, etc.)........................ 102. Do you carry any crop insurance?........ (Yes or No) 103. Do you carry any livestock insurance?........ (Yes or No) 104. Check (√) the members of your family who carry life insurance; Husband......Wife......Children......

Remarks:..
....
....
....

FIG. 13D. INQUISITORIAL QUESTIONNAIRE, PAGE 4

author of this test, A. M. Crossley, has been highly successful in applying this form of questionnaire. Each of the four degrees of interest is defined. Thus, "indispensable" means "a magazine I could not do without"; "necessary" applies to "a magazine I read with regularity"; "interesting" means "a magazine I enjoy, but do not read regularly"; while "mild interest" covers "a magazine I approve and read occasionally."

The answer to questions should not be suggested in any way. It has been proved that this will influence the reply in a majority of cases. It is the same principle that makes the department store teach its salespeople to say, "Will you take this parcel with you?" instead of saying, "Will you have it sent?" Note the violations of this rule in Figure 13, as, for example, Question 55, "Do you buy Minute Tapioca?" or Question 62, "Do you know about the uses of Mapleine?" This long questionnaire illustrates also another point in forming questions. The style of questions here is distinctly inquisitorial, such as, "About what is the value of your buildings, including your home?" People do not normally take kindly to such abrupt methods. Nor do they particularly care to answer questions which will require any effort on their part. If they find difficulty in remembering exactly, they may be inclined to put down what comes to their mind as an approximation. There is the familiar case of the dealer who is asked what his best selling brand of a given article is. He is inclined to answer without making accurate investigation, often mentioning the brand which had the last sale.

As a rule, it is futile to ask general opinions in a questionnaire, unless the recipients belong to the class of experts, in which case the consensus of opinions is often used as the basis for a forecast.

The order of questions should be logical. The first question especially should be interesting to the reader so that he will be led to answer the others.

Figure 14 shows an excellent example of a consumer mail questionnaire—brief, explicit, and arranged in such a way as to make it easy for the recipient to write down his replies. In the case of a government questionnaire, such as this, there is more likelihood of receiving a high percentage of returns than in the case of an ordinary concern.

Fig. 14.—An Example of a Consumer Mail Questionnaire

BUREAU OF AGRICULTURAL ECONOMICS

Philadelphia Milk Questionnaire

(*Mail*)

Name ....? *Husband's Occupation* ....

Address ....?

1. What is the Average Amount of Milk Purchased Weekly? ....Pints
   What part is used for drinking.......................... "
   What is the average amount of condensed and evaporated milk purchased weekly............................Small cans

2. How Many Persons Are There in Your Family or Household? Total ....
   Infants...
   Children 3 to 6 years, Inclusive................
   Children 7 to 12 years, " ....
   Children 13 to 18 years, " ....
   Adults..

3. How Many Drink Milk in Your Family?

	Infants	Children			Adults
		3 to 6	7 to 12	13 to 18	
At every meal...	....	....	....	....	....
Every day......	....	....	....	....	....
Occasionally....	....	....	....	....	....
Never........	....	....	....	....	....

4. Why Do Those in Your Family Who Drink Milk Do so?
   Infants...
   3 to 6...
   7 to 12...
   13 to 18...
   Adults...

5. What Are the Reasons Why the Other Members of Your Family Do Not Drink Milk?
   ....
   ....
   ....

6. What Kinds of Food Are of the Greatest Importance to Your Family?
   Most important.................................
   Second...
   Third..
   Fourth...
   Fifth..

7. Where Have You Seen Fresh Milk Advertised? ....
   What Do You Remember About Advertising You Have Seen?..............
   What Special Features Do You Think Should Be Advertised?..............

The Interview

The interview is valuable chiefly where an intensive survey is made of a particular locality, or where information is desired beyond that obtainable in a brief questionnaire, or where it is desired to bring out underlying motives. The interview method is a much more elaborate undertaking. It requires a trained field staff, it normally involves the expenditure of much time and money, but it can be made the basis of a much more thorough investigation. The governing motive in choosing between a mail and a personal investigation will be the objects to be attained.

An interesting classification of interviews was made by C. E. Haring, of Barton, Durstine and Osborn, who said, in an address:

> Two methods are commonly used in conducting field surveys of this kind. The first method uses a very few leading questions and relies entirely upon the field men so to question the persons interviewed that the desired information will be obtained. The result is generally a running story of each interview. The second method uses more or less detailed and lengthy questionnaires, and the task of the field man is completed when he has obtained answers to these questions.
>
> Each of these methods has its strengths and its weaknesses. The running story method of reporting is especially valuable when the flavor of the interview is more desired than the facts, when local color and copy leads are the chief consideration. The questionnaire method reaches its greatest value when definite facts and statistical data are desired.
>
> For a number of years we have, in our agency, combined the two methods. The tabulated answers to the many definite questions give the statistical information required to reach proper conclusions, and the running stories reported on each field report give the flavor and local color which are so valuable in preparing advertising. If then the two sets of results are viewed with an open mind and studied with analytical honesty, the answer to your problem will almost write itself.
>
> It is only in rare instances that the interview produces only the statistical information. The person interviewed does not reply in the colorless words of "yes" and "no," or stop at the name of

the make of his belt conveyor or weigh lorry, or state only whether he reads business paper advertising or not. He talks. What he says becomes the comment that elucidates the answers to the categorical questions.

Technique of the Interview

The American Telephone and Telegraph Company has gone to great lengths in tabulating the requirements for its field survey work, and from its past records it can tell with approximate accuracy what it will cost and how long it will take to make a field survey of a given locality. The table in Figure 15 gives a specimen of the company's records and the diagram summarizes its experience.

The interview often proves a corrective of certain statistical findings. For example, at the time cord tires were being introduced, a mail questionnaire brought out the fact that the majority of people were using fabric tires on their cars, whereas a personal investigation would have brought out the additional fact that when these had to be replaced the next tires purchased would be cords.

It is important to employ trained investigators, or to coach the men who are to do the investigating with great care. It is considered poor practice to use salesmen as investigators; the sales and the research temperaments are too unlike. Within limits, however, sales reports serve as suitable sources of research information. Figure 16 shows a form used by the Jell-O Company, Inc., of Le Roy, New York.

Each investigator should put the same interpretation upon each question to be asked. He should also know what he is talking about so that he can answer intelligently any questions put to him. The interview method followed by the Parker Pen Company to determine the public reception for an oversize and smaller size pen is interesting in this connection. Each investigator was equipped with a dozen fountain pens, varying in style and size, and all black except two new models. These investigators visited towns and cities in Illinois, Indiana, and Ohio, and interviewed all classes in offices, in homes, and even

FIG. 15.—TIME REQUIREMENTS FOR FIELD SURVEY WORK
(R. R. Copp, Bell System General Commercial Engineers' Conference)

City	Date of Survey	Families Counted per Man-Day	City	Date of Survey	Families Counted per Man-Day
Atlanta	1914	153	Bridgeport	1920	189
Pittsburgh	1915	205	Indianapolis	1920	126
Kansas City	1916	172	Little Rock	1920	122
Providence	1916	118	Dallas	1921	131
Los Angeles	1917	123	Milwaukee	1921	153
Salt Lake City	1917	144	Minneapolis	1921	148
Sacramento	1918	122	Spokane	1921	97
Mobile	1918	116	Altoona	1922	101
Detroit	1919	143	Columbus	1922	98
Lincoln	1919	134	Denver	1923	167
Youngstown	1919	101	St. Louis	1923	203

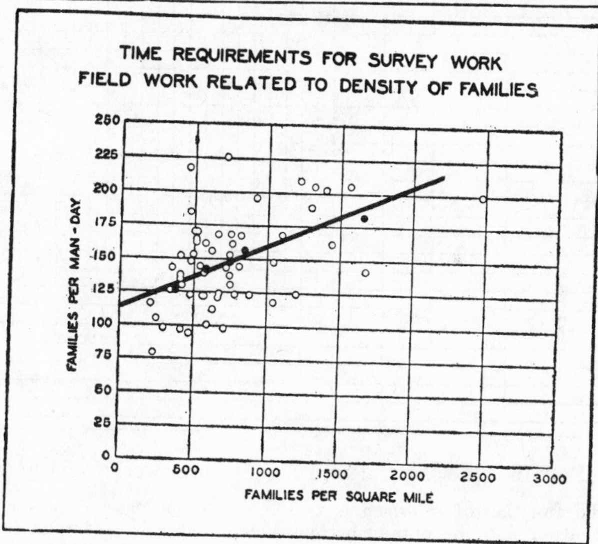

on the streets. Each investigator was instructed to display his tray of pens and ask:

"Will you pardon me, please, if I ask a question? I am not selling pens, I am merely finding out what kind people like. It will help me a great deal to have your opinion. Won't you try these pens and see which suits you best?"

The investigator was told to say nothing further, but to answer any questions put to him. He was to study the effect of each pen tried and also the effect of the price if it were asked of him. Each interview was recorded as soon as over.

The above instance is an unusual one. In the ordinary interview the field man must be almost as a good a salesman as

Trip No.______ **TRAVELER'S DAILY REPORT** Name of Hotel______

THE JELL-O COMPANY, INC., LE ROY, N. Y. Date______192___

Agent______ Town______ State______ Hours of Arrival______ A.M.______ P.M.

NAME OF GROCER	ADDRESS	BEST SELLING JELLY POWDER	NEXT BEST SELLER	Size of Store	No. Flavors Jell-O in Stock	No. Dozen on Hand	No. Cases Sold	[illegible]	No. Cases Sold	Inst. Jell-O Sold	D-Zerta Sold	[illegible]	Window Display	Panels	Small Cut Outs	Large Cut Outs	Danglers	Door Signs	Samples		Books	EXPENSE $ CTS.
																						BOYS HOURS
																						BOYS HOURS
																						BOYS HOURS
																						BOYS HOURS
																						ST. CAR FARE
																						R.R. FROM
																						R.R. FROM
																						CARTAGE ON GOODS
																						CARTAGE ON TRUNK
																						POSTAGE
																						OLD GOODS
																						TOTAL
	TOTAL																					...... Books Distributed / ...... Total Books Used

No.	JOBBER	ADDRESS	DIRECT TO JOBBERS Jell-O	DIRECT TO JOBBERS I.C.P.	Day of Week	ROUTE FOR WEEK	
							NEXT MAIL POINT
							REMARKS

FIG. 16. RESEARCH INFORMATION OBTAINED BY SALESMEN

The function of salesmen is to sell. In some cases, however, valuable information may be obtained from them, and such information may be invaluable in advertising research.

the man who actually sells the goods. He must secure a hearing from the individuals under investigation, and he must carry on his interview in such a way as to get the information without any bias. In many cases, he must conceal the identity of his employer until the end of the interview. He must ordi-

JOSEPH RICHARDS COMPANY
INCORPORATED
247 PARK AVENUE, NEW YORK
ADVERTISING
"Facts First—Then Advertising"
TRADE MARK

Date of Interview ....
Nature of Interview ....
Name of Investigator ....
Number of Interview ....
Edited by ....

Dealer Field Survey—Spark Plugs

1. Name of firm: ....
2. Address: ....
3. Kind of business:
   - Automobile accessory store 6–1
   - Public garage 2
   - Gasoline station 3
   - Service station 4
4. Name of individual interviewed: ....
5. Position of individual:
   - Owner or officer 7–1
   - Manager or foreman 2
   - Clerk or service man 3
6. What make or makes of spark plug do you sell and approximately what percentage of your total spark plug business is done with each make?
   - A. C. ....%
   - Bosch (Amer.) ....%
   - Bosch (Robert) ....%
   - Champion ....%
   - Splitdorf ....%
   - ....%
   - ....%
   - ....%
   - Total 100%
7. What reasons can you give for the .... spark plug being your best seller? ....
8. In your opinion, which of the following would most influence a motor car owner or operator to try a new make of spark plug?
   - Group 1. (Check one)
     - Reputation of manufacturer for quality product 8–1
     - Recommendation of automobile manufacturers 2
     - Recommendation of the accessory dealer 3
     - Recommendation of other users.. 4
   - Group 2. (Check one)
     - Indestructible porcelain 9–1
     - Replaceable porcelain 2
   - Group 3. (Check one)
     - Multiple spark 10–1
     - Single spark 2
   - Group 4. (Check one)
     - Plug with ordinary life electrodes, at regular price 11–1
     - Plug with long life electrodes, at a higher price 2
9. If you could purchase a plug that would remain efficient as long as the average car lasts, at what price do you think you could sell it retail?
   - 50c 12–1
   - 75c 2
   - $1.00 3
   - $1.25 4
   - $1.50 5
   - $1.75 6
   - $2.00 7
10. What discounts would you expect to receive when purchases were made in less than 100, 100, and 500 lots?
    - Less than 100 ....% 13–
    - 100 ....% 14–
    - 500 ....% 15–
11. Of the spark plugs you carry, what particular one has shown the greatest increase in sales during the last twelve months? .... 16 & 17
12. What reasons can you give for this increase? 18–
13. What percentage of the persons who purchase spark plugs from you ask for a particular make? ....% 19–
14. What particular make is most often called for? .... 20 & 21
15. What percentage of your customers purchase complete sets of spark plugs as compared with those who purchase plugs for immediate replacements or extras?
    - Complete sets ....% 22–
    - Replacements ....% 23–
    - Extras ....% 24–
    - Total 100
16. For what make of car do you sell the greatest number of plugs? 25–
17. To what classes of consumers do you sell the greatest number of plugs?
    - Owners 26–1
    - Chauffeurs 2
18. What do you consider the most frequent cause of spark plug troubles?
    - Short circuiting 27–1
    - Cracked Porcelains 2
    - Loosened electrodes 3
    - Compression leaks 4
    - Fouling 5
    - Burning off of electrodes 6
    - ....
    - ....
19. Approximately how many spark plugs do you purchase in a year? 28–
20. In what quantity and at what price do you usually purchase your best seller which you refer to in answering Question No. 6?
    - Quantity ....
    - Price ....
21. Would you consider stocking a spark plug of a superior quality, sold retail at a higher price than the ordinary plug but offering you a greater discount and a larger profit per plug?
    - Yes 29–1
    - No. 2
22. If "No," why would you not stock such a plug? 30–

FIG. 17A. INTERVIEW FORM FOR DEALERS, PAGE 1

narily keep his printed forms under cover and fill them out only after the interview is over.

Figures 17 and 18 are excellent examples of questionnaires for use by interviewers—one for dealer interviews and the other for consumer interviews. All questions are carefully detailed so that the work of the investigator in recording his ob-

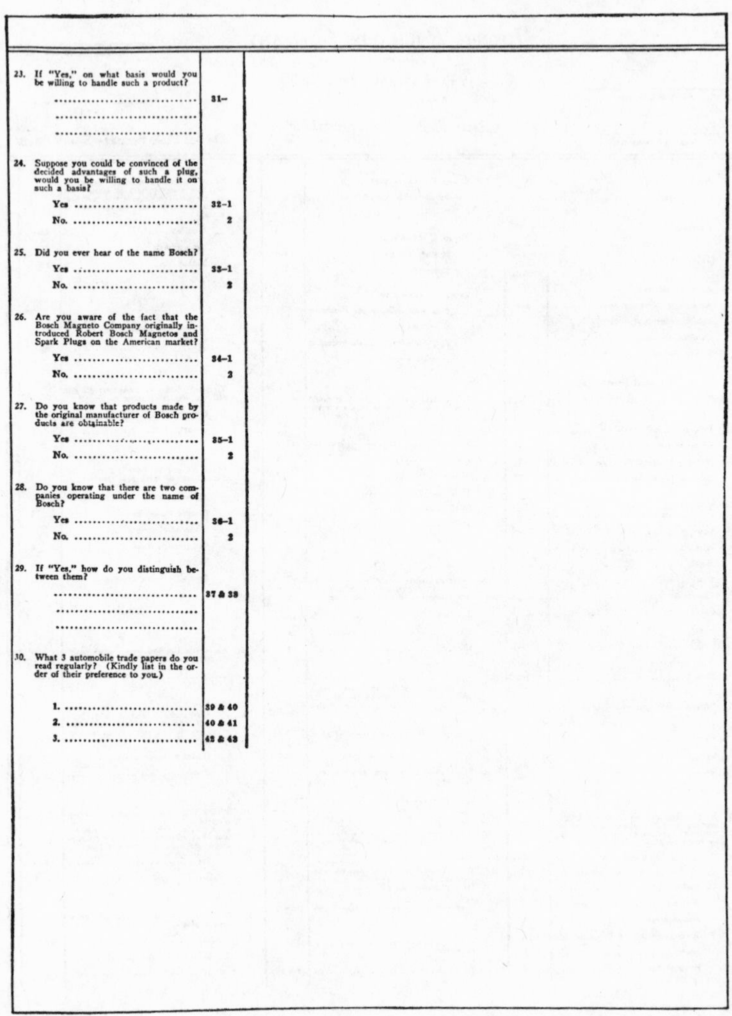

23. If "Yes," on what basis would you be willing to handle such a product?

....	31–
....	
....	

24. Suppose you could be convinced of the decided advantages of such a plug, would you be willing to handle it on such a basis?

Yes	32–1
No.	2

25. Did you ever hear of the name Bosch?

Yes	33–1
No.	2

26. Are you aware of the fact that the Bosch Magneto Company originally introduced Robert Bosch Magnetos and Spark Plugs on the American market?

Yes	34–1
No.	2

27. Do you know that products made by the original manufacturer of Bosch products are obtainable?

Yes	35–1
No.	2

28. Do you know that there are two companies operating under the name of Bosch?

Yes	36–1
No.	2

29. If "Yes," how do you distinguish between them?

....	37 & 38
....	
....	

30. What 3 automobile trade papers do you read regularly? (Kindly list in the order of their preference to you.)

1.	39 & 40
2.	40 & 41
3.	42 & 43

Fig. 17b. Interview Form for Dealers, Page 2

servations will be as easy as possible. No mention of the particular make of spark plug under investigation is made until almost the end of the interview, when there is an attempt to find out to what extent a specific company's products are known to the trade and to the public.

______ Date of Interview

______ Nature of Interview

______ Name of Investigator

JOSEPH RICHARDS COMPANY
INCORPORATED
247 PARK AVENUE, NEW YORK
ADVERTISING
"Facts First—Then Advertising"
TRADE MARK

______ Number of Interview

______ Edited by

Consumer Field Survey—Spark Plugs

1. Name of individual:
   ....

2. Address:
   No. ....Street..................
   City ....State ....

3. Make of automobile and year of manufacture:
   Make 6–
   Year 7–

4. Is this car a
   Passenger car 8–1
   Truck 2
   Taxi 3
   Bus 4

5. Is individual interviewed?
   Owner 9–1
   Operator 2

6. What make or makes of spark plugs were in this car when you bought it? 10 & 11
   A. C. ....
   Bosch (Amer.) ....
   Bosch (Robt.) ....
   Champion ....
   Fyrac ....
   Splitdorf ....
   ....
   ....

7. What make or makes of spark plugs are you now using? 12 & 13
   A. C. ....
   Bosch (Amer.) ....
   Bosch (Robt.) ....
   Champion ....
   Fyrac ....
   Splitdorf ....
   ....
   ....

8. If these plugs are all the same make, are they the identical ones that were in this car when you bought it?
   Yes 14–1
   No 2
   Some of them 3

9. If person interviewed answers "No" to Question 8, ask him:
   Why did you purchase other plugs of the same make and what price did you pay for them?
   15–
   ....
   ....
   Price $.................. 16–

10. If person is now using a different make of plug than that with which his car was originally equipped, ask him:
    What was your reason for changing from that make of plug with which your car was originally equipped to the make you are now using and what price did you pay for them?
    Make
    .... $.......
    ....
    Make
    .... $.......
    ....

11. What makes of plugs have you used since you have been driving automobiles? 17 & 18
    ....
    ....
    ....

12. Of all the plugs you have ever used which particular one do you like best? 19 & 20
    ....

13. Why do you like this make best?
    Does not carbonize quickly......... 21–1
    Porcelain more durable 2
    Porcelain replaceable 3
    Porcelain indestructible 4
    Prefer single spark 5
    Prefer multiple spark 6
    Less expensive 7
    Produces more power 8
    Electrodes last longer 9
    Lasts longer 0
    Make obtainable everywhere x
    More efficient in cylinders which are passing oil .... y
    ....
    ....

14. If you could purchase a plug that would last as long as your car, what price would you be willing to pay?
    50c 22–1
    75c 2
    $1.00 3
    1.25 4
    1.50 5
    1.75 6
    2.00 7
    Note to Investigator: First allow the person interviewed to answer the question before trying to raise the price.

15. Which of the following would influence you most to try a new make of spark plug?
    Group 1. (Check one)
    Reputation of manufacturer for quality products 23–1
    Recommendation of automobile manufacturers 2
    Recommendation of your accessory dealer 3
    Recommendation of friends 4
    Group 2. (Check one)
    Indestructible porcelain 24–1
    Replaceable porcelain 2
    Group 3. (Check one)
    Multiple spark 25–1
    Single spark 2
    Group 4. (Check one)
    Plug with ordinary life electrodes, at regular price 26–1
    Plug with long life electrodes, at a higher price 2

16. What particular spark plug trouble most frequently necessitates replacements?
    Short circuiting 27–1
    Cracked porcelain 2
    Loosened electrodes 3
    Compression leaks 4
    Fouling 5
    Burning of electrodes 6

17. Approximately how many spark plugs do you purchase a year?
    28–

18. How many extra plugs do you carry in your car?
    29–

FIG. 18A. INTERVIEW FORM FOR CONSUMERS, PAGE 1

Figure 19 illustrates the form of consumer field questionnaire used by government investigators in a survey of the Philadelphia milk market. This should be compared with Figure 14 to observe how the mail and interview questionnaires differ in make-up of questions.

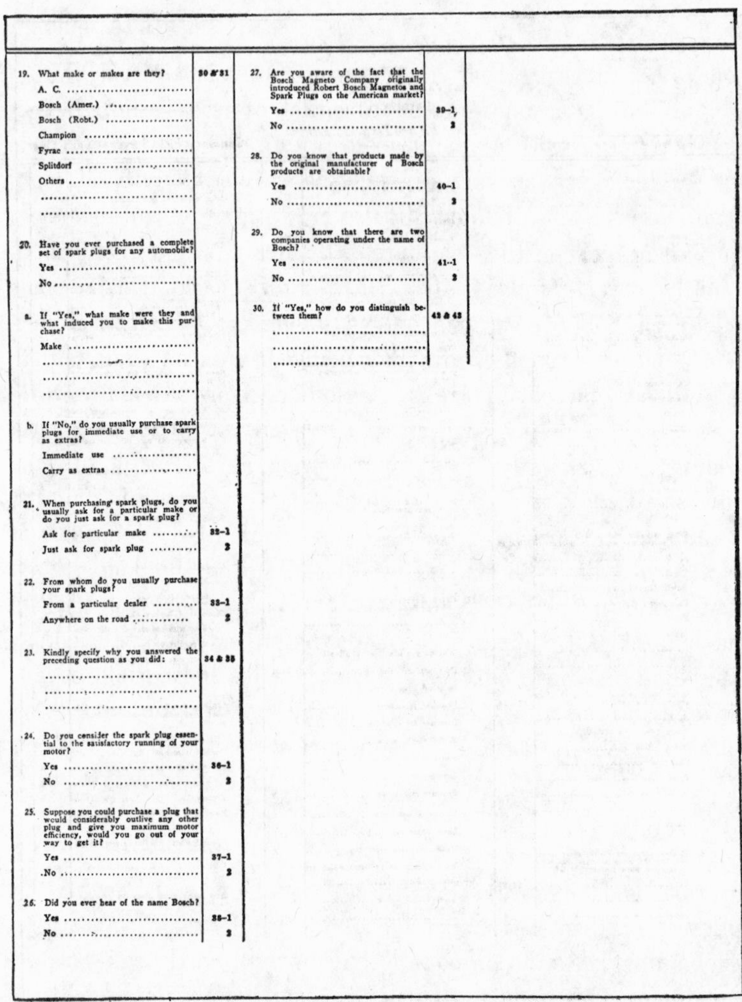

19. What make or makes are they? — 30 & 31

A. C. ....
Bosch (Amer.) ....
Bosch (Robt.) ....
Champion ....
Fyrac ....
Splitdorf ....
Others ....
....
....

20. Have you ever purchased a complete set of spark plugs for any automobile?

Yes ....
No ....

a. If "Yes," what make were they and what induced you to make this purchase?

Make ....
....
....
....

b. If "No," do you usually purchase spark plugs for immediate use or to carry as extras?

Immediate use ....
Carry as extras ....

21. When purchasing spark plugs, do you usually ask for a particular make or do you just ask for a spark plug?

Ask for particular make 32–1
Just ask for spark plug 2

22. From whom do you usually purchase your spark plugs?

From a particular dealer 33–1
Anywhere on the road 2

23. Kindly specify why you answered the preceding question as you did: — 34 & 35

....
....
....

24. Do you consider the spark plug essential to the satisfactory running of your motor?

Yes 36–1
No 2

25. Suppose you could purchase a plug that would considerably outlive any other plug and give you maximum motor efficiency, would you go out of your way to get it?

Yes 37–1
No 2

26. Did you ever hear of the name Bosch?

Yes 38–1
No 2

27. Are you aware of the fact that the Bosch Magneto Company originally introduced Robert Bosch Magnetos and Spark Plugs on the American market?

Yes 39–1
No 2

28. Do you know that products made by the original manufacturer of Bosch products are obtainable?

Yes 40–1
No 2

29. Do you know that there are two companies operating under the name of Bosch?

Yes 41–1
No 2

30. If "Yes," how do you distinguish between them? — 42 & 43

....
....
....

FIG. 18B. INTERVIEW FORM FOR CONSUMERS, PAGE 2

The Psychological Test

Experimental psychology as applied to practical advertising problems is growing rapidly in importance. Carried out under controlled conditions, it is possible to obtain exceedingly valuable results. A great many of these experiments have been carried on in schools and colleges because of the greater opportunity for such laboratory research, and the greater ease with which conditions may be controlled.

Psychological experiments may be differentiated according to their purpose, as being conducted according to the recognition method, the recall method, or collective opinion.

The recognition method is used most often to test the attention value of a given type of face, a slogan, a headline or an illustration. The method is always the same. The subjects to be tested are given a list of type faces, slogans, words, or whatever is being tested, and from this list they pick out the ones with the most attention value. For example, in measuring the memory value of a trade name, according to Richard B. Franken, 50 possibilities may be listed on sheets of paper and

FIG. 19.—AN EXAMPLE OF CONSUMER INTERVIEW QUESTIONNAIRE

Interviewer..........................
Date..............................

PHILADELPHIA MILK QUESTIONNAIRE
(*Consumer*)

Name......................*No*......*Street*..........................
City...............*State*.............*Occupation (Husband's)*..........
INCOME CLASSIFICATION...............

---

1. HOW MANY PERSONS ARE THERE IN YOUR FAMILY?
   Infants....3 to 6 Yrs. (Inc.)...
   7 to 12 yrs. (Inc.)...........
   13 to 18 " " ....
   Adults......................

2. HOW MUCH FRESH MILK IS USED IN YOUR FAMILY DAILY?
   What part for drinking?......
   Cooking?..............
   Cereal?...............
   Other (note what)?.........

---

3. WHAT GRADE MILK DO YOU PURCHASE REGULARLY?................
   Why?..

---

4. HOW MUCH OF THE FOLLOWING IS USED WEEKLY?
   Cream.............................
   Condensed or evaporated............ Cooking......In drinks.....
   Certified milk..................... Use..........
   Skimmed milk....................... Use..........
   Buttermilk......................... Use..........
   Cheese............................
   Ice cream (other than home-made).....
   Powdered Milk.......................
   Butter............................. Cooking......Table use.....
   Butter substitutes................. Cooking......Table use.....

Fig. 19—*Continued*

5. Who Drinks Milk in Your Family?

	Infants	Children			Adults
		3 to 6	7 to 12	13 to 18	
At every meal........	....	....	....	....	....
Every day..........	....	....	....	....	....
Occasionally........	....	....	....	....	....
Never..........	....	....	....	....	....

6. Is Milk Served at the School Where Your Children Attend?......
How many of your children drink milk at school?..................

7. Why Do Those in Your Family Who Drink Milk Do So?
(*a*) For health.............. Habit..........................
Like it.................. For food value...................
Urged to drink it......... Doctor's orders...................
Miscellaneous............ Do not know......................

(*b*) Why Do Not Members of Your Family Drink Milk?
Too fattening............ High priced......................
Do not like it........... Prefer coffee, tea, etc...........
Do not need it.......... Does not agree with them.........
Miscellaneous........... Do not know......................

8. What Would Cause You to Use More Milk?
Lower price................. Younger children.................
Larger family............... Better quality...................
More cooking................ Miscellaneous....................
Convenience................. Do not know......................

9. How Much Have You Increased..........or Decreased..........
Your Consumption of Milk Within the Last Three Years?
A great deal................ Moderately.......................
Not at all.................. Do not know......................

Why?
Price (Whether price is lower or not)..........................
Doctor's orders.............. For health.......................
Size of family...............

10. What Effect Does Price Have upon the Amount of Milk You Use?
None.......... Limits amount.......... Do not know..........

11. What Percentage of Your Budget for Food is Spent on Fresh Milk?..

12. How Does Milk Rank in Importance with Other Foods You Use?
First...... Second...... Third......
Other (note rank)........... Do not know......................

FIG. 19—*Continued*

13. WHY DO YOU USE CONDENSED, EVAPORATED, OR POWDERED MILK?

Price........................	Convenience........................
Cleanliness..................	Miscellaneous......................
Keeps without ice............	Do not know........................
Like it......................	(Number in order of preference)....

---

14. WHERE HAVE YOU SEEN FRESH MILK ADVERTISED?

Newspapers.................	Subway and elevated stations......
Movies.....................	Billboards........................
Street cars................	Dealers' wagons...................
Do not remember............	Stores and restaurants............
(Number in order mentioned)	Elsewhere.........................

---

15. WHERE AND HOW HAVE YOU HEARD OR SEEN THE USE OF FRESH MILK ADVOCATED?

	Schools	Other Places
Leaflets..............	....	....
Plays.................	....	....
Stories...............	....	....
Lectures..............	....	....
Cooking demonstrations	....	....

Did this reach you directly or some other member of your family?......

---

16. WHAT DO YOU REMEMBER ABOUT ADVERTISING YOU HAVE SEEN?

Price................	Cleanliness........	Miscellaneous........
Food value...........	Health.............	Do not know..........
Good for children....	Quality............	
Safe.................	(Number in order of preference)	

---

17. WHAT SPECIAL FEATURES DO YOU THINK SHOULD BE ADVERTISED?

Price...............	Cleanliness.......	Do not know........
Food value..........	Safe..............	Miscellaneous......
Health..............	Quality...........	
	(Number in order of preference)	

---

18. HAS SUCH ADVERTISING AND PUBLICITY INFLUENCED YOUR FAMILY IN CONSUMING FLUID MILK?

A great deal..........	A little............	Not any............
Do not know.........		

---

19. HOW DOES THE PRICE OF MILK IN PHILADELPHIA COMPARE WITH THE PRICE OF MILK IN OTHER LARGE CITIES?

---

20. HOW DOES YOUR MILK CONSUMPTION CHANGE BY SEASON?

Cold weather.........	No change.........
Warm weather.......	

What causes this change..............................?

---

21. REMARKS

....

....

....

distributed to 50 subjects. The next day these subjects are handed another sheet with 100 names, including the 50 given the day before, and 50 which they have never seen. They are asked to mark all those which they saw the day before.

The recall method consists of showing to certain subjects a list of trade names, for instance, and, after a given period of time, asking them to write down all those that they remember. The recall method is equally applicable to tests for the attention value of color, design, arrangement, or position.

A third method of testing is the so-called "order of merit" method. Some method of ranking must be devised and then a given group of subjects are asked to judge the various advertisements, appeals, motives, or whatever it may be, according to this method of ranking. Richard B. Franken used this method of testing direct impressions of various selling points or phrases for hosiery. Seventy-seven of these phrases were mimeographed on sheets of paper and distributed to four groups of students. These students were instructed to mark all the listed appeals according to the degree in which they appealed personally. The ratings were:

Mark very strong	3
Mark strong	2
Mark weak	1
Mark very weak	0

CHAPTER III

METHODS OF ANALYSIS AND COMPARISON

The previous chapter has dealt with the collection of data. The next step is to analyze them in such a way as to determine their meaning or significance. This is accomplished, at least in the majority of cases, by the use of statistical method, with the elements of which it is assumed that readers are acquainted. The attempt is made here to indicate in a general way how statistics and graphics are applied to the analysis of marketing data. In addition, this chapter deals with the editing, tabulation, classification, comparison, and correlation of the data required prior to the making of generalizations.

1. *Editing.*—Before any tabulation can be made, it is important to edit observations carefully for accuracy, bias, incompleteness, or other factors which would be likely to prejudice the validity of the statistical compilation.

2. *Tabulation.*—Observations are recorded as they come in on a tabulation schedule, or recapitulation sheet. This is made up, either in advance of the actual receipt of observations, where the type of answer is known, or as the answers come in.

3. *Classification.*—A number of classifications are usually possible, such as geographical distribution, age, sex, volume of business, or preferences expressed. Classification may be made from the basic records on the tabulation schedule, or results may be recapitulated later on special sheets.

4. *Computation and Comparison.*—The next step is to compare data in order to bring out causal relationships. It may be necessary to use computation at this point to reduce different sets of statistics to a comparable basis.

5. *Correlation.*—It is desirable, if possible, to establish

some relation between a specific set of statistics and the market. If a direct relation can be found, this is known as a "market index." Even where the precise nature of the causal relation is not understood, as in the case of market indices where one set of statistics has no directly traceable connection with another set, the causal relation may, nevertheless, be turned to practical account.

Statistical Analysis

The simplest form of statistical analysis is a mere enumeration of particular observations. In advertising research, however, the chief interest normally lies in the average and the aggregate rather than in the individual case. There are exceptions, of course, where it is desired to single out individuals whose observations carry special weight, such as the most prominent dealer in a town, or an authority on the subject which is being studied.

One of the great dangers in statistical analysis is that almost all sets of figures appear equally authentic to the person who merely scrutinizes them for the inferences which may be drawn from them. He will have no time to go back of the returns. Consequently, the statistical analysis of the observations should be made with strict attention to accuracy and to fairness of interpretation. While a profound knowledge of statistical method is not essential, since involved statistical forms are not generally required, it is desirable to have a fair working knowledge of it, such as may be obtained from any of the various texts on the subject.

Averages

Averages may be either arithmetic or weighted. The arithmetic average is obtained by taking the sum of the observations in any given class and dividing them by the number of observations. It has a fairly wide usage. It is of particular value where the numerical observations fall within a comparatively small range, and where there are not too many extremes to render the average unrepresentative of the whole. This does not necessarily hold true, however. Rates of pay may be properly averaged for certain purposes even though they range from $10 a week for the office boy to $1,000 a week for executives. Similarly, if dealers were asked how much of a certain article they sold in a year, it might be advisable to reduce the tabulation to the average number sold per dealer. It would make the result more complete if dealers were classified according to size, geographical location, and type of customer served, and an average obtained for each of these classifications.

The weighted average is employed to give proper emphasis to various factors of unequal importance. The question was asked, for example, "What are your three best selling brands of baking powder, named in order of importance?" Disregarding the method of selecting the weights for the moment, first choice was given a count of 5, second choice 3, and third choice 1. Here each choice is weighted in order of importance.

Out of the 100 grocers who replied to this particular question, 50 gave first choice to a certain brand, 30 gave it second choice, and 20 gave it third choice. The weighted average for the brand was made up, therefore, as follows:

50 (first choice) × 5 (weight for first choice) = 250
30 (second choice) × 3 (weight for second choice) = 90
20 (third choice) × 1 (weight for third choice) = 20

360

The weighted total for this brand was 360, which, when divided by the 100 observations, gives a weighted average of 3.6 for the group.

Suppose for a second brand 25 grocers gave it first choice, 50 voted second, and 25 third. Then the weight for this brand would be 25×5 plus 50×3 plus 25×1, which equals 300, or an average of 3.

By following out this method proper significance can be given to preferences for brands, appeals, qualities, or motives.

Modes and Medians

The mode, in a given series of numbers, is the number which is typical. In the ordinary case, this number would be the one which recurs the most frequently. Yet if a certain series had nine classes, all containing three items except one which contained four, this one class would not necessarily be the mode. In the series 4, 5, 6, 7, 7, 7, 6, 5, 4, the mode would clearly be 7. The mode, unlike the arithmetic average, discards extremes. It is often of value in advertising research because it points out the principal grouping, or, in other words, the principal market, appeal, or motive. There may, of course, be several modes in a series of numbers. For example, if dealers were asked at what price they thought a certain article should sell, there might be a number of price levels. Some might prefer an article to sell at $1.00; others at $1.50; and still others at $3.00. The arithmetic average would be misleading in tabulating the replies to such a question.

Median simply means middle point. The median is found by arranging a series of numbers in the order of their magnitude and choosing the middle one. It is not often used in market analysis computations, but is convenient in computing the results of psychological observations.

Graphic Interpretation

Whenever statistical tabulations can be reduced to simple forms, they may be graphed or charted to show relationships more clearly. The graph is a method of presentation which is of great importance in all market and advertising research because of the greater precision and ease with which generalizations may be made from these pictorial forms.

It is highly desirable for those engaged in research work to be familiar with the more ordinary forms of graphic presentation. This information is obtainable from any of the simpler textbooks on the subject. The pie or circle chart is more often used for pictorial effect than for accurate interpretation of statistical facts. It will serve to show component parts when they are few in number, and where their total may be considered to equal 100 per cent.

The bar chart, in addition to showing component parts, can also be employed to illustrate comparisons between two sets of data, and for showing comparisons over a period of time. It has an advantage over the circle chart in that the pictorial effect is not lost while the eye can readily grasp the quantitative relations involved.

The curve or line chart is, as a rule, the most valuable for research use. While it may not possess the same attention value as the more pictorial forms, the statistical facts are usually more readily understood in their relation to each other. It is especially valuable in showing variations over a period of time, or in forecasting probable trends. When plotted on so-called "ratio" or "semilogarithmic" paper, the numerical data appear in relative magnitudes, that is, according to the rate of increase or decrease, rather than in the actual amount.

In any study of markets, maps are naturally in frequent use. By the use of various colors, it is possible to show in vivid fashion at what points sales are satisfactory, where advertising or promotional effort is required, or other data of a geographical nature.

There has recently been a movement towards the standardization of colors used in market analysis charting. Committee Number III of the Distribution Conference of the Chamber of Commerce of the United States of America recommends following the order of the spectrum—red, orange, yellow, green, blue, indigo, violet. To quote Paul T. Cherington:

> Red should indicate the best, highest, richest, most immediate, or most conspicuous element to be graphed, and the others should follow in order (orange, yellow, green, blue, indigo, violet) as they occur in the spectrum, reserving white to indicate blank items, and black for special uses. Where less than seven colors are to be used, there is obvious advantage in selecting contrasting colors—such as red and violet, or red and blue, while for three colors, the three fundamental color sensations,—red, green, and violet blue offer simple choice. . . . The high spots should be red, the low spots blue, or one of the blue composites, the best territory would be red and the worst territory violet, while between these two would come the other grades, always in the same order, green always below yellow, and blue below green.

Examination and Editing of Data

A research job may have to consider statistics already available on the subject, such as those supplied by the government or other sources. It will also have to do with statistical observations gathered for the purposes of the investigation in hand. In either case, these statistics must be examined or edited for accuracy, reliability, relevancy, applicability, recency, and completeness. The editing of replies from mail questionnaires and personal interviews requires in some cases elaborate system and detail.

The person who does the editing of the material obtained from original observations must have a considerable knowledge of the subject being dealt with. Each particular questionnaire should be reviewed in relation to the matter as a whole. If, for example, he finds that certain of the questions are not being answered, he must ascertain the reason. If interviews are used, he should find out, by statistical comparison, whether one interviewer's results check with other's. There may be sound reason for discrepancies; but if bias is found throughout one interviewer's reports, then his observations must be set aside or allowed for. If a tabulating machine is used, the reporter's number can be punched on the interviews made by him, and his cards can quickly be sorted out for special analysis.

Editing should never become a mechanical process. Many times it is possible to discover new angles of approach through examination of the ways in which questions are answered or are not answered. The editor should be on the alert to note cases where the questionnaire does not bring out the exact results required, and should try to devise some new question or some better method of eliciting the information needed.

Tabulation of Data

There are a number of methods by which observations may be tabulated, depending primarily on the question asked and the nature of the reply. The simplest form of tabulation is that used in recording replies to inquiries which demand one answer only, such as "yes" or "no." Other forms of tabulation are used where a variety of answers is possible, as where the answer is in numerical form, or where preferences are registered.

1. *One Alternative.*—The tabulation of questions which may be answered by "yes" or "no" presents the easiest problem. Figure 20 is an example of such a tabulation. Here the question was: "Do you own a phonograph?" Postcards with this question upon it were mailed to a certain number of the subscribers to the magazine making the investigation, classified according to states.

FIG. 20.—AN EXAMPLE OF TABULATION OF REPLIES INVOLVING ONE ALTERNATIVE

(*American Legion Weekly*)

		Me.	N. H.	Vt.	Mass.	R. I.	Conn.	New England States
	Cards Mailed	100	70	50	480	50	90	840
	Returned	16	8	4	28	3	12	71
	Married	11	7	2	17	2	8	47
	Single	3	1	...	6	1	2	12
	Unanswered	2	...	2	5	...	2	12
Do you own a phonograph?	Yes	5	5	3	21	1	4	39
	No	10	3	1	6	2	8	30
	Unanswered	1	...	...	1	...	...	2

By glancing at the recapitulation sheet, it is possible to tell what the results were from each state. As a matter of fact, there were so few observations that the results, for any given state, would be of doubtful value. For example, 25 per cent of the replies from Vermont voted "no" while 66 per cent of replies from Rhode Island answered "no." But there were only four answers from Vermont and three from Rhode Island. Such a paucity of replies nullifies the value of any inferences which might be drawn from them. When, however, the figure for all New England is tabulated, the observations are sufficiently numerous to give a fairer basis, while those for the whole country should, of course, give a still more representative indication.

While the answers as tabulated here are straight numerical facts, it would have been possible to give them in the form of percentages, such as the percentage of subscribers owning phonographs in Maine, New Hampshire, etc.

2. *Order of Merit or Importance.*—A second tabular method of analysis is required when a question is asked which may be answered in a number of possible ways. For example, it was desired to find out what make of car was owned by car owners among Elks in six cities diversified in size and geographical area. Figure 21 shows how the results were tabulated in order of importance. The same form of tabulation might be used if the question had been: "What is your reason for drinking milk?" The various reasons would be ranked according to the number of votes received, *i.e.,* in their order of merit.

3. *Preferences.*—A further element of complexity is introduced into the tabular analysis when it is desired to determine the preferences for certain commodities, motives for purchase, or dominating appeals. In order to give each brand, commodity, or motive its proper rank, the weighted average is employed. Thus, in Figure 22, five points are allowed for first choice, four for second, three for third, two for fourth, and one for fifth. Each pen or pencil is given a certain arbitrary score when all the returns are in. Finally, the list is ranked in numerical order according to the total scores.

Preferences may be expressed graphically in many cases, as in Figure 23, which illustrates farmers' reasons for painting their houses. Here, in order to check results, information on the same subject was obtained from four sources—average farmers, county agents, dealers, and leading farmers—and the percentages were combined.

4. *Numerical Replies.*—It is often desired to obtain an-

Fig. 21.—An Example of Tabulation in Order of Importance
(*Elk's Magazine*)

An Analysis of Cars Owned, by Makes: 3387 Cars Owned by Elks in the 6 Cities Checked were Scattered Over 110 Different Makes of Cars

Ford	854	Grant	7	R & V Knight	2
Buick	443	Jeffrey	7	Westcott	2
Dodge	257	Briscoe	6	Borland	1
Studebaker	213	Premier	6	Columbia	1
Cadillac	197	Stutz	6	Crow Elkhart	1
Chevrolet	148	Cunningham	5	Day Elder	1
Nash	98	Mercer	5	Durant	1
Overland	89	Pierce-Arrow	5	Gordon	1
Oakland	79	Winton	5	Harroun	1
Reo	74	Anderson	4	Interstate	1
Hudson	73	Auburn	4	Jackson	1
Dort	67	Davis	4	Lexington	1
Franklin	65	Jordan	4	MacMore	1
Hupmobile	60	King	4	Maib	1
Maxwell	57	Saxon	4	McFarlan	1
Oldsmobile	54	Scripps Booth	4	Meteor	1
Chandler	50	White	4	Milburn Electric	1
Packard	42	Baker	3	Monitor	1
Paige	38	Case	3	Monroe	1
Essex	32	Gardner	3	Moore	1
Chalmers	29	Moon	3	Nelson	1
Liberty	21	National	3	Pan American	1
Detroit Electric	17	Ohio	3	Pilot	1
Paterson	15	Rauch & Long	3	R. & S.	1
Velie	14	Templar	3	Regal	1
Stephens	14	Wood	3	Roamer	1
Mitchell	13	Detroit	3	Sayer	1
Marmon	13	Marion	3	Standard Electric	1
Willys-Knight	12	Dixie	2	Stanley	1
Haynes	11	Empire	2	Stevens	1
Kissel	11	Apperson	2	Stoddard	1
Peerless	10	Garford	2	Texas	1
Cole	10	Leach	2	West	1
Cleveland	9	Moline Knight	2	Whitney	1
Elgin	8	Lafayette	2	Wilson	1
Milburn	8	Revere	2	Woods Electric	1
Stearns	8	Stearns Knight	2		

swers to question of "How much?" "How many?" or "How often?" The replies may be treated in a wide variety of ways. The arithmetic average may be obtained, either of all of them,

FOUNTAIN AND PROPELLING PENCIL ANALYSIS

COMPILED BY

THE AMERICAN LEGION WEEKLY

1867 letters mailed to Legionnaire Druggists — 245 letters returned

What make, or makes of FOUNTAIN PENS do you handle?
(Please list in order of volume sold.)

	Mentioned					★Total
	First	*Second*	*Third*	*Fourth*	*Fifth*	*Points*
Parker	84	50	18	3	2	682
Waterman	59	30	7	..	..	436
Sheaffer	34	12	4	1	..	232
Conklin	23	16	8	3	..	209
Dunn	9	5	18	5	1	130
Wahl	10	5	8	2	2	100
Moore	7	5	6	1	..	75
Monogram	3	8	5	2	..	66
Black and White	2	1	4	2	..	30
Ingersoll	1	2	2	2	1	24
Eagle	..	3	3	1	1	24
Century	1	3	..	1	..	19
United Drug Co.	1	1	2	1	..	17
John Holland	1	2	..	1	..	15
Aiken	..	2	2	..	..	14
Edison	1	1	1	..	1	13
Art Craft	2	..	1	..	..	13
Franklin	1	1	1	..	..	12
Diamond Point	..	1	1	2	..	11
John Hancock	..	1	..	2	..	8
Signet	..	1	..	2	..	8
Superite	1	..	1	..	..	8
Crocker	..	2	..	..	..	8
Salz	..	..	2	..	1	7
Snapfill	..	1	..	1	..	6
University	..	1	..	1	..	6
Peter Pan	..	..	..	1	3	5
Iridium	..	1	..	..	..	4
LeBoeuf	..	1	..	..	..	4
Liberty	..	1	..	..	..	4
Nu-Point	..	1	..	..	..	4
Shultz	..	1	..	..	..	4
Paul E. Wirtz	..	1	..	..	..	4
Maximum	..	..	1	..	..	3
Todd	..	..	1	..	..	3
Universal	..	..	1	..	..	3
Lambert	..	..	..	1	..	2
Unanswered						11

What make, or makes of PROPELLING PENCILS do you handle?
(Please list in order of volume sold.)

	Mentioned					★Total
	First	*Second*	*Third*	*Fourth*	*Fifth*	*Points*
Wahl	103	30	8	1	1	662
Ingersoll	39	33	10	5	1	368
Sheaffer	31	9	..	..	..	191
Parker	16	15	11	1	..	175
Conklin	16	8	5	1	..	129
Waterman	6	13	3	..	..	91
Signet	3	10	1	2	..	62
Superite	3	3	2	1	..	35
Eagle	1	4	..	1	..	23
Moore	3	1	1	..	..	22
Dunn	1	2	2	1	..	21
Pal	..	1	4	1	..	18
Ki-mi-o	..	2	2	..	..	14
Art Craft	2	1	..	..	..	14
Monogram	1	2	..	..	..	13
Rite-Rite	1	1	1	..	..	12
Edison	2	..	..	..	..	10
Tubit	1	1	..	..	..	9
Fynne-Point	..	1	..	1	..	6
Dixon	1	..	..	..	..	5
Acine	..	1	..	..	..	4
Dickens	..	1	..	..	..	4
Nu-point	..	1	..	..	..	4
Shur-rite	..	1	..	..	..	4
Venus	..	1	..	..	..	4
Kali-graf	..	..	1	..	..	3
Sal-rite	..	..	1	..	..	3
United Drug Co.	..	..	1	..	..	3
J. K. Wood & Sons	..	..	1	..	..	3
Yankee	..	..	1	..	..	3
Swan	..	..	..	1	..	2
Unanswered						22

★ In figuring the total points appearing beside a brand name, five points have been allowed if mentioned first, four points if mentioned second, three points if mentioned third, two points if mentioned fourth, and one point if mentioned fifth.

What proportion of customers ask for fountain pens and propelling pencils by brand names?

Fountains pens	50% average of 219 dealers
Propelling pencils	51% average of 200 dealers

What percentage of your sales is represented in the following classes?

Fountains pens	\$1.00—\$2.50	37% average of 150 dealers
	2.50— 3.50	38% average of 198 dealers
	3.50— 4.50	14% average of 162 dealers
	4.50 and up	24% average of 180 dealers
Propelling pencils	1.00 and under	52% average of 154 dealers
	1.00— 2.00	30% average of 149 dealers
	2.00— 3.00	13% average of 118 dealers
	3.00— 4.00	12% average of 79 dealers
	4.00— 5.00	6% average of 44 dealers
	5.00 and up	5% average of 14 dealers

22

FIG. 22. TABULATION OF PREFERENCES

Example of a concise tabulation of the results of a survey of readers' preferences.

or of various classifications of the whole. If typical answers are desired, it may be useful to employ the mode. The method of tabulation and analysis will depend on the nature of the material and the purpose of the investigation.

Classification of Data

The significance of statistical data is often not apparent until a number of different methods of analysis have been tried out. Since, in the ordinary course, much labor is involved in trying out new combinations, the mechanical tabulating machine, originally applied to census reports, and later adapted to statistical work of a business nature, is of unusual value. Where the information to be classified is numerically great, or where the process of statistical analysis is continuously proceeding, the expense of renting one of these machines, or of

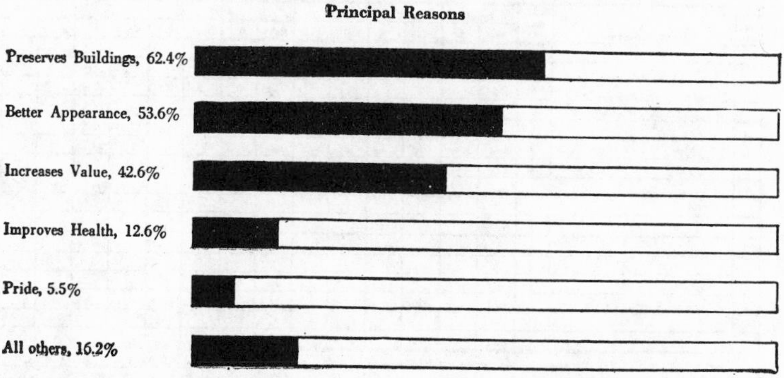

Principal Reasons

Preserves Buildings, 62.4%

Better Appearance, 53.6%

Increases Value, 42.6%

Improves Health, 12.6%

Pride, 5.5%

All others, 16.2%

Fig. 23. A Graphic Summary of Questionnaire Results

Reasons for the use of paint on farms are tabulated here in graphic form, on a percentage basis. (*Farm Journal.*)

having it done by a company specializing in tabulating work, is more than paid for by the increased speed of classification, and the freedom from clerical errors. Where the job of analysis is small and temporary, the mechanical procedure would have to be abandoned in favor of the recapitulation sheet, and hand methods. Simple punched-card systems, such as the "Findex," may, of course, be useful for special purposes.

R. O. Eastman, Inc., market analysts, have made excellent progress in mechanical methods of tabulation and classification. On the questionnaire, as it is made up by this concern, each question is coded for subsequent tabulation on punched cards. It is arranged in advance that every fact reported will be recorded by means of a hole punched on a card.

The same method of tabulation is used by the Joseph Richards Company, Inc. This concern, however, claims to have carried the process a step further by developing a chart upon which the results of the mechanical tabulation can be entered. For simplicity's sake, let it be assumed that each of the 45 columns contained on the Hollerith tabulating card is assigned to a different question and that each of the ten figures, from

Tab. by M. L. W. Coded by J. M. M. Question No. 14

Shaving Cream Questionnaire Account Alpha Mfg. Co. Classification By territories

Ord. of Imp.	Identification	Col. No. 6	Total		New Eng.		Middle Atl.		South Atl.		E. N. Central		W. N. Central			
			No.	%	No.	%	No.	%	No.	%	No.	%	No.	%	No.	%
		B														
	Not asked the question	Y	9		4		2		1		1		1			
	Could not remember	X	36		8		10		12		5		1			
	Shaved by barber	0	21		10		7		1		1		2			
4	Alpha	1	84	9.9	46	15.9	12	8.9	7	4.4	9	7.0	10	7.6		
2	Beta	2	276	32.7	99	34.0	40	29.6	54	34.2	35	27.1	48	36.6		
1	Delta	3	289	34.3	98	33.8	46	34.1	58	36.7	45	34.9	42	32.1		
3	Gamma	4	106	12.6	19	6.6	22	16.3	26	16.5	19	14.7	20	15.3		
		5														
		6														
		7														
		8														
5	others	9	89	10.5	28	9.7	15	11.1	13	8.2	21	16.3	11	8.4		
6	Times mentioned		843	100%	290	100%	135	100%	158	100%	129	100%	131	100%		
		Total	909		312		154		172		136		135			

Remarks – The 9 persons who were not asked the question are not considered. Of the balance, 36 or 4% "could not remember" the make of shaving cream they were using, and 21 or 2% were shaved by a barber – hence did not use this article. Percentages are based on the number of men in each territory who could answer the question.

FIG. 24. CHART SHOWING RESULTS OF MECHANICAL TABULATION

Machine tabulation is greatly simplified if its results may be readily summarized and compared. The names of the various products (which should have been arranged alphabetically) are each given a number before being punched on the tabulator. In the same way, numbers are assigned to the various answers given by respondents.

zero to nine, is assigned to a definite answer for each question. Thus, the answers to the question "What make of shaving cream do you use?" may be tabulated in column six and to Alpha Shaving Cream numeral one can be assigned, to Beta Cream numeral two, to Delta three, to Gamma four, and so on.

After all the questionnaires have been coded and a card punched for each questionnaire, the cards are run through the tabulating machine and the results entered on the form shown in Figure 24. Percentages are then worked, the identification of the code numbers inserted, and the order of importance indicated.

Should the information be desired by population groups, age groups, or geographical locations, this information can also be shown on the form as reference to it will indicate.

In addition to the numbers which represent brands, in this case, "O," "X," and "Y," "O" indicates none and on this

Tab. by M.L.D. Coded by F.M.M. Questions No. 14 & 15

Shaving Cream Questionnaire. Account Alpha Mfg. Co. Classification All territories

Column No. 6 / Column No. 7	Identification		Not asked the question	Could not answer	Shaved by barber	Produces quicker lather	Produces thicker lather	Lasts longer	Cheaper						Times mentioned		Persons answering Question [illegible]
Identification		B	Y	X	0	1	2	3	4	5	6	7	8	9	Total		
	B																
Not asked the question	Y		9												9	-	
Could not remember	X			36											36		
Shaved by barber	0				21										21		
Alpha	1		2	10		34	19	31	2						84		72
Beta	2		12	20		78	100	29	44						276		244
Delta	3		11	31		125	106	7	15						289		247
Gamma	4		5	12		18	14	64	-						106		89
	5																
	6																
	7																
	8																
Others	9		14	17		29	16	6	10						88		55
			44	92		284	255	137	71						843		707
	Total		53	128	21										909		

Remarks – Figures in Column marked "Times Mentioned" correspond to those in "Total" Column on Chart No. [illegible] and represent the number of individuals using each brand of shaving cream. Since a number of individuals gave more than one reason for choice, the total number of reasons given for each brand exceeds the figure shown in the extreme right-hand column.

FIG. 25. CROSS ANALYSIS OF THE SAME DATA

One purpose of the tabulating machine is to simplify the process of cross-analyzing—that is, the arrangement of data in divers ways, so as to discover any peculiar or significant groupings or relationships between them.

particular question, would apply to the number of individuals who do not use any make of shaving cream (men who are shaved regularly by the barber); "X" indicates those individuals who could not remember what make they were using; "Y" would indicate those individuals of whom this particular question was not asked, for some reason or other.

The remaining symbol "B" is used only in cases where an answer is dependent on some previous question. For example, the question is asked: "Do you like smoked herring?" and the possible answers are "yes" or "no." This question is followed by asking a dependent question of those who liked smoked herring, "Why do you like it?" In tabulating the answers to this latter question, as many "B's" will be shown as there are individuals who do not like smoked herring.

Practically the same procedure is followed in using the cross-analysis form as is used in filling in the straight analysis form. The only difference in the latter case is that information is shown by individual classifications. Going back to the question "What make of shaving cream do you use?" here can be shown the reasons why those persons now using Alpha Cream do so and the same for Beta, Delta, and Gamma. Although no percentages are shown on the cross-analysis form the numbers can be interpreted in percentages and entered on a separate sheet. (See Figure 25.)

Whereas most features may be precoded or set down in advance, such as questions which may be answered only by "yes" or "no," or where the definite possible answers are known in advance, the scope of other answers cannot well be predicted, and must be left uncoded until replies come in (such as replies as to uses of a product). In such cases, a special code is made up as the answers come in.

Interpretation symbols are used so that the reporters, the editors, and any others having to do with the question may know exactly what it is about. For example, the following are the code symbols used by R. E. Eastman, Inc.:

A. One answer only

B. More than one answer possible, such as "What brand used in the past?"

C. Answer in percentage

D. Actual figures ("How many stock turns per year?")

E. Both amount and per cent

F. Do not suggest answers

G. Answer may be suggested, as "Which of the following have you used in the past?"

H. Answer dependent on some previous question, requiring a check back, etc.

Cross-Analysis

The process of analysis requires careful cross-tabulation to bring out various relations for purposes of comparison. There are three main ways of making cross-analyses, according to:

1. *Characteristics of the Unit of Observation.*—These may be either qualitative, such as race, health, social position, and religion, or quantitative, such as income or size of business. Figure 26 shows how answers to the question of why other foods were used instead of meat were cross-analyzed according to race and income. Fifty-five per cent of the Italians interrogated used other foods instead of meat because they were fond of them, while only 22 per cent of native Americans gave this as a reason.

FIG. 26.—AN EXAMPLE OF CROSS-ANALYSIS BY CHARACTERISTICS OF THE UNIT OF OBSERVATION

(U. S. Bureau of Agricultural Economics)

Reasons for Using Other Foods Instead of Meat; Percentage of Reasons Mentioned

	Variety	Fond of it	Health	Religion	Food Value	Economy	Other Reasons
NATIVE WHITE AMERICANS:							
Poor	27.9%	24.6%	10.4%	8.3%	2.1%	13.8%	12.9%
Middle	38.2	17.1	16.0	10.9	8.7	4.7	4.4
Well-to-do	32.1	22.8	13.6	6.0	8.4	2.2	14.9
Total	33.0%	22.0%	13.0%	8.0%	7.0%	6.0%	11.0%
COLORED	34.7%	33.3%	21.3%	.0%	1.3%	2.7%	6.7%
POLISH	22.7	43.2	3.0	23.5	.0	3.0	4.6
ITALIAN	18.0	55.3	8.7	2.7	3.3	2.7	9.3

Product classes must often be subdivided and cross-analyzed according to consumer demand, territorial demand, appeal, class of trade, or other characteristics. For example, in analyzing the market for an adding machine, it is desired to know in what type of businesses it is most used, the average size of the business, the models used most frequently, whether there are territorial differences, and the reasons for purchasing.

2. *Geographical Arrangement.*—It is frequently necessary to analyze replies according to the geographical region from which they were received. This will bring out the sectional differences in demand, strength of buying motives, or volume of business. Answers are frequently classified according to whether they come from rural, suburban, or city districts.

3. *Special Classification.*—It is often necessary to devise methods of cross-analysis to suit the particular case in point. For example, if a questionnaire brings out the fact that 75 per cent of answers give economy as a motive for purchase, it is desirable to cross-analyze this motive and to see what class of respondents stresses economy, and what class stresses other motives.

It is important, for all cross-analysis work, to make sure that the data secured are complete enough to permit the necessary classifications. That is, there must be enough observations under each classification to be representative of that class. This, of course, is a problem both of questionnaire make-up and of obtaining enough responses.

The process of cross-analyzing should not be carried to too fine a point. Advertising research, for the present, is concerned mainly with aggregates, not with narrow distinctions. Except in the case of direct advertising and advertising in trade journals with strictly delimited fields, advertising aims to reach the "average" consumer, and the principal purpose of cross-analysis is to sift out from the general classification those markets, appeals, sections, or other factors which apply to the majority.

Computations

Before comparisons can be made it is frequently necessary to make computations so that the causal relationships between two sets of statistics will become evident. When the returns are in dollars, or in population, or in millines, it is a simple matter to measure one quantity against the other; but often one is not able to obtain data which are homogeneous and hence comparable. It is then necessary to reduce them to some sort of common denominator.

The simplest and most commonly used method of computation is the percentage basis. Figure 27 shows how such a reduction to percentages permits comparison which could otherwise not be obtained. Here it was desired to compare the number of brands handled by dealers from whom farmers buy according to geographic division. To compare by the actual counted number of dealers in each section would have given no comparison, while taking the percentage of each group permits accurate measurement and comparison of various territories.

FIG. 27.—AN EXAMPLE OF COMPARISON ON A PERCENTAGE BASIS

Showing the Number of Brands of Paint Handled by Dealers from whom Farmers Buy in the Various Sections of the Country

(Farm Journal)

	One Brand, per cent	Two Brands, per cent	Three Brands, per cent	Four Brands, per cent	Five Brands, per cent
New England and Middle Atlantic	55.1	24.6	13.0	7.3	
East North Central	55.4	28.7	12.9	2.0	1.0
West North Central	61.9	25.7	8.9	3.5	.....
South Atlantic	44.6	29.3	16.9	4.6	4.6
East South Central	58.3	29.1	8.3	2.0	2.0
West South Central	57.1	31.0	11.9	.....	.....
Mountain	65.8	23.7	7.9	.....	2.6
Pacific	71.7	24.5	3.8	.....	.....
U. S. average	58.2	27.3	10.8	2.8	1.1

Where a number of factors, when combined, will give a truer reflection of a given phenomenon than would any one fact, the use of index numbers is indicated. From the standpoint of pure mathematics it is anomalous to combine statistics of literate population, number of automobiles per square mile, and the number of individuals making income tax returns. The requirement for each set of statistics used in making up the index, however, is simply that it should have a relation to the purpose. The data above mentioned might be used to develop a standard of prosperity of a given territory over several time periods or for several territories at a given time.

The simplest type of index number consists merely of taking some statistical fact as a base, assigning it a weight of 100, and measuring all other data in terms of this base, or as a percentage of this base. For example, the average number of passenger cars per 100 families in all counties of the United States is 53.4. This is taken as the base figure. The number of passenger cars per 100 families in Genesee County, New York, is 75. The index number for this county, therefore, is as 75 is to 53.4, or 140, showing that it has a much larger number of cars than the average county.

The Crowell Publishing Company has prepared a tabulation of national market values by counties. Separate index numbers for purchasing power, standard of living, and accessibility were made up. The average of all counties in purchasing power, standard of living, and accessibility is taken as the base of 100. Each separate county is measured in relation to this base figure. For example, the average purchasing power of all counties is $15,371,000. In Isabella County, Michigan, it is $11,541,000, giving a purchasing power index of 75.

Purchasing power is taken as the total wealth created annually in each county from manufactures, mines and fisheries, crops, and livestock.

Standard of living is measured by the number of passenger car registrations per 100 families, and the number of income tax returns filed per 100 families, the index numbers of these two factors being averaged for the final standard of living index. These two factors were chosen because they tended to compensate for inaccuracies in each other. The number of income tax returns in urban areas is higher, in proportion to actual wealth, than in rural areas. The number of automobiles, however, is greater, in proportion to actual wealth, in the country than in the city.

Accessibility is measured by the number of dwellings per 100 square miles, and the number of retail outlets per 100 square miles.

Counties were then classed as best, good, fair, and poor, according to the following schedule:

Best Counties.—Over 100 in Purchasing Power.
Or over 50 in Purchasing Power and over
100 in Standard of Living and Accessibility.
Good Counties.—Over 50 in Purchasing Power.
Or over 20 in Purchasing Power and over
100 in Standard of Living and Accessibility.
Fair Counties.—Over 20 in Purchasing Power.
Or over 10 in Purchasing Power and over
50 in Standard of Living and Accessibility.
Poor Counties.—Under 10 in Purchasing Power.
Or under 20 in Purchasing Power and under
50 in Standard of Living or Accessibility.

Purchasing power is taken as the most important factor, although usually high purchasing power is combined with high scale of living and high degree of accessibility.

To take another case of index numbers, Figures 28, A, B, and C, illustrates graphically an index classification of states with a view to determining the intensity of sales effort required. Here two factors are used—accessibility and purchasing power. This index was formulated by F. N. Merriam.

Accessibility is made up from density of population and percentage of urban population to rural, with results as shown in Figure 28A.

Buying power (Figure 28B) is determined by the percentage of population filing income-tax returns, and the number of passenger cars per 100 families.

Figure 28C illustrates the final classification into four groups. In the first class are those states with high accessibility and buying power which will respond to intensive cultivation. In Class II are states which rank slightly less than Class I but which are still worthy of intensive cultivation. In Classes III and IV are states which should be treated accord-

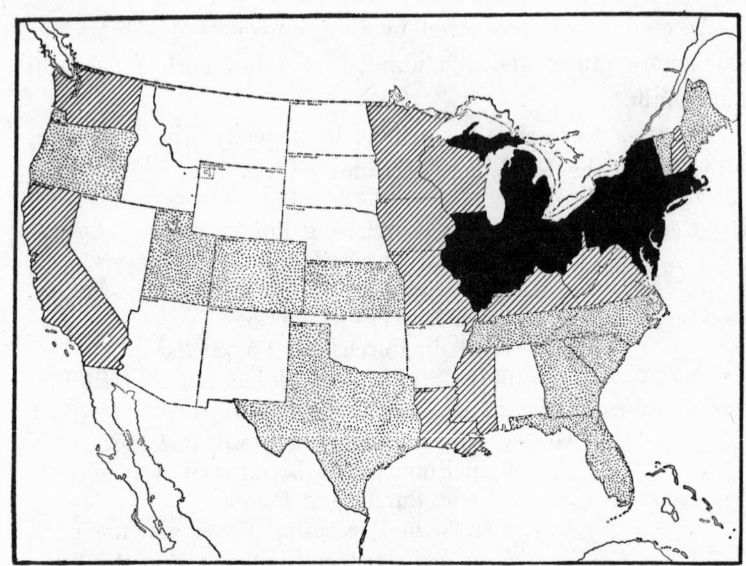

FIG. 28A. STATES INDEXED ACCORDING TO ACCESSIBILITY
Accessibility is based upon the ratio of urban to rural population.

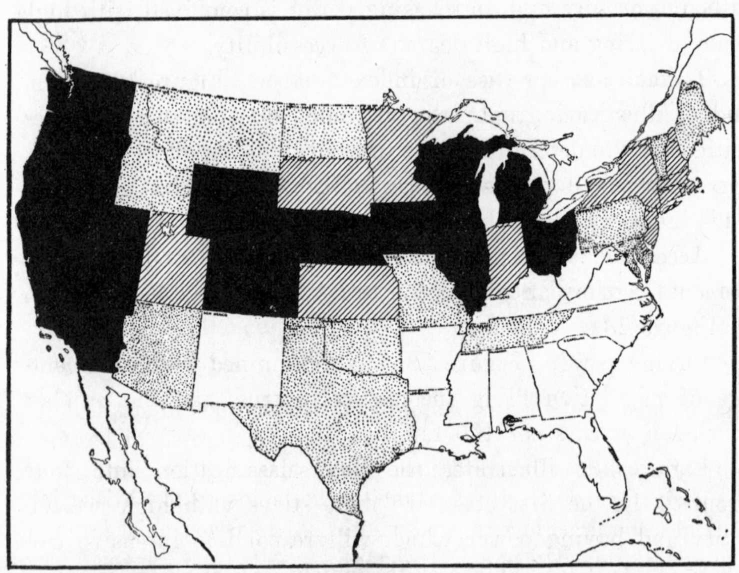

FIG. 28B. STATES INDEXED FOR BUYING POWER
This index is based on the percentage of the population filing income-tax returns and the number of passenger cars per 100 families.

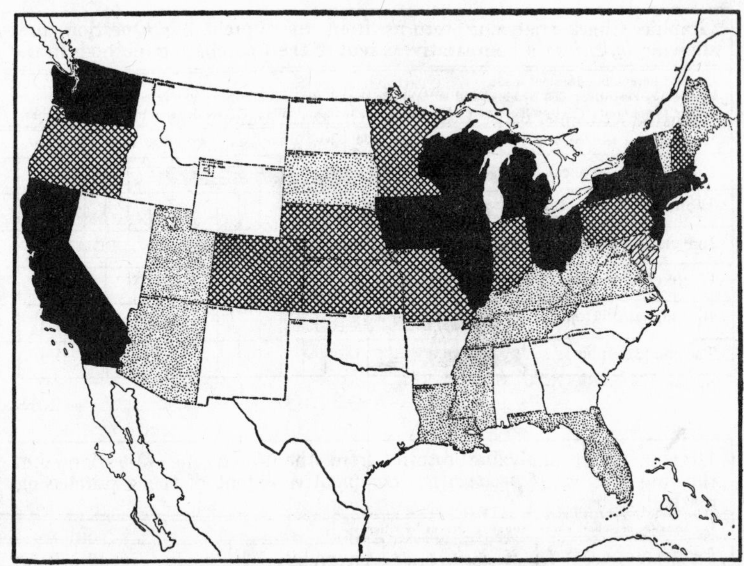

FIG. 28C. INDEX OF STATES COMBINING SEVERAL ELEMENTS

Here the states are rated according to a combination of the indices illustrated in Figures 28A and B, with a view to indicating the intensity of merchandising effort required in any given locality.

ing to the "high spot" method, that is, the centers of population should be covered in preference to an attempt to cover the whole state.

Comparisons

When the statistics have been reduced to a common denominator, they are ready to be compared. The method of comparison chosen, whether tabular or graphic, should bring out the comparative relations so clearly that chance of error in interpretation is reduced to a minimum.

Figure 29 shows how data may be analyzed and compared in two different ways—geographically and by class of product. The percentage basis is used as a method of computation.

In Figure 30 the method of comparing ratios is somewhat different. Here the circulation of various newspapers is measured in proportion to the population of the territories which

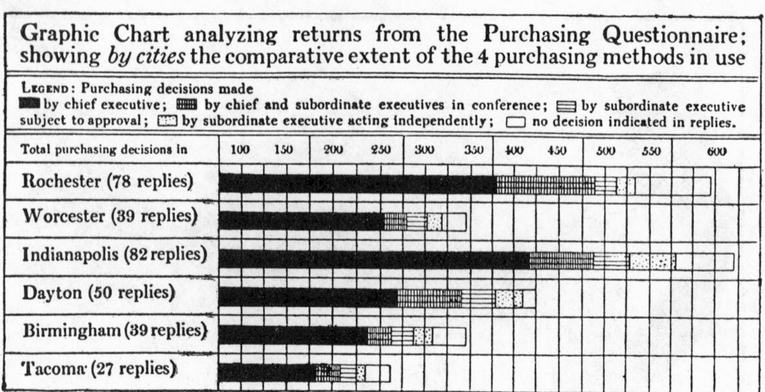

Graphic Chart analyzing returns from the Purchasing Questionnaire; showing *by class of product* the comparative extent of the 4 purchasing methods in use.

For LEGEND, see chart above, showing returns by cities

Decision in respect to choice of 25 50 75 100 125 150 175 200 225 250 275 300 325 350

Typewriters

Engineering Counsel

Building Materials.

Sprinkler Systems

Delivery Cars or Trucks

Tires

Banking Connections

FIG. 29. DATA ANALYZED GEOGRAPHICALLY AND BY CLASS OF PRODUCT (Barton, Durstine & Osborn.)

they cover. Of course, the value of such a comparison depends upon the character of the facts used and the representative nature of the sources. One journal might have a large urban circulation and little suburban, while in another city the paper might circulate mainly outside of the city. If the population were taken as within the city limits, the results would hardly be comparable, for such a case. Seldom is it possible to find a single measure which will apply fairly to all cases. Various *methods* of comparison should be employed.

It is sometimes desirable to combine a number of factors for purposes of comparison. In Figure 31, for example, race

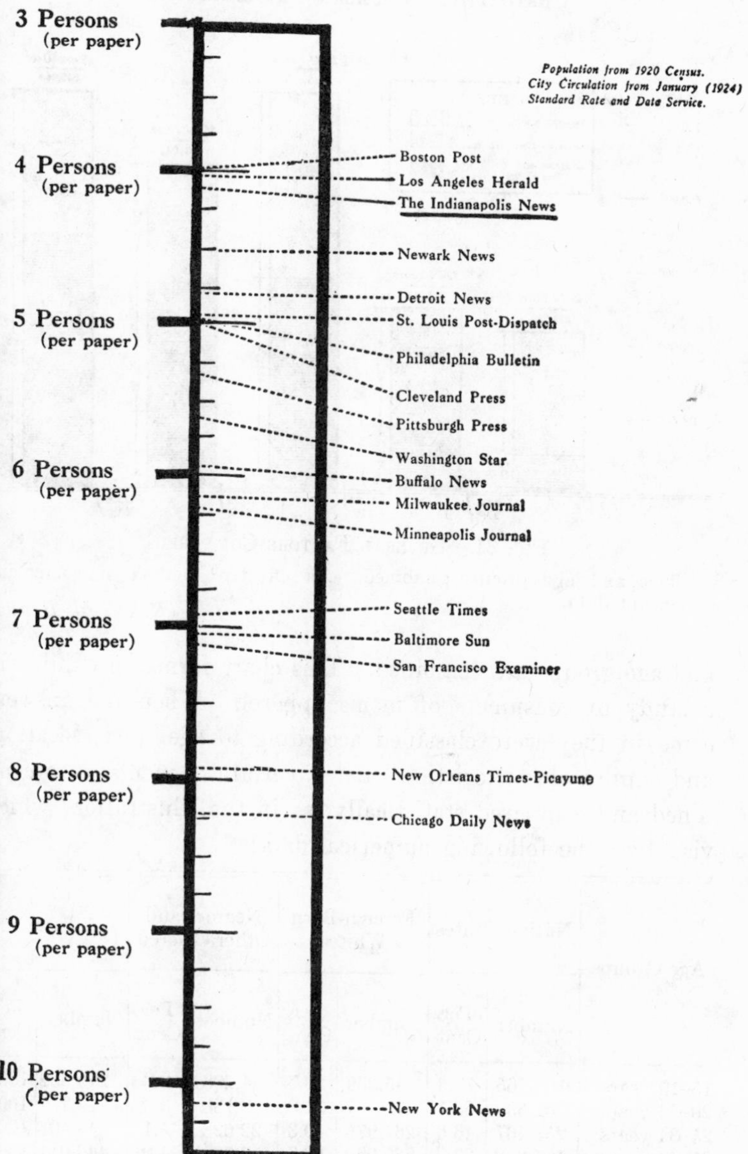

FIG. 30. METHOD OF SHOWING THE "PENETRATION" OF A MEDIUM

A graphic method of comparing ratios. Circulation in proportion to population.

(*Indianapolis News.*)

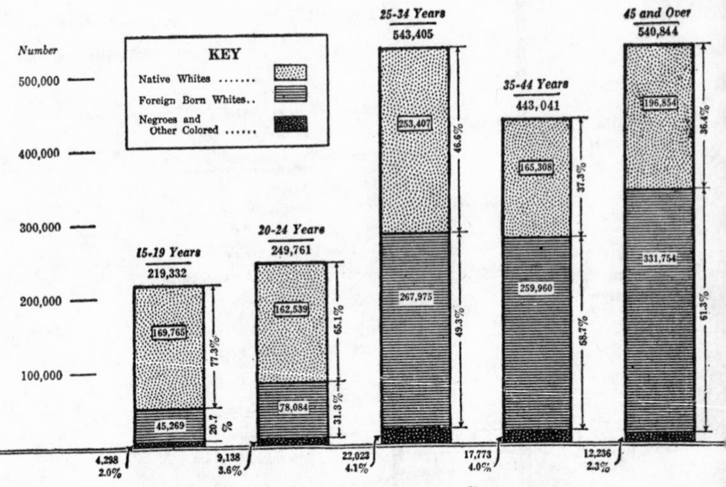

Fig. 31. Several Factors Compared

Race and age groups combined. An effective method of comparing significant data.

(*New York Herald*

and age groups are combined. This chart forms an exhibit in a study of consumers of men's apparel. When the answers came in they were classified according to age, race, location and similar characteristics. Later, certain elements were combined and compared statistically, as in the illustration, which visualizes the following numerical data:

Age Groups	Native Whites		Foreign-Born Whites		Negroes and Other Colored		Total	
	Number	Per Cent	Number	Per Cent	Number	Per Cent	Number	Per Cent
15–19 years..	169,765	77.3	45,269	20.7	4,298	2.0	219,332	100.
20–24 years..	162,539	65.1	78,084	31.3	9,138	3.6	249,761	100
25–34 years..	253,407	46.6	267,975	49.3	22,023	4.1	543,405	100.
35–44 years..	165,308	37.3	259,960	58.7	17,773	4.0	443,041	100.
45 and over..	196,854	36.4	331,754	61.3	12,236	2.3	540,844	100.
Total.....	947,873	47.5	983,042	49.2	65,468	3.3	1,996,383	100.

It is seen at once that the percentage of foreign-born white s steadily increasing as the ages increase. Seventy-seven per ent of the white population between 15 and 19 years is native-orn, while only 36.4 per cent of consumers 15, and over are ative-born whites. Comparisons of this nature may prove ighly significant, especially in the study of markets and media.

orrelations

Many business concerns have found that certain relations xist between some specific set of statistics and the potential narket. In the simpler cases there is a direct relation between he outside index and the company's market. The concern vhich makes electrical equipment is limited to houses wired or electricity, whether the current is supplied from central tation or storage battery. Car registrations, either by them-elves or in conjunction with other series of statistics, will nable the maker of automobile accessories to obtain a fairly ccurate idea of his potential market.

The population index is the simplest, considered from the oint of view of availability of statistical information. But nless the product is in universal use, sales will not be pro-ortionate to the number of inhabitants. Automobile registra-ions, the possession of telephones, home ownership, and maga-ine circulation are frequently used as indices of purchasing ower, but these too are ordinarily of a rather general nature. t is often necessary to modify them for certain territories.

The manufacturer should be able, as a rule, to find some nore concrete index of potential markets. To accomplish this esult, he frequently chooses an arbitrary standard which has roved to bring satisfactory results. If he makes adding nachines, for example, he may notice that in well-covered ter-itories there is one adding machine for every certain number f office files, or typewriters, or telephones, or stenographers, r some other unit which can be secured in statistical form.

It is not generally enough to develop a standard for the vhole territory. A standard should be developed for each ter-itory, as well as the comparison of one territory with another,

FIG. 32.—AN EXAMPLE OF EXCESSIVE COMBINATION OF DATA

Summary of Amounts Spent by Men and Girl Students on a Yearly Basis

Items	Average Number Items per Year		Total Number Items Bought Yearly		Average Price for Each Item		Average Amount per Person Yearly		Total Amount Yearly	
	Boys	Girls	Boys	Girls	Boys	Girls	Boys	Girls	Boys	Girls
Hats	2.75	6.3	2,134	4,177	$5.40	$13.00	$14.85	$81.90	$11,523	$54,300
Suits	2.5	0.7	1,940	232	40.50	52.00	101.25	36.40	78,570	12,012*
Overcoats	0.7	0.67	543	444	42.50	107.00	29.75	71.69	23,086	47,530
Shoes	3.0	7.2	2,328	4,773	9.00	10.90	27.00	78.48	20,952	52,032
Socks (hose)	18.0	15.75	13,968	10,442	0.86	2.60	15.48	40.95	12,012	27,150
Gloves	1.0	2.0	776	1,326	3.30	4.90	3.30	9.80	2,559	6,497
Underwear (suits)	7.3	......	5,664	......	1.65	......	12.05	......	9,346	......
Lingerie	......	......	......	......	......	......	......	81.00	......	53,703
Shirts	8.5	......	6,596	......	3.00	......	25.50	......	19,978	......
Skirts	......	2.0	......	1,326	......	11.40	......	22.80	......	15,116
Fur pieces	......	......	......	......	......	......	......	60.00	......	9,960*
Clothes pressed	......	......	......	......	......	......	12.75	5.50	9,900	3,630
Toilet articles	......	......	......	......	......	......	16.30	52.20	12,649	34,608
Beauty parlor service	......	......	......	......	......	......	......	57.12	......	18,906*
Candy	......	......	......	......	......	......	2.75	4.70	2,128	3,122
Downtown meals	......	......	51,480	25,600	......	......	33.20	16.30	25,740	10,800
Moving pictures	......	......	29,080	22,440	......	......	22.00	5.30	17,078	3,529
Majestic shows	......	......	18,066	11,826	......	......	26.30	3.00	20,464	1,954
							$342.48	$627.14	$265,985	$354,849

* 50% of the girls buy coat suits; 50% patronize beauty parlors; 25% buy fur pieces.

or one time period with another. In other words, it is necessary to determine how many adding machines there should be for a given number of files, typewriters, etc., in a given territory.

The work which is being done in regard to forecasting the business cycle is not without advertising interest. If it is possible to correlate available statistical compilations with statistics regarding the company's own activities, this should be done, and the proper generalizations made therefrom.

Opportunities for Error

It has frequently been observed that statistical tabulations and graphs can be made to serve any purpose while still appearing to present a true picture of the facts. Hence it is highly important to make sure that these tabulations represent things as they are.

The editing process is a guard against the admission of evidence which would distort the final result. Obscure or biased records of observations are either thrown out entirely, as are defective ballots on election day, or further investigation is made to see why the mistake, if it is a mistake, has been made.

Bias should be eliminated without exception, although this is sometimes a difficult task. For example, there was an investigation carried on among housewives to determine the preferred ingredients for bread, with a view to announcing them in the advertising. Since this investigation was carried on among the general population of the United States, and since lard was one of the substances included, there was obviously a racial factor to be considered.

An even more elusive form of bias is that where the answer to a question has been forced. For example, in a certain consumer investigation, those who brought with them to an office a questionnaire, properly filled out, were given a basket of sample foods. The condition precedent to obtaining one of these baskets was to state a brand preference. This was required in a number of classes of products. Naturally, the

Fig. 33.—An Example of Failure to Present all Essential Facts

Do You Buy Fresh Pineapple?

100% = Total Replies to the Question

Buy Fresh Pineapple.... 36%
Average number dozens bought per family yearly.... 3.3

Heart States	Per Cent Buy Fresh Pineapple	Average Number Dozens Bought per Family Yearly
Illinois	36	3.4
Indiana	41	3.3
Iowa	37	3.3
Kansas	20	3.6
Michigan	45	3.4
Minnesota	36	3.1
Missouri	16	3.9
Nebraska	33	3.4
North Dakota	22	4.5
Ohio	53	3.3
Oklahoma	16	4.6
South Dakota	35	3.1
Wisconsin	42	3.1
Total	36	3.3

Do You Buy Canned Pineapple?

100% = Total Replies to the Question

Buy Canned Pineapple.... 35%
Average number cans bought per family yearly.... 10.4

Heart States	Per Cent Buy Canned Pineapple
Illinois	45
Indiana	33
Iowa	42
Kansas	49
Michigan	23
Minnesota	34
Missouri	31
Nebraska	45
North Dakota	50
Ohio	32
Oklahoma	32
South Dakota	53
Wisconsin	19
Total	35

FIG. 33.—*Continued*

Brands

100% = Total Buy Canned Pineapple

	Per Cent
No preference	68
Hawaiian	8
Del Monte	3
Triangle Club	1
Montclair	1
Libby's	1
All Others	19

housewife would rack her brain to think of some brand, even though she may have been accustomed to buying in bulk or without consideration of brands. It is questionable whether the answers in such a case are representative of the true state of affairs. It sometimes happens that the answers to questionnaires are of such a nature that they cannot be tabulated accurately. In such a case they should be taken for their suggestive value, as when a place for general remarks is left on the questionnaire.

It does not always pay to recapitulate facts too much, or to combine them to such an extent that comparisons become forced. Figure 32, for example, illustrates a summary of two questionnaires, one to boys and the other to girls. The summary would have been clearer had each questionnaire been summarized by itself. Two separate tabulations would have been preferable. The one advantage of combining seems to be to compare the boys' purchases with those of the girls; but actually there is little basis for comparison. Boys' suits and girls' suits are inherently different things, the suit being the universal and continuous form of masculine, but not of feminine, attire. Nor are boys' hats and girls' hats comparable. In fact, the majority of products mentioned ought to be tabulated separately and considered separately.

One of the worst and least excusable types of error in tabulation is where the reader is misled by failure to present all data. For example, an investigation was made of the kinds of food used by farmers in certain states of the Middle West. Among the questions asked were the following: "Do you buy fresh pineapple?" and "Do you buy canned pineapple?" with a space after each question for the amount purchased and consumed. Figure 33 illustrates the form of tabulation as presented in the report. The average number of fresh pineapples bought per family yearly appears as 3.3 dozens, or about 39 pineapples for each family. In addition, there are 10.4 cans of pineapple purchased.

It appeared, upon further investigation, that the figures given in the booklet were based only on the replies from families which actually reported their consumption of fresh and canned pineapple. When based on the *total* number of replies to the questionnaire, the figures were, respectively, 1.2 dozen for fresh pineapple (instead of 3.3) and 3.7 cans (instead of 10.4). This should have been made unmistakably plain, especially since the method of tabulation shows a result more favorable to the magazine making the investigation than the other alternative would have done.

CHAPTER IV

METHODS OF GENERALIZATION

The process of generalization depends for its accuracy largely upon the way in which the previous processes of observation and comparison have been carried out. If a careful and extensive study has been made, for example, of consumers and their buying motives, and if the results of these observations have been properly tabulated and compared, the inferences to be drawn should be to a large extent self-evident.

Generalization and Applied Logic

The purpose of generalization is to reduce the mass of tabulated observations to a usable form, that is, to interpret them, and make them ready for application. Here the human element assumes a position of primary importance. No step here can be made purely mechanical. The brain is the only tool which will serve. Precedent must be avoided. The purely factual stage of the research work has been passed. Routine no longer has a place. The present step requires the exercise of reasoning powers. Generalization is wholly and exclusively a mental process.

The opportunities for going astray at this point are great. Mistaken correlations, confusions of cause and effect, and failure to weigh all the contributing factors are errors of frequent occurrence and often of disastrous results. To avoid these errors, it is desirable to have some knowledge of the science of reasoning, that is, of logic. Logic shows how certain premises may be taken and formed into a conclusion. It also deals with the various types of fallacies which lead to erroneous conclusions.

There are three recognized types of reasoning: First, the analogical inference, which argues that because two things resemble each other in certain particulars, therefore they will resemble each other in further particulars; second, the inductive inference, which reasons that because in a number of observations certain things are true, then these same things will be true of all things of that class; and, third, the deductive inference, which takes a general principle and assumes its applicability to specific cases.

Generalization begins when one attempts to interpret the facts gathered. The most natural method to suggest itself is the method of analogy. After this, it often becomes desirable to carry the process a step further, by passing beyond the obvious similarities to the more fundamental causes which are at the basis of the facts revealed. Thus the methods of causal analysis come into use. The final step is to formal reasoning, which depends upon the use of the syllogism.

Reasoning by Analogy

Analogy is the application of one particular case to another particular case. It is assumed that if two or more things agree with one another in one or more respects, then they will probably agree in other respects. The degree of this probability will depend upon the number and importance of the agreements, and these must be demonstrated.

Reasoning from analogy is a dangerous practice, as a rule, because no two cases are exactly alike, or even closely enough alike to permit an unequivocal inference. For example, a manufacturer might say, "My chief competitor advertises in the *Saturday Evening Post*. He is successful. Therefore, if I advertise like him in the *Saturday Evening Post,* I too shall be successful." Here the essential points of agreement may not be sufficiently complete to justify such a conclusion.

Analogies are, however, constantly used, because they offer a quick and easy method of arriving at inferences. Even though it is impossible to duplicate conditions exactly, it is often possible to tell about what margin should be allowed for error under certain conditions. Accordingly the analogical inference, with a suitable margin of safety, is a favorite method of reasoning with the business man. His difficulty lies chiefly in the fact that he sometimes fails to make proper allowance for error, because he is not sufficiently acquainted with the factors of variability between the two specific cases under comparison.

It is not possible to state definitely, for example, that if two identical advertisements are run in two periodicals of a similar type, under seemingly similar conditions, the results from both will be the same. Nor can a department store infer that the results from an advertisement run on Tuesday will bring similar results if run on another day of the week.

The following example shows how analogy is used in the advertising literature of a certain advertising agency. It reads as follows:

> There are several possible ways to harvest a field of ripe wheat. The old-fashioned way—a few of us still remember it—was to cradle it, and lay the wheat in an even swath. It was slow, hard work, and the acreage harvested was tiny judged by present standards.
>
> Another way is to hitch a tractor to a modern binder and drive over hill, valley, and washout, while the neat, tight bundles drop methodically in regular piles from the carrier. The binder misses a few heads here and there. But it will cut over a whole farm in a week.

In other words, the best method of harvesting a field of ripe wheat is to use a tractor and binder. This forms the example on which the analogy is based. To quote further:

> Many agencies (and many advertisers) are still in the cradle stage. They never miss a head. Like European peasants gleaning a field, they patiently stoop to count noses in Pittsfield, Mass. They questionnaire the Bronx. They cater to the sectional peculiarities of New Orleans. They perspire freely—as well they may—in trying to reduce intangible values to mathematical terms.

Here, the supposedly less efficient methods of harvesting are compared to the methods of approach used by those advertisers whose ways are said to be antiquated. The analogical inference is then drawn, as follows:

> The simple and sober fact which has escaped most of us is this: advertising isn't a hand sickle. It is the greatest harvesting machine in the world. It knows no seasons, for human nature is always ripe for it. It goes over ravines and washouts like a caterpillar tractor, for human nature is unaware of the Mason and Dixon line, the Mississippi River, the Rocky Mountains—even the salubrious climate of sunny California.
>
> Every advertising campaign, and every advertising agency, must stand or fall by the intelligence and skill it demonstrates in applying that force we call "advertising" to the mind of that greatly underestimated individual we call the "ultimate consumer."

That is, since extensive methods of harvesting wheat are superior to intensive methods, the same must be true of advertising, it being assumed that wheat harvesting and advertising are analogous. As a matter of fact, such analogies are so far-fetched that they can be considered as mere figures of speech. The argument is rhetorical, rather than logical. Even at best, the analogical inference is rather an unsafe guide.

Reasoning by Induction

Induction concludes that what is true of certain individuals of a class is true of the whole class. It is simply a development and an improvement upon the method of analogy. Instead, however, of using one particular instance from which to draw the inference, a number of instances are used. In fact, the more observations there are used as the basis of the induction, the more universally applicable the resulting inference will be.

The major task in inductive inference is to gather the observations and to make sure that they are sufficient in number, and that they are representative of the whole. It is then possible to apply the various methods of inductive reasoning:

1. *The method of agreement* consists of finding out what antecedents are always present in observations when a certain result follows. Suppose, for example, that 100 successful out-

door advertisements are analyzed. In each one of them color is used. The induction therefore is drawn that color is an essential element of the success of outdoor advertising.

2. *The method of difference* consists of ascertaining the antecedent which is invariably present when the phenomenon occurs, and invariably absent when it does not occur, and of reasoning, therefore, that this antecedent is the cause of the phenomenon. The utility of this method, according to Jevons, depends upon the precaution of only "varying one circumstance at a time, all other circumstances being maintained just as they were." Note, for example, the following method of induction, developed by Stanley I. Clark, of the Joseph Richards Company:

As a result of a recent mailing of 5,000 questionnaires the following information concerning the relative value of baronial versus government envelopes was determined. Since the New York Social Register was used as the mailing list, many of the persons to whom the questionnaires were sent were out of town. This probably accounts for the very small percentage of returns. The following figures, however, speak for themselves concerning the value of the two kinds of envelopes enclosed:

	Baronial	Government
Number questionnaires sent	2500	2500
Number returned unanswered	39	21
Total number delivered	2461	2479
Number returned answered	127	94
Number returned unanswered	9	12
Total returned	136	106
Per cent of returns answered	.0516	.0379
Per cent of returns unanswered	.0036	.0048
Total percentage of returns	.0552	.0427

Reference to the foregoing figures will show that the returns in baronial envelopes were 30 per cent higher than those in government stamped envelopes and that the unanswered returns in government envelopes were 33 per cent higher than those in baronial envelopes. Since the letters and questionnaires were identical in every other respect, the difference in returns must have been due to the type of envelope used.

3. *The joint method of agreement and difference* is used when one circumstance cannot be varied at a time without changing the circumstances, thus making the method of difference difficult of application. It consists of applying the method of agreement, first to a number of instances where an effect is produced, and second to a number of instances where the effect is not produced. Suppose, for example, that a study of 100 outdoor advertisements was made. Fifty of these were successful and 50 were not. In practically every case of the successful 50 advertisements, the length of copy did not exceed 10 words, while in the unsuccessful group a majority used over 10 words. The induction is that brevity of copy is an element in the success of outdoor advertising.

4. *The method of concomitant variations* is defined by John Stuart Mill as follows: "Whatever phenomenon varies in any manner whenever another phenomenon varies in some particular manner, is either a cause or an effect of that phenomenon, or is connected with it through some fact of causation." It is this method of induction which is used in formulating a market index or barometer of sales potentialities. If the cause varies in intensity, the effect will vary in intensity: *e.g.,* if income tax returns are higher in this territory, our sales will be higher in this territory.

5. *The method of residues* is used when there are several causes acting at once. When the effect of certain causes is known, these may be subtracted from the whole and the remainder will be due to the remaining causes. This method is used when quantities may be measured, having been used originally mainly for astronomical purposes. It is in constant use in modern research. If one asks, "Do you use cranberries?" and 60 per cent of those questioned reply "Yes," then by the method of residues 40 per cent do not use cranberries.

It is important to remember, in making any induction pertaining to advertising, that advertising often goes by contraries. The moment the attempt is made to reduce it to a standard, a sameness is produced which is detrimental. Advertising is most striking and possesses the most attention-compelling qualities when it departs from the norm. Color is striking, but if all advertisements in a magazine use color, the black-and-white effect might have better attention value. Thus, successes in advertising are often seeming exceptions to established principles.

Reasoning by Deduction

The deductive method takes a universal law and applies it to particular cases. Once having found a rule which holds true generally, it can be applied to the case in point. Deduction gives explicit application; induction gives general principles. For example, "The dealers in this line of trade are not receptive to new products, particularly during the holiday season; therefore it will not be wise for us to go ahead with this campaign until the spring." Here the premise is a generality—that is, dealers are not receptive to new products during the holiday season. It is applied to the company's own business and the deduction is made not to proceed with the campaign until spring.

Similarly, a company might reason as follows by deduction: "The design of our product should be changed in order to meet competition of Blank and Company, since the trade will not stock a line of higher price." Here the premise is: "The trade will not stock a line of higher price." To cite another case, "Dealers object to irregular shapes which will not fit on their shelves; therefore the shape of my package should be changed"; or, "A small advertising appropriation will have no effect on the general public; therefore my advertising will have to be restricted to the trade."

The great danger in using any deduction is that it may not be based on a fundamental truth. It may, and in many cases it is, purely a "glittering generality." Not only must it be a true principle, but it must be applicable to the case, and the application must be properly made.

A deduction may prove exceedingly valuable if it is constantly tested. The truth of the deduction may be substantiated by inductive methods. In fact, induction serves to bring out truths which will serve as the bases of deductions. In practice, the two processes are simultaneous.

The Combined Method

Advertising as yet has not reached a scientific standard which will permit stating irrevocable laws. There is nothing so universal about advertising as to justify making unqualified deductions, in the sense that deductions are made in mathematics or in astronomy.

This does not excuse the habit, altogether too common, of classifying, comparing, and graphing the observations secured, and then of allowing the reader to arrive at his own conclusions. It often happens, of course, that the appearance of the situation is such as to permit only one inference. The research task, nevertheless, is not completed until the inductions have been drawn from the observations made, and the resulting deductions established. As Jevons expresses it: "The first process consists in such a rough and simple appeal to experience as may give us a glimpse of the laws which operate, without being sufficient to establish their truth. Assuming them as provisionally true, we then proceed to argue to their effects in other cases, and a further appeal to experience either verifies or negatives the truth of the laws assumed."

In practical research work it is often necessary to start with a deduction as an hypothesis. Observations are then made which will, by the use of the inductive method, corroborate or nullify the original deduction. The inferential process views every plan as an induction, which will be verified or refuted in actual practice. This plan, in its original state, is based on a few observations, and is maintained because it works. As soon as this plan becomes standardized by verification and by the discovery and analysis of further observations, it may be said to have reached the deductive stage, and may then be applied to any case at hand.

The science of advertising can progress only in measure as organizing ideas can be suggested which will serve to classify the observations and experiments as they are made. That is, hypotheses must be formulated which will accord with observations, and which, furthermore, will serve as the bases of deductions and general laws.

The Syllogism

A syllogism consists of three propositions, of which the first two are called the premises, and the last the conclusion. The conclusion necessarily follows from the premises; so that, if the premises are true, the conclusion must be true, and the argument is tantamount to demonstration. Thus:

Major Premise: National distribution should be the objective of every large manufacturer.

Minor Premise: Magazine advertising is the most effective way to obtain national distribution.

Conclusion: Therefore, magazine advertising should be used by every large manufacturer.

The premises may, of course, be questionable, as in the above case; but if the syllogism is regular, the reasoning is valid, and the conclusion, whether it be true or false, is correctly derived.

Inference is the process of forming a judgment upon some other judgment which is essentially related to it. The relation of one judgment to another judgment, to which it bears a causal relation, warrants the formulation of a third judgment, or conclusion, which expresses a universal and necessary connection between the first two judgments, or premises. The process of inference, therefore, consists in exhibiting a judgment as the necessary result of the combination of two other judgments.

It is the function of the major premise to exhibit some phase of general and accepted belief. That of the minor premise is to exhibit some more particular phase of general knowledge, or of some particular case. The function of the two combined (*i.e.,* of the syllogism itself) is to apply universal knowledge to a special instance, so as to interpret it fully and truly.

This process consists of eliminating what is known as the middle, or common, term. In the following syllogism:

a equals *b*
b equals *c*
therefore, *a* equals *c*

b is the middle, or common term, and is eliminated from the syllogism. The importance of the middle term, as the key to the syllogism, may be illustrated by the following diagram:

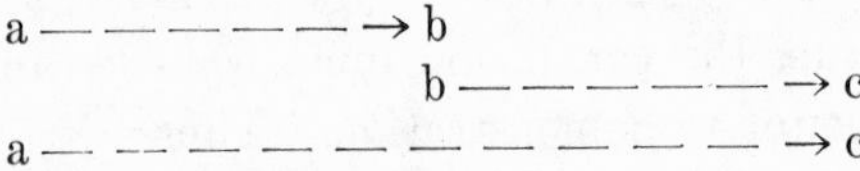

It is important to make sure that the middle terms are the same, and not two different terms. If they are not identical, the validity of the syllogism is lost. Most fallacies of reasoning result from an improper treatment of the middle term.

Analysis of the Syllogism

The first step in analyzing a syllogism, with a view to testing its validity, is to divest it of all but its essential parts. The following is a case in which the premises are already quite plainly and simply stated:

Ninety-four different makes of passenger cars were sold in Metropolitan New York during 1923.

Of these:

Seventy-one advertised in evening papers
Sixty-six advertised in Sunday papers
Sixty-four advertised in week-day morning papers
Seventy-six advertised in New York newspapers—evening, morning or Sunday
The evening newspapers published the advertisements of as many passenger cars as did the morning and Sunday papers combined

This preference for evening papers is based on the greater results which evening papers produce.

Even more condensed would be the premises in the following form:

1. Evening papers are the choice of most automobile advertisers.
2. This preference is proof of the superiority of evening papers as an advertising medium for automobiles.

The conclusion, of course, is as follows:

3. Therefore, evening papers constitute the best medium for advertising automobiles.

No matter how diffuse an argument may be, it is reducible to lowest terms, and this is the sure way to test its validity. It frequently happens that the most treacherous argument is hedged about with the greatest amount of verbiage.

The science of logic has suffered somewhat by reason of the unnecessarily abstruse and involved treatment which it has received. It is one thing to understand the theory of pure logic and another to analyze arguments used in advertising, whether they are one's own or those of another. This difficulty is enhanced by virtue of the fact that the significant propositions in the argument are often omitted entirely. In fact, it is seldom that a complete syllogism is to be found in the ordinary course of work. The reason for omitting any part of the syllogism is not because that part is of no importance but rather because it is usually self-evident. The syllogism in its partial or condensed form is known as the *enthymeme.*

The omitted portion of the syllogism is usually the major premise. Following is an example of enthymeme in which the major premise is omitted:

The results of the investigation of the Bureau of Business Research of Northwestern University and of the National Association of Retail Clothiers shows a remarkable increase in recent years in the percentage of total advertising expenditure that is appropriated for newspaper advertising. This is proof of the effectiveness of this form of advertising.

The omitted major premise would read as follows:

> Widespread adoption of a business expedient is proof of its effectiveness.

It should be remembered that in analyzing the validity of an argument, the omitted premise of the syllogism is as susceptible to error as are the other two parts. In fact, it is a common subterfuge to introduce a fallacious premise by suggestion only, so that a merely superficial examination of the discourse will not reveal the error.

Sometimes the two premises are stated and the conclusion omitted, as in the following statement by Earnest Elmo Calkins:

> The only way the manufacturer can obtain distribution is by being able to assure the local dealer who buys the goods that he will be able to sell them. And the only way to give that assurance is by advertising to that portion of the public which constitutes the customers of that particular dealer's store.

The Fallacies

Fallacy is a term given to a mistaken statement used in argument, and, in logic, "an argument which violates the laws of correct demonstration." An understanding of the principal fallacies is important if correct generalizations are to be drawn. The individual making the generalizations may well scan the list of fallacies to make sure that he has not, by chance, made some mistake in his reasoning process:

1. *Verbal fallacies* are due to the wrong use of words.
2. *Logical fallacies* are concerned with the process of reasoning.
3. *Material fallacies* are due to misstatement of facts.
4. *Miscellaneous errors,* mistakes, and bias of various types complete the list.

The Verbal Fallacies

Verbal fallacies are those which occur through an improper or ambiguous use of words. They must be carefully guarded against. In fact, every precaution should be taken to see that no ambiguity can possibly exist in the generalizations.

Verbal fallacies fall into the following classifications:

1. *Equivocation* consists of employing the same word in two senses.

2. *Ambiguity* of grammatical structure (amphibology) may sometimes occur, as in the position of the adverb "only."

3. *Composition and division* result from ambiguous usage of collective or distributive terms. The classic example is "The angles of a triangle are less than two right angles," which might refer to the angles added together or considered separately.

4. *Accent* is important when generalizations are read out loud. It is possible by a slight shift in emphasis to give an implied meaning totally at variance with the real significance. For example, in speaking of a certain advertising policy, the generalization might read: "This is a fairly good method," which would normally mean that there was some excellence in it. But if accent is placed on "fairly" it immediately implies there may be some other better method.

The Logical Fallacies

The logical fallacies, or formal fallacies, are those which result from errors in the reasoning within the syllogism itself. Such fallacies can be avoided for the most part by being sure of the facts, stating them in their clearest and most elementary form, and guarding against inferences which are too sweeping. It is helpful to remember that the minimum number of propositions which can be used as a basis for a process of logic is three, and that all logical processes can be reduced to steps having no more than three propositions. The mind, especially at first, can deal most effectively with the minimum number of elements, and it is wisest to reduce any doubtful arguments to this form.

In searching for formal fallacies, the fundamental importance of the middle term must be kept in mind, since it is by use of this middle, or common, term that the logical progression is made possible. The various fallacies of the middle term result from the failure to maintain its identity. In other words, the basic fallacy of the middle term is that in which there are actually two middle terms which are not identical. The ambiguous use of words gives an opportunity to use two middle terms which, though apparently identical, are in effect different. (See previous section.)

A subtle fallacy is that in which the middle term is not correctly distributed. A term is said to be distributed when it is used in the universal sense, and is said to be undistributed when used in a limited or partial sense. Thus the rule, "Any subject term which means *some* is undistributed, while any that means *all* is distributed." In other words, the word "distributed" is regarded as being synonymous with "universal," for the reason that it is the nature of the universal to distribute, or to apply the full force of its significance, to every particular case to which it relates. In the phrase, "All the advertising men present were good salesmen," the subject (advertising men) is distributed, while the predicate (salesmen) is undistributed.

The middle term must be distributed at least once in order to provide a common point of connection between the two premises. The following syllogism is an illustration of the so-called fallacy of the undistributed middle:

All the consumers interviewed were radio owners.
All patrons of the X store were radio owners.
Therefore, all consumers interviewed were patrons of the X store.

This conclusion does not, of course, follow necessarily. It should be remembered, to use the words of Dr. F. S. C. Northrop of Yale University, that:

If no middle term is distributed, then the middle terms refer only to parts of the class in question. Since there is nothing to indicate or necessitate that each refers to the same identical part, it follows that two undistributed middle terms, referring to the same class, are really not identical terms but are two different terms.

There may be a fallacy of the non-middle terms as well as the middle terms, the rule being that the non-middle terms in the conclusion must never be distributed if they are undistributed in the premises. This means nothing more than the obvious point that the conclusions must contain the same terms that were involved in the premises. To use a distributed term in the conclusion, when it was undistributed in the premise, is to use a different term, since a distributed term refers to the whole of the class in question, whereas an undistributed term refers to only a part.

Material Fallacies

Following Aristotle, students of the reasoning process have defined a number of fallacies having to do with the correctness and completeness of the observations.

1. *The fallacy of accident* results from making an inference from a general rule to a particular case without taking into consideration other factors which have a material bearing on the outcome. For example:

> The negative appeal tends to have an unpleasant effect on the reader; therefore, it should not be used in our advertising.

In this case the major premise may be true, but there are other factors which may nullify it in particular cases. It may be desirable to bring out the unpleasant effect to emphasize the virtues of the product, as in the advertising of Philco batteries, Weed chains, or the "halitosis offensive" of Listerine.

Accordingly, if the general law does not apply to all cases, it should be qualified suitably, or the exceptions fully explained.

Following is another case in which the fallacy of accident may be found:

> Every year the number of persons per car becomes smaller and the ownership of automobiles becomes more wide-spread among American families. Every year brings a closer relationship between population and registration. Some day the point will be reached when the number of automobile owners can increase only as the number of people increases—when everybody who can own a car is a car owner. With every passing year it becomes more and more true that the larger the population—the larger will be the sales opportunities for the automobile manufacturer.

And for this reason the advantages of New York's huge and constantly growing population will become more pronounced every year.

This is tantamount to saying that the sales opportunity for automobiles will be greater after the saturation point has been reached. The fallacy lies in not taking into account the fact that the fewer the cars which a community has per capita, the greater the market, other things being equal. The above quotation refers only to the replacement market for motor cars, and ignores the original market.

2. *The converse fallacy of accident* argues from a special case to a general law. For example:

I am now reaching a certain audience through the X magazine. It is possible for me to reach practically the same audience by combining the Y and Z magazines, and at a lower price; therefore, I shall be able to get the same advertising effect by using the combination, and at a less cost.

Obviously, in the above case, a great number of factors must be considered, in media research, beside the mere reaching of the audience. Here something may have been left out of the major premise which will have a pronounced effect on the result.

3. *The fallacy of begging the question (petitio principii)* or arguing in a circle *(circulus in probando)* consists of confusing the cause and the effect. For example:

We have run this piece of advertising copy 52 times with good results. Therefore, an advertisement which has such a record must be inherently excellent.

Here the inference is brought out by means of a premise which presupposes this inference.

4. *The fallacy of the consequent* occurs when a conclusion is drawn from premises which do not support it. For example:

There has been no case in my experience where interviews have checked with questionnaires. Therefore, interviews are more satisfactory than questionnaires.

Will you tell us, by making a check mark in one of the spaces below, whether you, personally, use a cake shampoo or a liquid shampoo to clean your hair?

I use ☐ ***a cake shampoo for my hair.***

☑ ***a liquid shampoo for my hair.***

Name ....

Address ....

R. F. D. or Street No. *City or Town* *State*

FIG. 34. THE FALLACY OF MANY QUESTIONS

Sometimes known as the "fallacy of the double question." No allowance is made for the subject who does not use either kind of shampoo mentioned. A common error in pseudo-research.

The premises might equally well have shown that questionnaires are more satisfactory than interviews; actually they prove nothing.

5. *The fallacy of false cause (non sequitur)* takes place when the cause which has been assumed for a certain phenomenon actually has nothing to do with it. For example:

I ran a classified advertisement in the New York paper and made three sales in San Francisco. Therefore, the best way to secure sales in San Francisco is to advertise in New York.

While the above example is obviously fallacious, there are other cases where it is difficult to detect the fallacy.

6. *The fallacy of many questions* results from combining several questions into one. In advertising, this fallacy frequently occurs. For example, this question was asked in a certain investigation, by post-card questionnaire:

Will you tell us, by making a check mark in one of the spaces below, whether you, personally, use a cake shampoo or a liquid shampoo to clean your hair?

Two spaces follow, one for a cake and the other for a liquid shampoo check (see Figure 34).

This is a perfect sample of the fallacy of many questions. No safe generalization can be made from the data, because they are self-evidently insufficient. Presumably the recipient would not care to admit that he did not wash his hair at all. The question compels him to choose between a cake shampoo and a liquid shampoo. It excludes automatically any other answer. Not only are comparisons from these answers themselves of doubtful value; but the form of the question might easily have prevented some of those addressed from answering at all.

Miscellaneous Errors

Errors are of many kinds, and of common occurrence, in advertising. Errors have been classified as those of perception, of judgment, of the imagination, and of the conceptual process. One value of classifying errors is that it puts the classifier on the alert for them. Doubtless the errors enumerated by such logicians as Aristotle, Bacon, and Mill would be easily applicable to advertising research. Or, perhaps, it would be as well to devise a new classification.

One of the errors not specifically recorded by the classicists, but of great importance in this work, is that due to the intrusion of what is called "salesmanship." Errors arising out of this cause must constantly be guarded against. If there is any attempt to sway the feelings or sentiments of those for whose sake the generalizations are made, the whole scientific aspect of the research is defeated.

A careful distinction must be made between advertising research and advertising itself. The advertiser must be careful not to get caught in his own net. It is the aim of advertising to influence its audience, and direct its desire into specific channels, not so much by pure argumentation and the principles of logic as by appeals to what is known as "fundamental buying motives," these often being based on instinct and emotion, as much as upon reason. Those who practice research must guard against employing such methods, and against being influenced by them.

One must be constantly on the guard for the irrelevant

conclusion *(ignoratio elenchi)*, especially when regarding the claim of pseudoresearch. The practical advertising man is continuously being assailed with statements which are beside the point. The advertising solicitor states: "If you use our medium, in place of the So-and-So medium, you will get the minimum of duplication; therefore the change will give you the best possible results." The assumption here is that duplication is undesirable; but if the space-buyer has doubts on this score he will first have to settle the question of whether or not duplication for his purposes is desirable, before accepting the conclusion that the recommended change would be for the best.

Bias

In making generalizations from data, the obvious, striking, and outstanding inferences should inevitably be drawn and recorded. Where such inferences are not drawn, it is fair to assume either that the person doing the work is lacking in ability, or that there is an ulterior reason for emphasizing minor conclusions and ignoring those which to the unprejudiced mind appear most significant.

A great deal of work done under the name of research is faulty in its generalizations. When such work is done with an ulterior purpose, many of the natural inferences are not recorded, but are censored out, since they would not tend to strengthen the argument, and an argument is always at the back of such pseudoresearch.

If, for example, in the course of an investigation it is found that 73 per cent of the business of a certain town is handled by the subscribers to a certain group of trade papers, and if it is found, also, that 74 per cent of the merchants in that town are readers of those papers, the obvious conclusion is that those who subscribe to (or read) those papers do not have quite so large a share of the business as the other merchants (see Figure 35). In other words, the conclusion which springs to the normal mind is that those who read these particular papers do less business than those who devote their time to other things—possibly to reading competitive papers. Cer-

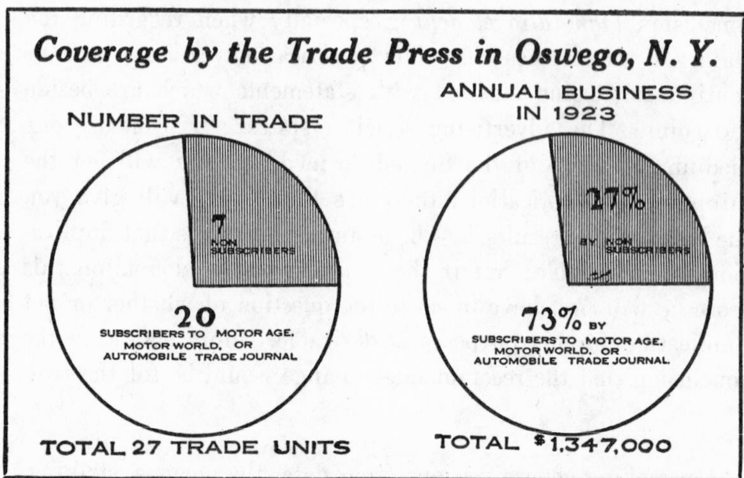

FIG. 35. INADEQUATE EXPRESSION OF DATA

The chart at the left, if it had been marked in percentages to be uniform with the one at the right, would then have shown more clearly the fact that the 74 per cent of the retail units which subscribe to these papers do 73 per cent of the business in this locality. The normal inference is that the nonsubscribers have the greater share of the business.

tainly, no one would find an argument in these data alone to indicate that reading this group of papers proves of the slightest help in getting business for the merchants of this town. But the following excerpt is taken from the generalizations published by this group of papers:

THE INFLUENCE OF THE AUTOMOTIVE TRADE PRESS

As in other parts of the country, ..., ..., and ...... trade papers are read by most of the worthwhile trade units in Oswego. There are 27 members of the retail automotive trade in this town, and 20 of them, or 74 per cent, read one or more of the above publications. Eleven out of 15 of the car and truck dealers are regular subscribers, and 15 out of 22 of the automobile repair shops are also subscribers. Of even greater consequence, however, is the fact that the 22 subscribers to these three papers sold about 73 per cent of the automotive merchandise handled in Oswego in 1923.

The whole emphasis in this paragraph is one-sided; the outstanding generalization is that the nonsubscribers get more than their share of the business.

The question of fallacy is of foremost importance in advertising research. In this field, the opportunity to digress from the truth is so great as to discourage any attempt at generalizations except those which are admittedly tentative, inexact, and approximate. So great are the chances for error that a large part of the research effort must be spent guarding against it. The study of fallacy is the obverse of the process of inductive or deductive reasoning, and supplements it.

The Presentation of Data

Willard C. Brinton says:

> After a person has collected data and studied the proposition with great care, so that his own mind is made up as to the best solution for the problem, he is apt to feel that his work is about completed. Usually, however, when his mind is made up, his task is only half done. The larger and more difficult part of the work is to convince the minds of others that the proposed solution is the best one—that all the recommendations are really necessary. Time after time it happens that some ignorant or presumptuous member of a committee or a board of directors will upset the carefully-thought-out plan of a man who knows the facts, simply because the man with the facts cannot present his facts readily enough to overcome the opposition. It is often with impotent exasperation that a person having the knowledge sees some fallacious conclusion accepted, or some wrong policy adopted, just because known facts cannot be marshalled and presented in such a manner as to be effective.
>
> Millions of dollars yearly are spent in the collection of data, with the fond expectation that the data will automatically cause the correction of the condition studied. Though accurate data and real facts are valuable, when it comes to getting results the manner of presentation is ordinarily more important than the facts themselves.

It is desirable to present the conclusions of a report in a brief and simple manner, even though it may appear to the writer that they are self-evident from an examination of the data which appear in the report. Figure 36 is an excellent example of the conclusions which are arrived at in the study of the farm market for paint.

FIG. 36.—AN EXAMPLE OF CLEARNESS IN SUMMARIZING CONCLUSIONS

(*Farm Journal*)

CONCLUSION

From the standpoint of advertising value, a number of facts in this report seem to be of special importance.

1. A great proportion of farms are owned by the occupants, so that the most important motives for better painting—preservation, appearance, increased value, happiness of family—are all very strong. This is particularly important since the desire for a good appearance apparently leads to more frequent painting than is required for preservation.
2. By far the greater proportion of farm paint is purchased by the owners, so that most farmer readers of the advertising are prospective buyers.
3. A large part of the farm painting is done by the farmers themselves, so that all the desirable qualities of paints are of more intimate interest.
4. The trend of farm conditions—education, wider circles of friends, better roads, automobiles—and the mental attitude of farmers, all tend toward better painting.
5. Future prosperity of farmers is indicated by the rapidly growing population of the country and thereby increasing demand for foods. These foods can be supplied only by the increased production of present farm lands. This undoubtedly means larger incomes per farm and per farm worker.
6. A very marked improvement in farm purchasing power has been made in the past few months.
7. With farm people desiring to buy more paint, and able to buy more paint, a long stride may be taken toward increasing farm purchases from 30,000,000 gallons yearly toward the potential farm market of 100,000,000 gallons yearly.

It is the experience of many research men that those to whom a report is submitted are interested only in the conclusions. Once these men have satisfied themselves that the work is founded upon adequate information and has been done by a properly qualified staff of investigators, their only requirement is a concise statement of findings. This may advisedly be placed at the beginning of a report in order that it may receive the immediate attention of the reader.

CHAPTER V

METHODS OF VERIFICATION

If the first three processes of observation, comparison, and generalization have been complete and accurately carried out, the process of testing and verifying the results might seem to be purely perfunctory. This may be true in the case of a mathematical science. The less exact a science becomes, however, the more necessary it is to verify the results. In the case of advertising research, which has hardly any body of scientific doctrine, it is essential to develop methods by which every step may be tested.

It is probably a safe assertion that no great credence will be given to advertising research until its methods have been perfected sufficiently to allow testing. As a matter of fact, little progress has thus far been made in this direction. Many phases of advertising do not lend themselves readily to testing. The greatest test of all—increase in sales directly attributable to advertising—in most cases cannot be considered accurate, because of the difficulty of tracing returns, and because they are distributed over so long a period. The excellent results obtained in selling by mail, based on actual orders booked, shows what can be done when the results of the advertising are directly traceable.

Efficiency in verification depends first upon the man, then upon the method. Tests must be applied to all three processes of observation, analysis and comparison, and generalization.

Requirements for Testing

There are certain requirements which should be observed in making tests. While these are not invariable, they hold true as a general rule.

In the first place, the person who makes the tests should not be the same one who makes the original observations or generalizations. This is no reflection on the observer. It has been determined, however, in other scientific research, that any individual is unconsciously affected by the work he has done. However much he intends to keep his mind open, he cannot help being affected. Faraday has pointed this out as a supreme difficulty. The person who comes freshly to the problem, who takes the results and subjects them to analysis, is more likely to discover errors than the person who is directly responsible for the original solution of the problem.

In the second place, the test should be made by a different method from the original, if this is possible. If the auditing method is employed, for example, different index numbers may sometimes be used. If a questionnaire analysis has been carried out by mail, the check may be by interview.

In the third place, new sources should be consulted, whenever feasible, as a check on the original results. Accordingly, if the possible sources for investigation are limited (*e.g.,* experts on sugar-making machinery) some of them should be left untouched to serve as later verifications of the original results.

Finally, it is desirable to ascertain whether the methods originally used still apply. Most research work is done in fields where conditions are constantly changing. To use results which were originally correct but which no longer apply will have unfortunate consequences. The results of research work, therefore, should be constantly tested for changes which may affect their application.

Tests can be divided roughly into laboratory tests and working tests. The former can usually be retested by actual experiment.

The Mental Attitude

A test is a method of verifying any scientific result, whether in the field of observation, analysis of data, or generalization. Most things which are done in science lend themselves to verification. The fundamental requisite in all testing is to be able to view the work done with a different mental attitude. Up to this point the work has been constructive, leading to the formation of certain hypotheses. If these hypotheses are to be put to practical usage, it is important to know in advance that they will prove satisfactory. It is now essential to apply the engineering-critical type of analysis to them.

Like the checker in the drafting room, who goes over all the figures of the draftsmen and submits them to careful analysis, there should be somebody in the research organization who will go over its results and check them from all angles. He should be permitted to ask all sorts of questions, however inconvenient they may prove to answer. He should be able to devise methods of testing out inferences which have been based upon observations.

A test, in the scientific sense, applies only to verification of observations, analyses, or generalizations. It should be clearly distinguished from the word *test* as applied to an original series of observations. Thus a test of attention value carried out upon a group of college students is not a test in the sense of verifying any scientific finding. To test out such a series of observations would require a submittal of the same *test* to other groups, or trying out the results on a small section of the market, or some other method of checking up the original observations.

Methods of Verification

There is no standard formula by which any series of observations or generalizations may be tested. The word *test* is very broad. It can apply to the least result or to the entire findings of a large research. Its purpose is to discover error wherever it may exist and in whatever form. The following methods are in common usage:

1. *The Check Method.* Obviously, the simplest form of verification is to go over the entire process and to check up each step. This will often serve to bring to light many errors of computation which have crept into research results, or even

to uncover bias unconsciously acquired as the research progressed.

2. *The Auditing Method.* Testing often may be carried out much after the fashion of the auditor who draws up a trial balance to see whether the calculations made are correct. The research results are verified by arriving at the same end through use of a different method, different groups of statistics, or some different plan of arrangement.

3. *The Referendum Method.* In the case of qualitative results, or where it is a question of possible trends, good results are often obtained by submitting findings to a group of experts qualified to express an opinion. This is a sort of test.

4. *The Trial-and-Error Method.* Wherever it is possible to test results on a small scale directly on the market, this should be done. There are a number of possible ways: (*a*) The test campaign. This is usually restricted to a particular territory, and is used for verifying a complete plan. (*b*) The sampling method. This is largely used in verifying direct-mail methods. (*c*) The coupon method.

The Check Method

The check method of verification is nothing more than carefully going over the methods and results obtained. It applies equally to the preceding three phases of the research process.

All observations used as the bases of comparisons or generalizations should be checked as a final guard against error. Here it is particularly important that the checker should be a different person from the original observer or tabulator. For example, the investigator with a fresh mind will be better able to judge whether the percentage of replies to a questionnaire offers a representative picture of the entire field. If he sees that only a small percentage of replies have been received and that most of these have come from a particular class, he can send some one out in the field to verify results and if a calculable margin of error is found, he can apply this as a coefficient to the original results, as a corrective.

Even interviews are not infallible. Here there are two

possible human factors of error. In the first place, the man interviewed may be biased, or may try to give the answers which he thinks are desired. In the second place, the interviewer himself must be checked just as any scientific observer is checked, by another observer. After he has made a dozen interviews, he probably knows what the outcome of the investigation will be, or at least he can make a good guess. Even if he gives no verbal information to the person interviewed as to what he already knows, he may find it difficult to prevent his attitude from disclosing the essential facts.

Analyses and comparisons should be carefully checked for possible errors. Generalizations also should be checked to see that none of the possible fallacies has crept in.

Checking alone is rarely sufficient proof of accuracy of results. Usually results should be audited.

The Audit Method

The process of auditing entails actual testing of results by the application of other methods, or new observations, or the investigation of new sources. It is conducted according to laboratory methods, however, and reflects solely upon the accuracy of data and generalizations prior to their application and use.

The simplest method of auditing is to take the results of one observation, or series of observations, and to compare them with those of another. If there is a marked difference, then the reasons for this should be investigated. For example, mail questionnaires and interviews may be compared as to results. Field interviews are too expensive, as a rule, to permit of nation-wide application. Furthermore, the field survey may require more time than can be allowed for this purpose. It is often customary, therefore, to conduct field research on a small scale and check for accuracy by a mail questionnaire in other sections of the country.

Figure 37 shows how the Joseph Richards Company (Stanley I. Clark) tests and compares the results of mail and field investigations. Here the question was as to what type or brand of spark plug was preferred by Ford owners and other car

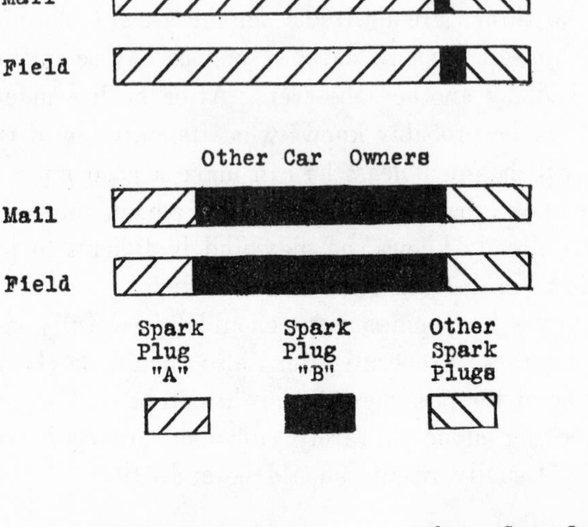

	Ford Owners			Other Car Owners		
	Spark Plug "A"	Spark Plug "B"	Other Spark Plugs	Spark Plug "A"	Spark Plug "B"	Other Spark Plugs
Mail	77%	3%	20%	20%	59%	21%
Field	78%	6%	16%	19%	60%	21%

Fig. 37. The Audit Method of Verification

A simple and satisfactory way of testing the results of mail and field investigations.

owners. With the exception of Spark Plug "B" and "Other Spark Plugs" in connection with Ford owners, the four other pairs of percentages check within 1 per cent. The variations and discrepancies were explained by the fact that the numbers were so small that one or two replies one way or another changed the percentage to a marked degree in the case of Spark Plug "B" for Ford owners.

The accuracy of results from interviews may be audited by selecting a certain percentage of interviews as they come in, and sending back the results to the persons interviewed, asking them if this was exactly what they said on or about a certain date.

The Referendum Method

The referendum method often proves a good way to verify generalizations. This consists of sending copies of the conclusions to different people who are qualified to judge them, and to ask them to express their opinions and to criticize. It is also possible to submit data without generalizations and have each authority consulted make up his own generalizations. In some cases this can be done in the office itself by having different individuals state their conclusions.

One advantage of asking for criticisms of generalizations is that most minds are critical. They are able to catch faults although they cannot themselves arrive at generalizations. The danger in the referendum method is from radicals with decided views of their own, and therefore biased, and also from those who do not wish to take the trouble to render any real criticism and who, therefore, merely write a polite letter saying they find the generalizations excellent and they feel unable to add anything further.

While the generalizations included in the referendum should, for the most part, be as sound and conservative as possible, as a matter of test some erroneous statement may occasionally be included. If this is noted, it shows that the generalizations have been carefully studied, and that the person who points out the defect is more competent to pass judgment than he who ignores the error.

As in all results obtained through the mail, it is important to make the task of criticizing as easy as possible, as by encouraging the use of marginal notations. Returns may sometimes be increased by offering an incentive of some kind. Normally, experts or authorities will be interested to know what others of similar position in the industry will have to say, and, consequently, they will be glad to give their opinion in return for a digest of all the opinions received.

Following is an example of the referendum method. The question at issue in a certain research job was as to probable future methods of placing outdoor advertising. There were few material facts available upon which to base a prediction, nor was it possible to gather facts and specific data which would give a well-rounded result. All facts available were gathered and a thorough study of trends made. Then the soundest exposition of the situation was written as was possible, and these results submitted to practically every person whose opinion could be considered authoritative. The replies from this referendum verified the original findings in practically every detail, and this corroboration constituted a body of evidence against which argument was futile. Without this verification, however, there would have been nothing tangible to warrant making a radical change in outdoor advertising policy.

The Trial-and-Error Method

In many ways, the most satisfactory method of verification of results is to try them out in practice. In fact, this is the only way by which it is absolutely certain that the right policy is being followed. It is particularly effective when there are a number of possible alternatives, or when it is desired to find out whether a certain appeal is as effective in practice as it is in theory. There are a number of methods of making such tests:

1. *The Trial Campaign.*—Before an expensive advertising campaign is launched, but after the preliminary work of analysis has been done, it is often advisable to try it out on a small but fairly representative section of the market. A certain city, for example, may be picked out for the test campaign, and the procedure as mapped out for the whole programme may be applied to this one section. By carefully noting results, and by allowing a suitable factor of safety, it is possible to tell approximately what results will be obtained from the complete campaign. If anything is radically wrong, this method of test ordinarily reveals it. The name of the product, the appeal, or the style of copy may be altered to suit actual working conditions. This subject is treated at length in Chapter XIX.

2. *The Sampling Method.*—The method according to which a small-scale investigation is used to indicate complete results

is normally known as sampling. The test campaign is really sampling a portion of the market; but the ordinary process of sampling can be applied to any phase of the advertising program. For example, if it is desired to find out certain things by questionnaire, a test mailing may be sent out and from the returns it will be possible to tell not only what percentage will reply but also whether the questions are worded correctly, and whether the results will be valuable enough to warrant the expense. The same thing is true of interviews. After making 20 or 30, the reports can be examined and it will be possible to see whether the whole investigation is going to bring in adequate data.

Sampling is invaluable as a means of finding out the relative value of direct-mail sales literature. A number of standard questions may be answered in this way. For example, it is desired to know which of two form letters will be most effective, whether the address should be filled in, whether a postcard or envelope should be enclosed, the best day of the week on which to send it, the type of mailing envelope, and similar questions.

By scattering the test material over the field to be covered, and by carefully tabulating returns, it is possible to estimate approximately what returns will be received from each type of material. By varying one factor at a time the effect of each may be measured.

Figure 38 shows how two sets of letters were tested and the results combined to make a more efficient series. A certain number of accounts were selected, according to B. W. Griffin, Assistant to the President, Gotham National Bank of New York[1] covering the cost of an $8.50 mail-order article. Two sets of letters were made up and keyed B-1 to B-6 and C-1 to C-6. Of the B series, 2,909 letters were mailed, with 936 returns. Of the C series, 2,668 letters were mailed and returns were 93 per cent. The letters in each series which brought the most results were then shifted around and combined into a

---

[1] *Printer's Ink,* June 5, 1924.

Fig. 38.—An Example of Testing by Sampling

Results of Testing Two Series of Collection Letters and their Combination into a Third Series

Form X

Key	Number Letters Mailed	Total Amount	Number Returns	Total Amount of Returns	Per Cent
B–1	1000	$8500.00	284	$2414.00	28.4
B–2	716	6086.00	225	1912.50	31.4
B–3	491	4173.50	123	1045.50	25.1
B–4	368	3128.00	145	1235.56	39.5
B–5	223	1892.44	112	950.00	50.2
B–6	111	942.44	47	401.48	42.6
Totals	2909	....	936	$7959.04	......

64 accounts uncollected

Form Y

Key	Number Letters Mailed	Total Amount	Number Returns	Total Amount of Returns	Per Cent
C–1	1000	$8500.00	280	$2380.00	28
C–2	720	6120.00	320	2723.40	44.5
C–3	400	3396.60	128	1086.91	28.5
C–4	272	2309.69	78	658.26	32
C–5	194	1651.43	112	953.53	57.8
C–6	82	697.90	17	149.86	20.9
Totals	2668	....	935	$7947.96	......

65 accounts uncollected

Form Z

Key	Number Letters Mailed	Total Amount	Number Returns	Total Amount of Returns	Per Cent
B–1	1000	$8500.00	284	$2414.00	28.4
C–2	716	6086.00	319	2711.50	44.5
C–3	397	3374.50	127	1079.50	32
B–4	270	2295.00	107	909.50	39.5
C–5	163	1385.50	94	799.00	57.8
B–6	69	586.50	29	246.50	42.6
Totals	2615	....	960	$8160.00	......

40 accounts uncollected

Fig. 39.—An Example of the Pratt "Bull's-Eye Sheet," an Elaborate Method of Testing Direct Mail Advertising

"HISTORY OF THE GREAT WAR"—$45 Set

TEST MAILING
5,000
Group Four

J. JONES CO.
N. Y. C.

1st MAILING (JULY 15th, 1922)

Mailing List Cost (5,000)	Putting on Cards	$40	Number of orders from 1st mailing necessary to make total sales-cost:
Four Page Letterheading	Printing, Stock, Pwk., Photos and Cuts	140	
Processing, Filling-in	Complete, signed	40	
Return Card Contract	Printing, Stock	15	
Envelopes, Number Nine	Printing, Stock	30	
Stamps, 2c	On Window Envelope.	100	10% 20% 33⅓%
		$415	92 46 28

2nd MAILING (JULY 25th, 1922)

One Page Letterheading	Embossed head	$45	Number of orders from 2nd mailing necessary to make total sales-cost:
Processing, Filling-in	Complete, signed	40	
Return Card Contract	Printing, Stock	15	
Envelopes, Number Nine	Printing, Stock	30	
Addressing on Envelopes	Typewritten	25	
Stamps, 2c., Applying	On Number Nines	120	10% 20% 33⅓%
		$275	154 77 46

3rd MAILING (AUGUST 1st, 1922)

Mailing Broadsides, Four Folds	Printing, Stock	$320	Number of orders from 3rd mailing necessary to make total sales-cost:
Addressing on Broadside	Typewritten	30	
Stamps, 1c., Applying	On Broadside	60	10% 20% 33⅓%
		$410	246 123 74

4th MAILING (AUGUST 7th, 1922)

One Page Letterheading	Embossed head	$45	Number of orders from 4th Mailing necessary to make total sales cost:
Processing, Filling-in	Complete, signed	40	
Four Page Folder	Printing, Stock, Folding, Pwk	140	
Return Card Contract	Printing, Stock	15	
Envelopes, Number Nine	Printing, Stock	40	
Stamps, 2c., Applying	On "Window" 9's	120	10% 20% 33⅓%
		$400	336 168 101
	Total	$1,500	336 168 101

new series. Whereas the uncollected accounts in the previous series had been 64 and 65 respectively, in the new series they were estimated to be only 40 in number. The procedure is described as follows:

By taking the letters of the two series which brought the biggest results, and working out a set of figures indicating the possible returns if the letters were to be used on the same number of accounts, we get the following results: 2,615 letters would be mailed; 960 accounts collected, totaling $8,160. Here only forty accounts remain unpaid; or in other words, the composite series would collect twenty-four accounts more than the "B" series, and twenty-five more than the "C."

Figure 39 shows an elaborate method of testing in advance whether a certain series of mailing will produce profits. Here it is necessary to know the costs of the mailing and from that it can be computed how many returns must be secured to return a profit. (V. E. Pratt.)

3. *The Coupon Method.*—It is sometimes possible to measure advertisements in different ways by using a keyed coupon

POSITION VALUES OF MAGAZINE and FARM JOURNAL PAGES

	Front Right	Front Left	Middle Right	Middle Left	Back Right	Back Left
		7% less response than right front	20.1% less response than right front 13.1% less response than left front	70.3% less than right front 50.2% less than right middle 65.3% less than left front	91.0% less-R.F. 70.9% less-R.M. 84.0% less-L.F. 20.7% less-L.M.	

Percentage scale: 95, 90, 85, 80, 75, 70, 65, 60, 55, 50, 45, 40, 35, 30, 25, 20, 15, 10, 5

FIG. 40. RESULTS OF TESTS AS TO POSITION

The development of test technique is the best single indication that advertising is becoming scientific. (*Sales Management.*)

system. The type of copy, the size of copy, the number of insertions, the position, and the value of a particular medium are some of the points frequently tested in this way. Obviously, the most accurate coupon testing results from advertising which solicits orders direct. Here it is a question of dollars and cents. But it is also possible to measure the advertising by offering, by means of a coupon, a sample of the product, or a booklet describing the uses of the product.

Coupons may be keyed by changing the street number, or by adding a desk or department number. This will identify the particular piece of copy from which the coupon was clipped, and the publication in which it appeared. It is important to remember that, if results are to be accurate, the conditions for the test must remain the same. Thus, if size is to be measured, the size of the advertisement should be the only factor changed. Position, copy, illustration, and all other features must remain the same, in so far as possible. This is in keeping with the principle of altering but one variable at a time.

Figure 40 illustrates the results of tests carried on over a period of 11 months to find out the value of position. This test covered 95 magazines and farm journals. A sample product was offered for the return of a coupon, and returns from 757 advertisements in these 95 periodicals were tabulated.

Each publication was divided into three equal parts—front, middle, and back. This, in turn, was divided into right-hand and left-hand pages. Results showed that the right-hand pages of the front section were the most valuable, with the left-hand pages of the same section a trifle behind them in value.

PART II

THE PRODUCT TO BE ADVERTISED

CHAPTER VI

PRODUCT ANALYSIS

A product, from the advertising point of view, may be either tangible or intangible. The raw material, the agricultural or technical product, or the manufactured product for consumer use, will serve as the basis of an advertising campaign. The intangible product, however, such as a service, or the idea behind an institution, can be used with equal success as the substance of the advertising.

All advertising is based on the product, and centers around it. Advertising research, therefore, properly begins at this point. The more that is known about the product, what it does, what it looks like, how much it costs, or its other distinguishing characteristics, the better able the advertising department or agency will be to do its work.

The product must be analyzed with two ideas in mind:

First, there is the influence which the product has upon the marketing programme as a whole. The seasonal character of the product, the sources from which it comes, the conditions surrounding its production or manufacture, the competition encountered, and similar product problems are all vital factors in formulating the advertising campaign. In fact, a campaign undertaken without a knowledge of these factors would depend largely upon chance for success.

Second, the product ordinarily furnishes a great part of the sales ammunition to be used in the advertisements. The advertiser wants to talk about his product and give any information about it which will help to sell it. He explains why his product will help the purchaser, and why it is better than other competing products on the market.

Research Procedure

In analyzing the product, there are certain elements which should always be subjected to analysis and others which may be peculiar to the case in point. While there is no definite order of procedure, the following is recommended unless there are particular reasons which render it inadvisable:

1. *Classification of Product.* The scope of the product investigation can be narrowed down by placing the product in one of the various possible classes, such as agricultural or technical products, raw materials, manufactured goods for consumer use, or intangible products, such as services.

2. *Constructional Qualities.* As soon as the product is classified, it becomes essential to analyze the various factors which enter into its construction and the qualities resulting from this. The materials of which it is made, for example, are important in the case of technical and manufactured products for consumer use. The degree of quality, or the grade, perhaps determined by laboratory test, should be ascertained. The various characteristics of the product resulting from its construction such as design, serviceability, endurance, reliability, weight, or other particular qualities, should be analyzed.

Figure 41 is an interesting example of a "Construction Points Chart," contributed by Robert L. Blanchard, an officer of the company for which the chart was made. In preparing this chart, the essential features of an efficient device in the particular field in question were analyzed and set down in columns on the left-hand side. Competing products, classified by general types, were then analyzed in columns from left to right. The analysis immediately clarified the points of superiority.

3. *Appearance.* Closely allied with the question of construction is the appearance of the product, and its size, its shape, and its color. These provide the appeal to the eye which forms so important a part of all display. Since the product is normally reproduced in advertising, it is desirable, for this reason alone, that its appearance should be an asset rather than a detriment.

Analyses of Co

Firm Name	Combustion Specialties Corporation	All Ot	
Trade Name	Combusto Draft System	Oxy Blast Hot Point, Little Wonder - Etc	Craigulator, Boynton, Etc
No. of Basic Styles	34	5	2
Capacities: Number of different fixed air capacities provided to meet range of grate areas, rates of combustion and kinds of coal	Unlimited Spray Outlets drilled to meet specific requirements	1 to 5	2
Mixture: Maximum number of outlets provided to effect intimate mixture of air with the combustible gases. PER DEVICE	Single Door 117 Double Door 234	1	1
Preheating: Approximate maximum heating surface in Square Inches with which air is caused to come in contact	1422	380	350
Preheating: Approximate maximum length of air travel in inches from point of inlet to discharge opening or openings.	180	20	18
Exclusive Features ~ Patent Status	1. Air Heating Chamber 2. Air Control Channel Structure. 3. Multiple Discharge Openings 4. Spray Air Indicator Valve 5. Coal Gas Detector, 6. Draft Indicator 7. Controlled Balanced Air Delivery rendering operation AUTOMATIC. 45 Patents Issued 3 Pending	⟹	⟹
Illustrations	  DRAFT COMBUSTO SYSTEM Description 1. Air Inlet. 2. Heating Chamber. 3 to 8. Control Channels. 9 to 11. Control and Distributing Chambers. A Few Combusto Styles Spray Air Valve Coal Gas Detector ~ Draft Indicator	 THE Oxy-Blast-HOT-POINT-Fuel Saver Little Wonder 	The Craigulator 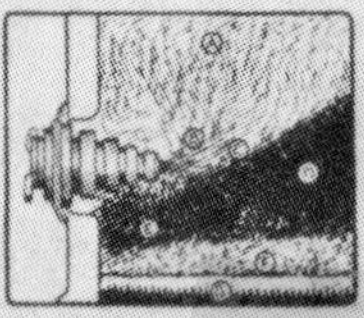 

FIG. 41. COMPARISON OF BASIC

...nstruction Points

...er Types Manufactured

Burnrite, KingKoal Karburetor, ...avcole, Master Carburetor, Etc	Crown, Star, Etc.	Savir, Lescole, Etc	Blaske, Royal Kendall, Burnall, Wolff Etc.
1	3	3	1 (Burnall Door Device*)
1	3	3	1
8	1	8	12
40	328	60	45
6	18	20	8

...ote:- It will be observed that the devices here described ...ach embodies features of design which are copies of ...r are similar to features found in one or more other ...devices. It cannot be said that any embody exclusive ...features. Patents on this character of equipment ...re of little importance generally covering minor ...details of construction which are easily surmounted ...This doubtless accounts for the tendency to imitate ...and for the similarity of design here recorded.-

*Stack outfits have no place in this analyses.- Their effect on plant operation is limited to service rendered by any ordinary Cold Air Check Damper

K. K. K. For BOILER or FURNACE

BURNRITE

THE CROWN FUEL SAVER

SAVIR

HEATED AIR OUTLETS

HOT AIR HEATER

The Royal-Kendall Blue Flame Coal Saver

BLASKE FUEL SAVING DEVICES

4. *Units of Sale.* It is necessary to know at the outset of the investigation how many types of product are made, and in what sizes and styles. The family of products, the line of products, or the single specialty will require different advertising treatment. Standardization of sizes and styles would naturally be investigated as a possible aid to better marketing.

5. *Uses of Product.* All uses of the product should be tabulated, both those recognized as major uses and those of a supplementary character. In addition, the investigation may well look into possible new uses for the product.

6. *Price.* The price placed upon the product by the seller, its relation to production costs, and the percentage of profit made, should be compared with the actual and potential market range and also with prices of competitors.

7. *Competition.* No product can profitably be studied by itself alone. It must be analyzed in connection with competing products and the relative position which each occupies in the market. There are a number of possible variations of the situation, such as competition from products made of other materials, products of cheaper construction, products protected by patents, and foreign products.

8. *Company Policies.* Lastly, it is necessary to survey the policies of the company in so far as they affect the product. The production schedule with its seasonal fluctuations, the attitude of the company towards the introduction of new styles or models, the measures which have already been taken to discover the effect of the product on the market, are only a few of the problems which will come under this heading.

The question of correlating product and market, or the selection of appeals, will be taken up in the following chapters. The appearance of the product in package form, the use of labels, and the choice of trade-marks will be studied in Chapter VIII.

Classification of the Product

Raw Materials. Raw materials are products which have to undergo a manufacturing or converting process before being marketed. Raw materials also include products which have undergone some change from the original form but are neither technical products nor products for consumer use. Agricultural products are in a sense raw materials, but they have so many properties peculiar to themselves that they are usually considered as a separate class. Such articles as cotton and wool, while technically agricultural products, are usually classed as raw materials. Agricultural materials are confined chiefly to goods consumed as food.

In making any analysis of a raw material, there are certain conditions to be considered:

1. Ordinarily speaking, the maker or producer of one type of raw material has little advantage over other makers or producers of the same type of raw material, as far as the product itself is concerned. Chemical analysis may show that his product falls in a certain grade, but in all likelihood there will be competitors whose product will fall in the same grade. His product has little or no distinguishing characteristics. There are, of course, many exceptions to this rule, as in the case of certain marble quarries.

2. Where the raw material is heavy or bulky, as it often is, transportation difficulties and expenses limit its distribution. The markets for raw materials are, therefore, often restricted to certain areas, depending upon competition and demand.

3. Demand and price are likely to fluctuate within a wide range.

The above factors have exercised a profound influence upon the advertising of raw materials. The fundamental problem is to bring together product and market. The owner of a gravel pit wants people to be familiar with it. The operator of a coal mine knows about what he can sell if he can make a low enough price. All that he has to do is to spread the information. He does not have to explain about his product, because everybody knows what coal is.

Because of the lack of distinguishing characteristics, raw materials have often been advertised coöperatively to increase their use. This has proved particularly successful where other

A·F·B·A
USE FACE BRICK
—it Pays

Entrance Detail, Sanitarium, Chicago. Otis & Clark, Architects

What could be more delightful than the simple and effective pattern work here rendered by means of the always adaptable brick units? The patterned tympana over the windows, the basket weave door jambs, the soldier and rowlock belt courses, and the field of Flemish Bond unite in a chaste mosaic of which the eye never tires.

Example of Artistic Brickwork

THE illustration above represents one of the plates in our Portfolio of Architectural Details in Brickwork. The collection at present embraces thirty-two de luxe half-tone plates of the finest type of brickwork, assembled in an enclosed folder, with printed tab, ready for filing.

These examples cover a wide range of interior and exterior subjects, and will be useful in the drafting room for suggesting many interesting methods of treating the wall surface. This portfolio will be added to from time to time with further examples, with data on brick and its uses, and with monographs on the treatment of the mortar joint in connection with the blending of the brick color tones.

A set of these plates in the folder will be sent to any architect requesting them on his office stationery, and his name will be placed on the list for future mailings.

AMERICAN FACE BRICK ASSOCIATION

1153 WESTMINSTER BUILDING · CHICAGO, ILLINOIS

FIG. 42. ADVERTISING OF BUILDING MATERIALS

raw materials can be used for the same purpose. The walls of a house, for example, may be made of wood, stucco, stone, or brick. Advertising may be used to induce the architect, or the builder, or the owner of the house to use one material rather than another. Figure 42 shows an advertisement intended to indicate to the architect that face brick is one of the more suitable materials.

Product analysis, therefore, of a raw material involves, first of all, research as to the uses to which the material is put. There are 70 specified uses for lime and a great many unspecified ones. Any new uses which are discovered will increase the market. Sometimes the chief obstacle to increased use of a certain material is price. The Mahogany Association, Inc., of New York City, carried on a campaign to correct the impression that mahogany is beyond the price-range of the normal purchaser.

Under average conditions, the ultimate consumer is little concerned with the raw materials of which the products which he himself buys are made. The difficulty of trade-marking or branding such products is usually such that the identity of the original producer is lost in the manufacturing processes through which the product is put. This is a serious obstacle, from the advertising viewpoint, and one which the research man can help overcome.

Analysis of an Agricultural Product.—Agricultural products, with some exceptions, are seasonal. Some have a comparatively brief period during which they must be marketed; others can be secured at almost all times of the year. Figure 43 shows the seasonal production of fruit for the entire United States; the season for particular localities would, of course, be considerably shorter.

In analyzing an agricultural product, therefore, the first step is to find out when it comes on the market, and during what period it must be marketed. If the period is brief, as for Bartlett pears, demand must be greatly stimulated, or else the market will be flooded. During a recent year, California Bartlett pears were heavily advertised in the season, with the result that a much larger proportion of the crop was marketed than is usually the case.

When the agricultural product can be stored over a fairly long period, the problem has often been to prevent demand from being seasonal. Lemons, for example, are as procurable in winter as in summer, yet the demand falls off in cold weather. Advertising has done much to correct this. Cranberries are bought chiefly around the holiday season; yet they are obtainable all winter. Coöperative advertising campaigns have done a great deal to spread demand for such products over a longer period of time.

In the case of a given class of agricultural products, there are practically no distinguishing characteristics which would, for example, differentiate one "make" of melon from another "make." While packaging may be resorted to, to lend individuality to some particular product, such as Sunsweet Prunes, the logical use of research in this field is to discover methods of increasing demand for the product as a whole rather than for any particular brand. Coöperative advertising, while featuring the brand of the association, increases demand for the product in general as well.

The Technical Product.—The technical product may be defined as all equipment and supplies used in manufacturing which have been fabricated beyond the raw material form but which do not enter the end product in its marketed form. This category includes such goods as machinery, surgical instruments, and textile soaps.

In analyzing the technical product, it is again necessary to answer the question, "What will it do?" The buyer is interested, first of all, in performance. His profit is directly or indirectly connected with the question of what the technical products which he purchases will accomplish.

In many technical product fields, competition is exceedingly keen. Advertising here often tends to stress the service which is rendered by the advertiser rather than the product itself. This is a wise thing to do in cases especially where ability to secure spare parts or new equipment, for example, is impor-

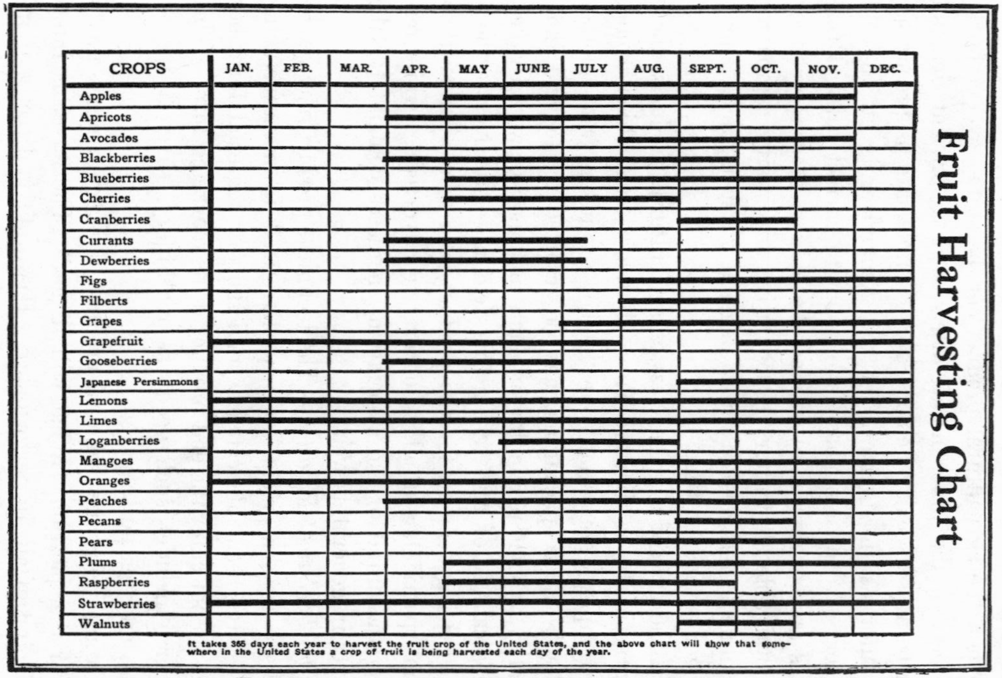

Fruit Harvesting Chart

CROPS | JAN. | FEB. | MAR. | APR. | MAY | JUNE | JULY | AUG. | SEPT. | OCT. | NOV. | DEC.

Apples
Apricots
Avocados
Blackberries
Blueberries
Cherries
Cranberries
Currants
Dewberries
Figs
Filberts
Grapes
Grapefruit
Gooseberries
Japanese Persimmons
Lemons
Limes
Loganberries
Mangoes
Oranges
Peaches
Pecans
Pears
Plums
Raspberries
Strawberries
Walnuts

It takes 365 days each year to harvest the fruit crop of the United States, and the above chart will show that somewhere in the United States a crop of fruit is being harvested each day of the year.

FIG. 43. ANALYSIS OF AGRICULTURAL PRODUCTS
The seasonal problem presents unusual difficulties in the advertising of fruits.

BYERS PIPE
GENUINE WROUGHT IRON
WHENEVER you see pipe marked with a spiral stripe, remember it is Byers. No other pipe is so marked. This conspicuous spiral stripe is painted on all Byers Pipe to the end that all purchasers may easily identify it and be protected against substitution of inferior pipe.
The similarity, in outward appearance, between Byers Pipe of genuine wrought iron, and pipe made of cheaper, less durable metal, has always been a source of confusion, frequently leading to the installation of pipe which in the end proved very costly to the owner.
For over half a century, Byers Pipe has been specified and installed in America's finest residences and large buildings of every character. Its record of rust resistance, after generations of service, is one of universal satisfaction. As a result, experienced engineers and architects protect their clients' interests by specifying Byers. They know that few materials entering into the construction of a building have greater possibility for harm, for the cost of replacing a network of pipe installed in walls, ceilings and other inaccessible places is staggering.
Nipples marked, too
Even Byers Nipples are now plainly marked—the Byers name and year of manufacture being plainly stamped in the metal. So the 100% genuine Byers installation has become an easily attainable ideal. You may now specify Byers Pipe and Byers Nipples with full confidence that they will be furnished.
Literature on Request
A. M. BYERS COMPANY Est. 1864 Pittsburgh, Pa.
Distributors in all Jobbing Centers
New York Philadelphia Boston Chicago Houston Los Angeles
the Spiral Stripe on Byers Pipe
also look for name and year rolled in metal

FIG. 44. IDENTIFICATION OF TECHNICAL PRODUCTS

This example shows how closely the question of product identity is to that of advertising.

tant in maintaining the production schedule of the manufacturer.

In conducting research for a technical product, performance facts may be obtained through testimonial letters, requests for information addressed to users (perhaps in questionnaire form), or by means of personal interviews with users. It is also important to find out who does the actual buying, so that this class of individual may be reached through the proper media.

One trouble which has been experienced with technical products is that of identification. Figure 44 illustrates how the A. M. Byers Company, of Pittsburgh, identifies its product by painting a spiral stripe on its wrought-iron pipe, and then advertises through a general medium. In the past few years there has been much advertising of technical products in media reaching the ultimate consumer, notably in the field of automotive parts.

Manufactured Articles for Consumer Use.—The majority of advertising research is concerned with the manufactured product for consumer use. This main classification can be subdivided in a number of ways. In the first place, there is the standard "necessity-luxury" method of division. A necessity is a product that is required to maintain the standard of living of any particular class of purchasers. Thus an automobile is a necessity to some; a luxury to others. Naturally the appeal will differ in the two cases, the necessity being merchandised on the price-utility bases; the luxury on the appeal of beauty, quality, appearance, or similar inducements.

Products for consumer use are sometimes classified as staples or novelties, particularly when they fall within the same line of goods. Thus some lines of shoes are staple while others are new each season and therefore classed as novelties.

Products may also be classed as well known, or little known, or unknown. In the case of the well-known product, the market does not have to be educated as to its uses; it has merely to be reminded. Where the product is little known, the market must be broadened, and where it is unknown, as in the case of a new product, the advertising must usually build demand from the ground up.

A still further method of dividing consumer goods is to arrange them according to the type of demand. Thus convenience goods are bought from the nearest outlet, regardless of

Westport---Baltimore's Central Station for Electric Power
POWER
PUBLIC SERVICE
Baltimore manufacturers know—or ought to know—that it is cheaper to buy power than to make it.
When a decision is made to share in the benefits of Central Station production instead of footing the bills for the waste that accompanies the use of an isolated plant, the power user begins to save money, and get better service; but he does more than that.
He does something for his city as well as for himself and for the power Company. He makes his city cleaner and more habitable.
In this advertisement are two pictures—one, the Central Power Plant at Westport; the other the artist's conception of a city of chimneys, a settlement of smokestacks and showers of soot.
Use Central Station Power for two reasons—
1—It is cheaper for you.
2—It is better for everybody.
Good Public Service---Good for You, Good for the Public
Good Public Service
THE GAS & ELECTRIC CO.
Is Your Service Good? If Not, Please Let Us Know
Telephone Plaza 8000 Industrial Power Department

FIG. 45. ADVERTISING REMOVES PREJUDICE AND MISUNDERSTANDING

brand. In this class would fall cigarettes, groceries, candy, and notions. Shopping lines are usually bought after comparing values at different stores, as is done by women, especially when buying clothing. Specialty goods are those for which manufacturers have created such a strong demand that purchasers will go out of their way to buy them, and will refuse to accept substitutes.

Products might conceivably be classified in still further ways, and this would be justified if it should make the process of analysis easier. While all attempts at classification are obviously only partially successful, they do serve to narrow the product investigation. If, for example, a product falls in the convenience classification, the advertiser knows that he will probably have to secure as many retail outlets as possible, and the most he can hope to do is to secure brand recognition. This will have a bearing upon the media used, the type of copy, and the whole campaign.

Any characteristics which will serve to distinguish the manufactured product for consumer use from competing products will supply ammunition for advertising purposes.

The Intangible Product.—The intangible product often lends itself better to advertising purposes than the tangible product. The transportation services of the country have found a wealth of information suitable for copy purposes. The public utilities have discovered that the service which they offer the public can be explained better in advertising than through annual reports, and that advertising will help to remove prejudice and misunderstanding. (See Figure 45.)

Many cities and towns have spent large sums in advertising, notably the cities of Florida and California, featuring palm trees and colorful text. The State of Maine Publicity Bureau has persistently advertised to vacationists, with excellent results.

The so-called institutional advertising, wherein the company sells itself, has become a recognized expedient. The company's name is then the *product* to be advertised. The department store, for example, has to convince the public of its stand-

Question: Where will he shop from now on?

Mark Twain loved to tell about a man who languished in prison for years. Then he had an inspiration, opened the window, and got out . . .

Mr. E. F. Garwood, able railroad executive, is chief clerk to the General Superintendent of the Long Island Railroad. He sits in the Pennsylvania Station, only a few steps from Macy's. What a chance, you will say, to shop efficiently!

But Mr. Garwood won't mind our quoting one sentence from a letter he has just written. "It is only recently," he says, "that I have had an opportunity to test Macy's promise to sell merchandise at prices lower than elsewhere; it is gratifying to know that there is a concern doing business on such principles."

The test transaction was a modest one—a pair of radio ear phones, on which Mr. Garwood saved 40 cents more than he thought he could save. But it called forth one of the most enthusiastic letters Macy's has received in weeks.

Hundreds of thousands of people, all over America, know that Macy's makes good its promise to save your money. Isn't it strange that a man who spends his days so near Macy's building has only just made this discovery!

Copyright, 1924, by R. H. Macy & Co., Inc., 34th Street & Broadway

"When, if ever, will you be big enough?"

In 1858, Rowland H. Macy opened on Fourteenth Street a store so small he could be proprietor, buyer, bookkeeper and salesman, all in one. His first day's sales were less than $10.

In 1902, the Macy store moved uptown and built on Herald Square the largest department store building in the world. Sales that year were $10,755,064.

In 1922, that big building had become so crowded that a 19-story addition had to be planned. Sales that year were $49,615,229.

"How long will this impressive progress go on?" you may ask. "When, if ever, will Macy's be big enough?"

If Macy's were merely offering merchandise on credit, your question might be answered. But Macy's is offering more. By buying and selling dependable merchandise at lowest prices for cash, it offers freedom from high prices, from extravagance, and from debt.

No institution which offers this freedom is ever likely to be big enough.

Copyright, 1923, by R. H. Macy & Co., Inc. Herald Square, New York

How much, in money, is the Macy Saving?

During its last fiscal year, ending February 2, 1923, the total sales made by R. H. Macy & Co., Inc., were $49,615,229.

It is the policy of Macy's to undersell all other stores by at least 6 per cent. Very often the saving is much greater.

But if you calculate the total Macy Saving at only 6 per cent, it means that Macy's enabled its customers to save last year $2,976,913.

It is not by mere size, or volume of business, that a great institution entrenches itself permanently in the life of a city. Macy's is not merely a big store; it is a big asset to families that want to make their money go as far as possible.

And that means most of us!

Copyright, 1923, by R. H. Macy & Co., Inc., Herald Square, New York

What kind of writing do you do?

Pope scribbled on the backs of old envelopes. Walpole sat elegantly at a satinwood escritoire. Thoreau dispensed with all comforts in his cabin at Walden Pond.

Frederick Palmer is a seasoned campaigner, and can write anywhere, bestrewing a whole room with his MSS. Bruce Barton writes his common sense editorials in a comfortable Windsor chair. Rupert Hughes wrote his most widely known story in a parlor car.

Whatever your writing habits, Macy's has furniture that will fit them—maybe reform them.

Prices are startlingly less than you would pay elsewhere; whether your taste runs to Macy's fumed oak table at $16.94, which would have seemed sinfully luxurious to Thoreau, or to Macy's Colonial secretary at $312, which would have appealed to the fastidious heart of Walpole.

Copyright, 1924, by R. H. Macy & Co., Inc., 34th Street & Broadway

FIG. 46. THE ADVERTISING OF THE "INTANGIBLE PRODUCT"

How a store uses institutional copy to build up goodwill.

ing. Figure 46 shows a number of the advertisements of R. H. Macy and Co., Inc., which won one of the Harvard Advertising Awards. These advertisements show the application of the news appeal. The institutional idea has also been applied by manufacturers whose products are well known to the public, in the endeavor to increase the value of the goodwill already existent in their names.

Constructional Qualities

When the product has been placed in its proper class, and the characteristics of that class are thoroughly understood, it is time to analyze the various characteristics of the product. The first thing to find out is how it is made, what materials enter into its manufacture, what are the outstanding features of its design, and what resulting qualities it possesses. Inquiry along all of these lines will help to furnish material for advertising copy.

Many people are interested to read about the materials of which a manufactured article is made, or about the conditions under which an agricultural product is grown, or to read the description of a service. Such details supply a news element which is valuable in arousing interest. The methods of manufacture of a product often prove stimulating to a lay mind, particularly when they are explained in a popular manner. In the case of the technical product, of course, the manufacturing details are all-important.

Grades and qualities in various products are gradually becoming standardized. The Bureau of Standards is publishing a National Directory of Commodity Specifications, covering 6,000 commodities. Many agricultural products are already standardized. Even in the consumer field, numerous articles are virtually standardized. Many companies have resorted to laboratory tests to discover qualities which may prove suitable for advertising purposes. Food products, for instance, are analyzed for calories and vitamines. A varnish proves under test to be resistant to the harmful effects of water, even when poured on it in boiling form. The furnace manufacturer shows how he has succeeded in reducing the heat losses due to poor insulation.

A more difficult task for product research comes when the product appears to have no special features connected with its construction. In durability, serviceability, endurance, or performance it may be matched by competing articles. Chemical or physical tests disclose little that is new. In such a case, it is necessary to examine further.

Appearance

More and more attention is being paid to the appearance of products. It is realized that many purchases are made almost wholly because of the appeal to the eye and that, between an attractive and an unattractive product, the choice is almost invariably for the former, given approximately the same price range.

Size and shape often exercise great influence in determining the sale. Much experimentation along these lines has been done by the makers of electric flatirons. Here also the question of weight plays a part.

Design and color are particularly important because of their attention value, especially when the package is reproduced in the advertisement. Much heed has been paid to having the appearance of the product in harmony with the use to which it is put. Thus, articles for use by women will be designed with especial care to attractive appearance. Artistry of design, which is of little importance in advertising a technical product, takes on added influence in the case of consumer products. The question of appearance is treated in Chapter VIII, on "The Product as its Own Advertisement."

Units of Sale

When a company makes a number of products, there is often a tendency to cater to market demand while varying styles and sizes. Even where only one product is made, the number of sizes is often considerable. In order to direct advertising stimulus in the right direction, it is essential to determine which unit or units of sale are best fitted to market demand. There are several possible methods.

In the first place, the sales records will ordinarily show at what point the bulk of demand centers. If a company makes a dozen different sizes, in all probability demand will be found chiefly for a few of these sizes. The same is true of the demand for styles.

It is not sufficient to determine the best selling line; it is necessary to find out the reasons behind the preference. One method is to interview dealers, and to ascertain from them their reasons why one size or line sells better than others. Another method is to find out from actual users what they think of the product, and why they buy one size or style rather than another.

A point to note in the product analysis is the suitability for sampling purposes. This would include sampling in miniature form through the mail and also the possibility of putting goods up in small packages for sale through such outlets as the five-and-ten-cent stores.

The unit of sale and the price are closely connected. It is always a difficult problem to determine whether the price should be changed or the quantity in the package altered. One good way to solve such a problem is to test both methods on a small scale.

Uses of the Product

The uses of the product determine its market. Under normal conditions, the market is broadened by finding new uses, the important thing being to be careful not to overemphasize uses which are filled better by some other product.

Since each market ordinarily requires a different advertising approach, uses must be carefully tabulated and given an approximate quantitative rating. The same product, for example, may be used in a number of industrial markets as well as for consumer use. Steel wool, as a cleaner and polisher, is used both in the factory and in the home.

Companies are always looking for new uses. Sometimes letters are written to them telling of new uses and asking why they are not being advertised. At other times, advertising is conducted, offering rewards for letters describing new uses.

Examples of products which have graduated from the one-use to the many-use column are numerous. Lux, for instance, started as a flake soap which would not shrink woolens or cause delicate silks to change color. Its advocacy as a soap for dishwashing, for washing machines, and for toilet purposes came later. The Climalene Company sold its product as a water softener for years before it could induce people to use it as a cleaner also. In fact, a questionnaire sent to 2,000 housewives in its territories showed that it had been sold so well as a water softener that the idea of using it for something else never occurred to the average consumer. The advertising was then made to emphasize the fact that Climalene "does more than soften water."

Even though the design of the product may have to be altered somewhat to suit a new market, this might prove profitable.

Price

The uses to which the product can be put determine its potential market; the price at which the product is sold serves to restrict the actual market range. While every householder would be interested, presumably, in owning an electrically operated or gas operated refrigerating system, the price at which such a product is sold automatically limits the market to certain income groupings.

Closely connected with the original selling price is the cost of upkeep. This is particularly important in selling technical products, or such articles as automobiles or electrical household equipment.

A number of factors should be examined in connection with the price situation, such as patent rights, the price of competing products, degree of monopoly in the territory, and the excellence of the sales methods. It is always valuable to obtain the reaction of the market to the price at which the product is sold.

The question of putting the price in the advertisement has long caused great discussion. There is general agreement that in the case of low-priced goods it is better to have the price appear, but that where luxury or quality are more important than price, it is just as well to omit the price. One difficulty lies in determining in which class many products fall. The general assumption of the consumer often is that, if the price is omitted, the article is beyond his means. But this is all a matter for research.

Competition

No product investigation is complete which fails to take cognizance of the competing products in the field.

In the first place, there are usually products made of the same materials and serving exactly the same purpose, differing perhaps only in some small feature. All electric toasters, for example, are approximately the same, but each one has some feature of its own, such as a special turnover arrangement, a plug that pulls out easily, or a rack for keeping the toast warm. Each one of these special features provides a talking point for the product, and the competitor who keeps adding new features supplies his advertising department with fresh ammunition each time an improvement is made.

In the second place, there is the question of substitute products. Shall the walls of the house be finished with lath and plaster, wall board, plaster board, or some of the other materials on the market? The advertising campaign must take cognizance of the competitors who serve the same market, even though with a product made of different materials.

In the third place, there is the problem of competing with cheaper grades of the same product. A manufacturer may, for example, be competing with himself if he makes two grades of product. The automobile manufacturer, again, always has his own secondhand products to consider. The makers of high-grade branded articles have the competition of low-grade unbranded articles which, on the surface, appear much the same to the consumer.

The analysis of the product, therefore, will also include a study of competing products of all kinds, perhaps with a tabulation of their selling points, prices, materials of construction, and advantages and defects.

Company Policies

In the majority of cases, after the process of making the product analysis has been completed, it will be desirable to scrutinize the product policies of the producer, manufacturer, or seller. A brief historical synopsis should indicate quickly whether the company has been progressive or overconservative, whether it has underestimated the merits of its product, or whether it has made claims which have not been actually substantiated.

If the survey discloses that the product has been constantly mproved, this is an excellent sign. In the case of a product vhich cannot be improved in quality, there may be improvenent in package design, manufacturing methods, or methods of listribution.

A defective product often does a great deal of damage beore any one discovers what is wrong. The test campaign, herefore, may serve to reveal flaws in the product, as well as n the method of marketing it.

Production schedules and plans should be analyzed and tudies made of the correlation between production and sales. f service is needed with the product, what steps have been aken to render it satisfactory?

he Product and the Market

A great part of product analysis is concerned with a study f the product in relation to its intrinsic qualities and to the ompany which sells it. It is equally important, however, to nd out what the buyers think of it. This is not always an easy iatter, because even the mention of the name of the product ay bias the results of the investigation.

Figure 47 shows the form used in an investigation to dermine what books are read and enjoyed by children of various

		Reading Score	
Complete title of book........			
Author's full name........			
Publisher			
Child's name........	*Age*........	*Boy or Girl*........	
School........	*Grade*........	*Teacher*........	
One of the best books I ever read ☐	Too easy ☐		
A good book, I like it ☐	Just about right ☐		
Not so very interesting ☐	A little hard ☐		
I don't like it ☐	Too hard ☐		

Write on the other side of this slip what you like best about this book, or why you like it.

FIG. 47. AN EXAMPLE OF PRODUCT ANALYSIS

A test of this sort, simple as it is, gives endless valuable informatio[n] of marketing value and supplies the advertiser with much "ammunition." (*The Publishers' Weekly*

ages and reading ability, carried on by the Carnegie Corpora[-]tion, through the American Library Association, with th[e] coöperation of public and private schools. The results of suc[h] a test as this will indicate what the market requires.

In the case of a product never before put upon the market careful advance analysis is necessary to determine the prope[r] appeals, the correct price range, and the best outlets.

CHAPTER VII

DETERMINATION OF APPEALS

The efficacy of any advertisement depends upon the corre-
tion of a number of factors, among which is the choice of the
ppeal which will bring about the most sales. The advertise-
ent may attract attention and arouse interest without having
e right appeal, but it will not stimulate the desire to buy.
nless it creates or accelerates the buying impetus, the adver-
sement will be almost worthless. Every salable product has
number of possible appeals. These may be ascertained and
easured in accordance with certain standards, just as may be
ne with the product's physical properties, such as breaking
rength, elasticity, elongation, or other index of utility.

Appeals may be variously approached, according to whether
ey are directed at perception, discrimination, emotion, or
eation. Then, there is the important factor of association
be considered. There is the problem of the negative and
sitive appeal, the general or selective appeal, the major and
e minor appeal.

Many advertisers go on the principle that once a success-
l appeal has been found it should be maintained. This policy
s undoubtedly proved successful in many cases. In others,
nditions arise which would make it desirable to change ap-
als. Improvements in the product, competitors' advertising,
tered business conditions, variations in the market, change
the company's own policies, all may make it desirable to
ter the appeal. Constant variety attracts attention, but it is
ssible, of course, to attain variety with change of appeal, as
devising different copy.

The testing of appeals, to measure their efficiency, is as

yet comparatively new. Enough results have been secured, however, to show that it is entirely feasible to develop researcl methods by which the appeal may be measured as to its "sell ing" power.

Classification of Appeals

It is not always an easy task to find one of a group of selling appeals which will prove effective. The best results may com from careful research or they may come from experimentation but the fundamental purpose is to strike the line of least re sistance. Generally speaking, the appeals for any given prod uct may be to perception, discrimination, emotion, or ideation

Perception includes all appeals to the senses. It is th simplest and most fundamental method of selling where prod ucts can be seen, handled, tasted, or listened to. In advertising most perceptional effects must be registered through the eye The flavor of foodstuffs, the odor of perfumes, the music fror the phonograph, the "feel" of fabrics, must all be conveye through the eye by what is known in psychological terms a "association."

The *discriminative* appeals are those which will lead th prospective purchaser to select one product rather than anothe Price, quality, durability, and service are all appeals whic are definitely directed at these rational buying motives.

Under the head of *emotion* come those generally known a "human interest" appeals. Curiosity, pride, fear, joy, thrif shame, and hope all exercise a powerful influence in the d rection of demand.

Ideation is the appeal to an idea. The electric appliance for example, makes house work easier. The idea of gift-givin at Christmas is such an appeal. A new product for consume use must normally be introduced by an ideational appeal. I is preliminary to any appeal for the purchase of a particula article. The educational and preparatory work may advisedl be done by using the ideational appeal.

FIG. 48. THE USE OF ASSOCIATION

Association

In the majority of cases, successful appeals depend upon the use of correct association. The advertiser of a product wants to put it before the public in its best light. He wants to give it an "atmosphere." If it is a bargain, and if the appeal is to price, he wants his advertisement to create the bargain

FIG. 49A. PRESTIGE THROUGH ASSOCIATION

How a "quality atmosphere" is created by classing the advertised product with an idea which connotes the highest craftsmanship.

atmosphere. If, on the other hand, he desires to create a quality atmosphere, he may use an artistic setting to attain this end.

In the case of appeals based on perception, association predominates. The advertiser must show graphically or convey verbally the reflection of a sensation, and usually a pleasurable sensation. He cannot actually reproduce the aroma of coffee,

Fig. 49b. Another Example of Association

(*a*) Brussels lace is the result of consummate skill. (*b*) Adler-Rochester clothes are likened to Brussels lace. From these two premises, the reader is led to but one conclusion. The method is simple but well executed.

but he can create the illusion through illustrative art, and let the memory and imagination of the reader do the rest.

Association is often used to assist the discriminative appeal. Figure 48 shows how the appeal of distinction is carried out by associating the hardware advertised with a building of a high type, and one which is favorably known. "Trading-up" or putting the product in a quality atmosphere, is a well-known expedient in advertising. Figure 49 illustrates the association of the art of the garment maker with that of the vase makers of Sèvres and the lace makers of Brussels. The appeal is carried out indirectly. Association is often more powerful than a direct statement that an article is "best" or of "superlative quality." Association allows the reader to draw his own inferences, and, if the stage is set correctly, the inference will be to the product's advantage.

Emotions, like perceptions, must be effected in advertising by means of association. So also with ideational appeals, for idea and product must be associated if the appeal is to be carried out successfully and with profit to the advertiser.

Appeals to Perception

The appeals to the senses, as already mentioned, are fundamental, being directed at such desires as hunger and appetite. It is, however, always a problem to determine to how great an extent the illusion, for it is no more than that, will prove effective. Can the association be made powerful enough to induce action, or will the picture merely arouse the reader's artistic admiration and leave his buying habits unaffected?

Appeals to perception are directed to the reader's sight, taste, hearing, smell, and touch, sight being most important.

An appeal to the eye would include beauty first of all. Hence the illustrator and designer of a product which lends itself to art treatment is progressing along rational lines when he makes it as attractive as he can. Color is likewise a powerful appeal. So also may be any unusual design or arrangement of layout, but these may easily degenerate into mere devices for catching the reader's attention.

Taste is a fundamental appeal in selling food. Figure 50 shows how the illustration can be made to convey the idea of taste, especially when color is used, as was done in the original. Such an appeal shows the product to best advantage.

The illusion of hearing is more difficult to reproduce in advertising, but it can be done by association with the proper

FIG. 50. AN APPEAL TO PERCEPTION

A successful attempt to make the subject "feel the taste through the eye."

atmosphere. In other words, if the fundamental appeal of a phonograph is the pleasure people get in listening to the music, this effect can be produced.

The sense of smell, as associated with the odor of a perfume or of a beverage can be described and it can also be illustrated. The same is true of touch.

Appeals to Discrimination

In selling raw materials, technical products, services, and even consumer goods, the practical appeals are of paramount importance. If it is desired to sell a machine by advertising, it is almost always necessary, somewhere along the selling process, to tell what the machine will do, and in this way appeal to the desire of the prospect to obtain the greatest performance in return for his money. Figure 51 shows graphically the results of an investigation carried out by Ernst and Ernst, and illustrates the almost universal desire in the industrial field to secure performance facts.

How performance facts may be used as the basis of appeals for a technical product is indicated in Figure 52. Describing this chart, Robert L. Blanchard, its originator, says:

> In the left-hand column you will note that we have gone to the foremost technical authority in our field for information as to the principles to be kept in mind in the production of an efficient product. In the right-hand column we have analyzed the construction features of the product, as it relates to these principles. Surely a similar analysis of any product must render an accurate index as to its efficiency in actual performance.

Because of the multitude of possible appeals to discrimination, it is ordinarily feasible to obtain the reaction of the consumer to them in order to ascertain which is the most powerful in determining the actual purchase. The strength of the ideational and emotional appeals cannot be measured in this way so successfully, since few people are capable of such introspective psychology as would be required. The discriminative appeal, being directed at rational motives, can, however, be determined by referring the matter to possible buyers.

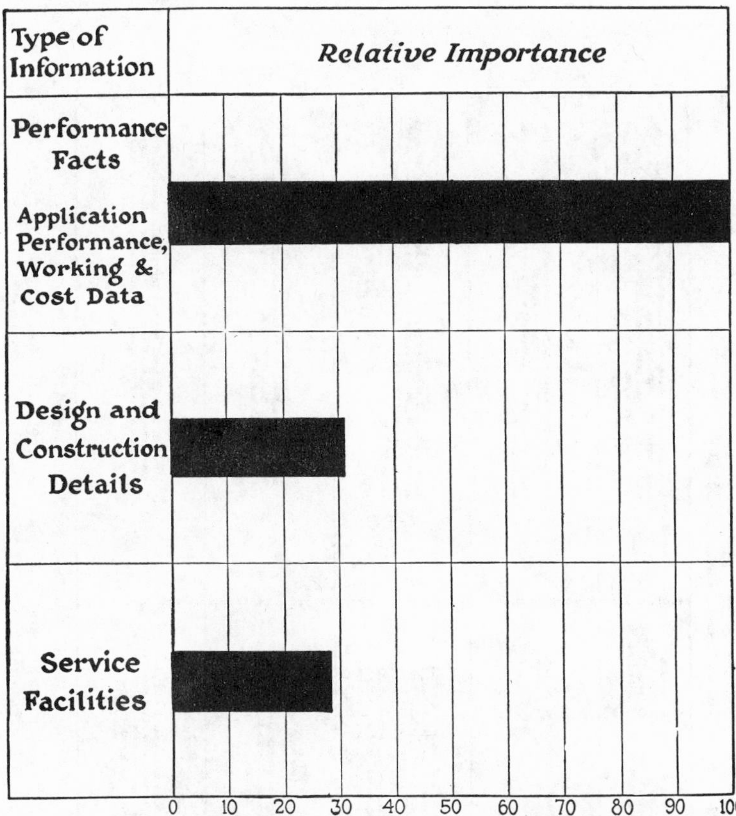

FIG. 51. ADVERTISING REQUIREMENTS OF INDUSTRIAL BUYERS
Discrimination plays a more important part in the purchase of goods for use in the mill and factory than for those used by the general public. This chart shows how various appeals to discrimination are classified.

The National Automobile Chamber of Commerce sent out a questionnaire to car owners, asking them their preferences in the selection of an automobile, and giving them a list of twelve qualities from which to choose. Over 2,000 replies were received. Figure 53 shows the tabulation of results for three different car-price classes. It also gives a tabulation of the appeals used in 40 current advertisements.

Many advertisements studied stressed speed and hill-climbing; but these appeared to be of relatively little importance in determining the car purchase. Forty-eight per cent of those

What Do the World's Foremost Combustion Engineers Say ?			
U. S. Bureau of Mines	The United States Bureau of Mines in Bulletin 135, Page 134 discussing the conditions essential for efficient combustion in hand fired heating plants, tabulate the four following conditions which are definitely defined by further quotations.	Combusto Draft System	It will be noted that the principles of construction incorporated in Combusto Draft System as outlined below conform in detail to the requirements of the United States Bureau of Mines as defined in left hand column. These principles of construction found in Combusto Draft System are exclusive features not incorporated in the product of any other heating plant or accessory manufacturer.
1st	"Enough Air" "Of the air necessary for complete combustion of the fuel only about one half can be supplied through the grate. The other half must be supplied above the fuel bed." Technical Paper 139, Page 7.	1st	Over thirty-four basic designs of Combusto drilled to meet specific requirements assure the correct volume of air supply over the fire. This is accomplished without hand operation and with absolute automatic control.
2nd	"Air and the Combustible Gases Thoroughly Mixed." "The ideal way to supply additional air over the fuel bed is to introduce it as close to the fuel bed and in as large a number of small streams as possible." Technical Paper 137, Page 55. "Mixing is probably the most important single factor and the one most frequently responsible for poor combustion. A large excess of air and high temperature will do no good unless the air is mixed with the furnace gases and the oxygen and combustible gases brought into contact." Bulletin 135, Page 134.	2nd	Air admitted to combustion chamber through Combusto Draft System is sprayed over the fire in from 30 to 234 fine streams at surface of fuel bed, assuring perfect distribution and intimate mixture of gases and air.
3rd	"A Furnace Temperature Above the Ignition Point of Gases." "Maintain a temperature high enough for the ignition of the combustible while the combustible is mixing with the air." Technical Paper 80, Page 55.	3rd	Air in passing through Combusto Draft System travels a distance of from 60 to 180 inches, coming in contact with from 880 to 1422 square inches of heating surface. Due to this length of travel and contact with heated Combusto channels, the air is obviously highly preheated.
4th	"Enough Time for Combustion to be Complete". "The air must be supplied as near to the surface of the fuel bed as practicable and be thoroughly mixed with the combustible matter, in order that the combustion may be completed in a short time and a small combustion space made effective." Technical Paper 135 - Page 131.	4th	Air is admitted at point furthest from flues in manner described under Paragraphs 2 and 3 above. This maximum time is allowed for gases and air to mix and complete combustion is the result.

FIG. 52. PERFORMANCE FACTS AS BASIS FOR APPEALS

A matching of the product's performance against the requirements as stated by the foremost authority, and the results of the comparison used for advertising purposes.

FIG. 53.—AN EXAMPLE OF INVESTIGATION OF APPEALS TO DISCRIMINATION

Factors Influencing Purchasers of Cars, in Order of Choice, Compared with Emphasis in Current Car Advertising

CLASS I (*Fords*)	CLASS II (*Medium priced*)	CLASS III (*Above* $3000)
1. Economy	1. Endurance	1. Endurance
2. Price	2. Comfort	2. Comfort
3. Endurance	3. Price	3. Economy
4. Service	4. Appearance	4. Appearance
5. Comfort	5. Economy	5. Hill Climbing
6. Appearance	6. Service	6. Service
7. Hill Climbing	7. Flexibility	7. Price
8. Flexibility	8. Hill Climbing	8. Flexibility
9. Indorsements	9. Indorsements	9. Indorsements
10. Speed	10. Specifications	10. Specifications
11. Specifications	11. Speed	11. Appointments
12. Appointments	12. Appointments	12. Speed

IN 40 CURRENT ADS

1. Economy	7. Comfort
2. Appearance	8. Endurance
3. Price	9. Flexibility
4. Speed	10. Service
5. Hill Climbing	11. Appointments
6. Indorsements	12. Specifications

replying said they were not interested in special features, such as engines, axles, frames, and shafts; only 23 per cent expressed interest, while 29 per cent were noncommittal. In other words, the car buyer wants performance rather than appointments or specifications.

Lee H. Bristol, advertising manager, Bristol-Myers Company, manufacturing chemists, says:

We all love to vindicate ourselves for any decision or any position we have assumed in our thinking on a particular subject. This brings out clearly that explanatory and argumentative copy should be balanced by sound, plausible, reasonable arguments.

Let us assume, therefore, that a reader of an advertisement of this character becomes convinced of the case presented in the advertisement. He arrives at that decision by mentally agreeing with the logical points that bring him to a definite conclusion. As a result, this reader becomes a user of the product. Now, after a period of some time has elapsed, let us assume that new and competing arguments from competitors are brought to the attention of that same converted reader. Aside from the intrinsic quality or merit of the original product itself, he can best be retained as a user of that product, in spite of the new and plausible competitive advertising appeals, if he is still able to find that the soundness of logic and reasoning whereby he was *first* influenced to purchase the product will still hold true and therefore vindicate his original decision. Any change, by specious reasoning, to some newer competitive argument would present a sharp bit of inconsistency in his own reasoning, in marked contrast to the known predisposition on the part of the human mind to rationalize and justify its previous decisions.

Appeals to Emotion

Emotion includes any feeling of joy, grief, love, fear, or in other words, feelings of pleasure, pain, activity, or repose. There has been much debate as to whether emotional copy is good advertising ethics, that is, whether it is good policy to avoid an appeal to reason in favor of an appeal to instinct or emotion. Those in favor of the emotional appeal argue that statistics can be falsified more easily than emotions. Those against maintain that it is possible to use emotional copy and illustration to sell goods which ought to be bought purely because of rational motives.

To illustrate the emotional method, the advertising of some insurance companies will serve as examples. One company bases its appeal on the discrimination of the reader, and appeals to his reason by means of statistical tables and charts of death rates. Another company uses an appeal which reads in part:

The first day of the month, and every month, comes this love letter to her. For over two years now she has been receiving it and it will come with the same regularity as long as she may live. "It was a thoughtful, loving husband and father who made this arrangement. His love letters really come from Beyond to the little family, for by a provision made years before he died, The London Life was to send his wife $100 a month as long as she should live."

A third company pictures the still burning remains of a house and a family group gazing at it in consternation. Here the appeal is also emotional, but it is to fear rather than love—the fear of what would happen if the house burned up without any insurance upon it.

An appeal to the emotions is closely connected with the ideational appeal, because it is difficult to connect the purely emotional appeal directly with the product. The problem of securing this connection is an important one.

The Ideational Appeals

If it is possible to use a basic idea as an appeal, then an approach is obtained to the entire market rather than to any particular division of the market. For example, the idea of motoring for pleasure might be advertised to the whole field, while the particular sections of the field each might have its own peculiar likes and dislikes, as far as discriminative appeals are concerned. The institutional copy run by General Motors Corporation falls in this class.

The importance of the discriminative appeal is that in the final analysis it is the appeal which determines the sale of the brand of product advertised. But before an individual buys any particular product, he must be convinced that he wants a product of that general description. In many cases, it is, of course, unnecessary to emphasize the idea behind the product, because the educational work has already been done. Thus the advertiser of a furnace emphasizes its beautiful design, or its saving in coal consumption, or the convenience of running it, but, when all is said and done, the fundamental appeal behind the sale of all furnaces is the idea of keeping the house warm. Similarly, clothes are used to protect the body, soap for cleansing purposes, and food for nourishment. There may be hundreds of other appeals but they are all subordinate to the one dominant appeal which is the reason why that general type of product is bought at all. Parenthetically, it may be noted that some appeals used in advertising are even broader than the normal and obvious appeals. Thus, Lifebuoy soap uses the health appeal, while Palmolive stresses the appeal of perennial beauty.

Figure 54 illustrates one of the most successful combinations of the ideational-emotional appeals. Here the idea is suggested; and the appeal made to fear. The illustration is made to express the emotion. The copy begins by being emotional, it is later ideational, finally, it is discriminative.

Figure 55 shows a somewhat different treatment of the ideational appeal. Here it is desired to overcome a misconception that silk is too expensive and not economical. The appeal takes for granted that silk underwear is desirable and aims to remove the impression that it is expensive.

Often it is difficult to classify appeals by any clear-cut system. Most products appeal, in other words, in different ways to different people. For example, W. Moede gives the following motives for purchase of a certain book, as found by a German publishing form in an investigation, a questionnaire being used:

36.2 per cent........Newspaper critiques
24.1 per cent........Publishers' prospectus
20.5 per cent........Purchased on recommendation
12. per cent........Acquaintance with author's other works
2.4 per cent........Hearsay and reports
3.6 per cent........Through study, reading, reference in other books
.8 per cent........Acquaintance with author himself
.4 per cent........Because of binding.

Negative versus Positive Appeals

There was once a time when it was considered poor advertising to dwell on the unpleasant factors connected with a product. This theory was based on the assumption that the unpleasant or negative idea would tend to identify itself with the product itself, through association. It was, therefore, assumed that if any suggestion of hardships, or misfortunes, or unpleasantness could be avoided, and if the emphasis were placed only on the pleasant aspects, then the results would likewise be satisfactory and positive.

This is good theory only so long as it sells goods. Beau-

FIG. 54. IDEATIONAL-EMOTIONAL APPEAL

tiful faces, perpetual smiles, "happiness" *ad infinitum,* these bores of advertising are, for the most part, justified. But in many cases it pays to accentuate the unpleasant factors—the time the battery failed, the mistake in etiquette, the radio apparatus that would not tune out interference. In other words, "If you buy my battery, you won't have any more of those

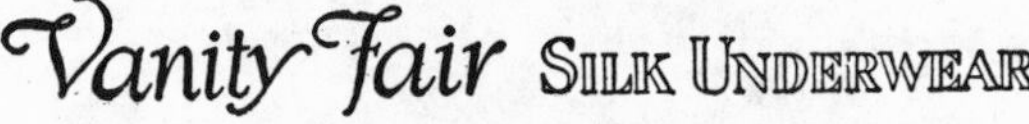

"I Used to think Silk Underwear a luxury,"
remarked one of our customers the other day, "but, I find that anything you can wash out yourself as you can Vanity Fair, is the most economical thing to buy!"
Unlike the under-apparel which must be boiled, blued and bleached, you can wash your Vanity Fair silk underwear yourself in the bathroom bowl. You need not even press it, unless you wish, for Vanity Fair is soft and smooth after washing.
Come in and let our salesgirls help you figure just what Vanity Fair will save you in actual laundry expense and in the wear and tear to which a laundering subjects your clothes. You'll be surprised to find that Vanity Fair will soon pay for itself!
You'll need only one type of underwear too, for Vanity Fair is worn the year round by well-dressed women.
There are special features about each article of Vanity Fair silk underwear—let us show them to you.
Vanity Fair Silk Mills, READING, PA.
Makers of Vanity Fair Silk Underwear and Silk Gloves
Vanity Fair SILK UNDERWEAR

FIG. 55. THE IDEATIONAL APPEAL

embarrassing moments when the car has to be cranked by hand in the middle of traffic"; or "You won't make any more of those mistakes in etiquette if you buy my book on the subject."

Naturally, if all advertising were negative, it would quickly lose its force because the novelty now characteristic of negative appeals would be lost. At certain times, however, it is highly useful. Figure 56 shows the use of the negative appeal to

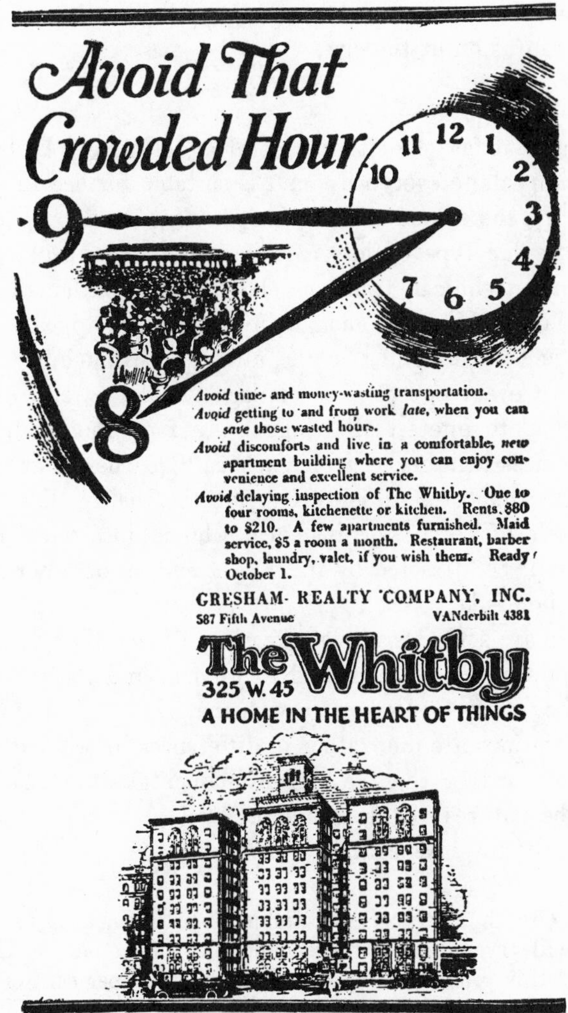

Avoid That Crowded Hour
12 1 2 3 4 5 6 7 8 9 10 11
Avoid time- and money-wasting transportation.
Avoid getting to and from work late, when you can save those wasted hours.
Avoid discomforts and live in a comfortable, new apartment building where you can enjoy convenience and excellent service.
Avoid delaying inspection of The Whitby. One to four rooms, kitchenette or kitchen. Rents $80 to $210. A few apartments furnished. Maid service, $5 a room a month. Restaurant, barber shop, laundry, valet, if you wish them. Ready October 1.
GRESHAM REALTY COMPANY, INC.
587 Fifth Avenue VANderbilt 4381
The Whitby
325 W. 45
A HOME IN THE HEART OF THINGS

FIG. 56. THE NEGATIVE APPEAL

Like so many other forces used in advertising, and like advertising itself, the negative appeal can be used or misused. It can succeed or fail. All depends on the skill with which it is applied.

induce people to live in the city. It points out the unpleasantness of traffic conditions around eight and nine in the morning, and how this may be avoided by living in the city itself. If the apartment house had been located in the suburbs, it might have used the negative appeal equally well by pointing out the restless confusion of the city.

Selectivity of Appeals

An appeal may be either general or selective. In the first case, it appeals to everybody, and is suitable for use in general media. In the second case, it is specialized and prepared for one particular type of buyer. The selective appeal is often found in a technical, trade, or class journal, although, where the special type is large enough in numbers, it appears also in general periodicals going to the ultimate customer.

Almost every appeal is specialized to some extent. It does not pretend to interest all readers. In fact, the small advertisement uses a large headline such as "Deafness," frequently merely for purposes of selectivity, on the theory that the one person out of forty, for instance, who is interested in that subject will be attracted by it. The attention of other readers may be ignored.

There are some broad classifications of selectivity. For example, the appeals to men and to women, and the manner in which they are presented, often vary materially. It may be that these variations are due rather to differences in occupation and experience, rather than to any fundamental dissimilarity between the natures of the two sexes.

Mr. Bristol says again:

> Using tooth paste as an example, even a most casual market survey will reveal the vast preponderance of women as the purchaser of this product. Possibly as much as 70 per cent or 80 per cent of this purchasing market consists of women. This does not mean that men and children do not use tooth paste, but it does clearly indicate that the purchasing of this product is largely done by women.
>
> It follows obviously, therefore, that the copy appeal should first address itself to women. That, in turn, begins to limit the advertisable traits to be looked for in the product. For instance, with a woman appeal it might be based on the sense of beauty to be created by the use of the product, or it might be of the essence of fear through which the appeal could be made.

Therefore, if you take all the possible points of advantage of your product and balance these off against the character of the market to be addressed, the advertisable traits begin to become apparent. If such an analysis does not lead to an obvious or easy solution of determining these traits, two other methods may be adopted to clarify any confusion.

One is the method of sending a questionnaire to consumers, offering them a modest prize or sample as an inducement for them to indicate which one of certain appeals listed would be of greatest value, from their standpoint. Again, two small local advertising campaigns might be instituted simultaneously in territories remote from each other, using separate copy appeals in each case. By a careful check-up of results, the proper information might be obtained.

One of the biggest determinations of our own advertising policy on a new product was the fact that the copy appeal decided upon should not be based on anything but a broad, sound, fundamental argument which would not prove essentially subject to change or subject to the variations of whim, fancy, style, or any other advertising foundation of a changeable quality.

Appeals may be selective, as to age. The appeals to the child are made within its comprehension. Sloan's Liniment, on the other hand, has been successful by appealing to people past fifty. It will be seen that the selective appeal should be based upon a classification of buyers, *i.e.,* upon market analysis.

Appeals differ with occupation also. The farmer and the banker, the college man and the ditch digger, have different outlooks on life. Differences in appeals to the rich and to the poor are naturally great. Social position, intelligence, disabilities, all offer themselves as opportunities for selected appeals, addressed to a particular audience.

Changing Appeals

In making any analysis of the appeal to use, it should be remembered that appeals are rarely static. Indeed, they are constantly changing.

In the first place, the appeal is likely to change with a variation in fundamental business conditions. An economy appeal may not be so effective as a quality appeal at a certain period of the business cycle.

In the second place, improvements or changes in the product naturally bring with them changes in appeals. Time also brings about changes in national habits, ideals, and living standards.

In the third place, the buying motives themselves may undergo change. This is well illustrated in the radio apparatus field. According to a survey made by Freling Foster, of the *New York American,* tonal quality, which was a fairly new appeal compared with distance and volume, has now come to the front as the leading appeal in selling radio sets. The factor of selectivity had also become more important because in population centers such as New York it is essential that sets should not overlap. The appearance of the set has become of importance in the last year or so, much as was the case with the phonograph. The radio set is rapidly becoming part of the furniture of the house, and, as such, must be in keeping with its surroundings. Distance and volume have both decreased from factors of primary importance to factors of practically no value (see Figure 57).

It is worth while to check the relative importance of appeals from time to time by analysis, through either the dealer or the consumer. It is a good idea to list appeals in the order of their importance as determined by experiment, and then to try out combinations of them. If competitors are using one type of appeal, it is often wise to shift appeals and to try something new upon the market.

Selection of Appeals

The chapter up to this point has dealt with the various classes of appeals. It is now necessary to subject these appeals to certain comparisons and tests. No comprehensive rules can be given for doing this, but the following list is suggestive:

1. Various possible appeals should be tried out on the purchasers, to find which are the most powerful in determining the purchase. Other things being equal, the result of such test may be taken as conclusive; but there are several modifying factors which may make it desirable to act otherwise.

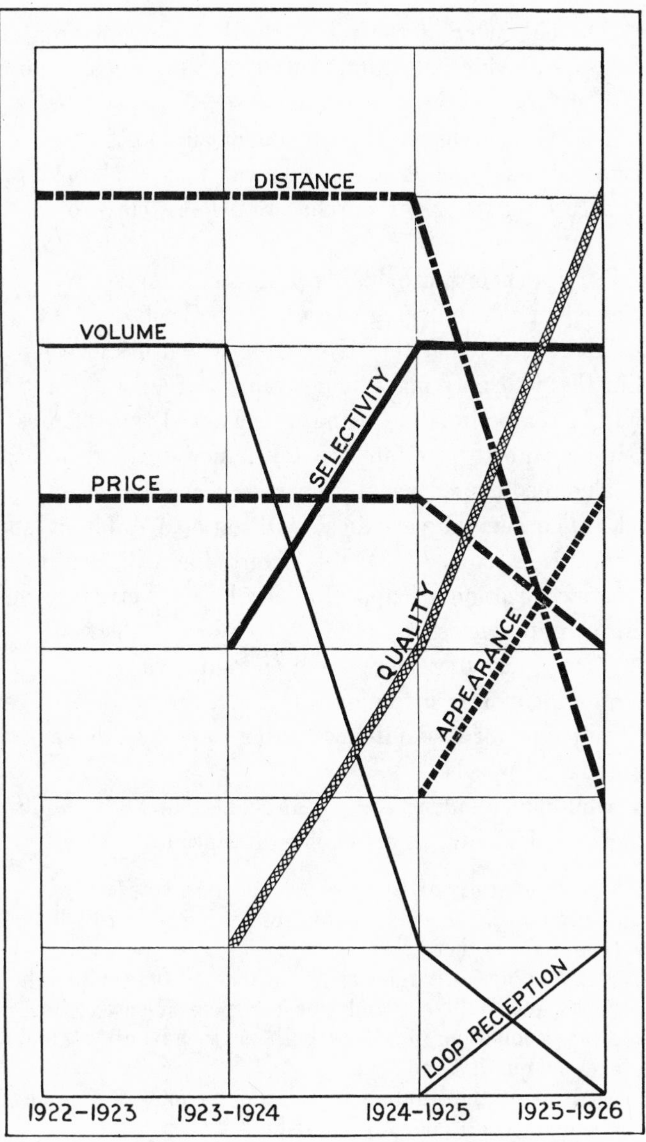

Fig. 57. An Example of Changes in Appeals
(*Radio Retailing.*)

2. The character of the product will have a marked effect on the appeal which should be used, notably such factors as price, quality, and exclusive features.

3. The type of buyer is an element supplementary to the character of the product. Appeals vary, as explained previously, according to age of purchaser, income, class, or occupation.

4. Buying habits are highly important for study. These are treated in the following section of the book.

5. The character of the advertising which has already been done in the field may make it desirable to follow out a special policy. If competitors are using a hackneyed type of presentation, it may prove profitable to try a new method of attack.

6. The media used usually exercise a marked effect on the appeal. The general periodical will carry a different appeal from the trade journal. Direct advertising will require, perhaps, a modification of appeal. Outdoor advertising, again, has its own problems.

7. The advertising policy will, perhaps, cause the appeals to be presented in a particular way, such as one in each series of a campaign, or a dominant major appeal with variations in secondary appeals.

A well-known advertising man contributes the following points as fundamental in the choice of appeals:

1. Thorough study of the product and its manufacture.

2. Study of consumers to determine the degree to which they really need the product.

3. Study of price in relation to income to determine who are the Canbuys and Willbuys, and who the mere Wishwecoulds.

4. Study competing products both as to advantages and disadvantages in quality and price.

5. Analysis of the product in relation to jobbers and retailers —what competitive or novelty advantage it has.

6. Study of profits to determine margin that can be spent in selling.

7. Analysis of repeat market.

"In my opinion," says this contributor, "the advertising man must reach many of these facts by actual contact with consumers and dealers—in other words practically selling the article to strangers. Opinions of one's own family, friends, or associates are often misleading. It is never entirely safe to sit at a cloistered desk and merely imagine the application of an article to a flesh and blood market."

Measuring Effectiveness of Appeals

In the case of direct-mail selling it is possible to measure the effectiveness of one appeal over another by the percentages of returns received from each. In the majority of cases, however, this is not possible, as where ordinary periodical or newspaper advertising is concerned (though there are exceptions, as in the case of some retail advertising). Where advertisements are tried out in a small way for test purposes, it is rarely possible to separate the effect of the appeal from the other elements in the marketing campaign which may be confused with it and which may have great influence in producing sales. It is desirable, therefore, to find some other method of measurement.

One of the simplest methods of finding out what appeals most to a given class of consumers is to use a questionnaire, and then arrange the appeals according to their order of merit. One difficulty with this method is that of getting any measurable uniformity of response. This can be overcome to some extent by printing the appeals on the questionnaire and then asking the persons used as judges to arrange them in order. Even under such conditions it is difficult to measure more than a limited number of appeals.

To avoid the above difficulties, Richard B. Franken, of New York University, tried out the method of direct impression. Seventy-seven somewhat overlapping selling points of phrases were selected from hosiery advertisments in leading national magazines, mimeographed on sheets of paper and distributed to four groups of students of the psychology of advertising. If the selling point appealed very strongly to the reader he marked it 3, if strong 2, if weak 1, and if very weak 0. The appeals follow: [1]

[1] Richard B. Franken, *Journal of Applied Psychology*, June, 1924.

ANALYSIS OF ARGUMENTS FOR HOSIERY

1. The best of service
2. Made of tested combed yarn
3. Specially dyed
4. Finished to retain the yarn in its greatest natural strength
5. Reinforced heels and toes
6. Specially constructed to guarantee long wear
7. Maintain original high quality
8. Don't speculate with the money you invest in silk stockings
9. There is a certain satisfying value
10. They're garter proof. "No run that starts above can pass the gold stripe"
11. Silk stockings that wear
12. Good as they look
13. You get what you pay for
14. Washing won't hurt them (don't get a cheap silk—it goes in the first wash)
15. Be sure you get fresh stock when buying silk hose (new shipments just arrived in all desirable colors)
16. All the qualifications of a guaranteed hose at half the price
17. Quality first
18. Don't wear out as quickly
19. Value for the price
20. Long staple yarn
21. Single sole with triple heel and toe
22. Prolong the life by changing daily or oftener for summer. Change your socks and your *shoes*—it's a very restful thing to do
23. Full fashion fits shape of the foot
24. Do not hang baggy
25. No seam to chafe or rub the skin
26. Snug fit prevents chafing the feet
27. Fit like a glove
28. Tested for strength
29. Strong threads
30. Absolute fast colors guaranteed (new pair or your money back)
31. Guaranteed 6 months
32. Guaranteed to give satisfaction
33. Wear well
34. Fit well
35. Stylish
36. Pure silk
37. Fast colors
38. Fast colors guaranteed
39. Double heel and toe
40. Seamless
41. More stitches per inch

42. Closer knit (or woven)
43. Reinforced where the wear comes
44. Best for 50 years
45. Made in daylight plant
46. Every pair will fit and wear satisfactorily
47. Snug fit at the ankle
48. The sheer beauty of ———
49. *Wears* as well as it *looks*
50. In many weights and shades
51. Pure thread silk
52. The first socks in America to be knitted by machinery were made at ——— in 1822
53. 97 years ago
54. More than 50,000,000 pairs of ——— that gave satisfaction last year
55. Doing one thing well for almost a century
56. Satisfying the needs of human feet
57. Oldest and one of the largest hosiery mills in the United States
58. Why have holes in your hosiery?
59. Reinforced hosiery for men, women, and children
60. Makes a sensible gift for men or women
61. It furnishes the kind of service that justifies the purchase
62. Dependable wear and snug clean-cut appearance
63. Hosiery satisfaction
64. There's real comfort for tired or tender feet in ——— fashioned hose
65. The method of knitting these stockings is different
66. Patent machines that "knit in" the proper shape and fit, without seams
67. No homely stitching up the back of the leg
68. No seams to walk on
69. Just a soft smoothness that gives real comfort
70. The fit is snug and firm everywhere
71. There's no room for wrinkles in ——— hose
72. Extra elastic, narrow tip, prevents garter runs
73. Style, quality, and sound value
74. Fascinating new designs in ——— silk hosiery for summer are certain to delight you
75. Hosiery—each the best of its kind
76. Home knit for our soldiers
77. For those whose needs demand the essential combination of style, quality and sound value

Figure 58 illustrates the method of tabulating the appeals, Column 1 giving key number of each appeal in reference to mimeographed sheet, Columns 2, 3, 4, and 5 giving ratings for males and females separately, Column 6 the total score for each

Fig. 58.—Tabulation of Results of Investigation of Sales Appeals

A Tabulation of the Rankings of 77 Hosiery Appeals by 160 Males and 75 Females, Listed According to the Strength of the Appeals as Indicated by the Results of the Study

Appeal Key Number	Ratings 0	Ratings 1	Ratings 2	Ratings 3	Total Score *	Average	Average Final Rank: Males	Average Final Rank: Females	The Sales Appeal
5	1	6	55	98	410	2.56	1	....	Reinforced heels and toes
	0	4	25	46	189	2.51	....	1	
31	18	14	32	86	346	2.16	2	....	Guaranteed six months
	6	17	16	36	157	2.09	....	10	
21	12	26	47	65	335	2.08	3	....	Single sole with triple heel and toe
	3	13	26	33	164	2.19	....	6.5	
39	5	27	79	70	334	2.08	4	....	Double heel and toe
	5	2	39	28	164	2.19	....	6.5	
43	7	26	78	49	309	1.93	5	....	Reinforced where the wear comes
	3	6	27	39	177	2.36	....	4	
6	10	42	62	46	303	1.88	6	....	Specially constructed to guarantee long wear
	2	14	31	28	160	2.13	....	8	
17	14	40	64	42	294	1.83	7	....	Quality first
	6	14	25	30	154	2.05	....	12	
38	24	26	61	49	293	1.81	8	....	Fast colors guaranteed
	6	8	16	45	176	2.34	....	5	
36	21	42	60	37	273	1.71	9	....	Pure silk
	8	9	29	29	154	2.05	....	12	
32	27	41	57	35	260	1.62	10		Guaranteed to give satisfaction
	5	14	28	28	154	2.06	....	12	

* The total score, Column 6, is figured as follows: For example, appeal No. 5, which ranked first by the males and females was rated 1 by 6 males 2 by 55; and 3 by 98; so that $1 \times 6 = 6 + 2 \times 55 = 110 + 3 \times 98 = 294 = 6 + 110 + 294 = 410$; etc. $410 \div 160$ (the number of cases) = 2.56 (Column 7), average score given to the appeal by males.

appeal, Column 7 the arithmetic average, Columns 8 and 9 the final rank for males and females, and Column 10 the sales appeal. One objection to the method was that only college students were studied, and they might not have been typical of the general consumer.

The Product and the Appeal

Before an appeal is used, it should be analyzed to determine whether it is suited to the product. One of the first questions in this respect is the degree to which the market is familiar with the product. If it is a comparatively new article, it may still be necessary to sell the idea behind it rather than to resort to selective or discriminating appeals.

The price at which the product is sold must also be considered. The price factor cannot always be measured advantageously by the same methods used in testing for the other most effective appeals. Yet, if a product sells at a price less than other products in its class, the price consideration is bound to be important. Furthermore, its strength is usually relative to quality, which is normally the converse of price.

Methods of merchandising the product may influence the appeal. For example, if sold direct from factory to consumer, it would be natural to emphasize the savings to the consumer achieved by this method of distribution.

If the product is of the convenience type, the appeal will be for an immediate sale. If, however, the product belongs in the shopping class of goods, the appeal will probably be discriminative. In the former case, the buying process will take place as soon as the need arises; in the latter case there will probably be a certain period after the need is first felt until the time that it is satisfied.

The type of buyer and his buying habits, also influential factors in determining the appeal, are treated in Chapter XI.

Competitive Advertising Appeals

Final choice of an appeal should always be preceded by a careful analysis of the appeals used by competitors in their advertising. In the first place, this will give some idea of what appeals are being used. Some idea of their relative success may often be obtained from a knowledge of results.

In the second place, it may be desirable to use an appeal which is not being employed by competitors. Thus, if the general tendency in the field is to advertise the idea, it may be best to employ discriminative appeals.

The advertising of competitors is an interesting and profitable study, because it serves as a source of observation and also a basis of analysis and comparison. The appeal will be, of course, but one of the factors examined.

Media and Policy

The type of appeal used will vary with the media, because the markets will also vary in accordance with the media used. A single company may advertise in general periodicals, local newspapers, trade journals, and use direct mail, with different appeals stressed in each.

The advertising policy is another of the major factors to be considered in connection with appeals. The appeal must be suited to the policy of the company and be in keeping with the reputation which it has created for itself. Thus an appeal to price would not be in keeping with the policy of a company which all its life had stressed quality. It would tend to remove the product from the atmosphere which had been created for it. Abrupt changes in advertising appeal, therefore, should be carefully considered before being put into effect.

In many cases, the leading appeals are scheduled for use in a series of advertisements. Some of them may be split up into several sections, as when a product has a number of uses.

CHAPTER VIII

THE PRODUCT AS ITS OWN ADVERTISEMENT

In many ways, the product is its own best advertisement. In making an advertising analysis, the manner in which the company identifies itself with its product, and the effect of its packing and trade-marking policies are important. In addition to certain physical, economic, and legal requirements, the product as an advertising factor should fulfill four conditions satisfactorily:

In the first place, it should serve as a link between the maker of the product and the consumer. That is, it should serve as a mark of identification. The name of the maker and the brand name of the product should be linked together almost automatically.

In the second place, the product and its package and trade-mark should be suited to each other. The carton or container should express the individuality and underlying characteristics or uses of the product as closely as possible.

In the third place, the package and trade-mark should be acceptable and pleasing to the market. It may have great attention value but this may sometimes be a disadvantage rather than an advantage. It must not only be remembered, but it must be remembered in a pleasing way.

Finally, the package and trade-mark should have good memory value and freedom from misleading associations. Unless it is remembered and associated properly a great part of its value is lost. To obtain good memory value, its size, shape, color, copy, illustration, typography, and general design should be submitted to the most careful test.

The Package

The package suited to any given product will be determined by studying the physical, the economic, and the psychological factors which bear upon the problem.

The physical requirements for a package often determine its size and the materials of which it is made. The use to which a product is put will also have an influence. A tooth powder can, for example, should be made so that it will fit easily into a medicine closet, and also serve as a convenient container for the powder.

In making up a carton or container, it is important to remember that display value is an essential element, and the physical form, while dependent upon mechanical and physical conditions, should be adapted for this display value in so far as possible. It will not often be possible to have containers so fitted to the product and to convenient usage as the Log Cabin Syrup can; but it is frequently possible to avoid the stereotyped form.

The advertising value of a container which later can be made to do further duty in the hands of the consumer is not to be ignored. The tobacco can which is placed upon the drawing-room table, the automobile oil container which is later used about the house, the coffee tin which is useful for household purposes when it is emptied of coffee, are only a few examples. Obviously, not many products would lend themselves to such treatment, but the idea is worth bearing in mind when making a product analysis. When articles which are packed in glass jars are used up, the containers are often kept for further usage. If these can be utilized for advertising purposes, the effect may be well worth while.

In making an analysis of the package, it is of value to see whether the package design or appearance is capable of exercising its maximum selling force. The perfumery industry is an example of a field where the physical form of the container is being constantly altered, to obtain variety. While the unusual package serves to stimulate sales for a short time, it quickly loses effect. The package is changed at frequent intervals. Some advertisers use a novelty package for purposes of introducing the product, and then supplant it with a permanent form. Figure 59 shows a novelty package for soap used by Houbigant in the shape of a miniature case for three books.

There are a number of economic limitations which will restrict the choice of a carton. The price at which the product is sold will affect the quality of the carton. Similarly, the

Fig. 59. A Novelty Package
(*Printers' Ink Monthly.*)

market in which the product is sold will have its influence. A large package for a small amount of money may sell well in poorer sections, while the same package in a wealthy locality might make little headway.

A valuable work sheet, used by the Blackman Company in dealing with packaging problems, is shown in Figure 60.

Psychological Basis of Packaging

Wholly aside from the practical and economic aspects of the package, there are certain psychological considerations of

FIG. 60.—WORK SHEET FOR USE IN DEALING WITH PROBLEMS OF PACKAGING

THE PACKAGE	Comment
Factors which affect SIZE	
1. Does package contain quantity of goods consumer is in the habit of buying?..........	
2. Does it suggest quantity?..........	
3. Does it suggest quality?..........	
4. Is it convenient to handle by consumer?..........	
Factors which affect SHAPE	
1. Does it conform to the goods packed?..........	
2. Is it distinctive?..........	
3. Is the shape of the package familiar to the public?..........	
4. Is it convenient to display by dealer?..........	
5. Is it convenient to handle by consumer?..........	
Factors which affect COLOR	
1. Is package of color appropriate to product packed?..........	
2. Is color attractive to consumer?..........	
3. Does color give high visibility on display?..........	
4. Is color distinctive from competitors' packages?..........	
Factors which affect DESIGN	
1. Does label design suggest commodity within?..........	
2. Does design show product in use?..........	
3. Is design distinctive?..........	
4. Is it easily remembered?..........	
5. Does it "stand out" on display?..........	
6. Is label correctly placed on package?..........	
Factors which affect TYPE	
1. Is type legible on display?..........	
2. Is it distinctive?..........	
3. Does it invite reading?..........	
Factors which affect TRADEMARK	
1. Is trademark prominently displayed?..........	
2. Will it be visible as packages are displayed by dealer?..........	
Factors which affect DISPLAY VALUE	
1. Is package large enough to attract attention?..........	
2. Is it tall enough to be seen when smaller packages are piled in front of it?..........	
3. Is it designed for convenience in display handling?..........	
4. Is it designed for visibility on display?..........	
Factors which affect CONSUMER USE	
1. Is package of size convenient for home use?..........	
2. Is package fitted to the hand?..........	
3. Is it designed for carrying by consumer where necessary?..........	
4. Is it easy to open?..........	
5. Is it convenient to use?..........	
6. Does package protect contents?..........	
7. Does it prevent wastage?..........	

great importance. A successful package must do three things: first, it must secure attention; second, it must possess memory value; and third, it must have the power to induce action.

A package should secure attention under normal conditions. If it does not possess this quality, then the eye of the prospective purchaser will pass over it to some more distinctively packaged product. The best method of obtaining attention is not necessarily to invent a fantastic package, but rather to strive for simplicity in layout, shape, design, and in other ways. The package should be made to suit the product, however, and to express its individuality if possible.

It will not be feasible to place ten-cent perfumery in a five-dollar bottle, expensive candy in a cheap package, or a high-grade soap in a newsprint wrapper. The package should convey to the prospective buyer a favorable and fitting impression of the product which it contains. In some cases it can do this by its shape. Figure 61, for example, shows how this can be done in the perfumery field. The luxury appeal is used to suggest the quality of the perfume inasmuch as this cannot be sampled. Since much perfume is bought by men for women, the package must also be suited to the masculine idea of what a woman would wish in the way of a perfume package.

Memory value is the second psychological necessity. The package, therefore, should carry the trade-mark of the manufacturer of the goods, or some other distinguishing mark, such as a picture, which will serve to link together products made by the same manufacturer, and also products with the advertising carried on in their behalf.

The third factor, action value, is in many ways the most important. As in the case of all advertising, it is comparatively easy to attract attention and to arouse interest—these are chiefly questions of advertising technique. But when it comes to the task of getting the prospect to buy, in other words, to induce action, the problem becomes more difficult.

Action may be induced in some cases by the use of a trade character. The Gold Dust Twins, for example, are excellent exponents of this theory, so much so that their action value on the retailer's shelves is an asset of untold price. Action is often induced because of the goodwill which the advertiser has built up through his advertising. When the purchaser sees the well-known trade-mark or package design, there is recogni-

Fig. 61. The Package as an Advertising Expedient

The bottle in the small leather case sells because of its novelty. The one at the bottom has the dignity and choiceness which make it desirable for the dressing table. The third is individual and unusual.

(*Printers' Ink Monthly.*)

tion and sales resistance is lessened. She is ready to "Let the Gold Dust Twins do *her* work." Between two packages, one of which is familiar and the other unfamiliar, the choice will naturally go to the first, unless there is some important price or quality differential, or some cause for aversion.

Among the devices used both to produce action and to fur-
ıer memory value is the seal. In some cases also, it has con-
derable attention value. The gold seal, for example, stands
ıt from the package, and conveys the idea of quality. For
ıis reason it is frequently used on candy packages. Figure 62
lustrates some seals which have proved successful.

Fig. 62. Examples of Seals

These give an idea of the wide variety of products and purposes to hich seals can be put. (*Printers' Ink Monthly.*)

'he Package and the Family of Products

The manufacturer of a number of products, when he ad-
ertises, wishes to take full advantage of any demand he cre-
tes. He may, at the time, be occupied in pushing one par
icular article, but he wishes also to have some of the advertis-
ng effect react to the benefit of the rest of the line. The
ommon link between all the products made by a company is
he package, label, or trade-mark. Therefore, in making an
ıdvertising analysis, if the company has a number of products,
he question should be asked whether they are related in some

way so that a purchaser, looking at any one of them, would be able to say that it belongs to the family of a company toward which he has a feeling of goodwill.

The importance of the package as a unifier of demand should not be underestimated. If, for example, a woman in the habit of buying Campbell's soups were intending to purchase a can of pork and beans, she would be favorably inclined towards the Campbell's brand and would recognize it immediately because of the family resemblance, even though she had never seen Campbell's Pork and Beans advertised. The National Biscuit Company ties its line together by means of its trademark. Heinz has a keystone. Beech-Nut has an oval. Other companies have distinctive colors or designs on their labels.

Testing Package Design

That some package designs are not well fitted to the product and to the market is well known. It is surprising, therefore, that so little work has been done towards the scientific selection of package design by actual test. The proper size can usually be told by an analysis of the sizes which sell best, taken from the sales records. But the influence of the package design in selling the product can be told only through testing. The seller may take the greatest pains in preparing his design, and may turn out a result which is highly satisfactory to himself, both from an artistic and economic point of view; but this does not tell him whether he is using the design which will lessen sales resistance, increase popularity, and strengthen the memory value of his product.

The package can be tested in two ways. By the first method, a questionnaire is sent to dealers, or interviews are had with dealers, with the end in view of finding out what they think of packages for the product in general, what their objections to packages on the market are, and what they think the ideal package should be like.

The second method is to test a number of designs, prepared after careful study, upon the consumer. The Beech-Nut Packing Company, for example, used trained investigators, who took sets of the proposed cartons to different grocery stores, and interviewed customers, first as to which carton was preferred as most appropriate to Beech-Nut Macaroni, next as to the most suitable design, and finally as to the most effective color combination. About 15 or 20 judgments an hour were secured, 500 being regarded as sufficient to be representative of any given group. Since the number of designs to be tested was large, they were divided up into groups. Each group was tested and the winners of the groups then retested in reference to each other. The final standing is shown in Figure 63.

A bulletin of the Blackman Company states:

> After deciding on a new package, it is often wise to keep on investigating the facts surrounding the acceptance of the new package by the trade.
>
> A large importer of citron, orange, and lemon peel long sold their products in bulk. They experimented with the package idea. They packed a one-pound carton containing an assortment of the three peels. During the first year the new package met with approval of both wholesalers and retailers. During the second year the new carton was giving national distribution under a well-known trade name. A careful check was made which brought about a change in the proportions of the products packed. Sales were very satisfactory but thorough investigations were still made at regular intervals. It was found the package put out by the manufacturer was rather arbitrary. The pound package was too large. The real demand was for smaller quantities. One-quarter pound packages of the three products were put out. And the size of the slices of peel was altered to conform to the housewife's requirements. Facts were substituted for fancy in the final development of these packaged goods.

Changing Package Designs

With the increased recognition of the importance of the package as a merchandising and advertising aid has come the realization that certain old package designs may not be so fitted to the product as had been supposed. Furthermore, it was formerly a custom to have a different package design for different products in the line, so that there was no or little apparent connection between them.

Fig. 63.—An Example of Testing Package Designs

Results of Tests of Cartons, Designs, and Color Combinations for Packaging Beech-Nut Macaroni

Note that the table is divided into two sections, Table of Averages, an Table of Ranks. These two complement each other. For instance, compa the category, "General Appropriateness," Column III for women, and no that the average for carton X is 1.8, and therefore ranks 1; carton N, averag 2.33 ranks 2; carton I, average 3.47 ranks 3; and so on.

Table of Averages (Lowest Average Best)

Set	Package	General Appropriateness		Color		Design		Final Average	
		Women	Men	Women	Men	Women	Men	Women and Men	Fina Ran
I	B	5.67	5.85	5.13	5.35	5.43	5.85	4.14	5
III	E	6.03	4.95	5.93	4.9	5.97	5.85	4.56	6
III	G	8.77	8.35	8.8	8.15	8.23	8.7	5.89	9
V	G¹	8.87	9.05	9.1	9.1	8.87	9.15	6.76	10
V	H	7.2	7.45	7.63	6.15	8.1	7.35	5.54	8
III	I	3.47	3.25	3.47	4.1	3.4	3.15	2.6	3
IV	N	2.33	3.5	3.33	4.2	3.17	3.45	2.42	2
IV	P	6.77	6.25	5.87	6.35	6.37	6.45	4.76	7
II	X	1.8	2.2	2.1	2.5	1.67	1.75	1.48	1
II	Z	4.1	4.15	3.63	4.2	3.73	3.4	2.9	4

Table of Ranks (1 Best, 10 Poorest)

Set	Package	General Appropriateness		Color		Design		Fina Ran
		Women	Men	Women	Men	Women	Men	
I	B	5	6	5	6	5	5.5	5
III	E	6	5	7	5	6	5.5	6
III	G	9	9	9	9	9	9	9
V	G¹	10	10	10	10	10	10	10
V	H	8	8	8	7	8	8	8
III	I	3	2	3	2	3	2	8
IV	N	2	3	2	3.5	2	3	2
IV	P	7	7	6	8	7	7	7
II	X	1	1	1	1	1	1	1
II	Z	4	4	4	3.5	4	4	4

Figure 64 illustrates how the package of Adjusto-Lite was hanged at the time the name of the product itself was altered s the result of a psychological test. Figure 65 shows the new nd the old package used by the makers of Sem-pray toilet rticles. The package was changed from a green box with pink abel to a pink and green mosaic box with a black and gold abel.

An important factor in making any change, and one which ny advertising analysis should take cognizance of, is that the hange should, as a rule, be made slowly. However inartistic r inappropriate the old package might have been, it had a ertain recognition value. This can be retained by altering nly one feature of the package at a time. The Lux package as altered so gradually that few consumers noticed the difference. Wheatsworth Whole-Wheat Graham Crackers were nade far more attractive by gradually altering the design of the ackage.

The hold of any particular package or label on its market nay be strong, yet it is a fact that standards change, and the abel that was effective twenty-five years ago may prove lifeless o-day. It may keep its popularity among the former generaion but the new generation will turn to products whose labels re more modern.

Package Copy

A special technique of package copy has been developed. The amount of copy which will go on the package depends upon he type of product, the purpose of the package, the degree to vhich the product is known, and the number of the uses to vhich the product is put.

If the purpose of the package is merely to serve as a conainer, such as a milk bottle, then the copy would be brief. If he package were well-known, a great deal of copy would be uperfluous and would detract from the attention value of the ackage. If the product is relatively unknown, then the package might well be used to carry some of the selling message. If the instructions as to use are simple, as, for example, in the case of Campbell's soup, then the copy may advisedly be brief.

Printers' Ink Monthly quotes four methods of treating the copy on the package:

1. To put very little on the carton and to use no package insert.
2. To put little on the package, thus getting a carton of good

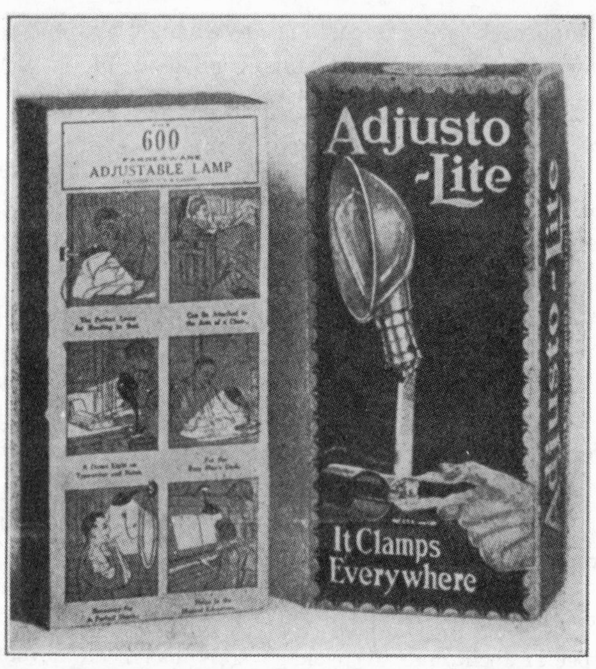

Fig. 64. A Profitable Package Change

For its new package the manufacturer of this product changed its name, redesigned the package, and printed it in colors. The value of the change was reflected in increased sales. (*Printers' Ink Monthly.*)

display value because of simplicity and beauty, and to use inserts for directions as to use.

3. To put a great deal of copy on the package and do away with the insert, as is often done with food products.

4. To put fair amount of copy on outer carton, repeat on insert, and repeat again in simple form on inside package which also serves as container. This is the usual practice in the toilet goods field (see Figure 66). The usual rule in deciding how much copy is needed is to use what is essential and no more. Too much copy

invariably means a loss in attention value or selling appeal. It may be desirable, of course, to link up the package copy with national advertising. This is usually done by reproducing the package in the advertising.

The ability of the package to make itself remembered is important on account of the great number of packages on the market. It is more important, in some ways, than the advertising itself, because it is actually handled by the buyers and stands on their shelves. It is the last opportunity which the

FIG. 65. ANOTHER PACKAGE CHANGE

On the left, the old powder box with the severe green color and the pink label with only the name Sem-Pray used. On the right, the new powder box with the pink and green mosaic pattern which was followed by the new cake container to link the entire Sem-Pray line.

(*Printers' Ink Monthly.*)

manufacturer has of telling the consumer how the goods should be used.

In analyzing the package, or in preparing a new package, care should be taken to see that no overstatements are made. The claims for a product about to be put to the test of usage should be conservative. Furthermore, it is ordinarily of little value to describe the virtues of the product at great length on the package. What the consumer ordinarily wants to know is how to use the product, told in a clear, concise, and interesting fashion. For this reason, the old-fashioned method of crowd-

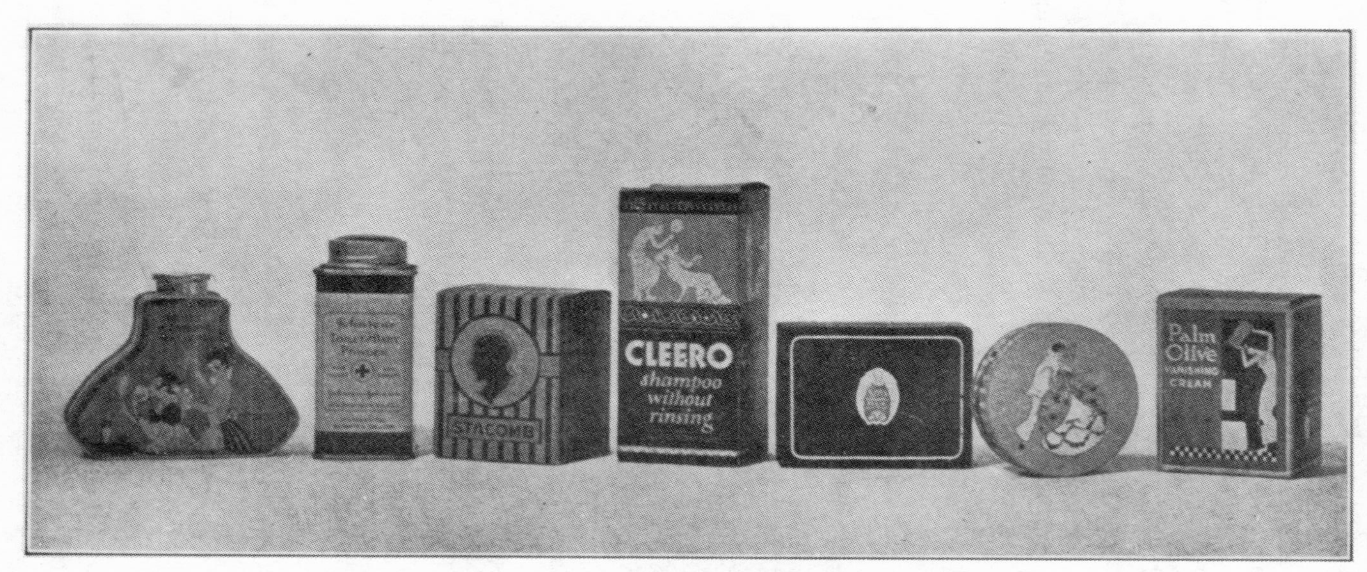

Fig. 66. Packages Designed for Maximum Display Value

These packages carry a comparatively small amount of copy. The Johnson & Johnson can is the exception. The copy is inserted in the package. This plan permits a maximum of display value with no distracting elements, such as directions or selling talk.

(*Printers' Ink Monthly.*)

ing on as much copy as possible is not to be recommended, under ordinary conditions.

Package Illustration

An illustration exerts a powerful influence on attention value, but it does something more. Color alone will attract attention but it will not hold it. Consequently the pictorial element of the package should be carefully studied.

One of the usual methods of illustrating the package is to use some common feature such as a trade-mark, a trade character, or a common design, which is also used in advertising.

Another method is that shown in Figure 67, where the uses of the product are shown pictorially. This, of course, is not possible for all types of products, but offers an interesting alternative to descriptive copy where other factors permit.

The use of a picture on the package has a sound foundation in psychology, because tests have proved that pictures are most easily remembered, forms next, words next, and meaningless combinations of letters last. Pictures have the further advantage of being universally understandable, whereas the text on the package would have to be changed for each foreign country in which it was used.

Highly colored lithographed labels have largely disappeared in favor of flat tones with vivid contrasts. A label which reproduces the goods is often successful in overcoming prejudice, as in the case of canned goods. This was the case with grapefruit in cans, which encountered much prejudice until the label was made to show the grapefruit, one half with juice running from it; the other showing segments of the fruit with skin and membrane removed.

Points for Study in Package Analysis

Given certain mechanical, economic, and physical conditions regarding the product which will restrict the package to certain limits, it is possible to enumerate a number of points to be considered in choosing a carton. The following are suggested by Richard B. Franken:[1]

---

[1] *Scientific Selection of Package Designs* (Robert Gair Co.).

FIG. 67. USES OF PRODUCT SHOWN PICTORIALLY

Each of these packages suggests to the buyer the uses of the product and thus becomes its own salesman. A manufacturer who uses this kind of package to break into new markets has gained a powerful ally.

1. *Practicability.* Is it practical to pack the commodity in a carton? (This depends largely on the buying habits of the consumer, and other factors following.)

2. *Shape.* The shape should be as familiar to the consumer as possible, yet not too familiar to be commonplace, nor too unique to be radical. The best possible shape of a carton often depends on the shape and size of the commodity and also, as aforesaid, on the buying habits of the consumer. The gable shape top of the C. N. Cleanser may be thought of, to illustrate this point.

3. *Size.* As convenient as possible. This also depends largely on the size and shape of the commodity.

4. *Color.* The color should be appropriate to, and suggestive of, the contents of the carton. A hot color combination, such as yellow and red, is appropriate for pepper and spices, whereas a cool color combination such as light blue or light green is appropriate for cold cream.

5. *Design.* The design should be appropriate and suggestive of the commodity or its use. Sometimes it is preferable to show the commodity in use, as macaroni en casserole, toast on an electric toaster, or canned heat being used.

6. *Type.* The type should be as legible as possible. Lower case (small) type is more legible than upper case (capitals) type. The color of the carton (back-ground) also affects the legibility of the type, and should receive some consideration.

7. *Trade-mark.* The trade-mark should be placed so that it will not destroy the balance or unity of the design.

8. *Individuality.* The carton should be made as distinctive looking as possible, so that it can readily be recognized and recalled. The memory value of different kinds of facts should be given consideration. Faces and figures such as the Gold Dust Twins, are more easily remembered than initials such as Q. R. S. *Do not imitate competitors.*

9. *Relationship.* Show or suggest the relationship of the commodity contained in the carton to other products that are sold by the same concern. Do not have this relationship so closely resemble the other products that it will cause confusion to the consumer and to the dealer.

10. *Describability.* The package should be designed so that it can readily be described to another person in directing him to buy the commodity; *i.e.,* the package of macaroni with the picture of the casserole on it.

11. *Display Value.* How will the carton look on the shelf alongside of competitive cartons? Its design and color should invite handling and examination of its contents.

12. *Atmosphere.* The carton should be agreeable to look at. There should be a harmony and unity of all the factors that make for unity, shape, color, design, and type. The carton should be suggestive of the goods it contains.

Trade-Marks

A trade-mark is a name, monogram, character, or other symbol which is used for purposes of identification. Its value is based on memory and association. While such symbols are hard to appraise, they are often rated at extremely high valuations. The trade name Uneeda, the trade symbol Inner Seal, and the boy in the oilskin coat, used by the National Biscuit Company, are rated in the millions of dollars.

For advertising purposes the trade-mark identifies, protects, and associates. More and more companies are changing their corporate names to coincide with the name used on their trade-marks. Years ago, before the rise of advertising, the company name was all-important and the name given to the product was usually chiefly in order to describe its grade or quality. Now, advertising has given the product an identity which the company desires to capitalize. Hence the Central Oil and Gas Stove Company changed its name to the Florence Stove Company, the Genesee Pure Food Company to the Jell-O Company, Inc., the Hendee Manufacturing Company to the Indian Motorcycle Company, the Channell Chemical Company to the O-Cedar Corporation, and the B. F. Johnson Soap Company to the Palmolive Company.

One of the best methods of finding out whether the company name is satisfactory is to ascertain how dealers and customers term the company in speaking of it. In 1917, the General Roofing Manufacturing Company found that it was being referred to as the Certain-Teed Company, and accordingly changed its name to the Certain-Teed Products Corporation.

In addition to identification, the trade-mark must fulfill certain requirements before it can be registered. It cannot be the name of a person, the name of a place, or descriptive of the goods, or even of the quality of the goods. Before decidng on a trade-mark care should be taken to find out whether it s registrable.

The association value of the trade-mark is in many ways ts most important asset. If a certain company's trade-mark s habitually confused with those of other manufacturers or ther products, much of its value is lost. Figure 68 shows ertain well known trade-marks which have been advertised in ational magazines. Figure 69 shows a number of trade-marks vhich have become especially well-known and whose association alue is high.

The Trade Name

Of the various types of trade-marks, the trade name is the nost commonly used and the most important. There are certain well-defined types of trade names:

1. The trade name and the name of the firm or maker are the ame, such as Sherwin-Williams paint, Packer's Tar Soap, Studeaker cars, or Kleinert's Rubber Goods.
2. The trade name may be taken from a geographical locality, uch as United States Gypsum, Paris or Boston garters, Hartford ire Insurance Company, and Ipswich Hosiery.
3. The trade name may reflect the quality of the goods, such s Standard Plumbing fixtures, Royal typewriters, or Royal Baking owder, Perfection heaters, or Nonesuch mincemeat.
4. The trade name may be formed artificially, either with a uggestive value or a more or less meaningless combination of yllables. In the first class come such names as Cream of Wheat, Jneeda, Hotpoint, Eversharp, Sunsweet, and Swan's-Down cake lour. In the second class come Kodak, Crisco, and Mazola.

Assuming that identification with the company and proection by registration can be secured, the most valuable trade name is the one which can be associated most easily with the roduct, and which cannot be easily imitated or confused. Figure 70 shows the results of a test of 40 trade names and logans, carried out on several groups of students at the University of Iowa.[2] The slogans or trade names were written

---

[2] *Advertising and Selling.*

Premium Ham and Bacon have been advertised for 33 years. Swift & Company has spent over $500,000 a year advertising these and other products in magazines.

85% of the advertising of Icy-Hot has been in magazines since the trademark was adopted 15 years ago.

Campbell's Soup was first advertised in 1899. The manufacturer is the most extensive user of magazine space, and gives national periodicals at least 90% of his annual appropriations.

Holeproof Hosiery

This trademark has been used for 20 years, and more than 75% of the advertising has been in magazines.

This trademark has been used since 1915, and approximately $100,000 a year for the past 5 years has been spent to cover the magazine appropriation.

The HOOVER
It BEATS... as it Sweeps as it Cleans

40% of the advertising appropriations of the Hoover Suction Sweeper Co. has gone to magazines in the 10 years they have used this trademark.

The name Bull Durham was adopted in 1865 Within the past 10 years magazine advertising has run over $120,000 a year. Pall Mall, Tuxedo and Lucky Strike are consistent users of magazine space. All are products of the American Tobacco Co.

FIG. 68. WELL-KNOWN TRADE MARKS
(*Periodical Publishers' Association.*)

out on sheets of paper and the students were to answer what specific article was referred to. The reasons responsible for wrong associations are given as follows:

Fig. 69. Trade-Marks with High Association Value

1. Variability in frequency of being seen.
2. Variability in nearness to students' interest.
3. Nearness to some other slogan.
4. Variability in inherent interest or "catch" of slogan.
5. Forces not yet known.

The test of merit in the above case is the relative frequency of correct association between the slogan or trade name and the

Fig. 70.—Results of Tests of Trade Names and Slogans to Determine Attention Value and Aptness

Slogan or Trade Name	Right	Nearly Right	Wrong	Omitted	Total	Mistakes
20-Mule Team	280	1	13	27	321	Tractor; drugs.
Sunkist	305	2	9	5	321	Raisins; peaches; biscuits.
Community Plate	291	0	3	27	321	Raising money for poor.
Liberty Six	266	0	4	51	321	Cigars.
The Road to Wellville	75	4	30	212	321	Tanlac; Sulphur Springs; Campbell's Soups.
Green River	292	2	8	19	321	Song; drinking water.
Bevo	304	0	2	15	321	Bouillon.
Bon Ami	264	27	16	14	321	Washing windows.
Listerine	189	20	48	64	321	Salve; patent medicine; vaseline; hand lotion; lubricating oil; shaving lotion; soap.
Good Year	319	0	1	1	321	Flour.
The Hoover	262	4	22	33	321	Vacuum cleaner.
Canthrox	211	13	37	60	321	Healing ointment.
Crisco	249	21	29	22	321	Biscuits; breakfast food; a book.
Hoosier	145	1	35	90	321	Indian's nickname; shoes.
Shur-On	101	0	86	134	321	Tacks on shoes; shoe polish
Ever-Ready	222	0	34	65	321	Rubber heels; stocking; pencils.
Valspar	231	2	19	69	321	Repair for car; flashlight; rock.
Lustrite	79	0	68	174	321	Scouring substance.
Have you a little fairy in your home?	181	88	36	16	321	Pear's Soap; the Good Fairy; Ivory.
Sonora	118	1	10	92	321	Essence; mattress; soap.
Eventually, why not now?	166	66	52	37	321	Home-building; Occident flour.
Time to retire	116	71	72	62	321	Clock; a yawning youngster in night clothes; Goodyear tires; U. S. tires; Goodrich.
The Universal Car	260	5	18	38	321	Coach; Overland; Packard; Hudson; Paige; Studebaker; Congress; Playing Cards.
It Floats	308	5	5	3	321	Puffed wheat; a boat.
His Master's Voice	294	2	21	4	321	Movie; Edison; Columbia
Roll Your Own	153	51	103	14	321	Quaker Oats; cigarette papers; Velvet.
Smith Brothers	283	0	8	30	321	A grocery; typewriter.
We Put the World to Sleep	26	0	38	257	321	Blankets; universal night garment.
Makes Kids Husky	10	43	157	111	321	Grape Nuts; shredded wheat; castor oil.
See That Hump	63	0	222	46	321	Camels; hairpins; dromedary dates.
You can feel its goodness	0	0	13	308	321	Coca-cola.
The National Drink	1	0	8	312	321	Coca-cola; Bevo.
The National Joy Smoke	100	8	94	119	321	Velvet; Girard; Robert Burns; Tuxedo; Bull Durham.
Raybestos	0	0	3	318	321	Electric light.
Aladdin	5	0	4	312	321	Cigarettes; lanterns; a lamp.
Brenlin	3	0	0	318	321	None.
Covers the Continent	21	14	70	216	321	Coveralls; telephones.
Bluebirds	6	0	3	312	321	Carpets; cards; novel; a café.
Never Gets on Your Nerves	17	6	19	279	321	Work; Postum.
Hasn't Scratched Yet	248	2	25	46	321	A crayon.

product. Four degrees of answers were recognized—right, nearly right, wrong, and omitted.

Lawrence A. Adams, of the United States Chamber of Commerce, conducted a survey of brand names for butter in Washington, D. C. The investigation was conducted by mail questionnaire. The findings of the survey are given as follows:

> Among the total of 79 brands which were mentioned, it was noted that there was considerable confusion in the minds of the housewives about the exact name. Several brands that use two words have one word the same. Thus they differ only in one word and, in addition, may have a meaning very similar to other brands. Several brands have attempted to choose names which will bring up in the mind of the consumer a picture of a bright sunny meadow. Another favorite picture is a combination of the thought of meadow with bright yellow or golden-colored butter. Judging by the resulting confusion in the minds of the housewives, there are too many names which are similar in words or in the thought picture which the words call up.
>
> The question has been raised whether the distributors of butter are pursuing the wisest policy in the use of such a large number of brands. One plan suggested to reduce the number is the co-operation of distributors handling the same grade and having only a limited market. They could put out the butter under a similar brand and thus unite in advertising.

Selection of Trade Names

The importance of having a good trade name for the product is so well recognized that many companies are willing to pay money for a suitable solution to their name problem. Hence the considerable number of companies which carry on contests for names most descriptive of the excellence of their product or of the service which it renders. This method is dependent for success upon securing public interest and upon the judgment of the individuals who select the name from those offered. Unfortunately, however, judgment is a poor substitute for measurement.

Tests for memory value may be carried on according to the recognition or the recall method. The preceding illustration, Figure 70, shows the recognition method, whereby a list of selected trade names are written down and handed out to a certain number of individuals for identification. Obviously the trade name having the highest score should possess the greatest memory value.

When it comes to a new product, the recall method is possible. On one day 50 names are submitted for examination for a few moments, on the next (or lapse of few days) these same names plus 50 new ones are submitted, and the individuals asked to write down those they remember having seen before.

Trade names, according to Franken, should possess four distinguishing qualities. First, they should have atmosphere, so that they will arouse feelings appropriate to the nature of the commodity; second, they should possess utility value (distinctive, easily pronounced); third, they should be euphonious; and fourth, they should possess good memory value, but memory value should always be correlated with the preceding factors because silly and valueless names may have good memory values.

In deciding on a new name for an adjustable lamp, six professional psychologists eliminated all names submitted during the contest which were general, cheap, absurd, unpronounceable, or otherwise unfitted. Ten psychologically trained assistants were then tested on the remaining names and the list reduced to 250 names. This list was submitted to 150 people, composed of buyers and college students, and 50 names picked out for semi-final testing.

A final test was made on 100 people, the test being divided into three parts:

1. Each name was presented on a mimeographed sheet and each person scored it 4, 3, 2, 1, or 0 for atmosphere and euphony.
2. Each name was then scored for utility, and the results of the two tests combined for a final value.
3. Two hours after the tests and without notice to those who had taken part, each one was given one minute to write down all the names on the list of 50 which were remembered, in the order that they came to mind. The following day, these same individuals were given a list of 100 names, 50 new ones and the same 50 which had been previously tested, and were asked to indicate by

the figure 2 all names they were certain of having seen the day before, and by the figure 1 all the names they thought they had seen, and all others by 0. The recognition and recall methods were thus used to verify each other.

In tabulating results, the best name was given a value of 100 per cent, and the other names given a value in terms of per cent of the best name. Results follow:

Order	*Name*	*Value Per Cent*
1	Adjusto-Lite	100
2	Comfort-Lite	98
3	Handy Lite	95
4	Adjustable Lite	85
5	Useful Lite	76
6	Angle Lamp	73
7	Every-use Lamp	72
8	The "Spot" Lite	70
9	Usefulite	70
10	Anywhere-Lite	69
11	Klamp-Lamp	66
12	Spotlite	63
13	Economy Lite	63
14	Fasten Lamp	61
15	Clasp Lamp	60
16	Klip-Lite	59
17	Clamplamp	50
18	Handy Bed Lite	47
19	Clamps Everywhere	45
20	Farber Spot Lamp	44
21	Clamplight	44
22	Farber-Lamp	43
23	Farber-Lite 600	39

The following thirteen qualities are suggested for the ideal trade name:

1. *Simplicity.* It should be simple enough to be readily remembered.
2. *Brevity.* It should be short. (Glycothymoline is too long.)
3. *Pronunciation.* It should be easy to pronounce. (Hyomei, Telekathoras.)
4. *Singularity.* Pronounceable in one way only. (Peb-e-co or Pee-be-co.)

5. *Euphony.* It should sound pleasant. Law: Easy to speak, agreeable to listen to. (Compare "Lemon Squash" and "Lemon Crush." Note Mazda, Kodak, Palmolive.)

6. *Aptness.* It should be apt. (Keen-Kutter, Shur-On, Walk-Over.)

7. *Originality.* It should be new—not imitative. (Moxie—Noxie; Uneeda—Uwanna; Peruna—Rupena.)

8. *Distinctive.* It should possess individuality. (Onyx, Crex, Jap-a-Lac.)

9. *Suggestive.* It should be suggestive of the article or its use. (Pianola, Holeproof, Shinola.)

10. *Sincerity.* It should not be silly. (No-Smellee, Fizza, O-Kid-O.)

11. *Memorability.* It should be easy to remember.

12. *Relationship.* It should lend itself to treatment as part of a family name. (Rubber-set, Beiset, etc. Note the Heinz, Keen-Kutter, Colgate products each built up around one name.)

13. *Registrability.* Personal, geographical, or descriptive names cannot be registered. Kantleek, Crystal Domino, Rubberoid, etc., have been refused registration. Foreign registrative requirements should also be considered.

Trade Symbols and Characters

The symbol was one of the earliest known devices for identification purposes. Watermarks were used as early as 1280; the guilds of the Middle Ages had their own distinctive marks, such as the hall mark of the silversmiths. Even in modern advertising, the symbol is still used, such as in the commercial trade-mark of the National Biscuit Company. Bakelite has adopted the mathematical symbol of infinity to convey the endless number of uses to which it may be put.

The trade character is a humanized symbol. It is often more useful in advertising than the plain symbol—such as the star, the butterfly, or the arrow—because it has higher impression value. When tied up with the product which it represents its power of association is high. Even though the consumer may not be able to ask for the product by its brand name, the trade character will often be remembered. For example, the Gold Dust Twins are among the most valuable trade characters on the market, and are inseparably associated with the product.

Figure 71 shows how the Coca Cola Company uses a trade character to carry its advertising message. The trade character often serves to humanize the campaign.

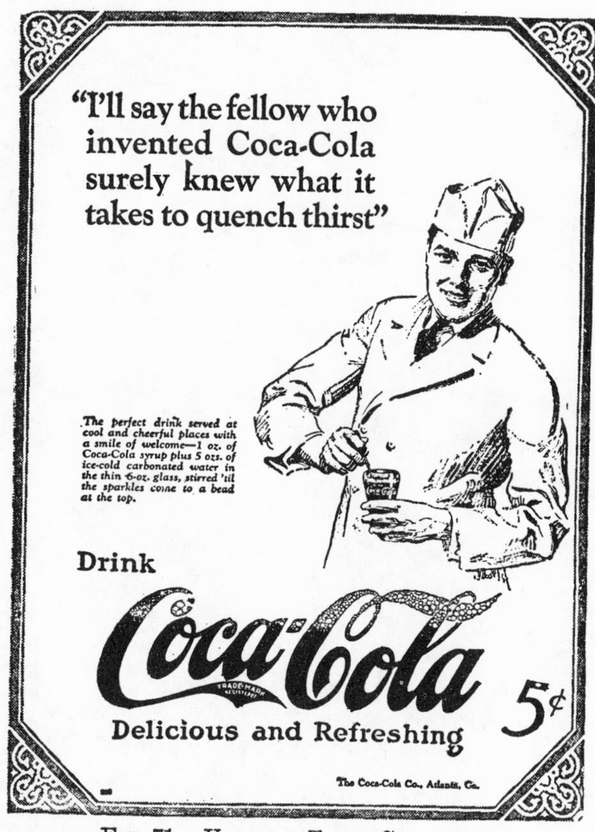

Fig. 71. Use of a Trade Character

In using any trade character, it is essential to remember that its value depends very largely upon the degree to which it is known and accepted.

PART III

THE AUDIENCE

CHAPTER IX

CONSUMER ANALYSIS

The consumer of any product is the one who uses it. For purposes of advertising research a consumer may be a mill, a mine, or an individual. The consumer and the reader of advertising may not be the same. The purpose of advertising is usually to reach as many consumers as possible through something which they read.

Since many may read who are not prospects, and since there may be many prospects who may not see the printed message, there is obviously a sharp distinction between the *market* and the *audience*. That is, if 1,000,000 copies of a magazine are used to reach a market of a thousand prospects, there is a waste circulation of 999,000. If the actual market is 2,000, and the medium reaches only 1,000 of them, the coverage, as far as that medium is concerned, is only 50 per cent. The audience, as far as this medium is concerned, is a thousand times as great as that part of the market which it reaches, and only half the market is covered.

To carry this illustration further, if it costs $5,000 for a page in the medium, the cost per prospect is not $5,000 divided by 1,000,000 (this being the audience) but $5,000 divided by 1,000 (this being the market, in so far as this medium covers it). That is, the use of this medium allows half the market to be covered at a cost of $5 per prospect.

The difference between the market and the audience must be kept in mind when the cost aspects of the advertising problem are being considered. Once the consumers have been located and the market analyzed, it is necessary to find what media will cover them to best advantage. The value of such calculations is that they reduce the choice of media to a cost basis, and cost must be the determining factor in the purchase of one medium as against another. In fact, cost must be the deciding factor in practically every advertising problem.

The Consumer as an Individual

The consumer is the individual whom the advertiser must, sooner or later, reach and satisfy. He may have to reach him through one or more intermediates, such as trade papers. He may have to display his message to a thousand readers before he finds a single prospect. Although this is a waste in one sense, in another way it shows the value of advertising, because advertising picks out of the great mass of readers, at a low expense, the comparatively few who will buy. There is also danger of confusing readers and consumers, but it is almost always the consumer who is to be sought after—the man who buys and uses the product.

In studying the consumer as an individual, there are a number of points which will affect him. He has certain buying motives which are important in determining what goods he purchases, and how. It is necessary to analyze them as well as the various factors which affect them, such as age, sex, occupation, class, race, or religion. It is also important to scrutinize buying habits and purchasing inclinations. Any prejudices which may exist against the product should be brought to light and examined as to their sources.

It is also important to ascertain who, in any particular group, does the actual purchasing. In the family, is it the husband or the wife that does the purchasing of a given product? In a company, is it the president, general manager, or chief engineer?

The individual characteristics of the consumer will also have to be correlated with the type of product sold. Consumers who are ignorant of the uses of the product must be educated before they can be sold. Consumer analysis and product analysis are closely interrelated; the latter ascertains what features of the product will appeal to the consumer; the former finds out what consumers want in the way of a product.

George H. Read, of Johnson, Read and Company, made an investigation of mail-order buying:

Without any effort to influence or to confine the replies to any specified subjects, it was interesting to see that practically 100 per cent of the answers to this particular question could be placed in one or another of the following three classifications:

1. Larger selection
2. Greater convenience
3. Better value

Four surveys were made, at different intervals. The following table shows how consistently and indisputably "Better Values" was designated throughout the four surveys as the primary reason for mail-order buying:

Time of Survey	Vote for "Better Value," Per Cent	Vote for "Larger Selection," Per Cent	Vote for "Greater Convenience," Per Cent
November	82	17	16
May	85	14	15
September	85	16	20
November	83	21	19
Average	84	17	17½

The Objective Viewpoint

Advertising problems should be approached from the point of view of the consumer. Copy, for example, should be written, not according to the way the advertiser feels, or as he desires, or as his own wants incline, but from the point of view of the person who buys his product. What sort of a man is *he?* What does *he* want? What are *his* tastes? How may *he* be appealed to?

Copy which appears poor to the expert often "pulls" because it is written in the language of some high-tension copy writer. Figure 72 shows how the General Cigar Company, Inc., is attempting, through general advertising, to approach the smoker on the ground of what the smokers want, not what the General Cigar Company thinks they want. The coupon in particular, should be noted: "Please send me your booklet 'What *Do* Smokers Want?' I know what *I* want and want to learn how to get it."

The consumer should always be analyzed for what he wants. An architect, for example, according to the Architectural Service Department of Sweet's Catalogue Service, wants ideas, mechanics, and economics, analyzed as follows:

Ideas

Permanent satisfaction. Simplicity
Conservation of man-time and energy
Compactness and sightliness
Safety for sidewalk pedestrians
Safety for operator
Quality of being in keeping with best modern development

Mechanics

Method of construction. Materials
Method of installation and operation
Capacity, speed, space occupied
Adaptability to varied needs

Economics

First and final cost of equipment
Cost of operation
Comparative cost as compared with other power hoists and with old hand method or freight elevator system
Promptitude of shipment to job
Freight rates

Industrial buyers, on the other hand, want performance facts first, last, and always, according to a survey made by Ernst and Ernst. They want to know what the product will do, all its possible uses, working and cost data, installations, and new features. The following 12 methods of presenting performance facts in industrial advertising are mentioned as most important:

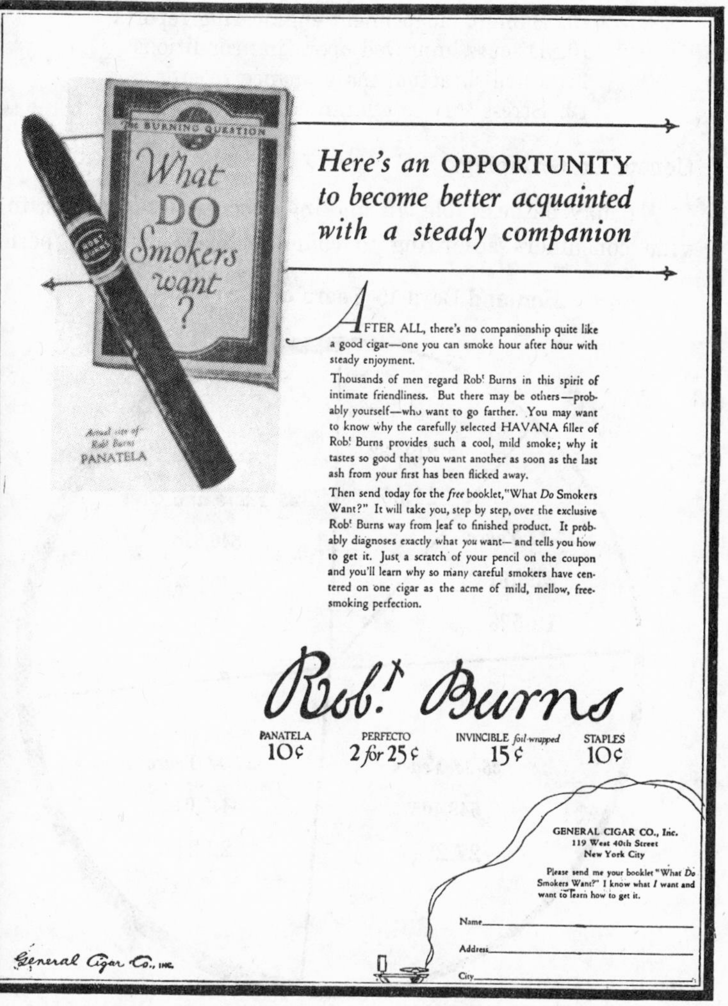

FIG. 72. THE OBJECTIVE VIEWPOINT IN ADVERTISING

1. Show new uses for the equipment
2. Feature installation photographs and figures
3. News stories of performance
4. Time studies on piece work
5. Performance testimonials from the field
6. Dramatic comparisons with manual labor
7. Present records of length of life
8. Demonstrate the return on investment

9. Submit independent engineering reports.
10. Discuss improved operating conditions
11. Furnish actual maintenance records
12. Stress service guarantees

Consumer Groupings

It may be desirable, in making a consumer analysis, to d
vide consumers according to common characteristics, perha

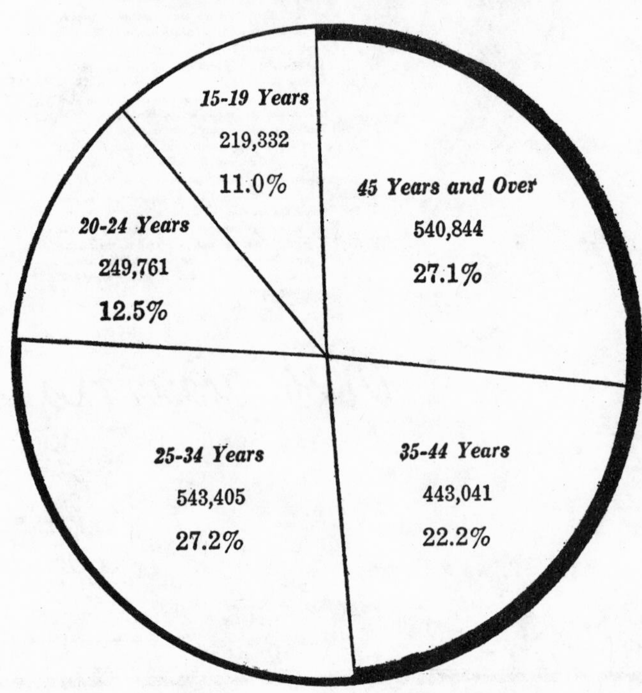

FIG. 73. CONSUMERS ANALYZED BY AGE GROUPS

A study of this sort indicates the proper appeals to use. It ser
as a point of departure for the copy man. (*New York Heral*

according to age, race, or religion, or perhaps according
occupation, place of residence, social standing, or educati
These classifications should be made if they will help to det

Store The Boston Store City Prov. R.I.

Department Ready to Wear

Name of person interviewed Mr. F. E. Flint

1. What percentage of all purchases are made by the following age-groups:

   a. Under 18 (flapper type) 15

   b. 18-30 yrs 40

   c. 30-45 yrs 30

   d. 45 yrs and over 15

   100%

2. What per cent of all purchases are "double" purchases. That is, the daughter and the mother, or a young girl and an older woman. 75

   a. When the mother and daughter come together and the purchase is for the daughter, does the daughter invariably make the decision for herself? Yes

   b. When the mother is buying for herself, does she like the advice of a younger person as to style, etc.? Yes

3. What is the average age at which a girl begins to buy for herself? 14

4. General remarks on the younger element in buying.

Price matters very little to the younger girl. She will often come in with her mother, pick out a dress which the mother feels is more than she can pay but nearly always the dress the girl picks out will be the one finally taken regardless of the price. The young buyer is very much inclined to be rattle-headed and buy whatever strikes her fancy regardless of value. These girls are however, usually good judges of style and goods which they purchase must be absolutely up to the minute or they will have nothing to do with them.

Mr. Flint thinks that the numbers of the young buyers are increasing rapidly and that they will continue to do so for some time.

G. 74. Questionnaire for Interviewing Retailers in Consumer Analysis mine the proper appeal, or to decide upon the media which may most effectively be used. The more important groupings are the following:

1. *Age.*—A number of products are used by all ages indiscriminately, but there is a large group of products, such as clothing, sporting goods, and toys, which are suitable for certain ages only. Figure 73 shows consumers in New York City analyzed by age groups. This analysis, which was made by the *New York Herald,* points out that the advertiser of men's wear directs too much of his advertising effort at the young man, whereas men of thirty-five and over form a larger proportion of the market. Even if a product is used by all men whatever their age, it may be important to vary the appeals to suit various age groups. One appeal may be used for men of one age, another for the next age group and so on. Figure 74 shows a questionnaire used for interviewing retailers, by Barton, Durstine and Osborn, in an investigation to determine the importance of the age factor in buying.

2. *Race.*—Owing to different standards of living, customs and habits, it is important to study the various racial groups which may use a given product. Figure 75 illustrates the wide variations which exist between white, colored, Polish, and Italian families in their methods of purchasing meats.[1] Marketing by telephone, for example, is practically confined to native whites. Such a study might prove important to the retail advertiser, in a campaign calculated to build up new business.

3. *Religion.*—Certain religious factors may enter the advertising problem, although to a less extent than a few years ago. There is still a vestige of feeling, however, against playing cards, theatres, and pool tables, not to mention golf or tennis as played on Sunday. An examination of the numerous religious papers will reveal examples.

4. *Occupation.*—The manner in which the consumer earns his living is reflected in his buying habits, and his outlook i

[1] U. S. Department of Agriculture report on "Influence of Method and Costs of Retailing and Consumers' Habits upon the Market fo Meat," June, 1925.

general. The point of view of a farmer is different from that of a broker in Wall Street; that of a clerk in a store from that of a factory worker. Since a great many trades and occupations have their own trade papers, much information about their peculiarities and customs may be learned from such sources.

FIG. 75.—AN ILLUSTRATION OF RACIAL VARIATIONS IN CONSUMERS' HABITS

Methods of Purchasing Meat Among Native Americans, Polish, and Italians

	Percentage of Families Buying Through					
	House-wife	Phone	Husband	Chil-dren	Servants	Other
Native Americans:						
White:						
Poor.	68.4	4.6	11.5	11.6	0.3	3.6
Middle.	63.7	17.4	10.6	4.9	.0	3.4
Well-to-do. . . .	51.1	36.8	8.7	1.2	9.7	1.5
Wealthy.	35.5	54.2	3.7	.0	4.9	1.7
Colored:						
Poor.	69.9	1.3	18.4	8.5	.0	1.9
Middle.	71.5	1.3	14.3	7.5	0.7	4.7
Polish.	88.0	.7	.0	8.6	.0	2.7
Italian.	74.9	.7	11.2	9.3	.0	3.9

5. *Class.*—Although class lines are not recognized in this country, nevertheless they exist. Some advertisers make their greatest success by appealing to consumers along class lines of exclusiveness, expensiveness, or taste. Publications themselves, although termed general periodicals, often circulate among particular classes. The Quality Group, for example, recognizes itself as going to a particular section of the population. *Vogue* and *Vanity Fair* are edited for the oligarchy.

6. *Education and Intelligence.*—Literacy is a factor of importance in rare cases only. The general standard of intelligence, however, varies widely. Certain sections of the population must be approached in terms of the greatest simplicity.

In general, however, the illiterate portion of the population is comparatively unimportant in purchasing power.

7. *Income.*—The economic status of the consumer has been a decisive factor in determining many markets. Luxury products, for example, are sold only to consumers who possess a certain amount of surplus income, over and above their necessary expenditures.

8. *Material Possessions.*—The consumer's ownership of goods is often the best possible index. Thus, the tire manufacturer will wish to know how many people of a certain group own motor cars. The manufacturer of lighting fixtures will want to know the number of houses wired. The manufacturer of roofing will want to know how many homes are owned by their occupants.

9. *Sex.*—One of the most obvious distinctions between consumers is that of sex. Women often buy many things which are not intended to be consumed by them. A study by Professor H. L. Hollingworth, of Barnard College, showed that the only articles of attire which men bought by themselves were collars, while men participated but little in the purchase of women's clothing. Obviously, it is important for the advertiser to find out to what extent his merchandise is bought by men or women. This is true not only of manufactured articles, but also in the case of firms which sell to department stores through women buyers, to hospitals through women superintendents, or to offices through women office managers.

To determine the proportion of its readers, by sexes, the service department of the *Cosmopolitan Magazine* analyzed its correspondence. The circles in Figure 76 indicate the relative response from men and women to the different types of services which it renders.

When the percentage of men and women buyers has been determined, the next step is to find out what differences exist in buying motives and what appeals are the strongest for each class. While there may be no inherent differences between masculine and feminine buying motives, as is maintained by some writers, nevertheless the distinctions due to environment and

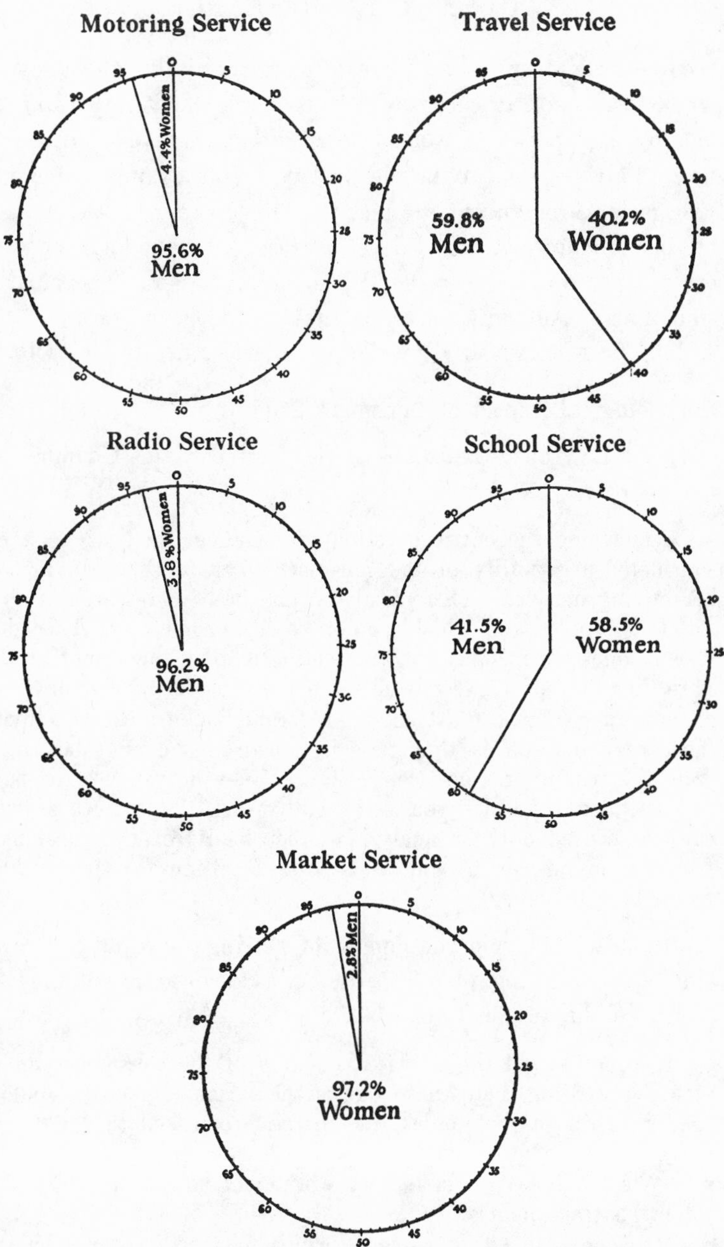

Fig. 76. Readers' Reactions to a Magazine's Service
The circles indicate the response from men and women to different advertising fields through the Service Department. (*Cosmopolitan.*)

occupation are sufficiently great to affect vitally the appeals which are made to each sex. It is particularly important to analyze the appeals to women because their motives for buying do not always appear on the surface. For example, one investigation brought out the fact that 95 per cent of the women buying talcum powder did so because of the odor, and the other 5 per cent because they liked the container. The purity, smoothness, and antiseptic qualities of the brand, which had so long been emphasized by the maker, were negligible factors.

Psychological Aspect of Consumer Studies

Says Lawrence C. Adams of the United States Chamber of Commerce:

Underlying the entire question of consumer analysis must be considered the ability of the consumer to state correctly his or her buying motives. There is always the need in research of this sort to secure answers which are not biased in some way. I wonder if consumers are sufficiently informed of their own motives to state that they purchase talcum powder because of odor or because of container. Price must enter and brand name must be important. My opinion is that reliable conclusions cannot be taken from the results of a question such as, "Why do you use the particular talcum powder you do?" but rather the correct answer can be secured only by analyzing other habits of the consumer, place of buying, price paid, and ways of calling for the product from the salesman.

In order to avoid the danger of getting a prejudiced reaction, the following plan of attack was devised by Stanley I. Clark, of the Joseph Richards Company:

In order to get the unbiased reaction of the consumers interviewed regarding their knowledge of the various makes of window shades on the market to-day, the investigator asked the following question:

"What articles of household equipment are sold under the following trade names?"

He then read off four names which may be indicated by the letters A, B, C and D. The figures appearing opposite each name indicate the number of persons who were able to associate that particular name with window shade products:

	Small Towns	Large Towns	Total
A..........	48	103	151
B.......	14	6	20
C..........	17	....	17
D..........	5	3	8
None......	395	343	738
Totals....	479	455	934

The investigator, in introducing himself, did not discuss the nature of the investigation in hand. He simply stated that he was securing information on household equipment and products so that there was no possible chance for the consumer to tie up his visit with window shades before the second question was asked which introduced the subject.

Buying Habits

The consumer, as an individual, is subject to certain reflexes and reactions, and responds to certain stimuli in certain ways. These are known as buying habits. The psychologist divides his consumer types of action into impulsive, habitual, and rational.

An impulsive purchase is made without forethought. A man is going along the street, sees a window display of razor blades, reflects that he needs razor blades, and makes the purchase. On his way home from the office, he stops to buy his wife a box of candy, or a toy for his child. A friend suggests to him that United States Steel is a good purchase, and he acts on the suggestion immediately. All these are impulsive purchases, and the three mentioned are reflexive, emotional, and suggested, respectively.

An habitual purchase results from the modification of a group of reflexes. A woman gets in the habit of buying a certain brand, or trading at a certain store. Unless there is some unusual event which turns her aside from the accustomed habit, she will continue in it. But if she becomes dissatisfied with the brand, or if the storekeeper offends her, then the habit may be broken. Similarly, if some advertiser succeeds in convincing her that his brand is better, the habit may be broken. The conventional buying habit is much stronger in certain lines of products than others.

A rational purchase, entered into only after due consideration, is probably the rarest of all, with consumer goods, because impulse or habit affect practically every purchase made. If the advertiser can create a buying habit, or if he can formulate his advertising so that readers will buy on impulse, his task is easier than to appeal to the reason of the reader. Technical products are probably bought for rational reasons more than any other type of article, but even here habit enters. The purchasing agent is accustomed to get his goods from a certain source, and he will normally go to that source unless dissatisfied or unless a new product is forcibly brought to his attention.

Lawrence A. Adams suggests the following methods of analyzing buying habits:

1. Personal interviews
2. Mail questionnaires
3. Coupon replies
4. Retailers' opinions
5. Listening to consumers' requests for merchandise

Buying Habits and Purchasing Inclinations

Both buying habits and purchasing inclinations are important subjects in advertising research. A buying habit results from custom and tradition. For years, New England considered white rubber goods superior in quality to red, while the rest of the country considered red rubber superior to white. Instances of sectional buying habits are many. Green asparagus in Boston, white in Chicago, rubber-stemmed pipes in New England, celluloid in the South, dark cheese in the South, light cheese in the North, cream of tartar in Maine, baking powder in the rest of the country—these are only a few cases.

Consumer purchasing inclination refers to the facility with which sales can be made in any certain territory. There is, for example, a marked difference between the purchasing inclination of the average thrifty New Englander and that of the inhabitant of the Pacific Coast, because of the differences in spending habits which have grown up in these sections. A salesman on commission, given a choice between New England and the Pacific Coast, would undoubtedly choose the latter if he were thinking of his income.

According to A. Heath Onthank, Chief of the Domestic Commerce Division, Department of Commerce, the question of consumer purchasing inclination is of growing importance. There has been a study recently made as to whether women in mill towns have the same group inclination to purchase silk stockings that women in cities have. Altogether, however, there has been little scientific work done on the subject.

Buying habits and inclinations are differentiated sometimes with difficulty. It may, for example, be the habit of an Italian to eat spaghetti three days a week and macaroni the other four, but his inclination to purchase cigars may be due to entirely different trends of thought. It may, on the other hand, be the habit of an American business man to smoke a certain brand of cigar after each meal, but his inclination to purchase a new hat will be based on different factors.

Reading Habits

The reading habits of consumers have never been studied with sufficient care, yet they are among the most important points for analysis in advertising research. If the advertiser is to get his share of attention in competition with the reading columns of the periodical or other medium, he must suit his advertising to the tone of the medium.

In general, reading habits have undergone a great change. There is much more for the reader to read than there is time to read it. Even if he had time, there are always rival diversions in the way of radio, moving pictures, and automobile rides.

According to Professor George Burton Hotchkiss, of New York University, there are five outstanding features in reading habits which should be considered by the advertiser:

FIG. 77.—AN INVESTIGATION OF MAGAZINE READING HABITS

Ranks of the Various States in Reading the Thirteen "High-Brow" Magazines: Their Ranks on the Ten Most Widely Read Magazines; and their Ranks on Both Groups

State	Per cent Which the Circulation of the Thirteen "High-brow" Magazines is of Population	Per cent Which Circulation of the Ten Most Widely Read Magazines is of Population	Rank on the Thirteen "Highbrow" Magazines	Rank on the Ten Most Widely Read Magazines	Rank on Both Groups of Magazines
Alabama	.29	4.36	47	49	49
Arizona	1.11	15.28	21	20	20
Arkansas	.27	5.69	48	45	45
California	2.34	25.83	2	2	2
Colorado	1.29+	17.97	14	8	9
Connecticut	1.61	17.27	10	10	10
Delaware	.85	12.32	33	34	34
District of Columbia	2.72	31.76	1	1	1
Florida	1.07	13.61	23	26	27
Georgia	.33−	5.12	46	47	46
Idaho	1.15−	17.09	20	11	12
Illinois	1.07−	14.43	24	24	24
Iowa	.90+	16.33	29	16	17
Indiana	.80	14.77	35	22	23
Kansas	.90−	13.60+	30	27	28
Kentucky	.39	5.97	43	42	42
Louisiana	.51	6.49	40	41	41
Maine	1.37	15.99	12	17	16
Maryland	.93	10.67	27	35	35
Massachusetts	1.62	17.89	9	9	8
Michigan	1.15+	16.43	19	15	15
Minnesota	1.08	15.54	22	19	19
Mississippi	.23	5.15	49	46	47
Missouri	.87	12.47	32	33	33
Montana	1.29−	18.56	15	7	7
Nebraska	.96	15.81	26	18	18
Nevada	1.94	21.25	3	5	5
New Hampshire	1.84	16.48	4	14	11
New Jersey	1.31	13.60−	13	28	25
New Mexico	.67	9.42	36	38	37
New York	1.53	14.66	11	23	22
North Carolina	.42	5.86	42	44	44
North Dakota	.81	13.59	34	29	29
Ohio	1.21	16.84	17	12	14
Oklahoma	.62	10.05	38	36	36
Oregon	1.76	24.99	6	3	3
Pennsylvania	1.00	13.34	25	30	30
Rhode Island	1.23	15.15	16	21	21
South Carolina	.33	4.77	44	48	48
South Dakota	.89	13.92	31	25	26
Tennessee	.33+	5.94	45	43	43
Texas	.50	9.43	41	37	38
Utah	1.16	13.08	18	31	31
Vermont	1.67	16.52	7	13	13
Virginia	.58	8.02	39	40	40
Washington	1.63	24.10	8	4	4
West Virginia	.64	9.00	37	39	39
Wisconsin	.91	13.04	28	32	32
Wyoming	1.78	20.85	5	6	6

FIG. 78.—AN EXAMPLE OF STRESS ON THE QUESTION OF READING HABITS

> HOME circulation. That's the thing advertising men have been hearing for years.
>
> But you can't have home circulation unless there is a home, and there are mighty few homes in New York.
>
> There are places to go back to, of course. Apartment life is quite different from home life, and apartment dwellers must go out for their recreation and amusement. But they don't go back to read.
>
> So home circulation is a pretty difficult thing to procure in New York. But this doesn't mean that you must abandon the idea of advertising to the people.
>
> Advertise to them where they are, and about 400,000 of them every week are in the theatres.

1. The reader desires to have action, preferably of the dramatic type. He will lend attention to pictures and to the pictorial element in words more quickly than to the educational matter.
2. Realism is required. There is a great fondness of biography, and for plain speaking in matters of sex. People want to read about the experiences of others.
3. The personal element is featured. The signed columns in the newspapers have their own special followings.
4. People want entertainment and not preaching.
5. There is great desire for self-improvement. People want to learn things if it is not too much trouble.

Circulation figures show how publications are consumed rather than how they are read, yet they offer the most reliable index available as to reading habits in various states and among various classes. Figure 77, from the *Educational Research Bulletin,* shows the ranks of the states as to the high-class magazines and also as to the 10 most widely read magazines. Figure 78 shows how one medium stresses reading habits.

Buying Control

It is essential in making a consumer analysis to determine who does the actual buying. In the household is it the husband or wife? In the manufacturing plant is it the executive or the engineer who has the deciding voice?

An investigation made for the McGraw-Hill Compan brings out some interesting facts in this connection. Figure 7 shows relative production and sales factors for various indu tries, the ones on the left being industries where there is large spread between production costs and selling price, th ones on the right being cases where production costs are th

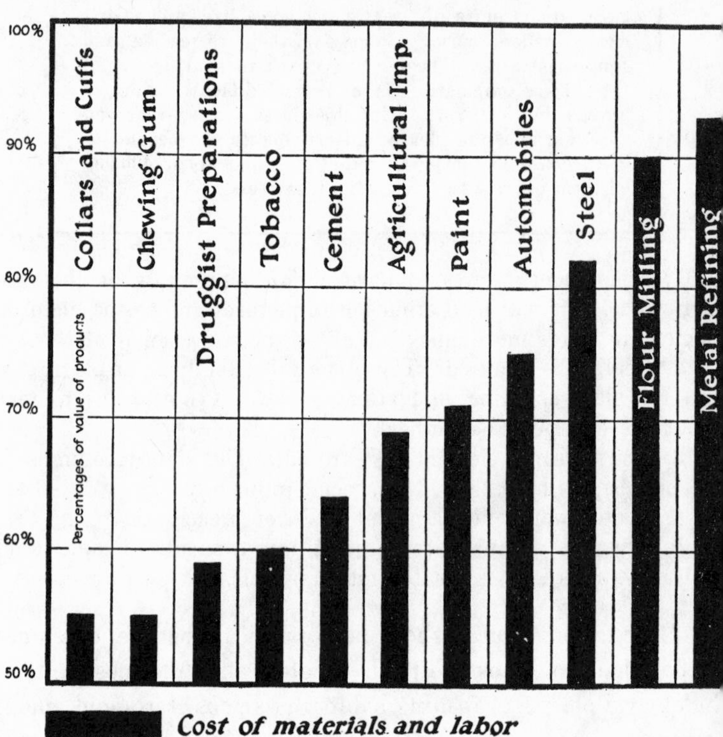

FIG. 79. PRODUCTION AND SALES FACTORS IN VARIOUS INDUSTRIES

The black bars represent the cost of materials and labor in percentage of the factory value of the products. (McGraw-Hill Company.

major consideration. In those businesses where sales strateg is the most important factor in profits, the general executive are merchandising men and take virtually no part in buying equipment. In those businesses where production costs ar paramount, general executives may take a part because of th important relation which this purchasing bears to profits.

Figure 80 shows the relative importance of various executives in buying, and the close correlation existing between men who initiate installations and those who specify the type and make of equipment. As is at once seen, the principal buying power lies with the production executives. The first three

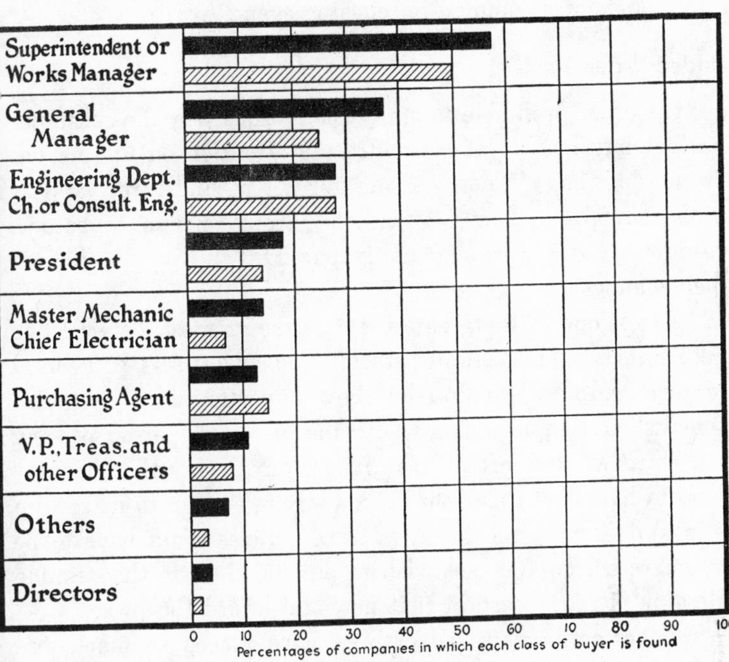

FIG. 80. IMPORTANCE OF VARIOUS EXECUTIVES IN BUYING

By "buyer" or "buying power," as indicated above, is meant the man who initiates the installation or specifies the equipment in the industrial field. It does not refer to the man who merely issues the formal order as a matter of routine. (McGraw-Hill Company.)

groups compose the operating staff of the company and are greatly in the majority when it comes to purchasing power. The president appears to be a general administrative official, taking little part in the choice of equipment.

A great many factors, of course, enter into certain special

fields. For example, if an investigation were made of the textile business, it would be found that in New England the agent is in entire charge of most mills, while in the South there are few agents and many general managers in control. Furthermore, southern mills often pool their purchases and place them in the hands of a common purchasing agent.

Hidden Sales Factors

It is often profitable to study the reasons why the consumer does not buy instead of concentrating attention on finding out why he does buy. These reasons for not buying rarely appear on the surface. They may not be strong enough to become prejudices, but yet be sufficiently powerful to divert sales into other channels.

Price is one of the greatest, if not the greatest, deterrent to making most sales. Manufacturers and advertisers in general are just beginning to find out how important it is that consumers should be acquainted with the price. A person passing by a store window often sees articles on display that he may desire to have, but this desire is not strong enough to make him go in and inquire the price. If the article would have to be demonstrated, he does not wish to put the clerk to this trouble unless he is fairly certain that he could afford the price.

Furthermore, many advertisers have placed so much emphasis on quality and service that the price appeal has been too much subordinated. Consumers have an idea that the quality is so high that the price will be beyond their pocket books and they purchase goods the price of which they know.

Another question to determine is whether the price is so high that the average consumer would not care to pay it all at once. In this case, the advertising might bring out the possibility of some time-payment plan.

Other hidden factors often come to light. The makers of gunpowder find that the great amount of posted property is a sales deterrent and advertise a plan by which owners of property will be glad to allow the hunting privilege. The makers of firearms find that women's inherent fear of having firearms

IF YOU SHAVE

–why not clip?

MEN who are as particular about the well-trimmed appearance of their hair as they are about clean shaving, use clippers regularly. They realize that hair around the back of the neck is just as untidy as an unshaven chin.

Of course you can't go to the barber's every day or even every few days, but you can own a pair of Brown & Sharpe clippers and use them at home to keep your hair well trimmed between hair cuts.

When you do buy a pair remember this—there *is* a difference in clippers. Nine out of ten professional barbers use Brown & Sharpe clippers because they have found that they stand up under the test of time and constant hard usage as no other clipper will. Many of them are using Brown & Sharpe clippers which they purchased twenty years ago and which are still giving steady, satisfactory service today.

Brown & Sharpe clippers are built with the precision, care and accuracy of a fine watch. You will only have to buy one pair in a lifetime; with a little care there is no reason why they should not last beyond the need of the average person.

The latest addition to the Brown & Sharpe line is the new, easy-action Dexter model—specially designed for all-round home use. The balance of the clipper is perfect and its cutting action is free and smooth. The blades operate as twenty tiny scissors and, being exceedingly sharp, they cut the fine hairs at the back of the neck without the slightest tendency to tug or pull. Like all Brown & Sharpe clippers, the Dexter does not coarsen the hair.

Get a pair of clippers today, and be sure to ask for Brown & Sharpe —the Dexter model for home use.

For all the family

Mother, too, will find Brown & Sharpe clippers a useful article to have at home—for the baby's first hair cut, for the children's Dutch clips, and for every bobbed head in the family. Hardware, barber supply and cutlery stores now have the Dexter clipper on sale—packed in a handsome, sturdy box with a hinge top, prominently marked for your identification. Price $4.50.

BROWN & SHARPE Mfg. Co.
Providence, R.I., U.S.A.

FIG. 81. ADVERTISING TO OVERCOME PREJUDICE

in the house prevents many sales. Consequently, the locking device is emphasized, as a safety precaution.

Prejudice

Among the hidden market factors the question of prejudice holds high rank. A prejudice, even though unfounded, may place a powerful check on any company's expansion. One of the most effective ways to combat and remove prejudice is by the use of advertising.

A prejudice may be due to several reasons. Most important, of course, is prejudice against the product itself. Figure 81 shows how the Brown and Sharpe Manufacturing Company is overcoming prejudice against the use of hair clippers.

There may also be prejudice against a process, as in the case of laundries and canning factories. Here the process is believed to be in some way deleterious. There is also prejudice against producers which reacts harmfully against their marketing policies. The prejudice against the meat packers is a case in point.

In making an advertising analysis, one of the first things to do is to find out what prejudices exist. This can be done effectively by means of personal interviews, both with dealers and consumers. A prejudice may be considered the converse of a buying habit—it might almost be called the habit of not buying. There are at least two methods of overcoming it, both of which have been used successfully.

The first method is to recognize the prejudice openly and then to combat it. Those who do not believe in negative forms of advertising frown upon this practice. Yet the unfortunate part of not recognizing specific prejudices is that they form the bases of attack on the part of manufacturers with competing products or services. For a long time, Postum was able to attack coffee virtually without response, this enhancing the already-existing prejudice against it. Finally, the coffee producer recognized that it was vital to meet Postum on the basic point of whether or not coffee was harmful to health.

The second method of overcoming prejudice is to use association and suggestion. Cigarettes, for instance, are shown being smoked by men whose faces and surroundings are supposedly indicative of their abilities and high social position. Talcum powder and union suits, often regarded as effeminate, are illustrated as being used by men of athletic build. Canned goods manufacturers have preferred to ignore prejudice and to stress the healthfulness of their products and the methods of manufacture.

The Average Consumer

There are two ways of picturing the consumer. One way is to study him as an actual human being—interview him, study him psychologically. Such studies, combined, will give a picture of the market.

The other plan is the converse of this; the market is studied first—statistically, of course. Then the market (consumers as a whole) is divided by the total number of consumers, and thus the "average consumer" is arrived at.

Advertising, in general, is a mass method of merchandising. It picks out a group of consumers with certain characteristics in common and directs its ammunition against them. A single consumer would not often justify the expense of an advertising message intended for him alone. The larger the group, and the more characteristics which it possesses in common, the greater the opportunity for the advertiser. Advertising analysis, therefore, separates the qualities and characteristics of the consumer, in order to find out what they are and what influence they exert.

For example, a publication makes an analysis of its subscribers. On the basis of the results, it plans to sell advertising space. If this analysis shows that subscribers constitute a logical market for products of a certain class, the publication proceeds to promulgate its space to manufacturers of those products. *Radio News* classifies its average reader as follows:

Is 27 years old.
Owns 1.9 radio sets.

Uses tools in constructing and building radio sets and apparatus.

Uses 3.8 tubes.

Has an audience of four persons listening to his set.

Spent $113.00 on radio during 1923.

Has read *Radio News* for the past two years.

Was influenced to buy 37 per cent of his radio apparatus through advertisements seen in *Radio News.*

Owns an automobile.

CHAPTER X

MARKET ANALYSIS

In the previous chapter the consumer was regarded as an individual; in this chapter the approach is to consumers collectively, commonly known as a market. The approach to the consumer is mainly psychological, while that to the market is largely statistical. The term consumer suggests buying motives and habits; while market connotes economic tendencies, the distribution of consumers, and channels of trade by which they may be reached. A study of consumers aids in determining the correct advertising message; that of markets in choosing suitable advertising media.

The most direct bearing, in fact, which market research has upon advertising is in relation to the choice of media. On this score alone, it is desirable to approach markets scientifically. In other words, markets must be classified and analyzed in as many significant ways as possible, since by this means the most efficient medium for reaching consumers may be discovered.

The primary market division is according to industries, trades, or classes, to which the product is sold. In other words, the first question in market analysis is as to the identity of the buyer. Following this, there are a number of methods by which the buyers, or the market, can be classified. The geographic method of division is one of the simplest. Purchasing power is often used; also class.

When the markets have been classified it is customary to compare the actual and the potential markets, measuring them according to the strength of competition in the industry. Potential market studies will include the various methods of broadening existing markets and of finding new ones.

Classification of Markets

Market analysis is a process of classifying and subdividing the market for a given product into its component parts. Beginning with broad groups, the process of analysis narrows these down until it has separated the entire field into subclasses. There are various methods of classification, the proper one to use being dependent upon the media which reach the market, and upon other considerations.

It is possible, for example, to divide the market geographically, according to districts. This is essential whenever media are to be used which are local in circulation, all media being, to some degree, local.

A geographical classification is rarely sufficient. The consumers of certain products, such as the more expensive luxuries, belong as a rule in a certain income class. This class is inclined to read magazines and other publications of a given type, such, for instance, as those numbered in the so-called "Quality Group." Some of these *class* media are almost exclusively confined in their circulation to those who have unusual buying power. While there is a distinction between social and financial status, it is difficult to draw such a line, in this country.

Technical and industrial products are usually classified according to the field which they serve, or according to the uses to which they are put, if they can be used in many industries. Figure 82 illustrates the buying structure of industry, divided according to major industries, and subdivided according to the main classes under each heading. The makers of some products, such as alloy steels, might profitably regard the whole field of industry as their legitimate market. The makers of such products as evaporators would probably look to the process industries for their principal markets.

Apart from industrial classifications, there are the various consumer types already discussed in the preceding chapter. Some manufacturers can profitably cultivate the whole field

FIG. 82. THE "BUYING STRUCTURE OF INDUSTRY"

The above chart is a skeleton or outline intended to classify the major industrial groups. It gives the individual enterpriser an opportunity to see his position in relation to the whole industrial market.

(McGraw-Hill Company.)

others will prefer to devote their efforts to some one section of the field. The farm population, for example, is the largest consumer unit, and there are many products which will be valuable for farmers as a whole. It may, however, be advisable to divide this farm market into wheat farmers, cotton farmers, dairymen, fruit growers, cattle raisers, and truck farmers. Each group will have its own problems and its own trade paper which will afford the most specialized approach.

Geographical Division of Markets

The simplest method of dividing markets is according to their location. This is of fundamental importance, of course, in selecting media with local circulations, but it is also valuable in determining what general magazine should be employed. Some of these, for example, have a stronger appeal, and a denser circulation in one section of the country than in another, and it is important to match circulation against markets, and against the distribution which has been obtained for the company's product.

In approaching a market, territorially, the broad questions which the investigator will set himself to answer, according to H. G. Lyall, director of the London Research and Information Bureau, are:

> (1) Are there already, or likely to be, a sufficient number of potential buyers of the goods in the area under review? (2) If so, how can the area be "sold" most economically? (3) What competition will have to be met and overcome? (4) What is the class distribution of the product? (5) What amount of dealer resistance may be looked for? (6) What is the "Peak" period of sales, and can it be altered to the advantage of the investigator's firm?

An investigation along the lines of determining relative magazine popularity was recently carried out. Interviewers went from house to house, asking for reader preferences as to magazines read and as to magazines preferred. This study was made in two cities, one in Kentucky and one in New Jersey. Approximately the same number of interviews was made in both places. In the Kentucky town, about 50 magazines were mentioned by those who were interviewed; while in the New Jersey town nearly three times as many magazines were mentioned, and a marked difference was found in the popularity of certain types of magazines in the two places.

Markets may be measured geographically in two ways. First, the volume sold in any given district or section can be figured from the sales records. This will supply figures as to the actual market at the moment. A market analysis, however, presupposes figuring the potential market also, and measuring the actual and potential markets in reference to each other to give the proportional amount of business secured by the company. A geographical division is also at basis of other types of market classification. Buying power, for example, must usually be divided territorially if it is to be of value.

Figure 83 illustrates a method of showing the potential market for paint on farms according to sections of the United

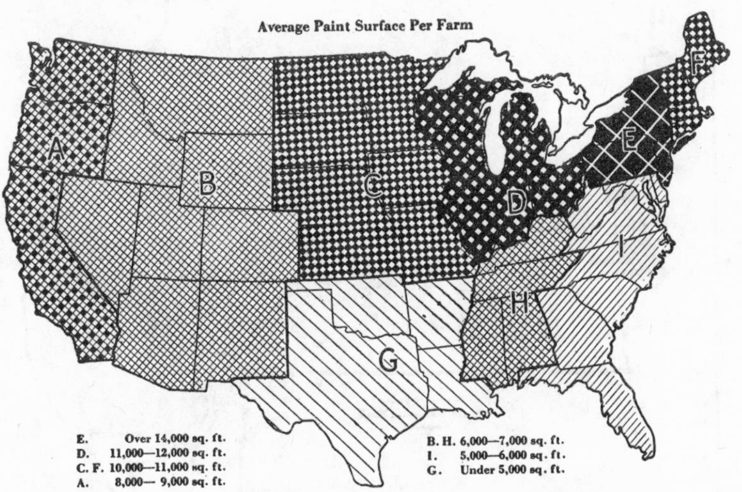

FIG. 83. A POTENTIAL MARKET SHOWN GEOGRAPHICALLY

States. A glance at the map shows that the average paint surface per farm in the E and D sections is larger than other parts of the country and hence offers a better market, judged purely on the basis of geographical potentiality. Other factors, of course, might enter the question which would modify the geographical factors. Buying habits, buying inclinations, climate, purchasing power, all might be influential in making some particular section better for advertising purposes. Many advertisers, such as manufacturers of silk hosiery, are interested in urban, rather than rural, markets. In such cases studies such as that indicated in Figure 84 are useful.

Markets by Industries

In certain cases it will be necessary to divide the market according to the industries represented. This will be true in all cases where a product's uses extend beyond a particular field. Dental supplies, for example, would be limited in all probability to dentists, but an indirect heat oven company would sell to many industries. See Figure 85, which illustrates the primary market for an indirect heat oven company.

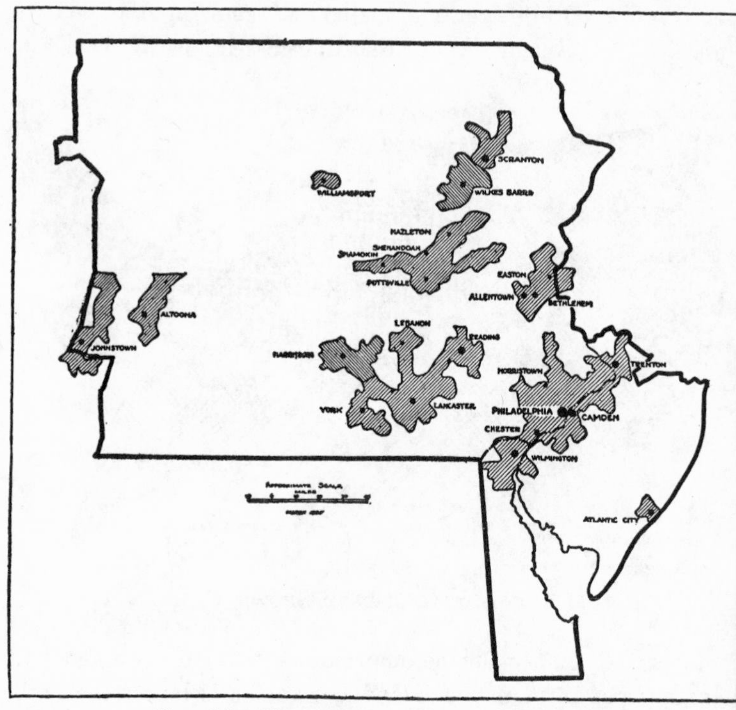

Fig. 84. Urban versus Rural Markets

The metropolitan areas of important cities are shown in this map. The shaded portions are the areas surrounding cities in which the density of population equals 150 persons or more to the square mile.

(U. S. Department of Commerce.)

In some cases, it is necessary to analyze other markets in addition to the primary market. For example, the following fields are consumers of heating apparatus:

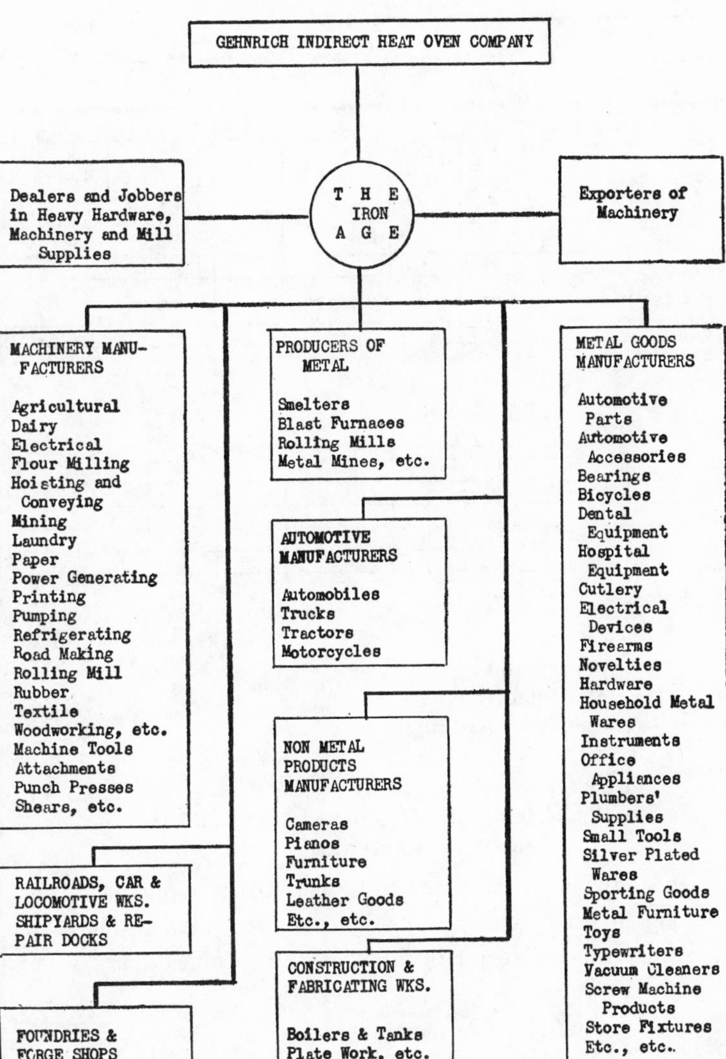

FIG. 85. TABULATION OF A PRIMARY MARKET
(*Iron Age.*)

1. Residential building owners
2. Hospitals
3. Hotels
4. Theaters

PAGE______ MILEAGE______ CORRECTED QUOTA—STATE TOTAL______
STATE______ DENSITY CORRECTION FACTOR______
STATE QUOTA______

NUMBER	CITY	POPULATION IN THOUSANDS	PROSPECTS												
			APARTMENTS	BANKS (TRUST)	BANKS (NATIONAL)	BANKS (SAVINGS)	CLUBS	DRY GOODS STORES	GENERAL	HOSPITALS	HOTELS	LIBRARIES	MUSEUMS	OFFICE BUILDINGS	RESTAURANTS
1															
2															
3															
4															
30															
31															
32															
33															

FIG. 86. A CONVENIENT FORM FOR

5. Office buildings
6. Apartment houses
7. Industrial buildings
8. Schools
9. Religious buildings
10. Public buildings (municipal, state, and federal)
11. Miscellaneous (laundries, stores, etc.)

In addition to these markets, there are a number of intermediary markets, which do not consume the product, but which are often responsible for installation and specification:

1. Architects
2. Building contractors
3. Building realtors
4. Heating and plumbing contractors—dealers
5. Sanitary and heating engineers
6. Building managers (on new construction)
7. Hardware dealers and jobbers

If the entire market is to be fully covered by advertising, both the primary and the intermediate markets must be examined to serve as a suitable basis for the selection of media.

PAGE________
STATE________

NEW BUILDINGS

No.______ YEAR______ No.______ YEAR______
No.______ YEAR______ No.______ YEAR______
No.______ YEAR______ No.______ YEAR______
No.______ YEAR______ No.______ YEAR______

	PROSPECTS																			
	RETAIL CLOTHIERS	STORES	Y. M. C. A.'S	Y. W. C. A.'S					TOTAL PROSPECTS	TOTAL PROSPECTS	DATE	BASIC QUOTA (NO OF DOORS)	ASSESSED VALUATION OF BUILDINGS (MILLIONS)	WEALTH CORRECTION FACTOR (PER CENT)	ANNUAL MEAN TEMPERATURE (DEGREES)	TEMPERATURE CORRECTION FACTOR (PER CENT)	COMBINED CORRECTION FACTOR (PER CENT)	SUPPLEMENTARY QUOTA FACTOR (PER CENT)	COMBINED QUOTA (NO. OF DOORS)	CORRECTED QUOTA (NO. OF DOORS)
1																				
2																				
3																				
4																				
28																				
29																				
30																				
31																				
32																				
33																				
15																				

MARKET ANALYSIS TABULATION

In practice, it is often necessary to analyze markets both by geographical divisions and by industries served. A good way of doing this is shown in Figure 86. The product in question here is revolving doors. Robert L. Blanchard, its originator, describes the scheme as follows:

These tables show our method of analyzing the market for Van Kannel Doors. The headings to the columns tell their own story. The first question was, "Who are our prospects?" A column was devoted to each class. The prospects who were listed in these columns were of course subjected to careful analysis. This analysis would of course be subject to wide variations according to the type of market to be analyzed. With us, it was first, the population of the town where the prospect was located, since we are not interested in the smallest cities, towns, and villages; second, the financial rating of the prospect. This market analysis forms the basis for our sales quotas as can be judged from the character of these additional columns.

Buying Power

The advertiser is constantly trying to find his most fertile markets. In many instances, these are indicated by the buying power of the communities in question. One way to estimate buying power is by the use of income tax figures.

The Life Insurance Sales Research Bureau has taken six sets of figures to measure the buying power of any given territory. For example:

1. The "insurable population" or the number of native white males over 20 years of age, excluding illiterates. This definition is quite strict and excludes some persons who are prospects for ordinary insurance. The figures are those of the United States Census of 1920.
2. The number of income tax payers, showing the total number of persons making a personal tax return for 1923, according to the Bureau of Internal Revenue.
3. The number of income tax payers, with incomes of $5,000 or over in 1923. Practically every one in this group is a good prospect for a sizable insurance policy.
4. Number of passenger automobiles registered in 1924. The possession of an automobile usually indicates sufficient wealth to buy life insurance.
5. Value added by manufacture by all industries. This is the difference between the cost of the raw materials and the price received for the products; it is the amount of money which comes into the industries of the county to be distributed as salaries, wages, profit, rent, and interest. Figures are taken from the Census of Manufactures of 1919.
6. Circulation of the *Saturday Evening Post,* the *Ladies' Home Journal,* and the *Country Gentleman.* Readers of these magazines usually have money to spend on life insurance as well as on reading matter. The sworn statement of 1924 paid circulation has been used.

Figure 87 shows how these statistics are compared for various counties.

Calculating Markets

It is not sufficient to count the number of units of the product which are in use, and to compare this with the amount sold

Fig. 87.—An Example of Statistical Compilation Indicating Buying Power

The Wealth in the Counties in the Detroit Agency Territory of the................Life Insurance Company

County Name	Insurable Population	Curtis Circulation	Number of Income Tax Returns	Incomes $5000 or Over	Number of Automobiles	Value Added by Manufacture (in thousands)
Bay............	12,851	2,830	3,021	217	9,340	$16,100
Clinton.........	6,371	1,280	428	34	4,920	1,300
Eaton..........	8,753	2,520	1,110	47	7,140	3,700
Hillsdale........	8,444	2,180	583	39	5,950	2,500
Huron..........	5,249	960	495	45	5,700	1,700
Etc............	....	.....	.....	.....	....	......
Total........	......	......	......	......	......	....

The Proportion of the Agency's Wealth in Each County of the Detroit Agency of the................Life Insurance Company

County Name	Insurable Population	Curtis Circulation	Number of Income Tax Returns	Incomes, $5000 or Over	Number of Automobiles	Value Added by Manufacture	Average
Bay.....	15%	14%	27%	28%	14%	32%	22%
Clinton...	8	7	4	4	7	3	6
Eaton....	11	13	10	6	11	7	10
Hillsdale..	10	11	5	5	9	5	8
Huron....	6	5	4	6	9	3	6
Etc......	......	......	......	......	......	......	......

The Ten Best Counties in the Detroit Agency

County	Proportion of Agency's Total Wealth in County	Number of Agents Operating in County	
		Whole Time	Part Time
Wayne.............	25%	6*	12*
Clinton............	12	2	5
Eaton..............	10	8	2
Jackson............	9	1	7
Monroe............	9	0	2
Lenawee...........	7	4	5
Ingham............	7	1	2
Huron.............	4	5	1
Bay...............	3	0	1
Saginaw...........	1	2	4
All other counties....	13	9	29

* These columns are to be filled in by the agency unless the necessary data have been urnished the Bureau.

by the company in question. It is necessary to go further and to find out those factors which limit market expansion, such as seasonal consumption, climate, weather, government restrictions, competition, and others.

The problem of calculating markets might well be divided into two parts. In the first place, there is the statistical problem of determining present consumption, comparing it with past consumption, and estimating future growth. In the second place, there are the tabulation and delineation of those factors which affect the market, of whatever kind they are. In other words, the market may be considered from the point of view of size, and also from the point of view of its potentialities and limitations.

The rapidly increasing volume of statistics relating to industries makes it possible, in most cases, to determine the consumption of any particular type of product. This preliminary information will serve as a standard by which to compare the performance of the company itself. Figure 88 shows a method of calculating market possibilities for an oil-burning farm engine, based on salesman's reports. It is interesting to note that market possibilities are closely correlated with sales each month. Here it is necessary to make allowance for renewal parts as well as for the sale of new engines.

In calculating any market, one of the first things to do is to estimate the replacement market. In some cases, of course, it may amount to practically nothing at the time, as in the case of a new product, but in other instances, the entire market may be to a large extent a replacement market.

Analysis of An Existing Market

An existing market can be appraised in two ways. By the first method, an actual count is made, either of the whole market, or of sections (samples) of it which are presumably representative of the whole, and which will permit estimation of the whole. The second method is to find some statistical set of facts which will vary in accordance with the market, and which constitute a market index.

EXHIBIT A-I

Sales Loading Form, as compiled by and maintained at each branch

The Burnoil Farm-Engine Company

SALES LOADING SHEET

'ear Ended Dec. 31, 1924 — Pittsburgh Branch

ngine Type	Total Demand	Burnoil Possibilities	Ratio B. P. to T .D.	Remarks
'ype X	$ 15,000	$ 5,000	80%	
'ype XX	10,000	2,000	33%	
'ype XXX	100,000	80,000	20%	
'ype XXXX	50,000	10,000	80%	
enewal Parts	25,000	20,000	20%	
thers *	150,000	- - -	- -	
'otals	$350,000	$117,000	33%	

* Detail in a separate attached report information pertaining to engines furnished by competitors which re not at present built by us.

Copy to General Sales Manager.

Copy to Branch Manager.

Signed—J. S. Smith Sales Record Clerk

'ote:—Analysis report on the above to be submitted by Branch Manager to General Sales Manager.

EXHIBIT B-1

SALESMAN'S RECORD

'ear Ended Dec. 31, 1924

'otal Demand, $300,000

urnoil Possibilities:

Type X	$20,100
XX	15,000
XXX	5,000
XXXX	35,500
Renewal Parts	20,400
Total	$96,000

M. S. Mowry, Salesman, Savannah Branch

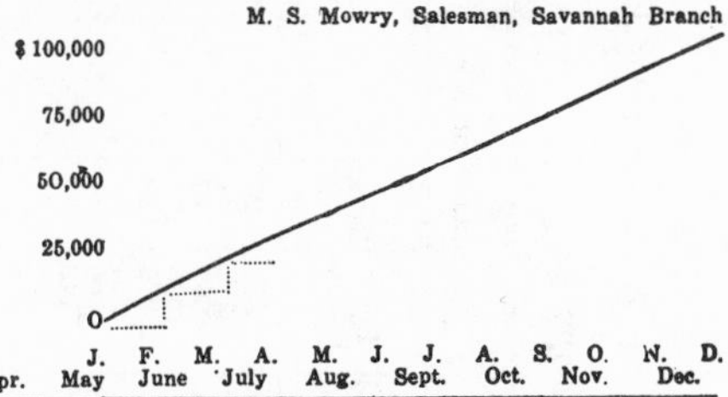

$ 100,000

75,000

50,000

25,000

0

J. F. M. A. M. J. J. A. S. O. N. D.

ctual Sales	Jan.	Feb.	Mar.	Apr.	May	June	July	Aug.	Sept.	Oct.	Nov.	Dec.
Type X	$2,500	$1,740	$ 620									
XX	720	·500	410									
XXX	600	1,220	1,330									
XXXX	3,200	4,170	2,750									
Renewal Parts	1,110	2,620	200									
Total	8,130	11,250	5,310									
Cum. Total		18,380	23,690									

Fig. 88. Market Computed from Salesmen's Records

(*The Pittsburgh Accountant.*)

One of the best examples of the counting method is the ystem used by the American Telephone and Telegraph Com- any in computing its markets. The steps in the analysis are s follows (E. I. Stone, Jr., *Harvard Business Review*):

1. Selection of the survey area.

2. Division of the survey area in homogeneous market sections. 'his requires a preliminary division of the community into small ections within each of which rental conditions are based on the ame economic considerations.

3. Determination of the method or scheme of classifying and rading family types and business firms. In the business market, elephone service is sold closely on a business firm basis, and may e analyzed by recording and classifying firms according to type f business done. The business market is also divided into general usiness firms, which are dependent upon the community as a

FIG. 89.—AN EXAMPLE OF THE COUNTING METHOD OF ANALYZING AN EXISTING MARKET

Resident Telephone Development

Rental Class, Private Residence	Families	Total Users	Per Cent	Users Of: Bell	Users Of: Ind.	Users Of: Both	Bell Service: Coin Box	Bell Service: One Party	Bell Service: Two Party	Bell Service: Four Party	Bell Service: Rural	P. B. X.: Users	P. B. X.: Trunks	P. B. X.: Station	P. B. X.: O. L	P. B. X.: O. S.	Ext.	Extra Service
100 Up	8,898	8,525	96	8,320	448	243	27	3434	1,873	3,008	26	22	25	177	1	5	3186	75
75–100	10,385	8,672	84	8,234	591	153	6	1118	1,819	5,272	21	...	...	...	...	4	703	6
55– 75	18,411	11,758	64	10,799	1152	193	1	989	2,041	7,697	73	...	...	...	...	5	396	7
40– 55	18,561	7,817	42	6,934	991	108	7	501	1,287	5,025	114	...	...	...	...	8	112	8
30– 40	14,085	3,848	27	3,117	776	45	1	263	509	2,209	132	...	...	...	...	6	39	3
25– 30	9,644	1,712	18	1,238	493	19	2	108	191	804	133	...	...	...	...	1	10	1
20– 25	8,127	974	12	633	353	12	...	36	88	365	144	...	...	...	...	...	5	...
15– 20	6,947	469	7	316	157	4	...	20	56	148	92	...	...	...	...	...	1	...
10– 15	4,513	144	3	109	35	...	...	3	14	58	34	...	...	...	...	...	1	...
Under 10	2,420	26	1	14	12	...	...	1	1	5	7	...	...	...	...	...	...	...
Total........	101,991	43,945	43	39,714	5008	777	44	6473	7,879	24,591	776	22	25	177	1	29	4453	100
Flats																		
100 Up	465	423	91	414	19	10	...	137	124	154	...	...	...	...	...	...	27	1
75–100	2,263	1,862	83	1,789	89	16	...	241	489	1,059	...	...	...	...	...	...	19	...
55– 75	10,328	6,311	61	5,730	632	51	8	413	1,191	4,119	...	...	...	...	...	2	48	3
40– 55	20,369	7,456	37	6,582	939	65	10	414	1,234	4,923	...	...	...	...	...	1	51	...
30– 40	23,004	4,045	18	3,205	888	48	7	234	653	2,309	1	...	...	...	...	1	31	...
25– 30	15,515	1,457	9	1,105	369	17	3	116	239	746	1	...	...	...	...	...	11	...
20– 25	13,684	794	6	559	244	9	5	38	118	393	5	...	...	...	...	...	5	...
15– 20	13,892	457	3	300	166	9	1	21	61	214	4	...	...	...	...	...	8	1
10– 15	9,046	129	1	75	58	4	1	2	9	63	...	...	...	...	...	...	2	...
Under 10	4,688	276	6	86	192	2	5	16	17	48	...	...	...	...	...	...	...	...
Total........	113,254	23,210	20.5	19,845	3596	231	40	1632	4,135	14,028	11	...	...	...	...	4	202	5

Rental Class, Private Residence	Fam-ilies	Total Users	Per Cent	Users Of			Bell Service											
				Bell	Ind.	Both	Coin Box	One Party	Two Party	Four Party	Rural	P. B. X.					Ext.	Extra Ser-vice
												Users	Trunks	Station	O. L.	O. S.		
Ap'rtm'nts																		
P. B. X.	471	471	100	471	1	1	1	4	3	1	....	7	32	577	....	....	....	−455
100 Up	1,663	1,540	93	1,530	27	17	5	655	484	389	....	....	....	....	....	....	137	3
75–100	1,631	1,353	83	1,331	28	6	4	284	419	626	....	....	....	....	....	1	20	3
50– 75	3,514	1,751	50	1,683	73	5	8	253	439	935	....	....	....	....	....	....	10	2
35– 50	1,855	440	24	407	33	....	5	61	92	249	....	....	....	....	....	....	3	....
25– 35	583	58	10	51	7	....	3	4	3	41	....	....	....	....	....	....	....	....
Under	211	43	20	38	5	....	3	1	8	26	....	....	....	....	....	....	....	....
Total........	9,928	5,655	57	5,511	174	29	29	1262	1,448	2,317	....	7	32	577	....	1	170	−447
Lodging Houses																		
Good........	414	343	83	335	24	16	104	86	88	107	....	5	18	205	....	4	23	59
Medium......	1,749	678	39	590	102	14	89	112	143	254	....	....	....	....	....	1	25	9
Poor.........	725	126	17	106	20	....	10	17	29	50	....	....	....	....	....	....	1	....
Total........	2,888	1,147	40	1,031	146	30	203	215	260	411	....	5	18	205	....	5	49	68
Light Housekeeping.	5,225	....	....	....	....	....	....	....	....	....	....	....	....	....	....	....	....	....
Grand Total..	233,286	73,958	32	66,101	8924	1067	316	9582	13,722	41,347	787	34	75	959	1	39	4874	274

whole for support, and neighborhood business firms, which depend on the immediate neighborhood for support.

In the residence market, telephone service is generally sold on a family basis. Families are graded into economic classes by first dividing the survey area geographically into uniform market sections and then by classifying each family by the rental value of quarters occupied. The final aim is to select the market sections in such a way that all families in each rental class in each section will be of similar type. Figure 89 shows a complete summary of a residence market in a certain city.

4. Preparation of record of existing subscribers and service by city blocks.

5. Field record and classification of existing families and business firms.

6. Summary of the field data.

The above method would be feasible only where a large portion of the population could be counted as belonging to the market. Obviously, such a method, due to its exhaustive character, is expensive. The ordinary way of making such a market analysis would be to count certain representative sections and to consider them as typical of other parts of the market.

The Market Index

The market index is a device by which certain sets of statistics are used as a "measuring stick" for market potentialities. The *Literary Digest* measures the market for its periodical by means of the home telephones of the United States. It prefers this index to income tax returns, for a number of reasons. In the first place, living expenses in rural districts are lower, so that money income goes further there. Therefore income tax returns underestimate the actual rural income, or at least do not give a well-balanced basis of comparisons. The telephone subscribers are a better index of the progressive members of the community. In the second place, metropolitan and industrial regions show up better as income tax payers than as telephone subscribers. Income is in cash, and tax returns tend to overestimate their buying power.

The Curtis Publishing Company states that its circulation

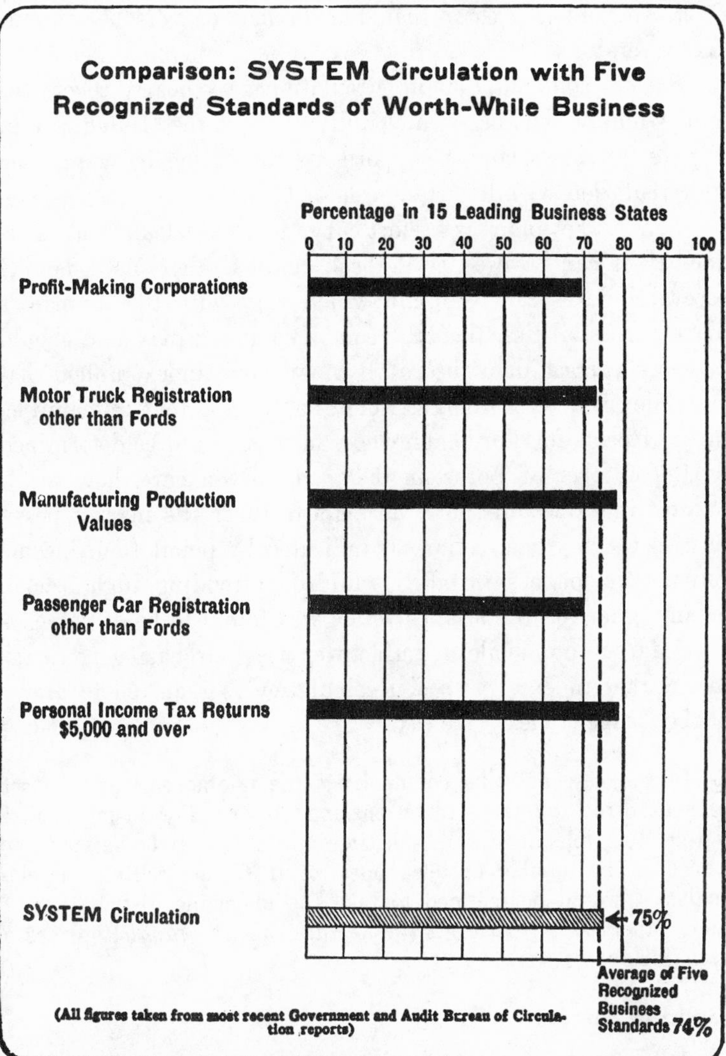

FIG. 90. MAGAZINE CIRCULATION COMPARED WITH BUSINESS INDICES

is a better guide to markets than income tax returns, based mainly on the reason given above. An income of $2,000 in a country town signifies a different scale of living from the same income in a large city. In more than four-fifths of the counties of the United States the circulation of the combined

Curtis papers is greater than the number of personal income tax payers.

System contends that its circulation very nearly covers the money-making businesses and individuals of the United States. Figure 90 shows how it supports its contention by comparing its circulation with five standards of business.

The market index is a short cut to market calculation. Frequently it can be used as a check against other methods. If several indexes can be found which vary with the company's market possibilities, then the combined index may and should be more correct than the result of any one index, unless that one index is determining, as would be the case for the manufacturer of parts for Ford cars, whose market would be determined by the number of Fords on the road. Even here, however, a market index would show the manufacturer the market possibilities for any one section, as indicated by population, income returns, telephones installed, children attending high school, or any other set of statistics which was found to be of value.

A large automobile manufacturer uses purchasing power as his market index. A special calculation is required to arrive at the correct index. He says:

> In the case of some commodities the quotas can best be set without direct reference to purchasing power. For instance, if I were selling telephone wall pads, it would obviously be better to go direct to the number of telephones, or if I were selling encyclopedias, I would be inclined to take the magazine distribution of such papers as *Atlantic Monthly*, *National Geographic*, etc., as a basis for quotas.

Limiting Factors

In making any market analysis, particularly for advertising purposes, the limiting factors must be determined. The most important among these are the following:

1. *Climate and Weather.*—The climate plays an important part in the sale of many commodities, from the automobile to the perishable food product. While it would seem so obvious as to be unworthy of comment, it is a fact that advertising cam-

paigns have been carried on in warm climates to sell articles used only in the North, and vice versa.

2. *Seasonal and Cyclical Characteristics.*—Almost every product has certain seasonal and cyclical peculiarities affecting its volume of sales at different times. Whether it is desired to increase advertising at dull seasons, or to concentrate advertising when sales resistance is at lowest ebb, it is important to define these seasonal limitations.

Figure 91 is taken from an Annual Report of the Cali-

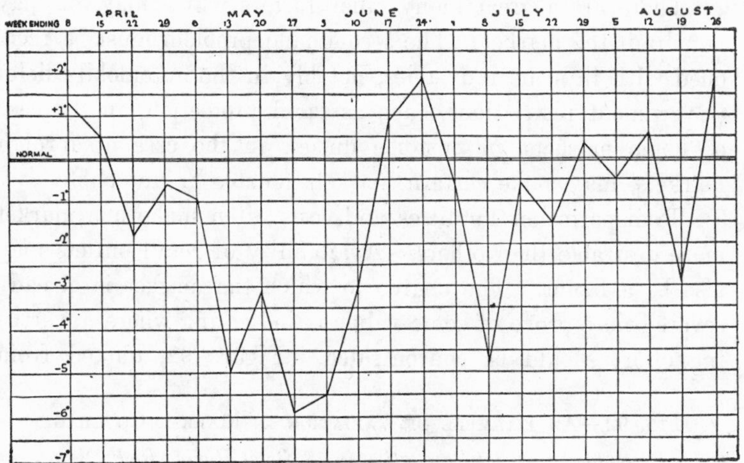

FIG. 91. TEMPERATURE AS A MARKET LIMITATION

This chart shows the average weekly temperature departure from normal for fourteen cities in the United States. Such fluctuations have a marked effect upon the demand for fruit.

fornia Fruit Growers Exchange. The market for lemons varies with the temperature.

3. *Sectional Peculiarities.*—It often happens that some particular sections of the country must be considered with particular care. Customs on the Pacific coast, for example, may differ from those along the Atlantic seaboard. Country and city are proverbially different, although these distinctions have been partly broken down in the past few years.

4. *Competition.*—Competition is a factor which is always important yet hardly ever the same. The company's standing

in the industry is dependent on so many varying conditions that preëminence one year does not mean that the following year will see the same superiority. Nevertheless, the ratio which the company occupies to the total sales in the field is an important thermometer of progress. It is customary to divide the market into its various component parts and to measure, if possible, the ratio in each of these sub-markets. When a company sells more than one product, it may be advisable to make separate computations for each product in each territory.

There are a great many other factors which may, or may not, limit the market. The secondhand problem must be reckoned with in some industries, notably in the automobile field. Government restrictions, such as tariff protection, in the case of home markets, or customs duties, in the case of foreign markets, may make certain markets tenable or untenable.

Transportation facilities and costs often make one market more desirable than others. Availability of retail outlets may also be a factor. The degree to which the market is already covered may prove of some value as indicating where advertising effort should be concentrated. Figure 92, quoted from

Fig. 92.—An Example of Variation in Market Coverage

Percentage of Rural Population in 13 States Having Radio Sets

	Per Cent
Iowa	18
South Dakota	12
Nebraska	22
Illinois	19
North Dakota	17
Minnesota	13
Kansas	14
Indiana	11
Wisconsin	10
Missouri	16
Ohio	12
Michigan	11
Oklahoma	4
Total	14

100% = Total Replies to Question

Radio Retailing, shows how the percentage of rural population having radio sets differs in 13 states. Obviously, in such a case as this, other factors would affect market possibilities, such as nearness to a sending station, buying power, or occupation.

Broadening Markets

A market analysis should do more than outline the markets which are already existent. It should indicate the possible methods for broadening markets, notably by the discovery of new fields, or by the use of new merchandising ideas.

The discovery of new uses for the product is valuable, not only because it increases the market but also because it provides a new advertising feature. In some cases, it has been imperative to discover new uses. With the coming of prohibition, for example, the United States Industrial Alcohol Company and its affiliated company, the United States Industrial Chemical Company, turned the attention of their chemists to the discovery of new uses for alcohol. The result was that alcohol and alcohol products now play a basic part, according to *Class,* in the making of such commodities as artificial musk, artificial silk, leather goods, imitation leather, motion picture films, dyestuffs, airplanes, explosives, motor fuels, fertilizers, preserved fruits, antiseptics, synthetic fruit flavorings, varnishes, lacquers, and perfumes.

The addition of new products to the line often serves to round out the marketing programme, especially where a company has hitherto been handicapped by seasonal factors. Such new products as are added should, however, be suited to production and merchandising facilities. The Harrisburg Pipe and Pipe Bending Company, for instance, found itself after the War with a greatly enlarged plant and no market for the pipe coils and bends which it could make. Analysis showed that it could use its lathes for the manufacture of forged seamless steel couplings and bull plugs for use in the oil industry. Various articles of forged steel for use in the oil industry followed. Next, extension was made to the automotive field. Finally, the alloy steel market was entered. The present line of products was arrived at after a great deal of experimentation, and after products which were unsuitable from a production or merchandising standpoint had been dropped.

A market analysis should bring to light any inefficient practices which exist in covering the present markets. If the advertising schedule is not reaching all markets, this will be brought to light and suggestions made for remedying the deficiency. The opening of new sales territories or outlets is another result of market analysis. This opens a wide range of possibilities. It may uncover the advantages offered by foreign markets. It may show how markets exist at home in different industries or in different classes of consumers. Tool makers, for example, within the last few years have found an unsuspected market in the household.

A rarer possibility is the discovery of a new sales idea. The product and the use remain the same as well as the user, but the new sales idea serves to increase the consumption. The National Lamp Works had great success in selling the idea of lighting rather than lamps. This organization made a survey of industrial lighting which established that better lighting had recognized effects on production, spoilage, and the number of accidents which occurred. An appraisal was made by manufacturers of advantages to be gained from efficient industrial lighting, the results of which were as follows:

Percentage First Choice	Reasons
80	............Increase in production
70	............Decrease in spoilage
60	............Prevention of accidents
50	............Improvement of discipline
40	............Improvement of hygienic conditions

These replies provided a basis for an industrial advertising campaign which was founded on facts rather than conjectures.

CHAPTER XI

CLASSES OF MEDIA

After analysis has been made of the product, the consumer, and the market, it is necessary to select the particular advertising medium or media which will most effectively fulfill the determined requirements. There are two parts to this problem: first, the selection of a particular class of advertising media, and second, the choice between the various available media in any particular field.

Any arbitrary division of advertising media will naturally be imperfect. It is essential, however, to make some sort of classification at the beginning, such as the following:

1. Magazines:
   (*a*) General periodicals with national circulation, such as the *Saturday Evening Post, Literary Digest,* or *Scribner's.*
   (*b*) Special magazines, circulating among readers differentiated by age, sex, class, avocation, or other common characteristic. In this class would come the *Ladies' Home Journal, American Boy, House and Garden,* and *Popular Mechanics.*
2. The business press, which may be subdivided into the following:
   (*a*) Trade papers, circulating among middlemen.
   (*b*) Industrial publications, devoted to the needs of a particular industry, such as *The Iron Age.*
   (*c*) Class publications, circulating to institutions, professions, or any particular class of business consumer.
   (*d*) Executive periodicals, circulating primarily among those who influence the general policy of the business, or among business men as a class. In this division would fall such publications as the *Nation's Business, System,* and *Management and Administration.*

3. Newspapers
4. Direct-mail media
5. Outdoor advertising
6. Street-car cards
7. Miscellaneous, media, such as specialties, samples, theater programs, films, point-of-purchase advertising, radio, and "publicity"

Magazines

The magazine offers to the advertiser a medium with broad geographical distribution, as well as with opportunity for art work and often the use of color. In addition, it is considered the primary medium for educational advertising to the consumer.

There has been little research done on the subject of general magazine advertising. The majority of that which has been done has been carried out with selected and homogenous groups of periodicals. It is, in point of fact, extremely difficult to conduct an investigation of the whole magazine field, so widely variant are the conditions to be encountered. Furthermore, such investigations, to be impartial, must be carried out by a disinterested research organization rather than by the magazine itself.

An extremely interesting experiment with magazine research was carried out by the New York University Bureau of Busincss Research. Advertisers were divided into four classes for the purposes of the investigation: constant advertisers, new advertisers, intermittent advertisers, and advertisers who had dicontinued magazine advertising. Six hundred questionnaires were sent out, from which 23 per cent returns were secured. The questionnaire sent to the group which had stopped advertising is illustrated in Figure 93.

An investigation tending to bring out the group characteristics of magazines would hardly be of great value, because the findings would rarely be applicable to the individual medium. Specific research would, however, be possible of application to such groups as women's magazines, or children's magazines, especially along psychological lines.

FIG. 93.—AN EXAMPLE OF MAGAZINE RESEARCH

Advertising Mortality Questionnaire of the New York University Bureau of Business Research

1. During the time you were advertising in magazines (between 1914–1921) approximately what per cent of your advertising appropriation was devoted to magazine advertising?..............per cent. About what per cent to newspaper advertising?.............per cent. To outdoor advertising?...............per cent. Mention others ....
2. In the case of your own product which of the following policies do you consider brought the best results in general magazine advertising? Indicate by checking one of the following:
   (*a*) Relatively larger advertising expenditures at first, decreasing gradually as the market is being developed.
   (*b*) Relatively light advertising expenditures at first, increasing gradually as the market is developed.
   (*c*) Constant expenditures as the market is developed.
   (*d*) Alternate "waves" of advertising with periodic peaks.
3. To which of the following causes is the apparent discontinuance of your magazine advertising due:
   Indicate by checking one or more of the following points:
   (*a*) Reduction in advertising appropriation?
   (*b*) Change in policy as to type or class of media used:
      (1) Change from magazine to newspaper?
      (2) Change from magazine to trade papers or class media?
      (3) Change from magazines to direct-mail advertising?
      (4) Change from magazines to outdoor advertising?
      (5) Change from magazines to car-card advertising?
   (*c*) Insolvency of business?
   (*d*) Production of your product lagging behind demand?
   (*e*) Expenditures in advertising your particular product not justified by results:
      (1) Because of excessive competition?
      (2) Because of nature of the advertised product?
4. Indicate which, if any, of the foregoing causes arose from change of ownership?

   ....

   ....
5. (*a*) What per cent (approximately) of your advertising was handled by your own organization?...........per cent.
   (*b*) What per cent (approximately) of your advertising was handled by an agency?..........per cent.

Product *Signed*......................

Advertised...................... *By*......................

Farm and Special Consumer Magazines

There are a number of publications circulating among consumers which are limited to special classes. The most important of these, perhaps, is the farm field, where buying is done both for the home and for the farm. A number of farm papers are national in distribution and partake almost of the nature of general periodicals in editorial make-up and scope of advertising.

A second type of farm papers are those with sectional distribution, such as the *Rural New Yorker* or the *New England Homestead.* Farming problems are so differentiated by sectional and local conditions that such sectional papers often seem to have a permanent lease of life and are of practical utility to the communities which they serve.

A third class of farm paper is that which is devoted to some particular branch of farming, such as the *Breeders' Gazette,* or the *American Poultry Journal.*

One of the important points to consider in reference to the choice of farm papers is that the farmer will buy by mail more readily, perhaps, than other classes of the population. Certain farm publications are accordingly particularly useful as mail-order media.

There are many other papers and periodicals circulating among particular classes of the consumer population. There are, for example, the religious press, journals devoted to sports, and those to moving pictures and other amusements, such as radio and motoring.

The Business Press

The business press, as mentioned earlier in the chapter, may be divided into trade, industrial, class, and executive periodicals. There has been much confusion in regard to the terminology of the various business papers, and it is not always possible to state definitely that they fall in a certain classification. Nevertheless, for purposes of convenience this fourfold division has the advantage of simplicity.

'rade Publications

A trade paper circulates among middlemen, sometimes to etailers or wholesalers separately, and sometimes to both. There s practically no trade which does not have its journal supplyng it with news of the trade as a whole, the conditions affecting t, the events which are taking place, and other news of paricular interest.

Closely connected with the trade papers are the professional eriodicals, such as circulate among physicians, architects, the dvertising men, or builders and contractors. In such narrow ields as these it is possible to do a great deal with research. For example, Paul T. Cherington, Director of Research, J. Walter Thompson Company, wanted to determine certain facts n regard to the architectural press. He sent mail questionnaires to practically all the important architects in the country, 2,000 of whom replied.

It was found that five of the papers in the field were read regularly by a fairly large percentage of the architects, the percentages being as follows:

Magazine A	........72%	Magazine D	........56%
" B	........67%	" E	........52%
" C	........61%	" F	........24%

It is interesting to compare these returns with those along similar lines compiled by the Kewanee Boiler Company, shown in Figure 94. When a second question was asked as to the time which was spent on a particular paper, the same papers were reported, but the order was changed as follows:

Magazine A by 37%	Magazine C by 21%
" B " 24%	" D " 17%

And in reply to a question as to which paper was found most useful by the chief designer and specification writer respectively, the results came out differently again:

Chief Designer	Specification Writer
B—41%	C—31%
C—26%	B—25%
D—23%	— —
A—19%	— —

FIG. 94.—AN INVESTIGATION OF THE RELATIVE VALUE OF MEDIA

Double Post-card Questionnaire on Architectural Publications Issued by the Kewanee Boiler Company

Gentlemen:

As advertisers in several architectural publications we are continually called upon to decide where our patronage should be placed.

We are anxious to co-operate with architects in supporting the publications that perform a definite duty to the profession most creditably.

Your information on this return card will help us.

Many thanks in advance.

KEWANEE BOILER CO.

Is the Architectural field covered by too many publications?

Yes.................. *No*..................

MAY WE HAVE YOUR VOTE?

Which of these are *read in* your office or at home?

The American Architect — The Architectural Review
The Architect
Architecture
Architecture and Building
The Architectural Forum
The Architectural Record
The Architect and Engineer (San Francisco)
Buildings and Building Management.
The Journal of the American Institute of Architects
Pacific Coast Architect
Pencil Points
Southern Architect and Building News
The Western Architect
....
....
....

NAME......................................

Such research work as this is valuable as showing the degree of reader interest a periodical with relatively small circulation may possess, and which may make it a more valuable medium than others having a far larger circulation.

When there are two or more competing papers in the same field, it is often difficult for the advertiser to tell which one has the greater reader interest and is the better all-round medium. To solve this question for its own product, the Kewanee Boiler Company sent out return post cards to the number of 6,909, to which it received a 23 per cent volume of replies. The questionnaire and the tabulation of results are shown in Figure 94. The first six publications on the list are fairly close to-

FIG. 94.—*Continued*

Number of return post cards sent out	6909
Number reaching destination	6629
Number of cards returned	1841
Number returned by Post Office	280
Changes of address	249
Per cent responding	23.5%

TOTAL VOTES FOR PUBLICATIONS LISTED

Architectural Record	1113
Architectural Forum	1034
The American Architect (The Architectural Review)	977
Architecture	865
Pencil Points	847
The Journal of the American Institute of Architects	691
The Architect	397
The Western Architect	363
Southern Architect and Building News	133
Pacific Coast Architect	124
Architecture and Building	119
Architect and Engineer (San Francisco)	107
Buildings and Building Management	74

REMARKS

Scattering votes were cast for 66 other publications not mentioned in our post card. One hundred and eight architects went to the trouble of filling in the post-card comments on various publications and some wrote letters where the comments were too lengthy to be included on the card.

gether in popularity. After these there is a marked and rapid dwindling. It is interesting to note that 603 architects were of opinion that the field was covered by too many publications, while only 245 thought that the field was not overcrowded.

Industrial Publications

Industrial publications may cover one or a number of industries. *The Iron Age,* for example, circulates among nine major divisions of the iron industry as indicated in Figure 95, according to certain proportions.

In the textile industry there are a number of types of periodical. In the first place, there is the nationally distributed journal which covers the industry in all branches and in all phases. In the second place, there is the sectional paper, such as that which deals with the specific problems of the South. Thirdly, there is the specialized paper which deals only with

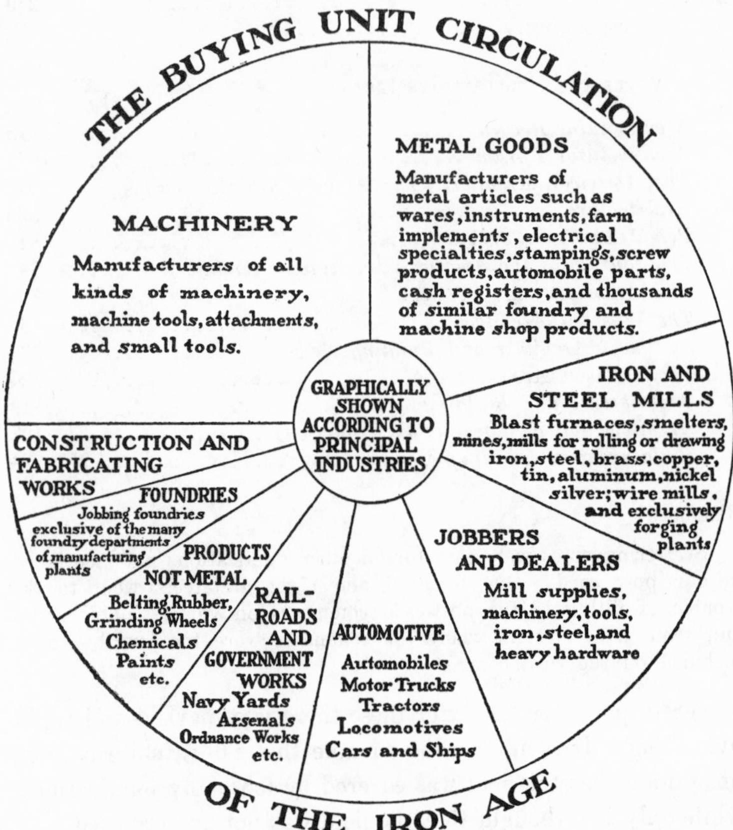

Fig. 95. Magazine Circulation Divided According to Industries Served

some particular phase of textile activity; and lastly there is the trade directory, which may be either general or specialized.

Class Publications

There are a certain number of business papers which do not fit in any other category, and are, therefore, called class magazines. In this division would be placed the journals which circulate to large consumers of an institutional nature, such as hotels, hospitals, office buildings, or greenhouses.

Executive Publications

Of increasing importance in recent years is the type of business publication which circulates chiefly among executives. As expressed by Walter Drey, of *Forbes Magazine,* they are not able to prove from the standpoint of scientific analysis what percentage of their total circulation is definitely major executive. As they increase in circulation, they must necessarily reach lower and lower into the business field to get the number of readers required. In general, however, this circulation is not a total waste, since the younger readers are likely to be the executives of the future.

The calibre of the executive publication as an advertising medium is determined largely by those who read it. Figures 96 and 97 show the tabulated results of a survey of part of the circulation of *The Nation's Business,* calculated to find out just what the executive factor in the circulation consists of.

This was done in an interesting way. The first of these charts shows the analysis of circulation in Pennsylvania, which was chosen because the well-balanced character of the state ought to present a good cross section of the country.

The second table illustrates the executive position of the 4,221 latest subscribers to the periodical. Comparison of the two would presumably show the character of the circulation as constituted at present, and the character of the incoming circulation.

The Newspaper

The newspaper exists chiefly to bring news to the public, and through its editorial columns to comment on this news. Newspapers carry the bulk of all advertising, they are local in appeal, quick in action, and can be adapted almost immediately to any particular requirement.

Almost every advertiser will find his problem so different

EXHIBIT L

Pennsylvania Summary excluding Philadelphia & Pittsburgh

	President	V. President	Secretaries	Treasurers	Sec.-Treas.	Gen. Mgrs.	Sup'tendents	Proprietors	Partners	Cashiers	Firms	Engineers & Sur.	Gen. Agents	Auditors & Acc.	Business Mgrs.	Sales Mgrs.	Advertising Mgrs.	District Mgrs.	Local & Br. Mgrs.
FINANCIAL & PROFESSIONAL																			
ACCOUNTING COMPANIES		1						1	1										
ADVERTISING AGENCIES			1		1	1		1			3								
BANKS & TRUST COMPANIES	103	32	9	71	2	3		2		266	81								
BROKERAGE HOUSES				1		2			2										
FINANCE COMPANIES	1	2	3	1	2	3		1			3								
INSURANCE AGENCIES	1					11	1	25	5		5								
INSURANCE COMPANIES	3	3	4	2	2	9	3	1	1		7		1					7	
INVESTMENT BANKERS	1					2			2		1					1			1
LAW FIRMS								1	2							1			
REAL ESTATE	6	1	1	1	1	2		12			2								
REAL ESTATE AND INSURANCE				1		3		39	6		2								
TOTAL	115	39	18	77	8	36	4	83	19	266	104		1			2		7	1
ORGANIZATIONS & INSTITUTIONS																			
AMUSEMENT COMPANIES						1													
CHAMBERS OF COMMERCE	3		10								52								
CLUBS	2		8			2					14								
COOPERATIVE ASSOCIATIONS	5		5	2	1	3			1		19								
EDUCATIONAL INSTITUTIONS	9		1	1		2	21				19				1				
HOTELS	1			1		6		6			2			1					
THEATERS				1		13		3			2								
LIBRARIES											33								
TOTAL	20		24	5	1	27	21	9	1		141			1	1				
SUMMARY																			
MANUFACTURERS (Exhibit I)	462	81	87	202	67	447	164	134	28	6	412	73	6	15	5	15	2	12	18
WHOLESALERS (Exhibit J)	43	10	4	22	5	75	2	69	9		79					4			1
RETAILERS (Exhibit K)	161	13	16	71	17	313	5	510	47		427					2	4		2
FINANCIAL & PROFESSIONAL	115	39	18	77	8	36	4	83	19	266	104		1			2		7	1
ORGANIZATIONS & INSTITUTIONS	20		24	5	1	27	21	9	1		141			1	1				
MISCELLANEOUS	1			2		3	3	2			3	2							
GRAND TOTAL	802	143	149	379	98	902	199	807	104	272	1166	75	7	16	6	23	6	19	22

	Traffic Mgrs.	Misc. Mgrs.	Agents	Foremen	Salesmen	Executive Assts.	Editors & Educators	Doctors	Lawyers	Judges	Ministers	Architects	City Officials	Mayors	Public Officials	Undertakers	Directors	Farmers	Miscellany	Total
FINANCIAL & PROFESSIONAL																				
ACCOUNTING COMPANIES																				3
ADVERTISING AGENCIES																				7
BANKS & TRUST COMPANIES		1				17	3										3		2	595
BROKERAGE HOUSES																				5
FINANCE COMPANIES																			1	17
INSURANCE AGENCIES																				48
INSURANCE COMPANIES			10		1	2														56
INVESTMENT BANKERS					2														1	11
LAW FIRMS																				4
REAL ESTATE																				26
REAL ESTATE AND INSURANCE																				51
TOTAL		1	10		3	19	3										3		4	823
ORGANIZATIONS & INSTITUTIONS																				
AMUSEMENT COMPANIES																				1
CHAMBERS OF COMMERCE																				65
CLUBS																				26
COOPERATIVE ASSOCIATIONS			1																	37
EDUCATIONAL INSTITUTIONS			1				48													103
HOTELS																				17
THEATERS																				19
LIBRARIES																	1			34
TOTAL			2				48										1			302
SUMMARY																				
MANUFACTURERS (Exhibit I)	6	26	24	12	10	47	14		1								3		60	2439
WHOLESALERS (Exhibit J)		2	2		3	4													4	339
RETAILERS (Exhibit K)		2			6	5													5	1606
FINANCIAL & PROFESSIONAL		1	10		3	19	3										3		4	823
ORGANIZATIONS & INSTITUTIONS			2				48										1			302
MISCELLANEOUS								64	23	1	29	3	11	2	15	8		3	15	190
GRAND TOTAL	6	31	38	12	22	75	65	64	24	1	29	3	11	2	15	8	7	3	88	5,699

Major Executives 88.1% (President through Firms)

• This is a summary of 5,699 replies received from 9,536 NATION'S BUSINESS subscribers in Pennsylvania (excluding Philadelphia & Pittsburg) as of Feb. 1st 1925 •

FIG. 96. DETERMINATION OF EXECUTIVE FACTORS IN CIRCULATION
A study of a magazine's circulation in a single representative territory.

Financial & Professional Organizations & Institutions Summary

	Presidents	V. Presidents	Secretaries	Treasurers	Sec. Treas.	Gen. Mgrs.	Superintendents	Proprietors	Partners	Cashiers	Firms	Engineers & Sup.	Gen. Agents	Auditors & Acc.	Business Mgrs.	Sales Mgrs.	Advertising Mgrs.	District Mgrs.	Local & Br. Mgrs.	Traffic Mgrs.	Misc. Mgrs.	Agents	Foremen	Salesmen	Executive Assts.	Editors & Educators	Doctors	Lawyers	Judges	Ministers	Architects	City Officials	Mayors	Public Officials	Undertakers	Directors	Farmers	Miscellany	Total
FINANCIAL & PROFESSIONAL																																							
ACCOUNTING COMPANIES	2							1	3		1								1																			4	12
BANKS & TRUST COMPANIES	55	28	3	5	3	9		1		103	27										1	2			5											1		4	247
BROKERAGE HOUSES	3				1	2		2	12		6																												26
FINANCE COMPANIES	7	1	9	2	5	6		2	2	1	4							1																				2	42
INSURANCE AGENCIES	7	1	1	1	1	6		30	4	1	11									1																		1	65
INSURANCE COMPANIES	10	2	4			14	3	2			8		7					9	2	1		13						1										7	83
INVESTMENT BANKERS	4	2			1	5		3	10		7					2		1						1															36
LAW FIRMS	1							8			2																												11
REAL ESTATE	19	2	5	4	1	7	1	59	9		9	1				3		1				1		6															128
TOTAL	108	36	22	12	12	49	4	108	40	105	75	1	7			5		12	3	2	1	16		7	5			1								1		18	650
ORGANIZATIONS & INSTITUTIONS																																							
AMUSEMENT COMPANIES	2					5					2					1			2																				12
CHAMBERS OF COMMERCE	2		10								6																												18
CLUBS	1		3								9																											6	19
COOPERATIVE ASSOCIATIONS	4		6			10	1				10		1									1																	33
EDUCATIONAL INSTITUTIONS	11	1	1			3	20				14															27										1			78
HOTELS	2					18		12			3																												35
THEATERS	1		1	1		11		2																														1	17
LIBRARIES	3			1							48																											4	56
TOTAL	26	1	21	2		47	21	14			92		1			1			2			1				27										1		11	268
SUMMARY																																							
MANUFACTURERS	321	58	54	84	53	268	31	142	36	1	186	18	1	7	5	16		25	4	4	7	27	13	2	13	19										4		28	1427
WHOLESALERS	48	6	8	13	8	61	1	53	14		21					2			5		4			3	3													8	258
RETAILERS	186	16	17	46	24	180	1	518	91		130						1		2						5													6	1223
FINANCIAL & PROFESSIONAL	108	36	22	12	12	49	4	108	40	105	75	1	7			5		12	3	2	1	16		7	5			1								1		18	650
ORGANIZATIONS & INSTITUTIONS	26	1	21	2		47	21	14			92		1			1			2			1				27										1		11	268
MISCELLANEOUS	7	1	5	3	2	7	3	20	1		6	16	3	23										3	2	8	85	89	4	10	25	16	9	25	9	3	4	6	395
GRAND TOTAL	696	118	127	160	99	612	61	855	182	106	510	35	12	30	5	24	1	37	16	6	12	44	13	15	28	54	85	90	4	10	25	16	9	25	9	9	4	77	4221

Major Executives 3526 or 83.5%.

This Analysis seems to indicate to us as publishers that the steady circulation growth of NATION'S BUSINESS is both natural and healthy and that as long as the quality continues to run as high as indicated, each month will add strength to our Magazine just as certainly as each additional thousand widens the market for our Advertisers.

FIG. 97. ANALYSIS OF POSITIONS OF SUBSCRIBERS

Positions of 4,000 subscribers to the *Nation's Business* analyzed. An interesting and novel manner of indicating the nature of growth of a medium. This study shows that there is no end to the application of research to the problem of media selection.

that he will have to base his decisions on what he finds out through his own research activities. This has brought forward a great number of advertising policies based on empirical methods. For example, the Borden Company based its major advertising campaign on women's publications, and supplemented them with space in newspapers. It found that by running advertisements three consecutive weeks and staying out the fourth week, it could reduce its expenditure one-quarter without reducing the strength of the advertising commensurately. It also found better results from using all the morning or all the evening newspapers in a given city than from using both. Smaller papers are claimed to have a more loyal following than the dominant paper, and rates are usually appreciably lower.

A great deal of information can be gleaned from an examination of the particular newspapers in a town or city. The editorial and advertising content often indicate the market stratum to which the paper particularly appeals. One newspaper in a city may carry the bulk of the Help Wanted advertisements, showing that it circulates among the working classes. Another may carry the advertising for high-class real estate sales and rentals, or a quantity of financial advertising, showing that it is read by business men.

Where there are large foreign groups, as in New York City, Boston, or Milwaukee, it has been found that foreigners prefer newspapers published in their own language. In Philadelphia, there are Jewish, Italian, and German dailies serving their own particular population elements.

The newspaper also offers an excellent field for psychological research, such as that done by Richard B. Franken, of the Department of Advertising and Marketing of New York University. Figure 98 shows how preferences of business and professional men among 10 newspaper features are divided, compared with the preferences of other bodies of readers. Such an investigation is of the greatest value in determining the preferred position for various types of advertising in the papers.

Direct-Mail Media

About one-quarter of the country's advertising expenditures is supposed to be devoted to direct-mail activities, distributed in such varying forms as letters, booklets, bulletins, broadsides,

		Business Group	Professional Group
1	General News	8.72%	10.58%
2	Finance	12.21%	4.57%
3	Editorials	4.82%	6.71%
4	Politics	5.02%	6.14%
5	Foreign News	5.59%	4.42%
6	Sports	4.11%	3.48%
7	Local News	1.39	2.85
8	Business Page	2.27%	.87%
9	Special Articles	1.24	1.46
10	Cartoons	1.20	1.19
11	Accuracy	.81	1.42
12	Book Review	.45	1.13
13	Advertisements	1.09	.24
14	Moral Tone	.54	.68
15	Brevity	.40	.75
16	Theatrical	.48	.43
17	Music	.13	.43
18	Shipping News	.00	.49
19	Society	.10	.23

FIG. 98. PREFERENCES OF NEWSPAPER READERS

This chart shows the first 19 features of newspaper reading interest. It compares the reading interests of the business class with those of the professional class. The gray shows the business class (410 executives) and the white the professional class (136 doctors and lawyers).
(Franken, *Attention Value of Newspaper Advertisements.*)

folders, envelope enclosures, mailing cards, poster stamps, almanacs, and other miscellaneous forms.

Direct mail has an important use for making sales direct, and is perhaps equally important as a supplementary sales medium. It prepares the way for the sales force, and follows up prospects between calls. It is used to help increase sales in particular localities through local dealers. Much direct-mail literature is prepared to send out in answer to replies and inquiries from other forms of advertising, and for follow-up purposes.

Direct advertising has certain marked advantages. It embodies the personal appeal as distinguished from the more general appeal obtained through publication advertising. As its name implies, it goes direct to the prospect. It is one of the most elastic media, because its appeal and timeliness can be suited more adequately to market needs than can other forms. Finally, direct mail is within the reach of both the large and the small company. Lack of capital, which would effectually forbid the use of periodical media, is no bar to the use of direct mail. In fact, some of the large national advertisers started advertising in a small way with the use of direct advertising.

Direct advertising, especially when intended to make sales, has the further advantage of indicating exactly what effect the advertising message has had. In other words, returns from direct advertising can usually be tabulated so that it is possible to determine whether it has paid its way or not.

The success of any direct-advertising campaign depends mainly upon two factors: first, the quality of the mailing list and the percentage of logical prospects which it contains; and second, the actual selling power and suitability of the direct-advertising material and methods employed.

The mailing list is in many ways analogous to the circulation of a periodical medium; but for a long time there was no method of submitting the mailing list to the auditing procedure which has now become a part of the substantiation of magazine circulation. It was recently decided, at a convention of the Direct Mail Advertising Association, that an auditing service for mailing lists should be instituted. Leading mailing-list compilers were asked to submit to a questionnaire covering the following points:

A PRINTING QUESTIONNAIRE

that printers find helpful in building successful direct advertising

A. What is the nature of the merchandise or service to be sold?

1 New Product
New Service
New Market
Old Product
Old Service
Old Market
2 Utility
3 Luxury
4 Unit of Sale
5 Amount each Sale
6 Margin of Profit
7 Seasonable or all Season

B. What feature is there about this merchandise or service that will interest buyers?

C. What competitive literature already occupies the field?

D. Where are possible buyers or users located?

1 In Large Cities
2 In Small Cities
3 In the Country
4 North | East | South | West

E. Are the possible buyers:

Male | Female

F. What kind of people are they?

1 Refined
2 Average
3 Coarse
4 Studious
5 Superficial
6 Limited Education
7 Average Education
8 Broad Education
9 Technical Education
10 Professional Education

G. To what kind of appeal will they respond?

1 Aesthetic
2 Bizarre
3 Common-sense
4 Humorous
5 Scientific
6 Economical
7 Dominant
8 Subdued
9 Flashy
10 Conservative
11 Colorful
12 Quiet

H. What is their financial or social standing?

1 High
2 Good
3 Fair
4 Doubtful

I. Buying for whom?

1 Corporation
2 Company
3 Self
4 Family
5 Husband
6 Wife
7 Mother
8 Father
9 Children

J. What is their annual income, budget, or appropriation?

$1,000	$5,000	$15,000
2,000	6,000	20,000
3,000	7,000	25,000
4,000	10,000	Or over

K. Where will the printed piece be received?

1 Home
2 Office

L. When will the printed piece be received?

1 Day of Week
2 Time of Day

M. Where will the printed piece be read?

1 Home
2 Office

N. Who will open mail?

1 Office Boy
2 Mail Clerk
3 Secretary
4 Proprietor
5 Maid
6 Housewife

O. By what light will it be read?

1 Daylight
2 Artificial Light

P. Will it be handled by:

1 Clean Hands
2 Dirty Hands
3 Dainty Hands
4 Rough Hands

Q. Will the printed piece be submitted to:

1 Casual Observation
2 Continued Observation
3 Close Study

R. How much money can be spent on printing?

S. What specifically is the printed piece to do?

1 Bring Inquiries
2 Effect Sales
3 Introduce Product
4 Introduce Service
5 Introduce House
6 Introduce Salesmen

T. Is there a limit to the mailing weight or space to be occupied?

U. What should be the nature of the printed piece?

1 Book
2 Catalog
3 Booklet
4 Folder
5 House Organ
6 Envelope Stuffer
7 Illustrated Letter
8 Broadside

V. If a book, will it be carried in pocket?

Side | Vest | Inside

W. If a book, will it be kept for reference?

On desk
In desk drawer

X. What should be the nature of text?

1 Of Primary Importance
2 Secondary to Illustrations
3 Continuous Story
4 Series of Short Articles
5 Long Captions
6 Short Captions
7 Simple
8 Technical

Y. What type style does the nature of the appeal and of the printed piece suggest?

Z. Should the printed piece be printed in plain type or should it be decorated?

AA. What should be the nature of the illustrations?

1 Halftones from Photographs
2 Halftones from Drawings
3 Halftones, Highlight
4 Halftones, Vignetted
5 Halftones, Two Color
6 Halftones, Three Color
7 Halftones, Quadricolor
8 Combin. Halftone and Line
9 Delicate Line
10 Strong Line
11 Flat Color from Line Plates
12 Line and Benday

BB. What ink treatment does the character of the printed piece suggest?

1 Colored
2 Tints
3 Process
4 Black

CC. What Warren paper will best serve the purpose behind this printed piece?

1 Cameo Dull Coated Book
2 Cameo Post Card, Dull Coated
3 Cameo Cover, Dull Coated
4 Silkote, Dullo-Enamel Book
5 Silkote Post Card, Dullo-Enamel
6 Silkfold, Strong Dullo-Enamel
7 Warrenfold Strong Coated
8 Lustro Superfine Coated Book
9 Warrentown Coated Book
10 Cumberland Coated Book
11 Printone, Semi-Coated
12 Library Text
13 Olde Style
14 Cumberland Super Book
15 Cumberland Machine Book
16 Thintext (India Paper)

FIG. 99. ANALYSIS OF DIRECT-MAIL REQUIREMENTS
(S. D. Warren Company.)

1. Name
2. Address
3. Branch offices
4. Lists compiled
5. Guarantee on lists of business concerns: Describe fully
6. Guarantee on lists of the professions and consumers: Describe fully
7. Percentage of business in local lists
8. Percentage of business in national lists
9. Describe your list catalogue
10. What is your policy regarding minimum ratings in compiling lists? For example, do you include those rated $3,000 to $5,000 when those rated $5,000 or up are ordered?

The cost of the investigation was borne by the Association, but it was stated that all claims made by a mailing-list house would be carefully audited, and if claims were verified, the name of the concern would be placed upon an accredited list which was to be furnished to members of the Association. This auditing was done by an outside firm.

The limitations of direct-mail advertising are chiefly concerned with the mailing list. No way has yet been devised of taking the place of periodicals or outdoor advertising, which carry the mass appeals. Direct advertising can reach only the known and individualized market; there must always remain many logical prospects who are not on the mailing list, not to mention the added market to be found in the younger generation.

Figure 99 shows a questionnaire which, while frankly advertising propaganda for the S. D. Warren Company, is intended to be helpful to the printer in analyzing the needs of his client who wants to do direct-mail advertising.

Outdoor Advertising

In this somewhat elastic category are grouped posters, painted displays, and electric signs. The medium, in all its branches, has grown rapidly, causing somewhat irrational and inadequate methods of placement. As it is now, the outdoor advertising company is agency and medium combined.

Outdoor advertising is suited either to a nationally or locally distributed product. The one universal requirement is placement in a position where sufficient circulation will be obtained. There are, of course, a number of other major requirements. The copy must be brief enough so that it can be read during the time that it takes to pass by. If located along a railroad right of way, or on a highway, readability must be especially easy. The outdoor advertisement, in its very nature, can have but a brief moment in which to make an impression. It does, however, duplicate a great deal so that the force of repetition should be especially strong, perhaps to the point of non-attention.

An interesting investigation has been made as to whether the logical method of handling outdoor advertising is through the advertising agency or not. The research tended to indicate that either the advertising agency or the soliciting company could be employed, as circumstances warranted, with the likelihood that ultimately the agency would obtain the business. A summary of results was sent to two selected lists of outdoor advertisers, with a letter asking for their comments of favorable or unfavorable to the conclusions. The percentage of returns from each list was above 50 per cent. It was found that 80 per cent of the replies agreed with the findings of the report. This, in view of the controversial nature of the subject, was taken as sufficient corroboration.

Street-Car Cards

The street-car card occupies in many ways a unique position. Every card is practically able to secure equal attention with the other cards in the car. The ordinary passenger looks at the street-car card because he has nothing else to do. So large a proportion of the urban population rides in street cars that it may be said that street-car cards have as near a 100 per cent circulation as any medium, except painted bulletins and posters. They reach, furthermore, a stratum of population which would be unlikely to read newspapers, such as laborers.

A point which has been made much of is that street-car

cards are the last things seen by shoppers, and serve as reminder advertising at a time when this reminder will be most likely to bear fruit. There has been much discussion as to the relative importance of the street-car card, and whether it is a good supplementary medium for the national magazine or the newspaper.

An investigation was made in five large cities by well-known auditing houses with a view to finding out exactly what medium was noticed most frequently (see Figure 100). In San Francisco, Milwaukee, and Chicago, street-car advertising was first, and in Los Angeles and Minneapolis, it was second, to newspaper advertising.

Fig. 100.—An Investigation of Effectiveness of Media

Straw Vote on Kind of Advertising Most Frequently Noticed by Telephone Subscribers in Five Cities

Medium	City I	City II	City III	City IV	City V
Street cars	30.64%	30.49%	33.27%	23.88%	25.73%
Newspapers	26.90	29.11	23.19	37.86	35.27
Magazines	12.77	16.83	17.24	13.87	19.56
Posters	14.43	6.76	6.73	8.12	8.14
Electric signs	8.93	11.59	13.79	11.50	6.80
Painted bulletins	3.43	2.89	3.36	3.27	3.17
Signs on buildings	1.45	1.65	1.64	.90	.68
Theater programs	1.45	.68	.78	.60	.56

Miscellaneous Media

There are a number of types of media which are sometimes of value to the advertiser. These types do not ordinarily carry the major advertising burden as any of the preceding media are often called upon to do. But they may serve as valuable auxiliaries when properly utilized.

1. *Specialty Advertising.*—This may take a number of forms, usually for purposes of reminder. Specialty advertising usually fills a utility purpose. Blotters are one of the types used most frequently. At one time and another there has been a vogue for registered key tags, for calendars, and for almanacs. A specialty finds its chief use, perhaps, in serving a definite

purpose, and not indiscriminately distributed. The first specialty advertising, it is said, was done by a bank in 1880 when it distributed book bags to school children, as a way of approaching parents.

2. *Sampling.*—One of the favorite methods of food manufacturers of introducing their products, or of furthering their sales, is to distribute samples. Sampling often accompanies a local newspaper campaign, or some other method of calling public attention to the product and its merits, while, at the same time, giving people an opportunity to give it an actual trial. Sampling is also done with drug products, toilet goods, brushes, and many other articles.

3. *Theater Programs.*—It is urged by the publishers of theatrical programs that the theater audiences provide a discriminating market for advertisers, that during intermissions the theater program is read, and delivers its message when the mind is receptive. As far as is known, there has never been a test made of the relative efficacy of the theater program as an advertising medium, and there is no way recorded of checking up results concretely.

4. *The Film.*—The industrial film started out as a "stunt" when $25,000 is said to have been paid to have a great banner advertising a brand of smoking tobacco hung over the prize ring at the Jeffries-Johnson fight. From this it developed into a direct sales force, to be shown at conventions, retail store meetings, salesmen's meetings, and other places where an interested audience may be secured.

The Boston Woven Hose and Rubber Company was highly successful in its use of moving pictures as a method of stressing the quality of its rubber fruit jar ring (see Figure 101).

5. *Point-of-Purchase Advertising.*—This somewhat ambiguous heading covers all advertising which is seen by the prospective purchaser at the place where the purchase may be made. It includes window display, counter cards, show cards, dispensing devices, and even packages.

6. *Radio.*—While it is true that almost every new force for spreading news has sooner or later been utilized for adver-

tising purposes, the conditions surrounding radio broadcasting are so unique that it is impossible to tell at this stage of its development to what extent it will serve as an advertising medium. Certainly, it has proved efficacious in the case of the manufacturers of radio sets and parts, but whether it will serve equally well for department stores, hotels, and other broadcasters remains to be seen.

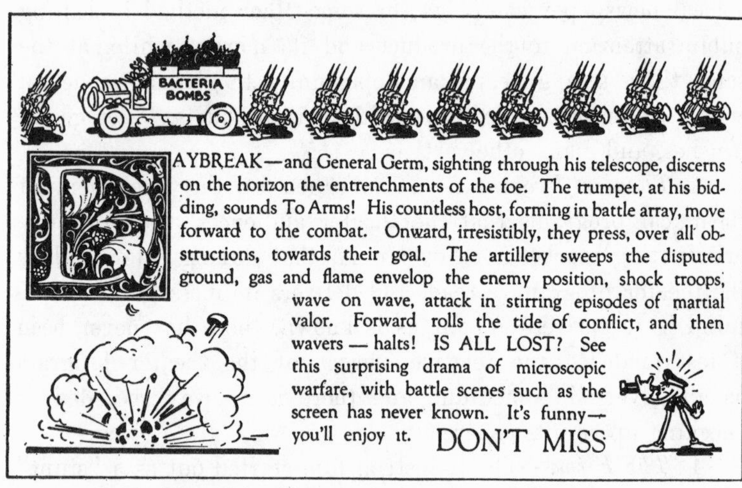

FIG. 101. USE OF THE INDUSTRIAL FILM

A sample of the literature which the Boston Woven Hose and Rubber Company uses to popularize its motion picture, "General Germ's Waterloo." The Company believed that an industrial motion picture could best show the selling points of its jar rubbers by showing in humorous style the activities of germs. (*Printers' Ink Monthly.*)

7. *Publicity.*—The last type of advertising is one that often proves highly important, namely, the publicity given the product outside of the regular advertising channels. This includes speeches by members of a firm, articles in print for public consumption, and diffusion of information through the daily press in the guise of news. The force of publicity, especially as organized propaganda, is tremendous, but there has been little progress in measuring it.

CHAPTER XII

ESSENTIAL CHARACTERISTICS OF MEDIA

The first point which comes up in the discussion of any particular class of media, or any special medium, has to do with the essential characteristics which make it fitted or unfitted for the purpose in hand. The study of media characteristics can be divided into three parts:

In the first place, there are the various facts to be ascertained about the publication itself, a great many of which must be passed upon by the personal judgment of the advertiser. This heading will include such questions as the editorial content of the publication, the reader interest which it arouses, the confidence which its readers feel in it, and the average life among subscribers and purchasers. It will also cover the advertising content, volume, distribution, and ratio to reading matter, and cost of publication compared with subscription price. Finally, there are certain mechanical requirements which must be known.

The second phase of the research work concerns itself with the stratum of population or field which the periodical covers, usually determined by a study of circulation, its volume, and the classifications of the readers according to the important factors. It might be advisable, for example, to divide circulation according to sex, age, buying power, business position, or geographical distribution.

The final division of the subject has to do with the relative cost of advertising in particular media, preferably measured in proportion to the amount of circulation, and also judged qualitatively.

Editorial and Mechanical Factors

Editorial Policy

Among the facts regarding the publication itself, editorial policy and content are regarded as of primary importance, since they affect the suitability of a given publication for a given advertiser's needs. The decision of the advertiser will be based on volume and variety of editorial matter, as well as on the appearance of the periodical or newspaper as a whole, and on its typography or art work. One advertising agency goes so far as to include the political attitude of the publication as one of the vital factors in its fitness as an advertising medium.

Editorial policy proves of particular importance when two or more media appear to have no decisive advantage over each other in circulation or rates. In this case, the degree to which the publication has secured a hold upon its readers by its editorial policy, the opinions it presents, and the standards which it sets up will prove important elements in determining choice. There is an undoubted tendency in magazines which have obtained large volumes of advertising and circulation to edit their reading matter to suit the demands of the advertisers rather than to serve the subscribers. Such a policy, while it may be apparently successful at the moment, may in the end result in a loss of renewals.

Publications in general recognize the weight which is given their editorial policies in making up advertising schedules. Hence, they are eager and willing to state their policies in definite terms. *Cosmopolitan,* for example, bases its policy on the elements of human interest, its major purpose being entertainment. In its sales literature, it points out that its reading columns contain the same basic factors as are existent in advertising of a human interest nature. For example:

Love—the home interest—the beauty appeal
Money—success—attainment—luxury—betterment
Health—comfort—self-preservation
Personality—self-interest—dread—thrill—hope—happiness
Humor

Help the Editors!

THERE has been a rather special effort to make this issue of the *Quarterly* more like the standard reviews. It would be helpful to know to what extent the contents of this issue are found interesting by its readers. Please tell us your reactions to these articles:

"A PUBLICLY OWNED INSTITUTION"

"MATHEMATICS IN INDUSTRIAL RESEARCH"

"THE STATISTICAL STUDY OF GENERAL BUSINESS CONDITIONS"

"COMMUNICATION ENGINEERING AND ELECTRICAL CURRICULA"

"THE 1924 STOCK ISSUE OF THE A. T. & T. COMPANY"

"WORLD'S TELEPHONE STATISTICS, 1923"

Mail this sheet with your general comments and suggestions to:

Information Department

AMERICAN TELEPHONE & TELEGRAPH COMPANY

195 Broadway

NEW YORK, N. Y.

*Name*______________________________

*Address*______________________________

FIG. 102. HOW READERS' DESIRES ARE DETERMINED

Interesting questionnaire used by a company magazine to find out the preferences of its readers for its various articles. This is a highly specialized example of the study of editorial content.

In other words, it wants to impress on advertisers that an editorial policy which is founded on entertainment along these lines will be useful for their advertising messages.

Business papers are glad to give advertisers statements of their editorial policies as well as general publications. The *Southern Ruralist,* for instance, emphasizes the fact that it serves every interest of the farm home and every member of the farm family, and covers every seasonal subject through special issues on the first of each month. The *Shoe and Leather Reporter* points out that it has the title of the most quoted business paper in the shoe and leather field.

Figure 102 indicates how it is possible for a publication to find out whether it is meeting the desires of its readers in the matter of editorial policy.

Charm, published by L. Bamberger & Company, of Newark, New Jersey, a department store, made an analysis of the reading features preferred by 17,000 of its readers, with the following results:

Recipes, diet, nutrition, home economics	3,449
Shirley's letter and society news	3,319
Fashion and style	2,694
Garden, flowers, and home decoration	2,657
Art, theatre and musical comments, educational	2,593
Fiction	1,430
Sports	1,113
Beauty hints	865

This information was obtained by the use of a letter and return form. This letter sent to those people who had been receiving *Charm* for a year is so carefully designed to achieve its purpose, and so well expressed that it not only obtained a high percentage of replies, but also assisted in creating the goodwill for which the magazine itself was started. The letter follows:

We have sent *Charm* to you gratuitously for a year. We wish now to take stock of our progress; to learn, if you will tell us, if we have succeeded in making *Charm* interesting and worth your while.

Have you been getting *Charm* regularly?

And has it interested you? Do you wish us still to keep it coming? It will continue to come to you, free of charge, if you wish it.

And if you do like *Charm,* will you help us with your suggestions to make it more interesting in the coming year?

We think we have noticed a great tendency abroad in America, one that is of particular interest to women like yourself—we mean an interest in the fine things that contribute to the graces of living—books, art, music, the theatre, the out-of-doors, tasteful dress and beautiful homes.

Don't you observe on every side a raising of our standards of good taste on all of these important matters, and a stimulation of our interest in them? It is because we believe that you love these things that we think there is a place in your home for *Charm.*

Most women's magazines are magazines of fiction and of practical service. *Charm* seeks to give both of these but something more, too. It is a monthly messenger carrying news of the local social activities of northern New Jersey and it is a magic carpet that transports the salons and ateliers of the Rue de la Paix and the smart shops of all the world to your reading table.

It is dedicated to the idea that Americans are becoming obsessed a little less with how to make a living and a little more with how to live.

Have we pleased you with *Charm?* Shall we continue sending it to you? Tell us on the attached sheet.

Reader Interest

Closely allied with editorial policy is the question of reader interest. How eagerly is the publication awaited by subscribers? Is there competition between members of the family to see which shall read it first? How shall this reader interest be measured?

Advertisers can measure reader interest in a number of ways, although there is no way of stating definitely the extent to which it is a factor in any given publication. The percentage of renewal subscriptions is often set up as an index of reader interest.

Archibald Crossley, formerly of the *Literary Digest,* thinks that editorial content determines character of circulation always, no matter how the magazine is bought. It is his opinion that it is possible to analyze news-stand sales from subscription analyses, provided the subscription percentage is high.

R. K. Leavitt, Secretary-Treasurer of the Association of National Advertisers, is in doubt as to the best indication of reader interest. He asks:

> Is it percentage of renewal subscriptions, or percentage of *newsstand* sales? Or is reader interest something which must be judged by each purchaser of space for himself from an inspection of the editorial contents of the magazine? Again, the editorial tone of magazines may be such as to make a considerable difference in the quality of readers. Thus, of two large women's magazines, one is admittedly better for mail-order advertising than the other, although it takes an expert to analyze the factors which bring out this result. Of two other magazines in the same field, one brings nearly twice as many inquiries to the advertiser per dollar expended for space, but these inquiries are of a lower grade and are found by advertisers who sell direct to the consumer to cost nearly twice as much to convert into sales as those of the other magazine.

Publications are constantly devising methods of sustaining and increasing reader interest. They may do this by expressing strong opinions which appeal to a particular class; they may offer cash prizes for articles or letters from subscribers telling of their experiences; they may distribute prizes for correct or best answers to contests which will lead to increase in circulation and to increase in reader interest.

The booklet published by the Audit Bureau of Circulations entitled "Scientific Space Selection" points out five indications of reader interest:

> 1. The subscription or single-copy price is sometimes an indication of reader interest. High price with small circulation would point to intense reader interest. High price and large circulation would suggest considerable merit in the publication. Low price and large circulation would indicate a general appeal with many classes of readers included. It is also of importance to note whether annual subscription prices are maintained when subscription is made for a number of years. If this price reduction is offered for reasons of economy to the publisher, it may be regarded as good business.

2. The second point is to consider whether inducements were offered in addition to the publication itself. If no premiums or other inducements were offered, then the conclusion would be that the periodical was bought for itself alone. If premiums were offered, it is important to see how large a part of the circulation was obtained in this manner.

3. The methods used by the publication in obtaining its circulation should be scrutinized from the standpoint of reader interest. Did the subscriber buy the publication because he wanted it, or because he was persuaded to do so by clever salesmanship?

4. Does the publication hold strictly to its price in dealing with subscribers, and does it stop subscriptions as soon as they have run out?

5. It is sometimes important to ascertain whether the publication is the official organ of some association. In this case, it is desirable to determine whether the members subscribe to the publication optionally, or whether the subscription is a part of their membership dues.

To measure the reader's interest in Metropolitan Life Insurance advertising, the *Literary Digest* sent a letter to subscribers asking whether they remembered having read and noted one or more of recent Metropolitan advertisements. Tabulation of replies showed that 75.4 per cent definitely remembered Metropolitan copy. This copy, of course, was particularly suited to the *Literary Digest,* as it dealt with news and facts.

The *Literary Digest* places high value on its Thermometer Test (described elsewhere) as a guide to reader interest. Another guide is the responsiveness to questionnaires. Thus in a certain test, the readers of Magazine A responded twice as well as the readers of Magazine B. The *Literary Digest* questionnnaires are usually expected to draw from 35 to 60 per cent. This betokens a high degree of reader interest.

Reader Confidence

The questions of editorial policy, reader interest, and reader confidence merge into each other gradually. One of the points any advertiser wants to find out about a medium is the degree of confidence its readers have in it. While this is closely tied up with reader interest, there is a definite limitation in the interest shown by the reader. As Harry Tipper, General Sales Manager of the General Motors Export Company, points out, surface attention is not depth of interest. Unless the reader is vitally interested in the magazine and believes in the information which it presents, he is not going to give the advertising columns more than cursory notice. He notes further that it would hardly pay to advertise a business in a golf magazine because the readers of this golf magazine are so interested in their special subject that they would pass by anything unconnected with golf.

Some periodicals maintain service bureaus for their subscribers. The degree to which these service bureaus are utilized will give some indication of the valuation placed upon the periodical by the reader. For example, *Cosmopolitan* inaugurated a motoring service in December, 1921. While intended to promote interest in automotive subjects, it also was employed to prove the interest of car owners and prospective car owners among *Cosmopolitan* readers. Inquiries from readers of the Motoring Service Page were invited, and 21 booklets were edited to answer readers' requests. In three years' time, 43,000 inquiries were received from readers, 95.6 per cent from men and 4.4 per cent from women.

Rate of Response

It is important to be able to estimate the rate of response to any advertisement inserted in a given medium. This is possible in direct selling by mail to a surprising degree. Much less attention has been paid to the same problem as applied to various types of publications.

G. Lynn Sumner, writing in the *Advertising and Selling Fortnightly,* contends that too little consideration is given to the life of a given periodical, that is, the period during which that magazine gives its advertisers a chance for attention from readers. While admitting that the life of a newspaper is but a few hours, the intensity of the message is greater than in the magazine which supposedly lives for a week or a month, and which may be gone through a number of times in leisurely inspection. Figure 103 shows the results he obtained from running keyed advertising in the various types of media—Sunday newspapers (magazine section), general weeklies, fiction weeklies, general monthlies, fiction monthlies, women's magazines, and fashion quarterlies.

FIG. 103.—AN INVESTIGATION OF RATE OF RESPONSE

Rate of Response on Seven Classes of Media

	Percentage of Total Inquiries Received within				
	10 Days	30 Days	90 Days	6 Months	1 Year
Sunday newspapers (magazine section)	81.4	94.8	98.7	99.3	99.8
General weeklies	44.2	74.1	89.7	84.8	99.0
Fiction weeklies	23.2	51.8	79.4	90.0	97.4
General monthlies	10.2	45.6	78.7	90.9	97.9
Fiction monthlies	11.5	42.3	76.1	89.7	98.0
Women's magazines	17.6	60.3	91.8	95.8	98.5
Fashion quarterlies	3.2	14.9	66.7	89.8	98.2

This table indicates in a general way the velocity of response which is brought about by various types of advertising media. The total volume is not indicated here and may mean something entirely different to the individual advertiser, but here at least is the order in which he may expect his returns to come in following the original advertising insertion.

The Sunday newspaper was more than 80 per cent finished in 10 days. General weeklies produced 44 per cent of total inquiries during the first 10 days, while the fiction weeklies showed only 23 per cent. At the end of three months, fiction weeklies were still producing inquiries. Women's magazines, perhaps because of the style and fashion elements, received 60 per cent of their inquiries during the first 30 days.

Mr. Sumner points out that the data in the chart, compiled from use of all these media by International Correspondence Schools and the Woman's Institute, show nothing about the value of the various media, but merely indicate the velocity of response. One type of medium might produce twice as many inquiries within the first 10 days as another produced within that period, yet fail in the end to produce an equal number of inquiries over a longer period.

Computing Life of Publications

A different method of investigation was used by R. O. Eastman, who checked up the magazines received at a junk dealer's establishment in Cleveland. Here magazines were received in carloads, bales broken in the car, and magazines delivered to stock rooms on a conveyor belt. Men were stationed along this belt and recorded name and date of issue of magazines on the "run-of-mine" principle. Since 4 per cent of the magazines were one month old or less, it was evident little time had elapsed since the magazines had been gathered. Returns from news-stands were not included, nor were magazines coming in file order, showing that they had been kept for some time. Allowance should also be made for the time that elapsed between the time the magazines were put aside for the call of the junk dealer and the actual time when he took them.

Weeklies were checked according to month and not week of issue. Of the 2,307 publications checked, 24 per cent were issued prior to 1924, and it was assumed that the active life of such magazines had passed. Hence they were not counted in figuring the age of publication. The principal reasons for keeping magazines are the following:

1. General carelessness in not discarding them when finished with them
2. General value, or feeling that magazine is too good to throw away, whether it is used or not
3. Kept for definite reference, as for patterns or recipes
4. Saving up continued stories
5. Decoration of reading tables
6. Date of issue of no significance, as in the case of the *National Geographic*

Mr. Eastman draws certain inferences from the data tabulated in Figure 104 [1]: The average useful life, with all classes of magazines, is not more than six months. Only one

[1] *Advertising and Selling Fortnightly.*

magazine out of six is discarded in less than three months, about one-third in less than six months, one-half in less than nine months, and two-thirds in less than one year. One-third of the magazines, whether they serve any purpose or not, seem to be kept for a year.

The ranking of age is in the following order: (1) farm and garden magazines; (2) women's and style magazines; (3) general monthlies; (4) story and movie magazines; (5) weeklies; (6) fraternal publications. There is less disparity in the age of women's publications than in other groups. The average life of weeklies approaches that of monthlies more nearly than might be expected. Certain publications, the contents of which do not get out of date, are kept longer than the average.

Merchandising Effectiveness

Merchandising effectiveness is a broad and comprehensive term, generally covering the willingness of the publication to coöperate with advertisers, and its ability to be of concrete assistance in matters of sales promotion. According to the Coolidge Advertising Agency, a publication should give information about trade conditions in the territory or in the field which it serves. The special representative who is most welcome is the one who can intelligently discuss marketing methods and market data with respect to the particular account which he is soliciting. The representative who devotes from 15 minutes to an hour to an argument as to why his paper has a few more subscribers than the other paper in the field is not so welcome as the representative who can tell how the market for a certain product, whether it is a saddle, a box of shoe polish, or a package of breakfast food, is best reached in his particular territory.

A point of interest to be noted in an investigation of the agency attitude towards periodical media is the growing willingness of the periodical to coöperate in merchandising. That is, the publication which can produce concrete facts about its market in relation to a definite product is going to be more seriously considered than the medium which can produce data

FIG. 104.—AN INVESTIGATION OF THE LIFE OF PERIODICALS

Average Age of Periodicals by Groups:

The weighted average represents the aggregate number of months of age divided by the number of publications counted. The mode is the age most frequently found. The ratio is the percentage that the weighted average of the group is of the average age of all publications counted.

Group	Number Counted	Weighted Average	Mode	Ratio
7 weeklies	716	5.7 mos.	2 mos.	90
15 woman's and style	455	7.0 mos.	7 mos.	111
12 general monthly	291	6.6 mos.	6 mos.	105
16 story and movie	121	6.1 mos.	2 mos.	97
6 farm and garden	56	7.6 mos. *	5 mos.	120
7 fraternal	35	4.6 mos.	2 mos.	73

* The greater age of farm and garden publications may be due to the fact that junk is gathered less frequently in smaller towns and rural sections.

Average Age of Individual Publications

These figures are given in group divisions for sake of comparison, with the average figure for the group repeated. Only publications counted ten or more times (issues for 1924 and 1925) are listed. The ratio figures represent the percentage that the average age of the individual magazine is to the average age of its class. Figures in parenthesis are the numbers of times counted.

Publication	Weighted Average	Mode	Ratio to Average for Group
WEEKLIES	5.7 mos.	2 mos.	....
Saturday Evening Post (406)	5.3 mos.	2 mos.	95
Literary Digest (103)	6.1 mos.	4 mos.	109
Collier's (96)	7.0 mos.	7 mos.	125
Liberty (79)	4.2 mos.	1 mo.	75
Judge (17)	5.4 mos.	4 mos.	96
Life (12)	5.8 mos.	5 mos.	103
Christian Herald (13)	11.9 mos.	11 mos.	208
WOMAN'S AND STYLE	7.0 mos.	7 mos.	....
Ladies' Home Journal (99)	7.6 mos.	7 mos.	110
Woman's Home Companion (72)	7.1 mos.	7 mos.	101
Delineator (72)	6.9 mos.	9 mos.	98
Pictorial Review (49)	7.2 mos.	5 mos.	103
McCall's (53)	7.3 mos.	7 mos.	104
Good Housekeeping (33)	6.1 mos.	6 mos.	87
People's Home Journal (16)	5.8 mos.	3 mos.	83
Harper's Bazar (13)	9.1 mos.	10 mos.	130
GENERAL MONTHLY MAGAZINES	6.6 mos.	6 mos.	....
American (100)	6.6 mos.	3 mos.	100
Red Book (39)	5.5 mos.	3 mos.	83
True Story (49)	5.5 mos.	3 mos.	83
Cosmopolitan (45)	6.8 mos.	....	103
Everybody's (17)	6.9 mos.	....	104
OTHERS COUNTED OVER 10 TIMES:			
Motion Picture News (11)	8.3 mos.	5 mos.	132
Photoplay (12)	7.3 mos.	....	116
Country Gentleman (19)	8.3 mos.	6 mos.	132
Farm Journal (12)	8.0 mos.	7 mos.	127
Elk's Magazine * (15)	5.1 mos.	1 mo.	81

* Probably the reason why fraternal publications are at the bottom of the list lies in their complete coverage of the fraternal group and hence the lack of necessity for passing such magazines along.

FIG. 104.—*Continued*

Percentage of Magazines Kept for Different Periods

The first division in the table which follows is of magazines counted 50 times or more; the second division of magazines counted from 19 to 50 times; the third division counted 10 to 18 times. Percentages can be accepted as indicative only as applied to the second and third groups.

Publication	Less than 3 Months, Per Cent	Over 3 Months, Per Cent	Over 6 Months, Per Cent	Over 9 Months, Per Cent	Over 12 Months, Per Cent
AVERAGE FOR ALL	16	84	65	49	34
1. *Saturday Evening Post*	25	75	48	32	18
Literary Digest	15	85	64	53	42
American	15	85	69	56	39
Ladies' Home Journal	7	93	82	54	34
Woman's Home Companion	11	89	75	61	46
Collier's	12	88	68	34	19
Delineator	9	91	71	55	34
Liberty	40	60	30	10	......
Pictorial Review	3	97	72	54	36
McCall's	6	94	73	56	34
Red Book	11	89	63	38	28
True Story	22	78	53	34	20
Cosmopolitan	16	84	60	46	26
2. *Good Housekeeping*	13	87	67	48	37
Country Gentleman	......	100	71	56	42
Farm Journal	9	91	76	69	60
People's Home Journal	17	83	64	51	34
Everybody's	21	79	53	47	36
National Geographic	5	95	95	78	73
Judge	21	79	41	36	10
3. *Harper's Bazar*	6	94	87	81	43
System	17	83	76	69	63
House and Garden	12	88	83	47	47
Motion Picture News	6	84	76	70	53
Elk's Magazine	31	69	44	24	12
Metropolitan	......	100	100	74	47
Outlook	......	100	100	100	100*
Photoplay	14	86	78	42	28
American Boy	......	100	100	100	100*
Review of Reviews	7	93	93	78	42
Christian Herald	......	100	100	100	62
Life	8	92	92	32	16
Success, Farming	......	100	92	76	42
Radio News	8	92	92	84	59
People's Popular Monthly	26	74	66	40	32
Wide World	......	100	90	81	81
Vogue	18	82	45	36	36
True Romances	30	70	50	40	20
Needlecraft	30	70	70	60	40
Physical Culture	20	80	80	60	40

* There were 14 copies counted of each of these two publications, all over 12 months old.

of a general nature only. One of the factors to be considered, therefore, is the specific nature of the information given by the publication as to its coverage of the market for a particular product.

Other Factors Affecting the Advertising Value of Media

One of the factors which may have considerable effect upon the selection of media is the mechanical make-up of the publication. Some periodicals use better grades of paper and ink than their competitors, which will allow the advertiser to make use of better art work. Another factor of importance is the size of the page. In one instance, a large concern weighs the value of various magazines, starting with the cost per page in the cities of such size as it must reach, and multiplying this figure by the number of pages of the magazine and the size of the page.

The effect of the volume of advertising carried by a periodical in proportion to the reading matter is a moot point. It is evident that increasing size in the advertising section decreases the attention value of the individual page. This makes it necessary for the advertiser to devise some means of attracting attention to his advertisement, such as the use of color, expensive art work, or other expedients. In a magazine with large advertising content, this factor must be considered in relation to circulation factors. If the advertisement will not be noted, the circulation of the periodical will have little effect.

Sometimes a periodical divides its editorial matter into departments, so that a given class of advertisement will be placed near reading matter which pertains to the same subject. Such a division might well prove a deciding factor between two media otherwise evenly matched.

There is a growing tendency among advertisers to doubt the efficacy of the publisher's argument as to volume of advertising carried, and to lay greater stress upon the degree of reader interest. Many publications, of course, maintain a certain ratio between editorial and advertising matter, but this ratio differs widely.

Another factor in advertising value, stressed especially by the Curtis Publications, is that the lower the price of a publication, the greater its value as an advertising medium. The reduction of the *Ladies' Home Journal* from 15 cents to 10 cents was emphasized as of great benefit to advertisers. The question immediately enters as to the vital effect of such a change in price to the advertiser. If more people buy the magazine because it is cheap, will this added circulation be of a type which are logical purchasers of the advertiser's wares? Or will advertising in a competitive woman's magazine, which maintains the 15 cent price, be equally or more effective?

The cost of printing and distributing such a magazine as the *Ladies' Home Journal* is probably around 40 cents for each copy. The difference between this cost price and the selling price of 10 cents must be borne by the advertiser and ultimately by the consumer. It is necessary for the advertiser to decide for himself whether his product is one that will benefit materially from the increase in circulation gained by lowering a low price to a still lower figure, and whether he is justified in paying the additional advertising rate based on the increased circulation which the publisher hopes the reduction will bring about.

Circulation Factors

Statistics in regard to the circulation of any given medium, when properly classified and arranged, should show four fundamental facts:

1. *Circulation statistics* will indicate how many buyers of the periodical there are. Figures may be obtained from the Audit Bureau of Circulations.

2. The *distribution of circulation* geographically will tabulate subscribers and buyers according to section of the country, and also acording to urban and rural residence.

3. The *readers* of the magazine, that is, the circulation treated individually, will be classified in a wide number of ways, depending on the important factors. Sex, age, influence, wealth, buying power, occupation, business position, and special

interests of any kind are among the ordinary bases of classification.

4. The various factors will be analyzed in relation to the *cost* to the advertiser, so that one medium in the same field may be compared with competing media.

These four primary tabulations can be subdivided and compared with each other in a number of ways. The aim is always to show how a particular medium is best suited to cover a

FIG. 105.—METHODS OF CIRCULATION ANALYSIS

Circulation Compared with Literate Population

State	Total White Literate Population	Total White Literate Families	*True Story* Circulation	Per Cent of White Literate Families Reached by *True Story*	*True Story* Read by One White Literate Family in Every
Alabama	973,208	324,402	10,368	2.9	32
Arizona	149,642	49,880	4,923	10	10
Arkansas	884,063	294,687	12,503	4.2	24
California	2,066,420	688,803	98,276	14	7

Circulation Compared with Income Tax Returns

	S. E. P.	L. H. J.	C. G.	Total	Personal Income Tax Returns
U. S. Total	2,353,266	2,180,650	804,023	5,337,939	7,685,900
New England	212,638	203,225	51,826	467,689	738,948
Maine	17,317	20,764	14,081	52,162	48,435
New Hampshire	10,587	11,938	4,642	27,167	36,876
Vermont	8,947	10,474	4,509	23,930	21,752
Massachusetts	120,661	106,032	18,604	245,297	415,100
Rhode Island	14,490	13,836	2,242	30,568	66,965
Connecticut	40,636	40,181	7,748	88,565	149,820
Middle Atlantic	577,342	515,501	127,406	1,220,249	2,255,635
New York	317,553	231,557	57,780	606,890	1,221,654
New Jersey	78,830	83,640	15,152	177,622	293,503
Pennsylvania	180,959	200,304	54,474	435,737	740,478
South Atlantic	191,819	200,262	62,941	455,022	606,830
Delaware	4,846	5,638	1,284	11,768	19,202
Maryland	26,236	30,591	6,824	63,651	127,770
District of Columbia	21,210	18,300	1,398	40,908	75,796
Virginia	25,439	32,441	14,913	72,793	77,451
West Virginia	19,384	21,701	6,087	47,172	89,263
North Carolina	21,111	26,417	14,498	62,026	68,191
South Carolina	10,882	12,351	6,161	29,394	28,225
Georgia	23,303	23,951	7,270	54,524	71,341
Florida	39,408	28,872	4,506	72,786	49,591
East North Central	508,916	476,294	183,112	1,168,322	1,862,459
Ohio	145,588	135,934	51,857	333,379	463,017
Indiana	62,107	67,512	29,491	159,110	178,831

FIG. 105.—*Continued*

Comparison of Subscription and News-Stand Circulation in Towns of Various Sizes

	Sub-scription	News-stand	Total	Sub-scription	News-stand	Total
	500,001 and Over			100,001—500,000		
Maine	...	...	...	...	...	...
New Hampshire	...	...	...	...	...	...
Vermont	...	...	...	...	...	...
Massachusetts	5,007	17,703	22,710	1,650	6,245	7,895
Rhode Island	...	...	...	884	3,516	4,400
Connecticut	...	...	...	2,336	6,287	8,623
New England	*5,007*	*17,703*	*22,710*	*4,870*	*16,048*	*20,918*
New York	21,040	71,927	92,967	3,756	10,708	14,464
New Jersey	...	...	...	4,257	10,821	15,078
Pennsylvania	14,225	31,929	46,154	2,008	5,469	7,477
Middle Atlantic	*35,265*	*103,856*	*139,121*	*10,021*	*26,998*	*37,019*
	25,000—100,000			10,000—25,000		
Maine	439	2,714	3,153	220	773	993
New Hampshire	181	848	1,029	258	1,346	1,604
Vermont	...	...	...	195	827	1,022
Massachusetts	1,213	4,902	6,115	1,232	3,256	4,488
Rhode Island	339	1,266	1,605	10	44	54
Connecticut	1,063	3,089	4,152	900	1,937	2,837
New England	*3,235*	*12,819*	*16,054*	*2,815*	*8,183*	*10,998*
New York	3,680	12,783	16,463	3,027	7,193	10,220
New Jersey	2,881	8,045	10,926	1,772	3,822	5,594
Pennsylvania	4,108	12,501	16,609	3,687	9,950	13,637
Middle Atlantic	*10,669*	*33,329*	*43,998*	*8,486*	*20,965*	*29,451*
	2,500—10,000			1,000—2,500		
Maine	422	1,458	1,880	314	827	1,141
New Hampshire	169	532	701	180	642	822
Vermont	331	932	1,263	212	489	701
Massachusetts	1,146	2,238	3,384	478	805	1,283
Rhode Island	160	278	438	57	78	135
Connecticut	713	1,139	1,852	452	408	860
New England	*2,941*	*6,577*	*9,518*	*1,693*	*3,249*	*4,942*
New York	3,477	5,816	9,293	1,913	3,925	5,838
New Jersey	2,517	3,478	5,995	662	641	1,303
Pennsylvania	4,951	9,111	14,062	1,986	2,917	4,903
Middle Atlantic	*10,945*	*18,405*	*29,350*	*4,561*	*7,483*	*12,044*
	Under 1,000			State Total		
Maine	436	397	833	1,831	6,169	8,000
New Hampshire	231	241	472	1,019	3,609	4,628
Vermont	325	242	567	1,063	2,490	3,553
Massachusetts	638	336	974	11,364	35,485	46,849
Rhode Island	148	40	188	1,598	5,222	6,820
Connecticut	434	377	811	5,898	13,237	19,135
New England	*2,212*	*1,633*	*3,845*	*22,773*	*66,212*	*88,985*
New York	3,601	2,834	6,435	40,494	115,186	155,680
New Jersey	1,221	651	1,872	13,310	27,458	40,768
Pennsylvania	2,892	1,310	4,202	33,857	73,187	107,044
Middle Atlantic	*7,714*	*4,795*	*12,509*	*87,661*	*215,831*	*303,492*

particular market. Knowing the market by analysis and the publication through similar statistics as to its coverage of the market, the advertiser is in a position to determine whether that particular medium is read by the type of individual who buys his product.

The number of buyers of a magazine, of course, rarely indicates the number of readers. In addition to the paid circulation, the medium has a secondary circulation which is difficult to ascertain, but which undoubtedly exercises considerable influence on the value of the particular medium. Among the foci of these secondary circulations are the library, the barber shop, and the physician's office.

Circulation Classifications

Practically all magazine circulation must be analyzed geographically and then subdivided according to the other factors included in the classification. Figure 105 shows a number of methods of circulation analysis used by publishers. In analyzing such statistics, it is essential to remember that such publications are presenting their figures in a way most favorable to themselves. This does not mean that the statistics are inaccurate, but that they are tabulated in such a way as to display the periodical to best advantage. In comparing a number of media, a common denominator of measurement should be found.

The first classification in the figure divides the population of the various states according to literate population and literate white families. It then shows the percentage of literate white families which read the magazine. The objection to this is that it is extremely difficult to determine the number of literate white families, from existing sources of information.

The second classification divides the country into sections and states, and compares the circulation of the magazine in each state and group of states with the personal income tax returns, the object here being to show the value of the media as indexes of purchasing power. It is interesting to note in addition that three separate media are added together in the

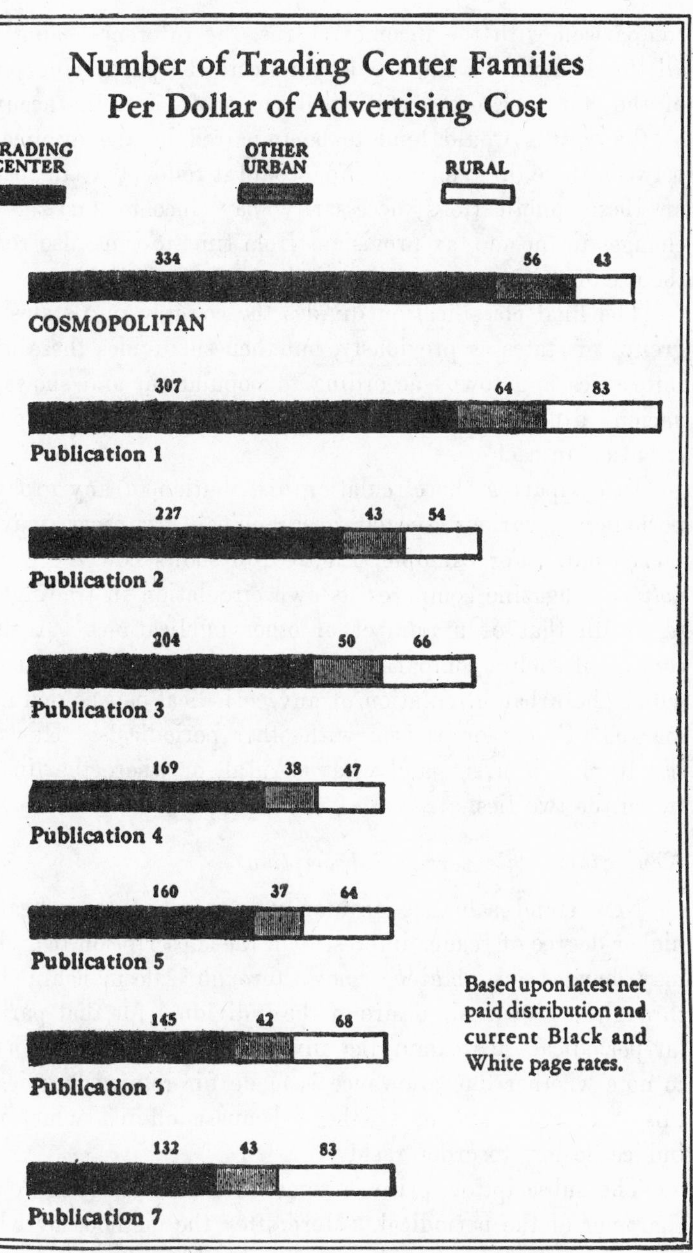

FIG. 106. CIRCULATION IN TRADING CENTERS

comparison with the income returns, the inference being tha all three should be employed to indicate the purchasing powe of the state. From a statistical point of view, the accurac of the results would tend to be impaired by the duplicatio between these three media. Nor would it follow that all reader of these publications necessarily pay income taxes. Th changes in income tax provisions from time to time also rende the use of the income tax as an index rather unreliable.

The final classification divides the country into states an groups of states as previously, but then subdivides these agai into cities and towns according to population, and shows th various differences between news-stand and subscription dis tribution in each case.

In comparing the circulation distribution of any group o periodicals, various special geographical groupings may b picked out. For example, Figure 106 shows how the *Cosmo politan* Magazine compares its own circulation in trading cen ters with that of a number of other publications. A short coming of such a comparison is that it provides no measure b which the urban circulation of any periodical can be definitel marked off for comparison with other periodicals. Nor doe it tell what is urban and what is rural, or where the line be tween the two lies.

News-Stand Sale versus Subscription

News-stand sale has ordinarily been taken to indicate higher degree of reader interest than the subscription list whic may have been obtained more through salesmanship tha through any intrinsic desire of the individual for that particu lar periodical. In examining any such figures, it is importan to note whether due allowance is made for returned copies, i this practice is used, or whether a bonus is offered, which ma induce dealers to order rashly.

The subscription price is sometimes an indication of th character of the periodical. More often the methods by whic the subscriptions were obtained will be the criterion. A grea many types of bait are used by media to obtain circulation

One of the commonest expedients is to use premiums. Hence, the percentage of subscribers obtained through premiums must be taken into consideration. Another method is to employ canvassers. Subscriptions may be made part of club offers, with certain material inducements.

Some periodicals find it necessary to maintain a constant series of contests in order to keep reader interest at high ebb and to keep circulation from falling. Periodicals running such contests should be examined to determine whether the emphasis is being placed on the contents of the periodical or whether interest is devoted entirely to the outcome of the contest. In the latter case, the value of the medium for advertising might be questioned.

The percentage of renewals, included on A. B. C. reports, is sometimes more of an index of reader interest than the entire subscription list. Some publications follow a policy of trial subscriptions. If considerable price discount is allowed, the resulting artificial increase in circulation might not be due to interest in the publication so much as desire to obtain a bargain.

Reader Characteristics

There are a great number of reader characteristics which may be analyzed in reference to a particular periodical. Some of these, such as income, or ownership of automobiles, or home equipment, indicate the buying power of the subscribers. Other characteristics, such as age, sex, character, occupation, or special interest, indicate the special fitness for a given medium to supply the conditions of adequate coverage.

Many publications are fully aware of the importance of securing such data in regard to their readers, and have adopted various methods of obtaining them, including the interview and the questionnaire. Figure 107 shows a method used by the *Literary Digest.* The purpose here was to find out the occupation of the readers, the number, sex, and age of *Digest* readers in a family, and the most popular magazine among the women of the family of a given number listed. In regard to this latter

QUESTIONNAIRE LETTER

The Literary Digest

Funk and Wagnalls Company, Publishers
354-360 Fourth Avenue
New York

Office of
THE VICE-PRESIDENT

March 21, 1924

Dear Subscriber:

It will give me pleasure to do a little friendly favor for you in return for your courtesy in answering this letter.

One of the important duties I am asked to perform as Vice-President is to keep in touch with the great public who make up the members of The Literary Digest family.

To know what path in life our readers pursue is of great value to us in the editing and promotion of our magazine. Also, does The Digest interest both father and mother? Is it read by the young people?

You will note that we offer to send to you without cost as a token of our appreciation of your courtesy a copy of "Faulty Diction", a helpful booklet containing invaluable information on the use of correct English.

With grateful appreciation of your favor, I am

Cordially yours,

W. J. Funk

Question No. 1

A. Please state your Business, Profession or other Occupation.

Cotton Seed - Products

Manufacturing

(Write on top line the *kind* of business, such as Automobile, Furniture, Drug, etc. On the second line, write the branch of the business, such as Manufacturing, Wholesaling, Retailing, etc. If Farming, state *branch* such as Grain, Produce, Dairy, etc. If engaged in Mining, state whether Ore, Coal, Oil, etc. If not in a business, state profession, such as Artist, Clergyman, Educator, Lawyer, Physician; or other occupation, such as Student, Retired, etc.).

B. Please state your Work or Position

V. P. & Gen Mgr.

(Are you a Member of a Firm, Official, Superintendent, Salesman, Advertising Manager, Buyer, Engineer (Civil, Electrical, etc.), Mechanic, Clerk, Bookkeeper or in other position).

Question No. 2

Please check below the number of Digest readers in your family.

Number of Women ... 1
Number of Men ... 1
Number of Girls (Under 17) ... 1
Number of Boys (Under 17) ... 1

Question No. 3

Which of the magazines listed below is most popular with the <u>women</u> of your family?

Vote for one only

....Delineator
....Good Housekeeping
....Ladies Home Journal
✓ Literary Digest ✓
....McCall's Magazine
....Pictorial Review
....Woman's Home Companion
....

Send Complimentary copy of "Faulty Diction" to this address.

Name T. W. McDonald
Street 1633 Victoria Ave
Town Los Angeles
State Cal.

Fig. 107. How One Magazine Learned About Its Constituency

Through the sale of books advertised in the pamphlet offered as a reward, the entire investigation paid for itself.

question, as explained earlier in this volume, the fact that the questionnaire was sent out under the letterhead of the *Literary Digest* would presumably tend to prejudice returns in its favor.

In order to check this point up, the same question was sent out on a card bearing the name Archibald M. Crossley, Box

103, Madison Square Station, New York City, instead of the *Literary Digest.* The results were found to check accurately.

The result of this survey was to give the *Literary Digest* definite information in regard to its subscribers. A total of 34,670 replies were received for classification. In 1922, 207,000 were sent out and 90,000 tabulated; in 1924, 100,000 sent out and 34,670 tabulated. There were 183 occupation groups, subdivided for executives and subordinates. The occupation analysis allows the *Literary Digest* to state definitely the number of readers which may be considered as direct prospects for a given advertiser, and to figure the page cost on that basis. A great deal of advertising solicitation is done on this basis. A company's direct *Digest* market is analyzed, as well as distributors of each class and advisory influences. Then sometimes it can be shown that the *Digest* reaches more of an advertiser's market at less cost than is possible through a group of trade papers.

Figure 108 shows the density of subscribers to the *Literary Digest* compared with the density of telephone subscribers, indicating the close correlation between the two. This has already been mentioned, the chart being included here to show how distribution and character of circulation have been analyzed to give a complete picture.

Figure 109 illustrates two methods of using the ownership of an automobile as an index of purchasing power. In the upper tabulation there seems to be no allowance made for ownership of two cars. In the second tabulation the *Rotarian* seeks to prove that its circulation is above the average because, of 618 Rotarians questioned, 583 owned 682 automobiles.

Figure 110 is interesting, when compared with the *Literary Digest* questionnaire. This was sent to 10,000 names, taken from the list at random. No inducement was given for a reply beyond the enclosure of a stamped return envelope.

Figure 111 illustrates a third questionnaire, used by *Physical Culture* to obtain information from subscribers. The method of investigation is interesting. Over 44 per cent of the 5,000 questionnaires mailed were returned. To ensure a rep-

Density of Telephone Subscribers in the United States Compared With Density of The Literary Digest Circulation

This map shows the percentage of telephone subscribers in each of the various groups of states and the percentage of Literary Digest subscriptions in each of these groups.

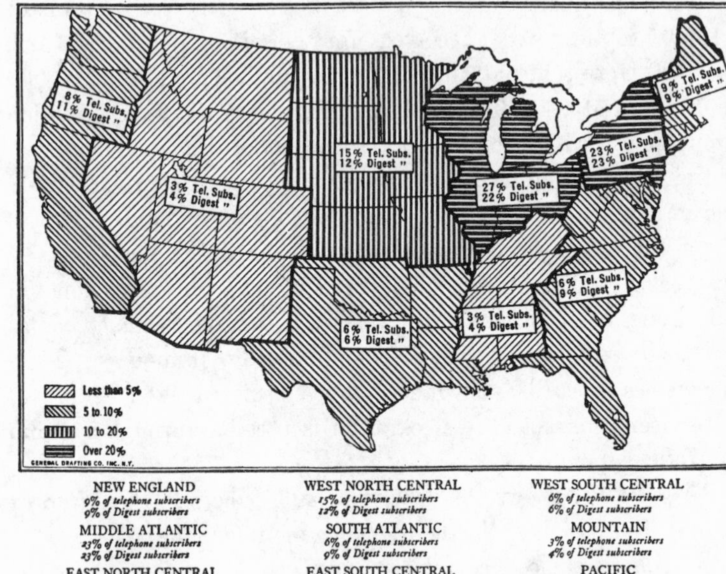

NEW ENGLAND
9% of telephone subscribers
9% of Digest subscribers

MIDDLE ATLANTIC
23% of telephone subscribers
23% of Digest subscribers

EAST NORTH CENTRAL
27% of telephone subscribers
22% of Digest subscribers

WEST NORTH CENTRAL
15% of telephone subscribers
12% of Digest subscribers

SOUTH ATLANTIC
6% of telephone subscribers
9% of Digest subscribers

EAST SOUTH CENTRAL
3% of telephone subscribers
4% of Digest subscribers

WEST SOUTH CENTRAL
6% of telephone subscribers
6% of Digest subscribers

MOUNTAIN
3% of telephone subscribers
4% of Digest subscribers

PACIFIC
8% of telephone subscribers
11% of Digest subscribers

A NINE-YEAR CAMPAIGN

The telephone market is the largest group of progressive purchasers that can be clearly defined, set apart, and reached directly.

During the past nine years, The Literary Digest has made 24 separate circular mailings to telephone subscribers, costing approximately $5,000,000. That nine-year campaign has been called the greatest selling achievement in the history of magazine publishing, for it has been the center of development in the sale to more than a million people of a weekly periodical at ten cents a copy, or $4.00 a year.

So large a distribution for a periodical at so high a price per year has never been obtained elsewhere.

There are in the United States 15,370,000 telephones. There are 12,000,000 telephone subscribers. For the purposes of The Digest, corporations and big business firms were omitted from the circularizing lists, the aim being to reach the homes of the individuals.

The Digest's telephone mailing list, therefore, contains the names of the 8,162,386 individuals who have telephones listed in their own names.

We present the above map as evidence of our success in building circulation among telephone subscribers in every section. WHERE A TELEPHONE GOES SO GOES THE LITERARY DIGEST!

Fig. 108. Circulation Compared with a Market Index

resentative division of replies, 8 per cent of the *Physical Culture* subscribers in each state were sent questionnaires. In addition, an advertisement was inserted in *Physical Culture* asking readers to write for the questionnaires. About 3,000 did so. A copy of the *Physical Culture Food Directory* was given in return for a filled-out questionnaire. The effective

Fig. 109.—Illustrations of the Use of Motor Car Ownership as an Index of Purchasing Power

1. (*Cosmopolitan*)

More than 28,000 of the 43,000 readers of *Cosmopolitan* who have written to *Cosmopolitan's* Motoring Service, named the makes of cars they own. It is interesting to compare an analysis of cars owned by *Cosmopolitan* readers with the United States' production during the last three years.

Of the passenger cars produced in 1921–1923, only 23.3% sold for $1,000 or more. An analysis of the cars owned by 28,000 readers of *Cosmopolitan*, show that 57.0% are in this price class.

	Owned by *Cosmopolitan* Readers	U. S. Production for 3 Years
Cars costing over $2000	7.5%	3.8%
Cars costing $1000 to $2000	49.5	19.5
Cars costing less than $1000	43	76.7

II. (*The Rotarian*)

Make of Car	Under $1000	$1000 to $2500	Over $2500	Make of Car	Under $1000	$1000 to $2500	Over $2500
Buick		106		Pierce-Arrow			3
Ford	75			Durant		3	
Studebaker		70		Stephens		3	
Dodge		63		Star	3		
Cadillac			42	Cole		2	
Hudson		39		Gardner		2	
Packard			29	Stearns		2	
Nash		24		Wills-St. Claire			2
Franklin			23	Kissel		2	
Willys-Knight		21		Apperson			2
Chevrolet	13			Dort		2	
Essex	12			King		1	
Paige		11		Velie		1	
Hupmobile		11		Elgin		1	
Chandler		10		R. & L. Electric		1	
Reo		9		Mitchell		1	
Marmon			9	Stutz			1
Overland	9			Case		1	
Jordan		8		White		1	
Peerless			8	Winton			1
Lincoln			7	Liberty		1	
Auburn		6		Locomobile			1
Oldsmobile	6			Murray		1	
Haynes		6		LaFayette			1
Oakland		5		Elcar			1
Jewett		5		National		1	
Maxwell	4			Bour-Davis		1	
Chalmers		4		Detroit-Electric		1	
Cleveland		4					
				Totals	122	431	129

Note.—In many cases the Ford was listed as a secondary car.

-3-

Success
The HUMAN Magazine
FOUNDED 1898 by Dr ORISON SWETT MARDEN

WALTER HOFF SEELY
EDITOR
CLARE E. MARDEN
ASSOCIATE EDITOR

251 FOURTH AVENUE
NEW YORK
GRAMERCY 6221

SUCCESS READER REFERENDUM

Explanation: SUCCESS is your magazine. In planning its content each month, I have only one thought in mind, and that is to give you the very best of those things that you want. But sometimes it is very difficult to decide just what are your desires, so I am trying to visualize you, for if I know the kind of man or woman you are, I can have a clearer idea of what SUCCESS ought to contain. Hence this, your referendum, my reader friend.

Walter Hoff Seely
Editor.

Sex

Age

Married Single (Check one)

Profession or Business What position do you occupy?

Do you own your home? Is it lighted by electricity?

Do you own an automobile? What make? Do you own a radio?

In what way has SUCCESS been of help to you?

What features of SUCCESS interest you most? (for example: stories of successful people, feature articles by Ellis Parker Butler or other writers, inspirational editorials, fiction, humorous section, pictorial section.)

Who else besides yourself reads your copy of SUCCESS?

What improvements or additions do you suggest to SUCCESS?

What other magazines do you read?

If you read other magazines what do find they have that SUCCESS lacks?

FIG. 110. ANOTHER QUESTIONNAIRE TO MAGAZINE READERS
Here no inducement to reply is offered.

returns from this questionnaire were presumably due to the great reader interest of subscribers in this publication.

The survey revealed that 71 per cent of the circulation was male, 55 per cent married, 43 per cent families with children,

23 per cent skilled workers, 13 per cent business owners and executives, 10 per cent agriculturists, 10 per cent professionals, 31 per cent own automobiles, etc. It is interesting to note that 34 per cent kept permanent files of the magazine.

An interesting analysis had been made by one of the large automobile companies of the reading habits of owners of automobiles. Readers here are divided into groups, not according to income or to the type of magazine read, or by any of the orthodox plans, but according to the type of car they drive. This is working from the product rather than from the market, or from anything less specific. One of the studies, for instance, shows what sort of magazines are read by owners of a certain make of car, and people of the same general income group. In this case it was found that six magazines per family were read. The aim of the investigation was to find out how to reach such people in the most effective manner, and the cost of reaching them through the magazines.

The method used was unusual. First, it was determined by means of a questionnaire mailed to car owners what percentage of them read each of the various magazines on a given list of about 35. The cost of reaching 1 per cent of the market for this car through each one of the magazines was then computed. This was done by using the page rates for advertising as given on the rate cards. Then, in order to test a theory that the more advertising the magazine carried, the less effective each advertisement might be, the proportion of advertising to reading matter in each magazine was calculated by actually counting and averaging the amount of space in six issues.

Using this figure as a coefficient, a further calculation was made whereby the magazine carrying a large proportion of advertising to reading matter stood in a less advantageous position than the magazine having a greater proportion of reading matter. In this way an index number was secured by which the various magazines could be ranked. Even this index number was modified further by making a calculation or allowance for the size of the page. Although it was felt a full page in the *Saturday Evening Post* would probably not make any better

FOR CONFIDENTIAL FILES ONLY

A QUESTIONNAIRE
for the
READERS of PHYSICAL CULTURE

(Answers to questions which you consider too personal may be omitted, but we shall appreciate as full and complete replies as possible.)

NOTE: As a reward for filling out and returning the enclosed questionnaire to us in the enclosed self-addressed, stamped envelope, we shall take pleasure in sending you free of charge a copy of the new PHYSICAL CULTURE FOOD DIRECTORY, which contains extremely valuable information on all kinds of foods and their specific effects on the body. This 152 page book tells you just what to eat in order to gain or reduce your weight, to promote growth, to increase vitality, to create energy and to prevent constipation. You can fill out the questionnaire in FIVE MINUTES, as many of the questions can be answered by a check mark or a simple "Yes" or "No."

Name .... Address ....

City .... State ....

Age? .... Sex? .... Married? .... Number of children in family ....

Children's Ages .... Occupation of head of family? ....

Executive? .... Employee? .... Average annual income of family ....
(Answer may be omitted if preferred)

How long have you read PHYSICAL CULTURE? ....

How many other members of your family read it? Men? .... Women? .... Boys under 18? .... Girls under 18? ....

How many borrowers outside family? ....

How long do you keep your copies? ....

Do you read the advertisements in PHYSICAL CULTURE? ....

Have you ever answered an advertisement in PHYSICAL CULTURE? ....

A classified advertisement? ....

What make of automobile do you or your family own, if any? ....

Do you expect to be in the market for a new car within a year? .... Within two years? ....

Do you own your home? .... Present estimated value? ....

Have you a home gymnasium? .... Do you own a piano? ....

If so, what make? .... A phonograph? .... Make? ....

A radio? .... Make? .... A Camera? ....

Please list your favorite magazines, in order of preference, including PHYSICAL CULTURE.

1. .... 3. .... 5. ....

2. .... 4. .... 6. ....

(OVER)

FIG. 111A. QUESTIONNAIRE FOR OBTAINING INFORMATION FROM SUBSCRIBERS, PAGE 1

impression than a full page in the *National Geographic,* a proportionately larger credit was given for the larger page.

Carried out in this manner, the investigation showed that the most economical way of reaching this market was through such magazines as the *Scientific American, Judge,* and *Life.* The objection, however, to these media was that they did not

Do you feel that you have been benefited by reading PHYSICAL CULTURE? ....

Can you offer any suggestions for improvement of the magazine? ....

....

Are you chiefly interested in regaining lost health? ....Or maintaining present health? ....

What are your chief interests, hobbies and recreations in life other than your vocation? ....

....

Place a check-mark (√) opposite the sports or athletic exercises in which you indulge.

____Hiking
____Baseball
____Football
____Basketball
____Handball
____Boxing
____Wrestling
____Gymnastics
____Pulley Weights
____Setting-Up Exercises
____Photography
____Camping

____Cycling
____Motorcycling
____Motoring
____Weight-Lifting
____Walking
____Running
____Tennis
____Golf
____Fishing
____Rowing
____Sailing
____Canoeing

____Motorboating
____Swimming
____Hunting
____Trapping
____Motor-Camping
____Riding
____Billiards
____Bowling
____Skating
____Tobogganing
____Snowshoeing
____Hockey

Any Others

In what kinds of advertising are you and other members of your family interested. Please check thus (√) in the list below, the various kinds of advertised goods or services for which you consider yourself or family logical prospects if convinced of their need or desirability.

____FOOD PRODUCTS
____BEVERAGES
____HOME EQUIPMENT
____Bathroom Fixtures
____Furnaces
____Ranges
____Gas Heaters
____Oil Heaters
____Electric Heaters
____Lighting Fixtures
____Furniture
____Carpets and Rugs
____Linoleum
____Hardware and Cutlery
____Kitchen Utensils
____Housefurnishings
____Household Brushes
____LABOR-SAVING DEVICES
____Vacuum Cleaners
____Kitchen Cabinets
____Refrigerators
____SOAPS AND CLEANSERS
____MEN'S CLOTHING
____MEN'S FURNISHINGS
____UNDERWEAR
____KNIT GOODS

____Sweaters
____Bathing Suits
____SHOES
____JEWELRY
____TOILET ARTICLES
____Hair Brushes
____Bath Brushes
____Soaps
____Shaving Creams
____Razors
____Tooth Pastes
____Tooth Brushes
____SANITARIUMS
____MUSIC
____Band Instruments
____Pianos and Players
____Phonographs and Records
____Sheet Music
____RADIOS
____AMUSEMENTS
____Moving Picture Advertising
____SPORTING GOODS
____CAMP EQUIPMENT
____BABY SUPPLIES
____SCHOOLS and COLLEGES
____Boys' Schools

____Girls' Schools
____Colleges
____Boys' Camps
____Girls' Camps
____Trade Schools
____Correspondence Schools
____Physical Culture Schools
____Dancing Schools
____Art Schools
____Chiropractic Schools
____Osteopathic Schools
____BOOKS
____TRAVEL
____AUTOMOBILES
____Tires
____Accessories
____HOTELS AND RESORTS
____INVESTMENTS
____Stocks
____Bonds
____Mortgages
____INSURANCE
____BUILDING MATERIALS
____OFFICE EQUIPMENT
____FARM EQUIPMENT

FIG. 111B. QUESTIONNAIRE FOR OBTAINING INFORMATION FROM SUBSCRIBERS, PAGE 2

have wide enough coverage, and any one of them would not begin to reach all possible prospects. It was necessary, therefore, to choose some medium in the general class, and in this group the *Literary Digest* seemed the most effective for this product, because it was second in its coverage of prospects and second in economy when ranked by the system just described.

Figure 112 illustrates a final questionnaire sent to automobile owners asking their opinion of automobile advertising. In the first place, an attempt is made to find out what general publications are read, and second, the number of hours a week spent in reading magazines and newspapers. The questionnaire also aims to determine what type of medium is likely to gain attention first, and the important determining factors in the purchase of an automobile.

Reading Habits

A few words are again necessary here in regard to the reading habits of the public, as regards magazines. It is logical to suppose that the total reading power of the public at large has been reduced by the radio, the moving picture, and perhaps the automobile. During this same period, however, the circulation of magazines has shown a tremendous increase.

No study, as far as is known, has afforded any definite knowledge as to the tendency towards increase or decrease in magazine reading as applied to the various classes of magazines. It is probable, of course, that the increase in magazine reading may be an increase in the habit of reading, rather than a concentration of reading upon certain forms of literature.

There are a number of tendencies constantly developing and changing connected with reading habits which are important for the advertiser to know, yet extremely difficult for him to determine. He would like to know what the public attitude is towards advertising, and to what extent it reads the advertising. He would like to know whether, even though the magazine is kept, the advertising columns are examined again. He would like to know more about the secondary circulation.

Such problems as these can be answered only approximately. There appears to be no method of research yet developed, even of psychological experiment, which can measure with accuracy the habitual attention given to advertising. People express interest in it; exclaim for a moment over an unusual bit of layout or art work, but apparently nobody knows just what the ultimate effect of this magazine advertising is.

FIG. 112.—AN INVESTIGATION OF THE EFFECTIVENESS OF ADVERTISING WITH READERS

Advertising Questionnaire Issued to Automobile Owners

A. Kindly check any of the following general publications that are read by you or your family: (Indicate by cross (X))

...*American Magazine*	...*House and Garden*	...*Review of Reviews*
...*Asia*	...*Judge*	...*Saturday Evening Post*
...*Atlantic Monthly*	...*Ladies' Home Journal*	
...*Century*	...*Liberty*	...*Scientific American*
...*Christian Herald*	...*Life*	...*Scribner's*
...*Collier's Weekly*	...*Literary Digest*	...*System*
...*Cosmopolitan*	...*McCall's*	...*Time*
...*Current Opinion*	...*National Geographic*	...*True Story*
...*Delineator*	...*Nation's Business*	...*Vanity Fair*
...*Designer*	...*Outlook*	...*Vogue*
...*Good Housekeeping*	...*Photoplay*	...*Woman's Home Companion*
...*Harper's Bazar*	...*Pictorial Review*	
...*Harper's Magazine*	...*Red Book*	...*World's Work*

B. Roughly, how many hours a week do you devote to reading magazines? (Check one of the following figures)

1 Hour....	3 Hours....	5 Hours....	7 Hours....	9 Hours....
2 Hours...	4 Hours....	6 Hours....	8 Hours....	10 Hours....

C. Do you read the morning newspapers?.... Evening newspapers?.... Both?....

D. Do you read the automobile section of your newspaper? Yes.... No....

E. Approximately how much time do you devote to reading your Sunday newspaper?

1 Hour... 2 Hours... 3 Hours... 4 Hours... 5 Hours... 6 Hours...

F. In your own case what type of advertising is most likely to gain your attention? (Check with a 1, 2, 3, 4, in order of value.)

Magazine....	Newspaper....
Billboard....	Direct by mail (Catalogs, Folders, etc.)....

G. When you buy an automobile, what are the most important determining factors? (Check with a 1, 2, 3, 4, 5, etc., in order of importance.)

Reputation of Manufacturer....	Price....
Reputation of Dealer....	Trade-in Allowance....
Local Service Facilities....	Appearance of the Car....
What other Owners say....	Comfort....
	Operating Costs....

REMARKS:

....

....

H. To what degree are you influenced by advertising?

Very much....   Slightly....   Not at all....

The psychological factor is undoubtedly of much importance in studying the reading habits of a particular group, especially in their reference to buying interests. The readers of any particular periodical, from the advertisers' point of view, should be mentally receptive to the selling appeal of the product. As expressed by John Hanrahan, there are the various factors of alertness, intelligence, open-mindedness, potential interest in the product advertised, heightened mental activity, directed and focused reader interest, all bearing upon the effectiveness of advertising in a given medium:

To illustrate: The readers of *The American Mercury* are open-minded in respect to many products, in the sense that their brand preferences in respect to those products are not solidly entrenched. They are alert people whose opinions may be readily formed by good advertising. They are, moreover, very much alert and enlivened, mentally awake, as it were, during a reading of *The American Mercury*. They may have a high potential interest in acquiring a competency and becoming financially independent and yet there being nothing to focus and direct their interest on financial matters during the reading of *The American Mercury,* the effectiveness of financial advertising in the magazine would be extremely doubtful in comparison to many another magazine of perhaps less natural potential effectiveness as an advertising medium. On the other hand, the advertiser of motorcycles in *The American Mercury* would be handicapped by the lack of a potential buying interest of motorcycles on the part of most readers of the magazine. In comparison to readers of *Field and Stream,* for instance, the medium would be distinctly poor.

Readers of *The American Mercury,* however, might be less open to conviction and to selling effort in respect to many commodities than newer, fresher material, such as readers, let us say, of *Liberty,* people whose buying habits are unformed, more open to direction.

Advertising Rates

Since the advertising appropriation is usually sharply limited, advertising rates are, to a definite extent, determinative of the media used. There is a growing emphasis, however, stressing the effectiveness of the medium for the particular purpose required, rather than its gross cost. A magazine or newspaper with high rates may be cheaper in the end than periodicals whose rates are much lower. Rates may be measured in at least three different ways:

1. *Page, half-page, or quarter-page.* Such a unit of measurement gives no further information than what it will actually cost to run an advertisement in a given medium. While this information is important for accounting purposes and for apportioning the budget, it does not permit any comparison, even with other media in the same class, the pages of which are of different size, or which have different circulations.

2. *The agate line.* This is also a unit of space, pure and simple, and does not take into consideration differences due to circulation. While the agate line may be slightly different in various publications, this variation is usually small.

3. *Combination of unit of space and circulation.* The milline is the unit of space of one agate line per 1,000,000 subscribers. It is also possible to take the agate line unit per 1,000 subscribers. Milline rates (rates per agate line per million circulation) differ widely, even among publications of the same class, but generally the average milline rate for a publication in a certain class will bear a certain relation to the average milline rate in another class. This average will depend upon the number of magazines included, and will, therefore, vary in the estimates of different calculators. The following figures, however, are fairly representative of the leaders in each group; the milline rate being for:

21 monthly general magazines	$7.61
11 women's magazines	6.16
8 weekly magazines	5.71
7 class magazines	9.75

Figures as to the median milline rate, given by Starch in *Principles of Advertising,* are based on a larger number of periodicals, and show decided differences in averages:

	Median Milline Rate
55 monthly publications	$11.72
18 weekly magazines	7.56
19 monthly women's magazines	6.36
30 foreign publications	7.50
185 business and trade publications	50.00

The rate is largest for the business publications and smallest for the women's magazines. Under general conditions, the smaller circulations have higher milline rates, due to the limited and specialized nature of the smaller circulations, and to the supposedly greater reader interest. Figure 113 shows varying rates per thousand circulation in the women's field.

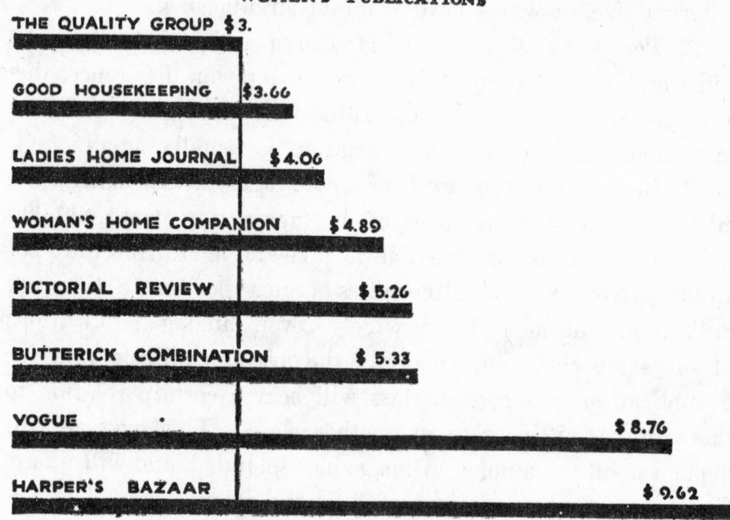

FIG. 113. METHOD OF COMPARING COSTS OF COMPETITIVE MEDIA

Although it is impossible to reduce such matters to a purely statistical basis, the above method gives at least some idea of differences in cost. (Quality Group.)

In the case of newspapers, the Bureau of Advertising of the American Newspaper Publishers Association estimates milline rates as follows:

Morning papers	$2.71
Evening papers	3.32
Sunday papers	2.29

The higher rate for evening papers is due to the greater number of small publishers, to a large extent. There is some claim that reader interest is greater for evening papers because of the greater leisure.

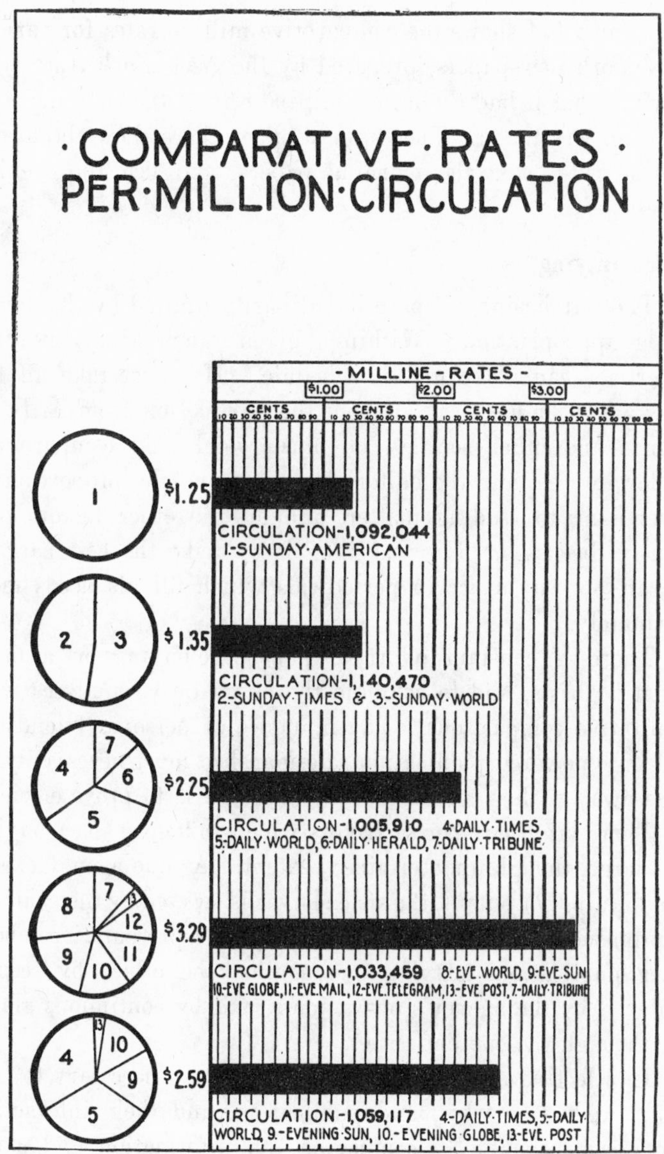

Fig. 114. Comparative Milline Rates

Another method of comparing media costs, especially useful in selecting newspapers.

Figure 114 shows the comparative milline rates for various New York newspapers, prepared by the *New York American,* showing that it had the lowest milline rate at the time the computation was made. The Sunday papers here show the lowest milline rate, next the morning papers, and last the evening papers.

Space Buying

The purchasing of space is ordinarily limited by the advertising appropriation. Within a given range of expense the advertiser can make up his schedule. He must take all the facts which he has secured about the publication from A. B. C. reports and other sources, he must weigh and compare the reader interest and the editorial content and the proportion of advertising to reading matter, and all the other factors previously discussed. His task then is to make the best bargain he can—to buy space in periodicals which fill his needs most adequately.

There is constant effort to put space-buying on a more scientific basis, and to combine the quantitative analyses with qualitative comparisons. The influence of personal friendship and high-powered publication salesmanship must necessarily be done away with if an advertising program is to prove efficient.

There are a number of factors which influence space-buying to a large, though undetermined, extent. As one agency executive (Mullally) puts it, the space-buyer is swayed by the example of prominent advertisers, by the gossip of representatives about other publications playing one against the other, by results achieved by the agency's own clients, and by continuous glancing through the current issues.

In selecting any one medium, it is always necessary to consider product, market, and publication, and their interaction upon each other. By comparing the information and statements obtained from a representative of one periodical with similar information and statments from a competitor, some idea of the relative standing of two publications can sometimes be obtained.

An investigation was undertaken among the more prominent advertising agencies to determine their practice in space-buying, and how they chose their media. The remarkable aspect of the result of this study was the total lack of uniformity of method. One authority on the subject says:

> An advertising agency selects first the class or classes of publications which appeal directly to the people he can naturally expect to make users of his client's goods. Then he begins the process of elimination until he has reached the figure appropriated for advertising in publications, always making comparisons as to relative costs, character of reading matter, printing, subscription price, etc. Publications that will pay well for one product will often fail completely for another. There is no hard and fast rule that can wisely be followed in selecting media or in selecting one publication in preference to another. The business of the agency is to know the class of publication and medium most suitable for each different product and the way to advertise in each. Two publications of equal circulation might be used for advertising the same product with the same advertising copy. One might prove profitable and the other fail completely, because it required a different style of copy to impress its readers to the extent of separating them from their money. The advertising agent should know what to recommend as to media, and what kind of copy each medium should have, to produce the best results; these things are not often left to the space-buyer, but are settled before the contract reaches the point of actually buying space.

The following example shows how a particular agency (C. Ironmonger) goes about the selection of media. All the facts regarding all the publications to be considered are tabulated in columns on large sheets. Then, applying judgment and experience, the publications are listed numerically in the order of their greatest value for the proposition in hand, everything considered. Finally, the schedule is prepared, within the appropriation, beginning at the top of the list. Sometimes deviation is made from the numerical order of the list, due to circumstances affecting localities or similar factor. In general, however, the agency begins at the top of the list and follows it down to the limits of the appropriation.

CHAPTER XIII

DUPLICATION OF MEDIA

Little has been written on the subject of duplication, that is, the extent to which the circulations of various media overlap each other. There is considerable difference of opinion as to the extent to which duplication is harmful or beneficial. On the one side it is contended that placing advertisements in two or more periodicals which cover the same ground is waste; on the opposite side it is alleged that duplication increases the chances of a given advertisement to be seen by a desirable audience.

J. Paul Maynard, advertising manager of the *Christian Herald,* presents his case as follows:

In the old days an advertiser used all the good magazines with small space. When more money was available, he would add other magazines rather than increase the number of insertions in the magazines being used, or rather than increase space. To-day, when an advertiser uses a magazine, he is trying to use it adequately. In other words, an advertiser does not feel that he is using the *Post* adequately until he can buy thirteen pages or more. The average advertiser is trying to reach, in most of the magazines he uses, every reader that it is possible to reach by the advertising message.

It is essential, therefore, that he should seek for new markets when more money is available; not that it will not pay him to hammer away at the old market, but that it will pay him more to strike out anew. For example, an advertiser is using the *Saturday Evening Post, Literary Digest, American Magazine, Ladies' Home Journal, Pictorial Review, Woman's Home Companion, McCall's,* and *Butterick,* with twelve pages in each magazine. With more money to spend, the question arises as to whether it is more worth while to reach the same people once again through another pub-

True Story duplicates:

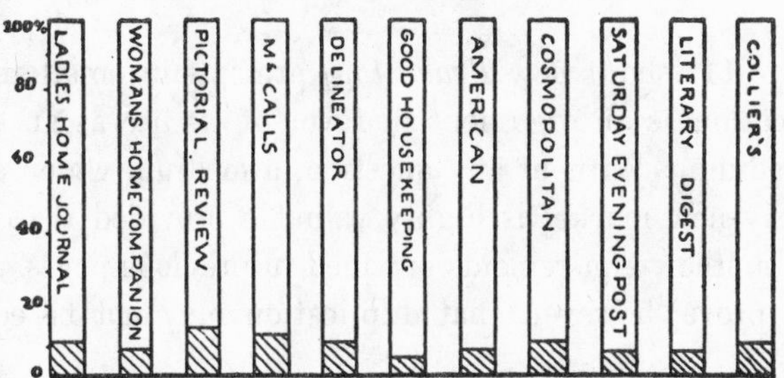

The shaded portion shows percentage of T. S. duplication

We have told you time and again that TRUE STORY experiences very little duplication with other magazines.

On this page we are showing you in a graphic manner how true this statement is with reference to several of the leaders—and the statistics which are used as the source of this information, were compiled by The Association of National Advertisers.

We could not state truthfully that TRUE STORY is 100% free from duplication. But up to a certain point, duplication is healthy and we do not believe that in any instance TRUE STORY'S two million passes this point.

If the subject of duplication interests you, we will be glad to hear from you and we will furnish other figures to make our point more emphatically.

True Story

"The Necessary Two Million"

"GREATEST COVERAGE—LOWEST COST"

FIG. 115. MINIMUM DUPLICATION HERALDED AS AN ADVANTAGE

lication, or to search for some field which is only partially covered by this group, if such a field can be found.

It is not a question of whether *Cosmopolitan, Red Book,* and *Quality Group* are offering value received from the money which space in them costs, but rather whether there are not good publications which will reach not only another group of people but a group in a market which is but sparsely covered by the aforesaid magazines.

Figure 115 shows how *True Story* presents its small amount of duplication as an argument in favor of its use as an advertising medium. Without any question, a medium which covers an entirely new market is highly valuable provided it can fulfill certain other requirements outlined in previous pages. This does not prove, however, that duplication may not be equally valuable.

The arguments in favor of duplication rest largely upon the cumulative effect of repetition. This is particularly important also where the advertisement is small and may have escaped attention in one medium. When the attention value of an advertisement is sufficient to ensure its being seen by the average person examining the periodical, the question of duplication becomes one of the added effect of seeing this same advertisement repeated in the different magazines.

Poffenberger points out that there are two types of attention: one which is attracted by what is different, and the other due to some traces of a previous stimulus, or memory. In attracting attention in advertising, it is desirable to preserve the proper balance between the new and the familiar to get the maximum results.

For the sake of memory value, which is not entirely coordinate with attention value, repetition is important, so that one might well use repetition for that purpose and depend upon newness or difference gained in some other manner for attention value. For the advertisement works as a whole and one of its functions must not be sacrificed in favor of another unless justified by the relative importance of the latter.

The Association of National Advertisers' Investigation

One of the most complete reports on duplication of magazines has been prepared by the Association of National Advertisers, Inc. The report states that three methods of studying duplication are possible: First, by checking comparative subscription lists of various magazines in certain test areas. Such a process is naturally limited to a small number of magazines, and takes no account of secondary or news-stand circulation. The second method is that of personal interviews, which is the most exhaustive but also the most expensive. The third method is the printed questionnaire. Although it does not permit the exhaustive study provided by the second method, it is less expensive and can be more quickly and easily carried out.

A letter was sent to all members of the Association of National Advertisers, enclosing cards, blue for executives, white for clerical workers, and pink for factory workers. Each of these cards listed 12 monthly magazines in the women's field, 12 general monthly magazines, and 4 weeklies, each leaders in their class. These cards were distributed and each person receiving a card was asked to place a cross before those magazines which were subscribed for or received regularly every month or week. The number of returns was in excess of 15,000.

As is stated in the report, there are certain limitations which must affect the accuracy of the returns, and which should be allowed for. These are:

1. It is an investigation of magazine readers only. No allowance has been made for the home in which no magazines are read. It is probable that in many cases where respondents did not fill out cards because no magazines were taken in their homes, the cards were passed on to other respondents who could fill them out.

2. The locality of this questionnaire is chiefly in urban and suburban districts closely surrounding industrial centers. On this account, the figures are a relatively better guide for those advertisers who sell in such districts, and a relatively less trustworthy guide for those who sell in rural districts.

FIG. 116.—AN EXAMPLE OF TABULATION OF DUPLICATION DATA

Percentage of Duplication of Circulation of 12 Monthly Women's Magazines in the Homes of 3000 Executives

	Magazine No. 1	Magazine No. 2	Magazine No. 3	Magazine No. 4	Magazine No. 5	Magazine No. 6	Magazine No. 7	Magazine No. 8	Magazine No. 9	Magazine No. 10	Magazine No. 11	Magazine No. 12
Magazine No. 1 is duplicated by (1297)	......	30.8	25.6	13.2	16.0	48.5	5.5	4.6	3.0	3.6	13.6	6.2
Magazine No. 2 is duplicated by (668).	60.0	......	32.0	19.6	20.0	50.0	8.8	6.7	5.2	4.4	10.4	5.4
Magazine No. 3 is duplicated by (583).	56.9	36.7	......	22.9	17.4	48.0	12.4	7.3	4.8	6.2	14.4	6.9
Magazine No. 4 is duplicated by (299).	57.2	43.7	44.7	......	31.4	47.5	12.4	8.7	10.4	7.0	13.7	7.7
Magazine No. 5 is duplicated by (327).	63.3	41.3	31.2	28.7	......	47.4	14.3	9.8	6.4	7.0	15.9	7.6
Magazine No. 6 is duplicated by (1161)	54.3	29.0	24.1	12.3	13.3	......	6.7	4.6	3.0	3.2	17.6	8.5
Magazine No. 7 is duplicated by (142).	50.0	41.5	50.7	26.0	33.1	54.9	......	12.6	9.8	16.8	18.3	9.8
Magazine No. 8 is duplicated by (89)..	67.4	51.0	47.2	29.2	36.0	59.5	20.0	......	16.8	19.1	19.1	15.7
Magazine No. 9 is duplicated by (68)..	57.3	51.5	41.2	45.6	30.9	51.5	20.6	22.0	......	22.0	14.7	11.8
Magazine No. 10 is duplicated by (79)..	59.5	37.9	45.6	26.6	29.1	46.8	30.4	21.5	19.0	......	15.2	10.1
Magazine No. 11 is duplicated by (397).	44.6	17.6	21.1	10.3	13.1	51.4	6.5	4.3	2.5	3.0	......	26.4
Magazine No. 12 is duplicated by (167).	47.9	21.5	23.9	13.8	15.0	59.2	8.4	8.4	4.8	4.8	62.9	......

3. No figures based upon a survey of part of the total magazine readers can be more than a general indication of the trend of conditions throughout the entire magazine-reading public. It cannot be proved, for example, that the duplication of one magazine by another among the respondents to this questionnaire will hold good throughout all readers of either magazine.

Figure 116 shows the method of tabulating and comparing the duplication of circulation of these magazines among the executive class, the table being limited, however, to the 12 monthly magazines in the women's field. The investigation indicated that the number of magazines read in the 15,000 homes averaged 3.54. The J. Walter Thompson Company calculated this at 3.52, showing close correlation.

While the calculations in the report merely give the extent of duplication between two magazines, there is also a possibility of calculating the effect of three or more magazines, described as follows by the Association:

Let us suppose a case of five purely imaginary magazines, A, B, C, D and E, whose circulations among the 15,000 homes of respondents are as follows, and which, in those homes duplicate each other as follows:

	Magazine				
	A Duplicates	B Duplicates	C Duplicates	D Duplicates	E Duplicates
Magazine A, 2000 circulation	.....	800	600	540	350
is duplicated by	.....	40%	30%	27%	17.5%
Magazine B, 1600 circulation	800	.....	600	400	400
is duplicated by	50%	.....	37.5%	25%	25%
Magazine C, 1500 circulation	600	600	.....	300	500
is duplicated by	40%	40%	.....	20%	33⅓%
Magazine D, 1200 circulation	540	400	300	.....	300
is duplicated by	45%	33⅓%	25%	.....	25%
Magazine E, 1000 circulation	350	400	500	300	......
is duplicated by	35%	40%	50%	30%	......

The advertiser using magazines in this list may use one or all of them. If he uses any one he will reach a certain number of homes once. If he uses two he will reach a certain number of homes once and a certain number twice, owing to the overlapping, or duplication, of circulation of the two magazines. A third magazine will yield him a certain amount of new circulation and a certain amount of circulation already reached by one or both of the previous two magazines.

If the advertiser wants to estimate how many of the 15,000 homes represented in this questionnaire he will reach by the use of a number of magazines, he may conceivably start with any one magazine which he regards for reasons of his own as the most desirable medium. Let him then figure out the additional circulation obtainable by the addition of other magazines, in order of desirability, as follows:

Suppose, for the moment, that his preference among the magazines of this list is governed by the size alone of their circulation among this market of 15,000 homes. In this case, he will start with Magazine A, as the largest.

Magazine A has 2,000 readers.

Adding Magazine B gives 1,600 readers, of whom 800 or 50 per cent also read magazine A.

This leaves 800 unduplicated readers.

Total homes for magazines A and B—2,800.

Adding Magazine C, gives 1,500 readers, of whom 600 or 40 per cent read magazine A. This leaves 900.

Of the 900, 40 per cent or 360 also read magazine B.

This leaves 540 readers of magazine C who do not read A or B.

Total homes for magazines A, B and C.

A	2,000	
B	800	additional
C	540	"
	3,340	

Adding Magazine D gives 1,200 readers, of whom 540 or 45 per cent also read magazine A. This leaves 660.

Of the 660, 33⅓ per cent or 220 also read magazine B.

This leaves 440. Of the 440, 25 per cent or 110 also read magazine C.

This leaves 330 readers of magazine D who do not read A, B or C.

Total homes—

A	2,000	
B	800	additional
C	540	"
D	330	"
	3,670	

Adding Magazine E gives 1,000 readers, of whom 350 or 35 per cent also read magazine A. This leaves 650.

Of the 650, 40 per cent or 260 also read magazine B.

This leaves 390. Of the 390, 50 per cent or 195 also read magazine C.
This leaves 195. Of the 195, 30 per cent or 58.5 also read magazine D.
This leaves 136.5 or 137 readers.

Total homes—			
	A	2,000	
	B	800	additional
	C	540	"
	D	330	"
	E	137	"
		3,807	homes reached

by a total circulation of 7,500 copies.

Another advertiser may take the magazines in order of desirability of editorial content, or of type of readers. If he lists the magazines, in the following order of desirability, E, C, A, D, B, then he will figure as follows, using E as his starting point:

Magazine E has 1,000 readers.
Adding Magazine C gives 1,500 readers, of whom 500 or 33⅓ per cent also read magazine E. This leaves 1,000.
Total unduplicated circulation of magazines E and C, 2,000.
Adding Magazine A gives 2,000 readers, of whom 350 or 17.5 per cent also read magazine E. This leaves 1,650.
Of the 1,650, 30 per cent or 495 also read magazine C.
This leaves 1,155 readers who do not also read magazines E or C.

Total homes—			
	E	1,000	
	C	1,000	additional
	A	1,155	"
		3,155	

Adding Magazine D gives 1,200 readers, of whom 300 or 25 per cent also read magazine E. This leaves 900.
Of the 900, 25 per cent or 225 also read magazine C. This leaves 675. Of the 675, 45 per cent or 304 (303.75) also read magazine A.
This leaves 371 readers who do not also read magazines E, C or A.

Total homes—			
	E	1,000	
	C	1,000	additional
	A	1,155	"
	D	371	"
		3,526	

Adding Magazine B gives 1,600 readers, of whom 400 or 25 per cent also read magazine E. This leaves 1,200. Of the 1,200, 37.5 or 450 also read magazine C. This leaves 750. Of the 750, 50 per cent or 375 also read magazine A. This leaves 375. Of the 375, 25 per cent or 94 (93.75) also read magazine D. This leaves 281.

Total homes—			
	E	1,000	
	C	1,000	additional
	A	1,155	"
	D	371	"
	B	281	"
		3,807	

Determining Duplication

A good method of determining duplication of media can be illustrated by describing an actual analysis made by Robert K. Leavitt, formerly with the Onyx Hosiery Company, for whom this investigation was made, and now Secretary-Treasurer of the Association of National Advertisers. The mailing list used was furnished by department stores in various cities, the names of the women being taken from the charge accounts of the store.

A questionnaire was sent out in each city, asking the recipient to make a check mark against the name of the magazines she read occasionally, and a cross against the magazine or magazines read regularly every month. Part of the work sheet for the city of Boston is shown in Figure 117. The names of magazines are given in the first column. Then the responses, as they came in, were recorded in the numbered columns.

To determine duplication, it is necessary merely to follow along the horizontal columns representing any two magazines. Whenever two marks are found under a given number, this counts for one duplication. Thus, respondent Number 20 reported that she read regularly (among others) both *Modern Priscilla* and *Good Housekeeping*. As far as this woman is concerned, these two magazines duplicate each other.

This method of tabulating duplication is applicable only where the number of names is limited. Mechanical tabulation

	Ladies Home Journal	Woman's Home Companion	Pictorial Review	McCall's	Delineator	Good Housekeeping	Modern Priscilla	Needlecraft	Designer	Woman's World	People's Home Journal	Fashionable Dress	Vogue	Harper's Bazaar	Theatre	American	Cosmopolitan	Red Book	Photoplay
1	X												X						
2	X					✓							✓				X		
3			X			X	X	X											
4	X					X										X			
5		✓				X		X		✓									
6	X	X	X			X	X												
7					X													✓	
8	X	X	X	✓	✓	X	X	X					✓			X			
9		X	X			X										X	X		
10	✓	✓	X			X	X	✓									✓	✓	
11																			
12	✓					✓										✓			
13			X	X	X									X		X			
14			X			✓	✓												
15																			
16	✓	✓	✓	✓		X							✓			✓			
17	✓	✓	X	✓	✓	✓						✓				✓	✓		
18	✓		X	✓			✓											✓	✓
19	X		✓			X										✓			
20	✓	✓			✓	X	X					✓	X			X			
21			✓			✓						✓				✓			✓
22			X		X	X							✓			X	X	✓	
23	✓	✓				✓							✓				✓		
24	✓	✓		✓	✓	X							✓			✓	X	✓	
25	X	X	X	X		✓	✓		✓					X		X	X	X	
26	X	✓	✓	✓	✓	✓	✓	✓					✓			✓	✓		✓
27	X		X	X	✓		✓		✓							✓		✓	
28	✓					X										✓			
29	✓					✓	✓	✓											
30		X		X	X	X	X												
31	✓																✓		
32	✓	X	X	X		✓										X		✓	
33	✓	✓	X			X	X	X								X			
34	✓	X	X	✓	X	X	✓		X							X			
35	X		X	X	✓	✓							✓			X			
36	X	X														✓			
37	✓	✓				X				X						✓			
38	✓	X	X		X	X	X	✓								X			
39																			
40	X		X			X								X					
41	X	X	X		✓	X	X	✓		X	X					✓	X	✓	✓
42	✓															✓	X	X	
43	✓	✓	X		✓	✓	✓						✓			✓	✓	✓	
44					X								✓				✓		✓
45	✓	X	✓			X										✓			
46	✓	✓	✓	✓	✓	✓										✓	✓		✓
47	X	X	✓	X	✓	X										X		X	✓
48	✓		✓	X	X	✓		X	X	✓	X	✓						✓	X
49	X	X	X	✓								✓	X			X			✓
50	X	X		X		X							X			X			
51	X	✓	✓		✓	X				✓			✓	✓		✓	✓	✓	✓
52	✓		✓	X		✓													
53			X	X	✓			✓	✓										
54		✓	X		X	✓			✓							✓	✓	✓	
55		X	✓	✓	✓	✓					X					X		✓	
56	✓				X	X							X	X		X			✓
57	X	X	✓		✓	✓			✓				✓			X			
58																			
59		X	X			X							X			X	X		
60		X	✓	✓				X			X					X			
61	✓	✓				X										✓			
62	X		X			X													

Fig. 117. Work Sheet Used in a Study of Duplication

This method is useful where the investigation is limited; otherwise, mechanical tabulation is preferable.

is almost essential where a large number of names or facts must be recapitulated.

Publications are constantly computing the extent to which they duplicate their competitors in the field. Figure 118, for

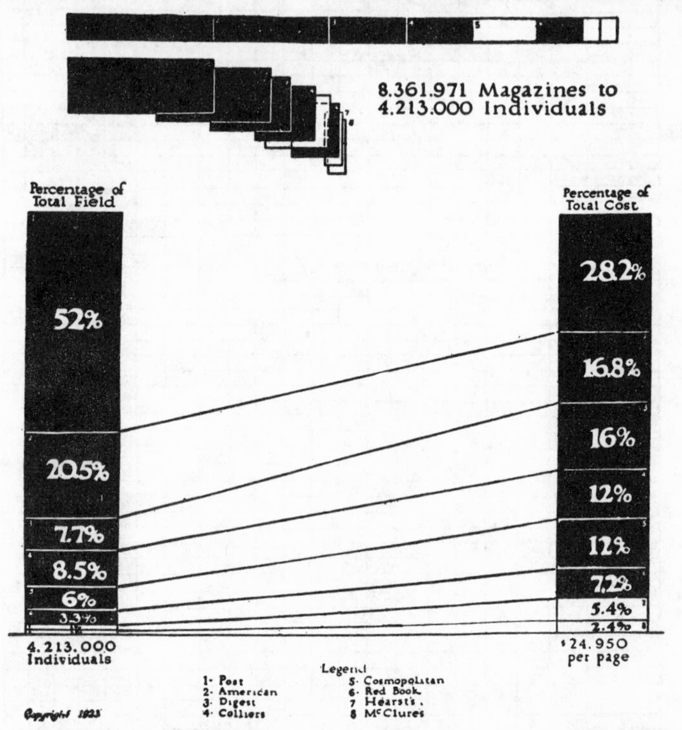

FIG. 118. DUPLICATION GRAPHICALLY SHOWN

An interesting method of indicating the overlapping of media. (Quality Group.)

example, shows how the Quality Group compares duplication of the *Post, Digest, American* and others. It is interesting to note that duplication among its own members is not indicated. Figure 119 illustrates the method of tabulating duplication of media which is employed by the *Farm Journal.*

Fig. 119.—The "Farm Journal's" Method of Tabulating Duplication

Small Duplication with the Farm Journal

Fifty-seven and eight-tenths per cent of the correspondents take only the *Farm Journal.* Only 42.2% reported taking any of these eleven other publications; 22.7% take only one publication besides the *Farm Journal.* Only 12.7% will see the advertisement of Del Monte in 2 publications other than the *Farm Journal.* Only 6.8% will see the advertisement in 3 or more of the magazines. The analysis shows:

General Analysis

	Number	Per Cent
Taking the *Farm Journal* only	535	57.8
Taking 1 other publication *	210	22.7
Taking 2 other publications *	117	12.7
Taking 3 other publications *	40	4.3
Taking 4 other publications *	13	1.4
Taking 5 other publications *	9	1.0
Taking 6 other publications *	1	.1
	925	100.0

* Only the eleven publications are considered in this analysis.

Analysis by Sections

	New England, Per Cent	Middle Atlantic, Per Cent	East North Central, Per Cent	West North Central, Per Cent	South Atlantic, Per Cent
F. J. only	38.3	49.7	59.9	52.1	70.3
1 other	28.3	26.8	21.3	27.9	17.2
2 others	20.0	13.4	10.1	16.3	9.4
3 others	10.0	6.1	5.1	2.3	3.1
4 others	3.3	2.0	1.8	.5	....
5 others	....	1.3	1.8	.9	....
6 others	....	.7	....	....	....

	East South Central, Per Cent	West South Central, Per Cent	Mountain, Per Cent	Pacific, Per Cent	Unknown, Per Cent
F. J. only	82.0	82.5	38.5	58.6	67.9
1 other	8.0	12.5	....	27.6	21.4
2 others	10.0	5.0	23.1	10.3	10.7
3 others	....	....	30.8	....	....
4 others	....	....	7.6	3.5	....
5 others	....	....	....	....	....
6 others	....	....	....	....	....

Somewhat more interesting than these are the following figures from the *Nation's Business,* based on preferences expressed by respondents to a questionnaire:

Out of the 800

650 receive *Nation's Business* on account of membership in Chamber of Commerce of the United States.

150 are paid subscribers.

				Per Cent
Nation's Business	duplicates	*Burroughs Business*	market	95
Burroughs Business	"	*Nation's Business*	"	17
Nation's Business	"	*Factory*	"	95
Factory	"	*Nation's Business*	"	14
Nation's Business	"	*Iron Age*	"	93
Iron Age	"	*Nation's Business*	"	13½
Nation's Business	"	*Industrial Digest*	"	94
Industrial Digest	"	*Nation's Business*	"	11
Nation's Business	"	*Industry Illustrated*	"	80
Industry Illustrated	"	*Industrial Management*	"	83
Nation's Business	"	*Nation's Business*	"	2½
Industrial Management	"	*Nation's Business*	"	14
Nation's Business	"	*Scientific American*	"	90
Scientific American	"	*Nation's Business*	"	29
Nation's Business	"	*System*	"	25
System	"	*Nation's Business*	"	13

Without analyzing the conditions under which this information was gathered, the important feature is the manner in which a comparison is made between the duplication of the various media with *Nation's Business.*

An analysis made by *Field and Stream* is interesting because of the checking of results. It was desired to find a basis for comparison between readers of the magazine and high-class sportsmen generally. The state of Pennsylvania was taken as the field for the survey, because of its representative nature. The same questionnaire was sent to the 20 rod and gun clubs as was sent to subscribers for *Field and Stream,* giving a total of 1,800 for both. Returns were received from 353, or 19.6 per cent, the results from both questionnaires being practically uniform. Figure 120 shows the magazine preferences and duplications as disclosed by the investigation. The evidence would seem to indicate that *Field and Stream* alone would give the advertiser 78 per cent coverage of sportsmen. There is

FIG. 120.—A CONTROLLED INVESTIGATION OF DUPLICATION

Some Interesting Side-Lights on Magazine References and Magazine Duplications

Magazine	Number of Sportsmen Readers	Percentage of Sportsmen Reached	Number of Sportsmen who Checked for Preferred Magazines	Number of Sportsmen Not Reached by *Field and Stream*
Total Sportsmen Replying	631	......	......	139
Field and Stream	492	78	259	......
Saturday Evening Post	414	66	188	78
National Geographic	387	61	97	71
Literary Digest	367	58	158	63
American	244	38	97	37
National Sportsman	213	33	84	17
Outers' Recreation	211	33	77	32
Cosmopolitan	188	30	60	35
Life	167	26	44	22
Country Life	152	24	50	1
Red Book	102	16	34	18
Collier's	99	16	30	22
Atlantic	90	14	37	17
Motor Life	88	14	31	13
Harper's	86	13	18	13
Scribner's	83	13	21	15
American Golfer	72	11	19	16
Century	67	10	15	8
Motor Boating	50	8	15	2
All Others	134	21	43	23

In the sportsmen's field, *Field and Stream* alone gives the advertiser access to 78% of his market.

The most that can be gained by adding any other magazine of any circulation whatever is 12% additional coverage—12% not reached through *Field and Stream* alone.

great duplication with the *Saturday Evening Post, National Geographic,* and *Literary Digest.*

Duplication of Newspaper Circulation

It is of great importance for newspaper advertisers to determine the circulation of newspapers in a given city and to find out the extent of duplication. While duplication in a magazine may, with some reason, be defended as not necessarily harmful, duplication of newspaper circulation is much more likely to result in waste. A newspaper has such a short life that the benefits of repetition are usually outweighed by the greater advantage of covering the entire market adequately without duplication.

The mere fact that a city has a number of morning newspapers does not, *ipso facto,* prove that there is great duplication. For example, the recent survey of the Philadelphia Marketing Area showed that one morning paper had only one-quarter of its circulation in Philadelphia, while another morning paper had 70 per cent of its circulation within the city. One evening paper had four-fifths of its circulation in the city. A knowledge of these circulation facts would be exceedingly important to an advertiser who had a product not likely to be used in the outlying districts. He would want to choose the newspaper with the largest urban circulation. Figure 121 is an interesting example of showing duplication graphically.

Much uncertainty has been felt as to the effect on circulation of the many cases of newspaper mergers which have taken place. Is the circulation of the new paper as large as the combined circulation of the original papers? This problem has been somewhat simplified by a study of the question by the Association of National Advertisers, Inc., which draws the following conclusions:

1. The first complete six-months circulation report after the merger generally shows a marked leap in circulation over the previous circulation of the larger of the two combining papers.
2. This point of circulation is usually equivalent to the circulation of the larger paper plus more than 50 per cent of the circulation of the smaller paper.
3. This point is generally the peak of circulation which the combined paper attains for a period of two years following the merger.
4. From this peak, circulation settles down to a point from which the paper grows or diminishes according to influences other than those of the merger.
5. The resultant circulation is hardly ever equal to the sum of

EXCLUSIVE AND DUPLICATED HOME DELIVERED CIRCULATIONS IN INDIANAPOLIS

To arrive at the total actual distribution to all homes, it is necessary to augment the figures actually found by applying to the homes where information could not be obtained the same ratio of relative circulations that was found to exist in the homes where information *was* obtained. The specific per cent. each figure is augmented is 34.9 per cent.—a carefully determined figure and one that is eminently fair in that it gives each of the three daily papers exactly the same share of the authentic allowable increase.

FIG. 121. AN INTERESTING METHOD OF SHOWING DUPLICATION

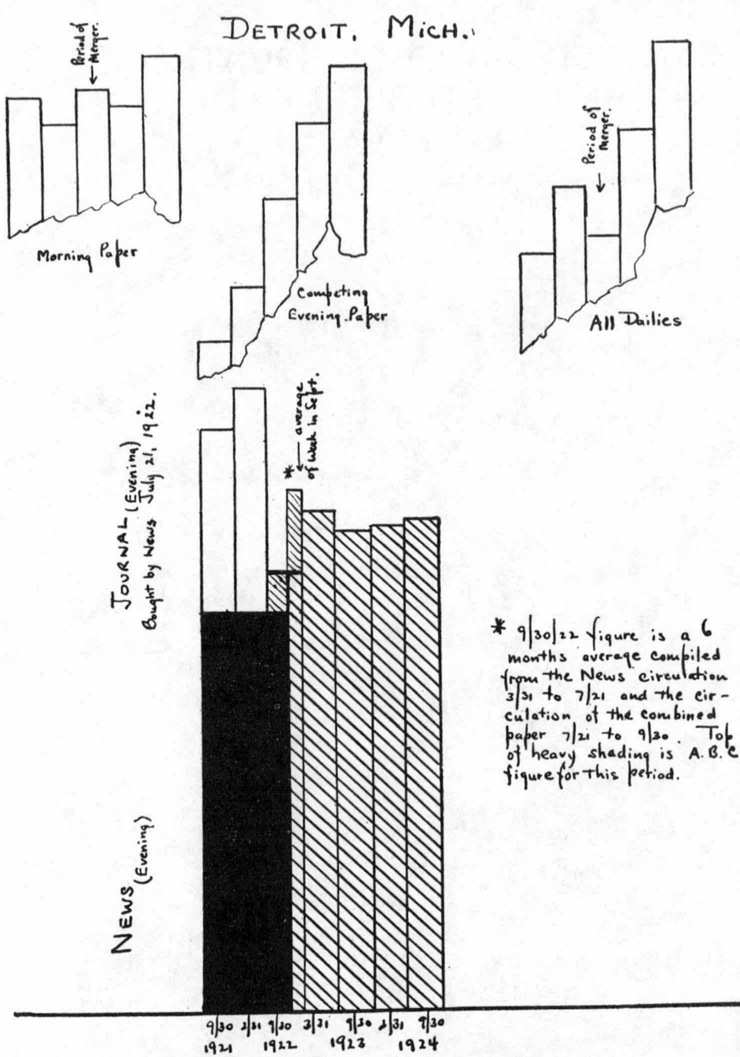

FIG. 122. RESULT OF THE MERGER OF TWO NEWSPAPERS (Association of National Advertisers.)

the circulation of the two papers when independent. Figure 122 is a typical example of what happens, as illustrated by the merger of the *Detroit Journal* and *News*. The average circulation for the two years following the consolidation is about 77 per cent of the total of the two papers when separate.

Duplication in a Single Issue

One of the most interesting practical uses of duplication is that of the International Correspondence School, which, after exhaustive tests, has adopted a policy of multiple advertising in several magazines. This has been possible to carry out profitably, and the advertiser has been able to figure out this profit by using box numbers in each advertisement's coupon. No distinctive box number is used again for four years, thus making almost certain the correct distribution of returns.

According to G. Lynn Sumner,[1] the former policy had been to increase the size of an advertisement in a given magazine which produced well, from a quarter-page, to a half, and finally to a full page, and rarely to a double spread. The first departure from this was to use two half-page units in the same medium, using different illustrations and copy for each. The result was that both half-pages produced as well as the single half-page had done previously, doing considerably better than the full page had done in this same medium. This policy was extended to three half-pages in the same medium, then four half-pages, and all of these pages were found to pay.

The test was extended to other media, particularly those which carried a large amount of advertising. The various advertisements were scattered throughout the advertising section. Tests proved that the number of duplicate advertisements which could be carried in a given medium varied from eight, which was the maximum, down to a single one. In magazines of the same general class, the number of multiple insertions was usually about proportionate to the total number of advertising pages in the publication.

The principal point which this investigation brings out is that duplication of advertising, in some cases at least, is beneficial to the advertiser.

---

[1] *Advertising and Selling Fortnightly.*

CHAPTER XIV

SELECTION OF MEDIA

One of the more difficult tasks confronting the advertising man is the selection of the media most suitable to the purposes of the campaign in question. The formulation of the advertising message, the art work, and all the other technique of advertising are contingent upon reaching that particular class of buyers which is known to constitute the logical market. The advertising man does the best he can on the basis of the facts before him. He admits that he cannot, under present conditions, make the choice on a scientific basis (although, unlike other phases of advertising, media research is most nearly reducible to a scientific basis). He is never in possession of all the facts, either concerning the medium, the market, or even the product.

There are several reasons why more facts are not available for use in media research. One reason is that the various trade publications which serve the advertising field do not care to make comparisons between various types of media. Since a comparison would be apt to imply that one medium is better than another, the publication adopts a policy of neutrality. The advertising agency is seldom in a position to give adequate information as to media, because, as a rule, it devotes itself mainly to a single branch of advertising. That is, the ordinary advertising agency is not able to supply unbiased facts concerning the relative merits of such diverse media as general magazines, outdoor advertising, car cards, and direct mail. A company engaged in street railway advertising claims that the average agency will not recommend car cards because of its lack of knowledge of the subject, or because the self-interest which leads it to stress the value of publications.

Factors in Choice of Media

The diversity of advertising media is such that it is almost impossible to pick out one type and say, "This is the best." In fact, it is more often true that certain types of media supplement each other, one reaching a certain section of the market which the others do not cover, or one presenting the message in a way which is more forceful than is possible for others. In choosing media, therefore, the empirical and the scientific methods are combined; experience and observation are reinforced by experiment and test.

Edwin E. Taylor, Vice President of the Postum Cereal Company, says that in his company the choice of media is a matter of evolutionary development. Only those are used which can be combined to form a good working whole. It is much like the organizing of a group of men into a company. One man does one thing, and his associates perform other functions. The division of the Postum advertising appropriation among the types of media varies for each product and varies yearly as well. Forty per cent of the advertising appropriation of one year may be placed in general periodicals for one product, but the next year it may receive only 20 per cent, while one of its companion products will have 50 per cent. Each medium has certain points of strength and usefulness. They cannot be used interchangeably, and certain requirements in one year will not be duplicated the next. This necessitates a constant shifting in the type of media employed.

In advertising Postum products, the general magazine is ordinarily the backbone of the campaign because, for the particular purposes of this company, the general magazine has proved itself the most economical as a missionary and educational force. But if Postum products are weak in some markets, then local media are used there, the amount of space used depending upon the degree of weakness. As a method of measuring the efficacy of the various media types used in local campaigns, the company sometimes employs checkers who count the packages on retail shelves before and after the campaign. Assuming that conditions are normal and equal, the increased sale will be attributable to the medium used.

There are five principal factors which are especially important in determining the choice of media:

1. The product itself
2. The market
3. The machinery of distribution
4. The advertiser
5. The medium

The Product

The classification of the product will in many cases determine the type of medium to be used. There are special types of publications, for example, available for makers of technical products, or producers of raw materials, or for manufactured goods sold in restricted fields. An agricultural product would naturally be given publicity in the various papers which cover the agricultural market. Thus the most obvious factor in the choice of media is to select a medium which covers the field for which the product is intended.

Products, of course, differ widely in price, even those products comprised within a single group. There are pianos, for example, which sell for $300, while more expensive instruments retail for $1,500 and over. This price differential may have an important bearing upon the selection of the type of medium. The cheap piano would be advertised in media which circulate in a certain class quite different from that to which the $1,500 instrument would prove suitable.

The physical features of the product often preclude certain forms of advertising. Sampling, for instance, is possible only where the nature of the product permits. Point-of-purchase advertising depends for its efficacy in large part upon the nature of the product.

The length of time a product has been on the market must usually be considered in choosing the type of medium. A new product must employ media which may be used satisfactorily to educate and instruct the market as to its value.

Closely connected with all product factors is the question of the basic appeal, or the combination of appeals which have proved efficacious. Thus, a special appeal, such as price, may prove more effective in local media and applied to a limited area than when published in general publications. The quality appeal will demand quality treatment and, as a rule, quality media.

All the factors which have been brought out in the process of analyzing the product should now be reviewed, in order to determine how they affect the type of medium to be chosen.

The Market

There are a number of selective factors connected with the market. In the first place, the classification of buyers, as determined by the consumer analysis, will indicate to some extent the type of media to be employed. There are specialized media, for example, to be used in covering the juvenile market, the racial market, the religious market, and many other markets, classified according to the consumer's occupation, buying power, sex, or other characteristic which may serve as the basis for a homogeneous market grouping.

A common interest, as in radio, or in tennis, or in boating, will provide a market to the manufacturer of products in these lines, and the peculiar aspects of such markets will have to be considered in choosing the media to reach them best.

Where there are both principal and secondary markets, the media will, in many cases, be different, just as the appeal will vary. In any case, the geographical distribution of the market will be fundamental in determining what publications will most adequately and at least expense cover the field. It will be of less importance in the case of direct mail. In the case of outdoor advertising, it will be determinative.

One of the most potent market factors is the degree and character of the competition. The advertising policy of the leader in the field often goes far toward determining the policies of the other members of the industry. Either they will follow the leader, or they will attempt to secure variety by choosing another line of advertising attack. It does not follow that a policy used with success by a certain company will prove successful when used by another.

Other market characteristics, such as seasonal variations in sales and climatic factors may, in certain cases, influence the choice of media. For example, a newspaper in the summer might be less advantageous than a general periodical which sold largely at vacation resorts.

Machinery of Distribution

The method of distribution employed by any company will have a great effect on its advertising policies, and hence on the media employed. A company which sells direct to the consumer may employ direct advertising by mail or it may use publications. The Fuller Brush Company sells from house to house, but it employs general publications to spread its advertising message.

A company which sells through middlemen always has to consider what effect the company's advertising will have on them. Some years ago, the New York University of Business Research sent out 506 questionnaires to the sales managers and advertising managers of advertisers spending $50,000 or more in magazine advertising. Of the 219 replies received, 93 per cent stated that their dealers were interested in the advertising plan. The second question, in regard to the type of consumer advertising preferred by the consumer, gave the following ranking:

1. Daily newspapers
2. Sunday newspapers
3. Weekly magazines
4. Monthly magazines
5. Women's magazines
6. Car cards
7. Outdoor advertising
8. Direct mail

   Window display was also mentioned in a number of replies.

Eighty-two per cent of the manufacturers, however, stated that dealers needed to be educated in order to demonstrate the value of advertising.

The size of the community may affect the type of advertising preferred by the dealer. Figure 123, prepared by the Dartnell Corporation, shows the popularity of three types of advertising among dealers in all lines, based on the size of the community. Whereas circulars are almost twice as popular

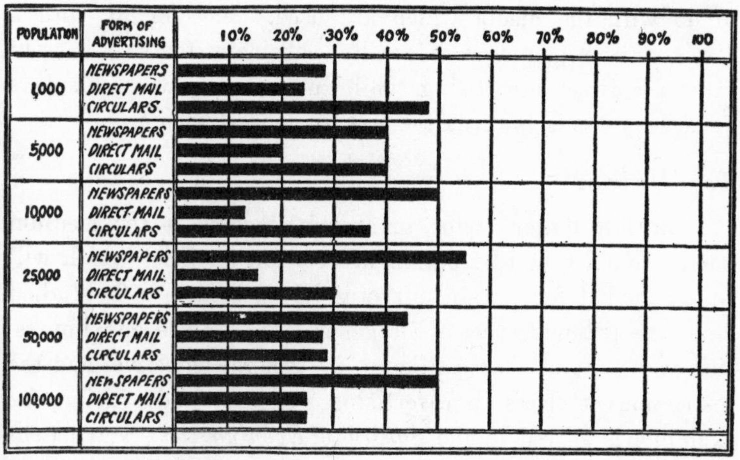

FIG. 123. ADVERTISING POPULARITY OF MEDIA VARIES WITH SIZE OF COMMUNITY

Results of a survey among dealers in towns and cities of various sizes to determine what form of medium they preferred.

(Dartnell Corporation.)

as other forms in the community of a thousand inhabitants, they are only half so popular in the community of a hundred thousand.

The Advertiser

The advertiser himself must not be left out of the calculation in choosing media. The capital which he has available for advertising purposes will affect his choice of media. Unless he has a considerable amount of money to spend, he cannot afford to use such media as the *Saturday Evening Post* or a large electric sign in Times Square.

The range of the company's distribution, and its strength or weakness in certain sections, should be considered. Mistakes have often been made in advertising too broadly, that is, in using media which cover wide stretches of territory in which the company is not represented at all. Such advertising is virtually wasted.

The facilities for handling advertising may have something to do with the media which are used. A company with a direct-mail department naturally considers that it is well fitted for direct advertising, while the company which employs an agency tends towards the use of general media.

The Medium

The last major factor in choosing media is the medium itself. Each type of medium has certain qualities which will recommend it for certain purposes. It will have to be studied from the point of view of its general appearance and impression value, its mechanical detail, its general objective, and the restrictions it places on advertising. Cigarette advertising, for example, is barred in the *Saturday Evening Post,* and patent medicines in the *New York Times.*

Analyzing the circulation of the medium allows the advertiser to judge whether his market will be covered adequately. A study of circulation should be both quantitative and qualitative. It should be carried out according to geographical location of subscribers, and according to the type of individual subscriber. A study of duplication of media may prove important.

If direct mail is being considered, it is essential to map out the mailing list or even to test mailings on a small scale. In the case of a general periodical, there are questions of editorial policy, reader interest, nature of other advertising carried, editorial content, secondary circulation, and similar problems, to be considered. These have already been discussed.

ources of Information

Information in regard to the types of media available may e obtained from a number of sources. First of all, there is e experience of the advertiser in his previous campaigns. If e has had a long record, he will doubtless have in his posession a quantity of data as to the media he has used. He ill also have acquired convictions as to which media are most seful for his purposes.

For information in regard to periodicals and newspapers e would be likely to consult first of all the facts supplied by e Audit Bureau of Circulations, which verifies the circulaon facts of over 96 per cent of the daily newspapers in the nited States and Canada and over 90 per cent of the pubshing and advertising business concerned in national adversing. When a publisher becomes a member of the Bureau, is books are subject to audit once a year and he must furnish statement of circulation every six months. These statements re duplicated by the Bureau and issued to advertiser and dvertising agency members. The "A. B. C. Blue Book" is a ompilation of all publishers' statements represented in the ureau, bound in book form. Figure 124 shows the informaion which should be secured in regard to media, the shaded ortions representing that furnished by the Audit Bureau of irculations.

The A. B. C. report seeks the answer to three fundamental uestions: (1) How many copies of the paper were printed? 2) Where were these copies distributed? and (3) How was his distribution obtained? Because of the fact that a pubisher member must answer these questions to remain a member of the Bureau, there has been considerable education among he publishers as to the accurate tabulation of circulation igures; they have sensed the value and advisability of accurate ecord keeping. Thus the Bureau has exercised an elevating nfluence by tending to enforce the standardization of records. he publisher knows that his statement will be checked by the nnual audit and therefore the tendency is for him to make

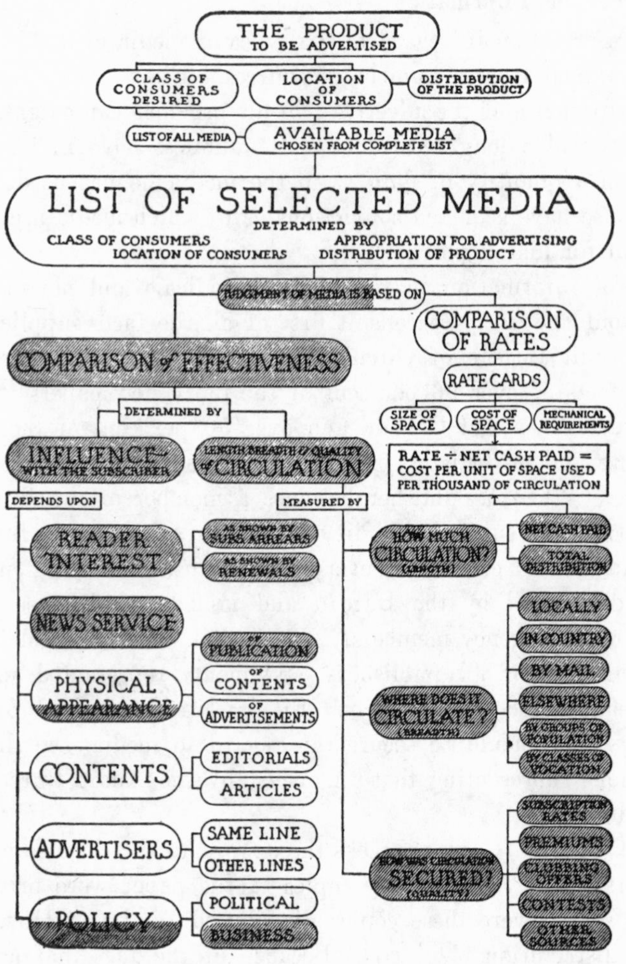

FIG. 124. INFORMATION NECESSARY IN SELECTING MEDIA

The shaded blocks represent information obtainable from the Aud[it] Bureau of Circulations.

his statements as accurate and dependable as is humanl[y] possible.

Figure 125 illustrates the form of auditor's report used f[or] a general publication. It differs slightly for a business pu[b]lication or a newspaper.

FIG. 125.—FORM OF AUDITOR'S REPORT OF THE AUDIT BUREAU OF CIRCULATIONS

AUDIT BUREAU OF CIRCULATIONS
CENTURY BUILDING, CHICAGO

AUDITOR'S REPORT

1. LIFE
2. New York
3. New York 4. *Year Estab.*, 1883
5. *Published* weekly
6. *Report for* twelve months ending Dec. 31, 1924

Date Examined, February, 1923

AVERAGE NET PAID	
1st Quarter, 1924......	131,301
2nd Quarter, 1924......	118,983
3rd Quarter, 1924......	123,276
4th Quarter, 1924......	123,544

8. Average Distribution for period covered by Paragraph 6 above:

Mail Subscribers (Individual)...	46,022	Correspondents...............	....
Net Sales through Newsdealers..	77,233	Advertisers..................	1,096
Single Issue Sales.............	55	Advertising Agencies..........	682
		Exchanges and Complimentary..	280
		Canvassers and Samples........	648
TOTAL NET PAID................	123,310	Employees.....................	50
Term Subscriptions in Bulk.....	804	File Copies...................	428
Single Issue Sales in Bulk.......	162	Canceled Credit Subs..........	20
TOTAL NET PAID INC. BULK..	124,276	TOTAL DISTRIBUTION.......	127,480

10. Net paid Circulation by States based on issue of August 28, 1924.

State	Mail Subscribers	News-dealers
Maine............	453	454
New Hampshire....	365	541
Vermont..........	244	294
Massachusetts.....	3,320	5,363
Rhode Island......	404	791
Connecticut........	1,383	1,077
New England.......	6,169	8,520
New York.........	7,251	16,683
New Jersey........	2,109	2,887
Pennsylvania......	3,832	7,651
Middle Atlantic.....	13,192	27,221
Delaware..........	120	213
Maryland.........	339	912
Dist. of Columbia..	393	1,409
Virginia..........	468	440
West Virginia......	278	571
North Carolina.....	372	307
South Carolina.....	419	209
Georgia..........	410	1,075
Florida...........	241	1,728
South Atlantic......	3,100	6,864
Ohio..............	1,988	4,822
Indiana...........	918	1,974
Illinois...........	2,661	4,607
Michigan..........	1,459	2,619
Wisconsin..........	814	772
East North Central..	7,840	14,794
Kentucky.........	401	522
Tennessee.........	370	532
Alabama..........	239	503
Mississippi.........	169	278
East South Central..	1,179	1,835

State	Mail Subscribers	News-dealers
Minnesota.........	736	1,769
Iowa..............	699	1,158
Missouri..........	673	1,646
North Dakota.....	61	181
South Dakota......	85	173
Nebraska..........	254	1,161
Kansas............	217	791
West North Central..	2,725	6,879
Arkansas..........	109	377
Louisiana..........	257	661
Oklahoma..........	145	773
Texas.............	708	1,987
West South Central..	1,219	3,798
Montana..........	168	381
Idaho.............	117	260
Wyoming..........	124	93
Colorado..........	447	995
New Mexico.......	126	55
Arizona...........	188	181
Utah..............	203	573
Nevada...........	23	128
Mountain..........	1,396	2,666
Washington........	443	1,349
Oregon...........	365	743
California.........	3,731	7,283
Pacific...........	4,539	9,375
Unclassified........	....	....
United States......	41,359	81,952
Alaska & U. S. Poss.	1,011	319
Canada...........	864	3,599
Foreign...........	2,182	893
Miscellaneous*.....	255	12
Grand Total........	45,671	86,775

* Miscellaneous—Sales other than mail subscribers or newsdealers.

FIG. 125.—*Continued*

11. CLASS, INDUSTRY OR FIELD COVERED?
Humor and Satire.

12. PERCENTAGES OF SUBSCRIPTION CIRCULATION BASED ON THE
OCTOBER 23, 1924 ISSUE IN CITIES OF

500,000 and over	21.11%	2,500 to 10,000	12.41%
100,000 to 500,000	14.56%	Under 2,500	19.89%
25,000 to 100,000	15.75%	Unclassified	6.57%
10,000 to 25,000	9.71%		
		TOTAL	100.00%

issue and do not include news-stand sales. This compilation of the
50,142 copies total subscription circulation for the October 23, 1924 issue and do not include news-stand sales. This compilation of the mailing list was tested by the auditor and found correct.

ANALYSIS OF CIRCULATION METHODS DURING THIS PERIOD

13. (a) SINGLE COPY PRICES 15C.
(b) REGULAR SUBSCRIPTION RATES:
One year $5.00, two years $10.00, three years $15.00, five years $25.00.
(c) SPECIAL SUBSCRIPTION OFFERS (INCLUDING TRIAL OR SHORT TERM RATES):

Period of ten weeks for $1.00
" " twenty weeks for $2.00
" " six months for $2.00
" " two years for $7.00
" " " " " $9.00

(d) CLUB RAISER'S RATES FOR THIS PUBLICATION ALONE.
None of record.
(e) SPECIAL RATES MADE FOR RENEWALS OR EXTENSIONS.
Two years for $7.00.

14. WERE RETURNS ACCEPTED?
Yes.
(a) PERCENTAGE OF TOTAL NEWSDEALER CIRCULATION SOLD ON RETURNABLE BASIS?
99.96%.
(b) PERCENTAGE OF TOTAL NEWSDEALER CIRCULATION SOLD ON NON-RETURNABLE BASIS?
0.04%.

In Paragraph 8 of this report all returns from newsdealers have been deducted and only net sales shown in Paragraph 8.

15–16–18 (b) PREMIUMS AND CONTESTS.

Records show a book entitled "Love Conquers All" with an advertised value of $2.00, was offered to subscribers in combination with one-year subscription to "Life" at $5.50.

Records show a book entitled "Skippy" with an advertised value of $2.00 was offered to subscribers in combination with a one-year subscription to "Life" at $5.50.

Records show that 126 subscriptions were received as a result of he above offers.

Records do not show any circulation contests to have been emloyed but "Life" offered a first prize of $250.00, a second prize of 125.00, a third prize of $75.00 and a fourth prize of $50.00 to the erson submitting the best articles on the subject "We Want Bigger nd Better Wars" which was run in the February 21, 1924 issue and ppeared in every issue thereafter up to and including the issue of April 10th, the closing date being April 15, 1924.

Records also show "Life" offered a first prize of $500.00, a second rize of $300.00, a third prize of $150.00 and a fourth prize of $50.00 o the person sending in the best title to a picture which was run in he October 23, 1924 issue and appeared in every issue thereafter up o and including the issue of December 18, 1924, the closing date eing December 20, 1924.

Anyone wishing to enter these contests was eligible, regardless vhether they were a subscriber or not. These offers were not based n any subscriptions, collections, club raising, etc., and did not directly ffect circulation.

17. (a) (b) CANVASSERS (IF EMPLOYED STATE WHETHER PAID BY SALARY OR COMMISSION OR BOTH).
None of record.

18. (a) 1. WERE SUBSCRIPTIONS RECEIVED FROM CLUB RAISERS PAID BY REWARDS OTHER THAN CASH?
None of record.

19. (a) WERE CLUBBING OFFERS MADE OF THIS AND OTHER PUBLICATIONS?

Yes. Records show a combination consisting of a ten weeks' subscription to "Life" and a four months' subscription to five other magazines with combined subscription rates of $8.80, was offered to subscribers for $5.00.

(b) PERCENTAGE OF SUBSCRIPTIONS RECEIVED THROUGH CLUBBING OFFERS.
00.20%.

20. (a) 1. WERE SUBSCRIPTIONS RECEIVED THROUGH OR FROM OTHER PUBLISHERS?
Yes.
2. PERCENTAGE OF SUBSCRIPTIONS RECEIVED THROUGH OR FROM OTHER PUBLISHERS?
22.86%.

(b) 1. WERE SUBSCRIPTIONS RECEIVED THROUGH SUBSCRIPTION AGENCIES?
Yes.
2. PERCENTAGE OF SUBSCRIPTIONS RECEIVED THROUGH SUBSCRIPTION AGENCIES?
44.82%.

FIG. 125.—*Continued*

21. WERE SUBSCRIPTIONS SECURED ON THE INSTALLMENT OR "PAYMENT ON DELIVERY" PLAN?

Yes. Subscriptions on the payment on delivery plan were received from another publisher acting in the capacity of a subscription agency who assumed the responsibility of collections and remitted to "Life" in thirteen payments.

(c) PERCENTAGE OF SUBSCRIPTIONS RECEIVED ON THE "PAYMENT ON DELIVERY" PLAN.
22.86%

22. (a) BULK SALES.

"Term Subscriptions in Bulk" as shown in Paragraph 8, averaging 804 copies per issue, represent subscriptions sold to various railroads, ships, hospitals, camps, firms and individuals in lots of from 2 to 15 copies at from $4.00 to $5.00 per subscription, copies being shipped in bulk to the purchasers for redistribution.

"Single Issue Sales in Bulk" as shown in Paragraph 8, averaging 162 copies per issue, represent a total of 8,432 copies and chiefly consist of 7,227 copies of the November 6, 1924 issue sold to various Girl Scout Organizations in lots of from 9 to 1,481 copies. These copies were sold at 10c. per copy and resold by the Girl Scouts at 15c. per copy; 1,000 copies of the December 4, 1924 issue were sold to an advertiser at 12½c. per copy, which were shipped in bulk to the purchaser for redistribution.

The balance of 205 copies represent sales to various individuals and commercial interests in quantity lots at from 12½c. to 15c. per copy, distribution being made by the purchasers.

(b) OTHER SOURCES (EXCEPT DIRECT AND THROUGH NEWSDEALERS) FROM WHICH SUBSCRIPTIONS WERE RECEIVED?
None of record.

23. (a) PERCENTAGE OF SUBSCRIPTIONS (OTHER THAN INSTALLMENT AND "PAYMENT ON DELIVERY") IN ARREARS.

As of the January 25, 1925 issue. Up to 3 months, 0.37%; 3 months to 6 months, None; Total, 0.37%.

(b) WERE TRIAL OR SHORT TERM SUBSCRIPTIONS STOPPED PROMPTLY AT EXPIRATION?
Yes, no exceptions noted.

(c) PERCENTAGE OF NEWSDEALER CIRCULATION IN ARREARS?
None, as of the August 28, 1924 issue.

24. PERCENTAGE OF MAIL SUBSCRIPTIONS RENEWED?
Actual figures not available.

25. IS PUBLICATION AN OFFICIAL ORGAN OF ANY ASSOCIATIONS?
Not the official organ of any association.

26. WAS EACH COPY OF EACH ISSUE UNIFORM AS TO CONTENTS AND QUALITY OF PAPER STOCK?
Yes, no exceptions noted.

28. Explanatory.

Included in "Mail Subscribers (Individual)" shown in Paragraph 8, there is an average of 183 first copies which represent copies delivered to subscribers by the agent of another publisher when securing subscription orders. These orders are usually payable in installments to cover twelve months. A subscriber therefore received 53 issues in all, paying to the canvassers for the first copy an amount equivalent to the pro rata price of the yearly subscription.

The average of 46,022 Mail Subscribers (Individual) shown in Paragraph 8, includes Gift Subscriptions.

"Newsdealer Distribution By States" for the August 28, 1924 issue was determined by pro-rating the returns from a state distribution of the gross draw, furnished by the American News Company.

The difference in net paid circulation as shown in this report compared with publisher's statements for the period audited, amounting to an average of 3,947 copies per issue, is accounted for by deductions made for: 1. Additional returns from newsdealers, publisher having underestimated returns in compiling semi-annual statements to the Bureau. 2. Clerical errors in the circulation records.

Net paid circulation for this period by issues follows:

1924		1924		1924		1924	
Jan. 3	139,008	Apr. 3	124,112	July 3	119,804	Oct. 2	122,060
10	132,202	10	123,868	10	118,514	9	123,809
17	128,894	17	125,389	17	117,491	16	124,455
24	124,265	24	121,705	24	116,816	23	125,299
31	132,546	May 1	117,239	31	122,245	30	121,775
Feb. 7	131,085	8	116,649	Aug. 7	120,729	Nov. 6	122,900*
14	131,065	15	117,163	14	126,373	13	124,583
21	133,716	22	114,669	21	123,931	20	123,023
28	125,833	29	117,925	28	132,446	27	123,976
Mar. 6	128,447	June 5	117,833	Sept. 4	125,046	Dec. 4	127,929
13	139.508	12	116,763	11	127,275	11	122,422
20	128,359	19	115,804	18	125,215	18	121,523
27	132,227	26	116,907	25	126,950	25	122,569

* (See Par. 22 (*a*)).

For comparative purposes we give below the net paid circulation by quarters as shown in audits for the previous three years, as well as the quarterly averages for the period covered by this report.

1st Quarter, 1921	185,467	1st Quarter, 1923	198,666
2nd Quarter, 1921	159,062	2nd Quarter, 1923	168,005
3rd Quarter, 1921	169,492	3rd Quarter, 1923	144,481
4th Quarter, 1921	181,879	4th Quarter, 1923	136,968
1st Quarter, 1922	234,646	1st Quarter, 1924	131,301
2nd Quarter, 1922	213,998	2nd Quarter, 1924	118,983
3rd Quarter, 1922	207,054	3rd Quarter, 1924	123,276
4th Quarter, 1922	192,010	4th Quarter, 1924	123,544

City—New York, N. Y.
Date—February, 1925. Audit Bureau of Circulations

How information of this nature can be used in comparing the merits of a number of publications is shown as follows (contributed by the Audit Bureau of Circulations):

COMPARATIVE RATES

OF THREE LEADING JOURNALS BASED ON CIRCULATION

	12-time-Rate per Page	Total Paid Circulation Dec., 1924 Issue	Rate per Thousand	Total Paid Professional	Rate per Page per Thousand Paid Professional	Total Paid Contractor Subscriptions	Rate per Thousand Paid
Magazine No. 1 Monthly......	130.00	117.52	11.07	9885	13.15	68.79	18.90
Magazine No. 2 Monthly......	130.00	65.00	20.00	4351	27.35	41.65	32.21
Magazine No. 3 Fortnightly....	115.00	77.53	14.83	6774	16.97	47.83	24.05

ANALYSIS OF CIRCULATION CONDITION

Percentage of Mail Subscriptions Renewed:

Magazine No. 1............................ 81.0 per cent.
Magazine No. 2............................ 65.0 per cent.
Magazine No. 3............................ 79.0 per cent.

Percentage of Subscriptions in Arrears:

Magazine No. 1............................ 18.0 per cent.
Magazine No. 2............................ 28.0 per cent.
Magazine No. 3............................ 14.0 per cent.

Percentage of Subscriptions Received through Canvassers, Subscription Agencies and other Publishers:

	From Canvassers	From Subscription Agencies	From Other Publishers	Total
Magazine No. 1....................	7.4	15.0	1.0	23.4
Magazine No. 2....................	5.5	16.0	3.0	24.5
Magazine No. 3....................	5.9	14.0	2.0	21.9

The first table is a comparison of the paid circulations and the rates per page per thousand for the three leading papers in a certain field. The second is a comparison of other details of circulations of these three papers, including renewal percentages and arrears.

It is often desired to obtain information in regard to publications not members of the Audit Bureau of Circulations. Here either the publication itself or the Standard Rate and

New York, N.Y. **LIFE**

Weekly
Rate Card—No. 5
Issued July 1, 1924
In Effect—Oct. 1, 1924

1—General Advertising

a. Per agate line. $1.70

b. Full page ......429 lines $725.00
LIFE ½ page....214 lines 363.80
LIFE ¼ page....107 lines 181.90
Single column...143 lines 243.10
Double column...286 lines 486.20

c. No time discounts.

e. PREFERRED POSITIONS Per Page
Second and third covers
four colors $1500.00
Two colors 1250.00
Fourth cover, four colors
only 2150.00

Special discounts on color, space to be used within one year.
7 pages or more...........10%
13 " " " 15%
26 " " " 20%

g. Minimum size of advertisements is five lines.

h. Deduction or rebate for error in the key number will not be allowed.

Orders for inside color and cover pages are not subject to cancellation. Cancellations for regular run-of-paper space subject to ninety days cancellation notice.

Advertisements containing black cuts, borders, etc., subject to stippling and resetting.

Orders stipulating position as a condition of the contract, other than preferred positions, are not acceptable.

2—Classifications

None.

3—Reading Notices

$3.00 per line.

4—Commissions and Cash Discount

a. Agency commission, 15 per cent.

b. Cash discount 2 per cent. on net amount, payable 10th of month following month of issue.

1M-1-25-B.

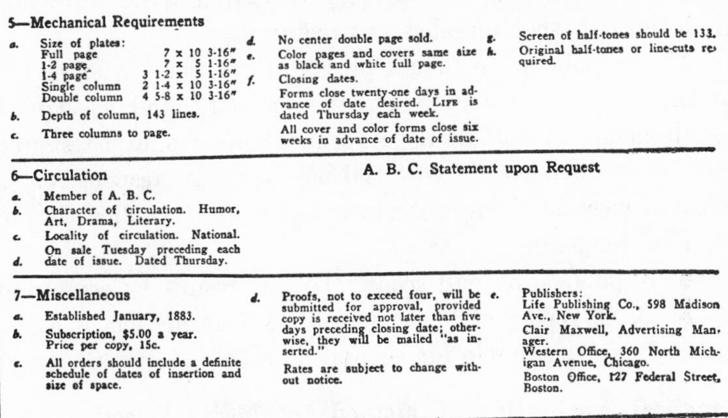

5—Mechanical Requirements

a. Size of plates:
Full page 7 x 10 3-16"
1-2 page 7 x 5 1-16"
1-4 page 3 1-2 x 5 1-16"
Single column 2 1-4 x 10 3-16"
Double column 4 5-8 x 10 3-16"

b. Depth of column, 143 lines.

c. Three columns to page.

d. No center double page sold.

e. Color pages and covers same size as black and white full page.

f. Closing dates.
Forms close twenty-one days in advance of date desired. LIFE is dated Thursday each week.
All cover and color forms close six weeks in advance of date of issue.

g. Screen of half-tones should be 133.

h. Original half-tones or line-cuts required.

6—Circulation

A. B. C. Statement upon Request

a. Member of A. B. C.

b. Character of circulation. Humor, Art, Drama, Literary.

c. Locality of circulation. National.

d. On sale Tuesday preceding each date of issue. Dated Thursday.

7—Miscellaneous

a. Established January, 1883.

b. Subscription, $5.00 a year. Price per copy, 15c.

c. All orders should include a definite schedule of dates of insertion and size of space.

d. Proofs, not to exceed four, will be submitted for approval, provided copy is received not later than five days preceding closing date; otherwise, they will be mailed "as inserted."
Rates are subject to change without notice.

e. Publishers:
Life Publishing Co., 598 Madison Ave., New York.
Clair Maxwell, Advertising Manager.
Western Office, 360 North Michigan Avenue, Chicago.
Boston Office, 127 Federal Street, Boston.

FIG. 126. FACE AND REVERSE OF A RATE CARD

By the use of such cards, the space buyer is able to keep information relative to media at his finger tips.

Data Service may be consulted. The latter organization also furnishes data as to advertising rates, a service not supplied by the Audit Bureau of Circulations. This information covers the newspaper, magazine, farm, and business fields. Comparative circulation analysis is given of all A. B. C. publications, showing the state and territorial distribution in its entirety. Rates by the line as well as units are given, cover and special position charges, size, half-tone screen required, and other data needed for use in preparing an advertising schedule and its subsequent operation.

The use of the Standard Rate and Data Service does away with the necessity of consulting a rate-card file or of waiting to secure rates on any particular publication not already in the file.

There may, of course, be special information in regard to a publication which can be secured only by going to the publisher, or, as in the case of editorial content, secured by personal examination of the publication. Figure 126 shows the rate card used by *Life*. A number of publications make most exhaustive analyses of their circulations which are available for use by prospective advertisers.

A recent study of the information desired by the advertiser from the publisher revealed two requirements:

1. The publication should present a complete, brief résumé of the facts concerning its circulation, rates, and mechanical requirements in standardized form. This should be supplemented by statements of editorial policy, reader responsiveness, and the merchandising assistance which the periodical is prepared to render.

2. A publication will secure the best results by combining an A. B. C. report with supplementary information of a specialized nature suitable for keeping in standard files.

Practical Application of Methods of Media Selection

Little work has been done along the lines of applying scientific methods to choice of media. One of the most interesting analyses was that carried out by Life Savers, Inc., and described by Merle P. Bates, the advertising manager of the company, before the Association of National Advertisers' Convention in Chicago, 1925. The method consisted of making up index numbers for market possibilities in the various states and for sales and advertising effort expended, and then correlating them into a final index percentage figure, showing relation between potentialities and effort.

Market possibilities were rated on the following factors:

1. Population, urban, suburban, and rural
2. Quantity of Life Savers sold in the past
3. Number of retail outlets
4. Number of jobbers or prospective jobbing accounts

The results were combined into an asset percentage figure for the whole country with which the figure for each state could be compared.

The next step was to budget anticipated fixed costs for various parts of the sales and advertising program for 1925. This was then distributed among the states according to a final index figure for each state.

The last step was to choose the media which would handle the situation most effectively in the light of conditions disclosed by the investigation. Newspapers were chosen for half the million dollar appropriation, while the other half was spent in 70 advertising automobiles, sampling, street-car advertising, and counter and store display material.

Change in Media Policy

One of the points to be stressed in all media research is that the choice of media at one time is not final or determinative. New developments in the field, testing and experiment, or financial reasons may make it desirable to shift the emphasis from one type of medium to another. Some exceedingly interesting points were brought out by an investigation made by the New York University Bureau of Business Research of mortality among magazine advertisers. Investigators checked advertisers in more than 40 weekly, women's, general, and national farm magazines for a period of seven years, and also secured answers to questionnaires from 150 national advertisers who had discontinued their advertising.

It was found that the chief cause for discontinuing magazine advertising was due to a change in policy as to type or class of media used. The table illustrated in Figure 127 shows the nature of the changes.

Fig. 127.—An Investigation of Media Policy

Changes in Policy as to Type or Class of Media Used

Change from Magazines to Newspapers	Change from Magazines to Trade Paper, Class or Technical Media	Change from Magazines to Direct Mail	Change from Magazines to Outdoor	Change from Magazines to Car-Card Advertising
Furnaces, Stoves and Ranges............ 3	Auto Trucks....... 2	Office and Store Equipment....... 2	Men's Clothing	—
Auto Accessories..... 2	Bicycle Tires	Trucks............ 2	Auto Accessories	
Men's Wear	Auto Tires	Notions........... 2		
Motor Cars	Seeds, Bulbs, and Plants	Storage Batteries		
Underwear	Auto Accessories... 2	Auto Accessories... 1		
Bicycles	Insurance	Tractors		
Hardware	Motor Boats	Metal Ware		
Hosiery	Overhead Cranes	Luggage Sundries		
Ammunition	Machinery and Belting	Paints and Compounds		
Chewing Gum	Boys' and Young Men's Clothing	Machinery and Belting		
Collars	Motion Pictures	Tires		
Agricultural Implements	Tractor Utilities	Furnaces		
Corsets		Motors		
Blouses and Suits		Food Products		
		Soaps		
		Knitted Wear		
Totals: 17	14	21	2	0

In addition, the following changes to a combination of media were made:

Change from magazines to newspapers and outdoor advertising: Flour, beverages, seed and seed-tape.

Change from magazine to newspaper, trade papers, and outdoor: Motion pictures.

Change from magazines to newspapers and direct mail: Tires (2), food products.

Change from magazines to newspapers and trade or class media: Hotels and resorts.

Change from magazines to newspapers, trade or class media and direct mail: Tires and tubes, office furniture, petroleum products, small tools.

Change from magazines to trade papers and direct mail: Greenhouses, moving pictures, auto accessories (5).

Evidently, the leading change has been to direct mail, 21 companies reporting a change to this form of advertising alone, and 14 others mentioning it in combination. Next most numerous have been the changes to newspapers, 17 companies mentioning this medium alone and 12 in combination. Very few companies changed from magazines to outdoor or car card advertising.

The reasons given for such changes are also interesting. In the case of advertisers who changed from magazine advertising to direct mail, the chief reasons were lack of complete national distribution, retrenchment in advertising expenditure, a limited market for the product, and the feeling that the mass appeal was not so good for their product as the special appeal provided by direct advertising.

Advertisers who abandoned general magazines for trade or business publications were usually manufacturers of products not used by the consumer, such as ball bearings and engines.

A number of advertisers who had discontinued magazine advertising stated that it had been used temporarily as a means of securing national prestige and goodwill. Other reasons were overselling by advertising agency, increased cost of magazine space, and excessive competition.

FIG. 128.—AN EXAMPLE OF PRELIMINARY TABULATION OF AVAILABLE MEDIA

Field	Name	City	Frequency	Circulation	Audit Sworn
All Chemistry and Metallurgy	*Chemistry & Metallurgical Engineering*	New York	W	10,000	Yes
Industrial and Engineering Chemistry	*Industrial & Engineering Chemistry*	New York	M	13,358	Yes
Coal Mining	*Black Diamond*	Chicago	W	10,292	Yes
Coal Mining	*Coal Age*	New York	W	10,042	Yes
Coal Mining	*Coal-Mine Management*	Chicago	M	13,000	No
Coal Mining	*Mining Catalog* (Coal Ed.)	Pittsburgh	Annual	14,000	Free—No
Chiefly Open-pit	*Excavating Engineer*	Milwaukee	M	17,000	Yes
General Mechanical Engineers	*Mechanical Engineering*	New York	M	22,000	Yes
General MIT Alumni	*Technology Review*	Cambridge, Mass.	M	6,107	Yes
General Industrial	*La Industria*	New York	M	9,150	Free—Yes
General Engineering, Spanish	*Inginiera Internacional*	New York	M	22 Spanish	
General Industrial Engineering	*Industrial Management*	New York	M	14,004	Yes
General Power Plants	*Industrial Power*	Chicago	M	30,500	Free—Yes
General Engineering Catalog	*Sweet's Engineering Catalog*	New York	Annual	15,000	Free—Yes
General Engineering Catalog	*ASME Condensed Catalog*	New York	Annual	18,000	Free—Yes
General Belt Engineering	*Belting Transmission*	Chicago	M	8,900	Yes
General Compressed Air Engineering	*Compressed Air Magazine*	New York	M	15,100	No
Metals Mining	*American Zinc, Lead & Copper Journal*	Joplin, Mo	M	4,240	No
General Iron Industries	*The Iron Age*	New York	W	12,900	Yes
Arizona Metal Mining	*Arizona Mining Journal*	Phoenix, Ariz	S-M	5,100	No
General Mining	*Engineering & Mining Journal-Press*	New York	W	11,200	Yes
Metal Mining and Quarries	*Mining Catalog*	Pittsburgh	Annual	5,800	Free—No
General Mining	*Mining & Metallurgy* (AIME)	New York	M	9,690	Yes
Limited Metal Mining	*Skilling's Mining Review*	Duluth, Minn.	W	1,300	No
General Safety Engineering	*Safety Engineering*	New York	M	5,480	No
Canadian General Mining	*Canadian Mining Journal*	Gardenvale, Quebec	W	1,880	No
Canadian General Mining	*Mining & Engineering Record*	Vancouver, B. C.	M	1,080	No
California Mining	*Mining & Oil Bulletin*	Los Angeles, Cal	M	5,900	No
General Power Plants	*Power*	New York	W	26,850	Yes
General Power Plants	*National Engineer*	Chicago	M	19,800	Yes
Steam Supply Equipment	*Steam*	New York	M	?	?

NOTE.—At least 70 per cent of all material and equipment purchased by mines is specified by the executive and engineering officials. Since mines are relatively isolated, these executives are much broader and more assiduous readers than the executives and engineers of other industries. Furthermore, the change of address of the American Institute of Mining Engineers averages 50 per cent each year. The desirability of reaching these equipment-specifiers through trade papers is evident.

FIG. 129.—AN EXAMPLE OF A FIRST SELECTION OF MEDIA FROM A LARGER LIST

Reference No.	Periodical	Frequency	Circulation						
			Total	Zone	Trade	Specifiers	Users	Active	$/Page/1000 Pros. Cir.
1	*Chemistry & Metallurgical Engineering*	W	10,000			1,000		500	$340
2	*Industrial & Engineering Chemistry*	M	13,358			1,100		550	175
3	*Black Diamond*	W	10,292			3,000 ?		3,000	38
4	*Coal Age*	W	10,042			6,500		4,000	37
5	*Coal-Mine Management*	M	11,000 ?			7,000 ?		3,500	38
6	*Mining Catalog* (Coal Ed.)	Ann.	14,000 ?			6,000 ?		3,000	*58
7	*Excavating Engineer*	M	17,000			2,000		1,000	80
8	*Technology Review*	M	6,107			1,000		700	114
9	*Inginiera Internacional*	M	22 Spanish 9,000			500		400	390
10	*Sweet's Engineering Catalog*	Ann.	15,000			1,000		500	*412
11	*ASME Condensed Catalog*	Ann.	18,000			1,000		500	*400
12	*Compressed Air Magazine*	M	15,100 ?			2,000		1,000	112
13	*American Zinc, Lead & Copper Journal*	M	4,240 ?			2,000		1,500	50
14	*Belting Transmission*	M	8,900			1,200 ?		600	210
15	*Engineering & Mining Journal-Press*	W	11,200			5,000		3,000	61
16	*Mining Catalog*	Ann.	5,800 ?			4,000 ?		2,100	*71
17	*Mining & Metallurgy* (AIME)	M	9,690			4,700		3,000	43
18	*Skilling's Mining Review*	W	1,300 ?			600 ?		400	150
19	*Power*	W	26,850			1,300 ?		650 ?	230
20	*National Engineer*	M	19,800			1,200		600	205
21	*Arizona Mining Journal*	S-M	5,106 ?			2,500 ?		1,100	51

* These media are referred to constantly during one year; their "cost" might be divided by 5.

Making Up Schedules

One of the simplest methods of selecting the media to be employed is to make out a tentative list of possible publications, and from these eliminate the poorer examples, leaving only those which will serve the purpose best. It may be necessary to revise the list a number of times in order to get it within the limits of the appropriation. Figures 128 and 129 show how this was done in one particular case.

When it is a question of one of the large advertisers, the schedule becomes exceedingly complicated. The following condensation of the Sunkist advertising plans for 1923–1924 will shed some light on the magnitude of the task. For this particular year there was an assessment of 4½ cents on each box of oranges, 7 cents on each box of lemons, and 4½ cents on each box of grapefruit, giving total appropriations for oranges of $806,000; lemons, $325,400; and grapefruit, $15,000. This was the program developed:

Magazines form the backbone of the campaign, since they reach the preferred customers for oranges and lemons, and are of greatest use for educational purposes. Advertising in magazines is directed principally to the attention of women, because women are the purchasing agents in the home. Color pages are used so that the appetite appeal can be given the greatest effect. Figure 130 shows the schedule of insertion dates, size of space, color, and circulation

Farm papers and class journals are used because of the promise for future development of this field. Medical journals are used to point out a few health facts in regard to oranges and lemons.

Newspapers are to be used to stimulate quick results, and are to be grouped in three campaigns:

1. December preholiday campaign (released from Lo Angeles)
2. Winter and spring campaign (released by District Managers)
3. Summer campaign (released from Los Angeles)

An attempt will be made to spread the campaign over the season so that advertising expenditures will bear a reasonable relation to shipments of fruit. The newspaper campaign will cover 150 large markets.

Poster advertising will consist of two showings, a month intervening between. There will also be a full showing on elevated station platforms in Chicago, Boston, and Philadelphia, as well as in New York, Brooklyn, and New Jersey points.

Street-car advertising will have a six months' run of cards in 11 states, cards appearing in every other street car.

Eight different booklets will be offered for distribution, covering all the more important uses of oranges and lemons.

General publicity work is carefully organized, such as recipe contests, and material secured in print through local connections.

SUNKIST MAGAZINE CAMPAIGN
SEASON 1923 - 1924

PUBLICATION	CIRCULATION	1923		1924										TOTALS	COMBINED CIRCULATION
		NOV.	DEC.	JAN.	FEB.	MAR.	APRIL	MAY	JUNE	JULY	AUG.	SEPT.	OCT.		
Saturday Evening Post	2,202,927	3rd Back Cover L	29th Back Cover O		23rd Back Cover O		19th Back Cover O		14th Back Cover L		9th Back Cover O		4th Back Cover L	7 Back Covers (4 Orange) (3 Lemon)	15,420,489
Literary Digest	1,389,539	24th Back Cover O		5th Back Cover O						19th Back Cover O				3 Back Covers (Orange)	4,168,617
Ladies Home Journal	1,895,240		L		O		L		O-L		L		O	2 Orange Pages 3 Lemon Pages 1 Orange & Lemon Page	11,371,440
Good Housekeeping	780,560	L				O	3rd Cover L		O	Back Cover O-L			O	3 Orange Pages 2 Lemon Pages 1 Back Cover (O-L)	4,683,360
Womans Home Companion	1,576,247					L		L			L			3 Lemon Pages	4,728,741
Pictorial Review	1,952,693					O		O		O				3 Orange Pages	5,858,079
McCalls	1,676,964					O		O		O-L				2 Orange Pages 1 Orange & Lemon Page	5,030,892
Peoples Home Journal	855,801				L		O			O				2 Orange Pages 1 Lemon Page	2,567,403
MacLeans	82,825							O		Back Cover O			O	2 Orange Pages 1 Back Cover (O)	248,475
TOTALS 9 Publications	12,412,796	3 Color Pages	2 Color Pages	1 Color Page	3 Color Pages	4 Color Pages	4 Color Pages	4 Color Pages	3 Color Pages	6 Color Pages	3 Color Pages		4 Color Pages	12 Back Covers 25 Color Pages	54,077,496

KEY: O—Orange Color Pages L—Lemon Color Pages

FIG. 130. AN ADVERTISING SCHEDULE

Insertion dates and other particulars which assist the advertiser in planning and keeping track of the advertising campaign.

Grocery trade papers are used that do not duplicate too much with other papers in the field that may be employed, and are used chiefly to point out the value of the consumer advertising to the dealer.

Wholesale trade papers are used to show how the Exchange helps the jobber.

Food fairs, conventions, and program advertising are usually not used.

Dealer service is very carefully organized from a number of headquarter cities, a great variety of dealer helps being supplied.

Factors in Choice of Direct-Mail Media

Any advertiser who decides to use direct-mail advertising can submit his proposition to at least six test questions. There may be more to be answered in his particular case, but these six will give some idea of the fitness of the particular media for the task in hand.

1. *What is the purpose of the direct advertising?* This is an exceedingly important point. If he intends to use this for selling purposes, the advertiser will consider carefully the possibilities of the catalogue, sales letter, and broadside. He will be perhaps less likely to use the booklet.

2. *What is the nature of the product or products?* The necessity of illustrating a product of large size, or great complexity, such as machinery, may make it desirable to choose a medium with a large page, or one which is suitable for the reproduction of color. A new product will require more explanatory copy. For this purpose the booklet is often used.

3. *What is the price of the product?* Direct-mail literature can readily be adapted to carry the price appeal effectively. A high-class product can be advertised on high quality paper, with good art work, and sent under first-class postage. The bargain appeal can be carried out successfully by the use of cheap paper, the featuring of price, the use of flashy color, and by other similar expedients.

4. *What is the nature of the medium?* Each of the various media of direct advertising has certain characteristics, which fit it particularly for certain purposes. The catalogue is kept for reference, the booklet is read during leisure moments, the broadside makes its effect immediately or not at all; so also the envelope stuffer.

5. *What is the margin of profit?* Direct advertising is often a matter of dollars and cents, especially when it is used for purposes of selling. (The distinction between direct advertising and mail-order advertising is arbitrary and difficult to maintain.) If there is a large margin of profit between cost and selling price, this permits a more elaborate treatment

of advertising literature. An article which depends on volume of sales and turnover for profits will naturally have to be advertised by means of the less expensive media and reproduction methods.

6. *What is the nature of competition?* The question of other advertisers in the same line of business is as important in direct advertising as in the case of periodicals. Figure 131 shows an analysis of what various companies which make food products put in their recipe books in the way of advertising. If a company were putting out a recipe book for the first time, this table would give an idea of what other companies had found to be a successful proportion of reading and advertising matter.

FIG. 131.—AN INVESTIGATION OF COMPETITIVE METHODS

Comparative Space Devoted to Recipes and Advertising in Specialty Cook Books

Speciality	Title	Recipes, Pages	Advertising, Pages
Pillsbury............	Pillsbury's Cook Book.......	72	2
	100 Delicious Foods.........	24	2
	Here's Health (bran recipes)..	6	15*
Knox Gelatine.........	Dainty Desserts............	35	2
	Food Economy..............	27	2
Shredded Wheat......	Health from Wheat..........	25	16†
	Fifty Ways of Serving.......	16	2
Postum Cereal........	101 Prize Recipes...........	33	5
	Better Breakfasts...........	11	8
Hawaiian Pineapple...	99 Recipes.................	28	2
Kraft Cheese.........	Ways to Serve Cheese........	28	2
Armour.............	Ways to Serve Ham..........	24	6
Carnation Milk.......	100 Favorite Recipes.........	29	2
Pet Milk............	Frozen Desserts.............	12	2
	Uses of Pet Milk............	12	2
	Superiority of Pet Milk......	9	1
H-O Cereal..........	Presto Flour Book.........	18	2
Sunkist.............	Every-Day Recipes..........	39	6
American Stove.......	Temperature Cooking........	115	2
Mirro Aluminum.....	Food Surprises..............	14	4

* Of these, most deal with the health value of bran, rather than with the Pillsbury product only.

† Other pages deal with health value of whole wheat.

One of the more difficult questions, of course, comes when it is necessary to make a choice between space and direct advertising. The S. D. Warren Company has prepared a comparison between the two shown in Figure 132, stressing, of course, the advantages of direct mail.

FIG. 132.—A COMPARISON OF SPACE WITH DIRECT ADVERTISING

Space Advertising	*Direct Advertising*
CIRCULATION: Inflexible. Mailing list is provided by the publisher. Advertiser must accept exactly the quantity offered. He cannot pick and choose except that he can select a magazine or a newspaper with a definite kind of editorial content, appealing to definite classes of readers.	CIRCULATION: Flexible. The advertiser can select his own circulation or mailing list by communities, by businesses, by professions, by social or executive positions.
MAILING DATES: These are set by the publisher.	MAILING DATES: These can be exactly suited to the work in hand.
TIMELINESS: Closing dates of magazines often prevent taking advantage of items of immediate news interest. The advertiser in the daily newspaper can use copy of immediate news interest.	TIMELINESS: Items of immediate news interest can be put into type and mailed while the interest is keen.
UNIT OF SPACE: Advertiser must use the units of space determined by the publisher.	UNIT OF SPACE: This can be whatever size and shape seems desirable for the presentation of the subject under discussion.
PRINTING TREATMENT: The advertiser must be guided by rules established by publishers regarding ink, type, and paper.	PRINTING TREATMENT: This can be whatever is necessary or desirable to promote the particular subject being promoted.
COST PER UNIT: The per unit per reader cost of space advertising is low—especially when each one of the entire reader group is a possible purchaser, or influences possible purchases.	COST PER UNIT: The per unit per reader cost of direct advertising may be low or high according to the character of the mailing. On envelope enclosures and package inserts, where carrying charges are already paid, for instance, the per unit charge can be very low.

Fig. 132.—*Continued*

Space Advertising

Advertising Competition: Magazines and newspapers carry advertising of competitors and of many other businesses.

Information to Competitors: In a space campaign the scope and character of the effort is usually apparent to competitors.

Direct Advertising

Advertising Competition: Direct advertising pieces usually are devoted exclusively to the business of a single advertiser.

Information to Competitors: In a direct advertising campaign, the scope of the effort is not apparent to competitors. The list may comprise one section of the country or all sections. It may comprise one hundred names or one million names.

This comparison *shows why space advertising and direct advertising can be combined to excellent advantage. Magazine and newspaper space can be secured at a comparatively low unit of reader cost. Direct advertising can supplement space advertising because a message can be exactly suited in wording, size, printing, treatment, and mailing date to the needs of individual groups—whether wholesaler, retailer, or consumer.*

PART IV

THE ADVERTISING CAMPAIGN

CHAPTER XV

ANALYSIS OF THE MARKETING FACILITIES

In the preceding sections, methods have been described for analyzing the product and the appeals by which it may best be advertised; the market has been subjected to analysis; the methods of locating those consumers upon whom the appeals have made their impression, and who are prospects for the product, have been indicated; finally, the media, which constitute the vehicle by which the appeals may be carried to the market, have been considered.

The product and the market are, to a degree, static and passive. Some *machinery* is required to bring them together; and if this machinery is highly efficient, the result will be maximum sales. The machinery consists of the marketing facilities, often highly organized, always delicate.

Ordinarily, it is made up of several components, which are often separate corporate bodies, thus making the whole system all the harder to coördinate for smoothest operation. The distributive mechanism may consist of manufacturer, wholesaler, retailer, and consumer. This is the classic system. All of these members must work in harmony, for the closest correlation is necessary in order to obtain the most efficient marketing of the product. The introduction of advertising as a major marketing force, and of the advertising agency as marketing functionary, have brought about additional complications. In the long run, the conformity or lack of conformity of the advertising with the marketing facilities will make or break the continued success of an advertising program.

Old-time copy men have sometimes said that they did not care to know anything about the subject. Given the product,

FIG. 133. THE METHOD OF DISTRIBUTION AFFECTS THE ADVERTISING
This manufacturer sells through the trade.

they would write copy which would sell it. This is not feasible, under present-day conditions. Before advertising can be prepared, there must be knowledge of the marketing machinery. An *analysis* of the company's own marketing facilities, and of the trade channels and outlets, and of the organizations which

FIG. 134. THE METHOD OF DISTRIBUTION AFFECTS THE ADVERTISING
This manufacturer sells through house-to-house canvassers.

handle and carry the advertising, are absolute prerequisites to the advertising plan.

The Distributive Channels

As far as the advertising is concerned, it makes a great deal of difference how the product is distributed. The emphasis in advertising will be determined by the policy of the company in directing its campaign at some particular group in the distributive chain, such as the dealers, or the consumers, or the jobbers. A company which desires to create consumer brand consciousness will try to make advertising serve its purpose, and will thus endeavor to make consumer demand react all along the line of distribution, causing each factor, such as dealer and jobber, to keep the product moving. Other companies will place major emphasis on the dealer, believing that he is the pivotal point in the creation of demand; that what he recommends the consumer will buy; and that what he orders the jobber will stock. In some cases, advertising is the backbone of the whole distributive system, the entire mechanism being useless as soon as the advertising becomes inoperative.

The method of distribution will, in many cases, determine the sort of copy used. Two identical products, distributed differently, must be advertised differently. For example, Figure 133 shows an advertisement of the Osborn Manufacturing Company, maker of brushes which are sold through the retail store. Emphasis is laid on the fact that brushes cost less at the retail store, and that Osborn brushes are never sold by house-to-house canvassers. Figure 134 illustrates an advertisement of the Fuller Brush Company, which advertises in the same types of media, but merchandises its product by an entirely different means—that is, by using the house-to-house canvasser.

Another example of the effect of distribution upon advertising is that of the Ford Motor Company in the introduction of its installment-selling plan. Whereas it had previously sold its cars without periodical advertising, it became advisable to explain its plan directly to the public through the columns of magazines and newspapers.

Choice of Channels

Since the channels of distribution do exercise an important influence on the manner of advertising, advertising research should cover them carefully. Figure 135 indicates the types of distribution used by 50 leading manufacturers in a number

		TYPES OF DISTRIBUTION					
		SALES MADE DIRECTLY TO					
Company Number	Product	Jobbers Wholesalers	Distributors	Sales Agents Brokers	Branch Houses	Retailers	Consumers
1	Automobile		▬				
2	Automobile		▬		▬		
3	Books						▬
4	Building Materials	▬				▬	
5	Building Materials					▬	
6	Clocks	▬				▬	
7	Clothing					▬	
8	Confectionery		▬			▬	
9	Dentifrice	▬					
10	Dentifrice	▬					
11	Dentifrice	▬				▬	
12	Drug Preparations	▬				▬	
13	Floor Covering	▬				▬	
14	Floor Covering	▬					
15	Food	▬					
16	Food	▬					
17	Food			▬			
18	Food	▬				▬	
19	Food	▬					
20	Food	▬		▬		▬	
21	Furniture	▬				▬	
22	Haberdashery					▬	
23	Heating Equipment	▬				▬	
24	Hosiery					▬	
25	Hosiery					▬	
26	Household Utility						▬
27	Luggage	▬				▬	
28	Magazines	▬				▬	▬
29	Magazine Advertising			▬			▬
30	Musical Instruments		▬				
31	Office Equipment			▬			▬
32	Office Equipment			▬			▬
33	Paint & Varnish				▬	▬	
34	Petroleum	▬				▬	
35	Photo Materials					▬	
36	Public Utility				▬		
37	Radio		▬				
38	Railroad (freight)						▬
39	Railroad (passengers)			▬			▬
40	Rubber Goods	▬				▬	
41	Soap	▬				▬	
42	Sporting Goods				▬	▬	
43	Steamship (freight)			▬			▬
44	Steamship (passengers)			▬			▬
45	Storage Battery		▬			▬	
46	Tires	▬				▬	
47	Toilet Goods	▬				▬	
48	Toilet Preparations	▬				▬	
49	Toilet Preparations	▬		▬		▬	
50	Toiletware	▬				▬	

FIG. 135. DISTRIBUTION PRACTICES OF FIFTY MANUFACTURERS
This chart shows interesting tendencies on the part of large advertisers. The trend is away from jobbing channels, and toward a more direct form of distribution. (Crowell Publishing Company.)

of lines. It is noteworthy that while jobbers are still an important factor, the majority of these manufacturers make their sales direct to retailers, in addition to selling through jobbers.

A somewhat different situation exists in the case of the manufacturers of technical products, that is, products for con-

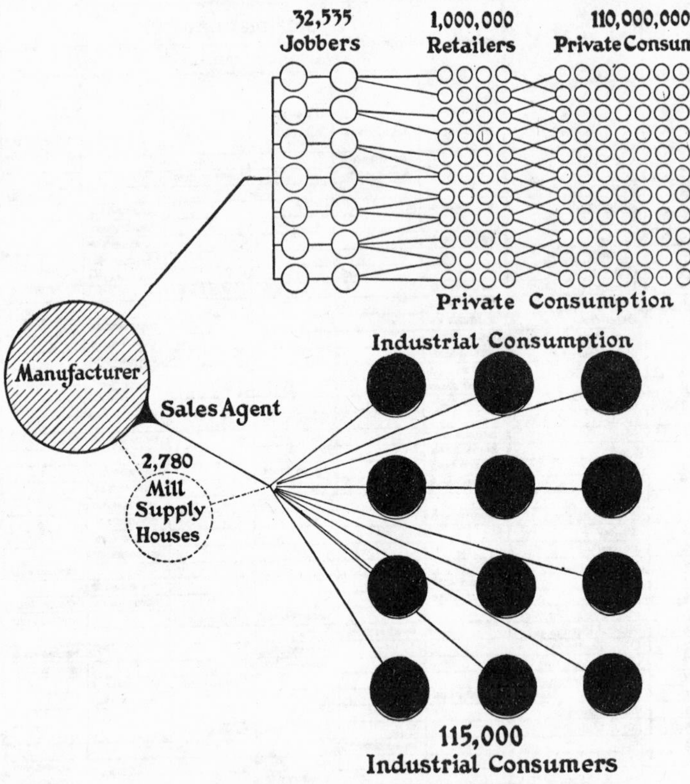

Fig. 136. "Flow Sheet of Distribution"

Comparing the differences in channels of distribution between consume products and technical products. (McGraw-Hill Company.

sumption in industry and not by the general public. Here the number of customers is comparatively small and the chan nels of distribution are correspondingly simpler. A compariso of the two systems is shown in Figure 136.

Different companies follow out different plans for develop ing their distributive channels. The ultimate goal is to dire sufficient advertising towards each of the links in the distribu tive chain to ensure maximum facility of movement and th least possible stoppage of merchandising momentum. Th Celotex Company, maker of a substitute for lumber, decide to market its new product through the retail lumber deale 'he secondary factors in influencing purchases were the con- 'actor and the architect. For the first few years, advertising 'as concentrated on these factors, mainly in business papers, ith direct-mail support. A moving picture film was part of ıe campaign for contractors. This gradually resulted in build- ıg up a feeling of goodwill and favorable comment. When ıe trade factors were sufficiently convinced of the value of elotex an intensive consumer campaign was started. Thus, hen a man about to build a house asked the architect or con- actor what he thought of Celotex, the replies were fairly sure be favorable, due to the long cultivation of the trade channels.

oördination of Sales and Advertising

It goes without saying that advertising and sales should perfectly coördinated. Yet, owing to the employment of lvertising agencies in some cases, and in others to the separa- on of sales and advertising activities in particular companies, has often happened that the two have not worked in harmony. ince the goal of each is identical—that is, the making of sales, ıy lack of balance is immediately reflected, if not in falling f in sales, at least in the failure to increase them in propor- on to the effort and money expended. Failure to coördinate les and advertising is one of the major causes of advertising aste.

The only way to determine the extent of a company's dis- ibution is to analyze the company's sales records in compari- n with actual distributive outlets available. In one case here this was done Arthur W. Sullivan, Vice President of oseph Richards Company, Inc., states the conditions which ere believed to be true and what actually was found to be ıe case:

1. Distribution was 30 per cent throughout the United States stead of 75 per cent, as the advertiser had claimed.
2. Eighty-two per cent of the advertiser's dealers were located ıtside of the trading areas in which the previous advertising had rculated.
3. There had been no advertising at all in 19 states where a ir percentage of the business came from.

4. Sixteen per cent of the dealers did two-thirds of the tot volume.

This may be an extreme case, but there are plenty of i stances where advertising and sales are no better coördinated.

Figure 137 illustrates the percentage of distribution of certain drug-store product, in a retail district. Data for th purpose were obtained by sending investigators to the vario drug stores, the investigators being routed as shown in Figu 138, through various sections of the city. By merely aski

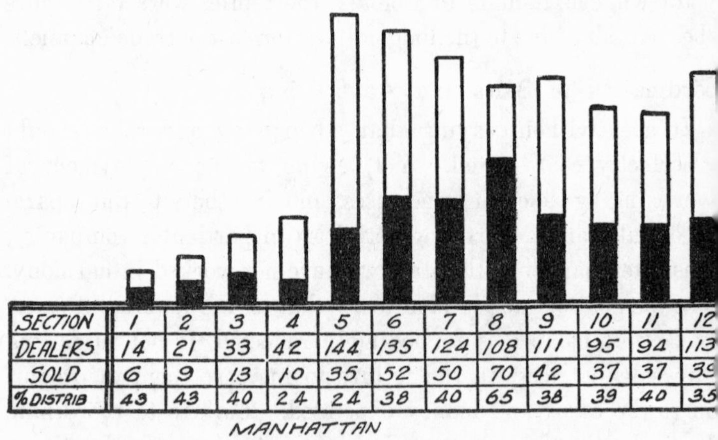

SECTION	1	2	3	4	5	6	7	8	9	10	11	12
DEALERS	14	21	33	42	144	135	124	108	111	95	94	113
SOLD	6	9	13	10	35	52	50	70	42	37	37	39
% DISTRIB	43	43	40	24	24	38	40	65	38	39	40	35

FIG. 137. DISTRIBUTION IN A RETAIL DISTRICT

This chart shows the percentage of distribution of a product in t drug field. The "Sections" are those districts of Manhattan shown the map in Figure 138. (*New York Evening Journal*

for the product in question, it is easy to determine whether is kept in stock, hence the calculation of the percentage distribution was simple. A percentage figure for the who district should, of course, be made.

Retailer Reactions

What does the retailer think of the manufacturer's adve tising campaign? A failure to answer this question proper may lead to much advertising waste. The trouble which mo researches have disclosed is that the advertiser failed to ta into consideration the needs of his distributors. One

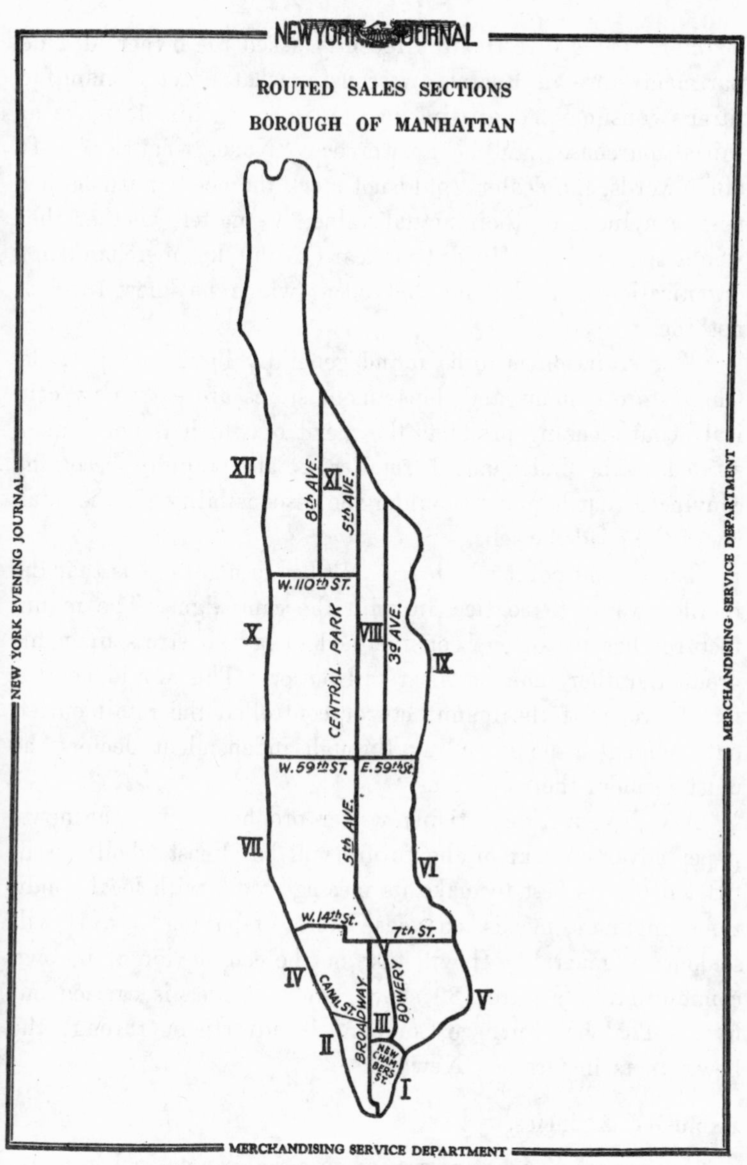

FIG. 138. ZONES OF A RETAIL MARKET

Otherwise known as "Sales Sections." These divisions of a district are used in planning the distribution of a drug-store product (see Figure 137). (*New York Evening Journal.*)

Printers' Ink's investigators recently asked the owner of a department store in Racine, Wisconsin, what effect a manufacturer's consumer advertising had in inducing him to make an initial purchase, and he answered: "None, whatever." In other words, the dealer would not stock the goods until he had been convinced of their actual value, no matter whether they would sell or not. He did not care to put his merchandising organization behind a product about which he knew little or nothing.

This situation is to be found generally in the retail trade. Chain-store systems and department stores are extremely critical about stocking products the merit of which is not demonstrated. The independent retailer is also rapidly becoming convinced that he must shoulder the responsibility for the quality of the goods he sells.

The second point which research has brought out is that the retailer wants to be tied in with the campaign. The manufacturer has too often been inclined to lay all stress upon his product, rather than on his retail outlet. This would be perfectly proper if the manufacturer controlled the retail outlet but as long as he is selling through independent dealers he must consider their opinions.

A well-known advertising writer prophesies that the newspaper advertisement of the future will be almost wholly local. "It will do its best to make its message mesh with local conditions, manners, moods, customs, habits of buying. . . . It will seldom be 'general.' It will take on the complexion of its own community." Figure 139 shows how this idea is carried out by the Thatcher Furnace Company in advertising through the newspapers in Orange, New Jersey.

Exclusive Agencies

An *agency* is usually granted to a retailer or jobber in return for an unusual degree of coöperation. Products handled in this manner are ordinarily exclusive in character, such as men's clothing, or automobiles, or radio apparatus. One radio manufacturer, for example, has exclusive outlets for a standard-

A South Orange, N. J. home heated with a Thatcher Round Boiler
THATCHER
THIS YEAR—
You Can Cut Those Mounting Coal Bills
"DOING AWAY" with high fuel bills is largely a matter of having the right heater—one that is especially designed to get the maximum amount of heat from your fuel.
The efficiency of the "Thatcher" Round Boiler has been demonstrated in a remarkable way. Careful competitive tests showed that actually more heat was transmitted with less frequent coaling.
In five series—with a size for every need. Specified extensively by architects.
SEND FOR CATALOG
"Your Warm Friend"
THATCHER HEATERS & RANGES
Since 1850
Made in Newark
Sold Everywhere
THATCHER FURNACE CO., Thatcher Building, St. Francis and George Sts., Newark, N. J.
New York Display Rooms 133-135 West 35th Street

FIG. 139. LOCALIZATION OF ADVERTISING

This company has taken the initiative in localizing its campaigns. Here, actual photographic copy is used as the basis and is then interpreted in pen and ink. Each advertisement is keyed to a community. The local dealer is pleased to find that some actual installation in his county or state or town has been emblazoned as the feature of the display.

ized five-tube set. He requires retail outlets to agree not to carry any other five-tube apparatus.

Some companies have both exclusive dealers and dealers who handle competitive lines. In such cases it is often customary to give the exclusive dealer special advertising assistance in the way of dealer helps, and mentioning his name in local advertising.

Undoubtedly the granting of exclusive agencies facilitates the manufacturer's local advertising problem. In a certain city he may have a sole retail distributor, or a number of distributors, each covering a particular section. But he is able to work with them in preparing and running the advertising campaign to an extent which would be impossible under other conditions. On the other hand, the manufacturer of a convenience product will naturally have to obtain as many outlets as possible, rather than resort to exclusive agencies.

From the point of view of research, the agency offers an excellent opportunity, because there is supposedly an unusual interest in the product on the part of the agent. The following questions illustrate the type of analysis carried on by the Devoe Paint and Varnish Company among its agents, with a view to finding out the degree of interest and coöperation which exists between agent and company:

DEVOE AGENT INTERVIEWED ....

ADDRESS ....

1. Has this year's Devoe Merchandising Plan been thoroughly explained to you?

   Yes..................
   No...................

2. In what year was the House of Devoe founded, or how old is the Devoe Organization?

   ....
   O. K.................
   Don't know..........

3. To what extent is the national market for Paint and Varnish Products developed?

   ....
   O. K.................
   Don't know..........

4. How do you determine the possibilities of your market for Paint and Varnish Products?

   O. K.................
   Don't know..........

5. How do you determine your share of the total sales of Paint and Varnish Products in this locality?

O. K................
Don't know..........

6. Approximately what percentage of the total sales of Paint and Varnish Products is represented by Outside House Paint and bulk goods such as Lead and Zinc, Turpentine, etc.?

..................%

7. Approximately what is your profit on your Paint Department?

..................%

8. How do you figure your profit on your Paint Department?

O. K................
Don't know..........

9. Has a Devoe representative ever made a "pigment test" or an actual "brush-out test" for you?

"Pigment Test"................
"Brush-out Test" ....
Neither ....

10. If tests have been made, what specific Devoe products have been tested?

Lead and Zinc ....
Velour ....
Mirrolac Enamels ....
Mirrolac Stains ....
Motor Car Finish ....
Devoe Wax ....

11. What do you think of this year's Devoe advertising campaign taken as a whole?

No opinion...........

12. What national magazines is Devoe advertising in this year?

O. K................
Don't know.........

13. Have you any criticisms or suggestions to make as regards this year's magazine advertising?

14. What do you think of Devoe's advertising in newspapers this year?

No opinion...........

15. Have you any criticisms or suggestions to offer as regards this year's newspaper advertising?

15 (*a*) In considering next year's newspaper campaign, would you prefer to have a campaign of say 40 or 50 small ads ($3\frac{1}{2}$ inches double column), or would you prefer a campaign of say 15 or 20 larger ads (8 inches three columns)?

15 (*b*) Regardless of whether you prefer large or small ads, which type of advertising would you consider best? (Show 1925 ads and "When you want to know ask Devoe Authorized Agent" series.)

16. Have you ever received a Devoe Flange Sign?

Yes...................
No...................

17. Are you displaying the Flange Sign on the front of your store?

Yes..................
No...................

18. If "no," why not?

19. Are you receiving an adequate supply of color cards from Devoe?

Yes..................
No...................

20. If no, what cards do you run short on?

21. Have you any suggestions or criticisms to offer as regards Devoe Color Cards?

22. What Devoe Paddle Racks have you and how are they being displayed?

23. Approximately how many times this year has a Devoe representative done some kind of missionary work for you?

.................Times
None.................
Didn't know of it..........

24. What was the nature of this missionary work?

25. Did you have a Devoe Demonstration in:

1924.................
1925.................
Neither..............

26. How did this year's Demonstration compare with last year's?

Better...............
On a par.............
Not as good...........

27. If "not as good," in what way did it fall down?

28. Approximately how many times this year have you made use of the Devoe Business Getter Letter Service?

................Times
None.................

29. How did you secure the names of prospects to whom you wanted Business Getter Letters sent?

30. Has the Business Getter Letter Service helped you to increase your sales of Devoe Products?

31. How do you know?

32. How do the Business Getter Letters this year compare with those of last year? Are they

Better...............
On a par.............
Not as good...........
No opinion...........

33. In what way are they "better" or "not as good" as last year?

34. Did you receive the Devoe Window Display Service during:

1924.................
1925.................
Neither..............

35. How does this year's service compare with last year's?

Better...............
On a par.............
Not as good...........
No opinion...........

36. In what way are this year's display "better" or "not as good" as last year's?

37. Supposing next year Devoe were to turn out at least ten complete window displays that were better than any displays in previous years, would you be willing to stand a small share of the cost of this service?

Yes..................
No...................

38. If yes, approximately how much would you be willing to contribute toward this better window display service during 1926?

39. Have you any criticisms or suggestions to offer regarding the Devoe Window Display Service?

40. Do you personally read the "Devoe News"?

Yes..................
No...................

41. How many other people in your store read the "Devoe News"?

....
None..................

42. Is the "Devoe News" of any real value to you?

Yes..................
No...................

43. If "Yes" what do you get out of the "News" that helps you?

44. Would you seriously object to have us discontinue the publication of the "Devoe News"?

Yes..................
No...................

45. If you want the "News" to be continued, what can we do to make it more interesting to you and to the people in your store?

46. How many times this year has a Devoe representative held a meeting of your clerks or sales persons?

................Times
None..................

47. Do you feel that these meetings are of any value to you?

Yes..................
No...................

48. Would you like to have more of them and would you help to organize such a meeting each time a Devoe representative calls on you?

Yes..................
No...................

49. Are you making use of the Devoe Home Improvement Plan?

Yes..................
No...................

50. How many jobs have you sold as a result of an inquiry on the Devoe Home Improvement Plan—either for "cash" or "on time"?

Cash................
Time................

51. If you are not using the H. I. P., what are your reasons for not doing so?

Don't understand ....
Economically unsound ....
Hdwe. Ass'n against it.............

52. Is there a difference between the H. I. P., and the Save-the-Surface Plan, and if so, what is it?

O. K.................
Don't know..........

3. Do you favor the idea of running a coupon in Devoe advertising?

Magazine advertising ....
Newspaper advertising ....
Neither ....

4. If yes, what do you think we should offer in this coupon?

Further information ....
Sample ....
Price concession ....

5. What are you doing to increase your sales in off-season months?

5*a*. Which form of chart is more understandable? (Show 1924 and 1925 "possibilities" and "profits" charts.)

5*b*. Do you think the institution (Devoe), the Devoe Line, or Individual products should be advertised in

(*a*) Newspapers
(*b*) Magazines

6. If Devoe were to make it possible for you to buy different kinds of specialty advertising such as painter's caps, paint paddles, yard sticks, putty knives, etc., at a lower price than you personally could buy them, would you patronize such a service?

Yes..................
No..................

7. Has a Devoe representative ever explained the Devoe Educational Course to you?

Yes..................
No..................

8. Do your salesmen use the Devoe Educational Course?

Yes..................
No..................

9. In your opinion, what steps shall be taken to secure a greater painter business?

0. Are there any other paint or varnish products you require that Devoe does not manufacture?

1. A number of suggestions for an advertising campaign have been offered for 1926:

Dramatizing the 171 years' experience back of Devoe Products and another based on a National contest awarding a Devoe Model House as a master prize.

Which do you think would do the most toward building up your sales of Devoe Products? Or do you think some other type of campaign would be more effective?

62. What discounts are you giving painters?

63. Have you any criticisms or suggestions to offer as regards the improvement of Devoe service to you or the products which they manufacture?

Analysis of Retail Outlets

If a company plans to direct its advertising at retail outlets, the first task is to determine what these outlets are, where they are located, and what their attitude is towards the company. If there are several types of outlet, the importance of each in merchandising the product must be studied, as well as the company's policies in doing business with retailers.

In certain lines, such as automobiles, the distributive plan is comparatively simple and uniform. In other industries, there may be a wide variety of retail outlets. In the radio field, for example, there are seven forms of retail outlet which are recognized as being important—the department store, the radio store, the electric appliance store, the battery or automobile-accessory store, the music store, the hardware store, and the sporting goods store.

All these types of retail outlet have filled the three requirements for satisfactory radio retailing. In the first place, they are able to demonstrate; in the second place, they are prepared to sell on a time-payment basis; and in the third place, they have proved their ability to give service. The volume of sales through each type of outlet is, however, not the same. Hence, the advertising appropriation should be apportioned with this in mind.

Figure 140 is a tabulation showing how each kind of radio retailer ranks in the sale of each kind of radio accessory. According to this particular study, the department store comes first as a radio distributor. Yet it is necessary to study the figures more closely, because other factors enter. While the individual department store may sell a great many more sets and accessories than any one of the other retail types, yet the number of radio stores compared with the number of department stores may show a decided numerical advantage in favor of the former, giving a greater merchandising value to the advertiser.

Fig. 140.—An Analysis of Retailing Efficiency

"Who are My Best Retailers?"

This tabulation of index numbers shows how each kind of radio retailer ranks in the sale of each kind of accessory. Horizontally the kinds of retailers may be compared with one another. Vertically they may be compared with themselves. The easiest way to understand this tabulation is to consider that while the average department store is selling 572 sets, the average radio store is selling 100 sets, the average electrical store 92 sets and so on across—and down—each column.

	Average Department Store	Average Radio Store	Average Electrical Store	Average Battery Store	Average Music Store	Average Hardware Store	Average Sports-goods Store
Complete Sets	572	100	92	36	100	94	32
Storage Batteries	540	89	86	255	46	87	35
Vacuum Tubes	375	137	86	44	59	40	63
Loudspeakers	495	135	89	39	62	68	62
Dry Batteries	845	124	91	79	43	55	47
Chargers	344	113	92	233	41	36	43
Headphones	220	137	108	34	41	67	50
Eliminators	58	120	70	174	29	87	0

This is brought out in Figure 141, where the area within a 40 mile radius of New York City was investigated by 20 surveyors who visited 1,675 stores, and reported on their value to the radio manufacturer. Here the combined sales of the 670 radio stores is many times that of the department store, and more than twice that of its nearest competitor, the electric store. The story as revealed by these two charts shows that the department store is the largest single retailer, judged as a unit, but that radio stores constitute the largest retail outlet, judged in the aggregate.

It is interesting to note how the various radio manufacturers are handling their distributive problems. The Mohawk Electrical Corporation pays particular attention to the retailer of musical instruments, looking upon him as the best demonstrator of a product which the company regards as a musical instrument rather than an electrical product. One large radio manufacturer is cultivating the general merchant in small towns.

The Radio Corporation of America sells to dealers through jobbers, but uses only "authorized" dealers. The Stromberg Carlson Telephone Manufacturing Company goes direct to the retailer. The Stewart Warner Company maintains its own distributing stations through which it supplies retailers with exclusive franchises. The Atwater-Kent Manufacturing Company is working entirely through jobbers.

Other factors may enter into the distributive problem, as where an influence is exerted on sales by architects, who are said to control 75 per cent of new building operations. In

Analysis of Radio Sales to Men, Women and Boys by Kinds of Stores

	Men	*Women*	*Boys*
670 radio stores	80%	8%	12%
Combined annual sales		$66,734,064	
300 electric stores	80%	8%	12%
Combined annual sales		$25,637,455	
375 music stores	72%	18%	10%
Combined annual sales		$25,618,883	
25 dept. stores	52%	36%	12%
Combined annual sales		$12,162,910	
140 au'motive sta.	76%	10%	14%
Combined annual sales		$9,561,301	
100 h'rdw're sto.	85%	5%	10%
Combined annual sales		$6,830,155	
65 sporting goods	79%	8%	13%
Combined annual sales		$3,359,695	

Boys

Women

Men

Totals

Men	$114,393,348	76%
Women	17,946,147	12%
Boys (under 18)	17,564,965	12%
	$149,904,460	100%

FIG. 141. INVESTIGATION OF STORES FOR THE RADIO MARKET

selling paints and varnishes, the painter must be considered, and must be convinced that the product will give satisfaction. The ordinary method of selling paints and varnishes is through hardware stores, with a certain percentage of sales, especially in rural districts, through general storekeepers, lumber dealers, and drug stores. Some paint manufacturers use wholesalers. Others establish their own warehouses, and from them supply retailers and, in some cases, consumers. It is obvious that the method of distribution will determine the advertising policy. Figure 142 illustrates distributive channels in the paint and varnish industry.

The Dealer and the Trade Papers

The average manufacturer who uses retailers as an outlet has two advertising problems to consider. First, he wants to know how to reach retailers with advertising; second, he wants to know what angle the copy should be written from.

The general consensus of opinion among retailers is that the trade paper is the best medium of approach, perhaps backed up by direct advertising and personal calls. M. P. Gould, writ-

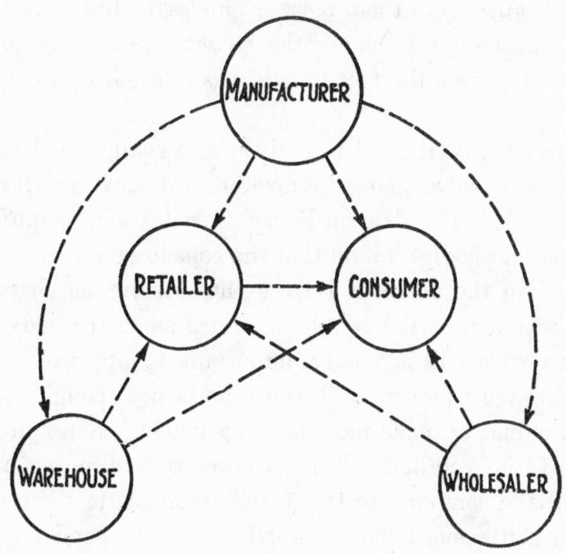

FIG. 142. DISTRIBUTIVE CHANNELS IN THE PAINT AND VARNISH TRADE (U. S. Department of Commerce.)

ing in *Class,* points out five reasons why trade paper advertising should be used:

1. It is the simplest method of securing wide distribution. This is especially important if national consumer advertising is being carried on, because "spotty" dealer distribution will react against the company.
2. It obtains better dealer display of advertised goods and advertising material for store display.
3. It increases productive selling ability of the manufacturer's sales force.

4. It protects against competition, and keeps the trade posted.
5. It shows the dealer that the advertiser recognizes the position of the retail outlet in relation to the general scheme of marketing.

Advertising in trade papers should be based on a knowledge of dealer conditions, and will take into consideration knowledge of selling costs, turnover, and other accounting problems.

Some companies have found it advisable to submit a number of advertising plans to retailers and ask them to pick out the one which appeals to them most. This gives the manufacturer a potent argument in using the chosen advertising plan, because he can stress the fact that it was selected by the retailers themselves.

There have been cases recently where companies have abandoned general advertising in favor of intensive cultivation of retail outlets. The Martin-Parry Corporation, manufacturer of commercial bodies, found that the consumer was not so much interested in the make of body as he was in the chassis, and that he would take the retailer's advice as to the body. Here is a case where it is not so important to approach the consumer through advertising, because he is not enough interested in the product to make him insist on getting it in spite of the advice of the retailer. Furthermore, it had never been the policy of the company to try to sell its goods to the consumer, and hence it seemed hardly worth while to spend large sums of money in advertising to him when the retail outlet was the critical factor in making sales.

Figure 143 is a pleasing example of an advertisement directed to the trade. Effort has been made, here, to coördinate all merchandising efforts and advertising efforts.

The Trade Influence of the Class Magazine

In ascertaining the type of advertising and the class of medium which will bring to bear the greatest pressure upon the distributors, it is natural to assume that the media most often used by competitors is the most valuable. As in everything else, there may be exceptions, and care should be taken

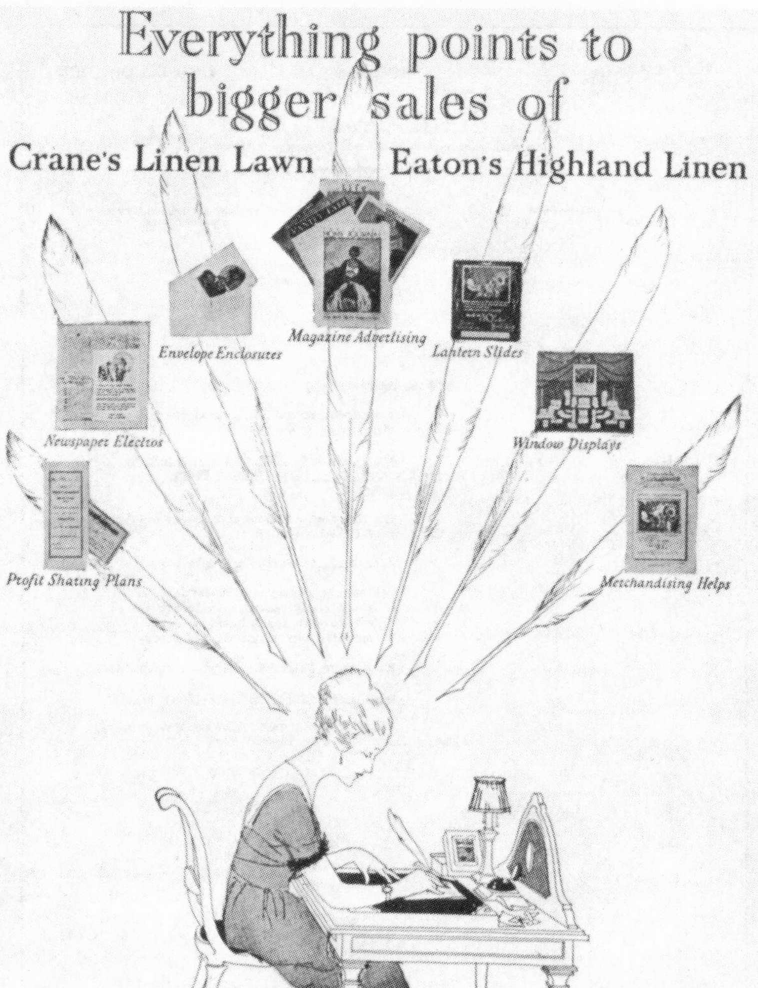

FIG. 143. AN ADVERTISEMENT DIRECTED TO THE TRADE

Excellent example of a plan to "sell the trade on the advertising." This helps in the all-important work of coördinating advertising with sales.

to investigate the relative standing which various media have with the retailers and jobbers, as described elsewhere.

It sometimes happens that a magazine with consumer circulation attains a high position of importance in trade circles. This is well shown in the influence of the Condé Nast publica-

VANITY FAIR VOGUE HOUSE & GARDEN

THE CONDÉ NAST GROUP

CONDÉ NAST, *President* FRANCIS L. WURZBURG, *Vice-President*

Telephone - Vanderbilt 2400

ADVERTISING OFFICES
19 WEST 44TH STREET, NEW YORK

EXECUTIVE AND PUBLISHING OFFICES
GREENWICH, CONN.

May 22, 1925.

Dear Miss Smith:

I am about to mail to you eleven folders setting forth:

the trade influence of the Conde Nast Group of magazines -- Vogue, Vanity Fair, House & Garden.

The argument of these folders is outlined on the flap of this letter.

Each folder develops a single point.

For many years we have known that we possessed a tremendously powerful influence on the trade. Now, for the first time, we have analyzed and measured the extent of its power.

This power is a tool ready for you to use,

with great profit to yourself.

May I ask your careful consideration of these folders soon to arrive at your desk?

Sincerely yours,

FIG. 144A. HOW A PUBLISHER CAPITALIZES HIS INFLUENCE WITH THE TRADE

tions on dealers, in such varied lines as department stores, specialty shops, jewelers, architects, interior decorators, and other trades where the class of the consumer is a factor of primary importance.

Figure 144 illustrates the introductory letter used by the Nast publications in capitalizing their influence with the trade.

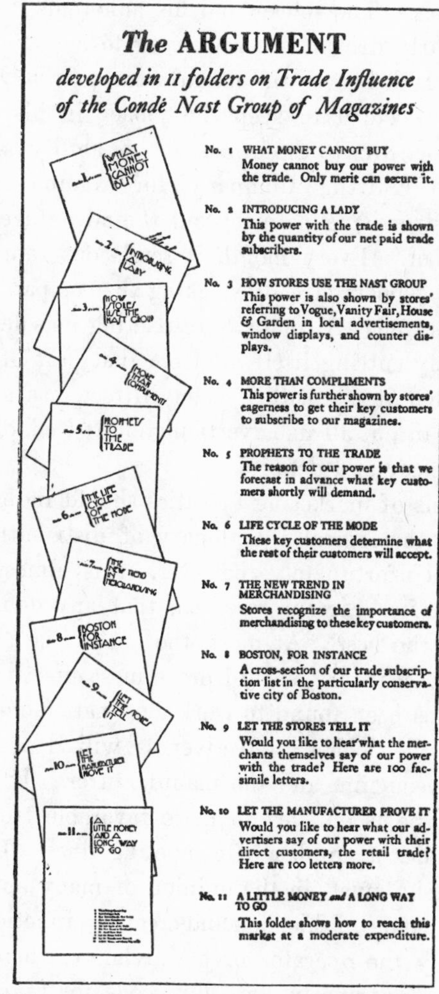

The ARGUMENT

developed in 11 folders on Trade Influence of the Condé Nast Group of Magazines

No. 1 WHAT MONEY CANNOT BUY
Money cannot buy our power with the trade. Only merit can secure it.

No. 2 INTRODUCING A LADY
This power with the trade is shown by the quantity of our net paid trade subscribers.

No. 3 HOW STORES USE THE NAST GROUP
This power is also shown by stores' referring to Vogue, Vanity Fair, House & Garden in local advertisements, window displays, and counter displays.

No. 4 MORE THAN COMPLIMENTS
This power is further shown by stores' eagerness to get their key customers to subscribe to our magazines.

No. 5 PROPHETS TO THE TRADE
The reason for our power is that we forecast in advance what key customers shortly will demand.

No. 6 LIFE CYCLE OF THE MODE
These key customers determine what the rest of their customers will accept.

No. 7 THE NEW TREND IN MERCHANDISING
Stores recognize the importance of merchandising to these key customers.

No. 8 BOSTON, FOR INSTANCE
A cross-section of our trade subscription list in the particularly conservative city of Boston.

No. 9 LET THE STORES TELL IT
Would you like to hear what the merchants themselves say of our power with the trade? Here are 100 facsimile letters.

No. 10 LET THE MANUFACTURER PROVE IT
Would you like to hear what our advertisers say of our power with their direct customers, the retail trade? Here are 100 letters more.

No. 11 A LITTLE MONEY *and* A LONG WAY TO GO
This folder shows how to reach this market at a moderate expenditure.

FIG. 144B. A PUBLISHER'S PROMOTION ARGUMENT
Attached to letter shown in Figure 144A.

his is an ingenious example of what can be done along these nes.

dvertising and the Jobber

The marketing situation is gradually growing less chaotic. he various factors are becoming grouped together within their natural confines. The jobber and his adherents, now that th issues are clearly drawn, are beginning to adopt more aggres sive tactics. It behooves the manufacturer or advertiser wh has definitely decided to keep the jobber in his distributiv ranks to support him to the utmost of his ability.

The Utica Knitting Company, for example, goes to th dealer with advertising pointing out the advantages of buyin from the jobber. Every month it sends out reprints of thi advertising to jobbers already stocking the company's line, an to prospects as well. A company restricting its sales to jobber while definitely cutting itself off from that part of the mark which feels that it is entitled to buy direct, has a certain a vantage. It can put all its advertising effort back of the jobbe The issue is clear and definite.

An analysis of marketing facilities should indicate wheth the jobber is the logical functionary of distribution, for an given case. Unfortunately, however, it is almost impossib to say, even after careful research, that any definite metho is ultimately the best. At most, the answer is a compromi between what, in theory, should prove most effective, and wha in practice, has been found to work most satisfactorily.

Much of the jobber's effectiveness will depend upon t relations between him and the manufacturer. If he is actin as sole agent he is entitled to more favorable treatment tha when he handles a number of competing lines. If the jobb is to survive, he must, in the opinion of many authorities, r tain at least some of his demand-creating functions, and n become merely the operator of a warehouse where the man facturer can conveniently store his goods for redistribution retailers.

Advertising and the Sales Force

Any study of marketing facilities of a company which e ploys a sales force should investigate the functions of adverti ing in relation to the salesmen.

1. What do the salesmen think of the advertising? Th is an important point. If the advertising is to reach its ma

mum effectiveness, it must be supported whole-heartedly by the sales force. It has been proved that a salesman who does not believe in what his company is doing rarely possesses enough confidence in the product to make sales. This applies especially in cases where the acceptance or refusal hangs in the balance and is dependent upon his own efforts. An increasing number of companies take particular pains to interest the sales force in their advertising programs, even going so far in some instances as to submit advertising to them for their approval.

2. How does the sales force use advertising in its selling? If the advertising is to prove helpful to the distributor, and it is presumed that the campaign will be planned with this in view, then the salesman should take full advantage of this fact in his approach. Analysis of marketing facilities may well include a survey as to the company's practice in this respect.

3. What is the effect of advertising which is intended to help the sales force? Good examples of what advertising can do in this respect are the Fuller Brush Company and the Real Silk Hosiery Company. Starting in business with the plan of house-to-house distribution, these companies had the problem of overcoming a long-rooted prejudice in the mind of the housewife against their method of selling. It is one of the best proofs of the power of advertising that the way has been paved for their sales force so that it can not only secure a hearing but sell its products more easily because of this advance publicity.

4. What is done with inquiries from advertisements? Where coördination is lacking between the advertising and the sales departments, it often happens that inquiries are not properly followed up. A great many advertisers seem to have included the offer of a booklet or catalogue largely as an afterthought, and without any adequate machinery for following up the interest thus aroused.

Methods of Research

The method of research as applied to marketing facilities differs in a number of particulars from the technique of product and market analysis. It is not the ultimate consumer, but the intermediate functionaries who are ordinarily sought as the sources of information. Questionnaires and interviews may be employed, preferably the latter where the number to be investigated is comparatively small, as is often the case with jobbing houses.

In the second place, this form of research is particularly difficult because it requires a thorough knowledge of the industry, its traditional methods of marketing, the success which has been obtained and the methods employed in realizing it, and the history of the particular business in its relations with distributors. It is not sufficient to make a study of distributors as they are at present. The research must go further and determine whether there are better methods which should be employed.

A great number of special factors are always coming up for consideration. Figure 145 shows the effect of two methods of distributing electrical appliances. In the first case, central stations are used for merchandising; in the second case, they are not. Specialty dealers selling from house to house may tend to replace the central station companies, and even the order of the other factors in distribution shows a change. It is the occurrence of such changes as these which make analysis of marketing facilities so difficult and of such vital importance.

The following account, contributed by Stanley I. Clark, of the Joseph Richards Company, Inc., indicates a method of applying research to the distributive mechanism, and shows how the advertising policy was changed, as a result:

Not long ago we were called upon to handle the advertising account of a prominent manufacturer of an article of clothing. The replies given by the client to our client's questionnaire seemed to indicate that his claim to national distribution was more or less a mere shell, so in addition to recommending a field investigation to determine the standing of his own product in relation to his competitors' we recommended an analysis of his sales. To both of these suggestions he readily agreed, whereupon we requested that he furnish us with a record of his actual sales to each and every customer during the past two years, by years. In addition, we requested that he indicate the kind of sales outlet that the dealer represented. All told, he had slightly over 500 sales outlets represented by three classes of dealers.

First of all, he controlled a chain of stores specializing in his own product which we may designate Class A dealers; the second, Class B was represented by approximately 10 stores having the

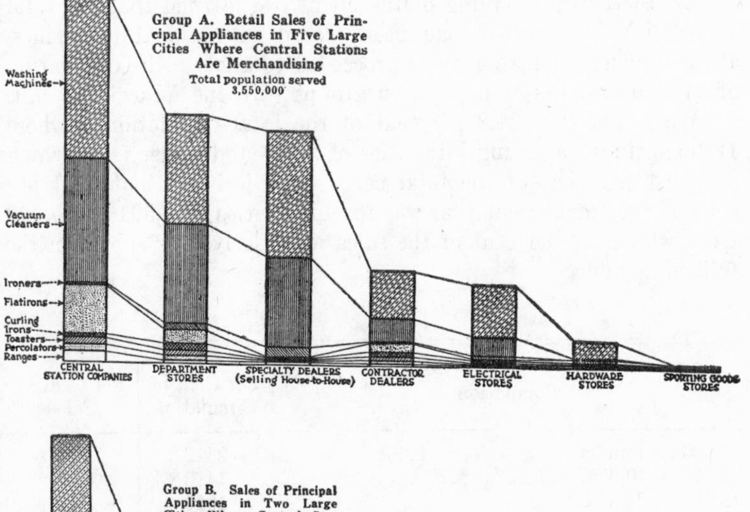

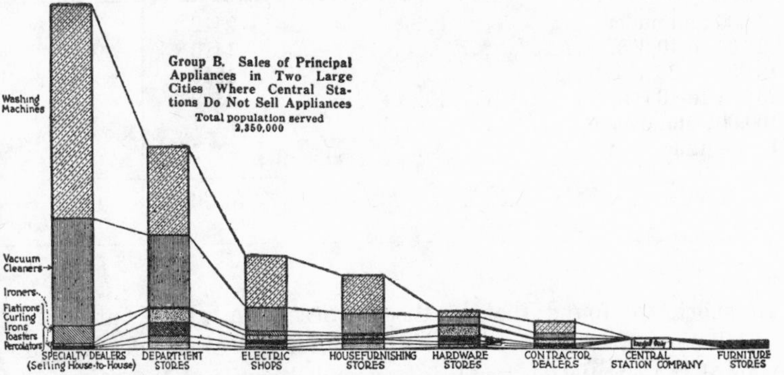

FIG. 145. A COMPARISON OF TWO METHODS OF DISTRIBUTION

exclusive agency and selling no other than his own product; the third and by far the largest group, Class C were independent dealers scattered throughout the United States, who were handling our client's product along with competitive products.

Our first step in this sales analysis was to have a Hollerith card punched for each and every dealer shown on the list submitted to us. This card was coded to indicate the state in which the dealer was located; the population group in which the dealer's town belonged; the kind of dealer (A, B, or C) and the sales for the two last fiscal years. From this information we were able to show what size cities and what sections of the country had shown an increase or decrease in sales. We were able to show, further, the percentage of business done by each class of dealer, totally and on a per capita basis.

On further questioning of the client, we learned that the total advertising expenditure had been placed in national magazines, 12 in number, and we at once proceeded to analyze the circulation of these magazines by population groups with the following result.

We found that 24.2 per cent of the total circulation of these 12 magazines was going into cities of 2,500 and under from which only 0.4 per cent of the total sales were derived; that 14.2 per cent of the total circulation was reaching cities of 2,501 to 10,000 from which 2.7 per cent of the sales were derived as shown in the following table:

Population	Per Cent of Circulation	Per Cent of Sales
2,500 and under	24.2	0.4
2,501 to 10,000	14.2	2.7
10,001 to 25,000	10.0	2.5
25,001 to 100,000	15.8	17.2
100,001 and over	34.1	77.2
Unidentified	1.7	....
Totals	100.0	100.0

In short, we found that in those cities from which but a very small portion of their total sales was derived a considerable portion of the circulation was being expended, while in the cities from which they were getting the bulk of their sales they had insufficient coverage. It might be well to state at this point that a newspaper campaign accompanying the national advertising was almost negligible in size of space.

From the field investigation we learned that although the product was giving satisfactory service it seemed to be better known to the older than to the younger generation. This fact, coupled with others, gleaned from nearly 1,000 interviews not only with users of the product but with persons using competitive products, and together with the data just set forth caused us to recommend that this client abandon national advertising for the present and concentrate all his efforts on the local newspapers in those cities where he had either a controlled sales outlet or an exclusive dealer.

Advertising as a Selling Force

Advertising itself can sometimes be made to take the place of other distributive elements. This is best illustrated in the case of products sold direct by mail. The large catalogue houses, for example, such as Sears, Roebuck and Company, and Montgomery Ward and Company, utilize the catalogue almost entirely as their selling force. There are countless instances of companies which are selling their whole production through the mail.

It is also possible to sell many types of products direct to the consumer through advertising in periodicals. The Estey Organ Company, for example, selling a product which retails for $10,000 and over, uses high-grade periodical media, and in answer to inquiries returns a brochure especially prepared for the inquirer.

There are other instances. Packer's Tar Soap, with the exception of two short periods in its history, has been sold entirely through advertising, and has a distribution of over 90 per cent. Pepsodent tooth paste was introduced in a highly competitive market and won distribution without the use of salesmen. Castoria is another example of a product sold by advertising without the aid of salesmen.

Other products, such as Crisco, have obtained distribution with the use of very few salesmen. The Campbell Soup Company employs its salesmen mainly to maintain friendly relations with the trade while its advertising serves to create the consumer demand.

It is to be noted in each of these cases, with the exception of the Estey Organ, that the product is one for which there is a large potential demand, and one which can be stimulated effectually by the use of nationally circulating media. In other

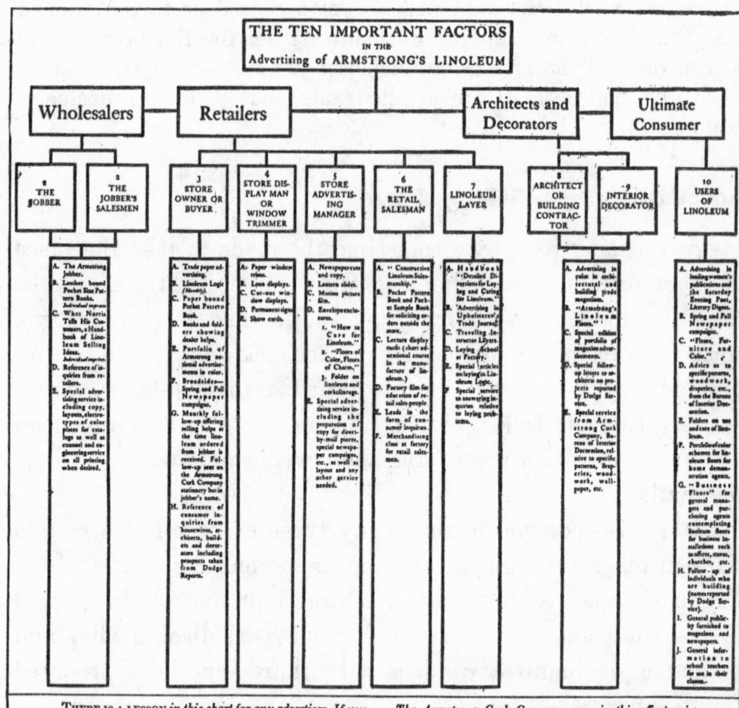

THERE IS A LESSON *in this chart for any advertiser. If you will examine the above chart, you will find that in the Armstrong selling machine there are nine factors between the Armstrong Cork Company and the ultimate consumer. Any one of these factors can sand or oil the bearings of the Armstrong selling machinery. The good work of every one concerned with sales from the Armstrong salesman down through the jobber to the retail salesman might be nullified by the linoleum layer who did not thoroughly understand his business. And their good work might also be spoiled if the architect or builder lacked understanding of the virtues of linoleum as a floor covering.*

Each factor can either help make the consumer WANT *Armstrong's Linoleum or put him in a mood to* ACCEPT *Armstrong's Linoleum for his flooring needs.*

The Armstrong Cork Company take care that these nine factors all know just why it is to their interest to pour oil into the bearings.

They do this through direct advertising and business paper advertising.

Note that they approach each factor from the standpoint of his individual interest and needs.

The Armstrong Cork Company uses in this effort principally direct advertising because of its flexibility. Each printed piece can be exactly suited to the work in hand.

For example, they issue two house magazines. The ARMSTRONG JOBBER *listed above in column 1 carries information written to interest the Jobber and to help the sale of Armstrong Linoleum from the Jobbing angle.* LINOLEUM LOGIC *is a monthly publication that carries material of especial interest to the Retailer.*

Both Jobber and Retailer receive portfolios showing the space advertising and carrying reprints of advertisements which the retailer can have in electro form or which he can use for copy suggestions. The Architect and Builder are furnished with complete printed data in filing size.

The Linoleum Layer receives a complete pocket size book of instructions. And so on.

This effort does not supplant the work of salesmen, but salesmen are better producers because of the material that paves the way for their intelligent selling. It is this consistent, careful dovetailing of the work of all factors that makes it possible to build sales with the greatest economy.

FIG. 146. AN EXAMPLE OF COÖRDINATION
(S. D. Warren Company.)

words, product, market, and media are aptly coördinated. A neat example of such coördination is shown in Figure 146.

CHAPTER XVI

PLANNING THE CAMPAIGN

First applied to production, and later to sales, scientific planning is only now coming into widespread use in relation to advertising. The first advertising efforts were largely unco-ordinated attempts. A body of experience was necessary before plans could be laid on a logical foundation.

The first question to be answered is as to who should make the advertising plans and policies. Should these be initiated and carried out by the company acting through its own department, or delegated to an advertising agency?

The second question is as to the relation of advertising activity to general business activity. When is the best time to advertise, and how frequently should advertising be done?

The third factor in planning has to do with the formation of advertising policies, the decision as to objectives, the overcoming of obstacles, and the elimination of wastes.

The fourth problem has to do with the layout of plans within the apportioned budget. This question will be taken up in the Chapter on "Budgets and Appropriations."

The fifth factor in planning is the formulation of the actual campaign plans. The campaign should be laid out as a whole, and not taken up piecemeal. Every piece of advertising should be designed to serve a purpose which is a structural element of the main objective.

Department cr Agency?

Planning will necessarily include consideration of the method of accomplishing the work. Much will depend on the answers to the following questions:

1. *How large is the company?* Ordinarily it will take

a fairly large company to run a regular advertising department with copy writers, illustrators, and space buyer. If the company is going to do a great deal of national advertising to the consumer, and if it can afford its own corps of specialists, it may be highly successful. A number of the larger companies virtually subsidize a small agency, giving it all of the business, apparently with a view to obtaining agency rates from publications. The agency then becomes virtually the company's advertising department.

2. *To what extent does the company control its sales activities?* The company which specializes on production, allowing its sales to be handled through a separate selling organization, would hardly care to set up its own advertising department, because it is not equipped to handle the selling function in its other aspects. On the other hand, the company which manages all the steps in distribution, and which devotes much of its efforts to sales, may well decide to have the advertising function handled by its own department. Even granted that the agency is functioning with a highly paid corps of experts, it cannot be expected to have quite the insight into the company's affairs that the company itself has, or should have. The agency, on the other hand, has a specialized knowledge of advertising procedure which is little understood by the ordinary advertiser. If a company is going to advertise extensively, it goes without saying that it must have a thorough knowledge of its business, and the entire industry, in addition to a grasp of advertising technique.

3. *Can the company obtain the necessary advertising talent?* Advertising is a special art. The novice is seldom able to purchase space economically or to produce effective advertisements; but there is no reason why the company should not build up its own staff of experts, and some companies have done so.

One of the principal arguments against the agency is that it is equipped mainly for periodical advertising, and that it is not generally fitted to give impartial advice about such media as direct mail, outdoor advertising, and other special forms.

The number of agencies functioning to-day is, however, an indication that there is a demand for the services which they have to offer, and that they serve the purpose, for most manufacturers, better than any other arrangement. On the other hand, the great turnover in advertising accounts shows that there is dissatisfaction in many quarters with the way the business is handled. It is extremely difficult for an agency to carry out a campaign according to its ideas of what it should be, and to coördinate these ideas with what the company thinks should be done. There is an especially difficult situation when an agency carries out a campaign which does not bring the results expected by the company, even though it is not the agency, but the company's lack of coördinated planning, which is at fault.

Advertising and the Business Cycle

There has been much discussion about the proper policy to pursue in regard to advertising during times of prosperity and depression. The monthly statistics of newspaper and magazine space show that over a long period of years advertising has increased and decreased in fairly close correspondence with the upward and downward swings of general business. Periods of prosperity have been accompanied by enlarged volume of publicity, while during periods of depression the volume has sometimes dwindled to proportions fatal to the weaker media. On the whole, newspaper advertising has been somewhat steadier than magazine advertising. During prosperity it has not always increased proportionately as much as magazine advertising; and during a depression it has not shown so marked a reaction.

The result of such an advertising policy has been that advertising has served to increase the spread of the business cycle instead of being used to retard it. Roger W. Babson, the authority on such matters, suggests that advertising should be one of the greatest forces in curbing the recklessness of booms and in stimulating recovery from the depths of depression. Control through advertising, when used in conjunction with control of bank rates and railroad rates, should have a decidedly beneficial effect.

The reason why advertising rates tend to be maintained practically constant, according to Mr. Babson, is that this policy is based upon precedent and tradition rather than upon sound economics and a sincere desire to improve business conditions. Under the present arrangement, where there is no flexibility of rates, the cost of advertising returns may soar during a period of dullness to a figure two or three times that prevailing in a period of activity.

Mr. Babson contributes the following statement:

Advertising rates, apparently made during a period of extreme expansion, are still maintained in periods of depression, when the cost of returns and results becomes so heavy as to be practically prohibitive. Basic rates should be established not when business is at an extreme peak, and not when it is at an extreme dip, but rather when it is in a middle stratum. Then, as a downward swing develops, this basic rate should be scaled down. Under the present system, the advertiser who wants to guide his business in accordance with fundamental conditions has to make the best of the situation as he finds it.

An advertiser who watches the trend carefully and who sees that business is being pushed up to speculative heights, can deliberately curtail his advertising and conserve his resources against the inevitable rainy day. When that day arrives, this advertiser has available the means which he has provided, and is in a position to stimulate his business at a time when it needs this stimulation most. Such a policy is far from ideal in the face of inflexible rates. Yet certain advertisers are carrying it out with success.

The Dennison Manufacturing Company at one time found itself in need of money for advertising during a slump in business and there was no cash available for the purpose. As H. W. Harney, their advertising manager, says:

It was slowly realized then that some of the money spent in days of prosperity would have been far more useful in the days of depression. The result was a "Five-Year Advertising Plan," calling for advertising appropriations with an outlook five years ahead, setting aside annual amounts, based on average conditions. It presupposes that the advertising department will spend less during days of business activity and more during slack periods. The plan never ends because, as it is finished each year, another year is added at the other end of the forecast. The plan is not made in detail, but looks forward to the extent of including the main provisions in our general calculations.

Figure 147 shows how the Dennison advertising is kept at low ebb during prosperous times, just enough to maintain the company's momentum and to keep its name and merchandise before the public. In periods of depression all forms of

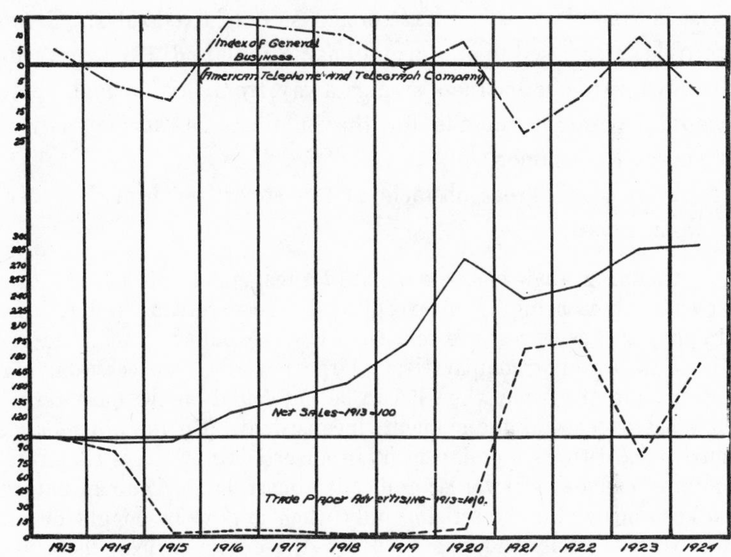

FIG. 147. CHART OF ADVERTISING ACTIVITY

Showing how the Dennison Manufacturing Company, of Framingham, Mass., charts its advertising against its sales and against an index of general business.

publicity are employed to the fullest degree, utilizing then to good advantage the advertising appropriations that were neither needed nor spent during periods of prosperity.

The broken line at the top of the chart gives the American Telephone and Telegraph Company index of general business. The solid line represents the company's sales, and the broken line at the bottom the trade paper advertising appropriations since 1913. During the good business period of 1915–1920 advertising was negligible. Late in 1920, when business conditions became bad, the advertising was materially increased and remained at a high level during the bad years of 1921 and 1922. With the improvement of business conditions in 1923, the advertising appropriation was materially reduced.

Obstacles to Cyclical Adjustment of Advertising

There are two principal obstacles to the adjustment of advertising volume to the cyclical conditions of business. The first is the inflexible and irrational system of fixed rates. Given flexible rates based upon normal business, and adjusted upwards or downwards as business swings away from this normal, there would be untold benefits for the publications, agency, advertiser, and consumer.

The second great obstacle is the advertiser himself. Mr. Babson says:

> Assuming that business is at a great pitch of activity, his advertising is bringing in exceptionally good returns and results. Inquiry and sales cost are relatively low. A dollar spent in advertising is bringing comparatively large rewards. To cease buying advertising at a time when it can be purchased on the most favorable basis seems, at the moment, inconsistent. On the other hand, during hard times a dollar spent in advertising produces the minimum of calculable rewards; and it is almost against human nature to keep on buying advertising only when it is to be bought on an unfavorable basis. Therefore, under the circumstances, there are not likely to be many concerns far-sighted enough to follow a policy of setting up advertising resources during the period of prosperity and expending these resources during the period of depression. The majority of concerns are alternately plunging and retrenching very nearly in proportion with the corresponding swings of business.

The Advertising Policy

Like the financial policy, or the production policy, the advertising policy is one of the fundamental guides in the conduct of the ordinary business. It has not always been defined so clearly as have the other policies; it has too often been regarded as a specialized and remote activity. This has often led to advertising wastes. No advertising can reach its maximum effectiveness without the formation of a definite policy.

There are certain conditions which underlie every advertising policy:

1. *Stability.* No advertising policy should be changed without due consideration and careful experiment. If general magazines have long been used, it would be unwise to drop them entirely and turn to some other media without the most careful investigation. Furthermore, the basic advertising policy should not change with every change in the personnel of the advertising department. Advertising should have a certain continuity, based upon a policy adopted in the beginning. The quality of stability is particularly important in relation to goodwill. Goodwill is so difficult to build up and so easily destroyed that any radical change in advertising policy should be effected gradually.

2. *Flexibility.* On the other hand, no policy should be inflexibly fixed. Conditions are constantly arising which require changes in advertising policy. An unforeseen fluctuation of the business cycle, for example, might require additional advertising. The policy should be so arranged that this could be carried into effect.

3. *A Basis of Facts.* A policy should always be formulated in accordance with the facts of the business. A national advertising policy would not be wise for a product having only local distribution, nor a campaign in farm papers when the chief users are city dwellers. These are absurd examples, but they are historical.

4. *Coördination.* Closely allied with the preceding factor is the necessity for coördinating the advertising policy with the other major business policies. It is not a separate factor by itself, but only one of the various policies which combine to form the rules according to which the business is carried on.

5. *Embodiment of Institutional Ideals.* Each business has a certain individuality which should be expressed, if possible, in its advertising. This corresponds to the effect which an individual business man has upon those with whom he

comes into contact. He has built up a certain reputation for himself. Advertising has the advantage in one way over personal reputation, because it can stress the good points about the institution which it represents, and can avoid mention of those features which might cause an unfavorable opinion.

6. *Preparation for Future.* A policy should, as much as possible, look to the future. Some companies do a great deal of advertising to children, not that they suppose these children will buy their product at the present time, but because they know they are going to grow up and form the market of the future. It is also advisable to prepare for competition before it actually comes. This is particularly the case when a company has long been protected by patent.

Objectives

Both major and minor plans are built around objectives. It goes without saying that the primary objective in the advertising campaign is to aid in making sales. If the product is new and as yet unknown to the majority of the market, then the major objective will be to see that the market becomes acquainted with the product. It is important to view the problem in this way, and not merely from that of the standpoint of the advertising itself. Each advertisement should be measured in accordance with the effect it will have in making the product better known and more desirable.

The objective in any particular case can be determined only after careful analysis of the product, market, and the distributive facilities. The result should indicate what the outstanding need of the particular business is in the way of advertising. A company may have a number of objectives; in fact, this is the usual case. A single company will utilize advertising to stabilize its seasonal fluctuations in sales, to introduce its salesmen, and to build consumer goodwill. To carry out these objectives it may have to use advertising in national media, in trade papers, and direct by mail.

It is more difficult to lay down far in advance the secondary objectives, with any degree of certainty. It is true that condi-

›ns may come up which will require changes. That is, while e fundamental plans will remain unchanged, the secondary ans will have to be altered to meet the current situation.

The first point, then, in actually making up an advertising .mpaign, is to decide on the objectives. Without this preminary step it will be impossible to coördinate the various ırts of the whole and to make them function in harmony with .ch other.

ecognition of Obstacles

A plan has not only positive phases, but it also has negative pects, which may prove of equal importance. A plan must ›t only consider the progressive factors, but also those factors hich tend to retard progress. It often happens that before ı advertising campaign begins to create demand, it is neces- .ry to conduct an educational campaign to do away with some :ejudice against the product, the company, or the use of the :oduct for some particular purpose.

Instances of this are exceedingly numerous. Slippers were ng associated with slovenliness. The advertising policy of ıe company was altered so that it met this objection, overcame , and increased its sales thereby. Pennsylvania Tires, because their peculiar vacuum-cup construction, make a humming ›ise when driven over the pavement. By calling this the sound of safety," the company forestalled adverse criticism ıd possibly a growing prejudice against this type of tread.

Fels-Naphtha Soap had two adverse factors to overcome, s dull color and the pungent smell of the naphtha. It adver- sed the "clean naphtha odor." It explains its color by stating ıat this is the natural color of the ingredients and does not :sult from any artificial coloring of the product.

The Upson Company, makers of wall board, sent investi- ıtors out into half a dozen states, and uncovered four prin- pal obstacles to sales, reported in *Printers' Ink Monthly:*

1. A prejudice against all wallboards was found because of ısatisfactory service given by cheaper articles. Out of 19 wall-

boards introduced between 1913 and 1921 only three had s
vived.

2. The use of wallboard in attics, chicken coops, and out-
the-way places had been emphasized so that contractors had
thought of using the product throughout the home.

3. Contractors had often installed the product poorly, usi
inappropriate trim, butting the panels, and employing other pr
tices which spoiled the appearance of the job.

4. Since every new building settles on its foundations slight
if the panels of the wallboard have been butted, the panels w
bulge or pull. This was often the reason for dissatisfaction.

It was decided to overcome these obstacles by dealer hel
direct mail, and periodical advertising. In addition, an arc
tectural service was started to solve problems connected wi
the use of wallboard. A complete merchandising service w
planned out, as follows:

1. The so-called "Blue Book," containing merchandisi
plans.

2. A campaign of three letters to carpenters and contracto
carrying the dealer's letterhead, to be sent by him to custome
and prospects.

3. Campaign of three letters to home owners, business hous
professional men, and other prospective consumers.

4. The national advertising is discussed and proofs shown.

5. The company's electro service for dealers is described a
illustrated.

6. Outdoor sign for dealer's buildings.

7. Large colored poster for dealer's office.

8. Blue Book lantern slides for the dealer's use.

9. "Reminder" stickers for attaching to the dealer's lette
envelopes, invoices and statements.

(All the foregoing features emphasize the Blue Book service

10. Promotional work for the dealer.

Elimination of Wastes

One important objection of the advertising plan should
the elimination of wasteful practices. The opportunity to avo
waste is present at every stage in the advertising process, fro
the preliminary work of analysis to the actual buying of t
space. For example, there has been little scientific analys

f the correct unit of space which will strike a balance between ttention value and diminishing returns. A great part of waste imination may be carried on through practical research.

G. Lynn Sumner, President of the Association of National dvertisers, illustrates the too common method of advertising rocedure by making the following analogy. The advertiser easons with himself thus:

1. You are going to advertise.
2. You are going to spend half a million dollars.
3. You are going to use the great publications, X, Y, and Z.
4. You are going to use full-page space.
5. You don't know yet what you are going to say in the copy.

Since copy is a sales force, this same line of reasoning, as pplied to a salesman would be:

1. You are going to hire a salesman.
2. You are going to pay him $8,000 a year.
3. His name must be Smith.
4. He must be six feet tall.
5. You have no idea whether he can talk or what he is going say.

A great deal of the efficiency of any plan is often due to e manner in which it is made, whether it is the result of a nference of men, or the work of a single individual. The tter method, once so prevalent in advertising procedure, is eing superseded by the conference system, whereby a better öördination of plans may usually be secured.

lanning the Campaign

Any advertising campaign presupposes a number of preminary steps. These steps often differ, there being no standrd procedure. H. K. McCann recommends the following rder:

1. Intensive study of the product
2. Investigation and analysis of the market
3. Determination of the plan covering:
   (*a*) The advertising theme
   (*b*) The copy and art treatment

(*c*) The choice of media
(*d*) Estimates of cost

4. Actual execution and release of the advertising in its fin form
5. Selling the advertising to sales organization and the tra

Henry Eckhardt, writing in *Printers' Ink,* puts his fund mental plan in the form of seven questions:

1. What result is to be accomplished?
2. What must be said to accomplish this result?
3. To whom should it be sold?
4. In what idea can this be summed up?
5. How should this idea be expressed?
6. How should the counter arguments be rationalized?
7. On what immediate objective should the advertising focus

After these have been decided upon, the operating pla consisting of schedules and particular copy and art interpr tations, can be decided upon.

The whole matter of planning as applied to advertisin may be summed up briefly as follows:

In the first place, there must be a basic advertising polic properly coördinated with the other policies of the busines. This is a permanent policy and will presumably continue fro season to season.

In the second place, there should be a thorough analysis c the product, the market, and the distribution. This will i clude a study of any obstacles which may exist, either in th market, or in the financial condition of the company, or els where.

In the third place, there will be a formulation of immediat objectives, as distinguished, perhaps, from the major objective embodied in the major policies. Immediate objectives wi cover the campaign for the coming year or other period, i accordance with the major policy, and also in accordance wit the results of product analysis, market analysis, and the analy sis of marketing facilities.

Finally, there will be the actual detailed schedule, cos estimates, choice of media, buying of space, and the prepara tion of copy.

Figure 148 illustrates points to be kept in mind when planing a campaign. The chart was prepared by Johnson, Read Co., who say:

The successful utilization of this chart requires a comprehensive rvice such as is rendered by the modern advertising agency, and, a protection to themselves, advertisers should insist that the eps in this chart be undertaken only in coöperation with a highly sponsible, completely equipped, fully recognized advertising ornization.

There is no attempt in this chart to cover the detailed requireents of every step. For instance, "Correct Copy" stands for erything that constitutes correct copy—including attractive lustrations, interest compelling display, pleasing typography, nvincing argument and other elements essential to the proper resentation. If every step of this chart is given proper considation, the essential details of each step are bound to receive due ttention.

isualizing the Plan

Once the market and the theme have been chosen, the next tep is to block out the operating plan. Figure 149 shows how e Lincoln Electric Company indicates graphically the various eople who have to be interested in the sale of electric motors, nd the various media best fitted to carry the message to them. here are four main classes of people to be influenced:

1. The company's own sales force, which uses the advertising s sales ammunition.
2. 2,500 machinery manufacturers with the various members f their organization, such as purchasing agents, engineers, salesen, etc., who must be convinced before they will use electric otors on their machinery.
3. 268,762 industrial plants who are users of machinery, toether with the various executives, workmen, etc., in their organations.
4. The experts and outside advisers, such as consulting engieers, contractors, architects and central stations, all of whom fluence and advise on the purchase of electric motors.

Industrial advertising has problems which are often totally ifferent from those met in consumer advertising. In planning out a sales program, the manufacturer of industrial produc aims to make certain that he covers all the fields of approac Figure 150 shows the part played by industrial advertising a compared with the other possible channels of approach to th industrial market.

When an industrial advertiser sells to a number of indu tries, it is important for him to determine in advance what th

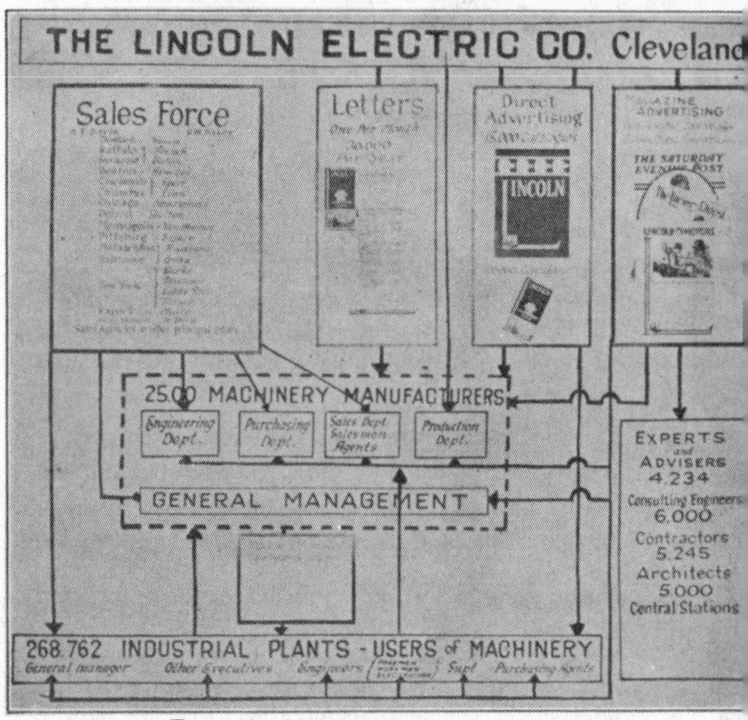

FIG. 149. VISUALIZATION OF A CAMPAIGN
The markets and the media graphically shown.

possibilities are in each field. He may find that the majorit of his sales prospects are in a few fields, and that he shoul concentrate his efforts in that limited market.

The Campaign and the Merchandising Scheme

It is extremely important in making plans to see that th advertising campaign fits in properly with the entire merchan ising program. The advertising plan of the Strathmore Paper ompany shows how this may be done logically:

According to Cy Norton, advertising manager of the company, the plan is based on a market for 35,000 people, composed of 20,000 printers, 10,000 large consumers (or advertisers), 2,000 advertising agencies, and 3,000 salesmen of the

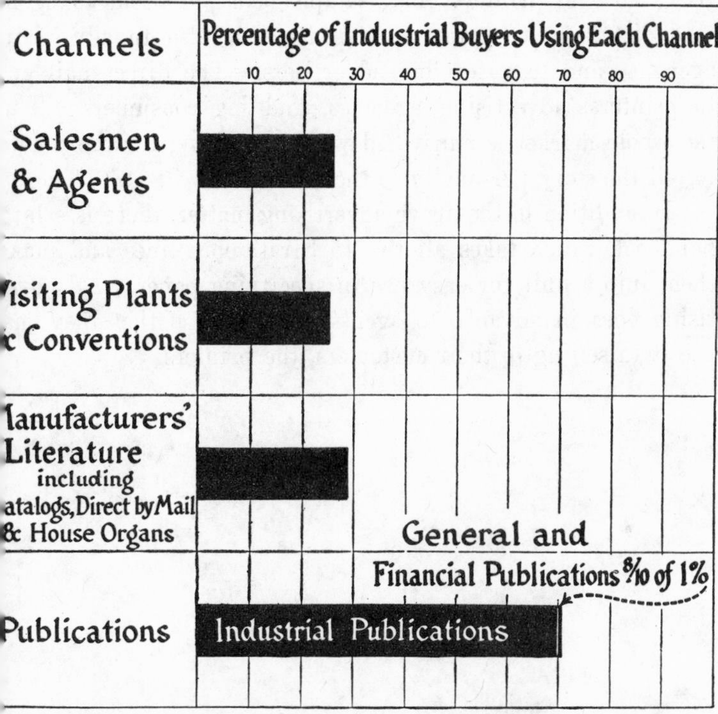

FIG. 150. CHANNELS OF APPROACH TO INDUSTRIAL BUYERS

The bars indicate the percentage of industry which uses each method. hese bars total more than 100 per cent, since the average industrial uyer uses more than one method. (McGraw-Hill Company.)

mpany's agents. Sales are made through agents to printers, ho do the printing and sell the paper in the form of printed terature to advertisers.

Strathmore advertising is of two kinds only—direct-mail nd magazine. Magazine advertising is limited to the trade ublications, such as *Advertising and Selling, Printers' Ink,*

Printers' Ink Monthly, American Printer, Inland Printer, Printing Art, and *Printing.*

Direct-mail advertising is of three types: First, a house magazine to printers entitled *Strathmore Town News;* second, sample books of the various Strathmore lines; and third, a direct-mail series called the Strathmore Town Series. The *News* goes to printers only, sample books are sent to agents who distribute to printers, and are sent also to advertising agencies, and to a few big advertisers. The direct-mail goes to printers, advertising agencies, and big consumers. Thus the whole market is cultivated without waiting for the printer to tell the story personally to the advertiser.

In addition to the above advertising matter, there is a large handbook which takes all the 45 Strathmore lines and makes them into a unit for easy use in specifying paper. All advertising goes in advance to agents' salesmen, so that they may use it in selling to their customers, the printers.

CHAPTER XVII

COMPUTING THE VALUE OF ADVERTISING

There are two attitudes toward the question of computing the value of advertising. One assumption is that since advertising benefits the company in a broad way, and that since the general results of advertising are necessarily good, it is not essential to know exactly how they are produced. Another theory is based on careful records of advertising, and the results which are attributable to it. The adherents of the first theory are apt to be advertisers with a broad, general aim. Very likely they are not selling merchandise themselves, but are trying to increase sales for their distributors, or to create consumer good-will. Their sole method of determining value is by the general increase or maintenance of sales volume. They may be able, by the coupon method, to estimate the pulling power of some one advertisement or medium; but they cannot be certain of the exact effect of advertising upon their businesses, particularly when the advertising is carried on in conjunction with high-powered merchandising through a sales force. The advertising and the selling must necessarily be judged together.

When an advertiser sets out to accomplish a specific purpose, such as to sell certain goods (as in a retail store), or to obtain new dealers, or to secure inquiries, the results are to some extent tangible and measurable. The advertising manager of a nationally distributed breakfast food says:

> In the case of a magazine advertisement, it is impossible to determine with any degree of accuracy the value of any particular advertisement of the type such as we run. In the case of newspapers, however, it is possible to appraise the approximate value of a newspaper campaign in any particular locality, after the campaign has run. Even then, trade or other conditions may affect

results, and all of these things must be taken into consideration in the light of past experience and practice.

Is Advertising Value Measurable?

In order to determine how advertising value may be measured, it is first essential to classify the various forms of advertising, and to indicate to what extent they permit of estimate. In the first place, advertising can be divided into two broad classes; for one of these the aims are definite, tangible, and measurable; for the other, the goal is indefinite and intangible, measurements of value being approximate only, in the present state of advertising science.

1. The *first type* of advertising, that where the aim is definite and results measurable, can be evaluated approximately by actual cost figures. It will include, among others, the following forms of advertising:

(*a*) Advertisements making specific offerings of merchandise, whether by mail, in catalogues, or through the columns of periodicals. It is necessary, of course, that the advertising be the sole means of merchandising employed. If a sales force is used in addition and in the same territory, it is still almost impossible to give the proper credit to each.

(*b*) Advertisements having a special and definite aim, such as the securing of dealers or agents, or the building up of a mailing list, or the securing of inquiries. By a system of keying or coupons, returns from individual media may be measured.

2. The *second type* of advertising, including the majority of so-called national advertising, and also such media as outdoor bulletins, electric signs, and direct advertising of a non-selling nature, is not readily susceptible of measurement. While coupons may be used, it is often felt that the fundamental purpose of the advertisement is lost if the emphasis is placed on the coupon. Consequently, many concerns measure results by the general stimulation of sales, compared with previous periods or with non-advertising periods. Advertising of the second class includes the following:

(*a*) General advertising, emphasizing the product, designed to increase sales, containing no offer of booklet or sample, except perhaps in an incidental fashion and without giving it any emphasis.

(*b*) General advertising, carefully keyed and containing offer of booklet or sample. Here the value of the advertising is usually measured by cost of inquiry, although a better measure is sometimes cost per sale. It is difficult, however, to use this latter measure because of the numerous other factors which enter the equation and which are not strictly due to the advertisement's merits or demerits.

(*c*) Advertising of an institutional character, designed to produce or increase goodwill. Such advertising is normally employed as a method of insuring the prestige of an established product. The success of such advertising would best be measured by the variations in volume of sales. Of all forms of advertising, it is, perhaps, the most difficult of measurement.

(*d*) Advertising to increase dealer business. This is a form of advertising which has greatly increased in recent years, with the recognition on the part of manufacturers that one way of increasing their business is to increase the business of the proper retail outlets. In some cases this plan has also been applied to the stimulating of jobbing businesses.

(*e*) Advertising applied to such intangible purposes as lessening the resistance encountered by the sales force. Here the composite result of the combined sales and advertising effort may, perhaps, be measured; but it is exceedingly difficult to award each its proper share of the credit.

Records of Inquiry

It is important for companies which rely on inquiries from advertisements for sales leads to keep records of the advertisements used, the media employed, the cost, and the actual sales resulting from the advertisements. Inquiries should be correlated with actual sales, because it has been found that a large volume of inquiries does not necessarily result in an equally large percentage of sales.

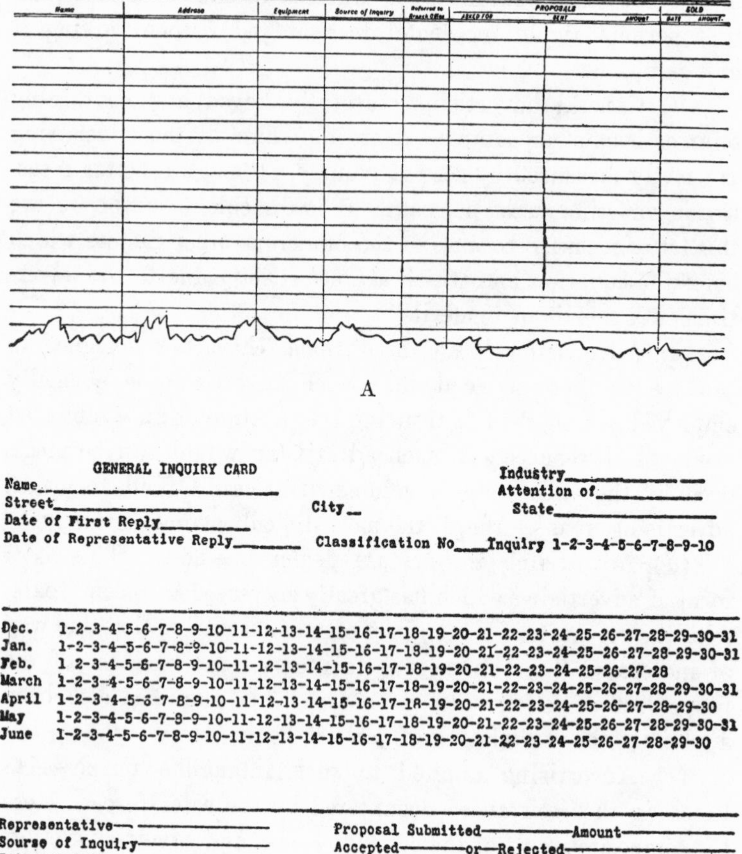

RECORD OF ADVERTISING RETURNS

DATE

Name	Address	Equipment	Source of Inquiry	Referred to Branch Office	Proposals: Asked for	Proposals: Sent	Proposals: Amount	Sold: Date	Sold: Amount

A

GENERAL INQUIRY CARD

Name ______ Industry ______
Street ______ City ____ Attention of ______
Date of First Reply ______ State ______
Date of Representative Reply ______ Classification No ____ Inquiry 1-2-3-4-5-6-7-8-9-10

Dec. 1-2-3-4-5-6-7-8-9-10-11-12-13-14-15-16-17-18-19-20-21-22-23-24-25-26-27-28-29-30-31
Jan. 1-2-3-4-5-6-7-8-9-10-11-12-13-14-15-16-17-18-19-20-21-22-23-24-25-26-27-28-29-30-31
Feb. 1-2-3-4-5-6-7-8-9-10-11-12-13-14-15-16-17-18-19-20-21-22-23-24-25-26-27-28
March 1-2-3-4-5-6-7-8-9-10-11-12-13-14-15-16-17-18-19-20-21-22-23-24-25-26-27-28-29-30-31
April 1-2-3-4-5-6-7-8-9-10-11-12-13-14-15-16-17-18-19-20-21-22-23-24-25-26-27-28-29-30
May 1-2-3-4-5-6-7-8-9-10-11-12-13-14-15-16-17-18-19-20-21-22-23-24-25-26-27-28-29-30-31
June 1-2-3-4-5-6-7-8-9-10-11-12-13-14-15-16-17-18-19-20-21-22-23-24-25-26-27-28-29-30

Representative ______ Proposal Submitted ______ Amount ______
Sourse of Inquiry ______ Accepted ______ or ______ Rejected ______
Interested In ______ Reason for Rejection ______
Date Called on ______ Additional Information ______

B

FIG. 151. RECORDING SYSTEM FOR INQUIRIES

A plan used by the Standard Conveyor Company. Figure A is the data sheet on which inquiries are entered. Figure B is the record card for each individual inquiry. (*Class.*)

The Standard Conveyor Company, North St. Paul, Minnesota, uses an interesting system for recording inquiries and keeping track of them until they result in sales or are discarded. Whenever an inquiry is received, it is recorded on a data sheet uch as is illustrated in Figure 151 A. This has spaces showng the name, address, industry, rating, product which the prosect is interested in, source of inquiry, whether inquiry is eferred to branch office, date of sending proposals, and the inal sale.

Figure 151 B shows the record card for each individual nquiry. The company has a carefully graded system of folow-ups, depending on the nature of the inquiry, whether it equires prices, special information, or necessitates a special etter from the company asking for further information. All nquiries are treated as potential sales.

After three letters have been sent out without effect, a o-called advertising inquiry questionnaire is sent, as follows:

ohn Smith & Company,
mithville, Illinois.
entlemen:

On December 5th, you asked us by letter for information on piler.

In order to determine our advertising costs and to give credit o the proper source of advertising, will you please tell us to what orm of advertising we can credit your inquiry?

We will appreciate your courtesy in replying and assure you ve will return the favor, whenever given the opportunity.

Very truly yours,
STANDARD CONVEYOR COMPANY
Advertising Inquiry Dept.

I inquired about an economical handling system because of:

Magazine Advertisement (name) ....
iterature Sent by Mail ....
ther Reasons ....

(Enclosed Stamped Envelope for Reply)

The following table shows the results over a certain period f months from follow-ups to inquiries, and also of the final uestionnaire. The inquiry questionnaires have proved parcicularly useful in revising the advertising list.

REPORT ON FOLLOW-UP LETTERS

Number of Follow-up	Number Sent	Number Returned	Per Cent of Return	Cost of Sending One	Cost of One Return
First "A"	1114	308	28	.11	.39
First "B"	60	18	30	.11	.37
Second..............	1018	182	18	.09	.50
Third...............	898	195	22	.10	.46
Questionnaire.......	3583	744	20	.08	.39
Total...........	6673	1447	21	.....	.....

When advertising is keyed, it is easy to analyze each day's mail as it comes in, and to credit the reply to the particular medium which is responsible. Figure 152 shows the form used by the Review of Reviews Corporation.

ANALYSIS OF CIRCULAR AND MAGAZINE EFFORT.
ADVERTISING EFFORTS AND TESTS

LIST
Mailing Date
Quantity
KEY
Accumulated Results
Dates

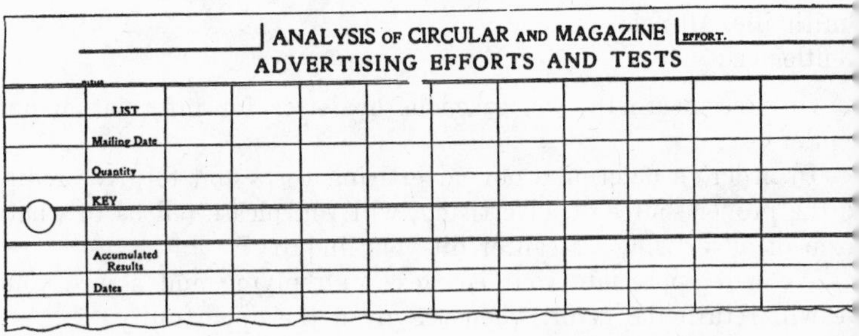

FIG. 152. KEEPING "TAB" ON KEYED ADVERTISING
This simple form is used by the Review of Reviews Corporation.

The Coupon

The use of the coupon to draw inquiries, and the further use of a key which allows credit to be assigned to the proper publication, has long been a recognized advertising expedient. There has been some hesitation, however, about using coupons as the sole method of determining the pulling power of an advertisement. In the case of technical products, for example, some companies feel that the coupon does not add materially to the effectiveness of the advertisement. Other companies believe that if advertising copy is written around the coupon the selling force is apt to be diverted from the main

Use this Coupon—
MISS JANE HILL, The H. W. Gossard Co.,
1008F So. Michigan Ave., Chicago, Ill.
Please send me your free book, "The Portrait of a Gentlewoman," and tell me what style corset to buy. I am ________ in height, weigh ________ pounds, waist ______ inches, bust ________ inches, hips ________ inches.
Name ________________
Address ________________
City ________ State ________

ARMAND
COLD CREAM POWDER
In The LITTLE PINK & WHITE BOXES

ARMAND—Des Moines
I enclose 25c coin / stamps for the Armand Week-end Package and "Creed of Beauty." A
Name ________________
Address ________________
City and State ________________
My dealer's name is ________________

MAIL *this coupon for* FREE BOOKLET *about life in California*·
THE GREAT VALLEY
SAN FRANCISCO BAY
California WHERE LIFE IS BETTER
Californians Inc·
Headquarters
SAN FRANCISCO
AUTHORITATIVE INFORMATION
140 MONTGOMERY STREET, ROOM 507
Please send me "California, Where Life is Better"
Name ________________
Address ________________

STACOMB
Trial
Tube Free
Standard Laboratories, Inc.
Dept 03, 750 Stanford Ave.,
Los Angeles, California.
Please send me free trial tube of Stacomb.
Name ....
Address ....
....
Dealer's Name ....

FIG. 153. FOUR EFFECTIVE COUPONS

These coupons are decorative. They have sales value. They invite he use of the scissors.

issue. Lee H. Bristol, advertising manager of Bristol-Myers Company, states that the investigations by that company on coupons show a marked difference in returns when the factors of color, cover, double spread, and inside or outside columns are taken into consideration.

Such variations as these make it difficult to compare coupon returns from different media. If a coupon is to be used, it should, of course, conform to certain well-known standards such as size large enough for name and address to be written in easily, and placed in a position where it is easy to clip. *Printers' Ink* quotes the following advice from a firm which has been using coupons for thirty-five years and has tested out the various possible practices:

A personality linked with a coupon doubles its appeal. The public reacts favorably to someone who speaks directly to the prospect. Thus, a coupon which merely asked the public to "please send for a booklet, free" was not as profitable as a later one which read: "Send for free booklet on artistic decoration by Emma Hendricks Fergusson."

A coupon, presented as an individual unit, accomplished less by far, than the one which was supported by several references to it and what it would bring, in the body of the message.

Invariably show a reproduction of the book or articles which the prospect will receive, in close juxtaposition to the coupon and in sufficient size to visualize it adequately.

Do not exaggerate the size of booklets or objects. The individual who sends for them will be grievously disappointed later on.

Allow the wording of coupons to intimate that the material forwarded will be of great value, great interest, and may prove of an exclusive character—and then make good on the promise.

People do not object to sending money or stamps for a thing which gives value received. But the wording of the coupon must very clearly indicate that this is true. One of the most successful coupons ever used explained that while the booklet sent cost the consumer seven cents in stamps, it cost the advertiser just nineteen cents per copy to publish.

The fact that there may be a limited supply of these coupon-offered articles seems to add reader zest.

If attention-compellers can be introduced into the advertisement which will assist in leading the eye down to the coupon, so much the better, and the cleverer they are the better.

FIG. 154.—AN INVESTIGATION OF THE VALUE OF COUPON INQUIRIES

TABLE I.—Ratings as to Coupon Inquiries

Magazine	Cost per Inquiry		Response to Free Appeal, Per Cent		Inquiry Rating	Resultant (.65 Considered as Normal)
A	$0.48	×	100	=	$0.48	1354
B	.56	×	90	=	.49	1326
C	.53	×	110	=	.58	1121
D	.58	×	105	=	.61	1066
E	.80	×	80	=	.64	1016
F	.52	×	125	=	.65	1000
G	.56	×	130	=	.73	890
H	.72	×	110	=	.79	823
I	1.16	×	75	=	.87	747
J	1.84	×	50	=	.92	707
K	1.35	×	70	=	.94	691
L	.88	×	110	=	.97	670
M	2.41	×	50	=	1.20	542
N	2.69	×	45	=	1.21	537
O	.76	×	160	=	1.22	533
P	1.45	×	95	=	1.38	471
Q	2.88	×	50	=	1.44	451

TABLE II.—Ratings as to Reader Value

Magazine	Reader Rating		Number of Columns per Dollar		Size Rating		Position Rating		Resultant
I	85	×	1427	×	100	×	100	=	1213
F	95	×	1218	×	100	×	85	=	1207
B	124	×	1200	×	90	×	90	=	1205
C	62	×	1840	×	70	×	100	=	1141
D	103	×	1182	×	90	×	90	=	986
A	100	×	1519	×	80	×	80	≐	972
G	80	×	1391	×	80	×	100	=	890
C	93	×	1132	×	90	×	85	=	806
E	135	×	900	×	80	×	80	=	778
L	86	×	1080	×	80	×	100	=	743
K	109	×	920	×	80	×	90	=	722
H	83	×	964	×	80	×	100	=	640
M	109	×	695	×	80	×	100	=	606
J	119	×	875	×	70	×	80	=	583
P	87	×	642	×	90	×	95	=	477
N	127	×	656	×	70	×	75	=	437
Q	116	×	610	×	70	×	75	=	372

FIG. 154.—*Continued*

TABLE III.—Combined Ratings

Magazine	Rating—$\frac{2}{3}$				Coupon Inquiry Rating $\frac{1}{3}$				Final Rating
B	1205	×	2	+	1326	÷	3	=	1245
F	1207	×	2	+	1000	÷	3	=	1138
A	972	×	2	+	1354	÷	3	=	1099
I	1213	×	2	+	747	÷	3	=	1057
D	986	×	2	+	1066	÷	3	=	1013
O	1141	×	2	+	533	÷	3	=	938
C	806	×	2	+	1121	÷	3	=	911
G	890	×	2	+	890	÷	3	=	890
E	778	×	2	+	1016	÷	3	=	857
L	743	×	2	+	670	÷	3	=	719
K	722	×	2	+	691	÷	3	=	712
H	640	×	2	+	823	÷	3	=	701
J	583	×	2	+	707	÷	3	=	624
M	606	×	2	+	542	÷	3	=	585
P	477	×	2	+	471	÷	3	=	475
N	437	×	2	+	537	÷	3	=	470
Q	372	×	2	+	451	÷	3	=	398

TABLE IV.—Rankings On All Bases

Magazine	Ranking as to Coupon Inquiries	Ranking as to Reader Value	Ranking in Combination
A	1	6	3
B	2	3	1
C	3	8	7
D	4	5	5
E	5	9	9
F	6	2	2
G	7	7	8
H	8	2	12
I	9	1	4
J	10	14	13
K	11	11	11
L	12	10	10
M	13	13	14
N	14	16	16
O	15	4	6
P	16	15	15
Q	17	17	17

Table I, Figure 154, shows how the relative values of inquiries are given a mathematical rating. The first column gives the cost per inquiry in 1923, the copy being the same in each issue, with coupon offering a sample, but no prominence given this sample offer. It is interesting to note the great difference in cost

FIG. 154.—*Continued*

per inquiry. The second column shows the response to the free appeal, giving magazine A the arbitrary value of 100 per cent. By multiplying the cost per inquiry by the response to the free appeal an *inquiry rating* is secured.

The fourth column reduces the values of the third column to a theoretical rating of $0.65, considered arbitrarily as normal, and made equal to 100 per cent.

In Table II, Figure 154, Column 1, an attempt is made to rate the individual reader of a certain publication in terms of value to the company. Such questions as the following entered the problem: Is it a home magazine? Is it read by women? What is its editorial viewpoint towards hygiene in general and towards oral hygiene in particular? What is the general level of intelligence of its subscribers? Are they influential among their friends? What is their average financial status?

This question of reader rating was submitted to 20 different agency executives who were considered authorities on magazine circulations. Each made an independent rating and results were averaged. Magazine A was again selected as 100 per cent.

Column 2 is the circulation divided by the single column rate, which gives the number of subscriber readers of a single column offered for $1.

Column 3 gives a size rating. It is recognized that the number of agate lines in a column increases the advertising value. Column 4 endeavors to rate the position factor, which is exceedingly important. The resultant figures in Column 5 come from multiplying the figures in the first four columns.

Magazines have now been rated according to cost of coupons and according to reader value. These two ratings are combined in Table III, Figure 154, the reader value rating being assigned a value of two-thirds and the cost of coupons rating a value of one-third.

Table IV, Figure 154, shows the rankings on all bases. Only magazines K and Q keep the same rating throughout.

Coupons are usually keyed by giving the firm a separate street address in each medium, or having replies directed to a special department. Figure 153 shows four effective coupons, showing the modern tendency to decoration, or to illustration of the sample or booklet offered. In the Armand coupon, the keys used consist of the letters of the alphabet, this particular example being A. The H. W. Gossard Company has a special address. Californians, Inc., has a room number. The Standard Laboratories, Inc., use the department system.

Obviously, a great many people reply to coupons merely out of curiosity, or from some other motives which enhance the difficulty of using them as indexes of value. Furthermore, the type of reader varies with the publication. Again, one sincere inquiry may be worth a great deal more than another. The following system, described by Paul Kenwood in *Advertising and Selling Fortnightly* (Feb. 13, 1924), was evolved by the manufacturer of a nationally advertised tooth paste:

While the possibility of error in such a complicated system as this is undoubtedly present, it does show an attempt to evaluate the various factors which render a particular publication valuable to the advertiser. By checking results by the use of two ratings, based on different factors, more accurate results are obtained.

Advertising to Lower the Cost of Selling

A company which markets a large line of goods through a great number of outlets normally has to rely on a comparison of total sales and total advertising expenditures as an index of the value received from its advertising. For example, the sales and advertising of the A. C. Gilbert Company, of New Haven, Connecticut, makers of toys, during the first seven years of its advertising history, show the following results:

	Sales	Advertising
1st year	$141,736.09	$12,000.00
2nd year	374,626.46	47,000.00
3rd year	831,049.78	110,000.00
4th year	1,182,236.20	124,000.00
5th year	771,802.11	82,000.00
6th year	1,053,843.47	100,000.00
7th year	1,710,086.23	130,000.00

One of the most interesting examples of the effect of advertising on a merchandising campaign is that of the Sun Maid

Raisin Growers of California. Its record from 1920 to 1924 has been as follows:

	Tonnage Sold	Advertising Charges per Ton
1920	110,644	.....
1921	102,919	.....
1922	128,037	$18.13
1923	121,144	12.39
1924	215,109	9.56

This is an interesting case of legitimate advertising expenditure, resulting in increased sales, and diminished advertising costs.

L. B. Jones, advertising manager of the Eastman Kodak Company says:

> On the whole, our advertising seems to pay, since our total selling expense is comparatively small, our volume of business is large, and our profits are large. When we advertise one specific item, however, diligently and continuously, and for a considerable period, we cannot point to that item and say that the publicity paid. It does increase the sale of that item, invariably and materially, but not sufficiently to warrant us in charging the advertising to that item. During 1925, we have been putting stress on a $26 camera. We greatly increased the sale of that camera, but not enough to justify the money we have spent on it. We believe two things—that such advertising has increased the sale of other cameras to some extent; and as this is not one of our cheapest cameras, we attribute to this advertising the fact that the public is buying higher priced Kodaks in 1925 than might be expected with general business conditions. We think this advertising did it; we do not really know.

Figure 155 shows an advertisement of the Tide Water Oil Sales Corporation used in the *Saturday Evening Post,* and costing $8,500. According to "Keyed Copy," the object of this advertisement was to get motorists into the habit of buying Veedol for their cars, and the success of the advertisement would depend largely upon the number of booklets that were sent for. The advertisement actually did bring in 17,000 inquiries for the booklet. The company realized that most

Fig. 155. An Advertisement Which Brought 17,000 Inquiries

motorists merely asked for a quart of oil, and the only way to get them to ask for a particular brand was to create in them a habit of buying it.

Advertising as Basis for Forecasting

For a company which sells entirely, or almost entirely, through advertising, it may be possible to use the returns as bases for determining what volume of business will be done for the year. To accomplish this, it is necessary, of course, that the company should have accurate records for past years. This plan has been followed by the Gordon-Van Tine Company, which sells through a series of catalogues. The company manufactures ready-cut houses and other buildings, and uses a large list of farm papers, women's magazines, and general publications. Each advertisement is keyed, and careful records kept of each inquiry and of the sales resulting therefrom.

The company finds that 10 per cent of its total sales volume cannot be traced to any specific advertising; the other 90 per cent is due to catalogue inquiries from publication advertising. Having ascertained this fact, a research was carried on of the records from each publication to find out what had actually been accomplished by each one.

The records, according to the account in *Printers' Ink* (Aug. 6, 1925), show that the first year's advertising in a new medium, or a different type of advertising in an old medium, does not yield net profit that year but that it does pay for itself. During the second year it exerts 60 per cent of its selling power, and during the third year 40 per cent. Accurate data on all publications used have been checked and compared. To accomplish this result, however, advertising must be continued in undiminished volume during the second year.

To show how this plan operates, suppose that the inquiries from a certain medium amount, in orders closed, to $12,000, during the second year it is used. Experience shows that this is 60 per cent of what will be received, leaving 40 per cent or $8,000 to come during the third year. But the advertising of the second year, which has already paid for itself, adds another $12,000 to the results of the third year, making the total return for that year $20,000. This $20,000, according to the company's reckoning, is a composite of the three years' advertising efforts. The advertising can be continued with a reasonable certainty that at least $20,000 will be secured in orders from year to year thereafter, with perhaps a small increase.

Orders can be divided according to months by simple tabulation of the records, and in this way it is possible to determine in advance just when orders will be large and when they will be small. This permits the company to reduce its inventories, and to control production according to the forecasted demand.

Calculating Value of Advertising to Help Dealers

While it is difficult to ascertain the value of advertising carried on by manufacturers to assist dealers, the example of the Dennison Manufacturing Company, as related to the Association of National Advertisers by H. W. Harney, shows what can be done along such lines.

The company started a definite advertising program in 1918. At that time it used small space, in the belief that advertising in a small way in a large list every month would create consumer demand, and help move the goods from dealers' shelves. An appropriation of $10,000 was laid out in advertisements about two inches square, each featuring a staple article, such as tape, glue, or sealing wax. Every advertisement offered a booklet or sample and referred to a Dennison dealer. Twelve hundred replies were received this first year, the cost per inquiry being $8.33.

In 1919, the size of the advertisement was increased by two lines and special holiday merchandise and information about hand crafts were included. A book of suggestions was offered. The cost of advertising that year was $19,337; replies 18,647; and cost per inquiry $1.03, as compared with $8.33 the year before.

Beginning in 1922, the size of the small advertisements was increased to 40 lines. Quarter-pages were also used. Also a policy was instituted of offering to send advertising material, at a price. Magazines with mixed circulation were discontinued. The company realized that its market depended largely on its ability to teach the public how to use its goods. A series of six instruction booklets was prepared, and sold to dealers for five cents and consumers for ten cents. While it is difficult to estimate the value of these books to the company, from questionnaires sent out to purchasers of the ten-cent books, it is believed that each book means the sale of at least a dollar's worth of merchandise.

During 1923, $24,000 were spent in advertising these booklets, bringing in a total of 64,267 requests, or a cost per inquiry of 38 cents. One of the company's 50-line advertisements entitled "How to Make Crêpe Paper Flowers," brought 4,170 replies at a cost of seven cents each. The "Flower" booklet costs five cents to produce; the total cost to the company was only two cents for each booklet placed in a consumer's hands.

Goodwill and Advertising

Goodwill often represents the most valuable asset in a business, yet is so difficult of measurement, and so intangible in value, that it is extremely hard to determine its true worth. Goodwill, according to A. C. Ernst, managing partner of Ernst and Ernst, accountants, "is the product of growth founded on the power and the will to serve. In the final analysis, it is value built up through outstanding service that is reflected in many ways. It is a reflection of quality of product or service, progressive methods, fair dealing, a high standard of character and efficient management and personnel."

The effect of advertising on goodwill is admittedly great. A number of observers have pointed out that a company which has always sold without advertising can keep on in this same way, but that once a company starts to advertise, its business falls off whenever it stops, even to the extent of dying altogether. It is also worthy of note that the department stores, which are the largest users of specific advertising, often devote much space to what is known as "institutional advertising," designed to increase goodwill.

Other companies, which have become well established in the field, continue advertising mainly to keep up the goodwill which they have gradually acquired. They believe it essential to do this, partly because of the new generations which are always coming to the fore and which must be told of their products, and also because the feeling of confidence in the company, which is such an integral part of goodwill, is best main tained when customers and consumers constantly see the nam of the company before them.

Public utilities have found advertising a great, althoug immeasurable, factor in the creation of goodwill. The Cana dian Pacific Railroad, always an extensive advertiser, find that a campaign emphasizing its history and economic impor tance is good business.

Returns from Direct Mail

As is, perhaps, natural, more work has been done in chart ing returns from direct-mail advertising than from genera advertising in publications. Some interesting results have bee obtained by Robert L. Blanchard, Vice President of the Va Kannel Revolving Door Company, who has instituted a simpl system of graphic charts as a means of deciding whether ad vertising pays and, if so, how much? It takes about thirty minutes each month to make up the charts shown in Figure 156

As described in *Printers' Ink Monthly* (April, 1925):

Chart No. 1 shows the percentages of inquiries received on mailings sent out. This permits the two factors of total mailings and total inquiries to be placed on a comparable basis. An average or normal figure is established for the business, in this case 5 per cent, because the unit sale is large. The horizontal line represents the normal return. Small figures at the left are percentages. Columns across the chart are numbered to indicate months, the chart represented here showing from May, 1923, to the end of 1924.

The inferences drawn from this chart are that there is no particular seasonal effect, that the mailings lists are not overworked, and the percentage of inquiries on mailings is generally satisfactory.

Chart No. 2 shows what percentage of inquiries results in estimates. Here 20 per cent of inquiries has been taken as the normal amount which will come to the stage of asking for estimates. In this chart, there is a decided seasonal trend with low points in the summer. On the whole, the results of the advertising are above the normal line.

The next point to chart is the percentage of estimates resulting from advertising which are turned into orders, based on the number of estimates submitted and the number closed. Here again the normal percentage is 20.

Chart No. 3 shows the percentage of all estimates rendered which are turned into orders, irrespective of whether they are derived from advertising or from other sources. Chart No. 4 shows the percentage of estimates closed due to advertising alone. Comparison of the two charts shows that advertising is proving effective, although in both cases there is a decided seasonal trend.

The final point to consider is the average value of the sales made to the prospects obtained by advertising. The answer to this is shown in Chart No. 5. The normal line represents an average sale of $100. In May, 1923, the average sale is at normal, but shows a decided increase during 1924.

A sixth chart is then prepared, Figure 157, which compares the sales volume of the company with Babson's Barometer of Business Conditions, in order to get an idea of what the potential business of the company is at a given time. In the years from 1920 to 1924 the averages have been charted on line A-A. If no advertising had been carried on, the sales of the company would have probably been represented by line B-B. In 1922, however, an advertising campaign began and sales actually followed line C-C. The difference between the lines B-B and C-C represents the effect of the direct-mail advertising on sales volume.

The percentage cost of advertising during 1924 was 4.5 per cent of gross sales, about 30 per cent less than the advertising cost the previous year.

Retail Advertising Analysis

The retail store, and particularly the large department store which advertises specific offerings, is in a position to calculate results from advertising with a fair amount of accuracy. It is necessary to remember, of course, that an advertisement for a particular department usually benefits the whole store, and also does something to build up future prestige for the institution.

The *Customer-Contact System,* illustrated in Figure 158, is a specialized method for analyzing the returns from daily newspaper advertising, originated and developed by Guy Hubbart, Retail Advertising Expert for the *Dry Goods Economist* and the Economist Group, and specialist in consumer demand. This system embodies in addition to the factor of drawing power of advertised price ranges on various types of items, the

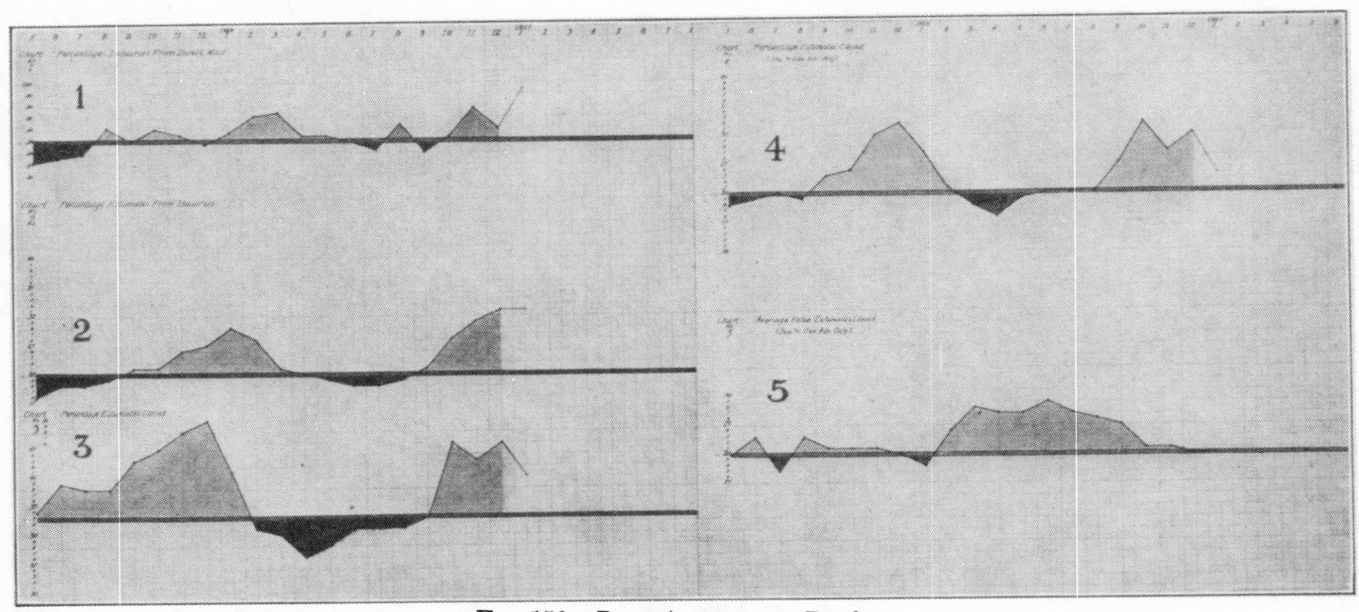

FIG. 156. DOES ADVERTISING PAY?
This series of charts tells whether or not it does, and how much.

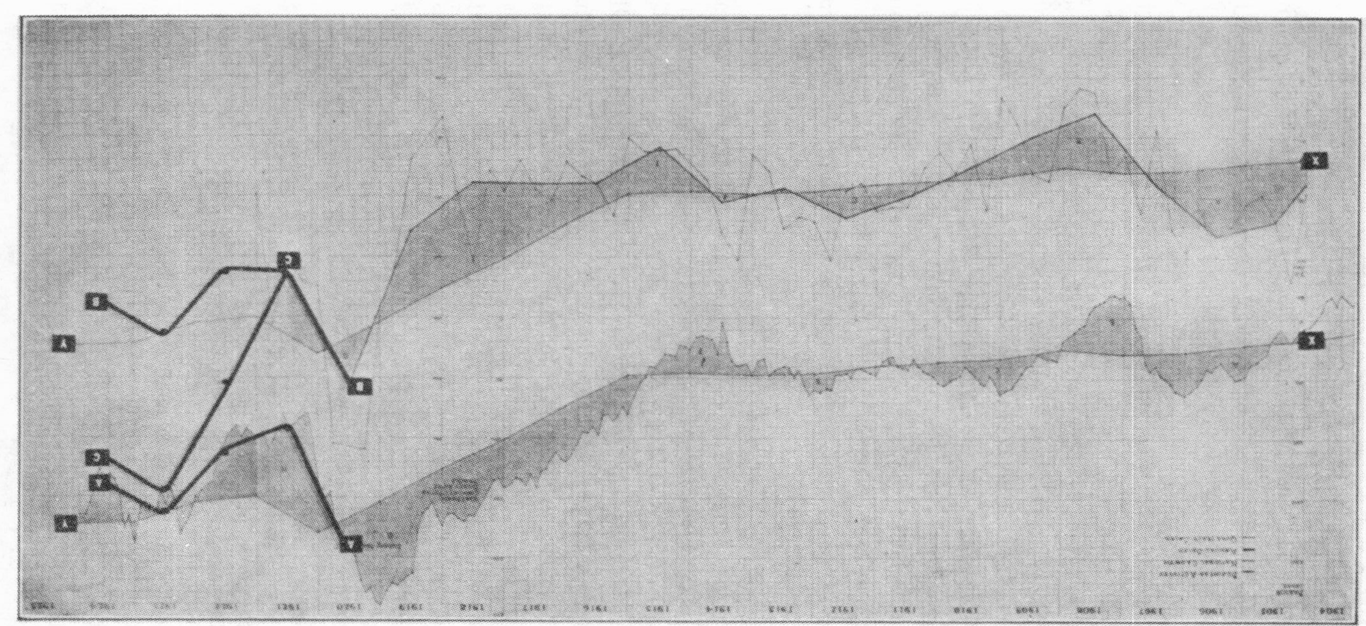

FIG. 157. SUMMARY OF ADVERTISING PROGRESS
The last of the series of charts shown in Figure 156.

factors of: (1) unit-price transaction returns from daily advertising on the basis of a given population; (2) the volume capacity of the store; and (3) the number of items advertised in a given amount of space. It is, therefore, while primarily a method of advertising analysis, a method of localized market and outlet analysis, furnishing the store a basis by which the selling power of a given amount of newspaper circulation may be computed in relation to store's total sales volume, by the day. It also indicates the percentage of population responding to the store's offerings on each price range advertised.

The system includes a set of forms with spaces for analysis and computation. Spaces are provided for the interpretation of the returns with reference to: (1) whole-store volume: (2) the volume of advertised departments and the number of average-sale transactions returned by each advertised item, and a corresponding form for recording the returns.

The basis of the method is the normal volume-movement of goods by types, as indicated on Figure 158, on an arbitrary standard of $2,800 daily volume. This standard is expressed in twenty-eighths in the left hand of Column S, and in dollars on the right hand. Volume on each type varies by the month and the variation is shown by the numerator of the fractions in Column S.

Mr. Hubbart gives the following explanation of computing method and recording of returns, with an actual analysis as an example:

Store data on which analysis was made:

Store No. 1266–2;
Date of advertisement, Jan. 8, 1924;
Total store sales for day following, $32,700;
Total sales of advertised departments, $12,137;
Number of transactions, 17,868;
Average sale transaction, $1.83;
Population of city, including trading area, 700,000.
The second column shows seven types of goods classified as to the kind of need each supplies.
Column E shows the number of items of each type advertised on Jan. 8.

RETAIL ADVERTISING ANALYSIS by the Customer-Contact System				Monthly Ratios January					Customer-Contact Basis of Average Sale for the day			Customer Contact Figures
		E	EE		S		SS	A	Whole Store	Advertised Dept.	Daily Prestige	
$2.00 to $30.00	Necessity Goods	15 Items	7	7/28 of 2800	=700	STORE	$8175.	$545.	297			.0029
						ADV. DEPT.	$2784.	$185.		101.		[.0035]
						DIFFERENCE	$5390.	$359.			196.	.0428
20¢ to $2.50	Utility Goods	29 Items	3	3/28 of 2800	=300	STORE	$3503.	$120.	66.			.0007
						ADV. DEPT.	$1193.	$41.		22.		[.0097]
						DIFFERENCE	$2310.	$79.			43.	.0084
$2.50 to $40.00	Convenience Goods	12 Items	2	2/28 of 2800	=200	STORE	$2335.	$194.	106.			.0126
						ADV. DEPT.	$795.	$66.		36.		[.0040]
						DIFFERENCE	$1540.	$128.			70.	.2001
60¢ to $2.40	Impulse Goods	8 Items	6	6/28 of 2800	=600	STORE	$7007.	$875.	478.			.0010
						ADV. DEPT.	$2386.	$298.		163.		[.0005]
						DIFFERENCE	$4620.	$577.			315.	.0041
$3.00 to $18.00	Personal-Identity Goods	6 Items	3	3/28 of 2800	=300	STORE	$3503.	$583.	319.			.0101
						ADV. DEPT.	$1193.	$198.		108.		[.0493]
						DIFFERENCE	$2310.	$385.			210.	.0600
$60.00 to $300.00	Luxury Goods	10 Items	2	2/28 of 2800	=200	STORE	$2335.	$233.	127.			.3000
						ADV. DEPT.	$795.	$79.		43.		[.0695]
						DIFFERENCE	$1540.	$154.			84.	1.5001
$20.00 to $120.00	Style Goods	4 Items	5	5/28 of 2800	=500	STORE	$5839.	$1459.	797.			.04
						ADV. DEPT.	$1988.	$497.		271.		[.0514]
						DIFFERENCE	$3850.	$962.			526.	.2801
	TOTALS	85	28	28/28	= 2800.	STORE	$32,700.					
						ADV. DEPT.	$12137.	$1366.96	2193.25	746.97	1446.28	[.1516]
						PRESTIGE.	$21,563.					
									2193.25	2193.25		

SUMMARY:—

I Advertising drawing power Relation of Whole-Store and Advertised returns in Advertised volume: Average Item drew ($384.71) for whole store: ($16.08) for Adv. Item Ratio (24.1)

II Population Response Relation of average sale to average-item volume: (a) Average Sale ($1.83) (b) Average Item Volume ($16.08) (c) Advertised Item Response (8.79) transactions per item. (d) Whole Store (2.10) transactions per item.

III Circulation Response (Newspaper) Relation of average advertised price to average-sale on basis of average-item volume. (a) Average Adv. Price ($63.72) (b) Average-Sale ($1.83) (c) Average-Item volume ($16.08). Ratio (4.1) on Circulation.

FIG. 158. METHOD OF COMPUTING RETURNS IN RETAIL ADVERTISING

Column EE shows correct number (the number actually needed to bring the store's average daily volume as a matter of record for the same day a year later).

Column S shows how each type of goods moves in relation to a total day's sales of $2,800 (the numerators of the fractions show the movement for January on each type—movement varies on each type in different months).

Column SS shows the amount of volume brought in by each type of goods for (1) the whole store, (2) the advertised department, and (3) the difference on the basis of the actual volume for the day.

Column A shows the amount done by the average item of each type of goods on (1) the basis of whole store, (2) advertised departments, and (3) difference.

Column "Customer-Contact" shows the number of transactions, at the average sale price, brought in by the advertised items on the basis of (1) whole store, (2) advertised departments, and (3) difference.

Column "Customer Contact Figures" shows the recording coefficients for each type of goods. There are three opposite each type of goods. The upper and lower figures are price-range coefficients, the upper one records the low price needed to beat the advertised day, the lower one records the high price. The middle figure records the population response.

In 1925 the store can refer to these figures, multiply them by the standard ratios in Column S, and get the price-range limits of the items in any type or group and get the advertised price which brought the returns (indicated in Column SS) from the advertised items of Jan. 8, 1923, in any type and any department classified under that type.

By multiplying the middle coefficient figure by the standard ratio, the percentage of population responding the previous year (1924 on Jan. 8) is shown. This indicates the number of transactions at the average sale for that day, in terms of population response.

The analysis of store No. 1266 shows the store management with reference to this specific advertisement the following points:

1. That the total number of items is too great and therefore reduces the drawing power of the advertisement as a whole.

2. That the correct number of items actually needed is 35 instead of 85.

3. That the volume done on the average item (whole-store basis) is $16.08. It should have been $178 which would have brought a whole-store days volume of 42,500. By selecting items with no regard for the normal movement of goods in its population, the store drew $9,800 less volume than its daily selling capacity warrants.

4. That the price ranges on the advertised items average too high in relation to the absorbing capacity of the population.

5. That advertised items drew $1,366.96 direct returns, and that the advertised departments drew $12,137, whereas they should have drawn, on the actual store volume, $14,930.

6. That the advertised items drew $23.90 volume on non-advertised departments to every dollar's worth on advertised departments.

7. That the average sale is too low because too many low-price

and high-price items and not enough medium-price items were advertised.

The store management of store No. 1266 can use this analysis to increase the productiveness of its daily advertising any month of the year and any day of the month:

1. By noting the drawing power of each type of item as indicated in Column A in relation to the volume done by that type on the standard of $2,800 and reducing or increasing, as needed, the number of items on each type.

2. By limiting the amount or sum of all advertised prices on all types of items advertised so as to bring the average advertising price (which is $63.72 in this advertisement) down to one-fourth of $63.72 which is $15.93 on any day's advertisement, in any advertisement, in the month of January.

CHAPTER XVIII

BUDGETS AND APPROPRIATIONS

Every budget presupposes a plan. It also presupposes careful coördination with other company activities. The budget is at once a rigid and a flexible instrument of control; rigid in that once laid out it should be followed exactly, and flexible in that it *may* be altered to make provision for unforeseen contingencies. It is customary to have the budget made up by some individual familiar with all phases of the subject, and then submitted to a committee for approval. Once approved, the budget becomes final, until reasons for change are submitted which appear strong enough to warrant altering the original plan.

A great many companies make appropriations which are not, properly speaking, budgets. More and more companies, however, are being converted to the budgetary system, as an effective aid in turning plans into practice. The effect of the budget is obtained through financial control. Where an advertising schedule can be laid out in advance, it is possible to make close estimates as to the amounts required.

The question as to how to determine an advertising appropriation is affected by so many elements that it has never been standardized. The modern trend is away from the arbitrary percentage-of-sales basis towards the formation of definite advertising objectives, and the appropriation of a sufficient amount of money to attain these objectives.

Advertising Policy

The advertising policy of the company naturally has a strong, if not a determining, effect upon the question of the appropriation. Certain companies, which have made small beginnings, and have gradually increased their market area, have policies which have been slowly evolved to fit their needs. These policies have been altered from time to time to suit the conditions of growth, both as regards copy, and also as regards the distribution of appropriations.

The type of advertising policy may have much to do with the kind of media used. For example, the American Multigraph Sales Company has prepared the chart shown in Figure 159, which divides advertising according to the goodwill or

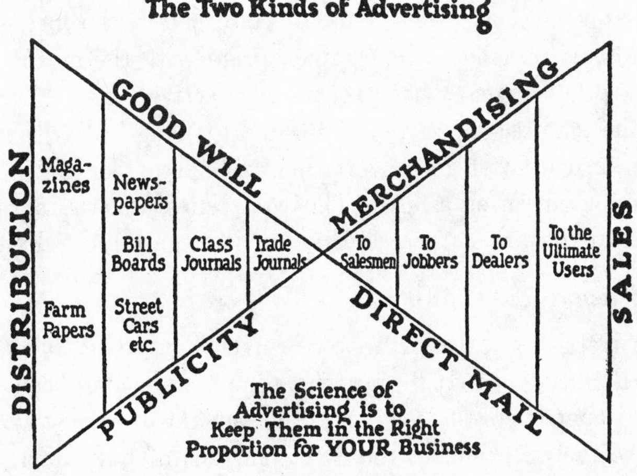

FIG. 159. ADVERTISING CLASSIFIED ACCORDING TO ITS USES
(American Multigraph Sales Company.)

merchandising functions performed. A company whose advertising policy leans towards the creation of goodwill, preferring to do actual merchandising by means of a sales force, would advertise through mass circulation at low cost per unit. The more specific the advertising task becomes, the more it requires a medium which will carry the message in the most forceful fashion.

The advertising manager, having set up his objective, and having figured the cost, as a rule has to convince the person or persons in authority over him that the expenditures he plans to make are justified by the facts. As a general rule, also, he has to explain the technique of his procedure to people unfamiliar with it. It is necessary, therefore, that the objective be clearly indicated, and that the means for reaching it be reduced to their simplest terms.

The Small Advertiser

In many ways the small advertiser seems to be handicapped in making his budget of appropriations. He sees the large advertiser spending hundreds of thousands of dollars, and almost believes that the size of the advertising appropriation is the criterion of success. This, of course, is by no means true. All advertising should be commensurate with the means which a particular company has to make it effective.

The small company, perhaps more than the large one, is inclined to scatter its advertising instead of concentrating it within a narrower scope. The companies advertising in national media are not necessarily paying the largest dividends.

Advertising Expenditures

Advertising expenditures, normally embodied in what is known as the advertising appropriation, have long been a subject of controversy. Obviously, the amount of money available will be the criterion, in the final analysis, of how much advertising can be done. A great many companies start at this point by saying, "We have so many dollars to use for advertising this year." Regardless of how they have determined the amount of money, whether by percentage of gross sales or profits, or merely a round sum based on previous years' expenditures, they are approaching the problem in a questionable manner.

Advertising, before anything else, is a part of the merchandising process. It serves the same function as do sales. A single company may perform its entire selling function by advertising; another may not advertise at all; the majority use both methods. In making up an advertising appropriation, therefore, the important thing to consider is the part which advertising plays in selling the product, and to make the appropriation for advertising in connection with the appropriation for sales, allowing each one an amount proportionate to its importance in the selling process.

Some products are particularly adapted to advertising; others are not. Chewing gum is sold almost entirely through advertising. Here is a case where economical results are obtained through increasing advertising and reducing sales expenses. Technical products, such as linotype machines and steel girders, are not sold by advertising so much as they are by personal solicitation.

Making the Appropriation

Generally speaking, there are two main methods of forming advertising appropriations: the first is to take a percentage of sales or profits; the second is to set up a definite objective, that is, determine what advertising is needed and then go ahead on that basis. In addition to these methods, there are a number of miscellaneous methods, such as appropriations based on the unit product, or on competitors' advertising programs.

Below are listed, by the Blackman Company, some bases for making up appropriations:

1. By taking out an insurance policy in the form of advertising investment to protect a company's accumulated goodwill.

2. By taking a certain percentage of the sales. Sometimes the sales figures for the past year are used, and in other cases the anticipated sales for the coming year form the basis of the computation.

3. By an assessment on each unit of the product. Here also the number of units sold in the previous year or the number of units that it is expected will be sold in the coming year may be used.

4. By putting all the money that can possibly be obtained into advertising as an investment in future sales. This is a demonstration of superior faith in advertising on the principle of casting bread upon the waters. The investment may be out of all proportion to the immediate sales or profits of the business.

5. The budget system.

6. By finding out how much advertising it takes to get a new user or a new dealer for a given product and then appropriating enough money to get as many as are needed that year.

7. By investing in advertising to buy inquiries or direct sales. This is the usual mail-order method.

8. By ascertaining the minimum job to be accomplished by the company and then deciding on the mediums and the size of space necessary to "put over" the task.

9. By appropriating a certain percentage of the previous year's profits.

10. By following in the footsteps of competitors. According to this plan an advertiser watches the activities of his competitors and then sets aside enough advertising funds to equal what they are doing, or go them one better.

11. Combining the percentage of sales and budget systems. When this plan is used, a definite percentage of sales is unfailingly appropriated each year—say 3 per cent. This is placed in an advertising fund. Then an advertising buuget is decided on. The budget varies according to the exigencies of the business. It may be more than the amount derived from the percentage of sales, but more often it is less. Where it is less, the difference piles up in the fund for use in those years where more advertising is needed than is provided by the current assessment on sales.

In common practice, the above methods usually narrow down to three. They are:

1. The appropriation is a definite percentage of sales in previous year.

2. A percentage of prospective sales in coming year. In other words, a production goal is set and the advertising and sales work toward that goal.

3. The arbitrary method. This is employed when a new product is brought out or when expansion is planned on certain lines or models, or when severe competition is to be met in certain territories. An appropriation made under these circumstances reflects the advertiser's belief in himself, his enthusiasm, and his willingness to take a certain amount of investors' risk on his advertising effort.

The Percentage System

The most commonly used plan in formulating an advertising budget is to take a percentage of gross sales. The simplicity of this system is its chief merit, although some companies have quite complicated methods of averaging past sales with anticipated sales for the future, and taking a percentage

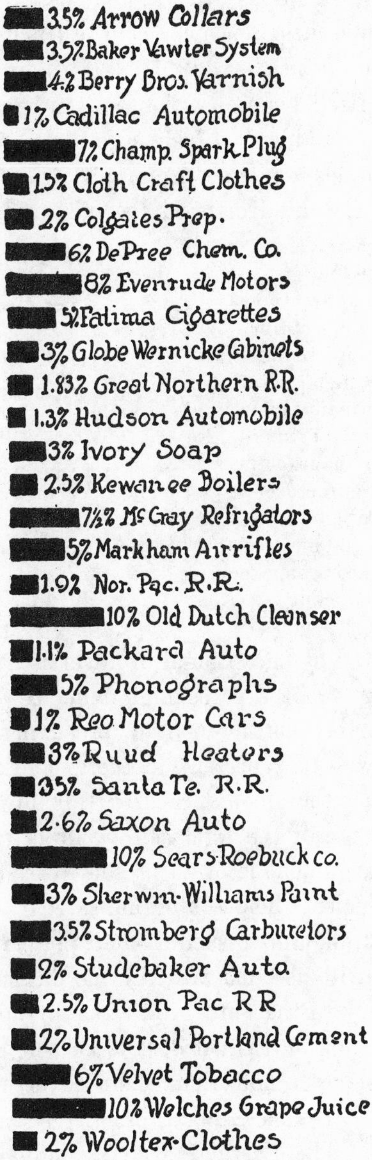

3.5% Arrow Collars
3.5% Baker Vawter System
4% Berry Bros. Varnish
1% Cadillac Automobile
7% Champ. Spark Plug
1.5% Cloth Craft Clothes
2% Colgates Prep.
6% DePree Chem. Co.
8% Evenrude Motors
5% Fatima Cigarettes
3% Globe Wernicke Cabinets
1.83% Great Northern R.R.
1.3% Hudson Automobile
3% Ivory Soap
2.5% Kewanee Boilers
7½% McGray Refrigators
5% Markham Airrifles
1.9% Nor. Pac. R.R.
10% Old Dutch Cleanser
1.1% Packard Auto
5% Phonographs
1% Reo Motor Cars
3% Ruud Heaters
3.5% Santa Fe. R.R.
2.6% Saxon Auto
10% Sears-Roebuck Co.
3% Sherwin-Williams Paint
3.5% Stromberg Carburetors
2% Studebaker Auto
2.5% Union Pac RR
2% Universal Portland Cement
6% Velvet Tobacco
10% Welches Grape Juice
2% Wooltex-Clothes

Fig. 160. Percentages of Sales as Basis of Budgets
(*Advertising and Selling.*)

of the resulting amount. Any system based on a percentage of sales or profits, either past, present, estimated, or combined, comes under this head.

It is recognized generally that percentages will differ for varying types of product. *Advertising and Selling* presents the following examples of advertisers, all of whom spend over $100,000 annually in advertising (see also Figure 160):

Business	Per cent
Collar manufacturer	3½
Paint manufacturer	3½
Spark plug manufacturer	7
Clothing manufacturer	1½
Clothing manufacturer	3½
Soaps and perfumes	2
Cigarette manufacturer	5
Soap manufacturer	3
Phonographs	5
Grape juice manufacturer	10
Refrigerator manufacturer	7½
Food products	5

It is suggested by one student of advertising that the reason for the prevalence of the percentage method is that some years ago the most expedient method of procuring an advertising appropriation was to represent to those holding the financial purse strings that the amount required for advertising was but a small percentage of the total sales volume.

This same argument is often presented by the salesmen for advertising agencies. The contention is that an increased appropriation will amount to such a small percentage of the sales volume that it will not matter. As one authority points out: "This is contrary to the natural law that it takes more energy to set a body in motion than it does to keep it in motion."

It is interesting to note that where advertisers use the percentage system there is a growing practice of making it as flexible as possible. The Eastman Kodak Company, according to L. B. Jones, prepares its advertising budget on the general basis of a certain percentage of sales for the previous year. But the company contracts only for such space as is necessary to contract for in order to obtain positions, that is, color pages, back covers, and the like. "We are thus able to increase or decrease our advertising during the year, according to the exigencies of the situation. Of course, the percentage that can be allowed for advertising depends greatly on the margin of profit on the goods, and how much can be allowed for selling costs—of which advertising is a part. If the gross profit is large, the advertising budget can be in proportion."

Vincent D. Ely, assistant advertising manager of the Pepsodent Company, advocates a budget based upon sales possibilities, and the determination of what per cent of gross sales can be allowed for advertising. The first step would be to analyze present sales, profits, and capital available for further extension.

According to N. O. Mick, advertising manager of the Burroughs Adding Machine Company, if the advertising appropriation is based on a percentage of gross sales, the advertiser confines his considerations to what kinds of advertising are essential. "This accomplished, he sets up a relative value opposite each kind of advertising to be undertaken. Then, setting aside a sufficient amount for administrative purposes and reserve, his budget should be fairly complete."

The Objective Method

The logical method of making an advertising appropriation is to decide on a *sales* objective for the year. To take again the classic example of chewing gum, the manufacturer would expect a large portion of the sales objective to be attained through advertising. On the other hand, a company building a machine tool would find it more profitable to depend upon personal salesmanship and correspondence, supported by descriptive literature, and limiting its advertising to a small portion of the selling expense.

It is admittedly difficult to determine the adaptability of any product to advertising purposes. One standard which has been suggested is the degree of deliberation required on the part of the purchaser. A convenience product, which is bought on impulse, and wherever the individual chances to be, would naturally lend itself to advertising. In such a case the advertisement could carry out all the steps in the sale, from the attracting of attention, the arousing of interest, and the creation of desire, to the actual sale.

There are many products which fall between the two extremes of making sales either entirely with or entirely without advertising. The automobile, for example, is advertised extensively, yet also must be sold in other ways as well. It is probably extremely rare that an individual buys his automobile from the advertising alone; he wants to see the car, to have it demonstrated to him, and to compare it with other cars in the same price class.

One advertising expert, in preparing his advertising budget, determines the objective of the advertising, the length of time required to reach the objective, and the general plan for reaching it. "This plan," he states, "has always been based upon using the cheapest means of reaching the individual for the widespread appeal and grading the method so that the appeal was segregated more and more definitely to the actual and potential customers as the cost of the method increased. In each case the factors were weighted so that the proportion of expenses was arranged with the least waste between the different methods of reaching the objective."

The most difficult part of the objective method, of course, is to estimate how much money will be required in order to attain it. If this is once determined, it is possible to fix upon the most economical methods by which to arrive at the goal, in other words, the selection of media process. Finally, the amount is distributed according to the individual media.

Frank A. Black, publicity manager for Wm. Filene's Sons and Company, points out several important factors in making up the budget. He says:

> The first thing will be to have the available funds. An advertiser cannot spend what he does not have; neither can he continue indefinitely to spend a larger amount for advertising than the difference between the cost and the selling price of the article.

The second consideration, providing finances are not limited, will be the planned achievement for a definite time. Where rapid growth is desirable, naturally the expenditure will have to be larger than where a slow gradual growth is satisfactory. The third point will be previous experience. Where an article has been advertised for some time, it should be possible to measure the cost of getting definite results, and this measure should be available as a guide for the future.

Miscellaneous Methods

There are still in existence a number of companies which base their advertising on the amount of money they happen to have left over from other purposes. Such practice, as far as it exists, is a relic of days when advertising had no basis beyond the belief that it produced results.

Certain companies, for one reason or another, base their advertising appropriation on a unit of their product. This has been the customary practice in coöperative campaigns. Orange growers, for example, are assessed so much a crate by the California Fruit Growers' Exchange. The National Canners' Association was financed by a contribution of so much per case. Units differ with the commodity, such as coffee by the bag, building tile by the ton, and metal lath by the number of square yards.

A number of businesses devote a certain portion of profits to advertising, as a means for development. The late Lord Leverhulme was a believer in this policy, holding that the goodwill created in this fashion would accumulate a reserve for hard times. In 1917, the American Sugar Refining Company put aside $1,000,000 as a reserve for advertising.

Lee H. Bristol, advertising manager of the Bristol-Myers Company, manufacturing chemists, says the first thing to do is to establish a fair and reasonable expected quota of sales for a year, and determine from this a net profit which would be considered adequate.

After this net profit figure has been fixed upon, the amount of the appropriation for advertising may be readily ascertained, and if such advertising should be sufficiently successful to produce results in advance of quota expectations, then the surplus thus accumulated above the normal quota of profit may be reinvested in added advertising. In this way a budget for advertising becomes a flexible amount in fulfilling the supporting function which it should play in any advertising sales program.

Competitors' Advertising

Among the factors which have often a great effect upon advertising appropriations is the advertising policy of competitors. Many manufacturers have gone to the extent of basing their appropriations on what leaders in the industry are doing. They believe that if they do not keep up their advertising, they will meet the same fate as befell the Pearline Company.

The disadvantage of governing advertising appropriations by what competitors are doing is apparent on the surface. It is not the amount of advertising which is done but its effectiveness which should be the criterion. A certain company may spend a million dollars and secure little benefit from it; another company may spend $100,000 and reap a greater reward.

This does not mean that the advertising of competitors should not be given great weight. It is always a factor of importance, whether it is taken into consideration or not. When there is much variety in the advertising carried on, as in the automobile field, a greater lesson can be learned from some of the advertising than from the rest. The advertising which is purely competitive has little to teach. The best advertising is that which broadens the market for the whole product, while aiming to take more than a proportionate share of the increased demand. In some cases this is very evident. In selling automobile tires, only a certain sales volume can be expected unless more automobiles are sold. The automobile tire advertiser, to take most complete advantage of his advertising, should try to sell automobile transportation as well as to convince the public that his tires are the best.

Starting to Advertise

There are certain difficulties connected with making up the appropriation for the first year. After a company has been advertising for a considerable period, it can estimate with a fair amount of accuracy what it will cost to obtain a certain result. But before any body of experience has been accumulated, it is essential to base calculations upon estimates.

After the price of the product has been set, and the net profit required allowed for, a certain amount will be left for selling expenses. This must be divided between selling and advertising, according to the adaptability of the product to advertising, as previously explained. If the margin between cost price and selling price is small, a large turnover will be needed. A product entering a highly competitive field often has the problem of obtaining quantity sales and large turnover immediately. This will require a large outlay in advertising to attain this objective, and will presuppose considerable capital reserve for advertising purposes.

In introducing a new product, it is also necessary to consider the resistance to be encountered from distributors and retailers, if these functionaries are to be employed. This resistance must be overcome, although advertising may not be the most effective means for doing so.

The question must be solved at the outset of whether the sales campaign is to be intensive or extensive, that is, is it going to cover the major markets, or attempt to cover the entire country? Is it going to start in the local market and gradually extend, or is it going to try to capture the whole country at once? The slow and steady method has almost everything to recommend it, and is the one which has been used most successfully. The advertiser gradually accumulates a body of experience which he can utilize as he broadens his market.

The second year's campaign can be based on the experience gained in the first year, to a certain extent. The advertiser can see how the goods are moving from the dealers' shelves and how many reorders he may expect. It is, however, a serious fallacy in a merchandising campaign to base future calculations merely on dealers' first orders. Not a few advertisers, judging wholly from such first orders, have not been able to move the goods as they had expected, and reorders fell below estimates, with the result that the manufacturer later found himself with an excessive inventory.

One point to emphasize in connection with the company just starting in advertising is that the size of the appropriation the first year may be extremely large, but this does not follow that the same appropriation will be needed other years. Breaking into a market is usually an expensive process, and it normally costs more to create demand than it does to continue it after it has once gained headway.

Distributing the Appropriation

It is impossible to give any general rules which will apply in all, or even a great many, cases for distributing the appropriation. The advertising manager of one company, the advertising program of which is nation-wide, says the first thing to bear in mind is adequate representation in the most important forms of media in the light of past experience, current conditions, and general indications as to what the year may bring forth. A sufficient balance should be left over for purposes of experiment, and to provide a reserve for any special occasions which might arise later in the year. The more flexible the budget, the better, because it may be deemed wise to take some of the contemplated expenditures from one medium and use it in another. This authority believes, however, that the budget should be something more than a forecast. It should be adhered to unless unusual circumstances arise which warrant making a change.

One of the most scientific schemes for distribution of an advertising appropriation is that described by C. B. Larrabee in *Printers' Ink* (March 12, 1925), as applied by Life Savers, Inc. This company sells a small five-cent unit confection in all parts of the United States, through many and varied outlets. The company wanted to spend its appropriation according to sales possibilities in the various states. The first job was the evaluation of the various states, by a regular process of market analysis, the following seven elements being determined:

1. Percentage of population compared with the total population of the United States.

2. Percentage of boxes shipped compared with the population of the state.

3. Percentage of boxes shipped compared with total boxes shipped to all states.

4. Percentage of retail outlets in the state compared with total number of retail outlets in the United States.

5. Percentage of jobbing outlets in the state compared with total number of jobbing outlets in the United States.

6. Population per retail outlet in the state. This item was then reduced to the percentage of retail outlets to total retail outlets in the United States.

7. Population per jobbing outlet in the state. This item also was broken down to get the percentage of jobbing outlets to the total number of jobbing outlets in the United States.

The total of percentages gives the weight factor for a single state. The total state weights give the figure for the United States, and in this way the percentage of each state can be compared with other states.

The next step was for the company to take the last twelve-month period of advertising and sales expenditure to determine what the effort had been in each state. This was done by studying the following 13 items:

1. Percentage of total advertising appropriation expended in each state to total expenditure.

2. Percentage of total sales appropriation expended in each state to total appropriation.

3. Sales expenditure to sales volume in each state on a percentage basis.

4. Percentage of advertising expenditure to sales volume in each state.

5. Advertising cost per 1,000 population.

6. Magazine cost per 1,000 population.

7. Newspaper cost per 1,000 population.

8. Street-car advertising cost per 1,000 population.

9. Outdoor advertising cost per 1,000 population.

10. Advertising car cost per 1,000 population. (This item refers to the automobiles used by salesmen. The bodies of these cars are made to appear like a package of Life Savers.)

11. Display case cost per 1,000 population.

12. Sampling cost per 1,000 population.
13. Sales cost per 1,000 population.

This will show, when figured as for the seven market elements, what percentage of advertising and sales effort has been expended for each state. When compared with the market figures, this will show whether the two sets of statistics are in line.

The above calculations have been comparatively simple because practically everybody is a prospect for Life Savers. The ordinary product would have to be sold to a certain percentage of the population in each state, and this figure would have to be determined in addition to the above.

Furthermore, the Life Savers plan requires no consideration of dealer advertising, which would require still further allowances in the calculations. It is important to note that in this case sales and advertising quotas were laid out together, on the principle that advertising is only a part of the selling function.

What Does Advertising Include?

It has often been the practice to include a great many border-line charges in the advertising account. An estimate has been made that until recently as much as 25 per cent of the money supposed to go for advertising really went to charity, was spent for entertainment, or for some other extension of advertising.

The following system is used by one of the members of the Association of National Advertisers (*Printers' Ink,* Nov. 23, 1922):

(*a*) Salaries.

(*b*) Printing and Stationery used in the Advertising Department.

(*c*) Postage expenses incurred by the Advertising Department.

(*d*) Office furniture and equipment, and repairs and renewals of same.

(*e*) Office expenses and supplies, which are not otherwise provided for and which cannot be definitely classed but are in the nature more or less of special expenditures.

(*f*) Telephone and telegraph expenses of the Advertising Department.

(*g*) Rent for office space, store-room, etc.

(*h*) Traveling and entertainment expenses of Advertising Department representatives.

(*j*) Advertising material—that is, catalogues, samples, copy illustrations, art work, cuts, express, freight charges, models, etc.—all these items in connection with publications or material prepared by the company.

(*k*) Publications which are not published by the company, but which the company uses, that is to say, periodical advertising, which includes trade and technical catalogues, general media, programs, guides, etc. Included in this item is the cost of copy, cuts, art work, etc.

(*l*) Expenses for exhibitions—all expenses in connection with conventions, associations, trade meetings, etc., including cost of material, traveling and entertainment expenses which are incurred in the interest of any specific convention or exhibit.

(*m*) Promotion work—We include under this item such material as lantern slides, motion pictures, and a little direct-by-mail material (letters and folders) which are sent out in the interest of some sales effort or educational work—all of which we consider in a measure indirect advertising.

Another company divides its appropriation under the following 16 headings:

1. Periodical advertising space	.2629
2. Periodical art work and plates	.0338
3. Direct-mail advertising	.1778
4. Catalogues and envelopes	.1903
5. House-organ	.0428
6. Samples and displays	.0405
7. Postage	.0761
8. Prints and negatives of jobs	.0043
9. Plates and photos for agents	.0146
10. Imprinting for agents	.0181
11. Stationery and office supplies	.0067
12. Freight, express and cartage outbound	.0045
13. Miscellaneous	.0169
14. Salaries	.0902
15. Traveling expense	.0090
16. Depreciation, taxes, insurance	.0108
	.9993

According to a leading agency, 121 national advertisers report the distribution of their advertising appropriations as follows:

Spent in magazines	58.58%
" " newspapers	12.1%
" " outdoor	1.7%
" " "other"	25.28%

The item "other" may include only such legitimate advertising items as direct-by-mail work, window displays, trade helps, etc. On the other hand, it is apt to be a sink into which is dumped odds and ends that cannot otherwise be easily charged off. Such items are:

Expenditures for entertaining
Rebates
Price-lists
Bonuses
Salesmen's calling cards
Show rooms
Catalogues
Sales conventions
Personal expenses
Press agents
Cartoons
Souvenirs
Labels
Picnics
Benefit and bazar programs
Free goods
Donations to religious, charitable, and fraternal organizations.

It is true that no one business would include all these items in the advertising account. It is equally true that several of them would be considered proper advertising charges in nearly every business. They form a heavy tax on advertising efficiency.

The great danger of such erroneous accounting, and the dire mistake of permitting any portion of the appropriation to be paid to press agents, should be realized by every advertiser.

Keeping Track of Expenditures

One of the most important features of any budgetary system is control. It is not sufficient to set up objectives, provide funds for reaching them, and to plan the campaign. All expenditures must be checked in accordance with a schedule, so that the advertising manager can tell at any moment how his account stands.

Printers' Ink suggests a loose-leaf system, with four separate forms of records, although all may be kept in one binder:

1. Dealing with details of expense by space and medium.
2. Dealing with results, cost per inquiry, etc.
3. Dealing with extras, cost of dealer helps, booklets, etc.
4. Dealing with car cards, posters, billboards, electric displays, etc.

The first set dealing with expenses is divided according to newspapers, magazines, and art work, engraving, printing, etc.

For newspapers, the names of the newspapers are written down the left-hand side and vertical rulings mark off on the right spaces for "lines ordered, lines used, cost per line, total cost, and remarks." Under remarks are put position of advertisements, type of printing, or any special feature. If advertisements are run daily, recapitulations may be made for the week.

The sheet for magazines is much the same as that for newspapers, except that it is kept monthly, and recapitulation sheets are made for the year or for the campaign.

On the third sheet, under costs, a record is kept of cost of electros, mats, art work, etc., for each advertisement, and these costs are added on each month to the other records. Advertisements are frequently keyed for reference by giving them a number.

Methods of keeping track of results have already been treated in the preceding chapter.

Records of extras are kept on an accounting form which shows total cost. These are useful for reference when planning any new work, and will give some idea of what a booklet, or series of dealer helps should cost.

Records dealing with car cards, outdoor advertising, and the like require separate sheets for each medium. The usual items required are cost of production (including art work, printing, lithography, painting, designing), number, rental, or monthly display cost, and method of cost comparison. With car cards, for example, the form shows total cost of cards, cost per card, cost per month of display, number displayed, frequency of change of renewal, and average number of persons per month estimated to see the cards.

For outdoor advertising, headings would be cost of designs, number of locations, total area of display, rental per month, rental per foot, frequency of change or renewal, population, cost per 10,000 population, cost in city, cost in state, and a space for a check showing whether the board has been inspected and when.

CHAPTER XIX

EXPERIMENTAL CAMPAIGNS

According to Jevons, all experience is the result of observation and experiment. To observe is merely to note conditions as they are. To experiment implies observation under controlled conditions. Tests or experiments may be of two kinds: the first a simple notation of what happens under certain conditions; and the second a quantitative measurement of what takes place. For example, a test proves that a certain sized advertisement is better for a given purpose than is one of another size. This test can be extended further to indicate the relative value of any given size of advertisement.

Scientific testing, strictly speaking, requires a separate experiment for each variation which occurs in conditions. If the size of an advertisement were to be tested, it would require theoretically an almost infinite series of tests, carried on in all types of media, in all sorts of positions, with and without color, with display heads and without, and so on. In practice, the number of tests may be reduced expediently to a comparatively small number, the important point being that only one condition should be changed at a time.

There is a constantly growing body of opinion in favor of testing all advertising campaigns. The period when an advertiser relied on his own judgment is becoming antiquated, although here and there individuals still have sufficient self-confidence. In the opinion of leaders in the profession, the experimental campaign is a virtual necessity, especially where competition is likely to be keen, and where it is essential to know what results will be obtained from the expenditure of certain sums of money.

Conditions of Testing

The value of any test is determined largely by the conditions under which it is carried out. There are some requirements applying to all such experiments, such as:

1. The market or markets in which the trial campaign is conducted should be as nearly representative as possible of the entire market area to be covered later. It should, in so far as possible, be typical as to amount and class of competition, character of population, and the other factors of importance connected with the market.

2. The trial campaign should be carried out under conditions which approximate those that will be used later. There is a tendency—a perfectly natural one—to overdo sales and advertising effort during a trial campaign. If sales are artificially inflated by extra efforts, the results obtained in this way will not be typical of the efforts carried out over a long range of time.

3. The trial campaign should be conducted, if possible, without letting distributors know that it is an experiment. This is naturally difficult, but if it is not done, there is danger that results will not be representative.

4. One factor should be tested at a time in the trial campaign. Price, package, method of merchandising, proper appeal, and similar factors, should be adjusted as closely as possible to the demands of the market and of the competitive situation, before the trial is instituted. Each one of these elements can then be tested out on the market under actual working conditions.

5. Careful records should be kept of all findings. This is at once one of the most important and most difficult parts of the program. If, for example, it is desired to know the effect of advertising in certain media, sales must be checked up immediately before the advertising, during the campaign, and afterwards. If two cities can be found, approximately comparable, it may be possible to try out two different types of advertising, or the effect of advertising in one place, and of not advertising in another.

Utilization of Experimental Campaigns

Tests can obviously be used for a great number of purposes, connected either with the product, the market, or the facilities used for reaching the market. The merchandising methods can also be experimented with. In some cases the test can be combined to obtain information concerning all factors. Where sales are made direct by mail, a careful check can be made upon the success of an entire campaign by testing a part of the market.

1. *The Product.*—A trial campaign may be used to indicate whether the price, the package, and the unit size of the product are suitable. For this purpose it is often desirable to use two similar markets. In one city a certain set of packages and prices may be used, while in the other city an entirely different combination may be tried out. If it is possible to use the same advertising effort in each case, then the difference in results should make it possible to weigh the advantages of the varying prices, packages, and sizes.

2. *The Market.*—One of the most important purposes of trial campaigns is to measure the market. Advance analysis may produce certain results, but it is never possible to be sure of their accuracy without trying them out on an actual market. Either extensive or intensive testing may be employed, depending on the particular case. In selling by mail, the extensive method is often best, while for a company which sells through the trade the intensive method is preferable.

3. *The Marketing Facilities.*—In the case of a new product, the advertiser is often at a loss to know how to apply his appropriation so that it will benefit the major outlets for his product. As C. C. Mosely, of the Manternach Company, advertising agents, points out:

In one case, the grocery outlet may be used entirely, while in another the drug store is the most important. In still another case, both outlets may be used, to ascertain whether competing channels can be employed without sacrificing interest on the part of jobbers and retailers in each channel. Sometimes an item which it would seem natural to clear through retail hardware stores may be found to do best in the department and house furnishing stores. In one instance, an article was found to sell far more readily through drug stores than through any other channel, although it was distinctly a hardware store item. The next best outlet was the department store, and following it the grocery.

4. *Merchandising Methods.*—Tests can be carried out effectively to determine the best method of reaching the consumer. They may be used to find out, for example, the value of house-to-house missionary work, the relative importance of store display, the benefits derived from demonstration, and the like. It is important to remember that repeat sales may prove a better index of the success of the trial campaign than the original sales. Consequently, the best form of testing implies waiting to see whether the article repeats satisfactorily.

It is generally felt that national magazines are not suitable for test campaigns because they cover too much territory. As Vincent D. Ely, of the Pepsodent Company, says:

> Tests are best conducted by selecting some representative communities. If coupons can be used in the advertising, test campaigns and their value are obvious. If the test is to be measured exclusively by sales, it is usually necessary to select a self-serving territory so the sales response can be accurately judged. For example, should the pulling power of 24-sheet posters be questioned, the only method of making a real analysis would be to select a state or a group of cities that have no outside jobber influence. Also, the jobbers in the territory selected should not extend in a large measure beyond the boundaries of the test territory. In this way, sales can be checked accurately, and the real results found.

The Tryout Market

It is difficult to give a definition of a tryout market which will suit everybody. Frank D. Webb, writing in *Printers' Ink* (Aug. 21, 1924), states seven requirements for an ideal tryout market:

1. Compactness, though not necessarily small population
2. Variety of activities
3. Average living conditions

4. Average wealth
5. Average, or nearly average, distribution of population by racial origin
6. Average competitive conditions
7. Reasonable proximity to supply of merchandise

Compactness is desirable because the market can be more quickly covered. A city with varied activities will not be dominated by any one industry. A city with large per capita wealth is not typical, while a preponderance of any one population group may cause special conditions.

If a number of manufacturers of nationally known products are struggling for mastery in a given territory, this would make it unsuitable for trial purposes. If there is a local brand which is in an exceptionally strong position in a given city, this also would unfit such a city for the test campaign. Proximity to supply of merchandise might be the deciding factor in choosing one of a number of suitable cities.

O. C. Mosely, of the Manternach Company, points out that territories or cities may be classified as difficult, average, or easy. For example, the city of Detroit is classified as an "easy market" in which to introduce a household specialty. St. Louis and Milwaukee are known as "difficult." Des Moines and Rochester are said to be "average." The classifications might be different for other commodities.

If the market area to be covered is large, then the best test would be to cover several average localities, watching the results for errors. For example, an "easy market" might show poor results through lack of coöperation on the part of the medium used, or a "difficult" territory might make an inordinately good showing through the great effort that the local newspapers put forth.

The care used in picking a representative market for test purposes may make the difference between success and failure. The object is not immediate sales, but to determine exactly what conditions will be met, how to overcome obstacles, and to pick out the appeal, methods of merchandising, and distributive outlets which are most effective.

In some cases, special investigators have been sent to selected territories to see what position the product occupies in each, and to classify them as difficult, average, or easy. It may be advisable to make a test in each type of market, thus giving a better idea of the appeal or medium best fitted for all purposes, or for special purposes.

The Westinghouse Electric and Manufacturing Company chose to carry out its campaign in Rochester, New York, on the basis of which the name of one of its products was changed, a new copy angle was adopted, and merchandising methods investigated.

Thomas J. Grace, sales manager of the Gorton-Pew Fisheries Company, describes (*Advertising and Selling Fortnightly*) how a market may be tested. In the first place, the possibilities are figured out on paper. A city of 120,000 inhabitants would mean 400 stores suitable for distribution of food products. This figure is obtained by estimating that there are about 300 population to the average grocery store (60 families with 5 to a family).

Twenty per cent of the 400 stores are eliminated as being too small, or run by foreigners. It is then estimated that 60 per cent of the 320 remaining stores should be sold in the first canvass. Forty per cent of these should buy about five cases, leaving 116 stores that would buy about one case. This preliminary work of distribution is, of course, necessary before starting the trial advertising campaign.

Testing by Sales

The success of the average trial campaign is measured by the volume of sales secured in response to the advertising and sales effort expended. A writer in *Advertising and Selling Fortnightly* maintains that a proper test would include at least six cities, so that abnormal conditions in any one would be offset by the average conditions for the total group. He also advises including a group of control cities in which no advertising is done, so that sales made with advertising may be compared with sales without advertising. This is particularly important where the test is carried on for a product which is already on the market.

This writer points out that in cities of from 15 to 50 thousand population, an average from 3 to 12 stores do the bulk of the business, depending on the type of retail outlet used for the product. If a salesman can take inventory prior to the campaign and then repeat this enumeration after the campaign, it is possible to tell how much sales have increased.

It is often important to determine the relative effectiveness of various types of advertising in a particular locality. L. H. Bristol, advertising manager of Bristol-Myers Company, suggests the following set of tests which could be applied to a particular locality;

1. Local newspaper advertising campaign
2. Local canvassing campaign, undertaken separately and not at the same time that the newspaper advertising is appearing
3. Newspaper and canvassing combined
4. Window display campaign
5. Window display campaign and canvassing alone
6. Newspaper and window display campaign alone
7. All three simultaneously

The Tryout Appropriation

A great many companies make the mistake of not spending enough on the trial campaign. Furthermore, they do not adopt the right attitude towards the test. A test is exactly what the name implies. Its purpose is to find out whether the product, the market, and the means of bringing the two together have been correctly planned out. *Printers' Ink* (Aug. 21, 1924) quotes the example of one of the largest corporations in the United States, which spent over $40,000 in a single market, with the ultimate result of finding that it was not possible to sell a certain product successfully. This company was satisfied with the expenditure of this money, because, had it not been for this trial campaign, it might have spent many times this amount trying to market a product which was not fitted for the purpose.

Mention has been made in a previous chapter of the method of making up an appropriation based on the advertising task to be accomplished. While it is difficult to set such a quota with definiteness, the trial campaign often affords an approximately accurate index of what it will cost to accomplish a certain result. Given a certain number of trial markets, the company has an opportunity to try out its various plans and compare results so that the most economical method may be adopted as its standard.

The importance of the trial campaign may differ a great deal, under varying circumstances. Where direct mail is used in any volume, it is good practice to test before every campaign. Where a company has been advertising for a long time, and has ascertained its most successful appeals, size of space, and other factors, it may feel that the trial campaign would be a useless expense. It is important to remember, however, that conditions are constantly changing, and the company which does not change also may find itself operating at a disadvantage.

Details of an Actual Test Campaign

After making a market analysis for its new Duofold model fountain pen, the Parker Pen Company decided that it would be best policy to test out the advertising campaign before going ahead with an expensive program. It had previously been decided to concentrate on the $7 model, and to mention the other two models only incidentally. No space at all was to be used for their ordinary line of pens or metal pencils.

It was decided to concentrate on the $7 model rather than the $5 pen because it was easier to sell the lower priced article on the reputation of the higher priced one, than to try to merchandise the higher-priced product on the basis of the reputation of the lower-priced article.

After careful consideration, Chicago was chosen as the trial market. It was recognized that this was not an easy market, because of the competition to be encountered there. The theory was, however, that if a success could be made there, less difficulty would be encountered in being successful everywhere.

Furthermore, it was decided to carry on the test during the supposed off-season of March and April.

The *Chicago Tribune* was chosen for the test medium, although it is now thought that a greater number of media would have been better. However, it was considered best policy to restrict the expenditure as much as possible while still making the test representative.

The test was to cover 12 weeks, with 12 insertions as follows:

1. 800-line advertisement first week
2. 360-line advertisement each week for three weeks
3. 360-line advertisement each week for eight weeks

Nine days previous to the publication of the first advertisement, 10 specially trained salesmen were assigned trading centers, and given dealer cards. Each salesman was equipped with samples of the pens, and a portfolio containing the following items:

1. Letter from the *Chicago Tribune* certifying to the receipt of a noncancellable order for the advertising.
2. Proofs of the newspaper advertisements.
3. Reproductions of posters of which 156 were to be posted throughout the city to show the black-tipped Chinese lacquer-red color of the Duofold, which could not be shown in the newspapers.
4. Reproductions of counter cards and window display cards, etc., which the advertiser would supply free.
5. Testimonial letters from dealers in other towns who had handled the Duofold with success.
6. A set of instructions to salesmen.
7. A map of Chicago with all trading centers numbered.
8. A set of cards each bearing the name and address of a stationery, drug, department, or jewelry store, and a number corresponding to the number of trading center on the map where the store was located. On the back of the card was the rating of each dealer.

The gross sales of pens in the first week exceeded the gross cost of the three months' advertising schedule. The Monday after the sales drive the first advertisement appeared, carrying the names of Chicago stores which had put the Duofold pens in stock. At the same time, as many window displays as possible were secured, because display was felt to be an essential part of the advertising campaign for a specialty article of this nature.

The objections encountered from the trade are interesting. It was felt, in the first place, that the advertisements would not be published. Dealers also felt the price of $7 was too high, or they did not like the color, or they thought their margin of profit was too small. As was natural, an especially strong sales resistance was met from retailers who had not previously been customers of the company.

At the end of five weeks, the campaign was so successful that it was decided to test out other major cities immediately. In each case, the coöperation of newspapers was secured to supply lists of dealers, routings for salesmen, and in some cases to deliver window displays. The campaigns in these cities were also successful.

Testing Direct Mail

Where sales are made direct by mail, it is possible to test out results in advance of the main mailing. The estimate may be made from intensive results in one city, or from an extensive mailing over the whole country. Estimates of costs should be corrected to allow for the savings in quantity possible in the main mailing.

It is important to select enough names to make the mailing representative of the whole list. There are many possible points to test. For example:

1. Best time for mail to be received
2. Address typed or hand written
3. Addressed return envelope or post card
4. Stamped or unstamped return envelope or postal card
5. Type of appeal to be used
6. Length of sales letter, or other literature
7. Number of enclosures
8. Type of product preferred

When the test fails to produce results warranting a full

FIG. 161.—AN INVESTIGATION OF CAUSES OF FAILURE OF A CAMPAIGN

Questionnaire

PLEASE RETURN THIS BLANK PROMPTLY

When you return this blank I will be pleased, in appreciation of your courtesy, to send you an attractive little gift which you will find very handy for daily use.

1. Did you receive a folder like the attached? Yes.... No.... (check)
2. If you received the folder, did the samples appeal to you?
   Yes.... No.... (check)
3. Did the prices appeal to you?
   Yes.... No.... (check)
4. Why did you not order?

REMARKS:

....

....

....

....

5. Will you order later?

   Yes.... No.... (check)

6. When? ....

Letter

Dear Mr————

I am in trouble and ask you to help me out as a brother business man. Perhaps, some day in some way I can do you a kind turn for your favor to me.

One of my customers is the ————. I got up for them the attached folder. It offered wonderful values. It should have brought a lot of replies. The returns have been disappointing.

Will you do this:

Simply check your answers on the attached sheet and return it to me in the enclosed envelope, so I can find out what is wrong?

When I get your reply I will send you, with my compliments, an attractive little gift you can use every day.

Sincerely yours.

campaign, it is possible to make up a new campaign and test this out again, or to find out why the original material did not bring sufficient volume of sales. For example, Edward H. Schulze, writing in the *Mailbag,* quotes the example of a New York cap manufacturer who desired to develop new retail accounts in small towns not covered by his retail sales force. A first mailing had produced 10 per cent results; a second and more ambitious campaign brought less than half of 1 per cent. The questionnaire and letter illustrated in Figure 161 was sent out to a hundred names on the list. Forty per cent replied that they had already placed their order for seasonal requirements, and consequently, no sales literature, however well carried out, would have been successful in making sales.

If this particular manufacturer had carefully tested out all the vital factors in advance, he would have determined the proper time to send out literature so as to produce the maximum results.

PART V

SCIENCE AND THE PRODUCTION OF ADVERTISEMENTS

CHAPTER XX

PLANNING THE ADVERTISEMENT

All the matters discussed up to this point have been of a preparatory nature. The next step is to put the results of this research into the advertisement proper. This must be done through the instrumentality of ink and paper. The preliminary operation in this process is to plan the advertisement as a whole.

The precise theme for the advertisement must now be selected, since it is around this fundamental idea that the whole advertisement is to be built. Not only must it serve as inspiration for the copy, but it must also give the clue to the technical and artistic treatment.

In planning the advertisement, most of the problems are reducible to a scientific basis. Much of the progress made in planning has been either of a laboratory nature, or is the result of empirical discoveries. The position which the advertisement is to occupy in the periodical or newspaper, for example, has a great deal to do with the attention value of the advertisement. Similarly, the position on the page, if the advertisement is less than full-page size, will have a measurable effect on attention value.

The size of the advertisement, and whether it is better to employ one large advertisement for one insertion or two half-size advertisements for two insertions, are problems of a similar nature. They must be dealt with in advance of the actual preparation of the advertisement. Such research as has been done along these lines and is available is mainly of a psychological character. Certain points have been brought out; but on the whole the progress made must be regarded merely as a beginning. The most the advertiser can hope to do is to make himself familiar with the results of such research, and to observe carefully his own experiences. He is not ordinarily in a position to carry on laboratory experiments of this nature himself, much as this is to be desired, although it is possible to have this work done for him.

The Advertising Theme

The advertisement, like the advertising campaign, should have a central theme if it is to prove consistently successful. This theme must be chosen with reference to three fundamental propositions:

1. The advertisement must attract attention, and in some way the attention value and the theme of the advertisement must be correlated.

2. The advertisement must arouse interest, and this interest must be centered on the theme, which should be, ordinarily, the strongest selling point.

3. The advertisement should attain a certain goal. The purpose of the advertisement, for example, may be to sell goods, or to secure action of some kind, such as inquiries from interested prospects. It may, of course, have no further aim than to create goodwill for an institution, or to increase consumer brand consciousness. The theme of the advertisement in any case must be chosen with reference to the central purpose it is to achieve.

Broadly speaking, the theme of the advertisement depends upon certain economic, psychological, and technical considerations. Each of these will exercise a determining influence upon the theme, and the result will be a compromise between the three. There may be cases where all considerations will point towards the choice of a single theme and a single treatment of it; but such conditions are not at all usual.

The economic aspect includes first of all the business conditions prevailing at the time of advertising. It will also be concerned with the product, the market, and the physical means of distribution.

The psychological aspect will have to do with the practical treatment of motives for purchase and with the appeals. It will also have to do with the size of the advertisement, its position in the periodical and on the page, and the number of times it is repeated.

The technical aspect is concerned with the presentation of the theme through the most suitable artistic and typographic treatment of it in the advertisement.

The Economic Aspect

The advertising theme should be chosen with due respect to the economic aspect, which has two phases: first, that which has to do with external conditions, and second, that which is concerned with the company and its policies. The main features of the economic aspect have to do with business conditions, with production and the product, and with marketing and markets.

How, one may ask, do business conditions affect the choice of a theme for an advertisement? The answer is that a theme which serves in times of prosperity may evoke no enthusiastic response in times of depression. The emphasis may shift abruptly from a luxury to a utility appeal. This is true not only of national conditions, but also of conditions within the industry, and even of the particular locality where advertising effort is being centered.

The business condition of the company itself will also have much to do with the choice of a theme. Is it planning for expansion? Can it afford to spend money in entering a new and competitive market? Has it ample working capital with which to enter upon planned developments?

The second economic factor to be considered in choosing a theme is production and the product. Each product has certain selling points which, other things being equal, may serve as the theme of the advertisement. Figure 162 illustrates advertising themes which have been found successful in industrial fields. The majority of these are based on product or production factors.

FIG. 162.—SUCCESSFUL ADVERTISING THEMES IN INDUSTRIAL FIELDS (McGraw-Hill Company)

Product	Field	Theme
Motors	Electrical	Improving power factor
Turbine	Power plant	Return on investment
Paint	Construction	Service suggestions
Dryer	Process industries	Installation data
Mechanical stoker	Power plant	Ability to burn low-grade fuel
Small steam shovel	Construction	"Earning" facts
Ball bearing motors	Industrial	Performance data
Hoists	Mining	Performance records
Mine cars	Mining	Endurance facts
Mechanical Ash Handling System	Power plant	Savings in labor
Roller bearings	Mining	Power and labor savings
High tension equipment	Electrical	Design service

Figure 163 shows an analysis of selling points, prepared by Robert L. Blanchard, Vice President of the Van Kannel Revolving Door Company. This chart was compiled only after many weeks of research, and from its beginning served as the basis of the Company's advertising campaign. During the six years that it has been in operation, no change has been found necessary. Under Appearance-Prestige it should be noted that an appeal to the pride of building owners is particularly effective in times of prosperity.

The third phase of the economic aspect is that which has to do with marketing and markets. The advertising theme of a concern which sells hosiery through the retail trade may differ materially from that used by a concern selling hosiery from house to house. Similarly, the theme of a concern selling quality goods will not be the same as that of a concern in the same line of business selling to a lower grade market.

The Psychological Aspect

The theme should be as broad as possible in its appeal to the class of prospects which may be reached through a given medium. A single theme, of course, may be treated in a variety of ways. There may also be a number of themes of almost equal importance in selling power.

One of the first things to determine is the relative importance of selling points in effecting the sale. For example, one investigation of figuring machines produced the following results:

1. Adaptability:	38 per cent	Machine purchased because it fits the work to be done.
2. Durability:	20 per cent	Considered secondary, but important and required due to high cost of product.
3. Service:	15.5 per cent	Vital to continuous, uninterrupted performance of the business, and so of tertiary importance.
4. Price:	14.5 per cent	Fourth in importance. Acceptable if comparable with kindred competition.
5. Accuracy:	12 per cent	Last in value because now accepted by all as an inherent feature.

If an advertising campaign does not seem to be proving profitable, an investigation should be made of the theme, assuming, of course, that the technical treatment is satisfactory. A Western central station, selling in about 60 towns, advertised washing machines on an economy appeal without great success. It then offered a free washing machine to the person who sent in the best reason why a woman should have a washing machine. Over 2,000 replies were received, divided as follows, according to an account in *Class:*

30 per cent wanted a machine because it saved time
25 per cent wanted a machine because it saved strength
14 per cent wanted a machine because it saved health
12 per cent wanted a machine because it preserved youth and beauty
8 per cent wanted a machine because it was more economical
7 per cent wanted a machine because it contributed happiness to the home

The theme of its previous advertising had been built around an appeal which was responsible for but 8 per cent of the sales

Armstrong's Linoleum *for every floor in the house*

A New Conception of Linoleum and a New Conception of Floors

PRETTIER rooms! Rooms of color! The last few years have brought in a growing vogue for brighter, more cheerful interiors.

Color and design in floors is part of this decorative trend. For in any room the floor is always the biggest expanse that meets the eye. The floor must complement or contrast with the other furnishings.

Eight years ago the makers of Armstrong's Linoleum established their Bureau of Interior Decoration. They had a new conception of linoleum. They saw linoleum not merely as a durable, sanitary, easily cleaned floor, but as a floor of beauty.

Today in all the finer patterns and colors Armstrong's Linoleum is designed and made with the idea—

First, that it shall be bought with an eye to its beauty,

Secondly, that it shall be laid for permanency, with cement, over a lining of builders' deadening felt (no

Thirdly, that it shall be waxed and cared for as any fine floor should be.

Very soon interior decorators saw the possibilities of color in floors. Architects, too, became interested in the idea. Women were quick to see what fine floors the newer and better designs in Armstrong's Linoleum would make for their best rooms.

Many interesting designs have been developed. There are rippling two-tone Jaspes (the living-room floor in the picture is the new Jaspé tile), dignified inlaids, rich marble tiles, quaint Dutch patterns, and attractive carpet and matting effects.

At good stores you can see these new designs and colorings and arrange for modern laying. If you want help and advice on particular problems of decoration, describe your rooms, and our Bureau of Interior Decoration will give you individual suggestions. No charge.

A new book on home furnishing and decoration

Mrs. Agnes Foster Wright of New York is an authority on interior decoration and a writer for House and Garden and other magazines.

Her recent book, "Floors, Furniture, and Color," includes color ideas for decorating different rooms, and gives advice that will help make your home more attractive. You may buy it from us for twenty-five cents. (In Canada, 60c.)

ARMSTRONG CORK COMPANY
Linoleum Division
844 President Ave., Lancaster, Pa.

FIG. 164. HOW AN ADVERTISING THEME IS CARRIED OUT
Each Armstrong advertisement tells approximately the same story, but always from a slightly different angle.

made. Changing the theme according to the results of the investigation resulted in greatly increased sales.

There are many examples of cases where the theme is connected with an intangible idea or conception, rather than the product or the institution. The American Stove Company sells its Lorain Oven Heat Regulator to women on the idea of time and temperature baking. This overcomes the objection from pride in culinary art based on good judgment in baking. The fundamental theme of the advertising of the International Silver Company has been the establishment of a social code for silver.

Fig. 165. A Successful Advertising Theme

The Armstrong Cork Company, some years ago, undertook to sell the idea that linoleum in proper design and coloring could be installed as a permanent floor for any room in the house over a lining of builders' deadening felt on a soft wood floor. Investigations showed that linoleum floors were so used in Europe, and were very satisfactory. This, according to S. E. Conybeare, advertising manager of the company, has been the theme of the advertising over a period of years, and will probably be continued. Figure 164 shows how the theme is carried out. Each advertisement tells the same story from a slightly different angle.

The American Saw Mill Machinery Company had been selling for a long time, according to *Keyed Copy,* on the basis

FIG. 166. THE THEME AROUND WHICH WAS BUILT THE ADVERTISING OF THE DIANA CAR

The famous St. Gaudens statue of Diana was so proportioned as to appear to advantage only when viewed from far below. So the statue reproduced here, the work of Miss Anne Hyatt, was used in its place. It serves as the keynote of this company's advertising. See also Figure 167. (*Advertising and Selling.*)

of "sawmills $200." After some research, this theme was changed to "Make money on your woodlots," with the result that sales were immediately increased (see Figure 165).

It is important that the whole treatment of the advertisement from the technical point of view should be carried out in accordance with the theme. This "theme" is shown in Figure 166. Attempt was made to build the advertising and the auto-

FIRST—After Twenty Years Research

No longer is mathematical balance a promise. Twenty years, and the industry's great quest is ended. Diana engineers have found *symmetrized design* and they reveal it in the first *Light* Straight Eight. It's a story of research without a parallel, steadfast, diligent, enthusiastic. ¶ *Symmetrized design* goes back to time remote, back to fundamentals, back to the Grecian vase, the basis of *all* design. And it brings to the Diana *Light* Eight the ultimate symmetry, the made-like-a-watch balance, mathematically correct, superbly true. ¶ But *symmetrized design* has given Diana more than a technical balance. It has added an amazing smoothness, a hushed operation, an even fullness of power, a pick-up like the snap of a whip. Diana for 1926 has 73 horsepower with a *pliant* flexibility of from 2 to 77 miles an hour. The acceleration is from 5 to 25 miles an hour in 6½ seconds. A new neutralizing force, the Lanchester Dampener, prevents synchronizing, stops vibration, prolongs the life of the car. ¶ Diana has the impudent swagger and dash of youth. She's clean limbed, light of foot, long and low. The newest, the very smartest, the most advanced type automobile. Engineers hail it, "The New-Day Motor Car." And Diana *is* new, crammed with new ideas, eager with new power. ¶ *Now get in and drive*—up hill, down dale, in the roughest going. Compare *this* performance with the best you have in mind, for comparison stresses Diana's leadership, points it out, isolates it, puts it in your memory forever.

DIANA

THE *LIGHT* STRAIGHT EIGHT

Diana Eights are sold and Serviced
By Moon Six Dealers *Everywhere*

PRODUCT OF A $75,000,000 COMBINATION

Roadster $1895 *Phaeton* $1895 *Standard Four-Door Sedan* $1995 *Cabriolet-Roadster* $2095 *Two-Door Brougham DeLuxe* $2095 *Four-Door Sedan DeLuxe* $2195 F.O.B. St. Louis
Built by the MOON MOTOR CAR COMPANY for the DIANA MOTORS COMPANY Stewart MacDonald, *Pres.*, St. Louis.

FIG. 167. THE DIANA THEME AS BUILT INTO THE FINISHED ADVERTISEMENT

mobile to the principles of "dynamic symmetery," taking the Saint Gaudens' statue of Diana as a model. The finished copy, embodying this theme, is shown in Figure 167.

The technical treatment of the theme as related to layout, typography, art work, and color are treated in subsequent chapters.

Position in the Medium

It is a well-recognized fact that the attention value of an advertisement is increased or decreased according to the position it occupies in the medium. Several experiments seem to indicate, for example, that the back cover of a periodical is worth about two and one-half times as much as the average inside page in black and white.

It is extremely difficult to secure accurate results from a study of reading habits. Nevertheless, some idea can be obtained of the most desirable positions from the point of view of interest in the reading matter. Few, if any, persons will say that their chief interest in a periodical or newspaper lies in its advertising contents. Yet there are few people who read either magazines or newspapers without being aware of at least some of the advertising.

Poffenberger (*Psychology in Advertising*) points out that different classes of individuals will have a varying distribution of interest in reading matter. Also he observes that an individual especially interested in some special department, such as finance, or radio, will be specially susceptible to the financial or radio advertising which appears in that department. The justice of these observations is borne out by the arrangement of advertising space in certain magazines.

The ordinary method of testing the relative merits of various positions is that of *recall* previously described. The first point to note in tests that have been made is that the ability to recall the advertisements seen steadily declines as the number of pages increases.

Starch (*Principles of Advertising*) conducted an interesting test of position value by giving the subjects of the test fifteen minutes to turn the pages of the advertising section, reading what they wished and skipping what they chose. The instructions were to turn every page. Corrections were made for familiarity with the advertisements so that position alone would be determining in the answers. The results are illustrated graphically in Figure 168. The value of the outside cover is taken as the basis, and the figures on the vertical scale are ratios of its value. Starch concludes from this:

1. That the outside cover is probably at least three times as valuable as an inside position.

2. That all positions within approximately eight pages from the end of the advertising section have greater value than other inside positions. These values gradually diminish as indicated by the drop of the curve.

3. That the positions facing the first and last pages of reading matter have approximately two-thirds of the value of the outside cover.

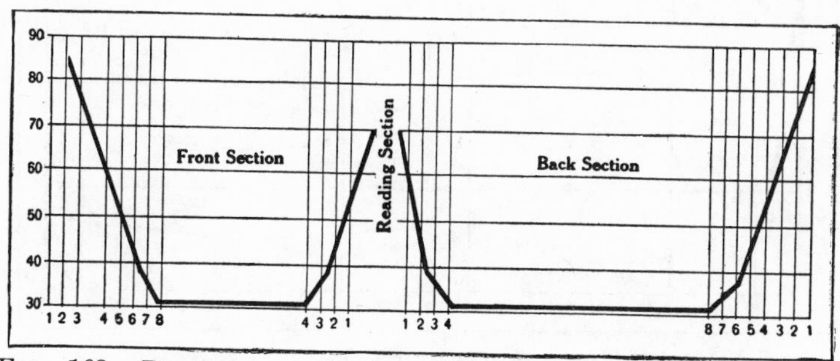

FIG. 168. RESULTS OF TEST TO DETERMINE RELATIVE POSITION VALUES FOR ADVERTISEMENTS IN THE VARIOUS SECTIONS OF A MAGAZINE

(Starch, *Principles of Advertising.*)

E. K. Strong (Bulletin of the Association of National Advertisers, No. 5) carried out a somewhat similar investigation except that there was no knowledge given those tested that the advertising content of the periodical was concerned. Those tested were merely told to read a certain article, and at the end of a week they were tested to see what advertisements they remembered in the magazine. The results of this test are shown in Figure 169.

Figure 170 illustrates the results as to position of a test made by George B. Hotchkiss and Richard B. Franken of New York University. The periodical used was an issue of the *Saturday Evening Post.* Here there is greater attention value at the beginning and end, but the spread is not so large as in the tests previously described.

Starch also made a test on the *Saturday Evening Post* issues between Aug. 8, 1914 and March 29, 1915. Each person tested was to look through one of these issues, turning every page, noting what interested him and passing over the rest. At the end of approximately 20 minutes each person was asked to write down the name of the advertisements remembered.

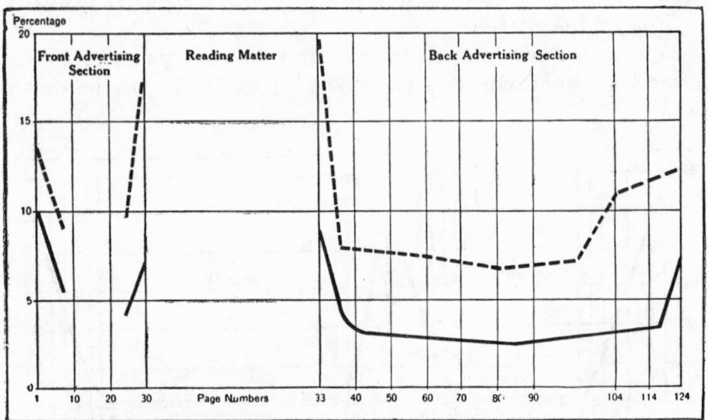

FIG. 169. RELATIVE ATTENTION VALUE OF PREFERRED AND NON-PREFERRED POSITIONS IN A STANDARD MAGAZINE (Starch, *Principles of Advertising,* after Strong.)

The average mentions of nonpreferred positions was taken as 100, and the following results then obtained:

	Percentage
Second cover	156
Facing second cover	140
Facing reading section	159
Average mention nonpreferred	100
Facing third cover	116
Third cover	147
Fourth cover	209

There has been some controversy as to whether there is any difference in value between right- and left-hand pages Strong in his test found that there was no difference. Hotchkiss and Franken (*Attention Value of Advertisements*) found that the average value of the right-hand page was 5 per cent greater than that of the left.

In planning where his advertisement shall go, the advertiser should ascertain:

1. Whether it is possible to insert the advertisement near text which pertains to the subject matter of the advertisement.

2. Whether the added cost of a preferred position is worth the added attention value gained thereby.

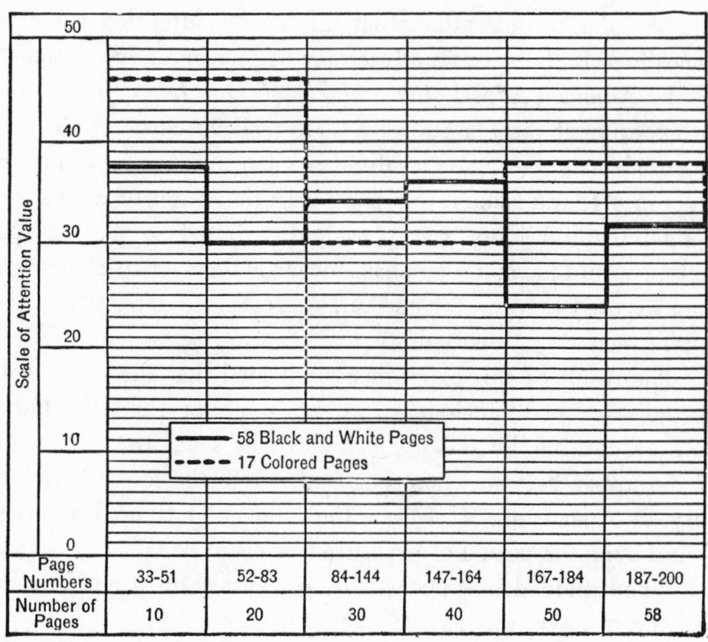

FIG. 170. ATTENTION VALUE OF VARIOUS POSITIONS IN A MAGAZINE WITH ADVERTISEMENTS "NEXT TO READING MATTER"
(Poffenberger, *Psychology in Advertising,* after Hotchkiss and Franken.)

Position on Page

It is important that all students of advertising should be acquainted with the experiments which have been conducted to show the relative value of different positions on the same page. While these various positions differ in attention value, the publisher rarely bases his rates on page position.

Early experiments tended to show that attention is closely connected with reading habits. The normal habit of the eye is to go to the upper left-hand corner of the page and travel to the right. When looking at pictures, the eye normally goes first to the so-called optical center—a point slightly above the middle of the page. However, since the eye, within the range of its vision, can take in the whole of an advertising page at one time, the specific attention value of some one advertisement on the page may overcome the disadvantage of inferior position.

In order to determine what the normal attention value is, regardless of the specific attractions of any one advertisement, H. F. Adams (*Advertising and Its Mental Laws*) conducted an experiment on 147 subjects. He took 92 cards of the size of an advertising page, and divided some into 15, some into 8, some into 4, and some into 2 parts. In the center of each space a small capital letter was placed, distributed so that no one section would have any emphasis over another. The cards were then exposed to view for one half second each, after which the letters seen were reported.

The result of this experiment indicated that the upper half of the page had much more attention power than the lower half. Counting by the number of times seen first, the score of the upper half was 85.5 per cent, while the lower half was only 14.5 per cent. However, the number of times both were seen during the period of exposure was about equal.

When divided in quarters, the percentage of attention each quarter received was as follows:

Upper left quarter	33 per cent
Upper right quarter	28 " "
Lower left quarter	21 " "
Lower right quarter	17 " "

The attention value of the various divisions of a page, according to the Adams tests is illustrated in Figure 171.

Starch conducted an experiment much like this, only substituting nonsense syllables for letters, and instead of cards, the pages were put in the form of a booklet. The subjects of the test read through the booklet and then reported all the

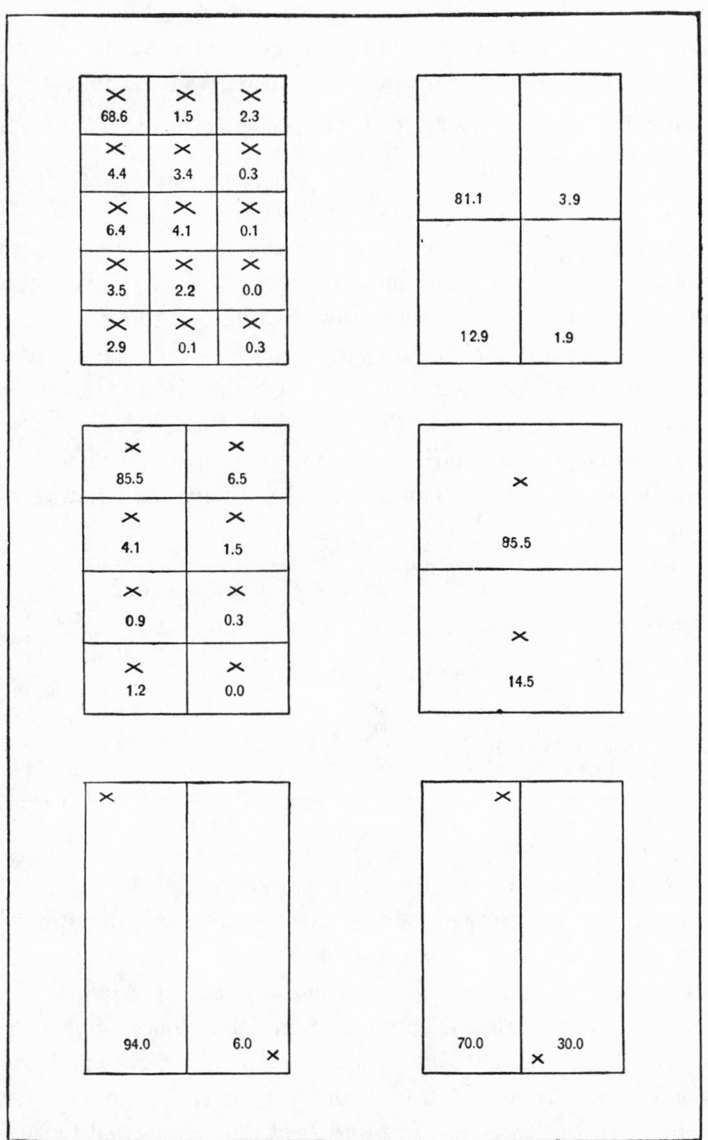

FIG. 171. THE ATTENTION VALUE OF VARIOUS POSITIONS ON A PAGE (Poffenberger, *Psychology in Advertising,* after H. F. Adams.)

nonsense syllables which were recalled. The results, in percentages of a perfect score for the position, were as follows:

Upper half	34 per cent	Upper left quarter..	28 per cent
Lower half	46 " "	Lower " " ..	16 " "
		Upper right quarter.	33 " "
		Lower " " .	23 " "

Other experiments have been conducted to determine the relative value of the right and left halves of a page. Hotchkiss and Franken found in their investigation of the position of advertisements in the *Saturday Evening Post* that the left-hand half had an 8.3 per cent advantage over the right half.

Franken, in his book *The Attention Value of Newspaper Advertisements,* summarizes the results of five experiments in the attention value of right- and left-hand pages as follows:

Attention Value of Right- and Left-Hand Pages

Name of Paper and Investigator	Number of Pages		Attention-Value in Per Cent		Per Cent Better
	Left	Right	Left	Right	
1. *The New York Times*—Strong...	7	6	5.6	7.3	.30
2. *The New York Times*—Roberts..	6	7	7.1	7.5	.06
3. *The New York Times*—Franken..	9	7	6.7	6.9	.03
4. *The* (Morning) *World*—Hough...	4	4	6.6	7.5	.14
5. *The New York Tribune*—Franken	10	9	7.4	7.7	.04
Final Average..............................			6.7	7.4	.10

In each case the right-hand pages show higher percentages of attention, the average for the five experiments being approximately 10 per cent. To illustrate to what extent advertisers utilize this fact, Henry D. Kitson (*Journal of Applied Psychology,* March, 1923) found that in 1082 consecutive pages of advertising in the *American Magazine,* the right-hand page was used five times as often as the left for full page advertisements. In the *Saturday Evening Post* they were used twice as frequently.

Repetition

Repetition is another of those factors in advertising about which comparatively little is known. Practically every advertiser would like to know whether it would be better for him to run a few large-sized advertisements or a greater number of smaller ones. The difficulty with psychological tests on the value of repetition is that it is almost impossible to separate attention from memory. Such tests as have been made indicate that with every repetition of the identical advertisement, the attention value decreases. This seems to be true regardless of the size of the advertisement.

In general, tests indicate that the second repetition adds about one-fourth, and a third presentation about two-thirds, to the

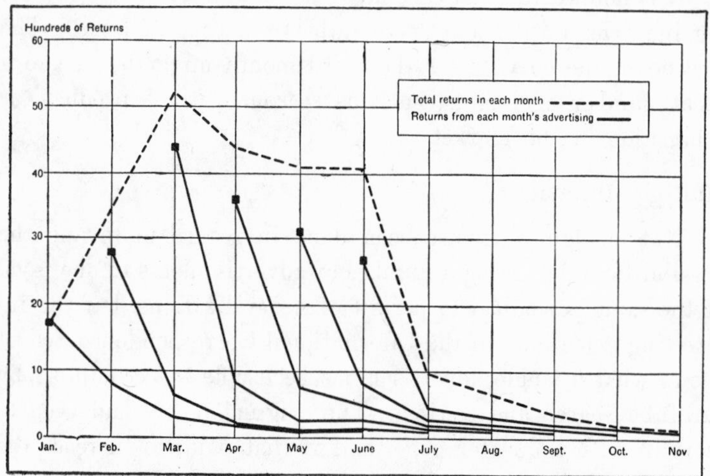

Fig. 172. The Effect of Repetition Measured in Returns (Poffenberger, *Psychology in Advertising,* after Max Freyd.)

value of the advertisement. Thus, if the same audience is to be covered, the larger sizes have an advantage over the smaller sizes twice repeated. As far as the effect on memory is concerned, there is an undoubted advantage in the repetition, but whether this is sufficient to offset the decreased attention power is not well established.

A number of advertisers have adopted the expedient of keeping part of their advertisement the same in every insertion, while varying the copy or illustration. In this way attention value is maintained while there are enough familiar features left in the advertising to make the repetitive effect of memory effective.

Not much experimental work has been done from actual advertising records, probably because the factors involved are so complex that they are difficult to analyze. Figure 172 shows the effect of repetition measured in inquiries to the first six advertisements in campaigns for two different products carried on in 15 different magazines. The study was made by Max Freyd in the *J. Walter Thompson News Bulletin,* August, 1923.

It is noteworthy that each advertisement does not stop drawing inquiries until about six months from time of issue. The decline in the curve after the third month might be due to a great number of factors, such as season, type of product, or exhaustion of the market.

Multiple Insertions

Not enough work has been done in regard to testing the possibilities of running a number of advertisements in one issue of the same periodical to permit of generalizations, but the interesting experience of the International Correspondence School shows what a single advertiser has been able to accomplish by careful research and testing. The original policy had been to start in with a quarter page, and if that paid, to increase the size to one half page, and then to a full page. It was noticed that the full page did not as a rule pull twice as many answers as the half-page advertisement. As an experiment, the company tried two half-page units in the same issue, with different illustrations and copy, but the same coupon. The company was surprised to find that both these advertisements paid as well as the single half-page had previously done. They did considerably better than the full page.

According to the account of the growth of this policy of multiple insertions by C. Lynn Sumner in *Advertising and Selling Fortnightly,* the tests were carried out in magazines with bulky advertising sections. Care was taken to scatter the advertisements. In three periodicals, it was found that as

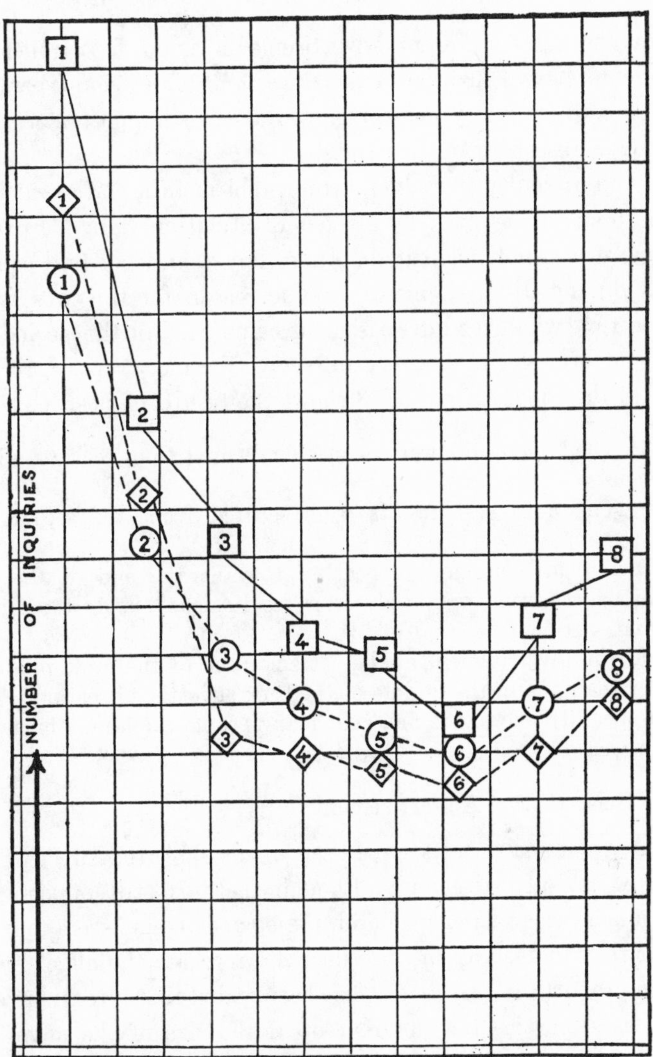

Fig. 173. Results of Position Tests

This chart represents a composite report on three years' advertising in one publication. Eight different pieces of copy were used in each issue, a total of 288 separately keyed insertions in 36 issues. Each of the three lines represents one year's advertising and each individual position represents the average number of inquiries produced each month in that year by the advertisement occupying the indicated position in the issue. For example, the first advertisement in the magazine is shown always to be the most productive and from there production declines directly in relation to position until the next to the last advertisement. (*Advertising and Selling.*)

many as eight different advertisements could be carried and made to pay. In other magazines, only four could be used, while a great many magazines could never support more than a single insertion in an issue.

The difficulty in reducing the problem to a statistical basis was to avoid the special emphasis of attention value. Furthermore, it was noticed that the same copy would not pull equally well during different months. The reason for this was found to be that whatever advertisement came first in the periodical, that advertisement was sure to receive the most replies, regardless of the copy. Figure 173 shows the results of position tests:

1. The best results were invariably secured from the first advertisements.
2. The next best results were secured from the second advertisement.
3. An advertisement appearing towards the end of the first advertising section produced better results than one in the middle of that section.
4. An advertisement at the extreme back of the issue produced better than one in the middle of the back advertising section. This is supposedly due to the fact that many people examine a magazine from back to front.

The Size of the Advertisement

A great many tests have been made upon the effect of the size of an advertisement, although there is still opportunity for much research. In general, these experiments seem to make clear that increasing the size does not increase the effect in the same proportion. In fact, it has been stated that attention value increases only as the square root of the size of the advertisement. Thus, a full page would be worth only twice as much as a quarter page.

There are, however, many factors which tend to make the full page particularly valuable. In the first place, it does not have to compete for attention with other advertisements on the same page. Also, experiments seem to prove that large advertisements are more easily remembered. So many other factors besides attention enter into the size of space to be used that it becomes, in many cases, an individual problem to be solved by experimentation. There is, for example, the greater prestige possessed by an advertisement of large size, the greater opportunity afforded for layout technique, and the increased memory value.

While it is true that a full page may not bring in four times as much as a quarter page, or twice as much as a half page, it might be that the full page could obtain orders that would never be obtained by the quarter or half page. The smaller size may attract the attention of those who are looking for the product, while the larger size may do the selling to those who are not so keenly interested in the product.

As shown by the experiments of Walter Dill Scott, there has been an almost constant increase in the number of full-page advertisements used. Up to 1890, only about one-fiftieth of advertising was in page size. In 1918, the ratio in the *Literary Digest* was found to be 45 per cent, whereas in 1910 it had been but 10 per cent.

The so-called "square-root law of effect" of increasing the size of an advertisement was verified by laboratory experiments. It has been claimed that the results between the experiment and the theory were so close that for all intents and purposes the law may be said to hold true.

The majority of experiments as to size have been made by memory tests. Strong and Franken have concluded from their tests that increase in space does not result in a corresponding increase in effect. Starch, on the other hand, contends that the full-page unit is the most economical space.

CHAPTER XXI

RESEARCH AS APPLIED TO COPY

In some form or other, copy is essential to every advertisement even though it be no more than the name of the advertiser or of his product. Copy itself can be classified in a great number of ways, such as the following 42 forms enumerated by *Printers' Ink:*

1. Reason why
2. Impressionistic
3. Sales talk
4. Institutional
5. "How to Use It"
6. Mechanical
7. Personification
8. Follow-the-leader copy
9. Dialogue
10. Question and answer
11. Signed statement
12. Testimonial
13. Exhortation
14. Reader notice
15. Sample offer
16. Blind copy
17. Geographical atmosphere
18. Historical
19. Poetical
20. Teaser copy
21. Dramatic
22. Odd forms of English
23. News
24. Timely advertising
25. Scriptural or philosophical
26. Incident
27. Scare copy
28. Slogan
29. Circus advertising
30. Statistical advertising
31. Personal efficiency
32. Epigram
33. Juvenile
34. Prestige
35. Quotation
36. Sense appeal
37. Playful copy
38. Editorial
39. Humorous copy
40. Plain facts
41. Association (atmosphere)
42. Story

Copy, in accordance with the laws of rhetoric, should supposedly conform to the principles of unity, proportion, coherence, and emphasis. Such questions as these, and the qualities of economy, force, beauty, euphony, and the like are treated in advertising textbooks.

The problem in this chapter is to outline briefly the possible methods of copy research, notably along psychological lines. It has been discovered that copy, like color, illustrations, and typography, has certain reactions on the audience, both in the form of separate words, and in groups of words, as in sentences.

It should be recognized at the outset that many able advertising men do not believe that the subject of copy is one for research, as it is at present practiced. The following comes from Leroy Fairman, of the Charles C. Green Advertising Agency, Inc.:

> Instead of evaluating an advertisement as you have instructed him to do, he [the consumer to whom a piece of copy has been referred] judges illustrations by the standards of what he thinks he knows about art; exercises his personal judgment as to what is appropriate display and typography; gives preference to flashy, flamboyant copy which he regards as "clever," and ends up by giving you the benefit of his quite worthless judgment as to what is "a good ad."
>
> One of the most striking illustrations of this type of result which has come under my notice was the case of a lady—one of a "class" upon which a consumer test was being made—who checked and graded for selling value the advertisements in a magazine.
>
> She gave the A mark to a handsome full page vacuum cleaner advertisement. Before she turned her magazine in, she was observed to make a memorandum in her note book, and inquiry disclosed the fact that she had written down the name and manufacturer's address of another vacuum cleaner, intending to write for further information concerning it. The advertisement was a quarter-page affair, none too attractive in appearance. The lady naïvely stated that the cleaner it advertised "sounded just like what she needed," and she wanted to find out all about it.
>
> I have participated in, or closely observed, quite a number of tests and questionnaires, some of which elicited information of much value; but consumer tests on the selling value of copy failed to impress me with anything except their utter futility.

The Copy Plan

Copy that is the product of pure inspiration may be artistically perfect, but the chances are that it does not take into consideration the practical requirements for selling the product to best advantage. Hence, it is desirable ordinarily to make a plan for the construction of the copy. Professor John H. Cover, in his book, *Advertising, Its Problems and Methods,* suggests the following example:

1. Theme; copper is the best metal for the plumbing of your house.
2. Kind of advertisement; complete.
3. Order of development; exposition, deduction.
4. Sequential order; historical.
   (*a*) Alloyed with tin, first metallic compound.
   (*b*) "Bronze Age" is term given era.
   (*c*) Mining has progressed from manual to machine production.
   (*d*) Exists in variety of forms.
   (*e*) United States largest producer.
   (*f*) Many modern uses.
   (*g*) Will not rust, corrode, or decay as will iron, steel and other metals.
   (*h*) Recently a copper pipe 2,500 years old was found in Egypt, as good as new.
   (*i*) Copper pipes will last as long as house with no replumbing, leaks, falling ceilings, or walls.

The first draft of the copy is then written, and checked with the following rules of procedure:

A. Introduction.
   (*a*) Is it direct?
   (*b*) Is it vigorous?
   (*c*) Does it properly develop theme?
B. Conclusion.
   (*a*) Does it assure unity of impression?
   (*b*) Does it recapitulate?
   (*c*) Does it appeal to action or memory?
C. Headline: "Copper Retains Eternal Youth."
   (*a*) Is it truthful?
   (*b*) Is it attractive?
D. Transitions: (1) between introduction, body, and conclusion; (2) between stages of thought.
   (*a*) Do they indicate distinctions?
   (*b*) Do they fill gaps?

This rough draft is then revised according to the following outline:

I. Qualities
  1. Economy
    (*a*) Must the reader interpret our meaning?
    (*b*) Can we substitute suggestion for exhortation?
    (*c*) Have we used æsthetic, congruous language effectively?
  2. Clearness
    (*a*) Have we exactness of expression?
    (*b*) Do our grammatical relationships cause ambiguity?
  3. Force
    (*a*) Have we been careful of the connotation of phraseology?
    (*b*) Have we obtained emphasis?
  4. Beauty
    (*a*) Have we tested euphony by reading aloud?
    (*b*) Can we add to effect by use of sound words and rhythmic phraseology?
    (*c*) Can we improve the feeling tone?

II. Structure
  1. Is our copy unified in impression?
  2. Is the proportion conducive to the most vivid impression?
  3. Is our copy coherent?
  4. Is there emphasis structually?

III. Functions
  1. Can we improve our device for attracting attention?
  2. Is our method of creating interest a natural evolution from attention?
  3. Is desire for our own brand likely to result?
  4. Have we established confidence?
  5. Is our appeal sufficiently strong to stimulate action or impress memory?

IV. Appeal
  1. Have we chosen the most appropriate emotional appeals?
  2. Have we backed the appeals with arguments?

V. Have we established a close, pleasant association?

VI. As a final check, before backing it with cash
    (*a*) Ask the family for criticism.
    (*b*) Ask the office boys what it means to them.
    (*c*) Prevail upon an eighth-grade teacher to submit it to her students.
    (*d*) Or, preferably, have a skilled psychologist conduct a test upon it.

Laboratory Tests

Starch, in his admirable book on the *Principles of Advertising,* from tests which he has made, contends that the attention value and the headline of an advertisement are each nearly twice as important as the text. He also reports a series of tests which measure the relative value of series of advertisements and the various elements in them.

174.—An Investigation of the Relative Value of a Series of Advertisements

Results of Tests of Seven Insurance Advertisements

(Starch: *Principles of Advertising*)

Advertisement	Attention Test		Headline Test		Test of Text		All Tests Combined	Final Rank According to Tests	Order According to Firm's Returns
	Median Rank	Order of Ranks	Median Rank	Order of Ranks	Median Rank	Order of Ranks			
A	2.2	2	2.3	1	2.2	1	2.2	1	1
D	1.9	1	3.5	3	3.3	3	2.9	2	4
G	4.0	4	3.2	2	3.1	2	3.4	3	2
B	3.6	3	3.9	4	4.3	4	3.9	4	3
F	5.4	6	5.2	6	5.0	5½	5.2	5	5
E	5.3	5	4.2	5	6.0	7	5.3	6	7
C	6.6	7	6.8	7	5.0	5½	6.1	7	6

For example, a set of seven insurance advertisements was tested for attention value, headline value, and convincingness of the text. The results are shown in Figure 174. The first column shows the letters given to each advertisement, the second shows median rank of each advertisement in the attention test, the third given median test rank for headlines, the fourth median for convincingness of text, the fifth tabulates medians of the three tests, and the sixth column enumerates the final order according to the results of the combined medians. The last column gives the order of effectiveness of the advertisements according to returns actually received by the advertiser.

There is a surprising amount of agreement between the laboratory test rankings and the actual results. The percentage of agreement between the two ranks, or the so-called coefficient of correlation, is 86.

This same experiment was carried out with 15 typewriter

advertisements, where the coefficient of correlation was 71. A third test of eight book advertisements sold entirely by mail shows a correlation coefficient of only 55. A fourth test of seven encyclopedia advertisements showed as coefficient of correlation of 71. Other tests were made up to 20, the results of which are shown in Figure 175.

FIG. 175.—A COMPARISON OF LABORATORY RESULTS WITH ACTUAL RETURNS

Summary of Correlation of Tests and Actual Return of 20 Sets of Advertisements

(Starch: *Principles of Advertising*)

Business or Commodity	Number of Advertisements	Attention Value	Headline	Text on the Ads	All Tests Combined
Life insurance	7	.68	.79	.88	.86
Encyclopedia	7	.90	.38	.30	.72
Typewriter	15	.48	.75	.46	.71
Book	8	.46	.75	.36	.58
Lumber	2	1.00	1.00	1.00	1.00
Spray pump	3	.83	.00	.00	....
Tooth paste	4	.40	1.00	.20	.80
Water heater	4	....	1.00	....	1.00
Filing device	8	.81	....	.53	.72
Filing device	8	.76	....	.55	.70
Filing device	8	.88	....	.02	.65
Condensed milk	2	1.00	1.00	.00	1.00
Coats and suits	2	1.00	1.00	1.00	1.00
Health exercise	5	.43	....	.78	.75
Correspondence instruction	6	.59	.60	.71	.71
Correspondence instruction	6	.49	.89	.34	.78
Addressing machine	3	1.00	.75	.50	1.00
Duplicating machine	6	.68	.90	.56	.87
Calculating machine	4	.40	.40	.40	.40
Calculating machine	5	.50	.45	.60	.80
Averages	.....	.70	.78	.48	.79

Headlines

The larger the volume of advertisements in periodicals becomes, the greater emphasis is laid on the importance of the headline to attract attention and arouse interest in the rest of the advertisement. A number of tests to determine the relative importance of the headline have been made by Starch (*Principles of Advertising*).

For example, 20 advertisements of the Savage Arms Company were secured, all much the same as to layout, size, and illustration, the chief differences being in text and headline. First, the headlines were taken by themselves and presented to 114 persons, who rated them according to strength, interest, and "gripping" qualities, in their order of merit.

After an interval of several months, when the headlines had been forgotten, the entire advertisements were presented to the same group, as well as to a group which had never seen any part of them. Figure 176 tabulates the results of both these

Fig. 176.—An Investigation of the Relative Importance of the Headline

Comparison of Effectiveness of Headlines and Text

(Starch: *Principles cf Advertising*)

Headlines	Rank of Headlines Separately	Rank of Texts as a Whole
1. A Match for Any Burglar	1	5
2. Shoot the First Shots	2	6
3. Banishes Night Fear	3	14
4. The Only Gun a Burglar Fears	4	3
5. Detective Burns Applauds It	5	2
6. Cold Steel *vs.* Cold Sweat	6	8
7. That Finger Will Save Your Life	7	1
8. Only the Burglar Need Be Afraid	8	9
9. No Wild Shots from This Gun	9	7
10. 3,000 Burglars Loose	10	12
11. Fights for Her Life Like a Fiend	11	4
12. Must a Burglar First Come?	12	17
13. There He Is—The Burglar	13	16
14. Woman's Turn Has Come	14	15
15. Why Live in a Haunted House	15	13
16. Chain Your Bedroom Doors	16	18
17. In the Hands of a Frightened Woman	17	10
18. Dr. Carver Banishes Burglar Fear	18	20
19. Is Yours an Egg-Shell Home?	19	19
20. Mrs. Dock—a Novice—Fires on Burglar and Tips Him	20	11
	Correlation	67

Men relate

this simple way to get

a new thrill in shaving

Men the nation over are awakening to the fact that there is a general switch to the Valet AutoStrop Razor.

Its sales have pyramided in an astounding manner.

All because men are discovering that a sharp blade *for every shave* is a genuine luxury.

The Valet AutoStrop is the *only* razor that sharpens its own blades. A few strokes on its strop restore a blade to new-like keenness.

Sharpen it, then shave, then clean—all in a jiffy, and without removing the blade from the holder.

This is a different principle. The blade doesn't get duller and duller until it must be thrown away.

Every shave can be with a blade of super-keenness.

Have you fallen into a habit? Do you continue your old way of shaving?

Then join the thousands upon thousands who have turned to a new and better way and whose enthusiasm never wanes.

A speedy, comfortable shave every time—uniformly perfect. An end to "pulling." An end to wasting time.

"There's no shave like it," men say. Why miss this supreme improvement?

Valet Auto-Strop Razor

REG. U. S. PAT. OFF.

$5 to $25
Other sets at $1
The RAZOR That Sharpens Itself
AUTOSTROP SAFETY RAZOR CO., 656 First Avenue, New York City

FIG. 177. HYPERBOLE MEANS WEAKNESS

Does the increasingly sophisticated advertising audience get a "thrill" so easily?

tests. The comparatively close correlation between these two tests shows what importance should be attached to the headline. There are a few cases where the ranking of the headline and the whole text is far apart, but in most cases they are fairly close together.

The same kind of test was applied to eight advertisements of Packer's Tar Soap. Here the correlation was again close except where a dominating illustration removed the emphasis from the headline.

A third test was carried out with five Turret Lathe advertisements, where the rank of the headlines was compared with the results actually produced. The headlines which ranked first and second belonged to the advertisements which produced best and second best results.

Tests made by Gale (*Psychology of Advertising*) tend to show that relevant words rank highest in attention value for headlines, their attention value increasing with the successive trials. Relevant cuts are next in order, while irrelevant words are at the bottom, tending to decrease in interest with each exposure. As in the case of illustrations, the irrelevant headline is often remembered, but rarely in connection with the product which it is intended to sell.

Figure 177 illustrates a headline which would be apt to fail of its effect because it would not be believed. It would be difficult to find a man who relates the thrills he gets from shaving. A test was made of for belief in connection with one of the Edison Phonograph advertisements, which pictures a well-known singer and the phonograph, and states that an audience could not tell when the phonograph was working and when the singer was performing, so perfect was the tone reproduction. It was found that 77 per cent out of 100 subjects questioned doubted the truth of the statements, believing that they could tell the difference between any phonograph and a human voice.

Is Advertising Copy Read?

E. K. Strong (Bulletin of the Association of National Advertisers, No. 9) some years ago made a test with the object

Fig. 178.—An Investigation of the Recognition and Identification of Advertisements

The Effectiveness of Copy

Advertisement		First Paragraph		Last Paragraph	
Number	Recognition	Recognition	Identification	Recognition	Identification
1	39	4	5	6	7
2	33	23	23	23	22
3	32	9	10	3	2
4	32	19	16	10	3
5	29	9	10	13	8
6	29	13	1	4	4
7	26	13	8	8	8
8	24	16	5	9	4
9	24	15	13	3	1
10	22	9	3	5	3
11	22	10	0	14	0
12	20	8	7	9	6
13	20	16	14	4	5
14	14	2	0	3	0
15	14	5	0	3	1
16	11	2	3	10	3
17	10	11	0	10	10
18	10	2	0	7	3
19	9	8	0	4	3
20	8	5	0	9	0
21	7	3	0	9	0
22	7	5	0	10	0
23	5	6	0	0	0
24	4	2	0	2	0
25	3	10	0	7	0
Average	18.2	9.0	4.1	7.4	3.7

of determining whether the copy of advertisements was read, or at least noticed so that it would be recognized. A group of subjects, 95 men and 53 women, were shown 25 full-page advertisements which had appeared during the preceding month in two magazines. It was then determined how many recognized having seen the advertisement before, how many recognized the first paragraph of the copy, and how many recognized the last paragraph. These first and last paragraphs were typewritten and presented separately.

The results of the test are shown in Figure 178. On the entire 25 advertisements an average of 18.2 per cent recognized the advertisement, 9 per cent the first paragraph and 7.4 per cent the last. The percentages which identified the product in terms of the trade name from the first paragraph was 4.1 and the last 3.7 per cent.

A study of the table shows that individual advertisements differed to a marked extent. Number 2, for example, shows an extraordinarily high percentage of recognition and identification, while Number 24 was recognized by few and identified by none.

Comprehension

It is a basic principle of advertising that the copy used should be understood by the audience. If the advertisement is to appear in a technical periodical, it may contain a great number of words which would not be suitable were this same product to be advertised in a general periodical. It is desirable to know what the level of intelligence of the audience is so that copy may be of a type which is readily comprehended.

The problem of comprehension may be divided into that of words and that of ideas. Some interesting tests have been made with regard to both of these questions. In one case[1] all the words were taken from 190 advertisements (excluding names of articles) in one issue of the *Saturday Evening Post, Ladies' Home Journal,* and *Woman's Home Companion.* After eliminating duplicates, 3,796 words were left, and these were checked against words appearing in the *Teacher's Word Book,* an alphabetical list of 10,000 words occurring most commonly in literature for children of various kinds. Only 4 per cent of the words in the advertisements failed to appear in the word book. Fifteen of the words appearing in both were chosen at

[1] Poffenberger and Goldstein, *Journal of Applied Psychology,* VII, 1923, pp. 364*ff*.

random and submitted to 37 individuals who had not gone through high school. They were asked to give the meaning of these words.

The average percentage of error for all the words was 12 per cent. It ranged as high as 73 per cent for the word *zest*. These same subjects were tested with six words appearing on the advertisement list but not in the *Teacher's Guide Book*, and the percentage of error was found to be about the same.

Dr. John T. Dorrance, president of the Campbell Soup Company, says:

Our educational advertising of soup has been continuous for more than 23 years. We have not aimed for advertisements that were brilliant in conception; rather we have favored plain, understandable statements which always carried answers to the consumer's questions: "What is the quality?" and "What is the price?"

Comprehension of Ideas

If the comprehension of the great public is comparatively limited as to single words, it is even more limited in its understanding of complicated phrases and sentences. Poffenberger, who has done much of the best experimental work in the psychology of advertising, reports the following test (*Psychology in Advertising*):

An advertisement in complete form, or simply the copy from it, was presented with a series of questions. Nineteen sets of material were tested on more than a thousand subjects, ranging in character from car cards to magazine advertisements. In one case, 107 passengers in the New York subway were asked to read the car card advertising a certain emulsion, and containing the following copy:

Milk is an emulsion. The ——— Emulsion is emulsified 550 times finer than milk and its fat content is eight times richer than the best milk. That is why physicians and druggists all over America, when asked to name the finest emulsion, answer The ——— Emulsion. Tastes good—No Cod Liver Oil—Protects and Builds Health.

It was found that 46 per cent knew an emulsion was fatty, but not one know what the essential characteristics of an emulsion were. One question asked what "emulsified 550 times finer than milk" meant to the subject, and 30 per cent said it meant the emulsion was 550 times better than milk.

A number of advertisements in general periodicals were shown to college students, who were asked to explain the operation of the products therein advertised. The majority of them were unable to do so, even by referring to the advertisement.

Testing copy on a sample audience is so simple, as compared with the other tasks of advertising research, that it is remarkable it is not done more frequently. In fact, almost any piece of copy, technical or not, would benefit by such a test. It is necessary simply to choose a certain number of subjects of the class which belong within the range of the market, show them the copy, and then ask them questions which will indicate whether they have thoroughly understood what they have read. If they have not understood, it will be of great profit to the effectiveness of the advertisement to rewrite it.

This is particularly important as there seems to be a growing tendency on the part of advertisers to "explain" not only about their product, but about themselves, and their policies.

CHAPTER XXII

RESEARCH AS APPLIED TO LAYOUT

The term *layout* covers the entire structure of the advertisement, ordinarily composed of the division of space, the illustration and decoration, and the typography. Its success is measured by the degree to which it attracts attention and directs this upon the theme of the advertisement, whatever this may be.

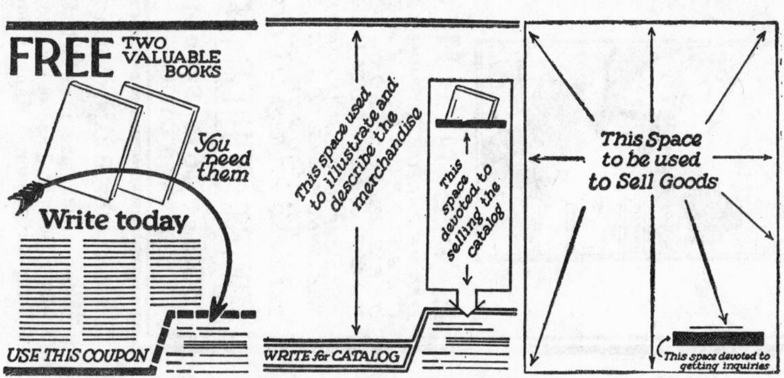

FIG. 179. THREE LAYOUTS

Reproductions of the three types of advertising layouts referred to in the text. The first one, making the literature of the company as alluring as possible and emphasizing the word "Free," is admirably calculated to coax inquiries, at the expense, however, of leaving the many thousands of non-inquirers in total ignorance of the line. The second layout gives about 25 per cent of its space to the obtaining of requests for the catalogue, which percentage is wasted upon those who do not inquire. The third advertisement aims toward selling the line to the total number of readers, even at the cost of an impressive inquiry return from the minority. (*Advertising and Selling.*)

Figure 179 shows how layout may be altered to effect different purposes. In the layout on the left, the emphasis is on the coupon; in the central layout only about 25 per cent of the emphasis is directed towards the coupon; in the layout on the right, the greatest part of the space is devoted to selling copy.

The BILTMORE
MADISON AVE., 43rd TO 44th STREETS
NEW YORK

Dancing in the Supper Room

Tea in Palm Room

Friday Morning Musicales

JOHN McE. BOWMAN,
President

86%

EIGHTY-SIX per cent of 10,000 children recently examined were found suffering from trouble with their teeth through improper care.

Ipana Tooth Paste makes brushing the teeth a pleasure. Its taste is smooth, snappy and delightful and its use results in clean, white, sturdy teeth.

Your druggist keeps Ipana Tooth Paste.

*IPANA
TOOTH PASTE

Bristol-Myers Co.
New York

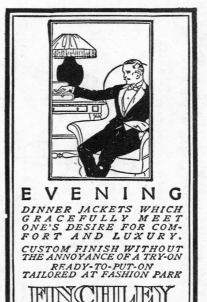

FIG. 180. EXAMPLES OF SMALL ADVERTISEMENTS

These three advertisements, reproduced here in the exact size in which they originally appeared, show what can be done by the judicious use of small space. Each small advertisement has to be as carefully prepared as its bigger brother. If it is so prepared it will build sales and hold good will for the advertiser. Many a small business has grown big because it has used small ads—and used them well.

Naturally, the major part of successful layout is due to artistic technique. Nevertheless, there are certain fundamental rules, verified by psychological tests, which must be recognized, and which form the basis of the principles of layout.

For example, the power to attract attention is based on contrast, obtained by white space, borders, typography, color, headline, or other means. Another factor in efficient layout

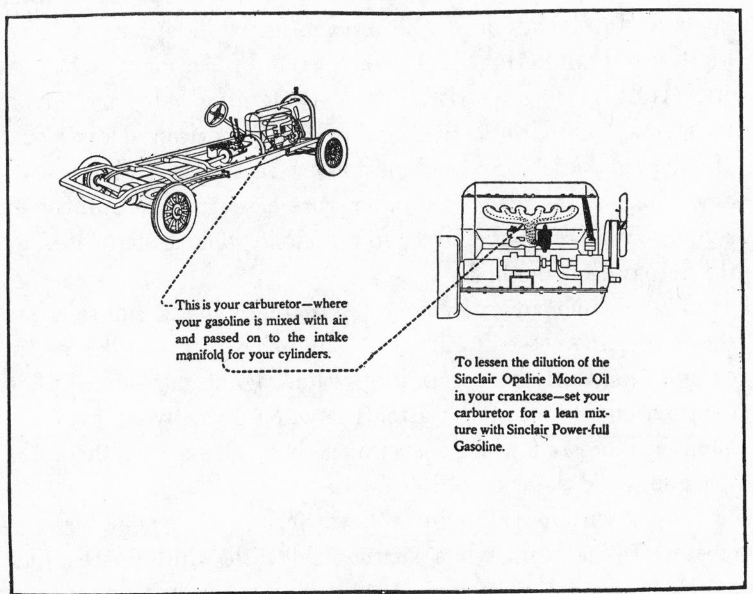

This is your carburetor—where your gasoline is mixed with air and passed on to the intake manifold for your cylinders.
To lessen the dilution of the Sinclair Opaline Motor Oil in your crankcase—set your carburetor for a lean mixture with Sinclair Power-full Gasoline.

Fig. 181. The Use of White Space
A simple and telling way of obtaining an effect.

is action, usually obtained by a novelty layout, in which the theme is given vitality through contrast.

The effect of layout on the small advertisement is particularly noticeable. Figure 180 shows three advertisements, which, although small in size, proved highly successful. Here the judicious contrast of white space, illustration, and decoration enhance the attention power of the advertisement many times over the normal effect produced by an advertisement of this size.

Contrast and Isolation

The aim of the layout man is to give his advertisement such attention power that it will compete favorably with other advertisements in the immediate surroundings, or that it will cause the reader to look further into the copy, rather than merely to give it a passing glance. Figure 181 shows the powerful effect of white space when used in a booklet. E. K. Strong made an investigation of this problem of white space, reported in Research Bulletin No. 1, Association of National Advertisers. He took 20 advertising pages containing half-page advertisements, half with vertical and half with horizontal divisions. He showed these one at a time to certain subjects, giving each advertisement an attention value score based on the number of subjects who remembered having seen it when tested later by the recognition method.

These same advertisements were then placed on separate sheets of paper (see Figure 182), and shown to another group of subjects, and the recognition value again tabulated. The supposition is that if the attention value of a given advertisement is increased when surrounded by white space, then this space must be the controlling factor.

The attention value for the vertical arrangement was increased 76 per cent when surrounded with white space; that of the horizontal arrangement 90 per cent. In the latter case, the advertisement on the lower half of the page received the greatest benefit. One advertisement in the whole series had its attention value decreased.

In connection with these results it should be remembered that doubling the size of the advertisement does not double the attention value *ipso facto.*

Simplicity versus Complexity

Layout, as already mentioned, is largely a matter of technique and artistic skill, to which research can add little. There are, however, certain points about layout which may be tested, notably its simplicity or complexity. Since the purpose of lay-

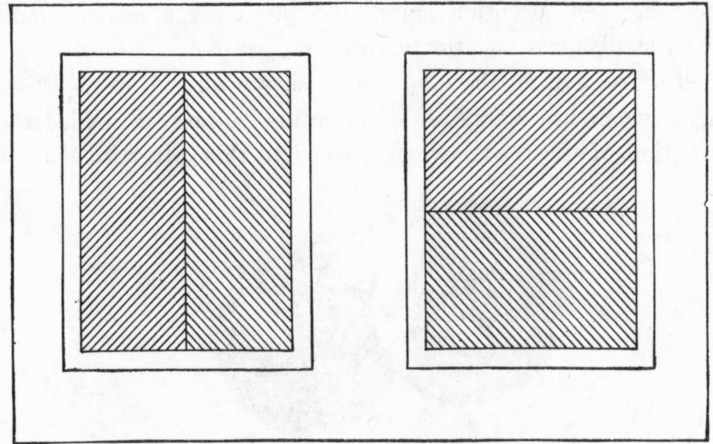

FIG. 182A. ARRANGEMENT OF HALF-PAGE ADVERTISEMENTS FOR AN EXPERIMENT IN ISOLATION

out is to attract attention and to impress the image on the reader's mind, it is highly desirable to know the best form to use.

Layout, of course, may vary from the excessively simple to the excessively complex. Figure 183 shows a type of advertising where the layout is of the utmost simplicity. Attention is undoubtedly secured by the liberal use of white space, but

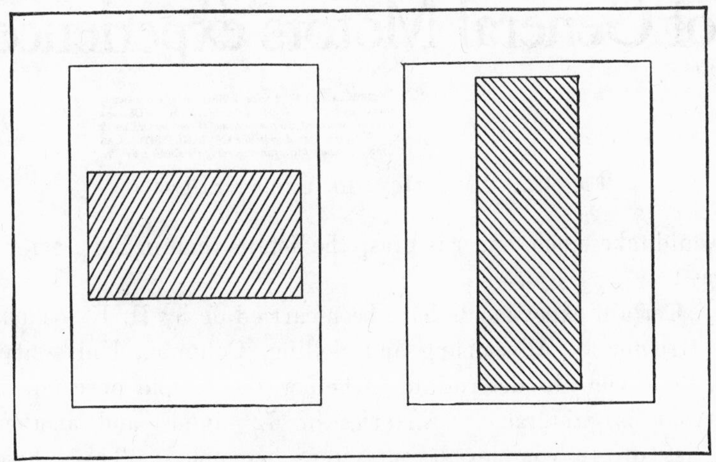

FIG. 182B. INDICATING REARRANGEMENT OF THE ADVERTISEMENTS OF FIGURE 182A

(Poffenberger, *Psychology in Advertising,* after Strong.)

there are few attention points and the average reader would undoubtedly pass on after a cursory glance.

Figure 184, on the other hand, shows a form of advertisement which has a number of attention points. Provided the attention of the reader were directed to this advertisement, it

PRODUCT
OF
GENERAL
MOTORS
A new Car–reflecting 17 years
of General Motors experience
A NEW name, a NEW value, a NEW car of tremendously broad appeal · · · It will be produced by the Oakland Division and marketed as a companion of the present OAKLAND SIX · · · Dealers should write the OAKLAND MOTOR CAR COMPANY, Pontiac, Michigan, regarding the double franchise.

FIG. 183. LAYOUT OF THE UTMOST SIMPLICITY

would take much longer to grasp the details than in the previous case.

Certain experiments have been carried on by H. K. Nixon, Instructor in Advertising and Selling, Columbia University, with a view to determining whether the simple or complex layout is preferable. A series of 42 simple and another series of 42 complex layouts were assembled. Then these were paired off, one simple and one complex layout, and presented to the subjects of the test. Record of eye movements was

Many a simple gift quickly achieves distinction with this smart LINEN THREAD

AN answer to every Christmas problem! The gay little gift, the useful gift, the gift unusual enough for the friend who has everything, lovely enough for the friend who has nothing—these are but a few of the delightful possibilities this new linen thread affords.

And all so quickly planned, so easily made!

A little cross-stitched motif—a few rows of linen feather-stitching—such uses as these shown on this page go far to transform the simplest of Christmas presents into something precious and exquisite.

And there is so much joy in the doing! The firm lustrous linen thread has won enthusiastic approval for this new linen needlework. There is such a satisfying quality in linen! All the firm strength that preserved the Egyptian tissues through the ages, belongs to each strand of Barbour's Art Needlework Threads.

And how they wash and wear! Linen worked with linen mellows and grows more beautiful with time. Months of testing and experimenting have proved the dyes used for Barbour's threads, sunproof and boilproof.

You will find these threads at the art needlework counters of the larger stores and the cozy little art shops—in balls of white, ecru, and natural, and in skeins of the most wanted colors.

Have you yet sent for this interesting book on needlework?

How to do Italian hemstitching, Swedish weaving and other interesting stitches with designs other than those shown here, is told with many simple diagrams in this helpful book. Send a dime with the coupon below—a copy will be mailed to you at once. The Linen Thread Company, Dept. G-23, 96 Franklin St., New York.

Sets for the buffet or for luncheon are quickly made of creamy linen with borders of plain mesh filet crochet. Then for the added touch that makes them quite the most delightful filet sets you ever made, darn in a simple design in color! This set has its pattern in yellow and gold and its edge finished with a row of gold buttonholing outside a row of yellow.

A charming cloth and napkins for bridge or tea are made like the popular drawn-thread handkerchiefs. The 36-inch yellow linen cloth has gold threads pulled in about 4 inches apart to form a border while gold colored squares are appliqued at the corners, and garlands of flowers decorate the middle of each side.

An apron of linen bound with contrasting linen has more uses than you can count! It has one big pocket and its fulness is held in place by rows of feather-stitching in contrasting colors (worked with Barbour's Linen Thread doubled to give a clear-cut, bold effect).

A gay touch of color for the simple cloth frock! Collar and cuffs of crisp white linen embroidered in China blue, red and black, adds a smart touch any girl will love. A little bag has a motif of real Russian cross-stitch worked on its side in red, blue, green, yellow and black linen thread. The Russian Princess made this also.

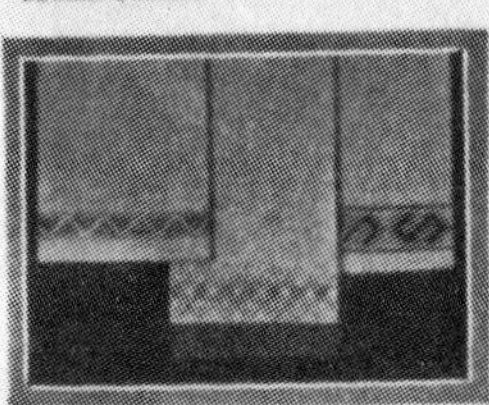

No one ever has too many towels, especially guest towels. The towel with coral colored linen border has its lacy pattern darned in shades of coral and red linen thread; the towel at the left has its simple pyramids darned in of clear blue linen; the towel at the right has a delightful pattern of cross-stitch designed for it by a Russian Princess.

Barbour's Linen Thread for Art Needlework comes in balls of white, ecru, and natural, sizes 12 to 50 inclusive; in skeins of black, white, coral, lavender, red, medium brown, gold, yellow, pink, willow green, China blue. Natural linen color of one size only.

BARBOUR'S
Linen Thread
FOR ART NEEDLEWORK

Send for this fascinating book today!

THE LINEN THREAD CO., Dept. G-23
96 Franklin Street, New York

For the dime enclosed herewith please send me your booklet showing how to do Italian hemstitching, Swedish weaving, etc.

Name ....

Address ....

City .... State ....

FIG. 184. LAYOUT WITH SEVERAL ATTENTION POINTS

kept, unknown to the subjects. From these observations it was found that the chances were 94 to 100 that the simple layout would be looked at first. This leaves out of consideration the special attention features, such as color or position.

At the end of 10 seconds, the ratio between the two layouts was 89 to 100 in favor of the simple group. The simple layout, while it attracts the attention first, cannot hold it long, and the eye shifts to the layout on the other page. Over a period of 30 seconds, the advantage lies with the complex layout in the ratio of 121 to 100.

In another experiment by this same investigator, subjects were shown about 40 simple layouts, paired with 40 complex layouts. They were then asked to recall as many of the advertisements as came to mind in 15 minutes. The simple layouts were favored in the ratio of 77 to 100.

From these tests, certain conclusions are reached as to human attention, according to the account in *Class*. The advertisement should have a simple layout, but at the same time it should provide several points of interest. Professor Hollingworth has given his opinion that there should be three units of attention (pictures, styles of type, masses of color, etc.). It is necessary to maintain a balance between the narrow limits of attention, and its constant fluctuations. Even though the conditions of the laboratory experiment may not be reproduced in actual advertising practice, the results of these tests are instructive as indicating the application of research to layout problems.

Division of Space

If attention is to be attracted, there must be one feature in the layout which will attract this attention. If there are two features, coequal in attention-compelling power, the total effect of the advertisement is weakened. Consequently, layout entails a study of the psychology of attention, as applied to artistic forms.

In dividing space, it is customary to observe a main division of 60–40, the smaller part of which may be divided again, while the larger part is kept for the dominating attention-attracting feature, whatever it may be. This smaller space is also divided on a 60–40 basis. The order of emphasis should follow the desired order in which the reader's attention should progress from point to point of the advertisement.

Martin Ullman and L. Leonard Heuslein, writing in *Mailbag,* recommend dividing the advertisement into various units with shapes and masses unlike each other. That is, if the focusing mass is square, the other elements should be oblong, round, or oval. Figure 185 illustrates divisions of space recommended by them.

Experiments in psychology have indicated that the so-called *golden section,* or rectangle with proportions approximately 5 to 8, is the most pleasing to the eye. It will be seen that the average magazine or newspaper space, by the page or quarter page, is approximately in the dimensions of this *golden section.* When single-column space is used, it is usually broken up into a series of sections. Booklets, street-car cards, outdoor bulletins, and electric signs are usually rectangular in shape, showing how widely recognized among advertising men this dimensional basis is.

When dividing up a given space, it is customary to observe a certain harmony. Thus, if curves are used in one part of the advertisement, they should be used in the others; and the same is true of straight lines.

The Novelty Layout

Since the principal purpose of the layout is to get attention, it is but natural to suppose that there should be a constant striving towards originality and novelty. The conventional scheme of layout is to have a picture at the top, then a headline, followed by copy, and the signature and the coupon, if one is used, at the bottom. Obviously, if all advertisers employed this same type of layout, there would be a distinct loss in attention value.

Figure 186 illustrates how the unconventional layout form, with unique arrangement of typography and white space, can

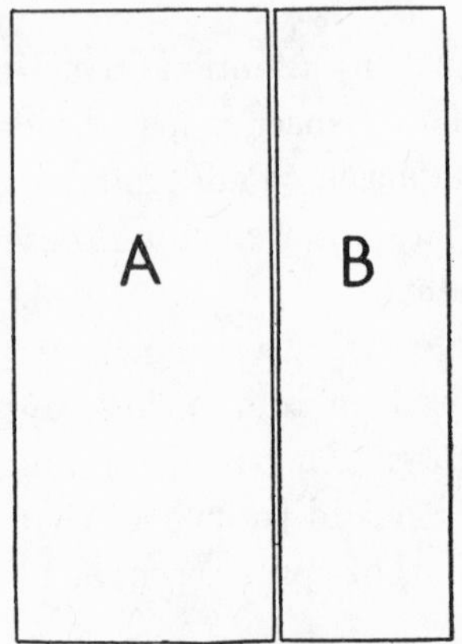

A—can be copy.
B—can be illustration.

Here the horizontal line is removed and the perpendicular one moved to one side for a good effect.

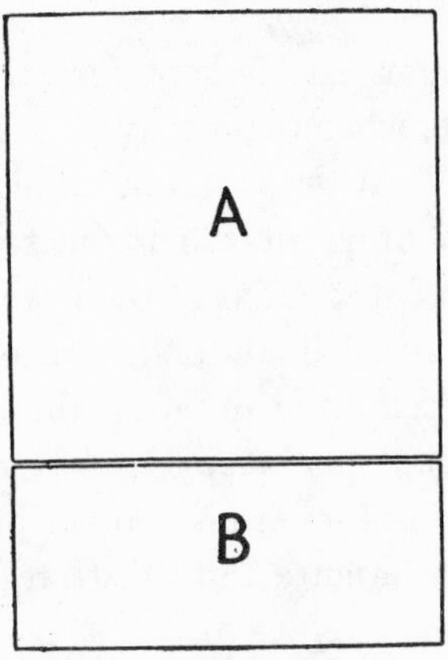

A—can be illustration.
B—can be copy.

Here the perpendicular line is removed and the horizontal lowered for another good effect.

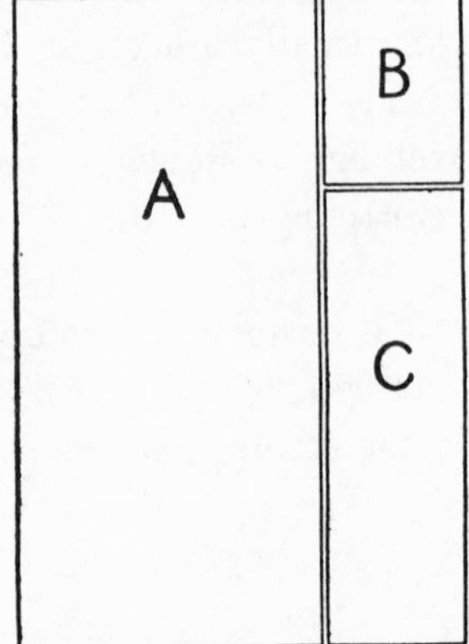

A—can be reason-why copy.
B—can be illustration.
C—can be detail copy.

This arrangement is good because one of the units is a dominant mass which attracts and focuses the eye. The other units appear related and belonging to the larger one.

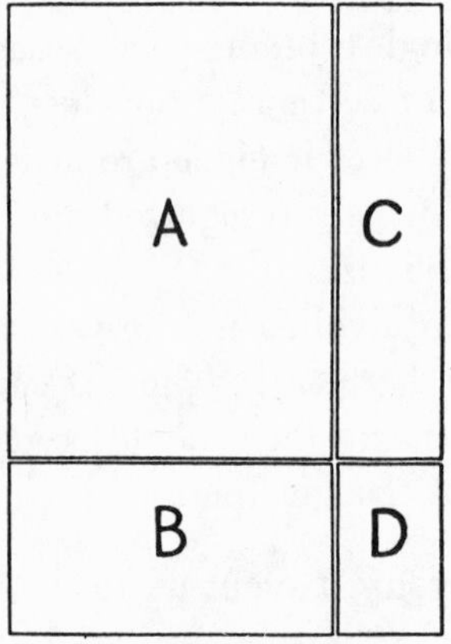

A—can be illustration.
B—can be copy.
C—can be copy.
D—can be copy or trademark, or illustration.

Here the perpendicular line is moved to one side and the horizontal one is lowered with the result of one dominant mass and three smaller units of different sizes but all related.

FIG. 185. DIVISION OF THE LAYOUT
(*Mailbag*)

produce an attention-compelling effect, at the same time tying in with the product.

The normal method of making a novelty layout is to change the distribution of the physical units, by rearranging them in some new fashion. An exceedingly simple novelty layout is the use of type alone, especially when combined with the proper amounts of white space to give attention qualities. Copy, of

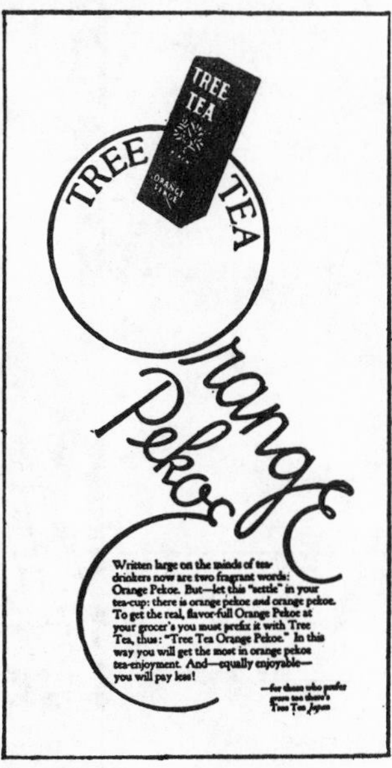

FIG. 186. NOVELTY LAYOUTS

These two samples for one product show a pleasing and unique layout and use of type. They are unusual and they attract attention.

course, may be placed ahead of the illustration, or by the side of it; illustrations may be put in peculiar shapes, or other changes made to transform the attention secured into interest and action.

The Single-Column Layout

Research does not invariably mean that something unprecedented must be discovered. It implies that full utilization should be made of what others have found. Research should

The line may linger, the line may falter, but the admiration of the gifts from Ovington's will linger long and falter never!
There goes the Bride!
THE smarter the wedding, the more likely you are to discover a multitude of Ovington gifts in the goods of the bride.
For when one person of good taste seeks gifts for another, then does the name of Ovington's fly quickly to the mind and to the lips.
And yet, the lips will testify and the mind will perceive that the prices are always very low.
OVINGTON'S
Fifth Avenue at 39th Street
What a lot of Receiving the Bride does!
AS the guests snake up to the receiving line, they talk of every subject in the world from how Aunt Nellie is, to the exquisite collection of the bridal gifts, and how many of them came from Ovington's.
OVINGTON'S
Fifth Avenue at 39th Street

FIG. 187. EXAMPLES OF SINGLE-COLUMN LAYOUT

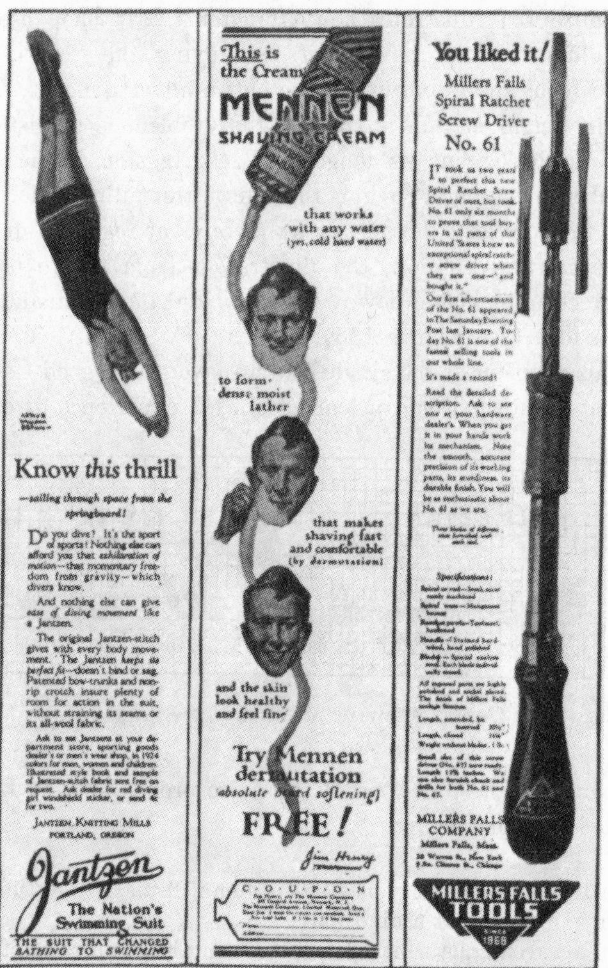

Fig. 188. Three More Examples of Single-Column Copy
Three different styles, but each effectively making use of a difficult form of layout.

always begin in the full knowledge of what others have accomplished along similar lines. This applies to the matter of single-column layouts which have often presented great difficulties to advertisers. Here the layout takes on a position of the utmost importance, because the illustration and typography must be arranged to suit the space at the advertiser's disposal.

Figure 187 illustrates how Ovington's Gift Shop uses the full column in the newspaper, employing the "continuity" idea to focus the attention on the entire advertisement. However the single column is treated, the problem is to distribute attention throughout its length. W. Livingston Larned cites a number of methods, such as the intermittent illustration idea, where the column is broken up by pictures at regular intervals, the serial story column, the illustration from top to bottom, the directing of vision downward plan, and the dominant illustration idea (see Figure 188).

This problem of the single-column layout is a good example of what an advertiser can learn from the experience of others.

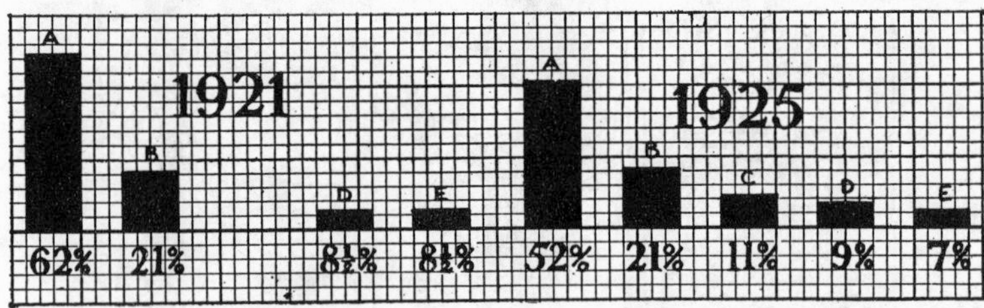

FIG. 189. CHART SHOWING CHANGES IN STYLES OF LAYOUT

For example, the following 10 rules are propounded by Larned for this type of layout:

In the large majority of single-column displays, the decorative border is nothing but a hindrance.

An art technique which permits of sparkling contrasts of black and white.

Simple composition (one figure where possible).

Hand-lettered headlines done in the modern, somewhat "jazzy" spirit. (These hand-lettered phrases are of great help, in themselves in bringing about distinctive display.)

Marginal white space, somewhere, in every layout.

Indented type set-ups.

Never more than two styles of type face to an advertisement—one if possible.

Shrewd apportionment of tone values in the composition of the space, meaning additional contrast.

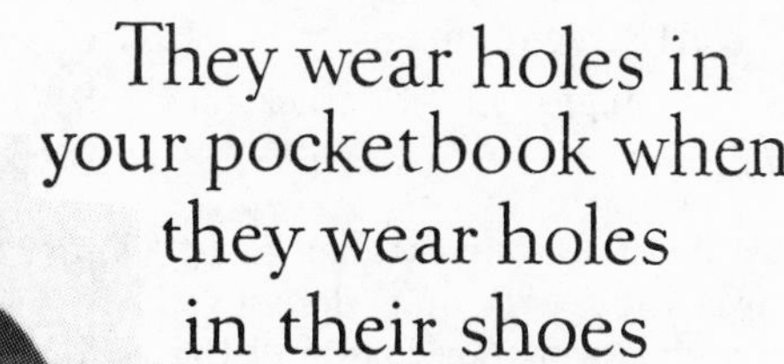

They wear holes in
your pocketbook when
they wear holes
in their shoes
A word to the parents of growing boys and girls, from the makers of "Better shoes for less money"
KEEPING healthy, active youngsters in shoes is no laughing matter. You know how all too frequently the subject of shoes comes up. "Isn't there some way of reducing this item of household expense?" you ask.
We have the answer for you: Endicott-Johnson shoes.
Endicott-Johnson shoes for boys and girls really are "Better shoes for less money." The reasons are not just the usual reasons of manufacture. They are fundamental—*institutional*. They lie deep in the policies and principles under which Endicott-Johnson operate.
Every worker a partner
Endicott-Johnson shoes are made by an industrial democracy unique in business history. "We" make them. And when we say "We," we mean 17,000 trained E-J Workers who have pooled their intelligence and their labor, their heads, their hearts and their hands, in a common enterprise. They are *partners* in this company. They share in the rewards and responsibilities of the business.
We make better shoes because we are all directly interested in every pair we turn out. We have high efficiency. We eliminate unnecessary costs between raw hide and finished shoe. We tan our own leather—by our own special processes, to assure maximum wear. We buy our materials direct, in large quantities and, consequently, at lowest prices. We use the best lasts, methods and machinery known to the industry.
The plan works! We do make better shoes. And our steady production and tremendous output enable us to sell them at very reasonable prices.
Test these shoes as we have tested them
Endicott-Johnson shoes for boys and girls are based on actual wearing test. We've put shoes of all kinds on hundreds of active boys and girls. Watched them day by day. Learned where shoes wear out first, and why. Strengthened them wherever more strength was needed.
Yet don't overlook the fine finish of these shoes. The trim, up-to-date patterns. The many styles from which to choose—for school, dress or play. *The extremely low prices*—only $2.50 to $3.50 (smaller size $1.50 to $2), according to size and grade. None more than $5. Fifty thousand stores sell Endicott-Johnson shoes. Look for the E-J trade-mark on the sole.
Equip each of your children with a pair and *mark the day* they start wearing them. See if through the service and prices of Endicott-Johnson shoes you haven't at last found the way to cut down your children's shoe bills.
If you don't happen to know where there's a nearby store selling Endicott-Johnson shoes, write us. We'll direct you to one. Endicott-Johnson, Endicott, N. Y.; New York City, N. Y., or St. Louis, Mo. —Largest manufacturers of boys' and girls' shoes in the world.

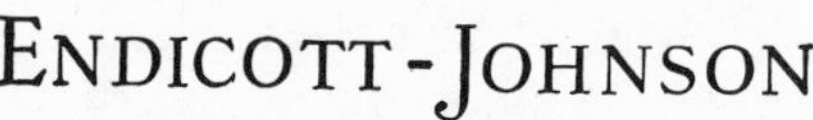

FIG. 190. EXAMPLE OF THE SEMI-EDITORIAL STYLE OF LAYOUT

Illustrations so placed that they never reach out to both sides of a display.

Action in both picture and drawn headings.

This gives an idea of layout technique as it has progressed to date. Further experience and research will corroborate or correct these findings.

Figure 189 shows how styles of layout changed between

1921 and 1925, according to a study of *Saturday Evening Post* advertisements made by S. H. Giellerup. The bar chart shows the changes in classifications, the latter being described as follows:

A—The *Conventional* style. Fairly short text set *en bloc,* this text being part of a design. The illustration is then set at the top or sweeps down around the right or left flank.

B—The *Poster* style. No description necessary.

C—The *Semi-Editorial* style. Fairly long text, set so as to be extremely readable, and not as part of a design. An obvious effort is made to make the page elegant and simple.

D—The *Full Editorial* style. Gives the text the place of honor. Contains subheads. Has news appearance. Illustrations are let into the text rather than the text being poured into the space left after the illustrations have been placed.

E—The *Eccentric* style. In these an effort is made. Sometimes this effort extends to the elements themselves, the pictures, the headlines, the type, but usually it stops with the *arrangement* of the elements. Often this unusual arrangement hinders reading.

Only one important change is evident in layout styles. The Semi-Editorial Layout, described and pictured in Figure 190, did not exist in 1921. To-day it claims one advertisement in nine. From the ranks of the Conventional Layout have come the converts. Surprisingly, the improvement in art has not brought with it an increase in Poster Layouts, the percentage of these having remained the same.

CHAPTER XXIII

RESEARCH AS APPLIED TO ILLUSTRATION

In the matter of illustration, artistic workmanship and the effect which can be obtained only through individual genius and talent relegate research to a secondary position. There are, nevertheless, certain phases of illustration which lend themselves to psychological experimentation. For example, the question of relevancy of illustration to text is one that may be tested. There is also the problem of whether the illustration should represent a person or a thing, should represent still life or motion, and similar considerations. While the intangible qualities of artistic treatment persist in making some advertisements exceptions to the rule, it has been found that research can be made to play an important part, although the work in this line is barely begun.

Illustration in advertising has had a rapid increase during the last fifty years. It has been recognized that the illustration serves certain purposes which nothing else will perform so efficiently. It visualizes the product, aids in the comprehension of the advertising story, produces atmosphere, lends human interest, increases attention value, familiarizes the public with the appearance of the product and its carton, supplies continuity, and helps to increase memory value.

Figure 191 shows the trend in the purpose for which illustrations are used. Those with primarily illustrative purposes have declined, while those combining attention-getting qualities with illustrative merit have risen steadily. More noticeable still is the fact that illustration designed mainly to attract attention has shown a sharp increase.

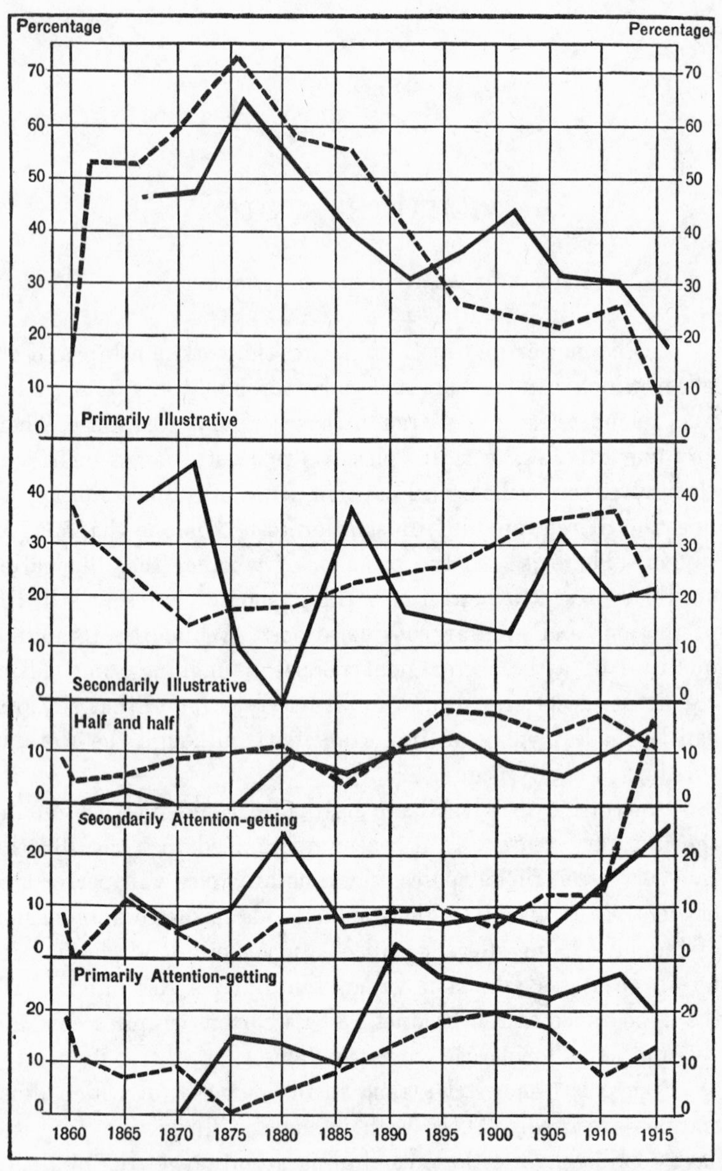

FIG. 191. THE TREND IN THE PURPOSE FOR WHICH ILLUSTRATIONS ARE USED
(Starch, *Principles of Advertising.*)

Bibliographical Research

When it is a question of artistic treatment, there is another phase of research which should not be neglected, namely, that which has to do with an exhaustive study of the product and the associations which surround it. The artist and the copywriter are both seeking constantly for ideas which will enable them to make their work more distinctive, and with greater attention and interest value.

The question of illustration is particularly important in making catalogues, booklets, or house organs. These must compete with the literature of other companies, and the recipient of them, more often than not, does not have time to look at them all. Hence, he looks only at those which particularly interest him or which compel his attention. Illustrated literature will, in almost every case, receive first attention.

Historical illustrations have often been used with telling effect, particularly if they are relevant to the product. Figure 192 shows one of a series of advertisements of Cheney Brothers, silk manufacturers, which resulted only after months of research work in books and in museums of fine art. In fact, the company adopted a policy of tracing all famous period designs back to their sources, in this way becoming an authority on the subject. The result was that the artists and interior decorators were deeply interested in the results of the research before the general public was approached.

With all due respect to artistic talent, it sometimes seems that more attention might be paid to what has already been done than to artistic inspiration alone. Art, unaccompanied by research, may be exceedingly beautiful, but, when unaided, it often fails to accomplish the result desired by the advertiser.

Attention Value of Illustrations

As a pure attention factor, the importance of the illustration is great. Every investigation made on the subject of the attention value of pictures has brought out the superiority of the advertisement with the illustration. The rapid increase in the use of pictures merely goes to show that advertisers have come to recognize this fact.

Edward K. Strong, Jr., found that of four newspaper advertisements selling watches, the ones with cuts were 124 per cent more effective measured in terms of inquiries, and 33 per cent superior, measured in terms of actual sales, than those without cuts.[1] Investigations of a similar nature carried on in direct mail have proved that the letter with a cut is considerably more effective than the one without a cut.

Richard B. Franken (*The Attention Value of Newspaper Advertisements*) made the following conclusions from his investigations:

1. Pictures in advertisements help to get attention.
2. Pictures of persons or animals are superior for purposes of attention to pictures of objects.
3. Picture plus headline is the most effective attention-getting combination, especially if the picture should contain figures of human beings or animals.

Relevancy

There has been much discussion as to the use of relevant or irrelevant illustrations in advertising. A relevant illustration, according to the accepted definition, is one that would allow the average reader to guess the nature of the product advertised from the illustration alone, without any copy. There are, of course, a great many grades of relevancy, ranging from that which reproduces the product exactly to that which has nothing whatsoever to do with it.

The advantage of using an irrelevant illustration is that it sometimes possesses more attention power than can be secured by an illustration of the product. Supporters of the theory that illustrations should be relevant claim that although readers may remember the irrelevant illustration they do not connect it with the product.

H. K. Nixon carried out an experiment on 30 subjects

[1] Association of National Advertisers, Bulletin No. 8, November, 1913.

"THREE GOLDEN BALLS"
THE origin of the ball-motif in decorative art and also in the accepted sign of pawnbrokers has been the subject of many speculative theories. It seems clear enough, however, to the student of Heraldry. He traces it to the pill of the apothecary who was the original "Medici", and so to the coat-of-arms of the great Medici family, those sublimated Florentine money-lenders whose agents were set in sixteen European capitals. Incidentally an interesting side-light is here discovered.
These agents combined the occupations of goldsmith, pawnbroker, banker; and to guide unlettered clients to their shops what could be more characteristic than to adopt a part of the Medici coat-of-arms? Or more natural that, in later days, the ancient pawnbrokers should display the sign of the Blue Ball, the Gold Ball, the "Three Blue Bowles", or even the "Three Golden Balls" familiar to our own streets?
To return to the field of decoration: the ball motif is not difficult to understand. Besides being the greatest of money-lenders—often taking from bankrupt nobles, fabrics, paintings and works of art as collateral for their loans—the Medici were unrivalled patrons of art and learning. Illustrious painters and sculptors, distinguished craftsmen throve in the generous noon-tide of their prosperity. Is it unnatural that the coat-of-arms of such great givers should be in part incorporated into beautied form?
Even Louis XI of France, himself, gave recognition of the potency of the Medici activities by conferring upon Piero, one of the Medici, permission to stamp the very lilies of France on one of the balls of the Medici coat-of-arms. So came the humble pills of the apothecary to become apotheosized in kingly edicts and on the walls of art; and so too, in Cheney Silks reflecting the spirit of the Florentine Renaissance.
CHENEY BROTHERS
CHENEY SILKS

Fig. 192. Results of Historical Research

An example of the Cheney Brothers' upholstery and drapery silk campaign, showing the elaboration of the borders accurately drawn in the style of the period referred to in the copy.

to see whether relevant or irrelevant illustrations had greater attention power and memory value, with the following results:

	Ratio Relevant to Irrelevant		
For primary attention	.95	to	1.00
For first ten seconds	.83	to	1.00
For thirty seconds	.80	to	1.00
For memory value	.66	to	1.00

Nixon explains the greater attention value of the irrelevant illustration by the theory that the reader must look further into the advertisement to see what it is all about. He explains, however, that the interest aroused by the irrelevant illustration is in something other than the product. Since the recall experiment was based on any feature of the advertisement, it was natural that the illustration on which most time had been spent should be remembered.

H. R. Laslett [2] also made a test of relevancy in terms of perception, time, and memory. Two copies of the *Saturday Evening Post* were built up with relevant and irrelevant illustrations taken from earlier issues. These were given to subjects with instructions to look through them without reading stories. At the end of five or seven minutes, they were removed. Two days later this was repeated. Five days after the second inspection a recall test was given them. For perception time, each advertisement was shown separately, and the time measured which the subject took to determine the firm name or product.

The results follow:

Particulars	Relevant	Irrelevant
Perception Time—Average..................	1.00	2.40
Recall—Magazine A. Class A................	1.00	0.29
Class B................	1.00	0.28
Recall—Magazine B. Class A................	1.00	0.38
Class B................	1.00	0.80

[2] "Value of Relevancy in Advertisement Illustrations," *Journal of Applied Psychology,* II, 1918, pp. 270*ff*.

The figures represent ratios, in each case the value of the relevant illustration is taken as 1.00. Class A covers the cases where the definite trade name and article were given; Class B provides for cases where enough description was given to make identification possible.

In every case in this experiment, the relevant illustration proves superior. In perception time it has great advantage. In recall value, the irrelevant illustrations are far inferior.

Illustration and Memory Value

Regardless of the merits of the copy, the typography, or the layout, in the final analysis, it is the illustration which remains longest in the memory. Repetition, of course, has a great deal to do with memory. For example, Horatio B. Moore[3] quotes a memory experiment in a university classroom. Sixty cards, containing widely advertised articles, were shown to the class several times, always in the same sequence. Each student was asked to write down: (1) the kind of product advertised; (2) manufacturer's name, trade-mark, or name of brand; (3) special features remembered.

The five cards best remembered were Onyx Hosiery, Arrow Collars, Hart, Schaffner and Marx Clothing, Haynes Automobiles, and Spearmint Chewing Gum. The women were found to remember details of illustrations better than the men. The cards at the end of the series had some advantage, showing the value of repetition.

A second experiment was carried on with 50 men and 50 women students. Certain cards and posters were exposed to them and they were asked to write down their impressions immediately after looking at them. Cards with large illustrations and small amount of copy were found to be remembered best. A 75 per cent average was obtained for illustrations of the product or phases of its use or manufacture.

Relevancy is an important feature in memory value, because the illustration may be remembered without the connec-

3 "Illustration in Advertising," University of Missouri Bulletin, Vol. XXV, No. 27.

FIG. 193. EXAMPLE OF IRRELEVANT ILLUSTRATION

Advertising is intended to help sell. If the advertisement does not link itself with the product to be sold, it represents a waste of money.

tion with the product or company. Figure 193 shows an illustration of an advertisement for an automobile ignition system. Several dealers in automobile supplies were asked by Mr. Moore to look at this advertisement and tell him what they thought it stood for. The most frequent answer was "perfume," while not one guessed correctly.

Effect of Pictures of People

The use of people as subjects of illustrations, commonly supposed to lend *human interest,* has not been investigated to any great extent to determine the increased attention value. For his reason, an experiment to determine the attention value of advertisements containing people, carried out by H. K. Nixon, is especially interesting.

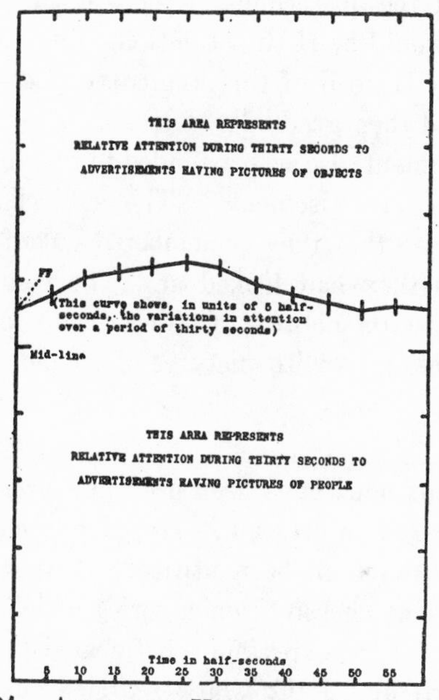

FIG. 194. ATTENTION VALUE OF ADVERTISEMENTS
Comparative effect of pictures of objects and pictures of people. (*Class.*)

Two groups of advertisements were studied, each containing 40 examples. The first group contained pictures of human beings; the second group, comparable in use of color, size of headline, and border, differed in that only illustrations of objects were shown. In other words, the advertisements were alike, in so far as possible, with the exception of the subject matter of the illustration.

Dr. Nixon's usual method of pairing advertisements was

followed, presented side by side as they would be seen in a magazine. The subjects, 30 men and women, were observed carefully as to eye movements. They had no idea that they were being tested for this purpose, merely thinking they were looking through the dummy magazine.

Figure 194 shows the results in graphic form. There is a marked tendency to give the greatest amount of attention to the advertisements having pictures of persons. In no case does the curve, over the 30 seconds of the test, descend to the mid-line where it would be if the attention value of the two groups was the same. Instead of this, the curve rises during the first 10 seconds, and then gradually decreases.

This experiment also was extended to test the memory value of the various advertisements. The subjects were asked to write down those that they remembered out of the total of 80 advertisements they had looked at. The result was that the advertisements with pictures of objects were recalled only half as frequently as those with pictures of people.

Facial Expression

Facial expressions have been used to a great extent to help convey the desired impression. Happiness, enjoyment, irritation, suspicion, have all been utilized. Figure 195 illustrates one advertisement chosen from a series which aroused nation-wide comment for the expressions delineated.

H. E. Burtt and J. C. Clark[4] carried out a test to determine whether the optimal degree of satisfaction in the facial expression varied with the particular commodity advertised, and whether apparent satisfaction in the facial expression of a photograph corresponded to actual satisfaction experienced by the model posing for it. The latter question was answered in the affirmative.

The test was carried out by taking pictures of 23 men's faces from advertisements which portrayed varying degrees of satisfaction. All copy was removed so that nothing was left

---

[4] *Journal of Applied Psychology*, VII, 1923, pp. 114*ff*.

EXCEPTIONAL RIDING COMFORT

Travel all day, and the next, and the next. Then you will begin to understand what Dodge Brothers, Inc. have accomplished with their long underslung spring equipment, balloon tires and low-swung body lines.

In touring, the master test of riding ease, Dodge Brothers Motor Car now acquits itself with a distinction you have learned to associate only with vehicles of the largest and most expensive type.

DODGE BROTHERS, INC. DETROIT
DODGE BROTHERS (CANADA) LIMITED
TORONTO, ONTARIO

FIG. 195. EFFECT OF FACIAL EXPRESSION

to suggest the nature of the product. Each subject tested was asked to indicate for which of 10 classes of products a particular picture would be most effective. The graphic results of this test are shown in Poffenberger, *Psychology in Advertising* (p. 288).

It was found that commodities differed to a considerable

. . . if every woman
could see—
This is the famous Eureka "High-Vacuum" test. See it performed on an apparently clean rug.

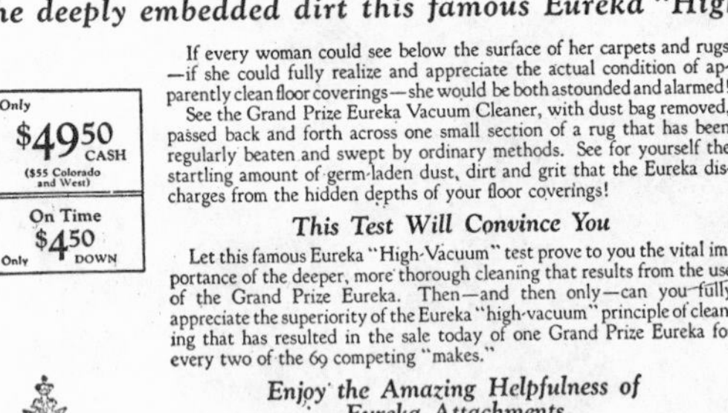

the deeply embedded dirt this famous Eureka "High-Vacuum" test removes!
Only $49.50 CASH ($55 Colorado and West)
On Time Only $4.50 DOWN
If every woman could see below the surface of her carpets and rugs —if she could fully realize and appreciate the actual condition of apparently clean floor coverings—she would be both astounded and alarmed!
See the Grand Prize Eureka Vacuum Cleaner, with dust bag removed, passed back and forth across one small section of a rug that has been regularly beaten and swept by ordinary methods. See for yourself the startling amount of germ-laden dust, dirt and grit that the Eureka discharges from the hidden depths of your floor coverings!
This Test Will Convince You
Let this famous Eureka "High-Vacuum" test prove to you the vital importance of the deeper, more thorough cleaning that results from the use of the Grand Prize Eureka. Then—and then only—can you fully appreciate the superiority of the Eureka "high-vacuum" principle of cleaning that has resulted in the sale today of one Grand Prize Eureka for every two of the 69 competing "makes."
Enjoy the Amazing Helpfulness of Eureka Attachments
And remember that the same astonishing effectiveness can be obtained in the use of Eureka "High-Vacuum" Attachments on mattresses, upholstered furniture, hangings, stair runners, etc.
Do not fail to have our dealer near you show you this convincing "high-vacuum" test. Then witness a complete demonstration of the Grand Prize Eureka and its attachments. Decide now to waste no further time and effort with old-fashioned or less efficient cleaning methods and devices. Get a Eureka today.

EUREKA
FREE $8.50 Set
of Eureka "High-Vacuum" Attachments with every Grand Prize Eureka purchased
[This offer may be withdrawn at any time.] Get your Eureka NOW and receive these wonderful attachments absolutely free.

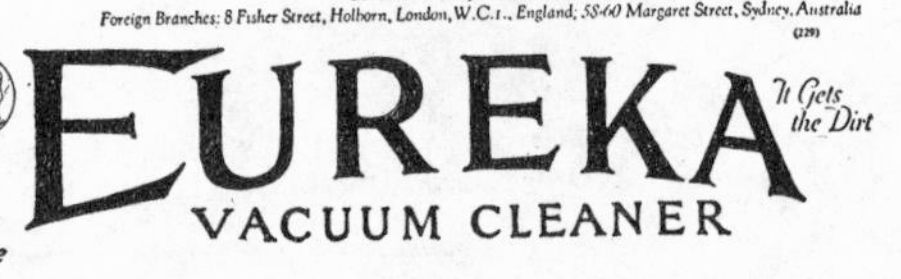

EUREKA VACUUM CLEANER COMPANY, DETROIT, U. S. A.
Makers of Electric Vacuum Cleaners since 1909
Canadian Factory, Kitchener, Ontario
Foreign Branches: 8 Fisher Street, Holborn, London, W.C.1., England; 58-60 Margaret Street, Sydney, Australia
EUREKA
It Gets the Dirt
VACUUM CLEANER
The Grand Prize

FIG. 196. A DEVICE FOR DIRECTING ATTENTION

extent in the degree of satisfaction thought to be most fitted to them. Maximum degree of satisfaction was thought proper for toilet articles and smoking supplies. A serious expression was considered most proper for clothing.

Such an experiment would be of value only when degree of satisfaction in facial expression was a factor in making the sale.

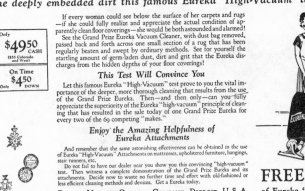

Opportunities for Research in Illustration

From the experiments which have been reported in this chapter, it is evident that the value of illustration to increase attention and interest is very great. There remains, however, a great deal to be done in the way of experimentation.

FIG. 197. THE EFFECT OF RETOUCHING

On the left is a balloon tire as it normally appears. On the right is the same tire enlarged and retouched for advertising purposes. This practice is typical of all tire advertising, and appears to be a necessary expedient. *(Printers' Ink Monthly.)*

There is the question of action and the effect produced upon the reader. Figure 196 shows how cleverly attention can be secured and directed to the theme of the advertisement by use of a pointed finger, an old device yet one which is still applicable.

Another point for research is the question of how much

exaggeration is permissible in portraying action in an illustration. If an automobile is pictured in motion, is it wise to show a line of white exhaust? Such a device undoubtedly creates the illusion of motion, but it would also tend to show something wrong with the way the engine was running.

Similarly, what is the effect psychologically on readers of retouching the illustration? Figure 197 compares a balloon tire as it normally appears and as it looks when retouched for advertising purposes. The result is greatly to enhance the appearance of the tire, but what is the effect upon the person who sees this super-tire and buys one on the strength of the illustration? Or does he notice the difference?

There is also the question of the setting for the illustration. Is it better to portray the product in its natural environment, or is it better to present it in an environment which is best suited to it, although perhaps not the one in which it is usually to be found?

CHAPTER XXIV

RESEARCH AS APPLIED TO COLOR

Color is a question of constantly increasing importance. A study made of the number of colored advertisements in the *American Magazine, Collier's, Ladies' Home Journal,* and *Country Life* shows that in 1905 these four magazines had only 1.1 per cent of their full pages in color, while in 1920 they had 20.2 per cent color pages. In 1922, 28 per cent of the full-page advertisements in the *Saturday Evening Post* were colored; by 1924 of the total lineage in this magazine, 31.75 per cent was in color.

In the women's magazines, color is even more often used. In 1924 the *Ladies' Home Journal* had 44.64 per cent of its total lineage in color. *Good Housekeeping,* which had the smallest color percentage of the group, amounted to 22 per cent. It is plainly evident, therefore, that color deserves a great deal of attention.

The use of color in advertising has two psychological aspects. In the first place, it is used as a device for attracting attention. It has been a general belief that a color page will attract the reader's eye more quickly than plain black and white.

In the second place, color has certain affective qualities. It has been found by experiment and test that certain qualities are expressed by certain colors or combination of colors, and the same often seems to be true of products. The psychological problem is to determine which color or combination of colors will produce the desired effect.

Color for Color's Sake

Among the principal uses of color in advertising are those which have to do with attention value. In such cases color is treated wholly apart from the effect produced upon the feelings. A series of experimental tests made by M. Luckiesh, and reported in *Advertising and Selling,* shed considerable light upon this matter.

Six pure colors (red, orange, yellow, green, blue, and violet), with their six medium shades and medium tints were chosen, making 18 colors in all. Taking them in pairs, there was a total of 153 combinations to be tested. The order of presenting these pairs was by chance so as to avoid any association of memory factors. The subjects were 115 male and 121 female college students in their first and second years. Over 35,000 individual records of preferred color of a pair were recorded, giving the following results:

COMPARATIVE ATTRACTION OF PURE COLORS, TINTS, AND SHADES

	115 Males	121 Females	Both
	Total Favorable Choices		
Pure colors	7309	6836	14,235
Tints	4906	5977	10,883
Shades	5064	5378	10,442
	Average Favorable Choices		
Pure colors	64.2	56.5	60.4
Tints	42.7	49.3	46.0
Shades	44.0	44.5	44.3

It is pointed out that the decided preference for pure colors is one that is found in primitive races and in children.

The following table shows the percentage of preference attributed to the respective colors by the average group, that is, the results of the total preferences for each of the 18 colors have been reduced to percentages of the average:

PERCENTAGE OF AVERAGE COLOR PREFERENCE

Color	Mean of 115 Males	Mean of 121 Females	Mean of 236 Subjects
Red—Pure	148	141	145
Tint	104	80	92
Shade	97	99	98
Orange—Pure	112	103	108
Tint	56	89	73
Shade	71	65	68
Yellow—Pure	93	91	92
Tint	68	97	83
Shade	55	44	50
Green—Pure	121	105	113
Tint	70	94	82
Shade	84	101	93
Blue—Pure	164	120	142
Tint	117	112	114
Shade	109	111	110
Violet—Pure	128	116	122
Tint	94	119	107
Shade	108	113	111

With the exception of one case, the pure color is preferred. The female subjects preferred pure red above all other colors, while the male subjects voted blue as first. The following table shows order of preference for pure colors, tints, and shades:

ORDER OF PREFERENCES FOR HUES, TINTS, AND SHADES

	Male			Female			Both		
	Pure	Tint	Shade	Pure	Tint	Shade	Pure	Tint	Shade
Red	2	2	3	1	6	4	1	3	3
Orange	5	6	5	5	5	5	5	6	5
Yellow	6	5	6	6	3	6	6	4	6
Green	4	4	4	4	4	3	4	5	4
Blue	1	1	2	2	2	2	2	1	2
Violet	3	3	1	3	1	1	3	2	1

From these data the author of the experiments draws certain conclusions, mainly that the pure or saturated colors are more powerful than tints or shades when colors are chosen on the basis of color alone and without reference to taste or harmony. Hence, when color is used in advertising to attract attention, or for a package or trade-mark, the pure color would normally have the advantage.

Attention Value of Color

Color is undoubtedly a valuable device for attracting attention. Since the cost of color advertising is so much more than plain black and white, it is exceedingly important that the relative efficiency in results should be measured. It is evident, of course, that the attention value of color is due to a considerable extent to contrast with surroundings, and if more than a certain percentage of the advertisements are in color, the attention value is greatly reduced.

Hotchkiss and Franken tested the relative attention value in dollars of colored and black and white space of the *Saturday Evening Post,* on the basis of the rate card of 1919. The results were as follows:

Page	Relative Cost, Per Cent	Relative Attention Value, Per Cent
One black and white (taken as base).....	100	100
One colored..........................	140	113
Two black and white..................	200	147
One colored, one black and white........	240	128
Two colored..........................	280	112

At the time this experiment was made, the colored page received only 13 per cent more attention than the black and white page, while the cost was 40 per cent higher. In this particular test, in other words, the authors conclude that the "use of colors for attracting attention, cost on the average $1,350 more than it was worth." Color, may, of course, be used for other purposes than attention value, in which case the added cost may prove highly profitable, but for attention value alone, color does not seem to add the effectiveness commonly attributed to it.

The large mail-order houses have been able to estimate accurately the value to them of color pages. For their black and white pages, they use the cheapest kind of catalogue reproduction, costing on a four million copy run, about $3,000 a page, including everything. When a four-color page is used, it will cost in the neighborhood of $17,000. This increased cost must be made profitable by a great increase in orders from the color page, and the mail-order houses, through long test and experiment, have worked out about what ratio of color to black and white should be used, and second, what items will sell from a color page and what will not. Clothing, shoes, and rugs bring excellent results in color. On the other hand, farm machinery and automobile accessories do almost as well in black and white.

A certain seed company found that the four-color process pages used for specialties brought in $9 in business where the black and white pages brought in one.

Experiments have brought out some interesting results in the use of color for direct-mail work. Figure 198 shows the results of a color test in a sales letter made by James H. Rothschild, of Barmon Brothers Company, Inc. Twelve thousand letters were sent out, 1,000 each of 12 letters. The same copy was used, the differences being in color of stock and use of cuts. The letters were multigraphed and filled in with typewriter to match. The plain white letter brought in 9 per cent returns; the letter on pink stock brought in 26 per cent returns. It is interesting to note that using a blue instead of a white return envelope increased the returns considerably. In every case the use of cuts of the product brought a substantial increase in returns.

The results of a study by H. K. Nixon seem, again, to indicate that the attention value of color is somewhat less than has ordinarily been supposed. The experiment was carried out by presenting a colored and noncolored advertisement to a subject at the same time and seeing which one was looked at

Fig. 198.—An Investigation of Color in Direct-Mail Advertising

Table I.—Results of Color Test

Letter Number	Quantity	Color	Cuts	Color Return Envelopes	Pull, Per Cent
1	1000	White	No	White	9
2	1000	White	No	Blue	12
3	1000	White	Yes	White	18
4	1000	White	Yes	Blue	22
5	1000	Corn	No	White	14
6	1000	Corn	Yes	Blue	26
7	1000	Green	No	White	16
8	1000	Green	Yes	Blue	28
9	1000	Gold	No	White	21
10	1000	Gold	Yes	Blue	34
11	1000	Pink	No	White	26
12	1000	Pink	Yes	Blue	48

Table II.—Duration of Pull

Number	1st Week	2d Week	3d Week	4th Week	5th Week	Total	Total, Per Cent
1	18	32	21	11	8	90	9
2	20	37	36	15	12	120	12
3	66	61	34	9	8	178	18
4	54	78	58	21	6	217	22
5	34	53	39	11	2	139	14
6	61	141	43	12	3	260	26
7	86	67	..	6	..	159	16
8	90	164	22	5	2	283	28
9	72	131	5	3	..	211	21
10	65	258	13	2	1	339	34
11	58	193	7	..	2	260	26
12	63	407	8	1	1	480	48

first, and for how long it held the attention. About 50 pairs of advertisements were used, taking care to vary the position, type of layout, and other factors. Enough subjects were used to make results representative.

The experiment, as illustrated graphically in Figure 199, shows two things:

1. Color has but a slight advantage in total attention. The upper half of the graph represents black and white; the lower half color.

2. The colored advertisements begin with higher attention value, but after about 10 seconds this advantage is lost, and the attention shifts to the black and white. At the end of

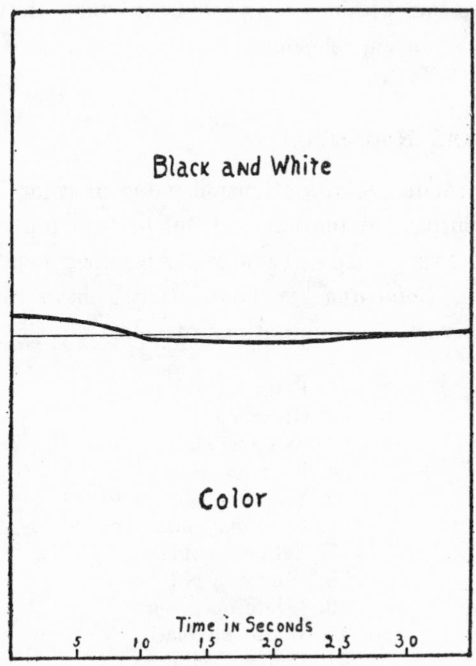

FIG. 199. EFFECT OF COLOR

A comparison of the attention value of black and white as against color. (*Class.*)

30 seconds, attention is almost equally divided between black and white and color.

The author of this experiment points out that its surprising feature is the failure of color to dominate attention at the start. The superiority of color was only about 8 per cent at the beginning and rapidly declined. However, as the percentage of color in the experiment was higher than would be the case even in a special holiday number, the attention value of a colored advertisement in an ordinary magazine issue would probably be greater.

Even more important, in his opinion, is the failure of color to attract interest. Color serves merely to attract attention, and the layout, illustration, or copy must serve to obtain the interest. Color, however, has certain valuable supplementary uses, such as to reproduce the product in more lifelike fashion, or to focus attention on some particular feature of the advertisement.

Legibility and Noticeability

Closely related to the attention value of color is the question of legibility. Attention will not be held unless the headline and copy are easily readable. An experiment quoted by M. Luckiesh (*Color and Its Applications*) shows the following legibility of various combinations of colors:

1. Black on yellow
2. Green on white
3. Red on white
4. Blue on white
5. White on blue
6. Black on white
7. Yellow on black
8. White on red
9. White on green
10. White on black
11. Red on yellow
12. Green on red
13. Red on green

The first color represents printed matter; the second background.

Luckiesh also reports an experiment made by Gale, whereby the attention values of a number of colors were studied by placing similar patches of these colors on a white background. The colors were exposed momentarily and the observer asked to record those he saw. Colors were rearranged between observations to remove error through memory. The following table shows the ratio of the number of times a color was noticed to the total number of times all colors were noticed:

PERCENTAGE OF NOTICEABILITY

Color	Men	Women	Both
Red	20	32	26
Black	34	12	23
Green	19	19	19
Orange	19	11	15
Blue	5	11	8
Purple	2	8	5
Yellow	1	7	4
	100	100	100

This experiment shows a greater difference between men and women than has been noted by other experimenters in this field.

In a tabulation of colored advertisements in periodicals, Starch found that 77 per cent used red, 19 per cent brown, 8 per cent blue, 6 per cent orange, 6 per cent green, 6 per cent yellow, and 5 per cent purple.

Color in Advertising

Affective Value

It is well known that certain colors and combinations of colors have varying reactions on the beholders. Although certain individuals, for one reason or another, may react in a particular fashion, test and experiment prove that the average human being has fairly definite and normal reactions to certain colors. It has been suggested by some authorities that the choice of colors preferred for a given purpose is due to custom and experience.

Certain attributes have been more or less arbitrarily given to the various colors and color combinations. M. Luckiesh (*Advertising and Selling*) for example, characterizes the principal colors as follows:

Red. In pure state—tragedy, anger, fire, hatred, passion, war, cruelty, power, destruction, danger, courage, blood. Tints may symbolize health, love, etc.

Yellow. Brighter colors—gaudy, gay, lustrous, enlivening, light, warmth. Gold with its additional qualities of brilliancy and metallic luster—glory, power, wealth, richness. Modifications of pure yellow—distrust, deceit, indecency, morbidness, decay, cowardice, jealousy, inconstancy, sickness, disease.

Green. Life, vigor, memory, immortality, youth, inexperience, faith.

Blue. Quality of coldness and its proximity to black—dignity, soothing, melancholy, subduing, cold, sedateness. Through association with sky or heaven—hope, constancy, fidelity, serenity, generosity, intelligence, truth.

Purple. Royal, stately, pompous, sedate, dignified, rich.

White. Light, purity, chasity, innocence, peace, modesty.

Black. Opposed to white—woe, gloom, darkness, dread, death, mourning, wickedness, crime, terror, horror, severity.

Gray. Humility, penance, piety, maturity, sobriety, fear, death.

Black and White. Humility, melancholy, resolution, solemnity, secrecy, prudence.

He reports an experiment made by N. A. Wells on a group of 63 college students, indicating three general influences of color, as follows:

PSYCHOLOGICAL INFLUENCES OF COLOR

Color	Exciting	Tranquilizing	Subduing
Crimson	41	0	10
Scarlet	56	0	0
Deep orange	59	0	0
Orange-yellow	55	6	0
Yellow	53	6	0
Yellow-green	14	39	5
Green	28	32	0
Blue-green	32	23	6
Blue	11	21	30
Violet-blue	0	17	45
Violet	0	6	54
Purple	3	1	48

The exciting colors are at the red end of the spectrum, the tranquilizing in the middle, and the subduing at the violet end.

Color Values

The memory value of a colored advertisement, according to the generally accepted theory, requires that the colors used arouse no antagonistic response on the part of the readers, and works better when an association has been formed between the article and the color.

An experiment to determine the values of color combinations was carried on at Columbia University by Nancy Tappan Collins. A series of 20 color combinations was prepared, and a group of subjects was asked to select which was most appropriate for the following list of abstract and concrete purposes:

1. Warmth
2. Coolness
3. Repose
4. Cheerfulness
5. Dignity
6. Cleanliness
7. Strength
8. Durability
9. Luxury
10. Economy
11. Building material
12. Jewelry
13. Breakfast food
14. Perfume
15. Coffee
16. Schools
17. Soap
18. Summer camps
19. Candy
20. Summer beverages

An assortment of all primary and usual secondary colors was used for the test, presented to the subject in the form of an abstract design (see Poffenberger, *Psychology in Advertising,* p. 454) reproduced on rectangles $8\frac{1}{2} \times 11\frac{1}{2}$ inches or approximating the size of an advertisement. The design was made up of two colors, in approximately equal areas.

The subjects were told to begin with the first word on the above list and find the color combination which seemed to fit the atmosphere or meaning of the word best, using the same color combination as often as was desired if it seemed to fit. The principal results of the experiment are tabulated in Figure 200.

Fig. 200.—An Investigation of Color Combinations

Choices of Color Combinations Best Adapted to Represent Certain Qualities and Commodities

	Red and yellow (s)	Red and yellow (w)	Red and green (s)	Red and green (w)	Red and blue (s)	Red and blue (w)	Blue and orange (s)	Blue and orange (w)	Blue and yellow (s)	Blue and yellow (w)	Blue and green (s)	Blue and green (w)	Yellow and green (s)	Yellow and green (w)	Yellow and purple (s)	Yellow and purple (w)	Yellow and orange (s)	Yellow and orange (w)	Red and orange (s)	Red and purple (s)
Warmth	7	0	4	2	30	2	1	1	0	1	2	0	0	0	0	0	1	0	31	11
Coolness	3	0	0	1	0	1	0	1	22	26	10	5	17	7	0	2	3	0	1	1
Repose	1	1	0	5	1	0	0	2	3	19	2	3	0	5	1	12	6	30	2	5
Cheerfulness	28	0	10	1	2	0	5	0	20	1	3	1	6	0	2	0	12	1	7	1
Dignity	2	2	3	7	4	3	4	3	6	5	8	1	3	13	13	0	1	14	1	10
Cleanliness	8	1	1	1	0	0	1	0	50	5	1	1	12	2	4	0	8	0	3	0
Strength	24	1	11	1	18	2	3	9	0	1	3	3	2	1	3	0	0	3	7	7
Durability	4	7	7	11	7	7	2	18	3	1	5	6	1	1	2	0	0	9	3	2
Luxury	1	0	7	1	11	5	11	2	5	4	1	1	0	0	20	4	1	2	10	12
Economy	2	11	2	3	0	1	2	3	6	11	2	2	9	9	1	4	9	16	1	1
Building material	10	14	3	7	1	5	1	6	0	4	0	3	2	5	11	1	5	24	4	1
Jewelry	5	1	2	1	4	3	7	2	9	5	4	1	5	2	18	8	8	1	3	7
Breakfast food	12	3	1	1	0	1	3	2	7	7	2	2	19	4	4	3	20	4	3	0
Perfume	2	0	2	2	4	4	7	2	10	9	7	1	5	2	12	13	7	0	5	5
Coffee	5	19	0	3	3	3	3	12	2	1	0	0	1	1	1	1	2	33	9	0
Schools	7	8	4	3	1	5	1	5	7	6	5	1	7	5	1	3	7	11	4	1
Soap	8	0	2	1	1	1	1	0	20	7	7	3	21	7	1	1	13	1	2	0
Summer camps	3	1	7	2	1	0	4	0	9	4	9	11	30	6	2	3	2	3	3	0
Candy	19	6	1	1	2	2	4	6	5	1	1	10	2	0	5	6	17	8	1	2
Summer beverages	6	1	4	2	0	0	1	0	13	11	7	3	25	6	2	3	10	0	5	0

(s) = saturated color. (w) = weak color.

The first question as to warmth brought out almost a tie between the combination of red and orange and red and blue. Another red combination with purples won third place. The atmosphere of cleanliness brings a decisive note of 50 per cent for blue and yellow. Dignity on the other hand brought a wide scattering of votes.

Great similarity between male and female preferences was found throughout, with the exception of jewelry and luxury. Here women chose purple and yellow 30 per cent of the time for luxury and 28 per cent of the time for jewlery. For the men the percentages were respectively 13 per cent and 12 per cent.

It was found that there were certain advertisements the memory value of which was so strong that when subjects were asked to choose independently, they unconsciously chose the colors used in the advertising. There is also the unconscious association of purple with "royal purple" to be reckoned with.

It was then desired to find out whether these preferences were temporary or had a certain permanence. To this end a special group of 20 subjects was tested twice, with an intervening space of time of from two to four weeks. The relationship between the two sets of choices was found to be the following, as expressed in coefficients of correlation, indicating the stability of color preferences:

1. Warmth	*plus*	.95	11. Building material	*plus*	.78
2. Coolness	*plus*	.82	12. Jewelry	*plus*	.82
3. Repose	*plus*	.66	13. Breakfast food	*plus*	.78
4. Cheerfulness	*plus*	.82	14. Perfume	*plus*	.58
5. Dignity	*plus*	.64	15. Coffee	*plus*	.86
6. Cleanliness	*plus*	.84	16. Schools	*plus*	.26
7. Strength	*plus*	.70	17. Soap	*plus*	.86
8. Durability	*plus*	.58	18. Summer camp	*plus*	.56
9. Luxury	*plus*	.76	19. Candy	*plus*	.84
10. Economy	*plus*	.76	20. Summer beverage	*plus*	.68

The average correlation is plus .73, most of the individual correlations showing a high percentage of agreement.

Poffenberger (*Psychology in Advertising*) makes certain inferences from the various experiments as to the feeling tone of colors which he has investigated, as applied to advertising:

1. Single colors do have definite feeling—tone values which are measurable, and which are stable and permanent in the individual.

2. There is agreement among the members of samples of the population as to the relative pleasantness of colors.

3. Colors have meanings or atmosphere which should be utilized wherever possible.

4. Combinations of color have feeling tones, which are stable and measurable, and which depend to a considerable degree upon the feeling tones of the component colors.

5. Certain colors and color combinations are more appropriate than others for a given purpose, and this appropriateness is fairly stable and can be measured.

6. The appropriateness of a color or combination of colors for a given purpose does not depend, entirely at least, upon the pleasantness of the colors when considered apart from that purpose, but on the contrary is a function of the purpose.

CHAPTER XXV

RESEARCH AS APPLIED TO TYPOGRAPHY

It has long been recognized that certain type faces are better for certain purposes than others. There are certain technical considerations of length of printed line, suitability of paper stock, legibility, and mechanical qualities which are fairly well known, and which must be followed if success is to be attained.

In addition to these there is what is known as the "feeling tone." That is, the style of type bears a certain relation to the commodity advertised. Among the first published experiments of the effect of typography and appropriateness of type faces was one by Dr. Anna Berliner.[1] By using the order-of-merit system, she found out the suitability of 18 hand-lettered types for the four commodities of fish, pork and beans, pancake flour, and orange marmalade. Four groups for one commodity will show the degree of agreement among these groups as to the fitness of the type faces to the product. It was found that the style of type most suitable for fish was least suitable for marmalade, but the results for fish and pork and beans were closely connected.

Figure 201 shows how the type face may be applied to such qualities, as cheapness, dignity, femininity, antiquity, nature, and elegance. The impression created on the mind of the reader will ordinarily reproduce these feelings.

Figure 202 shows the fashion of typography used by several well-known companies in advertising their product. It is in-

---

[1] "*Atmosphärenwert von Drucktypen,*" *Zeitschrift für Angewandte Psychologie,* January, 1920.

teresting to note here how the typography enhances the association normally connected with the products.

The Poffenberger-Franken Experiment

Professors A. T. Poffenberger and R. B. Franken, the former of Columbia, the latter of New York University, conducted a number of experiments with between 400 and 500 persons, under the following conditions:

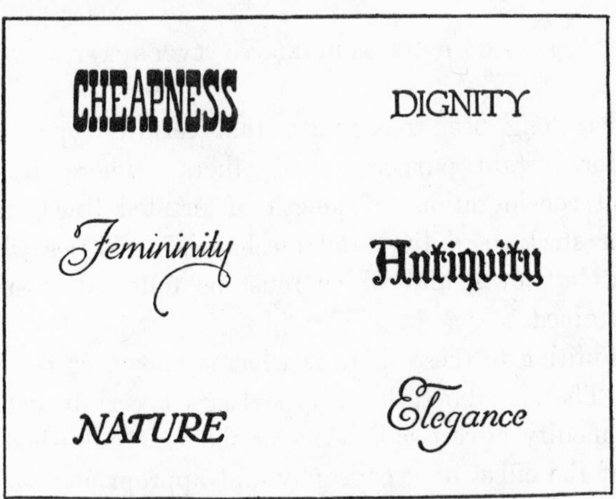

FIG. 201. TYPES AND THEIR CONNOTATIONS
(*Journal of Applied Psychology.*)

1. The material used consisted of 29 of the type faces commonly used for advertising work. This removed the objection against hand-lettered type which was applicable mainly to the concern using it.
2. The appropriateness of the type faces was measured for both abstract qualities and actual commodities. Thus, the results are suggestive of the most appropriate type faces, the records being kept separate, to find out whether any sex differences were present.
3. Both men and women were asked to judge the type faces, the records being kept separate, to find out whether any sex differences were present.
4. In only a few cases was the same person asked to judge more than one commodity, and then only after an interval long enough to minimize the effect of the memory of the previous arrangements.

5. A small group of type experts, members of the staff of one of New York's oldest and best-known print shops, were asked to judge the type faces for a number of categories. Their combined results coincided to a marked degree with the results obtained with the lay judges.

Each of the type faces illustrated in Figure 203 was mounted on a separate card and sorted into five piles, the first of which contained the most appropriate; the last the least

FIG. 202. ASSOCIATION VALUE OF TYPE FACES
(*Journal of Applied Psychology.*)

appropriate example. Then the relative order of merit within each of the five groups was determined and the entire number put together in a single order, headed by the most appropriate specimen. From 40 to 50 subjects were then tested as to their judgments on each of the following ten points:

Abstract Group	*Commodity Group*
Cheapness	Automobiles
Dignity	Building material
Economy	Coffee
Luxury	Jewelry
Strength	Perfume

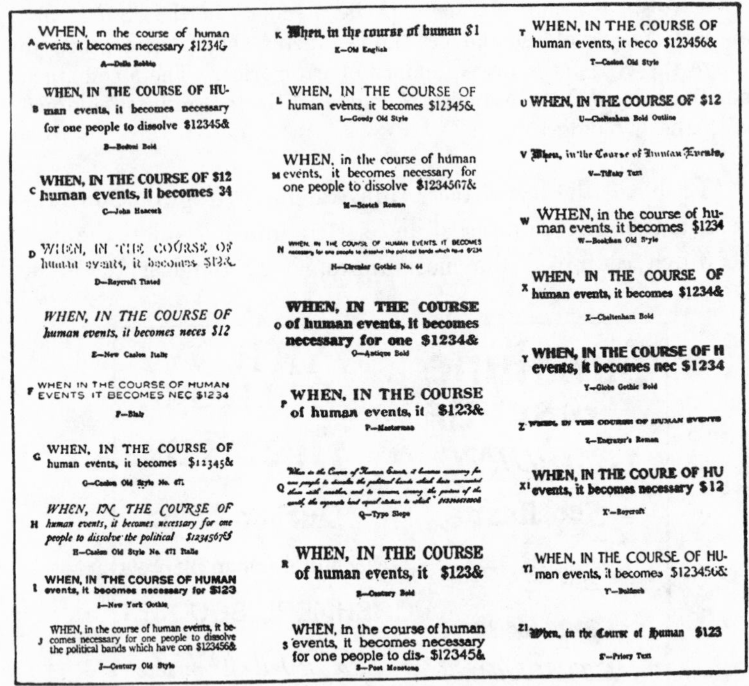

Fig. 203. Testing Suitability of Type Faces

These 29 type faces were chosen for a test to determine which ones best expressed cheapness, dignity, economy, luxury, and strength, and which would be most suitable to advertise automobiles, building material, coffee, jewelry, and perfume. The results are given in Figure 204.
(*Printers' Ink Monthly.*)

In the table shown in Figure 204 the results of the tests are set forth.[2] Position 1 in the table shows the most appropriate type face for any category. As there are 29 specimens, there are 29 possible positions. Specimen O, Antique Bold, ranks 1 for building material in the estimation of both men and women. Specimens V and Q are tied for the least appropriate type face to express cheapness, while specimen V is unanimously voted first place for luxury.

The percentage of agreement between men for the categories, luxury and dignity, luxury and jewelry, and luxury and per-

[2] *Journal of Applied Psychology,* December, 1923.

Fig. 204.—An Investigation of Type Faces

Results of an Experiment to Determine the Appropriateness of Type Faces to Represent Certain Abstract Qualities and Commodities

Key Letters	Technical Names of the Type Faces	Final Judgment for Each of the Five Abstract Groups										Final Judgment for Each of the Five Commodity Groups									
		Cheapness		Dignity		Economy		Luxury		Strength		Automobiles		Building Material		Coffee		Jewelry		Perfume	
		Men	Women	Men	Women	Men	Women	Men	Women	Men	Women	Men	Women	Men	Women	Men	Women	Men	Women	Men	Women
A	Della Robbia	17	12	14	11	5	2	12	11	16	18	12	21	16	14	16	7	12	11	6	12
B	Bodoni Bold	7	14	17	21	9	13	16	24	9	8	6	12	9	13	10	15	20	17	21	22
C	John Hancock	2	3	23	25	14	12	25	21	3	3	8.5	3	3.5	2	2	5	25	27	28	27
D	Roycroft Tinted	25	23	6	5	27	26	7	5	19	26	22	14	20	24	18	25	7	9	8	6
E	New Caslon Italic	15	19	12	13	19	21	11	10	17	17	7	18	19	19	19	17	19	14	10	8
F	Blair	21	20	7	6	11	15	10	9	21	21	23	19	22	20	22	21	8	8	11	7
G	Caslon Old Style No. 471	13.5	16	13	18	6	5	13	13	18	14	15	15	15	16	11	13	13	16	14	15
H	Caslon Old Style No. 471, Italic	24	22	8.5	10	24	24	6	7	27	24	17	23	25	22	27	19	3.5	1	2	2
I	New York Gothic	13.5	8	15	22	4	1	17	16	8	9	20	11	8	10	14	6	22	22	22	20
J	Century Old Style	11	17	22	14	2	8	18	27	24	22	24	22	18	18	21	22	15	13	12	13
K	Old English	22	25	4	4	28	28	4	4	15	19	25	25	23	23	23	24	11	7	16	11
L	Goudy Old Style	16	18	11	16	8	4	15	14	20	16	16	16	17	17	17	11	10	10	9	14
M	Scotch Roman	19	10	19	12	3	7	20	18	14	11.5	13	13	13	12	12	8	16	18	17	16
N	Circular Gothic No. 44	20	24	10	8.5	16	19	8	12	26	27	28	27	26	27	28	28	5	6	3	5
O	Antique Bold	1	1	27	27	18	18	26	28	2	2	3	4	1	1	3	14	28	29	25	29
P	Masterman	5	5	26	26	20	16	23	26	4	4	2	2	2	8	6	1	26	26	24	25
Q	Typo Slope	28	29	5	7	26	23	3	6	29	29	29	29	29	29	29	29	2	5	1	1
R	Century Bold	6	6	29	28	21	14	27	29	5	5	1	5	3.5	5	7	10	24	28	23	26
S	Post Monotone	12	9	16	15	7	3	21	17	10	13	11	9	11	7	9	12	18	19	18	21
T	Caslon Old Style	9	13	18	19	10	9	19	20	11	11.5	5	7	12	11	8	2.5	17	21	20	17
U	Cheltenham Bold Outline	26	21	8.5	8.5	23	22	9	8	23	23	21	20	21	21	20	20	6	12	7	9
V	Tiffany Text	29	28	2	1	25	27	1	1	28	28	18	26	28	28	26	27	3.5	2	5	4
W	Bookman Old Style	10	11	24	17	1	6	22	19	12	10	10	10	10	9	13	18	21	20	19	18
X	Cheltenham Bold	8	7	21	23	12	11	24	22	7	7	4	8	6	6	5	2.5	23	24	26	23
Y	Globe Gothic Bold	3	2	28	29	17	17	29	25	1	1	14	1	5	3	1	16	29	25	29	28
Z	Engraver's Roman	27	27	3	3	22	25	2	3	25	25	27	28	27	25	24	23	1	3	4	3
X	Roycroft	4	4	25	24	15	20	28	23	6	6	8.5	6	7	4	4	4	27	23	27	24
Y	Bulfinch	18	15	20	20	13	10	14	15	13	15	19	17	14	15	15	9	14	15	15	19
Z	Priory Text	23	26	1	2	29	29	5	2	22	20	26	24	24	26	25	26	9	4	13	10

fume, was 96, 93, and 88 per cent respectively. There was a positive agreement of 94 per cent between type best suited to jewelry and perfume, showing that the type suited to one would do well for the other also. Between such categories as luxury and building material there is a minus percentage of 94 per cent, showing their total unlikeness.

Hand-drawn Lettering

Hand-drawn lettering can be produced with the deliberate intention of reproducing the atmosphere of the product or of

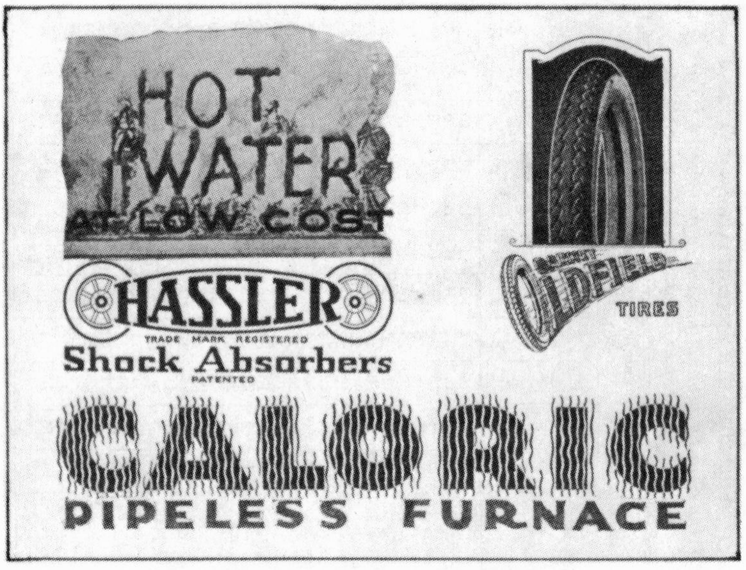

Fig. 205. Examples of Hand Lettering
(*Printers' Ink Monthly.*)

the message which is to be impressed on the public. These hand-drawn headlines have the advantage of helping the reader to visualize an idea. Figure 205 shows a number of these headlines which bespeak the idea behind the advertisement. Caloric pipeless furnaces, for example, have a logotype which fairly radiates head. The type used for Oldfield tires give the impression of speed.

Hand-drawn lettering also has an advantage, in the contrast which it offers to advertisements with straight type make-up. When the slogan or logotype is to be a continuous feature, its illustrative and active qualities will help to increase its memory value.

The Gorton-Pew Fisheries Company conducted a psychological test to select a suitable type face for the trade name "Gorton" before marketing its "Ready to Fry" Codfish Cakes. The test covered 18 hand-drawn type faces, and endeavored to find out which logotype was best for clearness, atmosphere, recognition, and æsthetic value. The final choice was inferior in beauty to many of the others, but it was felt that æsthetic beauty was not such an important feature of the type most suited to codfish.

Legibility

Since a feeling of pleasantness is highly desirable in the effect made by a given type face, it is essential to see that the legibility of the type is such as not to produce any eye strain. Tests which have been made indicate that the size of the letters and the blackness of the lines which make up the letters are more important for legibility than the form of the letter itself.

When the letters are grouped into words, the all-important factor in legibility becomes the amount of white space around the letter. The legibility for letters in groups is much less than for letters alone. The white space tends to increase this legibility because it makes the letters more isolated.

In choosing type, the factor of familiarity should also be considered. The normal person, for example, is more accustomed to reading in lower case type than in upper. Under ordinary conditions, therefore, lower case should be used.

Length of lines and spacing are also factors of importance in creating a pleasant impression. This matter of spacing was tested in a study of the New York Telephone Company among certain of its subscribers. It found that by inserting a one-point lead, an improvement in legibility of about 13 per cent was made. The degree of legibility was determined by measuring the average time required by a telephone user to find the number of the party he desired to reach.

Since a group of laborers was included among those tested, who were naturally slow in looking up the numbers, the average saving in time by inserting this lead was probably as high as 18 per cent to the average business user.

In regard to the best length of line to use, a study made by F. W. Dearborn [3] would seem to show that there is a certain length of line best suited to a given type face. The eye tends to develop a motor habit when the length of lines are the same. When lines are encountered which do not conform to the general standard, this motor habit does not function so efficiently. If the length of line differs in the advertisement, tests seem to prove that it slows up the reading process.

Starch reports an experiment designed to indicate the relative legibility of text on different colored backgrounds. Forty persons were tested to determine their natural rate of reading white type on a dark gray background, and black type on a white background. In the first case, the average number of words read per second was 4.26; while in the second case it was 6.06, a difference of 42 per cent in favor of the black type on the white background.

Continuity

It is almost universally agreed that it is valuable to have certain features in the advertisement which remain constant, no matter how the rest of the advertisement changes. This may relate to the style of copy, the illustration, or the typography of the logotype or headline. This is such an important feature that companies hesitate to make changes, and, when they do, carry out the changes gradually instead of making them all at once.

S. H. Giellerup reports the following changes in type face,

---

[3] "Psychology of Reading," *Archives of Philosophy, Psychology, and Scientific Methods,* 1906, p. 4.

as shown by comparing old and new copies of the *Saturday Evening Post:*

Type Family	Percentage of Advertisers Using It	
	1921	1925
Caslon	39	28
Bookman	23	8.5
Cheltenham	18	4.5
Garamond	0	11
Goudy	6.5	30
Kennerley	10	12.5

This particular magazine does not accept advertisements which contain type faces not on its list. This list, however, includes all of the most popular faces and it is interesting to note how advertising taste has changed with respect to these.

Three faces are no longer used to the same extent, two are used more frequently, and one new face appears to-day which was not present in 1921.

CONCLUSION

A CRITIQUE OF ADVERTISING

It is admittedly difficult to approach the broader aspects of advertising in the entirely objective manner which is to be recommended. Such an attempt, however, should be made, and the earlier in the experience of the user of advertising, the better. In many ways the attitude of the skeptic is safer than that of the convert, since those who profess a knowledge of advertising, and have broadcast that knowledge in the overwhelming mass of literature which they have produced, place little stress on the unfavorable aspects of the subject.

This chapter, by erring in the other direction, aims to be an antidote for such onesidedness, and to suggest some of the avenues of inquiry which may be followed in a more critical approach. But it should be realized that an attitude which is iconoclastic, or even wholly critical, will defeat the ends which science sets itself. Once aware of the shortcomings of advertising, the student should bend his efforts to improve it, and should take measures to apply it more effectively than can be done by those who have not been trained to recognize its limitations.

The Rise of Advertising

It is estimated that over a billion dollars annually is appropriated for advertising in the United States. Despite its meteoric development, however, and the publicity it has brought upon itself, advertising is still one of the less scientific of business activities. There are several reasons for this:

In the first place, the rapidity with which advertising has grown, and the profits which it has made possible, have made many of its supporters consider it unnecessary to carry on any widespread research. Advertising has thus far been cultivated, in the main, extensively; the period of its intensive cultivation is only just beginning.

In the second place, the ignorance concerning advertising has been profound, except on the part of advertising agents and publishers. Much advertising has been done because the business man has said to himself: "My competitors are advertising; therefore I also must advertise." As in similar cases, ignorance has been accompanied by reverence.

In the third place, advertising has hitherto been accepted largely upon faith. Not a few advertising men have been endowed with that same faith which, in earlier days, sufficed to move mountains. The miracles they have performed have increased their confidence and their veneration. The lifeless businesses which they have quickened are numbered in the hundreds, and are proclaimed far and wide. The failures of advertising, to be sure, are seldom recorded, except perhaps in the archives of a university, or in some other convenient burial place. This condition is natural and excusable.

Finally, little of the research work hitherto attempted in advertising has been scientific, in the true sense of the word. Armies of investigators have been sent out into the field to collect and tabulate statistics; yet the progress made and the methods developed are but rudimentary. The laboratories of advertising research are hardly established. Isolated individuals and groups, especially in universities, are attempting to formulate the laws and principles of advertising; but the work has only just begun.

The Advertising Fraternity

Advertising has outlived the bombast and claptrap of circus days, and has become a profession. As a profession, it is noteworthy for its solidarity, its coöperativeness, its aggressiveness, and its skill in salesmanship. Its leaders are brilliant and sincere men, believing fervently in themselves and in the cause which they champion. In some respects they are as a class more able than other business men. As executives they are powerful, since their commercial existence depends upon their powers of persuasion and leadership. Their decisions are rarely encumbered by scientific delays, but are intuitive and rapid. Furthermore, they have been obliged to rely mainly on their own experience as being final, and not without justice, since the present heads of the advertising business were in many cases its creators.

The advertising fraternity is well organized. It has local clubs, consolidated into state and national associations. It has developed its own trade language, a jargon almost unintelligible to the layman, which deals with millines, with media, and with a sort of lineage unknown to the genealogist. It is rapidly developing its own code of ethics. The "Truth in Advertising" movement is the result of the inevitable recognition that if advertising is to prove effective it must represent facts as they are. Laudable as this sentiment is, it implies, to the cynical, that truth in advertising is a thing to be proud of, that it is a positive rather than a negative virtue. In other pursuits such a slogan would seem out out of place. If financiers should make "Honesty in Banking" their slogan, they would do so against the advice of advertising men.

The advertising profession is, for the most part, frank to admit an ignorance of the nature of its subject. In fact, it is sometimes inclined to scoff at any one who attempts to formulate the definitions and principles of advertising. Advertising men wield an unknown force of tremendous power, but wield it somewhat blindly. They are only beginning to realize that only with the aid of scientific research can this force be directed logically and beneficially.

The Advertiser

Advertising normally proceeds from the advertiser, aided by his advertising manager and the advertising agency, to the publisher, and finally to the consumer.

The advertiser himself seldom has a thorough knowledge of the subject. He has, for the most part, put his faith in advertising and has profited thereby. He has been content to believe without inquiry, without research, and without test, other than the supreme test of satisfactory profits. There are, of course, brilliant exceptions to this rule, as in the case of the mail-order houses.

The advertiser has been willing to regard advertising as a thing apart from other business activities. He has not considered it, nor does he yet as a general rule consider it, as he considers production, or finance, or sales. He does not purchase it on specification, as he buys other goods. Advertising, with its special technique, has awed him. When he has much money he is prevailed upon to spend it in advertising. When his profits are small, he is inclined to cut down the advertising appropriation, even though the opposite procedure might prove more advantageous. In the matter of apportioning the amount of money he will invest in advertising, he shows himself less scientific and less shrewd than in making his other purchases. He may follow blindly the advice of those whose interest it is to have him spend as much money as possible. He may measure his appropriation by the volume of sales in previous years, or by the volume of profits secured. All too seldom does he apportion his expenditure to meet the requirements of a carefully planned sales campaign.

The Advertising Manager

The advertiser employs an advertising manager to be nominally in charge of advertising. In most manufacturing companies the advertising manager is, however, an executive of secondary importance. Ordinarily, he is subordinate to the sales manager.

His activities are largely of a routine nature, especially when an advertising agency is employed. It is his duty to take care of details. He must know what an advertisement of a given size will cost when run in a given periodical. He keeps records. He acts as a *liaison* officer. If he has charge of selecting the media to be used, he does not always choose them by scientific methods.

The Advertising Agency

The advertising function, for manufacturers at least, is carried on largely through a separate organization, known as an advertising agency. These middlemen have sprung up because of the specialized character of advertising. They have been highly successful in developing methods of creating and directing demand, and translating this demand into profits for their clients and themselves. Yet it must be admitted that many of them are more adept at producing advertisements than they are at producing advertising. Their status is open to criticism at several points, mainly as a result of conditions over which they have no control, and of which many of them disapprove.

The method whereby the agency receives payment for its services constitutes one of these conditions. Agencies are paid a commission by the publisher on the amount of blank space which they buy for advertisers. As one critic of this practice expresses it: "It is as though the physician received his pay from the druggist instead of from the patient." Obviously, the more space the agency persuades its client to purchase, the greater are its gross receipts. Regardless of whether the agency resists the temptation to buy the largest amount of space from the most expensive medium, it is laid open to such charges, and they are not easy to disprove. In the event that part of the commission is secretly rebated to the advertiser, the situation becomes worse rather than better.

The tendency of the system of payment, if not kept under control, would presumably be to bring agency and publisher into closer affiliation than agency and advertiser. The agency may, for example, find it more profitable to favor the national magazines than the newspapers. The natural tendency of anyone engaged in business is to follow the line of least resistance, and to do no unnecessary work. The task of preparing, placing, and changing advertising in enough newspapers to cover the country is more troublesome and expensive than the same work when confined to a few national magazines. It is interesting in this connection to note that agencies and associations of agencies have devoted much time to studies of magazine circulation. Less is heard about their investigations of other types of media.

Many of the most capable men in the advertising profession gravitate to the agencies, where they are paid handsomely for their services. In this way they become identified with the interests of the publisher. Once having accepted the views of the agency, it becomes their duty to promote them. If they did not, their stand would be inconsistent, if not untenable.

The Publisher

The publisher is the master link in the advertising chain. With him, again, a certain unfortunate situation exists. All large publications are dependent upon advertising revenues for their very existence. The *Ladies' Home Journal,* to cite an extreme instance, sells for 10 cents a copy, while the cost of manufacturing each copy is several times this amount. This overpowering burden may be considered as a tax which the advertiser must pay, and unless this tax is sufficient to defray a large part of the cost of the issue, the publishing enterprise will fall.

The publisher, therefore, gladly offers a generous commission to the advertising agent. He will do everything possible to aid the agent in selling advertisers the most expensive position available. The publisher will sometimes do more. There are instances where he has been persuaded to censor from the columns of his periodical any references which might tend to discourage the advertiser from spending his money, or which might disparage advertising in the mind of the public, or which might prove injurious to advertisers or to the advertising fraternity. The situation thus created explains why newspapers are loath to feature such news as elevator accidents in department stores.

For the protection of the agency, that is, for his own protection, the publisher sometimes goes so far as to refuse all advertising not offered through a "recognized" agency. There is nothing to prevent the advertiser from purchasing space direct from a national magazine; but the magazine protects the agency on the price of blank space, this being the same to the advertiser regardless of whether an agency is employed. It is the subtle delusion that he is getting agency service for nothing that has sent more than one manufacturer to the wall.

There have been, however, a few advertising agents courageous enough to depart from the commission plan of payment, and to charge for their services on a more professional basis.

The Consumer

In the last analysis, it is the consumer who pays the advertising tax. It may well be that advertising is a benefit to the consumer, even in the cases where the advertising tax is 300 per cent greater than the selling price of the magazine carrying the copy, and despite the fact that the publication, the agency, and the advertiser must all be paid a profit. Advertising, nevertheless, remains a tax, paid by the consumer. This does not necessarily mean that it increases the cost of advertised goods.

Advertising as a marketing function which increases the volume of sales of a necessary article, and thereby reduces the cost because of the economies secured, has been widely heralded as a beneficial force. When, however, this power is used to promote the sale of normally high-priced goods which become still higher in price because of the addition of the advertising burden, the benefit to the consumer becomes a negative quantity.

That the advertising tax is paid with so little discussion is perhaps due to the care taken by publications to exclude unfavorable comment on the subject. Hue and cry is raised by the press in its attack upon everything except its own interests, and those of its patrons. And since it has become next to impossible to fight a popular cause without the aid of the press, the position of advertising has so far been unassailed.

The Economic Aspect of Advertising

The average business man cares little about the economic aspect of advertising. Even if advertising were an economic loss, but he were assured, individually, of increased profits, he would, according to the prevailing business code, be justified in using it. The resultant higher cost to the consumer would not be his responsibility. The consumer's loss would be his legitimate gain.

There is much discussion of the high cost of distribution, but to the extent that artificial means are taken to stimulate an artificial demand for artificial wants, high marketing costs will continue. This is particularly true where a product passes through many hands, and where each functionary has a considerable advertising cost to meet.

It is hard to understand why the consumer should be expected to pay a higher price for oven glassware, for example, which had been advertised, if a nonadvertised product is demonstrably as meritorious. It is difficult to see what harm the consumer is doing himself in accepting something represented to be "just as good" as the advertised article is, provided he makes sure that it *is* just as good—and, after all, no product is intrinsically more useful to him merely because he has seen it advertised.

But possibly a comparison between advertised and nonadvertised articles does not mean much; the costs of both may be higher, or they may be lower, because of advertising. The unadvertised article receives little attention at the hands of advertising men, except as an opportunity for new business. To the agent the unadvertised product is the mark of an unprogressive manufacturer.

Yet there are still whole industries in this country which so far have survived and flourished without the use of advertising. The match, for example, is practically unadvertised in this country. Why does no one advertise matches, and build a business for himself in this virgin field? In England, matches are one of the most advertised commodities. Is it to be supposed that matches cost the consumer more in this country, where they are not advertised, than they do in England, where they are advertised?

The protagonists of advertising bring forth a number of

arguments to support the view that advertising is an economic good. They contend that advertising raises the quality of the merchandise, so that the consumer can rely on the advertised brand. Yet the mail-order houses, the chain stores, and even the department stores are selling millions of dollars' worth of goods at a lower price than that which they must charge for advertised brands, and they are building up goodwill by this policy. The public seems to want honest goods at honest prices, whether advertised or unadvertised.

Another argument frequently brought forward is the educational value of advertising. The *New York Herald,* however, in a laudable attack upon certain advertisers (none of whom used that particular paper as a medium) showed some years ago that many millions of dollars in mail-order frauds are perpetrated annually. This would indicate that the educational force of advertising can be applied to unrighteous as well as to righteous purposes.

Economists seem fairly well agreed that advertising cannot of itself increase the income of the nation, although there is room for doubt on this point. Advertising may induce the consumer to buy your goods instead of my goods; but the money he sets aside for the advertised product must be taken from that which would otherwise have been used for some other purpose. Advertising serves to shift the consumer's expenditures from one channel to a competitive channel, but it does not directly increase his total capacity to buy.

Psychologically considered, there is bound to be a definite limitation upon the value of advertising, even allowing for the educational and informative value which it undoubtedly possesses. There is a limit to the number of stimuli which advertising can imprint upon the mind. If there were twice as much advertising as there is to-day (and the advertising budget does double every few years), the responsiveness of the consumer's mind would certainly not also be doubled. Possibly his jaded perceptions would inhibit even more appeals than they do now.

Nor is it likely that a large proportional increase in all

advertising appropriations would bring about any economic good, or even a substantial gain to any individual advertiser. Thus it is conceivable that advertising may already have reached the point of diminishing returns, and that it has begun to be a drain upon the resources of the nation.

Advertising and Scientific Methods

The question of the economic status of advertising, however, is one of academic rather than of practical importance. The advertising agnostic may take the stand that, as far as the consumer is concerned, the wastes it incurs do not justify the benefits it bestows; but he will be forced to admit that advertising has at least one overwhelming practical advantage: it is a mighty weapon for fighting one's competitor, and for getting his business away from him. And he must appreciate that his greatest opportunity for correcting the economic waste is to apply himself to the less universal, but more practical, problem of building the advertising for some operating concern which really needs it.

There is undoubtedly a change for the better taking place in advertising, due to a number of factors. In the first place, the old order of advertising men is passing; a new generation is coming to the fore, trained systematically in business methods. In the second place, the rules according to which advertising has so far been conducted are not proving equal to the strain of changed conditions, and evolutionary development is overcoming many evils. Finally, there is the gradual introduction of research methods into advertising procedure.

The present attitude of advertising men towards research is divided. One advertising agency, for example, may attempt to sell its service on the basis of the research work which it conducts on behalf of the client. Another will stress the point that it has no research department, and that the advertiser will not be compelled to spend money uselessly for a mere counting of noses.

There is a great deal of work done which goes under the name of research, and which few can distinguish from true research, so carefully is it disguised. There are certain tests, however, which can be applied:

1. Does the research seek primarily to justify the present method of procedure, or does it attempt to find new and better methods?

2. Is the research work done with a view to persuading some one of something? Is there anything in it which would tend to create bias, either conscious or unconscious?

3. Does the research man draw conclusions only after he has collected, abstracted, and tabulated all adequate data in a thorough and scientific manner?

4. Do those conducting the research possess the necessary training and qualifications?

Scope and Limitations of Advertising Research

The demand for scientific advertising investigation is slowly increasing. Many business men and some advertising men are ready to search out the facts about advertising. Perhaps the most direct and efficient way to conduct this research is for the advertiser himself to do it. If this is out of the question, it may prove it expedient to have it done by some one engaged especially for that purpose.

One of the factors which has discouraged those advertisers who have experimented with research is that, even at best, it is slow, awkward, and often inferior in quick results to snap judgments. Another disadvantage of research in the minds of many advertisers is that it does not do away with thinking or planning. It is easier to conduct research than it is to apply the findings of research to the problems of an operating business. The results of research often leave executives more uncertain in mind than they were before. There are usually so many variables revealed by any careful investigation that the executive is often confused by the complexity of his problem. His present bewilderment is more dangerous than his former self-confidence.

A third, and perhaps the greatest, limitation upon scientific research is the general unpreparedness for it among those vitally concerned with advertising. There are business men to-day who advance employees because a handwriting expert has advised them to do so. There are other business men who rate their fellows according to the contour of their faces. There are even those who plan for "national distribution" in accordance with the advice of a magazine publisher.

Such men are not ready for research. They would not know how to use it, no matter how well it might have been carried out. A number of other advertisers have a vague notion that facts are valuable, so long as they do not upset established procedure. When they feel confident that research can find them such comfortable facts, they occasionally employ it, especially at those periods of the business cycle when they need it least. But these men cannot be called ready for research.

Again, a number of present-day advertising men, as differentiated from advertisers, are of a temperament which is unsympathetic, if not inimical, to true research. They do not understand the scientific attitude. They are likely to be intolerant of those who do not share their reverence for advertising. Not many of them are ready for research. The more successful of them are of necessity partisans, protagonists, special pleaders.

Even those who most earnestly and sincerely preach research are not entirely prepared for it. Many of the principles which they lay down are not thoroughly tested. They are too much concerned with methods and too lacking in vision. These men are perhaps less scientific than they suppose. They are inclined to be lacking in balance and mental symmetry. And they labor under the supreme disadvantage of being in possession of more advertising facts than any one else, though even these facts are pitifully inadequate.

It is the generation of advertising men yet to come that will be ready to approach their subject scientifically.

INDEX

(1)

A CENTURY OF MARKETING

An Arno Press Collection

Alderson, Wroe. **Marketing Behavior and Executive Action.** 1957

Assael, Henry, editor. **The Collected Works of C. C. Parlin.** 1978

Assael, Henry, editor. **Early Development and Conceptualization of the Field of Marketing.** 1978

Assael, Henry, editor. **A Pioneer in Marketing, L. D. H. Weld.** 1978

Bartels, Robert D. W. **Marketing Literature: Development and Appraisal.** 1978

Blankenship, Albert B. **Consumer and Opinion Research.** 1943

Borden, Neil H. **Advertising in Our Economy.** 1945

Breyer, Ralph F. **The Marketing Institution.** 1934

Breyer, Ralph F. **Quantitative Systemic Analysis and Control.** 1949

Clark, Fred E. **Principles of Marketing.** 1922

Clark, Lincoln H., editor. **Consumer Behavior.** 1958

Coles, Jessie V. **The Consumer-Buyer and the Market.** 1938

Collins, V[irgil] D[ewey]. **World Marketing.** 1935

Converse, Paul D. **The Beginning of Marketing Thought in the U.S.** *and* **Fifty Years of Marketing in Retrospect.** 1959

Copeland, Melvin Thomas. **Principles of Merchandising.** 1924

The Ethical Problems of Modern Advertising. 1931

Frederick, John H. **Industrial Marketing.** 1934

Frederick, J. George. **Modern Salesmanagement.** 1921

Hower, Ralph M. **The History of an Advertising Agency.** 1939

Longman, Donald R. **Distribution Cost Analysis.** 1941

Lyon, Leverett S. **Salesmen in Marketing Strategy.** 1926

The Men Who Advertise. 1870

Nystrom, Paul H. **Economics of Retailing.** 1930

Reilly, William J. **Marketing Investigations.** 1929

Revzan, David A. **Wholesaling in Marketing Organization.** 1961

Rosenberg, Larry J., editor. **The Roots of Marketing Strategy.** 1978

Scott, Walter Dill. **The Psychology of Advertising.** 1913

Sorenson, Helen. **The Consumer Movement.** 1941

Starch, Daniel. **Advertising Principles.** 1927

Terry, Samuel Hough. **The Retailer's Manual.** 1869

Tosdal, Harry R. **Principles of Personal Selling.** 1925

White, Percival. **Advertising Research.** 1927

White, Percival. **Scientific Marketing Management.** 1927